F.
PREMIERSHIP

POCKET ANNUAL 1996-97

Bruce Smith

4th Year of Publication

FA Carling Premiership Annual 1996-97

Copyright © Bruce Smith – Author 1996

ISBN: 1-898351-44-9

The right of Bruce Smith to be identified as the Author of the Work has been asserted by him in accordance with the *Copyright, Designs and Patents Act 1988*.

First published August 1996 by
Words on Sport Ltd

Typeset by Bruce Smith Books Ltd

Phone: 01923-894355
Fax: 01923-894366
eMail   BruceSmithBooks@msn.com

Cover photograph: SpedeGrafix

Printed and bound in Great Britain by
The Lavenham Press, Suffolk.

Cover Repro by Flame Limited

Words on Sport Ltd
PO Box 382, St. Albans,
Herts, AL2 3JD

Registered Office:
Worplesdon Chase, Worplesdon,
Guildford, Surrey, GU3 3LA
Reg. No.: 2917013

Disclaimer

In a book of this type it is inevitable that some errors will creep in. While every effort has been made to ensure that the details given in this annual are correct at the time of going to press, neither the editor nor the publishers can accept any responsibility for errors within.

We welcome comments, corrections and additions to this annual. Please send them to Bruce Smith at the address opposite or eMail them direct to him at: Bruce-Smith@msn.com

CONTENTS

Introduction...

The Premiership goes from strength to strength. Few players have been on the move between Premier League clubs during the close season as clubs hang onto what they have. Instead the influx continues from outside England with several notable signings from Serie A. The balance of power is shifting. The satellite TV money from BSkyB has further fuelled the fire of outrageous fortune now being earned by the playing staff of all concerned. With superb stadiums, ever improving facilities the FA Premier League is now not far off being the premier Premier League in the world.

These views can only be boosted by the spine-chilling atmosphere that was generated at Wembley for the majority of England's games. Anyone who had a chance to sample the uniqueness of it will have memories that are truly memorable. It is hard to believe they could ever be bettered – I hope that the spirit generated by Team England '96 will prevail. Glimpses of the possible were there to see but it should be remembered that only two of five games were won in the traditional sense, and that with home advantage. But it is the perfect foundation.

Season 1996-97 sees the return of Leicester and the baptisms of Sunderland and Derby. Regular Pocket Annualites will know I am all for penalty shoot-outs as a means to the end of deciding matches. However, it did strike me that a more subtle way to both break potential deadlock and ensure attacking football in the play-offs would be to bring League position to bear. In the event of a draw the team who finished higher in the League would prevail. The emphasis would therefore be on one side to attack, knowing they had to win. What made the First Division Play-off Final at Wembley so spectacular was the fact that Palace scored early on, thus forcing Leicester to attack. The same situation would have occurred using the League-bias option. It could also be used over the two-leg semi-finals, coming into play at the end of 90 minutes of the second leg.

From this season the clubs competing in the European competitions will be exempt until the third round. This important development is seen as a means of reducing the fixtures burden on top clubs whilst at the same time improving their chances of making progress in Europe. The effect of this move is that more clubs will have to be included in the first round of the competition in order to achieve the requisite number for the second and third round stages. The basic format of the competition remains unchanged. The participating clubs during the early rounds of the competition will be readjusted as follows:

Round One – Two legs   66 Clubs (18 Div. 1, 24 Div. 2 and 24 Div. 3)
Round Two – Two legs   54 Clubs (33 qualifiers + 6 Div 1, 15 FAPL)
Round Three   32 Clubs (27 qualifiers + 5 exempted clubs)

The exempted clubs for the 1996-97 competition are:

Manchester United	UEFA Champions' League
Liverpool	Cup-Winners' Cup
Newcastle United	UEFA Cup
Aston Villa	UEFA Cup
Arsenal	UEFA Cup

Back to the Premiership and in particular this year's annual. You'll notice that we've included maps and more detailed directions to each of the grounds, thus making the *Bible in your Pocket* even more comprehensive. On the subject of grounds, both Sunderland and Derby County continue with standing available until their new grounds are ready, probably for the start of the 1997-98 season.

Have a great football year and make sure you do your bit to keep the English atmosphere started at Euro96 rolling. Football must stay home!

List of Acknowledgments
Many thanks to everyone who has contributed to this year's Annual – not least the following: Phil Heady (Players), Dave Tavener (Reviews), Mark Webb (Copy Editing), Jacqui Meechan (Database Management) and Sarah Smith (Computations). Thanks also to Andy Porter.

Deadlines
After a relatively quiet close season on the transfer front things were starting to hot up just as we went to press. The cut-off date for this edition of the annual was July 20th 1996. Although many transfers were pending we have only included those that had actually physically taken place at this point.

Internet Site
Words on Sport are planning to launch an internet site on the World Wide Web during the autumn of 1996. An area specific to this Premiership annual will be included. If you have an internet account use a search engine to locate us later in the year. Search on either 'WOS' or 'Words on Sport'. Alternatively eMail us at the address below and we will let you know the details when the site is about to be launched:

BruceSmithBooks@msn.com

'95-96 Diary

August

As the start of the new season draws closer, fans get their first chance to see some of the expensive summer imports in action. Aston Villa parade £3.5m signing Savo Milosevic at West Bromwich Albion – Villa boss Brian Little has also spent close on £6m adding Mark Draper and Gareth Southgate to his squad – while Dennis Bergkamp, signed during the close season from Internazionale for £7.5m, scores freely for Arsenal during a tour of Sweden. Also getting to know the Gunners style under new manager Bruce Rioch is the England captain David Platt, signed from Sampdoria for £4.75m. Long serving Everton goalkeeper Neville Southall is around £200,000 better off following his testimonial match with Celtic at Goodison Park.

Middlesbrough fork out £5m to take home-sick Nick Barmby from Tottenham Hotspur, ironically Barmby's first ever goal for Spurs was against the north east club. Coventry City pay Derby County £1m for defender Paul Williams. Another transfer to finally be settled is that of Jurgen Klinsmann whose new club, Bayern Munich, have to pay Spurs £1.4m.

Just five days into August and already a cup has been decided with Sheffield Wednesday winning 3-1 at neighbours Sheffield United in the newly launched Steel City Challenge. Wednesday pick up £2.5m from Nottingham Forest for Chris Bart-Williams, a record fee set by a tribunal. Forest also agree to pay Arsenal the same figure for striker Kevin Campbell. Newcastle, following the £2.5m transfer of Frenchman David Ginola from Paris St. Germain, reach for the cheque book once more to secure the services of goalkeeper Shaka Hislop from Reading for £1.6m. Champions Blackburn Rovers are a touch more cautious and agree a fee of £200,000 for Darlington defender Adam Reed while Coventry pay Luton Town £1.15m for Paul Telfer.

One player not going anywhere is Eric Cantona, banned until October 1st the French international pledges his future to Manchester United. Queens Park Rangers and Wimbledon receive suspended fines of £25,000 from the FA following their poor disciplinary records the previous season. Collectively, the two clubs amassed 182 bookings and ten red cards.

Everton place the Charity Shield alongside the FA Cup as a second half Vinny Samways goal gives the Merseysiders victory over Blackburn Rovers in front of a crowd of 40,149 at Wembley. Just three days before the start of the Premiership season – one week after the Endsleigh League – Manchester United pull the plug on Kanchelskis' planned £5m transfer to Everton.

All the hype is consigned to the gossip columns on the 19th as the fourth season of the FA Carling Premiership gets underway. How does one justify a fee of £8.5m for a player yet to complete an international match? Stan Collymore does his best to do just that as he scores a stupendous goal to give Liverpool a single goal victory over Sheffield Wednesday at Anfield. Not to be outdone Tony Yeboah scores both Leeds United goals in a 2-1 win at West Ham United. Alan Shearer takes just five minutes to open his account, from the penalty spot, with the only goal against

Queens Park Rangers. Uwe Rosler and Teddy Sheringham ensure a share of the spoils between Manchester City and Tottenham Hotspur, Newcastle United move sweetly into form with a 3-0 win over Coventry City.

The shouts of 'Le Tissier for England' get an early boost with Matt scoring a hat trick at the Dell but Southampton still manage to lose to Nottingham Forest for whom Bryan Roy scores twice. Chelsea, complete with £1m signing Ruud Gullit from Sampdoria, and Everton draw a blank at Stamford Bridge but Manchester United come unstuck at the first hurdle as Aston Villa notch up an opening day 3-1 victory at Villa Park. New boys Bolton Wanderers come back from two down away to Wimbledon before succumbing to a 3-2 defeat. The first Sunday league match of the season sees Barmby score his debut goal for Middlesbrough before Ian Wright ensures equality for Arsenal at Highbury.

Yeboah follows up his brace at the weekend with a stunning strike from twenty five yards to see off Liverpool at Elland Road as Leeds United, on the 21st, are the first side to achieve maximum points from two games. Newcastle United follow suit twenty four hours later with Ferdinand grabbing a couple and Lee a single during a 3-1 win at Bolton Wanderers.

The Kanchelskis saga rumbles on and at last an agreement is reached with United helping Everton with the sell-on fee claimed by previous Kanchelskis' club Shaktor Donetsk.

Aston Villa maintain their winning start on the 23rd with a 1-0 victory at White Hart Lane while Manchester United are up and running following a 2-1 home win over West Ham United. Chelsea fans watch a second goalless ninety minutes, this time at the City Ground. Shearer scores again but he cannot stop Sheffield Wednesday from picking up their first points of the season as the Owls win 2-1 at Hillsborough but Queens Park Rangers are pointless after going down 3-0 at home to Wimbledon who, after just two games, are second in the table. Platt scores his first goal for Arsenal as the Gunners win 2-0 at Everton.

Leeds United are the first side to chalk up maximum points from three games as they end Aston Villa's winning start with a 2-0 triumph at Elland Road. Blackburn Rovers suffer a second away defeat with a surprise 2-1 reversal at Bolton Wanderers, a Simon Barker goal gives Queens Park Rangers their first victory over a Manchester City side which has eighteen year old debutant Michael Brown sent off. Middlesbrough's historic first match at the Riverside Stadium is a joyful occasion for the Teeside club as goals by Craig Hignett and Jan Fjortoft condemn Chelsea to their first defeat. Manchester United and Liverpool slip into gear with 3-1 wins over Wimbledon and Tottenham Hotspur respectively. John Barnes scores two excellent goals during Liverpool's win; he also scores an own goal. Southampton sit at the foot of the table as Anders Limpar and Daniel Amokachi score the goals that give Everton their first success. Coventry City, Arsenal, Nottingham Forest and West Ham United settle for a point each before, on the Sunday, Newcastle United go top on goal difference with a 2-0 victory over Sheffield Wednesday at Hillsborough. Ginola opens his account.

Referee David Elleray books seven players and sends off Manchester United's Roy Keane during a stormy encounter at Ewood Park on the 28th which sees United chalk up their third successive victory, but for champions Blackburn Rovers it's a third successive defeat.

Arsenal are still unbeaten after four games but a goal by Campbell on his return to Highbury cancels out a Platt effort and earns Nottingham Forest a point. The final Premiership match of the month sees Newcastle United move two points clear as a Ferdinand goal clinches victory over Middlesbrough at St James' Park. Leeds United lose their 100% start with a 1-1 draw at the Dell, a result which lifts Southampton one place and sends Manchester City to the foot of the table as Amokachi scores again during Everton's 2-0 win at Maine Road. Goals by Neil Ruddock and Dwight Yorke take both Liverpool and Aston Villa onto nine points. After three games without a goal Chelsea score twice in the opening ten minutes at home to Coventry City – Mark Hughes scores his first goal for his new club – but the Sky Blues rescue a point with Brazilian Isaias getting on the scoresheet.

As the country swelters in its hottest summer for over 200 years moves are made to bring a mid-season break into the English game. Premiership managers claim that the move is desirable to keep players fit and recharge their batteries.

September

The first weekend of the new month is a blank one for Premiership clubs as the national sides prepare for midweek qualifying games in the European Championship. Bolton Wanderers midfielder Alan Thompson is sent off for kicking during England U21's 2-0 defeat against Portugal in Santa Maria de Lamas. More bad news for Bolton supporters on the 4th as Liverpool reach for the cheque book once again this time to secure the services of Jason McAteer for £4.5m. The signing takes Roy Evans' spending since replacing Graeme Souness to £22m and it forces Blackburn to drop out of negotiations with Bolton skipper Alan Stubbs as the champions had wanted to sign both players in a £9m double swoop.

More money changes hands as West Ham part with cash and striker Jeroen Boere in exchange for the return to Upton Park of their former player Iain Dowie from Crystal Palace. Across London former Arsenal boss George Graham decides not to appeal against his one year ban from football.

Columbian goalkeeper Higuita grabs the headlines with an acrobatic 'scorpion kick' save during a goalless draw with England at Wembley. Most are pleased with England's performance but frustration mounts for Shearer as he completes a year without scoring an international goal. Shearer shows that he has no problem when it comes to Premiership football, though, as his goal on the 10th cancels out Savo Milosevic's first goal for Aston Villa during a 1-1 draw at Ewood Park. Newcastle United lose their 100% record as a Jim Magilton goal clinches Southampton's first win of the season. Tottenham also chalk up their first success, 2-1 over Leeds, while Manchester United gain revenge over Everton for their FA Cup Final defeat with a 3-2 victory at Goodison Park which takes the Reds into second place and level on points with Newcastle. Wimbledon leapfrog above Liverpool into third place with a Mick Harford goal securing victory at Selhurst Park. Biggest winners of the day are Sheffield Wednesday, 3-0 over Queens Park Rangers at Loftus Road. On the Monday, West Ham United and Chelsea evenly share eight bookings but the visitors take all the points with John Spencer scoring twice in a 3-1 win. Julian Dicks escapes further punishment by the FA despite television pictures suggesting that he stamped on the head of Spencer. Manchester City, bottom of the Premiership, swap striker Paul Walsh for Gerry Creaney in a deal which will eventually be worth £1m to Portsmouth.

English sides begin their annual assault on Europe but it is Ghanaian Yeboah who makes the biggest impact with a hat trick as Leeds win 3-0 in Monaco. Also in the UEFA Cup, Nottingham Forest go down 2-1 at Malmo, Manchester United draw 0-0 away to Rotor Volgograd while Liverpool return to winning ways with a 2-1 success at Spartak Vladikavkaz.

Blackburn fly the flag in the Champions' Cup but it is quickly lowered as their Group B campaign kicks off with a 1-0 home defeat by Spartak Moscow. In the Cup-Winners' Cup, Everton, thanks to a late goal by Daniel Amokachi, notch an unconvincing 3-2 win over Icelandic side Reykjavik.

England coach Terry Venables is advised that he is free to resume watching games at White Hart Lane after the Spurs chairman Alan Sugar removes the ban he placed on the former Tottenham manager. There is, however, sadness on the England scene with the death of 76 year old Harold Shepherdson who was trainer to the national team for 17 years.

Newcastle United and Manchester United stay neck and neck at the top of the table on the 17th with 3-1 and 3-0 wins over Manchester City and Bolton Wanderers respectively; Creaney scores his first goal for City. Blackburn join City and Bolton in the bottom four when going down 3-0 at Anfield in front of the largest crowd of the day, 39,502. Rovers defender Henning Berg is sent off but has his suspension quashed when referee Gary Willard, after watching television pictures, admits he made a mistake to dismiss the player. Third placed Aston Villa along with Arsenal and Nottingham Forest have the last remaining unbeaten records in the Premiership.

The 19th kicks off with news that plans are in hand to demolish Wembley and replace it with a £168m state of the art complex though the Twin Towers will survive the alterations. The day ends with shocks in 2nd Round 1st Leg matches of the Coca Cola Cup as Nottingham Forest go down 3-2 away to Bradford City, a last minute Lars Bohinen goal gives Forest hope of turning the tie around. Wimbledon come off second best, 5-4, in a nine goal showdown with Charlton Athletic at Selhurst Park while Manchester City, Sheffield Wednesday and Queens Park Rangers have to be satisfied with draws away to Endsleigh League opposition. Leeds United are held at home by Division Two Endsleigh side Notts County.

The biggest shock of all comes 24 hours later when York City take advantage of an experimental Manchester United side to win 3-0 at Old Trafford. There are no other major shocks and even Blackburn win away from home with Shearer scoring twice in a 3-2 success at Swindon Town. Biggest winners of the night are Aston Villa 6-0 over Peterborough United at Villa Park. Cup holders Liverpool repeat their 1992 FA Cup Final win over Sunderland, again by a 2-0 scoreline. There is joy in one quarter of north London as Chris Armstrong scores twice during Tottenham Hotspur's 4-0 win over Chester City, his first goals for the club.

Clubs show more than passing concern as the European Court of Justice declares that players out of contract can move on free of charge to a new club and that the club system of only being able to field three foreigners is illegal.

Yeboah becomes the first player to reach double figures in the Premiership by scoring a hat trick in Leeds 4-2 win away to Wimbledon. But Robbie Fowler goes one better by scoring four times as Liverpool maintain their 100% record at Anfield with a 5-2 destruction of struggling Bolton. This time it is the Highbury corner of North London that is celebrating as Dennis Bergkamp gets off the mark by scoring twice in Arsenal's 4-2 win over Southampton. Manchester United are held to a goalless draw at Hillsborough but it is sufficient to move a point clear of Newcastle, Liverpool and Arsenal at the top of the table. Andy Townsend is sent off for the third time in twenty six league games after scoring during a 1-1 draw with Nottingham Forest. With just a solitary point from seven games Alan Ball and his Manchester City side are three points adrift from the pack.

Newcastle United return to the summit twenty-four hours later with Ferdinand scoring twice in a 2-0 win over Chelsea at St. James' Park. Teddy Sheringham scores twice on the 25th as Tottenham come back from two down to win at Queens Park Rangers and move into the top half for the first time. Rangers began the day by signing Mark Hateley from Glasgow Rangers for £1.5m.

The final Wednesday of the month sees Premiership sides in European action with the 1st Round 2nd Leg ties of the UEFA Cup. Of four English sides in combat only one, Nottingham Forest, win on the night. Brian Roy's second half goal is enough to give Forest a 1-0 triumph at the City Ground and an away goals victory over Malmo. There is no such glory for Manchester United at Old Trafford where a last minute goal from goalkeeper Peter Schmeichel earns a 2-2 draw with Rotor Volograd but the away goals rule removes United from the competition. Liverpool are held goalless at Anfield by Spartak Vladikavkaz but victory in the 1st Leg is sufficient to take Liverpool through. Leeds United go down 1-0 to Monaco but Yeboah's hat trick in the first game takes them through.

More Euro misery for Blackburn Rovers in the Champions' League the next day though as a late goal sends them spinning to a 2-1 defeat away to Norwegian champions Rosenborg. With no points from their two Champions' League Group matches Blackburn are bottom of the pile. Playing their first European match at Goodison Park for ten years Everton move through to the 2nd Round of the Cup Winners' Cup with a 3-1 victory over Reykjavik. Amokachi is stretchered off suffering a head injury.

The doom deepens for Manchester City and Bolton Wanderers on the final day of the month with defeats against Nottingham Forest 3-0 and Queens Park Rangers 1-0, respectively, leaving them further entrenched at the foot of the table. Blackburn Rovers awayday problems persist as they go down to goals from Nick Barmby and Craig Hignett at Middlesbrough. Mark Hughes is on target at Stamford Bridge in a London derby as Arsenal suffer their first defeat of the season. In a midlands derby Dwight Yorke scores inside thirteen seconds as Aston Villa rout Coventry City 3-0 at Highfield Road with Milosevic grabbing a brace. Also scoring two is Sheringham with another couple in Tottenham's 3-1 win over Wimbledon who are slipping down the table at a rate of knots. A satisfactory week for Leeds United is completed with a 2-0 win over Sheffield Wednesday and a rise into fourth place.

October

For the first time since his outrageous actions at Selhurst Park in January, Eric Cantona pulls on a Manchester United shirt and scores from the penalty spot as United and Liverpool draw 2-2 at Old Trafford. But Cantona's return is overshadowed by Newcastle United's flying start to the campaign and on the back of a 3-1 win at Everton the Magpies open up a four point lead at the top of the table. Not everything is going the way of the Geordies though, as Ruel Fox departs for Tottenham for a fee of £4.5m. Matt Le Tissier plays his 300th League game for Southampton on a day which also sees him become a father for the second time but is again rejected by England as he is left out of Terry Venables' squad for the forthcoming match in Norway.

On the 3rd, Manchester United win 3-1 away to York City in the 2nd Round 2nd Leg of the Coca Cola Cup but it is not enough to save United from a humiliating 4-3 aggregate defeat. Wimbledon and Charlton Athletic serve up another six goal feast to go with the nine in the first meeting, a 3-3 draw after extra time at the Valley takes the Endsleigh League side through to the next round. No other Premiership sides crash out although there are scares for Bolton Wanderers, Leeds United and Queens Park Rangers. Ian Wright scores a hat trick and Bergkamp bags a pair as Arsenal complete an aggregate 8-0 win over Hartlepool United.

The following day three more Premiership sides say their farewells in the Coca Cola Cup. Everton, leading 2-0, are defeated 4-2 at home by Millwall who secure victory with two extra time goals. A last minute Ian Ormondroyd goal at the City Ground clinches a 2-2 draw on the night for Bradford City and an aggregate 5-4 success over Nottingham Forest. Chelsea, unbeaten at home in the league, concede a Paul Peschisolido goal at the Bridge and in a rematch of the 1972 League Cup Final go down 1-0 to Stoke City.

Fowler is once again on the mark as Liverpool complete a 3-0 aggregate victory over Sunderland but the Reds have Rob Jones sent off, Martin Smith is dismissed in the same incident. Shearer scores another brace at Swindon to give Blackburn Rovers a 5-2 aggregate win. Others scoring twice on the night are Sheringham as Spurs win 3-1 at Chester City and Uwe Rosler for Manchester City during a 4-0 win over Wycombe Wanderers at Maine Road.

Forest manager Frank Clark is none too pleased to see Lars Bohinen walk out of the club to sign for Blackburn Rovers for just £700,000. Rovers also sign Billy McKinlay from Dundee United for £1.75m and Graham Fenton from Aston Villa for £1m. Thirty two year old Arsenal defender Steve Bould is called up to replace Neil Ruddock in the England squad. Ahead of the forthcoming internationals there are no matches in the Premiership on the 7th but around 22,000 spectators turn out at Old Trafford to see Cantona play for United Reserves. The following Wednesday England are derided at the end of a tedious 0-0 draw with Norway in Oslo.

Newcastle United maintain their four point lead over Manchester United on the 15th when seeing off Queens Park Rangers 3-2 at Loftus Road while United win the Manchester derby with an early goal from Paul Scholes. Nine games played and City still have just one point. Arsenal move third with an impressive 3-0 win over Leeds United at Elland Road and Shearer scores again this time at the expense of his former club Southampton. The Gunners' victory mars the 400th League appearance of their former goalkeeper John Lukic. A fortuitous Steve Stone goal protects the last unbeaten record in the Premiership and earns Nottingham Forest three points at White Hart Lane. A Dennis Wise goal gives Chelsea victory at Villa Park and ends Aston Villa's unbeaten home record. Chelsea's new £2.3m signing from Sheffield Wednesday, Dan Petrescu, watches from the sidelines. Wednesday strengthen their squad with a double swoop on Red Star Belgrade, for a combined fee of £4m David Pleat signs Darko Kovacevic and Dejan Stefanovic. Struggling Bolton Wanderers and Everton are reduced to ten a-side during a 1-1 draw at Burnden Park; referee Paul Alcock is the centre of attention as Richard Sneekes and Barry Horne are controversially dismissed. Bolton boost their squad with the signing of Dragan Curic from Partizan Belgrade for £1m.

Two days later West Ham United move out of the relegation places with Tony Cottee's first league goal for six months seeing off Wimbledon at Selhurst Park. Not quite Beatlemania but there are huge crowds at the Riverside Stadium as

Middlesbrough unveil new signing Juninho. The Brazilian joins Boro from Sao Paulo for £4.75m having caught the British public's imagination when scoring for Brazil during a 3-1 win at Wembley in the summer.

On the 17th Leeds United go down 5-3 at home to PSV Eindhoven in the UEFA Cup during a remarkable night in Yorkshire; at one stage Leeds pulled level from 3-1 down. Forest, thanks to Stone, chalk up a fine 1-0 win over Auxerre in France and Liverpool return home with a goalless draw in Brondby behind them.

Blackburn Rovers manager Ray Harford makes a startling offer to allow his top scorer Shearer to miss the trip to Poland to face Legia Warsaw in the Champions League. Shearer neglects the offer but Blackburn are still pointless after three games as they go down 1-0. Everton, in an entertaining clash at Goodison Park, draw a blank with Dutch masters Feyenoord.

Almost six weeks after being accused of stamping on Spencer of Chelsea, West Ham United defender Dicks is banned for three games by the FA.

The top three all win on the 21st and Middlesbrough step up to fourth with a Hignett penalty accounting for Queens Park Rangers at Riverside. Ferdinand takes his tally with the Magpies to fifteen in twelve games on the back of his first hat trick on Tyneside as Newcastle thrash Wimbledon 6-1. The visitors have goalkeeper Paul Heald dismissed with Vinny Jones taking over between the sticks. Manchester United turn over Chelsea 4-1 at Stamford Bridge despite Hughes scoring against his former club. United's neighbours City double their points total following a goalless draw with Leeds United at Maine Road. City have notched up three Premiership goals compared to their neighbour's twenty one.

Aston Villa lose again, this time away to Arsenal who are London's top club sitting six points and six places above both Chelsea and Tottenham Hotspur. Goals by Bryan Roy, Jason Lee and Colin Cooper give Nottingham Forest a 3-2 win over Bolton Wanderers and a place in the record books as they set a new record of twenty three Premiership matches without defeat.

In the 3rd Round of the Coca Cola Cup, Premiership clubs show up well. Arsenal and Newcastle have convincing away wins at Barnsley and Stoke City respectively – Bergkamp and Ferdinand are again on target –β Blackburn Rovers leave it late to see off Watford at Vicarage Road, Leeds United notch up a fine win at Derby County but the comeback of the night is achieved by Coventry City who overturn a two goal deficit to put out Tottenham Hotspur at Highfield Road. Middlesbrough also come back from two down to force a draw with Crystal Palace.

On the final Saturday of the month Manchester City return to the scene of their Coca Cola Cup defeat and find Liverpool in even more clinical mood as Fowler and Rush score twice each during a 6-0 thrashing. Manchester United move level on points with Newcastle United by virtue of a 2-0 win over Middlesbrough, a game which sees Bryan Robson back at Old Trafford for the first time as manager. Southampton chalk up their first away win of the season with a 2-1 success at Wimbledon. Dowie scores his first goal since returning to West Ham United as the Hammers win at Sheffield Wednesday and a Gary McAllister hat trick for Leeds United pushes Coventry City into the bottom three. Twenty four hours later a David Ginola goal earns Newcastle United a point at White Hart Lane and takes Keegan's side back to the top of the table. Armstrong scores for Spurs but Ferdinand misses out on equalling the club record of scoring in nine successive games for the Magpies. On Monday 30th, Arsenal miss out on the chance to reclaim third place from Liverpool when a John McGinlay goal gives Bolton Wanderers only their second win in the Premiership.

George Graham is back in the news as Radio 5 Live announce that he will no longer be used as a guest summariser. On the final day of the month a crowd of 35,878 at Anfield give Brondby a standing ovation as they win 1-0 to dispose of Liverpool in the UEFA Cup. Leeds' exit is more emphatic as they are beaten 3-0 in Holland and lose 8-3 overall to PSV Eindhoven. At the City Ground Nottingham Forest play second fiddle to Auxerre but hold out for a goalless draw and an aggregate 1-0 victory.

Premiership clubs continue to invest in overseas players as Bolton Wanderers splash out £1.5m on Sasa Curcic from Partizan Belgrade. Closer to home Leeds United spend £1m on Richard Jobson from Derby County.

November

Blackburn Rovers find little cause for celebration on the 1st despite breaking their duck in the Champions League on the strength of a 0-0 draw with Legia Warsaw at Ewood Park. The stalemate means that, with two group matches still to be played, Harford's team are out of Europe.

Everton continue the English exit as a first half goal in Holland takes Feyenoord through to the 3rd Round of the Cup-Winners' Cup. Due to the failure of Premiership clubs to make an impact in Europe the FA plan a meeting for later in the month to discuss how to stop the fall from grace.

On the 4th, many of the big guns are back amongst the goals as Newcastle United move four points clear. Ferdinand scores the winner on Tyneside as Newcastle beat Liverpool 2-1 and Bergkamp gets the goal at Highbury that deals Manchester United their second away defeat of the season. Milosevic scores twice as Aston Villa trounce West Ham United 4-1 at Upton Park and Sheringham is also on target as Tottenham Hotspur return to the scene of their Coca Cola Cup exit to defeat Coventry City 3-2. An early Nicky Summerbee goal eases Manchester City to their first win of the season, 1-0 over Bolton Wanderers at Maine Road. City are now two points behind Coventry at the foot of the table but along with Bolton they remain the only Premiership and Endsleigh sides still without an away point.

Jan Fjortoft scores for Middlesbrough during a 1-1 home draw with Leeds United but 29,467 spectators only have eyes for one player as Juninho makes his debut. Frank Clark's 100th League game as manager of Nottingham Forest sees Forest climb into third place as Vinny Jones is sent off during Wimbledon's 4-1 away defeat – the Dons' seventh in succession. Wimbledon chairman Sam Hamman responds to his club's disciplinary record by threatening to compile a video showing where referees have been wrong to take action against his players.

A meeting between the reigning champions, Blackburn Rovers, and this season's favourites, Newcastle United, at St. James' Park has the expected outcome with a Robert Lee goal taking Keegan's side eight points clear of the pack. Rovers' away record shows just one point gained from seven outings.

Two Premiership sides are in Coca Cola Cup 3rd Round action on the 9th and both, Bolton Wanderers and Middlesbrough, overcome Division One opposition to move closer to Wembley. There are no Premiership matches the following weekend as Venables gets his squad together at Bisham Abbey in preparation for a friendly with Switzerland at Wembley. The national press continue to hound Venables regarding his off the field financial dealings but the England coach pledges his commitment to the job. Venables is not the only personality making the headlines for wrong reasons. Collymore, unable to regain his place at Liverpool, is fined in the region of £24,000 following an article criticising the club in a glossy magazine, the fine is the equivalent of two weeks' wages.

England U21s defeat Austria 2-1 on Teeside with goals from Fowler and Neil Shipperley but still bow out of the European U21 Championships at the qualifying stages. One day later the full national side, in front of less than 30,000 fans at Wembley, beat Switzerland 3-1.

The following weekend sees Newcastle United held at Villa Park, a result which allows Manchester United to reduce the gap to six points. United hammer Southampton 4-1 at Old Trafford after going three up inside eight minutes. Third placed Arsenal drift eleven points behind the leaders when going down 2-1 away to Tottenham Hotspur for whom Sheringham and Armstrong wipe out Bergkamp's early goal. It is also derby day at Anfield where Fowler's last minute goal is not enough to deny Everton a 2-1 victory with Andrei Kanchelskis scoring both Everton goals to end Liverpool's unbeaten home record.

West Ham United trounce Bolton Wanderers 3-0 at Burnden Park and the Lancashire outfit are now the only club without an away point in the Premiership as Manchester City draw with Sheffield Wednesday at Hillsborough. The most surprising result of all comes from Ewood Park where champions Blackburn Rovers end the twenty five match unbeaten run of Nottingham Forest. Not only that but, boosted by a Shearer hat trick, Blackburn inflict on Forest their heaviest defeat for thirty three years when slamming in seven without reply. A couple of dreary encounters are lit up by the sight of a couple of overseas players. Leeds United's new £4.5m signing from Parma, Swedish international Tomas Brolin, watches just the opening half of his side's 1-0 win over Chelsea before heading for the airport. Yeboah celebrates Brolin's arrival with his first goal in nine games, having scored a goal a game during the previous eleven outings. Juninho gets his first taste of Vinny Jones et al during a goalless draw at Selhurst Park. Aston Villa move into third place courtesy of Tommy Johnson's third goal in as many games which secures all three points at Southampton.

On the 21st, Middlesbrough, complete with Juninho, lose at the Riverside Stadium for the first time as Armstrong grabs the winning goal for Tottenham Hotspur. Spurs move up to fifth and Arsenal climb back above Aston Villa into third place when recovering from 2-1 down to defeat Sheffield Wednesday 4-2 at Highbury. Nottingham Forest continue their solitary march into Europe with a Paul McGregor goal at the City Ground earning Frank Clark's side a slender one goal lead to take to France for the 2nd Leg of this UEFA Cup 3rd Round tie.

Blackburn Rovers' sorry tale in the Champions Cup continues on the 22nd as they not only end the away leg of their programme with a 3-0 defeat at the hands of Spartak Moscow but also have Colin Hendry sent off. Inside the opening five minutes team mates David Batty and Graeme Le Saux have to be separated after coming to blows. On the domestic scene Manchester United move to within three points of Newcastle United with an emphatic 4-0 win over their former manager Ron Atkinson's Coventry City side at Highfield Road. Chelsea and Everton consolidate their midtable positions with respective victories over Bolton Wanderers and Queens Park Rangers while Manchester City send Coventry to the foot of the table with a second home win, this time over Wimbledon. Liverpool take a point off West Ham United at Upton Park to end a run of three successive defeats.

Two goals in as many minutes by Lee and Peter Beardsley wipe out a Brian Deane goal for Leeds United and allow Newcastle United to open up a six point advantage over Manchester United on the 25th. Kanchelskis scores again but Everton are held 2-2 at Goodison Park by Sheffield Wednesday for whom Mark Bright scores twice. Liverpool lose again, this time at Middlesbrough with Barmby notching the winner. Bolton Wanderers' problems increase with a Michael Hughes goal deciding the points in Southampton's favour at the Dell. Aston Villa's march up the table is halted by a resurgent Manchester City at Maine Road when Georgi Kinkladze's first goal for City takes the club out of the bottom three for the first time and Alan Ball's side have now kept four successive clean sheets.

Wimbledon end their run of defeats with a 3-3 draw at Highfield Road but it is Coventry City who earn the accolades for saving the game despite going down to nine men when Paul Williams and Richard Shaw are dismissed. Another heading for an early bath is Queens Park Rangers defender Karl Ready at Upton Park, Tony Cottee's late strike in that match takes West Ham United up to tenth. But there are no goals in another London derby at Stamford Bridge where Tottenham Hotspur maintain the only unbeaten away record in the Premiership. Most attention seems to be centred on the feud between Chelsea chairman Ken Bates and director Matthew Harding. Blackburn Rovers take a goalless point off Arsenal at Highbury. The Monday Match sees Manchester United fail to make much of an inroad into Newcastle's lead as the Reds draw 1-1 away to Nottingham Forest with Cantona scoring an equaliser from the penalty spot.

Blackburn Rovers fine both Le Saux and Batty two weeks wages in the wake of their disagreement live on TV in Moscow. UEFA announce that they will not be taking any further action against the two players.

Southampton's Coca Cola Cup dreams are ended in the 3rd Round at Reading. The following night, 29th, five more Premiership clubs are removed from the Coca Cola Cup. A stunning second half goal by Steve Watson earns Newcastle United victory over Liverpool at Anfield, first half strikes by Deane and Yeboah take Leeds United through at Elland Road at the expense of Blackburn Rovers, Wright and John Hartson get the goals that see off Sheffield Wednesday at Highbury, a goal on the hour by Andy Townsend puts Queens Park Rangers out at Villa Park and Coventry City are defeated by Endsleigh League neighbours Wolverhampton Wanderers at Molineux. A thrilling cup tie turns in Wolves favour when Sky Blues' 'keeper Steve Ogrizovic is dismissed.

The month ends with the FA announcing that BSkyB will continue to show live coverage of England matches through to the year 2001. It is also revealed that ITV will take over the role of the BBC regarding the FA Cup from 1998. Independent Television will show live Cup ties on Sundays from the 3rd Round onwards.

December

The start of the festive month kicks off with Manchester United being held to a 1-1 draw at Old Trafford by Chelsea in front of a gate of 42,019. Aston Villa and Arsenal also drop two points each when drawing 1-1 at Villa Park and on a day of six draws in the Premiership Nottingham Forest are grateful for Cooper's last minute goal which staves off defeat at Bolton. Fabian de Freitas' goal for Bolton is sufficient to send Coventry to the foot of the table. In eight games played only two sides, Blackburn Rovers and West Ham United, score more than once with a

Shearer hat trick going some way towards settling that match in Blackburn's favour by 4-2. Leeds slump to their third home defeat of the season as Creaney scores Manchester City's winner at Elland Road.

Goals flow on the Sunday as Wimbledon edge out of the bottom three by taking a home point off Newcastle United, Ferdinand and Dean Holdsworth both score twice during a 3-3 draw. There are seven more goals on the Monday and Dion Dublin nets three of them but still finishes on the losing side as Sheffield Wednesday recover from being behind three times to claim a 4-3 victory at Hillsborough. Wednesday's win lifts them two places and leaves Coventry City in bottom place.

On the transfer scene, Queens Park Rangers are on the verge of selling their record summer signing Ned Zelic to Eintracht Frankfurt. Coventry City are close to finalising a £2.8m deal with Crystal Palace for Chris Coleman and take veteran Chris Whyte on a months loan from Birmingham City.

Nottingham Forest are again the toast of English football as a patient 0-0 draw with Lyon in France takes them through to the quarter finals of the UEFA Cup. The curtain comes down on Blackburn Rovers' second season in Europe on the 6th but the Premiership champions go out of the Champions' Cup in style with Mike Newell netting a hat trick during a 4-1 victory over Rosenborg, a result which also sends the Norwegians out of the competition.

Peace breaks out at Chelsea where Bates and Harding build bridges and on Merseyside 10,432 Everton fans turn out at Goodison to herald the return of Duncan Ferguson after forty four days in Glasgow's Barlinnie Prison. Ferguson repays the locals' support by scoring twice in the Reserves' 5-0 victory over Newcastle United Reserves.

The north east rises to celebrate Juninho's first goal for Middlesbrough on the 9th as Boro, after being a goal down, end Manchester City's five match unbeaten run in impressive fashion. Also on target in a 4-1 win are Phil Stamp and Barmby with a brace. Another big money signing, Collymore, sets about proving himself with Liverpool's winner at Bolton Wanderers. Dan Petrescu opens his Chelsea account with the deciding goal against Newcastle United at Stamford Bridge but Manchester United again fail to take advantage of that slip and are held 2-2 at home by Sheffield Wednesday when Cantona's late goal rescues a point. An early Sheringham goal condemns Queens Park Rangers to a ninth successive winless match while Spurs' victory takes their record to just one defeat in fifteen outings and level on points with neighbours Arsenal in third place.

Arsenal are involved in the only goalless match of the afternoon and have skipper Tony Adams dismissed at Southampton. The most remarkable score comes from Highfield Road where Blackburn Rovers are the visitors. No, Rovers do not add to their miserable two points from nine away games or indeed boost their pitiful total of three away goals, the glory is all Coventry City's as the Sky Blues hammer in five without reply to move above Bolton at the foot of the table.

Ferguson's long, enforced, absence from the Everton First team comes to an end when he replaces Anders Limpar during a 3-0 victory over West Ham United at Goodison. Almost thirty two thousand sees Ferguson's return and the exit of Hammers' 'keeper Ludek Miklosko for felling Amokachi. The George Graham affair surfaces again with the agent involved in handing the former Arsenal manager the bung, Norwegian Rune Hauge, being banned from football indefinitely by FIFA.

The draw for the 1998 World Cup is made in Paris on the 12th and England are put in a group headed by Italy, and completed by old adversaries Poland and former Soviet Union countries Georgia and Moldova. England celebrate the draw by achieving a draw of their own, this time 1-1 with Portugal at Wembley. Steve Stone's remarkable season continues in the ascendancy when he scores the opening goal in front of another disappointing crowd of 28,592.

The following night sees Holland book their return ticket to England with a 2-0 European Championship Qualifying Play Off victory over Eire at Anfield, Patrick Kluivert scores both Dutch goals. Staying on the international front, the transfer system is thrown deeper into confusion with a ruling by the European Court of Justice regarding Jean-Marc Bosman's attempt to make transfer fees illegal. The Court rules that players transferring within the same country can be traded for a fee but those moving to another country at the end of their contract will be able to move without a fee changing hands. Clubs are concerned that time put into producing players through youth systems will be wasted as overseas clubs can then snap them up for nothing and the club's time, effort and financial commitment to that youngster will have been wasted. The ruling also means that more money will go out of the game and straight into the pockets of the players.

A first half goal by Ferdinand gives Newcastle United a ninth win in nine outings at St. James' Park and opens a seven point lead at the summit, Everton are the Magpies latest victims. A late Lee Dixon goal rescues Arsenal's unbeaten home record after Spencer puts Chelsea ahead. Fox scores the decider against Wimbledon as Tottenham Hotspur go third and Aston Villa move up to fourth with Milosevic ending his goal famine at Villa Park with a quick fire hat trick as Villa beat midlands rivals Coventry City 4-1. Another import getting on the scoresheet is Brolin for Leeds United, his first for the club, but the Yorkshire derby at Hillsborough is conclusively settled in Sheffield Wednesday's favour as Marc Degryse and David Hirst score twice each in a 6-2 thrashing. Queens Park Rangers' long wait for a win is over as Bolton Wanderers are beaten 2-1 at Loftus Road. Blackburn Rovers nightmare at Coventry is put behind them as Shearer scores the winner against Middlesbrough at Ewood Park but the champions' joy is marred by a broken leg suffered by defender Le Saux which is also likely to put him out of the Euro Championships.

Manchester United fail to close the gap on Newcastle on the Sunday as Fowler scores twice to give Liverpool victory at Anfield and only the brilliance of Schmeichel saves United from a heavier reversal.

On the same day Birmingham hosts the draw for the 1996 European Championship which pits England in the same group as Scotland, Switzerland and the highly fancied Dutch.

Rosler puts Manchester City ahead against Nottingham Forest but Kevin Campbell equalises with the first goal conceded by City at Maine Road for 594 minutes.

Following on from the Marc Bosman ruling, the Executive Commission of the European Union dictate that the 'three foreigners rule' in the three UEFA cup competitions must end. But the situation is not clear cut as the 'three foreigner rule' will still apply when playing against sides from outside the European Union. The English FA do little to clarify the matter at home by firstly announcing that the change will come into immediate effect in domestic football only to quickly reverse that decision and expect clubs to carry on as before until the end of the current season.

Two Premiership clubs are in Coca Cola Cup 4th Round Replay action on the 20th and both, Middlesbrough and Bolton Wanderers, are defeated by Endsleigh League opposition. Boro go down to two Kevin Francis goals at Birmingham City and Bolton, following a goalless draw, lose on penalties at home to Norwich City.

Bolton sign Welsh international Nathan Blake from Sheffield United for £1.2m, Mark Patterson leaves Burnden Park. Collymore misses out on a small fortune when an FA Premier League Board dismiss his claim for over £400,000, five percent of the fee following his move from Nottingham Forest to Anfield. An Englishman whose team has caused his homeland countless headaches during the past ten years calls it a day when Jack Charlton resigns as manager of Eire.

Newcastle United head into Christmas with a massive ten point lead over Manchester United and an eleven point lead over Liverpool and Tottenham Hotspur the third and fourth placed clubs. Newcastle condemn Nottingham Forest to their second league defeat of the season with a 3-1 win at St. James' Park while Fowler continues his personal assault on Arsenal with a hat trick against the Gunners at Anfield for the second successive season as Liverpool win 3-1. A Gavin Peacock goal clinches victory for Chelsea and ends Manchester City's revival at Maine Road. Two late goals earn Bolton Wanderers their first away point in the Premiership as they battle back from two down at White Hart Lane. West Ham United also grab two late goals but still go down 4-2 to a Middlesbrough side which climbs into fifth place. Wimbledon take a point off Blackburn Rovers at Selhurst Park but they are joined on fifteen points – five clear of Bolton – by Coventry City who see off Everton with a 2-1 home win. Sheffield Wednesday stay four points clear of Southampton following a 2-2 draw at Hillsborough.

There is no seasonal goodwill for visitors Manchester United at Elland Road on Christmas Eve as Howard Wilkinson's Leeds United romp home 3-1. Cole scores for the visitors but Ferguson sees his championship hopes diminish as Gary McAllister, from the penalty spot, Yeboah and Deane confirm the completion of the Reds' fifth consecutive match without a win.

Arsenal move level on points with Liverpool on Boxing Day with a 3-0 win over Queens Park Rangers at Highbury. Everton are also amongst the goals as Middlesbrough's fragile away form sees them go down 4-0 at Goodison Park. Chelsea's highly promising run is ended at Stamford Bridge by perennial party-poopers Wimbledon who overturn a goal deficit to win 2-1. Blackburn Rovers strengthen their outstanding home record with a 2-0 victory over Manchester City. Tottenham miss a chance to go second when drawing 0-0 with Southampton at the Dell. Lee's seventh goal of the season gives Nottingham Forest maximum points at home to Sheffield Wednesday.

Manchester United reopen the championship debate with a thoroughly convincing 2-0 victory over Newcastle United at Old Trafford and on the final Saturday of the year United close the deficit to four points with a less convincing 2-1 victory over Queens Park Rangers in Manchester. Cole and Giggs notch the decisive goals in front of one of two crowds on the day to exceed 40,000. Goodison Park plays host to the second biggest attendance of the day, which sees Everton move to within two points of their visitors with a 2-0 win over Leeds United. The Blues' win was achieved despite losing Dave Watson after eighteen minutes following a second bookable offence.

The year ends with Shearer scoring his 25th goal of the season as Blackburn Rovers end the last remaining unbeaten away record in the Premiership with a 2-1 victory over Tottenham Hotspur at Ewood Park. Sheringham scores his 16th goal of the campaign. Middlesbrough lose away again, this time to a Stuart Pearce penalty which enables Nottingham Forest to leapfrog the Teeside club. Spencer and Steve McManaman score twice each as Chelsea and Liverpool share the spoils at Stamford Bridge and Wimbledon spring another surprise victory in the capital when Arsenal are on the receiving end at Highbury. A last minute John Salako penalty at Burnden Park takes Coventry City eight points clear of bottom side Bolton Wanderers.

January

United's hopes of moving to within a point of Newcastle United are shattered on the opening day of the New Year as Armstrong scores twice during Tottenham Hotspur's 4-1 win at White Hart Lane. Liverpool join Spurs at just three points behind United with Fowler scoring a brace during a 4-2 victory over Nottingham Forest at Anfield, Forest were two up inside eighteen minutes. A spectacular goal by 5'3" Alan Wright sets Aston Villa on the path to a 2-0 win at Middlesbrough, the three points lift Villa above Boro, Forest and Arsenal. Two goals by Niall Quinn past the seventeen year old debut-making West Ham United goalkeeper Neil Finn take Manchester City above Queens Park Rangers. Fellow strugglers Coventry City and Southampton share the points with a 1-1 draw. Everton climb into the top ten as two goals from Ferguson, his first in the league for almost eleven months, clinch a 3-2 win over Wimbledon, Sheffield Wednesday's £2.5m import Darko Kovacevic and David Hirst also grab a pair each during a 4-2 success over Bolton Wanderers. The Lancashire club respond by dismissing joint manager Roy McFarlan while Colin Todd remains as manager and Ian Porterfield is recruited as coach.

The League Managers Association put their weight behind a mid-season break and are to put their suggestions to the FA and Premiership. A four week break is suggested although the timing of it is still in question.

League leaders Newcastle United make their first appearance of the New Year on the 2nd and, inspired by Ginola's early strike, brush Arsenal aside 2-0 at St James' Park. An injury time goal by Paul Furlong confirms Chelsea's improved form and gives the Blues a 2-1 win at neighbours Queens Park Rangers. It is Chelsea's first win in the west London derby for thirteen years.

The first Saturday of the year sees clubs in the top two Divisions join in the battle for the FA Cup but there are few giant killings in the 3rd Round. Just one Premiership club bites the dust, Sheffield Wednesday, who go down 2-0 to Charlton Athletic at the Valley. Ian Rush comes on as substitute and sets a new post war individual record of 42 FA Cup goals as Liverpool trounce Rochdale 7-0 at Anfield but Manchester United and Arsenal are both held at home, by Sunderland and Sheffield United respectively. Arsenal's neighbours Tottenham Hotspur also have problems in securing an unconvincing draw at Hereford United where the home side parade the famous Hereford Bull before the match but are denied permission to repeat the display during the replay in London. Blackburn Rovers and Wimbledon also face replays after drawing away to Endsleigh League Division One opposition.

A late Stuart Pearce goal salvages a replay for Nottingham Forest at Stoke City but Bolton Wanderers, Aston Villa, Middlesbrough, Coventry City, Queens Park Rangers and West Ham United are safely through.

Twenty four hours later Cup holders Everton are held to a 2-2 draw at Goodison Park by Division Two side Stockport County but there are no such problems on the south coast as Southampton breeze to a 3-0 victory over close rivals Portsmouth. Chelsea put in an excellent performance at home to Newcastle United but have Hughes' first half goal wiped out in injury time by Ferdinand. Division One leaders Derby County lead Leeds United 2-0 with two goals in the opening five minutes of the second half despite having had defender Gary Rowett dismissed. Leeds hit back with McAllister and Yeboah scoring during injury time to clinch a 4-2 triumph.

The FA Cup gives way to the Coca-Cola Cup in midweek and there is controversy at Highbury as Arsenal progress to the semi-finals with a 2-0 win over Newcastle United. Wright grabs two superb goals but Ginola is in the headlines following his dismissal for elbowing Lee Dixon. The Magpies assistant manager Terry McDermott is also in trouble as he clashes on the touchline with Arsenal boss Rioch. Elsewhere a Tommy Johnson goal eases Aston Villa past Wolverhampton Wanderers and Leeds United's exciting week continues with a 2-1 success over Reading at Elland Road.

Weeks of speculation is finally ended as the England coach Terry Venables announces that he will not continue in that position once this summer's European Championships are completed.

Just weeks after UEFA withdrew one of England's places in next season's UEFA Cup as punishment for English sides not taking seriously the previous summer's InterToto cup competition, Tottenham Hotspur and Wimbledon are banned from European football for a year – the ban is to run for the next five years should either club gain European entry in that time. The Premier League and the FA support moves to get UEFA's decision overturned.

On the 14th, Manchester United drop two points when held to a goalless draw by the side with the meanest defence in the Premiership, Aston Villa. Tottenham close the gap on United to just two points with a 1-0 victory over Manchester City at White Hart Lane. Rioch celebrates his return to his former club Middlesbrough by masterminding a 3-2 win for the Gunners at the Riverside Stadium – Juninho gets one of the Boro goals. Another overseas player amongst the goals is Brolin who scores twice in Leeds United's 2-0 home win over West Ham United. Blackburn Rovers' rise up the table is accentuated by a Shearer goal at Loftus Road which ends the champions wait of nine months for an away win in the Premiership; Rovers previous away win? At Queens Park Rangers! Despite rescuing a point with a late goal from Rush at Hillsborough, Liverpool slip to fourth behind Spurs. At the opposite end of the table Bolton Wanderers win for the third time in twenty three attempts as Wimbledon go down 1-0 at Burnden Park. Heading the bad boys list are Hughes who is dismissed during Chelsea's 1-1 draw at Everton, Wimbledon captain Robbie Earle, Middlesbrough's Alan Moore who had only come on as substitute and Lee Chapman. Recalled on loan by Leeds from Ipswich Town, Chapman survived just twenty six minutes before seeing red for elbowing Hammers defender Marc Rieper.

Blackburn Rovers' FA Cup dream is over as Ipswich Town win their replay at Ewood Park with an extra time goal while Cole heads a last minute winner for Manchester United at Roker Park as Sunderland are defeated. With that 2-1 success United avoid the embarrassment of going out in the 1st Round of all three of the cup competitions they entered this season.

On the day that former Burnley manager Harry Potts passes away at the age of 75 the row over the InterToto Cup lingers on with the Premier League voting not to compete in this year's competition.

Fortress St. James' Park is finally breached as an absorbing FA Cup replay ends with Chelsea proving to be better at taking penalties than Newcastle United after the two sides are level at 2-2 after extra time. An 88th minute goal from Gullit takes the tie into extra time after United forged into a 2-1 lead with Beardsley's 100th goal for the club, ironically a penalty kick.

Arsenal's indifferent season dips again as a second half goal at Bramall Lane sends the Gunners spinning to a 1-0 replay defeat at the hands of Endsleigh League side Sheffield United. Everton have a struggle at Stockport County but second half goals eventually clinch a 3-2 win. Elsewhere it is a good evening for Premiership clubs as Manchester City thrash Leicester City 5-0, Nottingham Forest see off Stoke City 2-0, Andy Clarke's goal gives Wimbledon a slender win over Watford while a Sheringham hat trick helps Tottenham Hotspur to a 5-1 victory over Bull-less Hereford United.

Newcastle United return to winning ways on the 21st as bottom side Bolton Wanderers are overcome 2-1 at St. James' Park. Newcastle are twelve points clear as Liverpool move into second place with a 5-0 thrashing of Leeds United at Anfield, Neil Ruddock and Fowler scoring twice each. Shearer celebrates his 100th successive league game for Blackburn Rovers, a 3-0 win over Sheffield Wednesday, by maintaining his record of scoring in all of Rovers' twelve home league games this season. Chelsea crown an outstanding week with a Spencer goal taking all three points off Nottingham Forest at Stamford Bridge, but the slide continues for Arsenal, Middlesbrough and Queens Park Rangers, who lose to Everton, Southampton and Wimbledon respectively. A Dion Dublin equaliser for Coventry City at Maine Road keeps the visitors above Alan Ball's side on goal difference. QPR and Bolton stay entrenched at the foot of the table. Gary Kelly is unfortunate to be sent off during Leeds hammering at Anfield while Mick Harford becomes the eighth Wimbledon player to depart before time this season. Dons' manager Joe Kinnear is pleased that referee Steve Dunn is prepared to look at a video clip of the incident before reporting to the FA.

The Sunday match sees Aston Villa move to within two points of their visitors, Tottenham Hotspur, when an outstanding goal by Dwight Yorke ensures a 2-1 Villa victory. Twenty four hours later it is a stormy night in the capital as Manchester United cling to Newcastle's tail by virtue of a gruelling 1-0 victory at Upton Park. Controversy surrounds the dismissal of United's Nicky Butt who gets a second yellow card after seeking retribution on Julian Dicks whose wild challenge on Cole goes unpunished by referee Steve Lodge. Cantona settles the issue with an eighth minute goal.

The row centring on the InterToto Cup reaches a satisfactory conclusion for English clubs as the combined weight of the FA and the Premier League convinces UEFA that their ban on Wimbledon and Tottenham Hotspur is unjust. Both clubs, should either of them win the FA Cup or finish in a high enough league position, are cleared to play in Europe next season.

The final Saturday of the month is a virtual ice-out in the 4th Round of the FA Cup with just three ties surviving the big freeze. Everton are pulled back twice by Port Vale who force a draw at Goodison Park thanks to Martin Foyle's last minute equaliser after Ferguson had put the Toffeemen 2-1 up with just two minutes

22

remaining. Manchester United canter to a 3-0 win over Reading at Elm Park. Sadly linesman Jeff Pettitt is struck by a 10p coin thrown from the crowd. Wolverhampton Wanderers force a replay with a 1-1 draw at White Hart Lane.

The Cup boils over on the Sunday as Aston Villa edge past Sheffield United with an elegant but controversially awarded Yorke penalty seeing Villa blunt the Blades and progress to the 5th Round. A cracking goal by seventeen year old Nigel Quashie is not enough to deny Chelsea a second victory at Queens Park Rangers this month.

Middlesbrough's Bryan Robson, one of the leading contenders for the England job, is fined £750 by the FA for bringing the game into disrepute following an incident at the end of Boro's match with Blackburn Rovers. Middlesbrough players Neil Cox and Nigel Pearson are fined £500 for the same offence. Manchester United are also fined £20,000, for poaching schoolboy David Brown from Oldham Athletic. An FA Commission clamp down on United as the club were reprimanded just two weeks earlier after allegedly attempting to entice young Matthew Wicks from Arsenal.

With a stunning display at Villa Park, Liverpool nudge Manchester United out of second place on goal difference with the Premiership's most prolific partnership, Collymore and Fowler, scoring the goals that earn the Reds a 2-0 victory. Nottingham Forest maintain their unbeaten home record with a 2-1 success over a Leeds United side which is fast slipping down the table. A goal by Dowie just four minutes from the end of West Ham United's match with Coventry City sends the Sky Blues into the bottom three. The Hammers 3-2 win takes them to seventh off the bottom. Two other lowly sides, Southampton and Manchester City claim a point each as a late Rosler goal clinches a 1-1 draw at the Dell.

The month closes with Newcastle United involved in an 'on-off' deal with Italian club Parma regarding Colombian striker Faustino Asprilla. If the deal goes through Parma will pick up £6.7m while the player will receive a tidy £21,000 per week. During the month four £1m plus deals were completed. Ilie Dumitrescu goes from Spurs to West Ham for £1.65m only to encounter work permit problems, his replacement at White Hart Lane is Andy Sinton a £1.5m signing from Sheffield Wednesday. Nigel Clough resurrects his career at Manchester City with a £1.5m move from Liverpool and Don Hutchison leaves West Ham for Sheffield United for £1.2m. The Hammers boost their squad with the loan signing of pin-up Dani from Sporting Lisbon. One other player to move during the month was veteran goalkeeper John Burridge who signed for his 22nd club in 28 years as a professional footballer.

February

As frozen grounds and snow drifts take their toll of pitches up and down the country the Football League announces that it will not support moves for a mid winter break. Understandably, Endsleigh League sides believe that they can cash in from increased attendances providing they keep playing when the Premier League clubs are taking a siesta.

One year and a handful of days after his infamous kung-fu kick at Selhurst Park, Eric Cantona scores twice as Manchester United defeat Wimbledon 4-2 at Selhurst Park to move two points clear of Liverpool who are held to a goalless draw at

Anfield by Tottenham Hotspur. Title favourites Newcastle United stay nine points clear, with a game in hand, by virtue of their 13th home Premier League victory in 13 outings as goals from Ferdinand and Lee Clark account for Sheffield Wednesday. Aston Villa move to within a point of Spurs with a with a three goal hammering of Leeds United who are without the dropped Brolin. Blackburn Rovers add to Bolton Wanderers problems thanks to one more Shearer hat trick at Ewood Park while Manchester City boost their survival hopes with a 2-0 win over Queens Park Rangers at Maine Road, Clough scores the first City goal. Coventry City, one place above bottom but one side Rangers, take a point off Arsenal at Highbury for whom Wright misses a penalty. The first Sunday match of the month sees Chelsea claim their largest victory in the top flight for over thirty years, 5-0, as Gavin Peacock scores three times during Middlesbrough's sixth consecutive defeat.

Seven Premier sides are involved in five delayed FA Cup ties on the 7th but none go through as Coventry City draw 2-2 with Manchester City, Wimbledon and Middlesbrough are goalless at the Riverside Stadium, Nottingham Forest rescue a late draw at home to Oxford United, Southampton come back from behind at home to Crewe Alexandra and West Ham United are held by Grimsby Town at Upton Park. There are no such problems for Tottenham Hotspur as early strikes from Ronny Rosenthal and Sheringham see off Wolves during a replay at Molineux.

Coventry City end Chelsea's fine run on the 10th with Jed Whelan's goal taking the Sky Blues out of the relegation places. Big Ron's side move above Manchester City who lose 2-0 at Everton, and Bolton stay well adrift of the pack as Yorke scores another brace to give Aston Villa a 2-0 win at Burnden Park. With the transfer of Asprilla safely concluded, Newcastle United give the Colombian his debut as a 67th minute substitute at Middlesbrough and the £6.7m signing quickly makes his mark by setting up Watson for the league leaders equaliser. Ferdinand clinches victory for Keegan's side who remain nine points clear of Manchester United following the Reds 1-0 win over Blackburn Rovers at Old Trafford. At the City Ground, Bergkamp scores a second half winner for Arsenal who end Nottingham Forest's 13 month 27 game unbeaten home record, just for good measure Forest have substitute Lee booked twice, and consequently dismissed, within 13 minutes of coming on. Liverpool consolidate their place in third position with a twelfth match undefeated, this time a 2-1 win at Loftus Road condemns Queens Park Rangers to an eighth reversal in nine games.

Leeds United stage a second half fightback to clinch a Coca-Cola Cup semi final 1st Leg lead over Birmingham City at St Andrews. Yeboah cancels out the towering Kevin Francis opener for City before a Chris Whyte own goal sets Leeds on the path to Wembley.

West Ham United move five point clear of the relegation a Dani scores the goal which gives the Hammers a 1-0 win at White Hart Lane to end Tottenham's four unbeaten home record. Wimbledon midfielder Vinnie Jones picks up his fifth fine from the FA in as many years for comments criticising Rudd Gullit. Premiership sides reaffirm their authority in the FA Cup twenty fours later, the 13th, as Southampton and Nottingham Forest win their 4th Round replays away to Crewe Alexandra and Oxford United respectively. A Dean Holdsworth goal sees Wimbledon to victory over a Middlesbrough side which cements seven successive league defeat with an FA Cup exit.

A day of shocks in the FA Cup on the 14th is overshadowed by the death of former Liverpool manager Bob Paisley at the age of 77. Paisley was the most successful manager of an English club throughout the games history.

Cup holders Everton are outplayed in a 4th Round replay in Burslem as they are defeated 2-1 by Port Vale, but Everton are not the only Premiership casualties as West Ham are well beaten 3-0 on Humberside by Grimsby Town. Manchester City set up an all Mancunian 5th Round tie when overcoming Coventry City 2-1 at Maine Road. Leeds United continue their good run of cup form with a first minute Rod Wallace goal removing Bolton Wanderers from the competition. Bruce Rioch eyes taking Arsenal to their first cup final under his leadership as two Bergkamp goals put the Gunners in the driving seat of their Coca-Cola Cup semi final against Aston Villa. A double blast from Yorke, however, ensures equality for the 2nd Leg in the midlands.

The backlog of fixtures caused by the lengthy freezing conditions sees just three 5th Round ties played on Saturday, 17 February, two games are played the following day. Aston Villa are the only victors with a 3-1 success at Ipswich. Southampton equalise in the latter stages away to Swindon while Wimbledon leave it until injury time for Efan Ekoku to clinch a 2-2 draw away to Huddersfield Town.

West Ham United continue their recovery in the Premiership with a 2-1 victory over Chelsea at Stamford Bridge and a bad day for the Blues is underlined as Eddie Newton breaks a leg. Middlesbrough sample an eighth consecutive league defeat, their equal worst record for 42 years, as Bolton Wanderers chalk up their first away victory of the season with an emphatic 4-1 success at the Riverside, four Bolton players get on the scoresheet. But Bolton stay five points adrift at the foot of the table due to Queens Park Rangers ending their poor run with an equally fine 3-1 victory over Sheffield Wednesday at Hillsborough, Simon Barker grabs two of the Rangers goal.

Liverpool show ominously good form in the FA Cup on the Sunday with a 4-0 4th Round hammering of Shrewsbury Town at Gay Meadow while at Old Trafford a controversial penalty cancels out Rosler's early strike for City and sets United on the way to the quarter finals. The Monday match is obliterated by a blizzard at the City Ground where Nottingham Forest and Tottenham Hotspur are goalless after 15 minutes as referee Gary Willard calls proceedings to a halt. Earlier in the day UEFA announces that it will be bound to end all restrictions on the number of European Union 'foreigners' that clubs can field in the same match.

Newcastle United's bid to maintain a nine point lead at the top of the Premiership falls off the rails at Upton Park on the 21st as the Magpies become the fifth successive side to lose to Harry Redknapp's rejuvenated Hammers, this time 2-0. Goals by Roy Keane and Ryan Giggs help Manchester United to cut the points deficit as the Reds see off Everton at Old Trafford. A crowd of close on 40,000 look on as Aston Villa successfully complete the first leg of their two pronged assault on Wembley with a goalless draw with Arsenal at Villa Park in the 2nd Leg of the Coca-Cola Cup semi final clash, Villa go through on the away goals rule.

Two FA Cup 5th Round ties fail to produce a single goal, at Elland Road it is Leeds United who are hanging on as Port Vale push for victory whilst at Blundell Park, Chelsea hold out for a draw with Grimsby Town.

League leaders Newcastle United equally share six goals with Manchester City on the final Saturday of the month but it is not Asprilla's first goal in England that grabs the headlines. The Colombian is caught on camera allegedly elbowing Keith Curle in the face and then head butting the same player in two separate incidents. Two goals for the in-form Collymore enable Liverpool to inflict on Blackburn Rovers their first defeat at Ewood Park for almost six months and move to within nine points of Newcastle. Collymore's first goal embarrasses England keeper Tim Flowers as the ball bobbles crazily off his illegal pitch marking and past the startled keeper. Two own goals and a penalty earn Aston Villa a point away to Wimbledon while Sheffield Wednesday and Southampton are dragged into the relegation frame with respective defeats against Tottenham Hotspur and Chelsea. Middlesbrough's search for a point is finally over as they draw 0-0 with Coventry City at Highfield Road. A John Hartson goal for Arsenal ends West Ham United's winning streak but the Gunners have 'keeper David Seaman to thank after saving a Dicks penalty. Bolton's hopes of following up their win at Middlesbrough with a rare home success are extinguished in the most emphatic way possible as Manchester United run in six goals without reply at Burnden Park.

Twenty three years after their famous FA Cup Final defeat by Sunderland, Leeds United are back at Wembley in the Coca-Cola Final after a 3-0 and 5-1 semi final aggregate victory over Birmingham City. Masinga, Yeboah and Deane score while Steve Claridge misses a penalty for the Endsleigh League side.

Just two days after the Asprilla and Curle clash at Maine Road the pair are charged by the FA with misconduct, one charge for Curle, two for Asprilla.

Division One side Port Vale again demonstrate their quality, which is well hidden when it comes to league matches, during an FA Cup replay with Leeds United on the 27th but a pair of second half goals by Gary McAllister wipe out Tony Naylor's first half strike to keep the Yorkshire club on course for a Wembley double. The Premiership is set to lose one of its greatest goalscorers at the end of the season with the news that Ian Rush is to leave Liverpool.

But as one goalscoring legend comes close to moving so two more continue to enhance their reputations as Fowler and Collymore score the goals that send Charlton Athletic spinning to a 5th Round defeat at Anfield. On an evening unspoilt by the elements, Nottingham Forest and Tottenham Hotspur are still locked together when two magnificent Ian Woan free kicks lead to another replay and further confusion regarding the quarter finals, Armstrong scores both Tottenham goals in the 2-2 draw. Middlesbrough turn to South American defender Branco to stop their slide as manager Robson signs the World Cup winner with 83 international caps on a free transfer. Coventry City are amongst the month's highest spenders as Liam Daish and Eoin Jess move to Highfield Road from Birmingham City and Aberdeen respectively for a combined fee of almost £3m. But after Asprilla's £6.7m move to Newcastle the Magpies get the cheque book out once more to give Blackburn Rovers £3.75m in exchange for David Batty.

March

The penultimate full month of the season gets off to a low key start although Bolton Wanderers raise a few eyebrows as a Gundi Bergsson goal boosts their outside chances of survival in a 1-0 win at Elland Road. Middlesbrough's woes continue as Everton win 2-0 at the Riverside Stadium, Branco is kept under wraps until coming on for the final eleven minutes. The Sunday match gets off to an explosive start with Liverpool blitzing Aston Villa with three goals in the opening eight minutes, two of which are courtesy of Fowler. Liverpool's win takes them to within two points of Manchester United but 24 hours later United throw the title race wide open when a Cantona goal, completely against the run of play, causes Newcastle

United to drop their first points of the season at St. James' Park. The Magpies stay top with a game in hand but are now just a single point clear of Ferguson's side.

A 3-1 midweek win for Arsenal over Manchester City includes two goals for Hartson who is deputising for the suspended Wright while a Steve Chettle goal in the Olympic Stadium restricts Bayern Munich to a 2-1 UEFA Cup victory over England's last European representatives, Nottingham Forest. Jurgen Klinsmann scores the first Munich goal. Queens Park Rangers slump deeper into relegation trouble as Yeboah scores twice during Leeds United's 2-1 win at Loftus Road and Sheffield Wednesday edge closer to the danger zone when two goals by Milosevic help Aston Villa towards a 3-2 victory. The one bright note for Wednesday is struck by new signing Regi Blinker with the Dutchman scoring both of the Owl's goals.

The second Saturday of the month, the 9th, sees the FA Cup start to take better shape as Nottingham Forest beat Tottenham Hotspur on penalties, following a 1-1 draw, to move through to the quarter finals. One Sixth Round tie is played but despite late goals from Gullit and Dean Holdsworth neighbours Chelsea and Wimbledon cannot be separated at Stamford Bridge as the close rivals draw 2-2. Referee Graham Poll sparks a storm by awarding Chelsea a free kick for an alleged back pass from which Gullit's deflected shot flies into the net.

In the Premiership Coventry City grab a vital point when recovering from two down at Everton but Queens Park Rangers stay four points adrift of safety when going down 4-2 at Aston Villa after taking the lead early in the second half. Branco and Juninho both come on as second half substitutes for Middlesbrough but the run of defeats continues with a 2-0 reversal at Upton Park, Dowie scores for the Hammers after just 67 seconds. On the Sunday a dull quarter final FA Cup tie sees Leeds United and Liverpool grind out a goalless draw at Elland Road.

Southampton put up a good performance at Old Trafford but cannot stop Manchester United from moving through to the last four of the Cup on the 11th as second half goals from Cantona and Lee Sharpe clinch the Reds' tenth successive victory. Chelsea are thwarted by Arsenal in their bid to sign Wright and then drop two points when held 1-1 at Stamford Bridge by Manchester City who move two points clear of the bottom three sides. Wimbledon also gain a valuable point in midweek when sharing four goals with Liverpool at Anfield while Leeds United become Blackburn Rovers' latest victims at Ewood Park. Forest old boy Franz Carr ends their hopes of a double cup triumph by scoring Aston Villa's winner in an absorbing FA Cup quarter final tie at the City Ground; it is Villa's ninth consecutive away tie in the competition.

Former Leeds defender Jon Newsome returns to Yorkshire with a £1.6m transfer from troubled Norwich City to Sheffield Wednesday who could still be sucked into the relegation battle. A last gasp goal by Cantona at Loftus Road on the 16th takes Manchester United above Newcastle United on goal difference and Queens Park Rangers' worries increase as Bolton Wanderers win 2-0 at Coventry City. Sheffield Wednesday and Middlesbrough ease their fears by picking up a win and a draw between them but two goals for Georgi Kinkladze send Southampton into the bottom three, the Saints have Gordon Watson dismissed.

Liverpool keep their outside title hopes alive with a 2-0 win over Chelsea and Shearer scores a hat trick as Blackburn Rovers beat Tottenham Hotspur 3-2 to take their away goals in the season to just nine. Three second half goals give Arsenal an away win over Wimbledon. Newcastle reopen a three point lead on the Monday night with a 3-0 victory over West Ham United who have Steve Potts sent off.

Klinsmann scores twice as Bayern Munich destroy Nottingham Forest at the City Ground to clinch a 7-2 aggregate win for the Germans and remove the last remaining British side from Europe in the quarter final of the UEFA Cup. Aston Villa's hopes of claiming a top three place are damaged as Middlesbrough collect a point from a goalless draw at Villa Park. A crowd of 50,028 sees Cantona volley the decisive goal against Arsenal and once again move the Reds level on points with Newcastle but the Geordies have two games in hand. Bolton Wanderers stage a fightback against Tottenham Hotspur but go down 3-2 while a first minute Mark Degryse goal gives Sheffield Wednesday a valuable win at Southampton. In the FA Cup it is the end of the road for Leeds United and Wimbledon who lose their respective quarter final replays against Liverpool and Chelsea by 3-0 and 3-1.

Newcastle United go down to a 2-0 defeat at Highbury for the second time since the turn of the year as early strikes from Scott Marshall and Wright further dent the visitors' title hopes. Wright's goal makes him the Gunners' third highest goalscorer in the club's history. Questions are asked about whether the unpredictable multi million pound signing Asprilla is upsetting Newcastle's pattern. Liverpool bow out of the race as a Steve Stone goal brings a smile back to the faces of Nottingham Forest supporters. Queens Park Rangers draw at Chelsea but Bolton Wanderers are off the foot of the table at long last with a 2-1 home win over Sheffield Wednesday. Wimbledon come from behind to storm to a 4-2 success at Goodison Park while West Ham United beat Manchester City by the same score with four goals coming after the interval; City also have Steve Lomas sent off.

The first Wembley showpiece of the season fails to fizz as Aston Villa condemn an out of form Leeds United side to a second 3-0 cup defeat in five days to win the Coca Cola Cup. Milosevic, Ian Taylor and Yorke score the goals that clinch a place in Europe for Villa. While 77,056 witness Villa's triumph, 50,157 see Manchester United gain a fortuitous victory over Tottenham at Old Trafford thanks to Cantona's fifth goal in five games. Southampton move above Coventry in the final Monday match of the month and push the Sky Blues into the bottom three with a Jason Dodd goal clinching a 1-0 victory at the Dell.

While the FA Cup takes centre stage from the battle for the Premiership crown at the end of the month Southampton are hauled back into the relegation picture with a 3-0 defeat away to Queens Park Rangers who are now just a point behind the Saints. Wimbledon ease their way towards safety with a late winner over Forest while Coventry take the lead at White Hart Lane before slipping deeper into trouble with 3-1 reversal. A John McGinlay goal rescues a point for Bolton at home to Manchester City but their survival hopes look slim. Everton close in on a place in Europe with a 3-0 win at Ewood Park which sees Gary Flitcroft dismissed just a couple of minutes into his Blackburn debut after a £3.2m transfer from Maine Road. Flitcroft is one of four players to join Premier clubs during March for fees in excess of £1m. Manchester City splash out £1.4m on Spartak Vladikavkaz player Mikhail Kavelashvili, Gary Croft signs for Blackburn from Grimsby Town for an initial fee of £1m while Newsome joins Sheffield Wednesday.

England's preparations for the Euro Championships receive a boost with a 1-0 victory over Bulgaria at Wembley, Les Ferdinand scoring the deciding goal after just seven minutes in front of a crowd of 29,708.

Injuries play a decisive part in the Cup semis as Chelsea's reluctance to replace Terry Phelan, at Villa Park, after picking up thigh strain allows Manchester United to overturn a Gullit goal and close in on the double with two goals in four minutes from Cole and David Beckham. Meanwhile at Old Trafford a strapped up Gareth Southgate tries unsuccessfully to stop Fowler from scoring the first Liverpool goal during a 3-0 victory. Two goals in the closing minutes, from Fowler again and McAteer, over emphasise the Reds' supremacy.

April

The first Premiership action of the month takes place on the 3rd and in an absorbing clash at Anfield the title challenge of Newcastle suffers another setback with a Stan Collymore injury time goal clinching a 4-3 victory for Liverpool. The lead changes hands throughout the match as Newcastle go down to their fourth defeat in six games and the final result leaves Manchester United three points clear while the Merseysiders' remote title hopes are still alive. Leeds add to Southampton's problems with a 1-0 victory at Elland Road; Brian Deane's goal is Leeds' first in over six hours.

Good Friday is just that for Middlesbrough who notch up their first home win since before Christmas with a 3-1 triumph over Sheffield Wednesday. The holiday weekend continues to throw up fluctuating fortunes for the top sides. Liverpool aid Coventry's survival bid with a Jed Whelan goal earning the Sky Blues all three points. Manchester United twice surrender the lead to lowly neighbours City before a late Ryan Giggs goal settles what may be the last Mancunian derby match for at least one season. Newcastle stay three points behind United with a game in hand by overturning a Queens Park Rangers' lead on Tyneside with two late goals from Peter Beardsley. With four games remaining Rangers are four points adrift of Manchester City, the side just above the relegation line. Bolton's plight looks even worse as goals from overseas players Hottiger, Kanchelskis and Amokachi take Everton into sixth place. Southampton dent Blackburn's hopes of qualifying for Europe with a Matt Le Tissier penalty deciding the points at the Dell. Aston Villa and Arsenal stay fourth and fifth with 2-1 wins over Chelsea and Leeds respectively. Wimbledon pick up a valuable point at Upton Park while Nottingham Forest inflict further damage on Tottenham with Ian Woan again on the scoresheet during a 2-1 win at the City Ground.

Easter Monday sees Bolton and Queens Park Rangers resurrect their hopes of avoiding the drop with good wins. Bolton come from one down to see off Chelsea while Rangers cruise to a 3-1 win over Everton but 3-0 defeats for Southampton and Manchester City add to the tension at the foot of the table. At the top end of the Premiership a crowd in excess of 50,000 celebrate as Cantona's seventh goal in eight games takes the Reds six points clear of Newcastle who concede two goals in the final five minutes of their visit to Ewood Park to slump to another defeat. Blackburn old boy David Batty puts the Magpies ahead.

Leeds United's troubled run continues with 71 year old chairman Leslie Silver standing down after 13 years at the helm. Matters fail to improve for Leeds on the pitch on the 13th as Mark Hughes scores his first hat trick for Chelsea during a 4-1 win over Howard Wilkinson's side at Stamford Bridge. But Chelsea are not the day's top scorers, an award that goes to Blackburn who get five different names on the scoresheet in a 5-1 thrashing of Nottingham Forest at the City Ground. Manchester United lose a chance to open a nine point lead at the top and also lose their shirts as Southampton run out 3-1 winners at the Dell. With the Saints three goals up at half time, United boss Alex Ferguson orders his team to dispose of their grey shirts for the second half, they do so and pull a goal back. Defeats for Bolton at West Ham and Queens Park Rangers just about spell the end for both clubs but Coventry are alive and kicking with a vital win over Rangers who have Andy Impey dismissed. It is also a good day for Manchester City whose 1-0 win over Sheffield Wednesday has David Pleat's team looking over their shoulders. Newcastle United take full advantage of United's slip up 24 hours later with a Ferdinand goal seeing off Aston Villa at St. James' Park.

The Monday match sees Arsenal and Tottenham share the spoils as Darren Anderton plays his first match in the Premiership for seven months. Attention switches to Goodison Park the following night as an early Kanchelskis goal is rubbed out by Fowler's late strike to ensure equality in the Merseyside derby. A busy week of midweek action continues, Manchester United and Newcastle United matching each other stride for stride with respective 1-0 victories over Leeds and Southampton. Following a spate of substandard performances, Leeds work tirelessly at Old Trafford and hold out for 72 minutes until Roy Keane beats stand in 'keeper Lucas Radebe who replaces the unfortunate Mark Beeney who is dismissed early in the game. Goals are in short supply but Coventry's goalless draw in Nottingham edges Manchester City back into the relegation places. But there is no lack of goals at Blackburn where Alan Shearer becomes the first player to achieve 30 league goals or more in three consecutive seasons when scoring twice in a 3-2 victory over a spirited Wimbledon side.

The penultimate weekend of the month is bereft of Premiership action, due to England's forthcoming friendly with Croatia, but Eric Cantona has cause for celebration as he is voted the Football Writer's Player of the Year. There is also a party atmosphere in the north-east where Peter Reid's Sunderland side are promoted to the Premiership.

Missed chances prove costly for England as Croatia, despite being on the back foot for most of the game, return home with a goalless draw following their trip to Wembley which attracted a crowd of 33,650.

The final Saturday of the Premiership season sees Queens Park Rangers' year long battle against relegation end in failure despite a 3-0 win at Loftus Road over West Ham. Coventry City, Manchester City and Southampton all gain away wins to put pressure on Sheffield Wednesday who could yet go down providing those three all win their last match and David Pleat's side lose. Wednesday's cause is not helped by Andrei Kanchelskis who scores a hat trick in Everton's 5-2 win at Hillsborough. A Stan Collymore goal clinches third place for Liverpool.

Manchester United close in on their third title success in four seasons with a 5-0 drubbing of Nottingham Forest at Old Trafford on the Sunday. Just under 54,000 spectators see goals from Scholes, Beckham 2, Giggs and Cantona take United to within one more victory of the championship, goal difference permitting. As the final week of the league season begins Newcastle, realistically, have to win all of their three remaining games in seven days to replace Blackburn as champions. The run starts on the Monday evening with a Keith Gillespie goal accounting for Leeds at Elland Road. An emotional outburst by Kevin Keegan live on Sky Sports at the final whistle and aimed at Alex Ferguson suggests that the loss of their one time 12 point lead has got to the Magpies' manager.

The following day Asprilla picks up a £10,000 fine and a surprisingly lenient one match ban for his part in the bust up with Manchester City defender Keith Curle who is acquitted by an FA commission.

The last four days of the league season kick off with speculation that Glenn Hoddle is set to be named as the new England coach once Terry Venables moves on at the end of Euro 96. Hoddle formally accepts the position on the 2nd.

On the same day that Chelsea say farewell to Hoddle, Newcastle United become outsiders for the championship when for the fourth time in six matches they surrender a lead and have to settle for a point at Nottingham Forest. Beardsley gives United the lead but Woan levels to light up the red half of Manchester. Leeds United equal their worst losing run for 49 years by going down 3-1 at home to Tottenham for whom Anderton strikes twice.

Three days before the curtain comes down on the league season, and possibly Manchester City's continued existence in the Premiership, former chairman Peter Swales dies of a heart attack.

Former Manchester United captain Bryan Robson and his Middlesbrough side stand between United and their third championship in four years on the final day of the season, Sunday, 5 May. Victory for Boro would open the door for Newcastle United to end a wait of 69 years since last taking the trophy to St. James' Park. Newcastle trail at home to a Jason Dozzell goal before Les Ferdinand equalises in the 71st minute but by then Alex Ferguson's side have taken a two goal lead at the Riverside Stadium through David May and Andy Cole who scores with his first touch. Ryan Giggs completes a 3-0 championship-clinching victory which takes the title to Old Trafford with a four point cushion as Newcastle are held by Spurs and fail to win at home in the league for only the second time this season.

While Manchester United celebrate, their neighbours across the city at Maine Road are heading for the Endsleigh League. Ian Rush scores his 346th goal for Liverpool in his final league match for the club to put the Merseysiders two up prior to the interval, goals from Uwe Rosler and Kit Symons offer hope of survival for City. A rumour goes round that a point will save City who, bizarrely, attempt to waste time only to discover that goalless draws for Coventry City and Southampton at home to Leeds and Wimbledon respectively condemn Alan Ball to the fifth relegation of his managerial career. Sheffield Wednesday also pick up a point with a last minute equaliser at Upton Park.

The two men who captured the headlines for Arsenal before the season started, David Platt and Dennis Bergkamp, both score in the closing stages to give the Gunners a 2-1 victory over Bolton Wanderers and a place in the UEFA Cup.

Hoddle's last match as a club manager, at least for the foreseeable future, ends in defeat as Blackburn Rovers win 3-2 at Stamford Bridge.

In the week-long run up to the FA Cup Final, Terry Venables announces his England squad to face Hungary a week later. Alan Shearer and Darren Anderton both receive call-ups while Tony Adams plays his first match since January when turning out in Paul Merson's testimonial, in which the rehabilitated Gunner collects around £400,000. Chelsea satisfy their supporters' wishes with the appointment of Ruud Gullit as their new manager.

Manchester United create football history on the 11th when a late second half goal by Eric Cantona gives United a 1-0 FA Cup Final victory over Liverpool at Wembley. Cantona's goal hands United the double for the second time in three years and they become the first club to complete 'the double double.' But the game itself is a damp squib with Liverpool being criticised for a negative approach. ∎

FINAL TABLES 1995-96

FA Carling Premiership

		HOME					AWAY				
	P	W	D	L	F	A	W	D	L	F	A	Pts
Manchester United	38	15	4	0	36	9	10	3	6	37	26	82
Newcastle United	38	17	1	1	38	9	7	5	7	28	28	78
Liverpool	38	14	4	1	46	13	6	7	6	24	21	71
Aston Villa	38	11	5	3	32	15	7	4	8	20	20	63
Arsenal	38	10	7	2	30	16	7	5	7	19	16	63
Everton	38	10	5	4	35	19	7	5	7	29	25	61
Blackburn Rovers	38	14	2	3	44	19	4	5	10	17	28	61
Tottenham Hotspur	38	9	5	5	26	19	7	8	4	24	19	61
Nottingham Forest	38	11	6	2	29	17	4	7	8	21	37	58
West Ham United	38	9	5	5	25	21	5	4	10	18	31	51
Chelsea	38	7	7	5	30	22	5	7	7	16	22	50
Middlesbrough	38	8	3	8	27	27	3	7	9	8	23	43
Leeds United	38	8	3	8	21	21	4	4	11	19	36	43
Wimbledon	38	5	6	8	27	33	5	5	9	28	37	41
Sheffield Wednesday	38	7	5	7	30	31	3	5	11	18	30	40
Coventry City	38	6	7	6	21	23	2	7	10	21	37	38
Southampton	38	7	7	5	21	18	2	4	13	13	34	38
Manchester City	38	7	7	5	21	19	2	4	13	12	39	38
QPR	38	6	5	8	25	26	3	1	15	13	31	33
Bolton Wanderers	38	5	4	10	16	31	3	1	15	23	40	29

Composite Table with Prize Money

	P	W	D	L	F	A	Pts	Prize Money	Psn
Manchester United	38	25	7	6	73	35	82	£989,300	1
Newcastle United	38	24	6	8	66	37	78	£934,135	2
Liverpool	38	20	11	7	70	34	71	£884,970	3
Aston Villa	38	18	9	11	52	35	63	£835,805	4
Arsenal	38	17	12	9	49	32	63	£768,640	5
Everton	38	17	10	11	64	44	61	£737,475	6
Blackburn Rovers	38	18	7	13	61	47	61	£688,310	7
Tottenham Hotspur	38	16	13	9	50	38	61	£639,145	8
Nottingham Forest	38	15	13	10	50	54	58	£589,980	9
West Ham United	38	14	9	15	43	52	51	£540,815	10
Chelsea	38	12	14	12	46	44	50	£491,650	11
Middlesbrough	38	11	10	17	35	50	43	£442,485	12
Leeds United	38	12	7	19	40	57	43	£393,320	13
Wimbledon	38	10	11	17	55	70	41	£344,155	14
Sheffield Wednesday	38	10	10	18	48	61	40	£294,990	15

	P	W	D	L	F	A	Pts		
Coventry City 38	8	14	16	42	60	38	£245,825	16
Southampton 38	9	11	18	34	52	38	£196,660	17
Manchester City 38	9	11	18	33	58	38	£147,495	18
QPR.............................38	9	6	23	38	57	33	£98,330	19
Bolton Wanderers 38	8	5	25	39	71	29	£49,165	20

Endsleigh League Division 1

	P	W	D	L	F	A	Pts		Pos
Sunderland 46	22	17	7	59	33	83	P	1
Derby County 46	21	16	9	71	51	79	P	2
Crystal Palace 46	20	15	11	67	48	75		3
Stoke City 46	20	13	13	60	49	73		4
Leicester City 46	19	14	13	66	60	71	P	5
Charlton Athletic 46	17	20	9	57	45	71		6
Ipswich Town 46	19	12	15	79	69	69		7
Huddersfield Town 46	17	12	17	61	58	63		8
Sheffield United 46	16	14	16	57	54	62		9
Barnsley 46	14	18	14	60	66	60		10
West Bromwich Albion 46	16	12	18	60	68	60		11
Port Vale 46	15	15	16	59	66	60		12
Tranmere Rovers.............46	14	17	15	64	60	59		13
Southend United 46	15	14	17	52	61	59		14
Birmingham City 46	15	13	18	61	64	58		15
Norwich City 46	14	15	17	59	55	57		16
Grimsby Town.................46	14	14	18	55	69	56		17
Oldham Athletic 46	14	14	18	54	50	56		18
Reading 46	13	17	16	54	63	56		19
Wolverhampton Wanderers	46	13	16	17	56	62	55		20
Portsmouth 46	13	13	20	61	69	52		21
Millwall 46	13	13	20	43	63	52	R	22
Watford 46	10	18	18	62	70	48	R	23
Luton Town....................46	11	12	23	40	64	45	R	24

Play-offs: Charlton v Crystal Palace   1st Leg: 1-2   2nd Leg: 0-1   Agg: 1-3
          Leicester City v Stoke City   1st Leg: 0-0   2nd Leg: 0-1   Agg: 0-1
Final: Crystal Palace v Leicester City   1-2 *after extra time*

Endsleigh League Division 2

	P	W	D	L	F	A	Pts		Pos
Swindon Town 46	25	17	4	71	34	92	P	1
Oxford United.................46	24	11	11	76	39	83	P	2
Blackpool 46	23	13	10	67	40	82		3
Notts County 46	21	15	10	63	39	78		4
Crewe Alexandra.............46	22	7	17	77	60	73		5
Bradford City 46	22	7	17	71	69	73	P	6
Chesterfield 46	20	12	14	56	51	72		7
Wrexham.......................46	18	16	12	76	55	70		8
Stockport County 46	19	13	14	61	47	70		9

Team	P	W	D	L	F	A	Pts		Pos
Bristol Rovers	46	20	10	16	57	60	70		10
Walsall	46	19	12	15	60	45	69		11
Wycombe Wanderers	46	15	15	16	63	59	60		12
Bristol City	46	15	15	16	55	60	60		13
AFC Bournemouth	46	16	10	20	51	70	58		14
Brentford	46	15	13	18	43	49	58		15
Rotherham United	46	14	14	18	54	62	56		16
Burnley	46	14	13	19	56	68	55		17
Shrewsbury Town	46	13	14	19	58	70	53		18
Peterborough United	46	13	13	20	59	66	52		19
York City	46	13	13	20	58	73	52		20
Carlisle United	46	12	13	21	57	72	49	R	21
Swansea City	46	11	14	21	43	79	47	R	22
Brighton & Hove Albion	46	10	10	26	46	69	40	R	23
Hull City	46	5	16	25	36	78	31	R	24

Play-offs: Bradford City v Blackpool   1st Leg: 0-2   2nd Leg: 3-0   Agg: 3-2
           Crewe Alex v Notts County   1st Leg: 2-2   2nd Leg: 0-1   Agg: 2-3
Final: Bradford City v Notts County   2-0

Endsleigh League Division 3

Team	P	W	D	L	F	A	Pts		Pos
Preston North End	46	23	17	6	78	38	86	P	1
Gillingham	46	22	17	7	49	20	83	P	2
Bury	46	22	13	11	66	48	79	P	3
Plymouth Argyle	46	22	12	12	68	49	78	P	4
Darlington	46	20	18	8	60	42	78		5
Hereford United	46	20	14	12	65	47	74		6
Colchester United	46	18	18	10	61	51	72		7
Chester City	46	18	16	12	72	53	70		8
Barnet	46	18	16	12	65	45	70		9
Wigan Athletic	46	20	10	16	62	56	70		10
Northampton Town	46	18	13	15	51	44	67		11
Scunthorpe United	46	15	15	16	67	61	60		12
Doncaster Rovers	46	16	11	19	49	60	59		13
Exeter City	46	13	18	15	46	53	57		14
Rochdale	46	14	13	19	57	61	55		15
Cambridge United	46	14	12	20	61	71	54		16
Fulham	46	12	17	17	57	63	53		17
Lincoln City	46	13	14	19	57	73	53		18
Mansfield Town	46	11	20	15	54	64	53		19
Hartlepool United	46	12	13	21	47	67	49		20
Leyton Orient	46	12	11	23	44	63	47		21
Cardiff City	46	11	12	23	41	64	45		22
Scarborough	46	8	16	22	39	69	40		23
Torquay United	46	5	14	27	30	84	29		24

Play-offs: Colchester Utd v Plymouth   1st Leg:1-0   2nd Leg: 1-3   Agg: 2-3
           Hereford Utd v Darlington   1st Leg: 1-2   2nd Leg: 1-2   Agg: 2-4
Final: Darlington v Plymouth   0-1

ALL-TIME TABLES
1992/93-95/96

Positions Based on Points

Psn		P	W	D	L	F	A	Pts	Yrs
1	Manchester United	164	102	40	22	297	132	346	4
2	Blackburn Rovers	164	90	35	39	272	168	305	4
3	Liverpool	164	74	42	48	256	181	264	4
4	Aston Villa	164	65	47	52	206	181	242	4
5	Arsenal	164	63	52	49	194	147	241	4
6	Leeds United	164	62	51	51	221	196	237	4
7	Newcastle United	122	67	26	29	215	125	227	3
8	Tottenham Hotspur	164	59	50	55	230	221	227	4
9	QPR	164	59	39	66	224	232	216	4
10	Wimbledon	164	57	45	62	215	243	216	4
11	Sheffield Wednesday ...	164	54	52	58	228	223	214	4
12	Chelsea	164	52	55	57	196	206	211	4
13	Everton	164	55	43	66	203	213	208	3
14	Coventry City	164	47	55	62	181	224	196	3
15	Manchester City	164	45	43	47	147	164	189	4
16	Southampton	164	46	47	71	198	242	185	4
17	Nottingham Forest	122	47	34	41	163	159	175	3
18	Norwich City	126	43	39	44	163	180	168	3
19	West Ham United	122	40	33	49	134	158	153	3
20	Ipswich Town	126	28	38	60	121	206	122	3
21	Crystal Palace	84	22	28	34	82	110	94	2
22	Sheffield United	84	22	28	34	96	113	94	2
23	Oldham Athletic	84	22	23	39	105	142	89	2
24	Middlesbrough	80	22	21	37	89	125	87	2
25	Bolton Wanderers	38	8	5	25	39	71	30	1
26	Swindon Town	42	5	15	22	47	100	30	1
27	Leicester City	42	6	11	25	45	80	29	1

Positions Based on Points-Games Average

Psn		P	W	D	L	F	A	Pts	%
1	Manchester United	164	102	40	22	297	132	346	70.33
2	Newcastle United	122	67	26	29	215	125	227	62.02
3	Blackburn Rovers	164	90	35	39	272	168	305	61.99
4	Liverpool	164	74	42	48	256	181	264	53.66
5	Aston Villa	164	65	47	52	206	181	242	49.19
6	Arsenal	164	63	52	49	194	147	241	48.98
7	Leeds United	164	62	51	51	221	196	237	48.17
8	Nottingham Forest	122	47	34	41	163	159	175	47.81
9	Tottenham Hotspur	164	59	50	55	230	221	227	46.14
10	Norwich City	126	43	39	44	163	180	168	44.44
11	QPR	164	59	39	66	224	232	216	43.90
12	Wimbledon	164	57	45	62	215	243	216	43.90
13	Sheffield Wednesday ...	164	54	52	58	228	223	214	43.50
14	Chelsea	164	52	55	57	196	206	211	42.89
15	Everton	164	55	43	66	203	213	208	42.28
16	West Ham United	122	40	33	49	134	158	153	41.80
17	Coventry City	164	47	55	62	181	224	196	39.84
18	Manchester City	164	45	43	47	147	164	189	38.41
19	Southampton	164	46	47	71	198	242	185	37.60
20	Crystal Palace	84	22	28	34	82	110	94	37.30
21	Sheffield United	84	22	28	34	96	113	94	37.30
22	Middlesbrough	80	22	21	37	89	125	87	36.25
23	Oldham Athletic	84	22	23	39	105	142	89	35.32
24	Ipswich Town	126	28	38	60	121	206	122	32.28
25	Bolton Wanderers	38	8	5	25	39	71	30	25.64
26	Swindon Town	42	5	15	22	47	100	30	23.81
27	Leicester City	42	6	11	25	45	80	29	23.02

PROMOTIONS and RELEGATIONS

1995-96	Promoted	Sunderland	Champions
		Derby County	Runners-up
			Play-Off winners
	Relegated	Manchester City	20th
		QPR	21st
		Bolton Wanderers	22nd
1994-95*	Promoted	Middlesbrough	Champions
		Bolton Wanderers	Play-Off winners (3rd)
	Relegated	Crystal Palace	19th
		Norwich City	20th
		Leicester City	21st
		Ipswich Town	22nd
1993-94	Promoted	Crystal Palace	Champions
		Nottingham Forest	Runners-up
		Leicester City	Play-off winners (4th)
	Relegated	Sheffield United	20th
		Oldham Athletic	21st
		Swindon Town	22nd
1992-93	Promoted	Newcastle United	Champions
		West Ham United	Runners-up
		Swindon Town	Play-off winners (5th)
	Relegated	Crystal Palace	20th
		Middlesbrough	21st
		Nottingham Forest	22nd
1991-92†	Promoted	Ipswich Town	Champions
		Middlesbrough	Runners-up
		Blackburn Rovers	Play-off winners (6th)

FA Premier League reduced to 20 clubs
†*Promoted from Division 2 to newly formed FA Premier League*

FA PREMIER LEAGUE

	Arsenal	Aston Villa	Blackburn Rovers	Bolton Wand'	Chelsea	Coventry City	Everton	Leeds United	Liverpool	Manchester City
Arsenal	•	2-0	0-0	2-1	1-1	1-1	1-2	2-1	0-0	3-1
Aston Villa	1-1	•	2-0	1-0	0-1	4-1	1-0	3-0	0-2	0-1
Blackburn Rovers	1-0	1-1	•	3-1	3-0	5-1	0-3	1-0	2-3	2-0
Bolton Wanderers	1-0	0-2	2-1	•	2-1	1-2	1-1	0-2	0-1	1-1
Chelsea	1-0	1-2	2-3	3-2	•	2-2	0-0	4-1	2-2	1-1
Coventry City	0-0	0-3	5-0	0-2	1-0	•	2-1	0-0	1-0	2-1
Everton	0-2	1-0	0-0	3-0	1-1	2-2	•	2-0	1-1	2-0
Leeds United	0-3	2-0	0-0	0-1	1-0	3-1	1-2	•	1-0	0-1
Liverpool	3-1	3-0	3-0	5-2	2-0	0-0	1-2	5-0	•	6-0
Manchester City	0-1	1-0	1-1	1-0	1-1	0-1	0-2	0-0	2-2	•
Manchester United	1-0	0-0	1-0	3-0	1-1	1-0	2-0	1-0	2-2	1-0
Middlesbrough	2-3	0-2	2-0	1-4	2-0	2-1	0-2	1-1	2-1	4-1
Newcastle United	2-0	1-0	1-1	2-1	0-0	3-0	1-0	2-1	2-1	3-1
Nottingham Forest	0-1	1-1	1-5	3-2	1-2	1-1	3-2	1-2	1-0	3-0
QPR	1-1	1-0	0-1	2-1	1-2	4-3	3-1	6-2	1-2	1-0
Sheffield Wednesday	1-0	2-0	2-1	4-2	0-0	1-0	2-5	6-1	1-1	1-1
Southampton	0-0	0-1	1-0	1-0	2-3	1-0	2-2	1-1	1-3	1-1
Tottenham Hotspur	2-1	0-1	2-3	1-0	1-3	3-1	0-0	2-1	1-3	1-0
West Ham United	0-1	1-4	1-1	1-0	1-1	3-2	2-1	1-2	0-0	4-2
Wimbledon	0-3	3-3	1-1	3-2	1-1	0-2	2-3	2-4	1-0	3-0

RESULTS 1995-96

	Manchester United	Middlesbrough	Newcastle United	Nottingham Forest	QPR	Sheffield Wednesday	Southampton	Tottenham Hotspur	West Ham United	Wimbledon
Arsenal	1-0	1-1	2-0	1-1	3-0	4-2	4-2	0-0	1-0	1-3
Aston Villa	3-1	0-0	1-1	1-1	4-2	3-2	3-0	2-1	1-1	2-0
Blackburn Rovers	1-2	1-0	2-1	7-0	1-0	3-0	2-1	2-1	4-2	3-2
Bolton Wanderers	0-6	1-1	1-3	1-1	0-1	1-0	1-0	2-3	0-3	1-0
Chelsea	1-4	5-0	1-0	1-0	1-1	0-0	3-0	0-0	1-2	1-2
Coventry City	0-4	0-0	0-1	1-1	0-2	0-1	1-1	2-3	2-2	3-3
Everton	2-3	4-0	1-3	3-0	2-0	2-2	2-0	1-1	3-0	2-4
Leeds United	3-1	0-1	0-1	1-3	1-3	2-0	1-1	1-3	2-0	1-1
Liverpool	2-0	1-0	4-3	4-2	2-0	1-0	1-1	0-0	2-0	2-2
Manchester City	2-3	0-1	3-3	1-1	2-1	1-0	2-1	1-1	2-1	1-1
Manchester United	•	1-0	2-0	5-0	2-1	2-2	4-1	1-0	2-1	3-1
Middlesbrough	0-3	•	1-2	1-1	2-1	3-1	0-0	1-1	4-2	1-2
Newcastle United	0-1	1-0	•	3-1	3-0	1-0	1-0	1-1	3-0	6-1
Nottingham Forest	1-1	1-1	1-1	•	2-1	0-3	1-0	2-1	1-1	4-1
QPR	1-1	1-1	2-3	3-1	•	1-3	3-0	2-3	3-0	0-3
Sheffield Wednesday	0-0	1-0	2-0	1-1	1-3	•	2-2	1-3	0-1	2-1
Southampton	3-1	1-0	1-0	3-4	2-0	0-1	•	0-0	0-0	0-0
Tottenham Hotspur	4-1	1-0	1-1	1-0	1-0	1-0	1-0	•	0-1	3-1
West Ham United	0-1	2-0	2-3	0-0	1-0	1-1	2-1	1-1	•	1-1
Wimbledon	2-4	0-0	3-3	1-0	2-1	2-2	1-2	0-1	0-1	•

FA PREMIER LEAGUE

	Arsenal	Aston Villa	Blackburn Rovers	Bolton Wand'	Chelsea	Coventry City	Everton	Leeds United	Liverpool	Manchester City
Arsenal	•	38,271	37,695	38,104	38,295	35,623	38,275	37,619	38,323	34,519
Aston Villa	37,770	•	28,008	31,770	34,922	28,476	32,792	35,982	39,332	39,336
Blackburn Rovers	29,834	27,084	•	30,419	27,733	24,382	29,468	23,358	30,895	28,915
Bolton Wanderers	18,682	18,099	20,253	•	18,021	16,678	20,427	18,414	21,042	21,050
Chelsea	31,048	23,530	28,436	17,495	•	24,398	30,189	22,131	31,137	17,078
Coventry City	20,081	21,004	13,409	17,168	20,629	•	16,638	22,769	23,037	16,568
Everton	36,047	40,127	30,097	37,974	34,968	34,517	•	40,009	40,120	37,354
Leeds United	38,552	35,086	31,285	30,106	36,209	30,161	29,425	•	35,852	33,249
Liverpool	39,806	39,508	39,502	40,104	40,820	39,079	40,818	40,254	•	39,267
Manchester City	23,994	28,027	29,078	28,397	28,668	25,710	28,432	40,390	31,436	•
Manchester United	50,028	42,667	42,681	32,812	42,019	50,332	42,459	48,382	34,934	35,707
Middlesbrough	29,359	28,535	29,462	29,354	28,286	27,882	29,407	29,467	29,390	29,469
Newcastle United	36,530	36,510	36,463	36,534	36,225	36,485	36,557	36,572	36,547	36,501
Nottingham Forest	27,222	25,790	25,273	25,426	27,007	24,629	24,786	24,465	29,058	25,620
QPR	17,970	14,778	13,957	11,456	14,904	11,189	18,349	13,991	18,405	14,212
Sheffield Wednesday	24,349	22,964	25,544	24,872	25,094	16,229	32,724	24,573	24,573	24,422
Southampton	15,238	13,582	14,793	14,404	15,226	14,461	15,136	15,212	15,245	15,172
Tottenham Hotspur	32,894	26,726	31,803	30,702	32,918	26,808	32,894	30,034	31,254	31,438
West Ham United	24,217	23,637	21,776	23,086	19,228	18,884	21,085	22,901	24,324	24,017
Wimbledon	18,335	12,193	7,105	9,317	17,048	15,540	11,121	13,307	19,530	11,844

ATTENDANCES 1995-96

	Manchester United	Middlesbrough	Newcastle United	Nottingham Forest	QPR	Sheffield Wednesday	Southampton	Tottenham Hotspur	West Ham United	Wimbledon
Arsenal	38,317	37,308	38,271	38,248	38,259	34,556	38,136	38,273	38,065	37,640
Aston Villa	34,655	23,933	39,167	33,972	28,221	27,893	34,059	35,666	26,768	26,928
Blackburn Rovers	29,843	27,996	30,717	27,660	25,932	24,732	26,780	30,004	26,638	24,174
Bolton Wanderers	21,381	18,376	20,243	17,342	17,362	18,368	18,795	17,829	19,047	16,216
Chelsea	31,019	21,060	31,098	24,482	25,590	23,216	26,237	31,059	25,252	21,906
Coventry City	23,344	17,979	20,553	17,238	22,916	14,002	16,822	17,545	17,448	12,496
Everton	39,496	40,091	33,080	33,163	30,009	35,898	33,668	33,629	31,778	31,382
Leeds United	39,801	31,778	38,862	29,220	31,504	34,076	26,077	30,061	30,658	27,984
Liverpool	40,546	40,782	40,702	39,206	37,548	40,535	39,883	40,628	40,102	34,063
Manchester City	29,688	25,865	31,115	25,660	25,710	30,898	29,550	30,827	31,966	23,617
Manchester United	•	36,580	42,024	53,926	41,890	41,849	39,301	50,157	50,326	32,226
Middlesbrough	29,921	•	30,011	23,392	29,293	29,751	29,188	29,487	28,640	29,192
Newcastle United	36,584	36,483	•	36,531	36,583	36,567	36,521	36,589	36,331	36,434
Nottingham Forest	29,263	27,027	28,280	•	27,509	27,810	23,321	27,053	24,024	20,810
QPR	18,817	17,546	18,254	17,549	•	22,442	17,615	15,659	18,828	11,837
Sheffield Wednesday	34,101	21,177	24,815	21,930	22,442	•	25,115	26,565	23,917	19,085
Southampton	15,262	15,151	15,237	15,165	15,137	12,459	•	15,238	13,568	15,172
Tottenham Hotspur	32,852	32,036	32,279	32,876	28,851	32,047	26,320	•	29,781	25,321
West Ham United	24,197	23,850	23,843	21,257	21,504	23,790	18,501	23,516	•	20,402
Wimbledon	24,432	13,780	18,002	9,807	9,123	6,352	7,982	16,193	9,411	•

FA PREMIER LEAGUE RECORDS 1995-96

SCORERS

Top Scorers – All Competitions

Player	Club	L	F	C	E	Total
Alan SHEARER	Blackburn Rovers	31	0	5	1	37
Robbie FOWLER	Liverpool	28	6	2	0	36
Les FERDINAND	Newcastle United	25	1	3	0	29
Dwight YORKE	Aston Villa	17	2	6	0	25
Teddy SHERINGHAM	Tottenham Hotspur	16	5	3	0	24
Ian WRIGHT	Arsenal	15	1	7	0	23
Chris ARMSTRONG	Tottenham Hotspur	15	4	3	0	22
Tony YEBOAH	Leeds United	12	2	2	3	19
Stan COLLYMORE	Liverpool	14	5	0	0	19
Eric CANTONA	Manchester United	14	4	0	0	18
Dion DUBLIN	Coventry City	14	2	0	0	16
Andrei KANCHELSKIS	Everton	16	0	0	0	16
David HIRST	Sheffield Wednesday	13	0	1	0	14
John SPENCER	Chelsea	13	1	0	0	14
Savo MILOSEVIC	Aston Villa	12	1	1	0	14
Robbie EARLE	Wimbledon	11	1	2	0	14

L=League, F=FA Cup, C=Coca-Cola Cup, E=Europe

FA Carling Premiership Top Scorers

Player	Club	Goals	All-time Total
Alan SHEARER	Blackburn Rovers	31	112
Robbie FOWLER	Liverpool	28	65
Les FERDINAND	Newcastle United	25	85
Dwight YORKE	Aston Villa	17	28
Teddy SHERINGHAM	Tottenham Hotspur	16	69
Andrei KANCHELSKIS	Everton	16	39
Ian WRIGHT	Arsenal	15	71
Chris ARMSTRONG	Tottenham Hotspur	15	38
Stan COLLYMORE	Liverpool	14	37
Eric CANTONA	Manchester United	14	58
Dion DUBLIN	Coventry City	14	29
David HIRST	Sheffield Wednesday	13	28

John SPENCER	Chelsea	13	36
Tony YEBOAH	Leeds United	12	29
Savo MILOSEVIC	Aston Villa	12	12
Robbie EARLE	Wimbledon	11	27

FA Carling Premiership Club Top Scorers

Club	Scorers
Arsenal	Wright 15, Bergkamp 11, Platt 6
Aston Villa	Yorke 17, Milosevic 12, Johnson 5
Blackburn Rovers	Shearer 31, Fenton 6, Bohinen 4, Sherwood 4
Bolton Wanderers	McGinlay 6, De Freitas 5
Chelsea	Spencer 13, Hughes 8, Wise 7
Coventry City	Dublin 14, Whelan 8, Ndlovu 5
Everton	Kanchelskis 16, Stuart 9, Amokachi 6, Rideout 6
Leeds United	Yeboah 12, Deane 7, McAllister 5
Liverpool	Fowler 28, Collymore 14, McManaman 6
Manchester City	Rosler 9, Quinn 8, Kinkladze 4
Manchester United	Cantona 14, Andy Cole 11, Ryan Giggs 11
Middlesbrough	Barmby 7, Fjortoft 6, Hignett 5
Newcastle United	Ferdinand 25, Beardsley 8, Lee 8
Nottingham Forest	Woan 8, Lee 8, Roy 8
QPR	Dichio 10, Gallen 8, Barker 5
Sheffield Wednesday	Hirst 13, Degryse 8, Bright 7
Southampton	Shipperley 8, Le Tissier 7, Watson 3
Tottenham Hotspur	Sheringham 16, Armstrong 15, Fox 6
West Ham United	Cottee 10, Dicks 10, Dowie 8
Wimbledon	Earle 11, Holdsworth 10, Ekoku 7

FA Carling Premiership Hat-tricks

Player	Goals		Match (result)	Date
M. LE TISSIER	3	(2p)	SOUTHAMPTON v N. Forest (3-4)	19/8/95
A. SHEARER	3		BLACKBURN v Coventry City (5-1)	23/9/95
T. YEBOAH	3		Wimbledon v LEEDS UNITED (4-2)	23/9/95
R. FOWLER	4		LIVERPOOL v Bolton Wanderers (5-2)	23/9/95
L. FERDINAND	3		NEWCASTLE U. v Wimbledon (6-1)	21/10/95
G. McALLISTER	3	(1p)	LEEDS UTD v Coventry City (3-1)	28/10/95
A. SHEARER	3		BLACKBURN v N. Forest (7-0)	18/11/95
A. SHEARER	3	(1p)	BLACKBURN v West Ham Utd (4-2)	2/12/95
D. DUBLIN	3		Sheff. Wed. v COVENTRY C. (3-4)	3/12/95
S. MILOSEVIC	3		ASTON VILLA v Coventry City (4-1)	16/12/95
R. FOWLER	3		LIVERPOOL v Arsenal (3-1)	23/12/95
A. SHEARER	3		BLACKBURN v Bolton Wdrs (3-1)	3/2/96
G. PEACOCK	3		CHELSEA v Middlesbrough (5-0)	4/2/96

A. SHEARER	3 (1p)	Tottenham H. v BLACKBURN (3-2)	16/3/96
M. HUGHES	3(1p)	CHELSEA v Leeds United (4-1)	13/4/96
A. KANCHELSKIS	3	Sheff. Wed. v EVERTON (5-2)	27/4/96

*p = penalty(ies),

Alan SHEARER – 5 Hat-tricks in a season – new Premiership record.

ATTENDANCES

Top Attendances by Club and Number

Club ... ... Posn	Total	Ave
Manchester United 1	791,940	41,681
Liverpool 3	751,501	39,553
Arsenal 5	713,797	37,568
Newcastle United 2	693,580	36,504
Everton 6	673,407	35,442
Leeds United 13	619,946	32,629
Aston Villa 4	619,650	32,613
Tottenham Hotspur 8	579,834	30,518
Middlesbrough 12	549,486	28,920
Manchester City 18	528,885	27,836
Blackburn Rovers 7	526,564	27,714
Nottingham Forest 9	492,395	25,916
Chelsea 11	486,361	25,598
Sheffield Wednesday 15	472,665	24,877
West Ham United 10	424,015	22,317
Bolton Wanderers 20	357,625	18,822
Coventry City 16	351,646	18,508
QPR 19	297,775	15,672
Southampton 17	281,615	14,822
Wimbledon 14	250,422	13,180
TOTAL	**10,470,973**	**27,555**

BOOKINGS & DISMISSALS

Players Sent Off

	Player	Match	Date	Official
1	FLOWERS	BLACKBURN R. v QPR	19-Aug-95	WILKIE
2	ATKINS	Sheff. Wed. v BLACKBURN R.	23-Aug-95	DANSON
3	BOOGERS	Man. United v WEST HAM	23-Aug-95	GALLAGHER

4	HOLDSWORTH	QPR v WIMBLEDON	23-Aug-95	POLL
5	BROWN	QPR v MANCHESTER CITY	26-Aug-95	DANSON
6	KEANE	Blackburn R. v MAN. UNITED	28-Aug-95	ELLERAY
7	UNSWORTH	EVERTON v Man. United	9-Sep-95	POLL
8	BERG	Liverpool v BLACKBURN R.	16-Sep-95	WILLARD
9	PEMBERTON	LEEDS UNITED v QPR	16-Sep-95	LODGE
10	EDGHILL	Newcastle Utd v MAN. CITY	16-Sep-95	WINTER
11	DICKS	Arsenal v WEST HAM	16-Sep-95	WILKIE
12	TOWNSEND	ASTON VILLA v N. Forest	23-Sep-95	DANSON
13	SPACKMAN	CHELSEA v Arsenal	30-Sep-95	BODENHAM
14	BRIGHTWELL	N. Forest v MAN. CITY	30-Sep-95	REED
15	HIRST	Leeds United v SHEFF. WED.	30-Sep-95	ALLISON
16	SNEEKES	BOLTON W. v Everton	14-Oct-95	ALCOCK
17	HORNE	Bolton W. v EVERTON	14-Oct-95	ALCOCK
18	SINCLAIR	CHELSEA v Man. United	21-Oct-95	WILKIE
19	HEALD	Newcastle U. v WIMBLEDON	21-Oct-95	POLL
20	Le TISSIER	SOUTHAMPTON v Liverpool	22-Oct-95	GALLAGHER
21	KEANE	MAN. UNITED v Middlesbrough	28-Oct-95	LODGE
22	FITZGERALD	Southampton v WIMBLEDON	28-Oct-95	WINTER
23	BARDSLEY	Southampton v QPR	4-Nov-95	DILKES
24	JONES	N. Forest v WIMBLEDON	6-Nov-95	ALCOCK
25	PATTERSON	BOLTON W. v West Ham	18-Nov-95	DURKIN
26	CHETTLE	Blackburn R. v N. FOREST	18-Nov-95	WINTER
27	WILLIAMS	COVENTRY C. v Wimbledon	25-Nov-95	HART
28	SHAW	COVENTRY C. v Wimbledon	25-Nov-95	HART
29	READY	West Ham United v QPR	25-Nov-95	ALCOCK
30	ADAMS	Southampton v ARSENAL	9-Dec-95	DANSON
31	BOULD	ARSENAL v Chelsea	16-Dec-95	·ASHBY
32	BERGSSON	QPR v BOLTON W.	16-Dec-95	LODGE
33	RICHARDSON	Aston Villa v COVENTRY C.	16-Dec-95	ALCOCK
34	WHYTE	Blackburn R. v MIDDLESBRO'	16-Dec-95	DANSON
35	BERESFORD	NEWCASTLE U. v Everton	16-Dec-95	DURKIN
36	HENDRIE	QPR v ASTON VILLA	23-Dec-95	WILKIE
37	JONES	Chelsea v WIMBLEDON	26-Dec-95	GALLAGHER
38	WATSON	EVERTON v Leeds United	30-Dec-95	WINTER
39	HUGHES	Everton v CHELSEA	13-Jan-96	HART
40	CHAPMAN	LEEDS UNITED v West Ham	13-Jan-96	DANSON
41	MOORE	MIDDLESBROUGH v Arsenal	13-Jan-96	POLL
42	EARLE	Bolton W. v WIMBLEDON	13-Jan-96	REED
43	KELLY	Liverpool v LEEDS UNITED	20-Jan-96	DURKIN
44	WHELAN	Southampton v MIDDLESBR'	20-Jan-96	BURGE
45	BUTT	West Ham v MAN. UNITED	22-Jan-96	LODGE
46	DICHIO	Manchester City v QPR	3-Feb-96	POLL
47	FRONTZECK	Everton v MAN. CITY	10-Feb-96	ALCOCK
48	LEE	N. FOREST v Arsenal	10-Feb-96	HART
49	MIKLOSKO	Everton v WEST HAM	11-Mar-96	REED
50	WATSON	Man. City v SOUTHAMPTON	16-Mar-96	WINTER
51	POTTS	Newcastle U. v WEST HAM	18-Mar-96	LODGE

52	LOMAS	West Ham v MAN. CITY	23-Mar-96	COOPER
53	FLITCROFT	BLACKBURN R. v Everton	30-Mar-96	WINTER
54	SUMMERBEE	Bolton W. v MAN. CITY	30-Mar-96	DILKES
55	IMPEY	Coventry City v QPR	13-Apr-96	COOPER
56	BEENEY	Man. United v LEEDS UNITED	17-Apr-96	COOPER
57	McKINLAY	BLACKBURN R. v Arsenal	27-Apr-96	COOPER

Referees by Number of Bookings Issued

Although the number of dismissals and bookings are down on the 1994-95 season,
with fewer games being played the average rate of dismissals and bookings have
increased on last season, rising from 2.8 to a little over 3.11 (see the All-Time
section for a year-by-year summary). Over half of the red cars raised were shown
by just five referees with messrs Danson and Winter notching six apiece, followed
by Lodge and Poll (last years chart topper) on five each. The 1995-96 season was
officiated using 20 referees which is two fewer than the 1994-95 season. The table
below lists referees in order of the average booking rate per game – red cards are
not included in the average.

	Referee	Matches	Yellow	Red	Average
1	LODGE, Stephen	18	76	5	4.22
2	WILKIE, Alan	18	72	4	4.00
3	POLL, Graham	20	78	5	3.90
4	DANSON, Paul	19	74	6	3.89
5	REED, Mike	23	79	3	3.43
6	JONES, Peter	18	61	0	3.39
7	WINTER, J	20	67	6	3.35
8	WILLARD, Gary	17	55	0	3.24
9	ASHBY, Gerald	21	64	1	3.05
10	DURKIN, Paul	24	74	3	3.08
11	DUNN, S	20	60	1	3.00
12	ALCOCK, P	18	54	6	3.00
13	HART, Robert	21	61	4	2.90
14	ELLERAY, David	21	61	1	2.90
15	BURGE, Keith	18	50	1	2.77
16	BODENHAM, Martin	22	57	1	2.59
17	GALLAGHER, Dermot	20	49	3	2.45
18	COOPER, Keith	22	51	4	2,32
19	DILKES, Roger	19	33	2	1.74
20	ALLISON, D	1	4	1	4.00
	TOTAL	380	1180	57	3.11

Disciplinary Record by Club

Club	Matches	Yellow	Red	Average	Psn
Arsenal 38		62	2	1.63	5
Aston Villa 38		46	2	1.21	4
Blackburn Rovers 38		70	4	1.84	7
Bolton Wanderers 38		64	3	1.68	20
Chelsea 38		66	3	1.74	11
Coventry City 38		58	3	1.53	16
Everton 38		67	3	1.76	6
Leeds United... 38		63	4	1.66	13
Liverpool 38		44	0	1.16	3
Manchester City... 38		68	6	1.79	18
Manchester United 38		52	3	1.37	1
Middlesbrough 38		74	3	1.95	12
Newcastle United 38		50	1	1.32	2
Nottingham Forest 38		51	2	1.34	9
QPR 38		76	4	2.00	19
Sheffield Wednesday ... 38		39	1	1.03	15
Southampton... 38		64	1	1.68	17
Tottenham Hotspur... ... 38		57	0	1.50	8
West Ham United 38		53	4	1.40	10
Wimbledon 38		56	7	1.47	14
TOTAL 380		1180	57	1.55	

Dismissals by Club

Club	No	Player(s)
Arsenal	1	Tony Adams, Steve Bould
Aston Villa	1	Andy Townsend, Lee Hendrie
Blackburn Rovers	1	Tim Flowers, Mark Atkins, Henning Berg, Garry Flitcroft, Billy McKinlay
Bolton Wanderers	1	Richard Sneekes, Mark Patterson, Gudni Bergsson
Chelsea	1	Nigel Spackman, Frank Sinclair, Mark Hughes
Coventry City	1	Paul Williams, Richard Shaw, Kevin Richardson
Everton	1	David Unsworth, Barry Horne, Dave Watson
Leeds United	1	John Pemberton, Lee Chapman, Gary Kelly, Mark Beeney
Liverpool		–
Manchester City	1	Michael Brown, Richard Edghill, Ian Brightwell, Michael Frontzeck, Steve Lomas, Nicky Summerbee
Manchester United	2	Roy Keane
	1	Nicky Butt
Middlesbrough	1	Derek Whyte, Alan Moore, Phil Whelan

Newcastle United	1	John Beresford
Nottingham Forest	1	Steve Chettle, Jason Lee
QPR	1	David Bardsley, Karl Ready, Daniele Dichio, Andy Impey
Sheff' Wednesday	1	David Hirst
Southampton	1	Matthew Le Tissier, Gordon Watson
Tottenham Hotspur	–	
West Ham United	1	Marco Boogers, Julian Dicks, Ludek Miklosko, Steve Potts
Wimbledon	2	Vinnie Jones*
	1	Dean Holdsworth, Paul Heald, Scott Fitzgerald, Robbie Earle, Mick Harford

Sent off three times but one reduced to a yellow card on appeal

Referees – Who They Sent Off

Referee	No.	Players
ALCOCK	6	Richard Sneekes, Barry Horne, Vinnie Jones, Karl Ready, Kevin Richardson, Michael Frontzeck
DANSON	6	Mark Atkins, Michael Brown, Andy Townsend, Tony Adams, Derek Whyte, Lee Chapman
WINTER	6	Richard Edghill, Scott Fitzgerald, Steve Chettle, Gordon Watson, Dave Watson, Garry Flitcroft
LODGE	5	John Pemberton, Roy Keane, Gudni Bergsson, Nicky Butt, Steve Potts
POLL	5	Dean Holdsworth, David Unsworth, Paul Heald, Alan Moore, Alan Moore
COOPER	4	Steve Lomas, Andy Impey, Mark Beeney, Billy McKinlay
HART	4	Paul Williams, Richard Shaw, Mark Hughes, Jason Lee
WILKIE	4	Tim Flowers, Julian Dicks, Frank Sinclair, Lee Hendrie
DURKIN	3	Mark Patterson, John Beresford, Gary Kell
GALLAGHER	3	Marco Boogers, Matthew Le Tissier, Vinnie Jones
REED	3	Ian Brightwell, Robbie Earle, Ludek Miklosko
DILKES	2	David Bardsley, Nicky Summerbee
ALLISON	1	David Hirst
ASHBY	1	Steve Bould
BODENHAM	1	Nigel Spackman
BURGE	1	Phil Whelan
ELLERAY	1	Roy Keane
WILLARD	1	Henning Berg

Tottenham and Liverpool headed the Fair Play table with clean sheets on the red card front. Sheffield Wednesday were the best behaved team in respect of bookings averaging fractionally over a booking per game throughout the season.

Both Wimbledon and QPR ended the season facing FA disciplinary action and heavy fines having had suspended sentences placed on them at the end of the 1994-95 season. QPR's booking average of 2 per game was the worse in the Premiership for 1995-96.

Club	Games	Red	Yellow	Ave
Tottenham Hotspur	38	0	57	1.50
Liverpool	38	0	44	1.16
Southampton	38	1	64	1.68
Newcastle United	38	1	50	1.32
Sheffield Wednesday ...	38	1	39	1.03
Arsenal	38	2	62	1.63
Nottingham Forest	38	2	51	1.34
Aston Villa	38	2	46	1.21
Middlesbrough	38	3	74	1.95
Everton	38	3	67	1.76
Chelsea	38	3	66	1.74
Bolton Wanderers	38	3	64	1.68
Coventry City	38	3	58	1.53
Manchester United	38	3	52	1.37
QPR	38	4	76	2.00
Blackburn Rovers	38	4	70	1.84
Leeds United	38	4	63	1.66
West Ham United	38	4	53	1.40
Manchester City	38	6	68	1.79
Wimbledon	38	7	56	1.47

SCORES

8	6-2	Sheffield Wednesday v Leeds United	16/12/95
7	7-0	Blackburn Rovers v Nottingham Forest	18/11/95
	5-2	Liverpool v Bolton Wanderers	23/9/95
	4-3	Sheffield Wednesday v Coventry City	3/12/95
	2-5	Sheffield Wednesday v Everton	27/4/96
	3-4	Southampton v Nottingham Forest	19/8/95
	6-1	Newcastle United v Wimbledon	21/10/95

Biggest Home Wins

7-0	Blackburn Rovers v Nottingham Forest	18/11/95
6-0	Liverpool v Manchester City	28/10/95
6-1	Newcastle United v Wimbledon	21/10/95
6-2	Sheffield Wednesday v Leeds United	16/12/95

Biggest Away Wins

0-6	Bolton Wanderers v Manchester United	25/2/96
2-5	Sheffield Wednesday v Everton	27/4/96
3-4	Southampton v Nottingham Forest	19/8/95

Highest Score Draw

3-3	Manchester City v Newcastle United	24/2/96
3-3	Wimbledon v Newcastle United	3/10/95
3-3	Coventry City v Wimbledon	25/11/95

Score Frequencies

Home Win		Away Win		Draws	
Score	No.	Score	No.	Score	No.
1-0	59	0-1	29	0-0	53
2-0	28	0-2	10	1-1	28
3-0	19	0-3	8	2-2	14
4-0	1	0-4	1	3-3	4
5-0	4	0-6	1		
6-0	1	1-2	14		
7-0	1	1-3	12		
2-1	32	1-4	3		
3-1	14	1-5	1		
4-1	5	1-6			
5-1	1	1-7			
6-1	1	2-3	12		
3-2	7	2-4	3		
4-1	1	2-5	1		
4-2	8	3-4	1		
4-3	2				
5-2	1				
6-2	1				

THE MANAGERS

Length of Tenure

Club		Manager	Arrived
1	Manchester United	Alex Ferguson	November '86
2	Leeds United	Howard Wilkinson	October '88
3	Wimbledon	Joe Kinnear	January '91
4	Newcastle United	Kevin Keegan	February '92
5	Nottingham Forest	Frank Clark	June '93
6	Liverpool	Roy Evans	January '94
7	Middlesbrough	Bryan Robson	May '94
8	West Ham United	Harry Redknapp	August '94
9	Aston Villa	Brian Little	November '94
10	Everton	Joe Royle	November '94
11	Tottenham Hotspur	Gerry Francis	November '94
12	Coventry City	Ron Atkinson	February '95
13	Sunderland	Peter Reid	March '95
14	Arsenal	Bruce Rioch	May '95
15	Blackburn Rovers	Ray Harford	May '95
16	Derby County	Jim Smith	June '95
17	Sheffield Wednesday	David Pleat	July '95
18	Leicester City	Martin O'Neill	Dec '95
19	Chelsea	Ruud Gullit	May '96
20	Southampton	Graeme Souness	July '96

See later in this Annual for full records of all Premiership managers

FA PREMIER LEAGUE ALL-TIME RECORDS

Premiership Titles by Win

3	Manchester United	1992-93, 1993-94, 1995-96
1	Blackburn Rovers	1994-94

Premiership Runners-up by Win

1	Aston Villa	1992-93
1	Blackburn Rovers	1993-94
1	Manchester United	1994-95
1	Newcastle United	1995-96

Championship Records

	Season	Champions	P	W	D	L	F	A	Pts	%
1	1992-93	Manchester United	42	24	12	6	67	31	84	66.67
2	1993-94	Manchester United	42	27	11	4	80	38	92	73.02
3	1994-95	Blackburn Rovers	42	27	8	7	80	39	89	70.63
4	1995-96	Manchester United	38	25	7	6	73	35	82	71.93

All-Time Biggest Home Wins

9-0	Manchester United v Ipswich Town	04/03/95
7-0	Blackburn Rovers v Nottingham Forest	18/11/95
7-1	Aston Villa v Wimbledon	11/02/93
7-1	Blackburn Rovers v Norwich City	02/10/92
7-1	Newcastle United v Swindon Town	12/03/94
6-0	Sheffield United v Tottenham Hotspur	02/03/93
6-0	Liverpool v Manchester City	28/10/95
6-1	Newcastle United v Wimbledon	21/10/95
6-2	Sheffield Wednesday v Leeds United	16/12/95

All-Time Biggest Away Wins

1-7	Sheffield Wednesday v Nottingham Forest	01/04/95
0-6	Bolton Wanderers v Manchester United	25/02/96
1-6	Crystal Palace v Liverpool	20/08/94
0-5	Swindon Town v Liverpool	22/08/93

| 0-5 | Swindon Town v Leeds United | 07/05/94 |
| 2-5 | Sheffield Wednesday v Everton | 27/04/96 |

All-Time Highest Score Draws

4-4	Aston Villa v Leicester City	22/02/95
3-3	Crystal Palace v Blackburn Rovers	15/08/92
	Sheffield Wednesday v Manchester United	26/12/92
	West Ham United v Norwich City	24/01/93
	Swindon Town v Norwich City	19/02/93
	West Ham United v Southampton	07/05/93
	Coventry City v Leeds United	08/05/93
	Middlesbrough v Norwich City	08/05/93
	Oldham Athletic v Coventry City	24/08/93
	Sheffield Wednesday v Norwich City	01/09/93
	Southampton v Sheffield United	02/10/93
	Leeds United v Blackburn Rovers	23/10/93
	Sheffield Wednesday v Leeds United	30/10/93
	Tottenham v Liverpool	18/12/93
	Sheffield Wednesday v Swindon Town	29/12/93
	Liverpool v Manchester United	04/01/94
	Everton v Chelsea	03/05/95
	Manchester City v Nottingham Forest	08/10/94
	Manchester City v Southampton	05/11/94
	Newcastle United v Tottenham Hotspur	03/05/95
	Manchester City v Newcastle United	24/02/96
	Wimbledon v Newcastle United	03/10/95
	Coventry City v Wimbledon	25/11/95

Fastest Goals in a Game

| 13 seconds | Chris Sutton | BLACKBURN ROVERS v Everton | 01/04/94 |
| 17 seconds | John Spencer | CHELSEA v Leicester City | 08/10/94 |

Fastest Hat-trick in a Game

| 4min 33 secs | Robby Fowler | LIVERPOOL v Arsenal | 28/08/94 |

All-Time General Records – Home & Away

Most Goals Scored in a Season	Newcastle United	84	1993-94	42
	Manchester United	73	1995-96	38
Fewest Goals Scored in a Season	Crystal Palace	34	1994-95	42
	Manchester City	33	1995-96	38

Most Goals Conceded in a Season	Swindon Town	100	1993-94	42
	Bolton Wanderers	71	1995-96	38
Fewest Goals Conceded in a Season	Arsenal	28	1993-94	42
	Manchester United	28	1994-95	42
Most Points in a Season	Manchester United	92	1993-94	42
	Manchester United	82	1995-96	38
Fewest Points in a Season	Ipswich Town	27	1994-95	42
Most Wins in a Season	Manchester United	27	1993-94	42
	Blackburn Rovers	27	1994-95	42
Fewest Wins in a Season	Swindon Town	5	1993-94	42
Fewest Defeats in a Season	Manchester United	4	1993-94	42
Most Defeats in a Season	Ipswich Town	29	1994-95	42
	Bolton Wanderers	25	1995-96	38
Most Draws in a Season	Manchester City	18	1993-94	42
	Sheffield United	18	1993-94	42
	Southampton	18	1994-95	42
	Chelsea	14	1995-96	38
	Coventry City	14	1995-96	38

* 38 or 42 refers to the number of games played in that season.

Record Attendances by Club

Club	Att	Opponents	Date
Arsenal	38,377	Tottenham Hotspur	29/04/95
Aston Villa	45,347	Liverpool	07/05/94
Blackburn Rovers	30,895	Liverpool	24/02/95
Bolton Wanderers	21,381	Manchester United	25/02/96
Chelsea	37,064	Manchester United	11/09/93
Coventry City	24,410	Manchester United	12/04/94
Crystal Palace	30,115	Manchester United	21/04/93
Everton	40,127	Aston Villa	05/05/96
Ipswich Town	22,559	Manchester United	01/05/94
Leeds United	41,125	Manchester United	27/04/94
Leicester City	21,393	Liverpool	26/12/94
Liverpool	44,619	Everton	20/03/93
Manchester City	37,136	Manchester United	20/03/93
Manchester Utd	53,926	Nottingham Forest	28/04/96
Middlesbrough	30,011	Newcastle United	10/02/96
Newcastle United	36,589	Tottenham Hotspur	05/05/96
Norwich City	21,843	Liverpool	29/04/95
Nottingham Forest	29,263	Manchester United	27/11/95

Queens Park Rangers	21,267	Manchester United	05/02/94
Sheffield United	30,044	Sheffield Wednesday	23/10/93
Sheffield Wednesday	38,668	Sheffield United	13/03/93
Southampton	19,654	Tottenham Hotspur	15/08/92
Tottenham Hotspur	33,709	Arsenal	12/12/92
West Ham United	28,832	Manchester United	25/02/94
Wimbledon	30,115	Manchester United	08/05/93

Top 10 Attendances

Psn	Att	Match	Date
1	53,926	Manchester United v Nottingham Forest	28/04/96
2	50,332	Manchester United v Coventry City	08/04/95
3	50,157	Manchester United v Tottenham Hotspur	24/03/96
4	50,028	Manchester United v Arsenal	20/03/96
5	48,382	Manchester United v Leeds United	17/04/96
6	45,347	Aston Villa v Liverpool	07/05/94
7	44,751	Manchester United v Liverpool	30/03/94
8	44,750	Manchester United v Everton	22/01/94
9	44,748	Manchester United v Wimbledon	20/11/93
10	44,745	Manchester United v Chelsea	05/02/94

Lowest Attendances by Club

Club	Att	Opponents	Date
Arsenal	18,253	Wimbledon	10/02/92
Aston Villa	16,180	Southampton	24/11/93
Blackburn Rovers	13,505	Sheffield Utd	18/10/93
Chelsea	8,923	Coventry City	04/05/94
Coventry City	9,526	Ipswich Town	10/10/94
Crystal Palace	10,422	Sheffield Wednesday	14/03/95
Everton	13,660	Southampton	04/12/93
Ipswich Town	10,747	Sheffield United	21/08/93
Leeds United	25,774	Wimbledon	15/08/92
Leicester City	15,489	Wimbledon	01/04/95
Liverpool	24,561	QPR	08/12/93
Manchester City	19,150	West Ham United	24/08/85
Manchester United	29,736	Crystal Palace	02/09/92
Middlesbrough	12,290	Oldham Athletic	22/03/93
Newcastle United	32,067	Southampton	22/01/94
Norwich City	12,452	Southampton	05/09/92
Nottingham Forest	17,553	Arsenal	17/10/92
Oldham Athletic	9,633	Wimbledon	28/08/93
Queens Park Rangers	9,875	Swindon Town	30/04/94
Sheffield United	13,646	West Ham Utd	28/03/94

Sheffield Wednesday	18,509	Oldham Athletic	24/11/93
Southampton	9,028	Ipswich Town	08/12/93
Tottenham Hotspur	17,452	Aston Villa	02/03/94
Wimbledon	3,039	Everton	26/01/93

Lowest 10 Attendances

Psn	Att	Match	Date
1	3,039	Wimbledon v Everton	26/01/93
2	3,386	Wimbledon v Oldham Athletic	12/12/92
3	3,759	Wimbledon v Coventry City	22/08/92
4	3,979	Wimbledon v Sheffield United	20/02/93
5	4,534	Wimbledon v Southampton	06/03/93
6	4,714	Wimbledon v Manchester City	01/09/92
7	4,739	Wimbledon v Coventry City	26/12/93
8	4,954	Wimbledon v Ipswich Town	18/08/92
9	5,268	Wimbledon v Manchester City	21/03/95
10	5,536	Wimbledon v Sheffield Wednesday	15/01/94

Top Appearances by Player

Maximum number of games possible is 164.

Player	Total	Start	Sub	Goals
SOUTHALL, Neville	161	161	0	0
FLOWERS, Tim	159	159	0	0
ATHERTON, Peter	155	154	1	1
IRWIN, Dennis	153	153	0	10
LE TISSIER, Matthew	153	153	0	67
DEANE, Brian	151	145	6	42
McALLISTER, Gary	151	151	0	25
SCHMEICHEL, Peter	150	150	0	0
SHERWOOD, Tim	149	148	1	15
BRUCE, Steve	148	148	0	11
RICHARDSON, Kevin	148	147	1	8
FERDINAND, Les	147	146	1	85
SEAMAN, David	147	147	0	0
WILSON, Clive	147	147	0	6
PALLISTER, Gary	146	146	0	5
PEACOCK, Darren	146	142	4	6
PALMER, Carlton	145	144	1	11
RIPLEY, Stuart	144	141	3	11
BEARDSLEY, Peter	143	143	0	52
FOX, Ruel	143	139	4	29
SPEED, Gary	143	142	1	22
BART-WILLIAMS, Chris	142	116	26	17

HUGHES, Mark	142	141	1	43
IMPEY, Andy	142	138	4	11
McGRATH, Paul	142	137	5	6
GIGGS, Ryan	141	131	10	34
DOWIE, Iain	140	138	2	33
SHERINGHAM, Teddy	140	137	3	69
WATSON, Dave	140	139	1	5
BABB, Phil	139	131	8	3
DIXON, Lee	139	138	1	3
HOLDSWORTH, Dean	139	134	5	53
KENNA, Jeff	139	136	3	5
McMANAMAN, Steve	139	134	5	19
SHEARER, Alan	138	132	6	112
WINTERBURN, Nigel	138	138	0	3
BRIGHT, Mark	137	117	20	48
TOWNSEND, Andy	136	135	1	10
BENALI, Francis	135	126	9	0
HENDRY, Colin	135	134	1	6
PEACOCK, Gavin	135	121	14	29

Top Substitute Appearances by Player

Player	Sub	Total	Start	Goals
CLARKE, Andy	50	99	49	10
BARLOW, Stuart	41	62	21	10
WATSON, Gordon	40	94	54	21
ROSENTHAL, Ronny	31	98	67	9
McCLAIR, Brian	30	130	100	18
HYDE, Graham	29	117	88	8
CORK, Alan	28	46	18	5
WALTERS, Mark	28	72	44	11
BANGER, Nicky	26	34	8	8
BART-WILLIAMS, Chris	26	142	116	17
FENTON, Graham	26	46	20	9
LIMPAR, Anders	26	97	71	16
ADAMS, Neil	25	92	67	12
WARHURST, Paul	25	79	54	8
GOODMAN, Jon	24	46	22	10
LEE, Jason	24	50	26	11
RADOSAVIJEVIC, Pedray	24	46	22	4
SPENCER, John	24	99	75	36
THOMAS, Michael	24	65	41	2
ATKINS, Mark	22	84	62	12
GUENTCHEV, Bontcho	22	61	39	6
STUART, Graham	22	126	104	24

BLISSETT, Gary	21	31	10	3
HEANEY, Neil	21	65	44	4
KANCHELSKIS, Andrei	21	120	99	39
MATHIE, Alex	21	37	16	6
SCHOLES, Paul	21	43	22	15
BRIGHT, Mark	20	137	117	48
BURLEY, Craig	20	73	53	5
FURLONG, Paul	20	64	44	13
PENRICE, Gary	20	62	42	17
QUINN, Niall	20	120	100	30
RIDEOUT, Paul	20	102	82	29
SUTCH, Daryl	20	55	35	3
WHELAN, Noel	20	69	49	15

Top Goalscorers by Player

Player	Goals	Total	Start	Sub
SHEARER, Alan	112	138	132	6
FERDINAND, Les	85	147	146	1
WRIGHT, Ian	71	132	130	2
SHERINGHAM, Teddy	69	140	137	3
LE TISSIER, Matthew	67	153	153	0
COLE, Andy	66	110	107	3
FOWLER, Robbie	65	108	105	3
CANTONA, Eric	59	120	118	2
HOLDSWORTH, Dean	53	139	134	5
BEARDSLEY, Peter	52	143	143	0
COTTEE, Tony	51	132	125	7
BRIGHT, Mark	48	137	117	20
SUTTON, Chris	48	132	122	10
RUSH, Ian	45	130	118	12
HUGHES, Mark	43	142	141	1
DEANE, Brian	42	151	145	6
KANCHELSKIS, Andrei	39	120	99	21
SAUNDERS, Dean	39	118	117	1
ARMSTRONG, Chris	38	111	111	0
COLLYMORE, Stan	37	69	66	3
SPENCER, John	36	99	75	24
GIGGS, Ryan	34	141	131	10
NDLOVU, Peter	34	134	122	12
DOWIE, Iain	33	140	138	2
EKOKU, Efan	31	92	78	14
QUINN, Niall	30	120	100	20
DUBLIN, Dion	29	77	69	8
FOX, Ruel	29	143	139	4

PEACOCK, Gavin	29	135	121	14
RIDEOUT, Paul	29	102	82	20
WALLACE, Rod	29	125	107	18
HIRST, David	28	74	70	4
YORKE, Dwight	28	111	92	19
BARMBY, Nicky	27	119	113	6
EARLE, Robbie	27	130	130	0
MORRIS, Chris	27	48	44	4
WHITE, David	26	100	86	14
CAMPBELL, Kevin	25	118	100	18
McALLISTER, Gary	25	151	151	0
OLNEY, Ian	25	44	42	2
QUINN, Mick	25	64	57	7

All-Time Player Most Goals in One Game

Gls	Player	Match	Date	Res
5	Andy COLE	MAN UNITED v Ipswich Town	04/03/95	9-0
4	Efan EKOKU	Everton v NORWICH CITY	25/09/93	1-5

Player: Consecutive Games with Goals

7	Mark Stein, Chelsea		1993-94		
	Dec 27	Southampton	Away	1-3	Stein
	Dec 28	Newcastle United	Home	1-0	Stein
	Jan 1	Swindon Town	Away	3-0	Stein
	Jan 3	Everton	Home	4-2	Stein x 2 (1pen)
	Jan 15	Norwich City	Away	1-1	Stein
	Jan 22	Aston Villa	Home	1-1	Stein
	Feb 5	Everton	Away	2-4	Stein x 2 (1 pen)

(Stein actually scored 9 goals – inc. two penalties – in this sequence)

Player: Most Hat-tricks in a Season

5	Alan Shearer, Blackburn Rovers	1995-96

Crime Count – Year-by-Year

Season	Games	Red Cards	Ave	Yellow Cards	Avg
1992-93	462	34	0.077	760	1.65
1993-94	462	25	0.054	599	1.30
1994-95	462	65	0.140	1294	2.80
1995-96	380	57	0.150	1180	3.11
Total	*1766*	*181*	*0.102*	*3833*	*2.17*

Final Table 1992-93 Season

		P	W	D	L	F	A	Pts	
1	Manchester United	42	24	12	6	67	31	84	
2	Aston Villa	42	21	11	10	57	40	74	
3	Norwich City	42	21	9	12	61	65	72	
4	Blackburn Rovers	42	20	11	11	68	46	71	
5	QPR	42	17	12	13	63	55	63	
6	Liverpool	42	16	11	15	62	55	59	
7	Sheffield Wednesday	42	15	14	13	55	51	59	
8	Tottenham Hotspur	42	16	11	15	60	66	59	
9	Manchester City	42	15	12	15	56	51	57	
10	Arsenal	42	15	11	16	40	38	56	
11	Chelsea	42	14	14	14	51	54	56	
12	Wimbledon	42	14	12	16	56	55	54	
13	Everton	42	15	8	19	53	55	53	
14	Sheffield United	42	14	10	18	54	53	52	
15	Coventry City	42	13	13	16	52	57	52	
16	Ipswich Town	42	12	16	14	50	55	52	
17	Leeds United	42	12	15	15	57	62	51	
18	Southampton	42	13	11	18	54	61	50	
19	Oldham Athletic	42	13	10	19	63	74	49	R
20	Crystal Palace	42	11	16	15	48	61	49	R
21	Middlesbrough	42	11	11	20	54	75	44	R
22	Nottingham Forest	42	10	10	22	41	62	40	R

Promoted:
Newcastle United – Champions
West Ham United – Runners-up
Swindon Town – Play-off Winners

Final Table 1993-94 Season

		P	W	D	L	F	A	Pts	
1	Manchester United	42	27	11	4	80	38	92	
2	Blackburn Rovers	42	25	9	8	63	36	84	
3	Newcastle United	42	23	8	11	82	41	77	
4	Arsenal	42	18	17	7	53	28	71	
5	Leeds United	42	18	16	8	65	39	70	
6	Wimbledon	42	18	11	13	56	53	65	
7	Sheffield Wednesday	42	16	16	10	76	54	64	
8	Liverpool	42	17	9	16	59	55	60	
9	QPR	42	16	12	14	62	61	60	
10	Aston Villa	42	15	12	15	46	50	57	
11	Coventry City	42	14	14	14	43	45	56	
12	Norwich City	42	12	17	13	65	61	53	
13	West Ham United	42	13	13	16	47	58	52	
14	Chelsea	42	13	12	17	49	53	51	
15	Tottenham Hotspur	42	11	12	19	54	59	45	
16	Manchester City	42	9	18	15	38	49	45	
17	Everton	42	12	8	22	42	63	44	
18	Southampton	42	12	7	23	49	66	43	
19	Ipswich Town	42	9	16	17	35	58	43	R
20	Sheffield United	42	8	18	16	42	60	42	R
21	Oldham Athletic	42	9	13	20	42	68	40	R
22	Swindon Town	42	5	15	22	47	100	30	R

Promoted:
Crystal Palace – Champions
Nottingham Forest – Runners-up
Leicester City – Play-off Winners

		P	W	D	L	F	A	Pts	
1	Blackburn Rovers....	42	27	8	7	80	39	89	
2	Manchester United ...	42	26	10	6	77	28	88	
3	Nottingham Forest ...	42	22	11	9	72	43	77	
4	Liverpool	42	21	11	10	65	37	74	
5	Leeds United	42	20	13	9	59	38	73	
6	Newcastle United ...	42	20	12	10	67	47	72	
7	Tottenham Hotspur ..	42	16	14	12	66	58	62	
8	Queens Park Rangers	42	17	9	16	61	59	60	
9	Wimbledon..........	42	15	11	16	48	65	56	
10	Southampton........	42	12	18	12	61	63	54	
11	Chelsea	42	13	15	14	50	55	54	
12	Arsenal	42	13	13	17	52	49	51	
13	Sheffield Wednesday	42	13	12	17	49	57	51	
14	West Ham United....	42	13	11	18	44	48	50	
15	Everton	42	11	17	14	44	51	50	
16	Coventry City	42	12	14	16	44	62	50	
17	Manchester City	42	12	13	17	53	64	49	
18	Aston Villa........	42	11	15	16	51	56	48	
19	Crystal Palace	42	11	12	19	34	49	45	R
20	Norwich City	42	10	13	19	37	54	43	R
21	Leicester City	42	6	11	25	45	80	29	R
22	Ipswich Town	42	7	6	29	36	93	27	R

Promoted:
Middlesbrough – Champions
Bolton Wanderers – Play-off Winners

Last Day Championships

The FA Premier League Championship has twice gone to the last day of the season to be decided.

1994-95

	P	W	D	L	F	A	Pts	GD
Blackburn Rovers	41	27	8	6	79	37	89	+42
Manchester United	41	26	9	6	76	27	87	+48

On the last day of the season Blackburn travelled to Liverpool needing a win to ensure the title. Manchester United went to Upton Park needing three points from West Ham and hoping that Rovers would fail to win. A last minute goal gave Liverpool a 2-1 win over Blackburn, but despite a succession of missed chances Manchester United could only draw and the title went to Blackburn Rovers.

1995-96

	P	W	D	L	F	A	Pts	GD
Manchester United	41	24	7	10	70	35	79	+35
Newcastle United	41	24	5	8	65	36	77	+29

At one point Newcastle lead the table by 12 points but a string of last minute reversals and a relentless attack by the Red Devils allowed them to peg the Magpies back. On the final day of the season the United of Manchester travelled to the North-East to play Middlesbrough needing a point to take the title. Newcastle entertained Spurs at home and need to win and look a few miles south for a result. The United of Manchester prevailed through winning 3-0 at the Riverside as Newcastle drew 1-1 with Spurs.

FA CHALLENGE CUP

1995-96 Sponsored by Littlewoods

Note: Dates given are for official date of round – games may have taken place on different dates. † = after extra time.

Third Round – 6 January 1996

Arsenal	v	Sheffield United	1-1	33,453
Barnsley	v	Oldham Athletic	0-0	9,751
Birmingham City	v	Wolverhampton Wanderers	1-1	21,349
Bradford City	v	Bolton Wanderers	0-3	10,265
Charlton Athletic	v	Sheffield Wednesday	2-0	13,815
Chelsea	v	Newcastle United	1-1	25,151
Crewe Alexandra	v	West Bromwich Albion	4-3	5,750
Crystal Palace	v	Port Vale	0-0	10,456
Derby County	v	Leeds United	2-4	16,155
Everton	v	Stockport County	2-2	28,921
Fulham	v	Shrewsbury Town	1-1	7,265
Gravesend & Northfleet	v	Aston Villa	0-3	26,321
		(at Aston Villa)		
Grimsby Town	v	Luton Town	7-1	5,387
Hereford United	v	Tottenham Hotspur	1-1	8,806
Huddersfield Town	v	Blackpool	2-1	12,424
Ipswich Town	v	Blackburn Rovers	0-0	22,146
Leicester City	v	Manchester City	0-0	20,640
Liverpool	v	Rochdale	7-0	28,126
Manchester United	v	Sunderland	2-2	41,563
Millwall	v	Oxford United	3-3	7,564
Norwich City	v	Brentford	1-2	10,082
Notts County	v	Middlesbrough	1-2	12,621
Peterborough United	v	Wrexham	1-0	5,983
Plymouth Argyle	v	Coventry City	1-3	17,721
Reading	v	Gillingham	3-1	10,324
Southampton	v	Portsmouth	3-0	15,236
Stoke City	v	Nottingham Forest	1-1	17,947
Swindon Town	v	Woking	2-0	10,322
Tranmere Rovers	v	Queens Park Rangers	0-2	10,230
Walsall	v	Wigan Athletic	1-0	5,626
Watford	v	Wimbledon	1-1	11,187
West Ham United	v	Southend United	2-0	23,284

Third Round Replays

Blackburn Rovers	v	Ipswich Town	0-1 †	19,606
Manchester City	v	Leicester City	5-0	19,980
Newcastle United	v	Chelsea	2-2 †	36,535
		(Chelsea won 4-2 on penalties)		
Nottingham Forest	v	Stoke City	2-0	17,372
Oldham Athletic	v	Barnsley	2-1	6,670
Oxford United	v	Millwall	1-0	8,035
Port Vale	v	Crystal Palace	4-3 †	6,754
Sheffield United	v	Arsenal	1-0	22,255
Shrewsbury Town	v	Fulham	2-1	7,983
Stockport County	v	Everton	2-3	11,283
Sunderland	v	Manchester United	1-2	21,378
Tottenham Hotspur	v	Hereford United	5-1	31,534
Wimbledon	v	Watford	1-0	5,142
Wolverhampton Wand'	v	Birmingham City	2-1	28,088

Fourth Round – 27 January 1996

Bolton Wanderers	v	Leeds United	0-1	16,694
Charlton Athletic	v	Brentford	3-2	15,000
Coventry City	v	Manchester City	2-2	18,709
Everton	v	Port Vale	2-2	33,168
Huddersfield Town	v	Peterborough United	2-0	11,629
Ipswich Town	v	Walsall	1-0	18,489
Middlesbrough	v	Wimbledon	0-0	28,915
Nottingham Forest	v	Oxford United	1-1	15,050
Queens Park Rangers	v	Chelsea	1-2	18,542
Reading	v	Manchester United	0-3	14,780
Sheffield United	v	Aston Villa	0-1	18???
Shrewsbury Town	v	Liverpool	0-4	7,752
Southampton	v	Crewe Alexandra	1-1	13,736
Swindon Town	v	Oldham Athletic	1-0	???
Tottenham Hotspur	v	Wolverhampton Wanderers	1-1	32,812
West Ham United	v	Grimsby Town	1-1	22,020

Fourth Round Replays

Crewe Alexandra	v	Southampton	2-3	5,579
Grimsby Town	v	West Ham United	3-0	8,382
Manchester City	v	Coventry City		
Oxford United	v	Nottingham Forest	0-3	8,022
Port Vale	v	Everton	2-1	19,197
Wimbledon	v	Middlesbrough	1-0	5,220
Wolverhampton Wand'	v	Tottenham Hotspur		

Fifth Round – 17 February 1996

Grimsby Town	v	Chelsea	0-0	9,448
Huddersfield Town	v	Wimbledon	2-2	17,307
Ipswich Town	v	Aston Villa	1-3	20,748
Leeds United	v	Port Vale	0-0	18,607
Liverpool	v	Charlton Athletic	2-1	36,818
Manchester United	v	Manchester City	2-1	42,692
Nottingham Forest	v	Tottenham Hotspur	2-2	18,600
Swindon Town	v	Southampton	1-1	15,035

Fifth Round Replays

Chelsea	v	Grimsby Town	4-1	28,545
Port Vale	v	Leeds United	1-2	14,023
Southampton	v	Swindon Town	2-0	13,962
Wimbledon	v	Huddersfield Town	3-1	7,015

Sixth Round – 9 March 1996

Chelsea	v	Wimbledon	2-2	30,805
Leeds United	v	Liverpool	0-0	24,632
Manchester United	v	Southampton	2-0	45,446
Nottingham Forest	v	Aston Villa	0-1	21,067

Sixth Round Replays

Liverpool	v	Leeds United	3-0	30,812
Wimbledon	v	Chelsea	1-3	21,380

Semi Finals – 31 March 1996

Aston Villa	v	Liverpool	0-3	39,072

(Old Trafford, Manchester)

Chelsea	v	Manchester United	1-2	38,421

(Villa Park, Birmingham)

Final – 11 May 1996 at Wembley Stadium

Liverpool	v	Manchester United	0-1	79,007
		Cantona (85)		

Liverpool: James, McAteer, Scales, Wright, Babb, Jones (Thomas 85), McManaman, Redknapp, Barnes, Collymore (Rush 74), Fowler. Sub not used: Warner (gk). Booked: Redknapp, Babb.

Manchester United: Schmeichel, Irwin, May, Pallister, P.Neville, Beckham (G.Neville 89), Butt, Keane, Giggs, Cantona, Cole (Scholes 83). Sub not used: Sharpe.

Referee: Mr DJ Gallagher (Banbury)

FA CHALLENGE CUP
FINALS 1872-1996

Year	Winners	Runners-up	Score
1872	The Wanderers	Royal Engineers	1-0
1873	The Wanderers	Oxford University	2-0
1874	Oxford University	Royal Engineers	2-0
1875	Royal Engineers	Old Etonians	1-1
	Royal Engineers	Old Etonians	2-0
1876	The Wanderers	Old Etonians	1-1 †
	The Wanderers	Old Etonians	3-0
1877	The Wanderers	Oxford University	2-1 †
1878	The Wanderers*	Royal Engineers	3-1
1879	Old Etonians	Clapham Rovers	1-0
1880	Clapham Rovers	Oxford University	1-0
1881	Old Carthusians	Old Etonians	3-0
1882	Old Etonians	Blackburn Rovers	1-0
1883	Blackburn Olympic	Old Etonians	2-1 †
1884	Blackburn Rovers	Queen's Park, Glasgow	2-1
1885	Blackburn Rovers	Queen's Park, Glasgow	2-0
1886	Blackburn Rovers**	West Bromwich Albion	0-0
	Blackburn Rovers**	West Bromwich Albion	2-0
1887	Aston Villa	West Bromwich Albion	2-0
1888	West Bromwich Albion	Preston North End	2-1
1889	Preston North End	Wolverhampton Wanderers	3-0
1890	Blackburn Rovers	Sheffield Wednesday	6-1
1891	Blackburn Rovers	Notts County	3-1
1892	West Bromwich Albion	Aston Villa	3-0
1893	Wolverhampton Wanderers	Everton	1-0
1894	Notts County	Bolton Wanderers	4-1
1895	Aston Villa	West Bromwich Albion	1-0
1896	Sheffield Wednesday	Wolverhampton Wanderers	2-1
1897	Aston Villa	Everton	3-2
1898	Nottingham Forest	Derby County	3-1
1899	Sheffield United	Derby County	4-1
1900	Bury	Southampton	4-0
1901	Tottenham Hotspur	Sheffield United	2-2
	Tottenham Hotspur	Sheffield United	3-1
1902	Sheffield United	Southampton	1-1
	Sheffield United	Southampton	2-1
1903	Bury	Derby County	6-0
1904	Manchester City	Bolton Wanderers	1-0

Year	Winners	Runners-up	Score
1905	Aston Villa	Newcastle United	2-0
1906	Everton	Newcastle United	1-0
1907	Sheffield Wednesday	Everton	2-1
1908	Wolverhampton Wanderers	Newcastle United	3-1
1909	Manchester United	Bristol City	1-0
1910	Newcastle United	Barnsley	1-1
	Newcastle United	Barnsley	2-0
1911	Bradford City	Newcastle United	0-0
	Bradford City	Newcastle United	1-0
1912	Barnsley	West Bromwich Albion	0-0 †
	Barnsley	West Bromwich Albion	1-0
1913	Aston Villa	Sunderland	1-0
1914	Burnley	Liverpool	1-0
1915	Sheffield United	Chelsea	3-0
1920	Aston Villa	Huddersfield Town	1-0 †
1921	Tottenham Hotspur	Wolverhampton Wanderers	1-0
1922	Huddersfield Town	Preston North End	1-0
1923	Bolton Wanderers	West Ham United	2-0
1924	Newcastle United	Aston Villa	2-0
1925	Sheffield United	Cardiff City	1-0
1926	Bolton Wanderers	Manchester City	1-0
1927	Cardiff City	Arsenal	1-0
1928	Blackburn Rovers	Huddersfield Town	3-1
1929	Bolton Wanderers	Portsmouth	2-0
1930	Arsenal	Huddersfield Town	2-0
1931	West Bromwich Albion	Birmingham	2-1
1932	Newcastle United	Arsenal	2-1
1933	Everton	Manchester City	3-0
1934	Manchester City	Portsmouth	2-1
1935	Sheffield Wednesday	West Bromwich Albion	4-2
1936	Arsenal	Sheffield United	1-0
1937	Sunderland	Preston North End	3-1
1938	Preston North End	Huddersfield Town	1-0 †
1939	Portsmouth	Wolverhampton Wanderers	4-1
1946	Derby County	Charlton Athletic	4-1 †
1947	Charlton Athletic	Burnley	1-0 †
1948	Manchester United	Blackpool	4-2
1949	Wolverhampton Wanderers	Leicester City	3-1
1950	Arsenal	Liverpool	2-0
1951	Newcastle United	Blackpool	2-0
1952	Newcastle United	Arsenal	1-0
1953	Blackpool	Bolton Wanderers	4-3
1954	West Bromwich Albion	Preston North End	3-2
1955	Newcastle United	Manchester City	3-1

Year	Winners	Runners-up	Score	
1956	Manchester City	Birmingham City	3-1	
1957	Aston Villa	Manchester United	2-1	
1958	Bolton Wanderers	Manchester United	2-0	
1959	Nottingham Forest	Luton Town	2-1	
1960	Wolverhampton Wanderers	Blackburn Rovers	3-0	
1961	Tottenham Hotspur	Leicester City	2-0	
1962	Tottenham Hotspur	Burnley	3-1	
1963	Manchester United	Leicester City	3-1	
1964	West Ham United	Preston North End	3-2	
1965	Liverpool	Leeds United	2-1	†
1966	Everton	Sheffield Wednesday	3-2	
1967	Tottenham Hotspur	Chelsea	2-1	
1968	West Bromwich Albion	Everton	1-0	†
1969	Manchester City	Leicester City	1-0	
1970	Chelsea	Leeds United	2-2	†
	Chelsea	Leeds United	2-1	†
1971	Arsenal	Liverpool	2-1	†
1972	Leeds United	Arsenal	1-0	
1973	Sunderland	Leeds United	1-0	
1974	Liverpool	Newcastle United	3-0	
1975	West Ham United	Fulham	2-0	
1976	Southampton	Manchester United	1-0	
1977	Manchester United	Liverpool	2-1	
1978	Ipswich Town	Arsenal	1-0	
1979	Arsenal	Manchester United	3-2	
1980	West Ham United	Arsenal	1-0	
1981	Tottenham Hotspur	Manchester City	1-1	†
	Tottenham Hotspur	Manchester City	3-2	
1982	Tottenham Hotspur	Queens Park Rangers	1-1	†
	Tottenham Hotspur	Queens Park Rangers	1-0	
1983	Manchester United	Brighton & Hove Albion	2-2	
	Manchester United	Brighton & Hove Albion	4-0	
1984	Everton	Watford	2-0	
1985	Manchester United	Everton	1-0	†
1986	Liverpool	Everton	3-1	
1987	Coventry City	Tottenham Hotspur	3-2	†
1988	Wimbledon	Liverpool	1-0	
1989	Liverpool	Everton	3-2	†
1990	Manchester United	Crystal Palace	3-3	†
	Manchester United	Crystal Palace	1-0	
1991	Tottenham Hotspur	Nottingham Forest	2-1	†
1992	Liverpool	Sunderland	2-0	
1993	Arsenal	Sheffield Wednesday	1-1	†
	Arsenal	Sheffield Wednesday	2-1	†

Year	Winners	Runners-up	Score
1994	Manchester United	Chelsea	4-0
1995	Everton	Manchester United	1-0
1996	Manchester United	Liverpool	1-0

Final Venues

1872	Kennington Oval
1873	Lillie Bridge
1874-92	Kennington Oval
1893	Fallowfield, Manchester
1894	Everton
1895-1914	Crystal Palace
1915	Old Trafford
1920-22	Stamford Bridge
1923 –1996	Wembley

Replay Venues

1886	Derby
1901	Bolton
1910	Everton
1911	Old Trafford
1912	Bramall Lane
1970	Old Trafford
1981	Wembley
1982	Wembley
1983	Wembley
1990	Wembley
1993	Wembley

* *Trophy won outright by The Wanderers, but restored to the FA.*

** *Special trophy awarded for a third consecutive win.*

† *after extra time.*

FA CHALLENGE CUP WINS BY CLUB

Manchester United (9)	1909, 1948, 1963, 1977, 1983, 1985, 1990, 1994, 1996
Tottenham Hotspur (8)	1901, 1921, 1961, 1962, 1967, 1981, 1982, 1991
Aston Villa (7)	1887, 1895, 1897, 1905, 1913, 1920, 1957
Arsenal (6)	1930, 1936, 1950, 1971, 1979, 1993
Blackburn Rovers (6)	1884, 1885, 1886, 1890, 1891, 1928
Newcastle United (6)	1910, 1924, 1932, 1951, 1952, 1955
Everton (5)	1894, 1906, 1933, 1966, 1995
Liverpool (5)	1965, 1974, 1986, 1989, 1992
The Wanderers (5)	1872, 1873, 1876, 1877, 1878
West Bromwich Albion (5)	1888, 1892, 1931, 1954, 1968
Bolton Wanderers (4)	1923, 1926, 1929, 1958
Manchester City (4)	1904, 1934, 1956, 1969
Sheffield United (4)	1899, 1902, 1915, 1925
Wolverhampton Wdrs (4)	1893, 1908, 1949, 1960
Sheffield Wednesday (3)	1896, 1907, 1935
West Ham United (3)	1964, 1975, 1980
Bury (2)	1900, 1903
Nottingham Forest (2)	1898, 1959
Old Etonians (2)	1879, 1882
Preston North End (2)	1889, 1938
Sunderland (2)	1937, 1973

Club	Year	Club	Year
Barnsley	1912	Ipswich Town	1978
Blackburn Olympic	1883	Leeds United	1972
Blackpool	1953	Notts County	1894
Bradford City	1911	Old Carthusians	1881
Burnley	1914	Oxford University	1874
Cardiff City	1927	Portsmouth	1939
Charlton Athletic	1947	Royal Engineers	1875
Chelsea	1970	Southampton	1976
Clapham Rovers	1880	Wimbledon	1988
Coventry City	1987		
Derby County	1946		
Huddersfield Town	1922		

FA CHARITY SHIELD
WINNERS 1908-95

1908	Manchester United v Queens Park Rangers	4-0
	after 1-1 draw	
1909	Newcastle United v Northampton Town	2-0
1910	Brighton & Hove Albion v Aston Villa	1-0
1911	Manchester United v Swindon Town	8-4
1912	Blackburn Rovers v Queens Park Rangers	2-1
1913	Professionals v Amateurs	7-2
1919	West Bromwich Albion v Tottenham Hotspur	2-0
1920	Tottenham Hotspur v Burnley	2-0
1921	Huddersfield Town v Liverpool	1-0
1922	Not Played	
1923	Professionals v Amateurs	2-0
1924	Professionals v Amateurs	3-1
1925	Amateurs v Professionals	6-1
1926	Amateurs v Professionals	6-3
1927	Cardiff City v Corinthians	2-1
1928	Everton v Blackburn Rovers	2-1
1929	Professionals v Amateurs	3-0
1930	Arsenal v Sheffield Wednesday	2-1
1931	Arsenal v West Bromwich Albion	1-0
1932	Everton v Newcastle United	5-3
1933	Arsenal v Everton	3-0
1934	Arsenal v Manchester City	4-0
1935	Sheffield Wednesday v Arsenal	1-0
1936	Sunderland v Arsenal	2-1
1937	Manchester City v Sunderland	2-0
1938	Arsenal v Preston North End	2-1
1948	Arsenal v Manchester United	4-3
1949	Portsmouth v Wolverhampton Wanderers	* 1-1
1950	World Cup Team v Canadian Touring Team	4-2
1951	Tottenham Hotspur v Newcastle United	2-1
1952	Manchester United v Newcastle United	4-2
1953	Arsenal v Blackpool	* 3-1
1954	Wolverhampton Wanderers v West Bromwich Albion	* 4-4
1955	Chelsea v Newcastle United	3-0
1956	Manchester United v Manchester City	1-0

1957	Manchester United v Aston Villa	4-0
1958	Bolton Wanderers v Wolverhampton Wanderers	4-1
1959	Wolverhampton Wanderers v Nottingham Forest	3-1
1960	Burnley v Wolverhampton Wanderers	* 2-2
1961	Tottenham Hotspur v FA XI	3-2
1962	Tottenham Hotspur v Ipswich Town	5-1
1963	Everton v Manchester United	4-0
1964	Liverpool v West Ham United	* 2-2
1965	Manchester United v Liverpool	* 2-2
1966	Liverpool v Everton	1-0
1967	Manchester United v Tottenham Hotspur	* 3-3
1968	Manchester City v West Bromwich Albion	6-1
1969	Leeds United v Manchester City	2-1
1970	Everton v Chelsea	2-1
1971	Leicester City v Liverpool	1-0
1972	Manchester City v Aston Villa	1-0
1973	Burnley v Manchester City	1-0
1974	Liverpool v Leeds United	1-1
	Liverpool won on penalties	
1975	Derby County v West Ham United	2-0
1976	Liverpool v Southampton	1-0
1977	Liverpool v Manchester United	* 0-0
1978	Nottingham Forest v Ipswich Town	5-0
1979	Liverpool v Arsenal	3-1
1980	Liverpool v West Ham United	1-0
1981	Aston Villa v Tottenham Hotspur	* 2-2
1982	Liverpool v Tottenham Hotspur	1-0
1983	Manchester United v Liverpool	2-0
1984	Everton v Liverpool	1-0
1985	Everton v Manchester United	2-0
1986	Everton v Liverpool	* 1-1
1987	Everton v Coventry City	1-0
1988	Liverpool v Wimbledon	2-1
1989	Liverpool v Arsenal	1-0
1990	Liverpool v Manchester United	* 1-1
1991	Arsenal v Tottenham Hotspur	* 0-0
1992	Leeds United v Liverpool	4-3
1993	Manchester United v Arsenal	1-1
	Manchester United won on penalties	
1994	Manchester United v Blackburn Rovers	2-0
1995	Everton v Blackburn Rovers	1-0
1996	Manchester United v Newcastle United	

* Each club retained Shield for six months

FOOTBALL LEAGUE
COCA-COLA CUP 95-96

Second Round

			1st	2nd	Agg
Aston Villa	v	Peterborough United	6-0	1-1	7-1
Birmingham City	v	Grimsby Town	3-1	1-1	4-2
Bolton Wanderers	v	Brentford	1-0	3-2	4-2
Bradford City	v	Nottingham Forest	3-2	2-2	5-4
Bristol City	v	Newcastle United	0-5	1-3	1-8
Bristol Rovers	v	West Ham United	0-1	0-3	0-4
Coventry City	v	Hull City	2-0	1-0	3-0
Cardiff City	v	Southampton	0-3	1-2	1-5
Crewe Alexandra	v	Sheffield Wednesday	2-2	2-5	4-7
Hartlepool United	v	Arsenal	0-3	0-5	0-8
Huddersfield Town	v	Barnsley	2-0	0-4	2-4
Leeds United	v	Notts County	0-0	3-2	3-2
Leicester City	v	Burnley	2-0	2-0	4-0
Liverpool	v	Sunderland	2-0	1-0	3-0
Manchester United	v	York City	0-3	3-1	3-4
Middlesbrough	v	Rotherham United	2-1	1-0	3-1
Millwall	v	Everton	0-0	4-2	4-2
Norwich City	v	Torquay United	6-1	3-2	9-3
Oxford United	v	QPR	1-1	1-2	2-3
Reading	v	WBA	1-1	4-2	5-3
Sheffield United	v	Bury	2-1	2-4	4-5
Shrewsbury Town	v	Derby County	1-3	1-1	2-4
Southend United	v	Crystal Palace	2-2	0-2	2-4
Stockport County	v	Ipswich Town	1-1	2-1	3-2
Stoke City	v	Chelsea	0-0	1-0	1-0
Swindon Town	v	Blackburn Rovers	2-3	0-2	2-5
Tottenham Hotspur	v	Chester City	4-0	3-1	7-1
Tranmere Rovers	v	Oldham Athletic	1-0	3-1	4-1
Watford	v	Bournemouth	1-1	1-1	2-2
		After extra time. Watford win 6-5 on penalties.			
Wimbledon	v	Charlton Athletic	4-5	3-3	7-8
Wolverhampton W.	v	Fulham	2-0	5-1	7-1
Wycombe Wanderers	v	Manchester City	0-0	0-4	0-4

Third Round

Aston Villa	v	Stockport County	2-0	17,679
Barnsley	v	Arsenal	0-3	18,429
Birmingham City	v	Tranmere Rovers	1-1	13,429

Bolton Wanderers	v	Leicester City	0-0	9,166
Coventry City	v	Tottenham Hotspur	3-2	18,227
Crystal Palace	v	Middlesbrough	2-2	11,873
Derby County	v	Leeds United	0-1	16,030
Liverpool	v	Manchester City	4-0	29,394
Millwall	v	Sheffield Wednesday	0-2	12,882
Norwich City	v	Bradford City	0-0	11,649
QPR	v	York City	3-1	12,972
Reading	v	Bury	2-1	10,329

First match abandoned after 25 mins due to rain with Bury leading 2-0

Southampton	v	West Ham United	2-1	11,059
Stoke City	v	Newcastle United	0-4	23,000
Watford	v	Blackburn Rovers	1-2	17,035
Wolverhampton W.	v	Charlton Athletic	0-0	22,481

Third Round Replays

Bradford City	v	Norwich City	3-5	8,665	
Charlton Athletic	v	Wolverhampton W.	1-2	10,909	aet
Leicester City	v	Bolton Wanderers	2-3	14,884	
Middlesbrough	v	Crystal Palace	2-0	16,150	
Tranmere Rovers	v	Birmingham City	1-3	9,151	

Fourth Round

Arsenal	v	Sheffield Wednesday	2-1	35,361
Aston Villa	v	QPR	1-0	24,951
Leeds United	v	Blackburn Rovers	2-1	26,006
Liverpool	v	Newcastle United	0-1	40,077
Birmingham City	v	Birmingham City	0-0	28,031
Norwich City	v	Bolton Wanderers	0-0	13,820
Reading	v	Southampton	2-1	13,742
Wolverhampton W.	v	Coventry City	2-1	24,628

Fourth Round Replays

Birmingham City	v	Birmingham City	2-0	19,878
Bolton Wanderers	v	Norwich City	0-0	8,736

(After extra time. Norwich win 3-2 on penalties)

Fifth Round

Arsenal	v	Newcastle United	2-0	37,857
Aston Villa	v	Wolverhampton W.	1-0	39,277
Leeds United	v	Reading	2-1	21,023
Norwich City	v	Birmingham City	1-1	13,028

Fifth Round Replays
Birmingham City   v   Norwich City   2-1   21,097

Semi-Finals First Leg
Arsenal   v   Aston Villa   2-2
Birmingham City   v   Leeds United   1-2   24,781

Semi-Finals Second Leg
Aston Villa   v   Arsenal   0-0   39,334
(After extra time. 2-2 on aggregate. Aston Villa win on away goals)
Leeds United   v   Birmingham City   3-0   35,435
(Leeds United win 5-1 on aggregate)

Final – 24 March 1996 at Wembley Stadium
Aston Villa   v   Leeds United   3-0   77,056
Milosevic (20), Taylor (54),
Yorke (89)
Aston Villa: Bosnich, Southgate, McGrath, Ehiogu, Charles, Wright, Townsend, Taylor, Draper, Yorke, Milosevic. Subs not used: Staunton, Johnson, Oakes. Booked: McGrath, Southgate.
Leeds United: Lukic, Kelly, Radebe (Brolin 65), Palmer, Pemberton, Wetherall, Gray, Ford (Deane 46), McAllister, Speed, Yeboah. Sub not used: Worthington. Booked: Wetherall, Ford.
Ref: R. Hart (Darlington)

† *after extra time*

FOOTBALL LEAGUE CUP FINALS 1961-1996

Year	Winners	Runners-up	1st	2nd	Agg
1961	Aston Villa	Rotherham United	0-2†	3-0	3-2
1962	Norwich City	Rochdale	3-0	1-0	4-0
1963	Birmingham City	Aston Villa	3-1	0-0	3-1
1964	Leicester City	Stoke City	1-1	3-2	4-3
1965	Chelsea	Leicester City	3-2	0-0	3-2
1966	West Bromwich Albion	West Ham United	1-2	4-1	5-3
1967	Queens Park Rangers	West Bromwich Albion	3-2		
1968	Leeds United	Arsenal	1-0		
1969	Swindon Town	Arsenal	† 3-1		
1970	Manchester City	West Bromwich Albion	2-1		
1971	Tottenham Hotspur	Aston Villa	† 2-0		
1972	Stoke City	Chelsea	2-1		
1973	Tottenham Hotspur	Norwich City	1-0		
1974	Wolverhampton W	Manchester City	2-1		
1975	Aston Villa	Norwich City	1-0		
1976	Manchester City	Newcastle United	2-1		
1977	Aston Villa	Everton	† 3-2		
	after 0-0 draw and 1-1 draw aet				
1978	Nottingham Forest	Liverpool	1-0		
	after 0-0 draw aet				
1979	Nottingham Forest	Southampton	3-2		
1980	Wolverhampton W	Nottingham Forest	1-0		
1981	Liverpool	West Ham United	2-1		
	after 1-1 draw aet				

Milk Cup

1982	Liverpool	Tottenham Hotspur	† 3-1		
1983	Liverpool	Manchester United	† 2-1		
1984	Liverpool	Everton	1-0		
	after 0-0 draw aet				
1985	Norwich City	Sunderland	1-0		
1986	Oxford United	Queens Park Rangers	3-0		

Littlewoods Cup

1987	Arsenal	Liverpool	2-1
1988	Luton Town	Arsenal	3-2
1989	Nottingham Forest	Luton Town	3-1
1990	Nottingham Forest	Oldham Athletic	1-0

Rumbelows League Cup

| 1991 | Sheffield Wednesday | Manchester United | 1-0 |
| 1992 | Manchester United | Nottingham Forest | 1-0 |

Coca–Cola Cup

1993	Arsenal	Sheffield Wednesday	2-1
1994	Aston Villa	Manchester United	3-1
1995	Liverpool	Bolton Wanderers	2-1
1996	Aston Villa	Leeds United	3-0

FOOTBALL LEAGUE CUP WINS BY CLUB

Aston Villa (5)	1961, 1975, 1977, 1994, 1996
Liverpool (5)	1981, 1982, 1983, 1984, 1995
Nottingham Forest (4)	1978, 1979, 1989, 1990
Arsenal (2)	1987, 1993
Manchester City (2)	1970, 1976
Tottenham Hotspur (2)	1971, 1973
Norwich City (2)	1962, 1985
Wolverhampton Wders (2)	1974, 1980
Birmingham City	1963
Leicester City	1964
Chelsea	1965
WBA	1966
QPR	1967
Leeds United	1968
Swindon Town	1969
Stoke City	1972
Oxford United	1986
Luton Town	1988
Sheffield Wednesday	1991
Manchester United	1992

FWA FOOTBALLER OF
THE YEAR WINNERS

Season	Winner	Club
1947-48	Stanley Matthews	Blackpool & England
1948-49	Johnny Carey	Manchester United & Rep of Ireland
1949-50	Joe Mercer	Arsenal & England
1950-51	Harry Johnston	Blackpool & England
1951-52	Billy Wright	Wolverhampton Wanderers & England
1952-53	Nat Lofthouse	Bolton Wanderers & England
1953-54	Tom Finney	Preston North End & England
1954-55	Don Revie	Manchester City & England
1955-56	Bert Trautmann	Manchester City
1956-57	Tom Finney	Preston North End & England
1957-58	Danny Blanchflower	Tottenham Hotspur & Northern Ireland
1958-59	Syd Owen	Luton Town & England
1959-60	Bill Slater	Wolverhampton Wanderers & England
1960-61	Danny Blanchflower	Tottenham Hotspur & Northern Ireland
1961-62	Jimmy Adamson	Burnley
1962-63	Stanley Matthews	Stoke City & England
1963-64	Bobby Moore	West Ham United & England
1964-65	Bobby Collins	Leeds United & Scotland
1965-66	Bobby Charlton	Manchester United & England
1966-67	Jack Charlton	Leeds United & England
1967-68	George Best	Manchester United & Northern Ireland
1968-69	Dave Mackay	Derby County & Scotland
	Tony Book	Manchester City
1969-70	Billy Bremner	Leeds United & Scotland
1970-71	Frank McLintock	Arsenal & Scotland
1971-72	Gordon Banks	Stoke City & England
1972-73	Pat Jennings	Tottenham Hotspur & Northern Ireland
1973-74	Ian Callaghan	Liverpool & England
1974-75	Alan Mullery	Fulham & England
1975-76	Kevin Keegan	Liverpool & England
1976-77	Emlyn Hughes	Liverpool & England
1977-78	Kenny Burns	Nottingham Forest & Scotland
1978-79	Kenny Dalglish	Liverpool & Scotland
1979-80	Terry McDermott	Liverpool & England
1980-81	Frans Thijssen	Ipswich Town & Holland
1981-82	Steve Perryman	Tottenham Hotspur & England
1982-83	Kenny Dalglish	Liverpool & Scotland
1983-84	Ian Rush	Liverpool & Wales
1984-85	Neville Southall	Everton & Wales
1985-86	Gary Lineker	Everton & England
1986-87	Clive Allen	Tottenham Hotspur & England

1987-88	John Barnes	Liverpool & England
1988-89	Steve Nicol	Liverpool & England
1989-90	John Barnes	Liverpool & England
1990-91	Gordon Strachan	Leeds United & Scotland
1991-92	Gary Lineker	Tottenham Hotspur & England
1992-93	Chris Waddle	Sheffield Wednesday & England
1993-94	Alan Shearer	Blackburn Rovers & England
1994-95	Jurgen Klinsmann	Tottenham Hotspur & Germany
1995-96	Eric Cantona	Manchester United & France

PFA AWARDS 1995-96

Player of the Year
Les Ferdinand   Newcastle United

Young Player of the Year
Robbie Fowler   Liverpool

Premiership Team
Goalkeeper	David James	Liverpool
Defenders	Gary Neville	Manchester United
	Tony Adams	Arsenal
	Ugo Ehiogu	Aston Villa
	Alan Wright	Aston Villa
Midfield	Robert Lee	Newcastle United
	Steve Stone	Nottingham Forest
	Ruud Gullit	Chelsea
Forwards	Davide Ginola	Newcastle United
	Alan Shearer	Blackburn Rovers
	Les Ferdinand	Newcastle United

ENGLAND 1995-96

Wembley, September 6th 1995 – Green Flag Friendly International

ENGLAND **COLOMBIA** **0-0 20,038**

Shearer (33, 40)

England: Seaman, G. Neville, Howey, Adams (capt), Le Saux, Wise, Redknapp (Barnes 75), Gascoigne (Lee 75), McManaman, Barmby, Shearer (Sheringham 75). Subs not used: Flowers (gk), Ruddock.
Second lowest attendance at Wembley for a full international.

Oslo, October 11th 1995 – Friendly International

NORWAY **ENGLAND** **0-0 21,006**

England: Seaman, G.Neville, Pearce, Redknapp, Adams (capt), Pallister, Barmby (Sheringham 68), Lee, Shearer, McManaman, Wise (Stone 68). Subs not used: Walker, Bould, Jones.

Wembley, November 16th 1995 – Green Flag Friendly International

ENGLAND **SWITZERLAND** **3-1 29,874**

OG (Quentin 45); Knup (41) HT: 1-1
Sheringham (56); Stone (78)

England: Seaman, G. Neville, Pallister, Adams (capt), Pearce, Lee, Redknapp (Stone 5), Gascoigne, McManaman, Sheringham, Shearer. Subs not used: Howey, Flowers (gk), Beardsley, Ferdinand.

Wembley, December 12th 1995 – Green Flag Friendly International

ENGLAND **PORTUGAL** **1-1 28,592**

Stone (44) Alves (58) HT: 1-0

England: Seaman, G. Neville, Adams (capt), Howey, Pearce (Le Saux 79), Gascoigne, Stone, Wise (McManaman 79), Barmby (Southgate 79), Shearer, Ferdinand (Beardsley 65). Subs not used: Flowers (gk).

Wembley, March 28th 1996 – Green Flag Friendly International

ENGLAND **BULGARIA** **1-0 29,708**

Ferdinand (7) HT: 1-0

England: Seaman, G. Neville, Southgate, Howey, Pearce (capt), Stone, Ince, Gascoigne (Platt 76), McManaman, Sheringham (Lee 76), Ferdinand (Fowler 76). Subs not used: Wright, Walker (gk).

Wembley, April 24th 1996 – Green Flag Friendly International

ENGLAND **CROATIA** **0-0 33,650**

England: Seaman, G. Neville, Wright, Pearce (capt), Ince, Stone, Gascoigne, Platt, McManaman, Sheringham, Fowler. Subs not used: Flowers (gk), Campbell, Ehiogu, Wise, Collymore.

79

Wembley, May 18th 1996 – Green Flag Friendly International

ENGLAND   HUNGARY   3-0   34,184

Anderton (39, 62); Platt (52)

England: Seaman (Walker 65), G. Neville, Wright (Southgate 11), Pearce, Ince (Campbell 65), Anderton, Lee, Platt (capt)(Wise 65), Wilcox, Sheringham, Ferdinand (Shearer 76). Subs not used: Beardsley, Barmby.

Workers Stadium, Beijing, May 23rd 1996

CHINA   ENGLAND   0-3   65,000

Barmby (30, 53); Gascoigne (64)

England. Flowers (Walker 65), G. Neville, Adams (capt) (Ehiogu 76), Southgate, P. Neville, Anderton, Redknapp, Gascoigne, McManaman (Stone 80), Barmby (Beardsley 72), Shearer (Fowler 72).

Wembley, June 8th 1996 – Euro96 – Group A Match

ENGLAND   SWITZERLAND   1-1   76,567

Shearer (23)   Turkyilmaz (83 pen)

England: Seaman, G. Neville, Adams(capt), Southgate, Pearce, Ince, McManaman, Gascoigne (Platt 75), Anderton (Stone 68), Sheringham (Barmby 68), Shearer. Subs not used: Flowers (gk), Campbell, Redknapp, Howey, Ferdinand, Fowler, P.Neville, Walker (gk).

Wembley, June 15th 1996 – Euro96 – Group A Match

ENGLAND   SCOTLAND   2-0   76,864

Shearer (53), Gascoigne (79)

England: Seaman, G. Neville, Adams (capt), Southgate, Pearce (Redknapp 45, Campbell 85), Ince (Stone 77), McManaman, Gascoigne, Anderton, Sheringham (Barmby 68), Shearer. Subs not used: Flowers (gk), Platt, Ferdinand, Fowler, P.Neville, Walker (gk). Howey injured.

Wembley, June 18th 1996 – Euro96 – Group A Match

ENGLAND   HOLLAND   4-1   76,798

Shearer (23 pen, 57)   Kluivert (78)
Sheringham (51, 62)

England: Seaman, G. Neville, Adams (capt), Southgate, Pearce, Ince (Platt 67), McManaman, Gascoigne, Anderton, Sheringham (Fowler 75), Shearer (Barmby 75). Subs not used: Flowers (gk), Campbell, Ferdinand, P.Neville, Stone, Walker (gk). Redknapp and Howey injured.

Wembley, June 23rd 1996 – Euro96 – Quarter Final

ENGLAND   SPAIN   0-0   75,440

England: Seaman, G. Neville, Adams (capt), Southgate, Pearce, Platt, McManaman (Barmby 108), Gascoigne, Anderton (Fowler 108), Sheringham (Stone 108), Shearer. Subs not used: Flowers (gk), Campbell, Ferdinand, P.Neville, Walker (gk). Ince suspended. Redknapp and Howey injured.

After extra time. England won 4-2 on penalties.

ENGLAND   GERMANY   1-1 75,862
Shearer (3)   Kuntz (16)

England: Seaman, Southgate, Adams (capt), Pearce, Ince, Platt,
McManaman, Gascoigne, Anderton, Sheringham, Shearer. Subs not used:
Flowers (gk), Campbell, Ferdinand, P.Neville, Barmby, Fowler, Stone,
Walker (gk). G. Neville suspended. Redknapp and Howey injured.
After extra time. Germany won 6-5 on penalties.

England Record 1995-96

P	W	D	L	F	A
13	6	7	0	19	5

Goalscorer Summary 1995-96

	Player	Goals
Alan	SHEARER	6 (1pen)
Teddy	SHERINGHAM	3
Darren	ANDERTON	2
Nick	BARMBY	2
Steve	STONE	2
Les	FERDINAND	1
David	PLATT	1
Paul	GASCOIGNE	1
	OWN GOALS	1

Post-War England Manager Records

Manager	Tenure	P	W	D	L	F	A
Terry Venables	01/94-6/96	23	11	11	1	35	13
Graham Taylor	08/90-11/93	38	18	13	7		
Bobby Robson	08/82-07/90	95	47	30	18	158	60
Ron Greenwood	08/77-07/82	55	33	13	10	93	40
Don Revie	10/74-07/77	29	14	8	7	49	25
Joe Mercer	04/74-10/74	7	3	3	1	9	7
Sir Alf Ramsey	01/63-03/74	110	67	26	17	224	98
Sir Walter Winterbottom	08/46-12/62	139	78	33	28	383	196
Venables Breakdown	Home	21	10	10	1	32	13
	Away	2	1	1	0	3	0

Euro96 games v Scotland, Holland, Spain and Germany officially listed as away
matches by UEFA, but listed as home by FA. Does not include abandoned match in
Dublin, although caps were awarded to players.

1995-96 APPEARANCE CHART

	Colombia	Norway	Switzerland	Portugal	Bulgaria	Croatia	Hungary	China	Switzerland	Scotland	Holland	Spain	Germany
ADAMS	*	*	*	*	–	–	–	*+	*	*	*	*	*
ANDERTON	–	–	–	–	–	–	*	*	*†	*	*	*+	*
BARMBY	*	*†	–	*+	–	–	–	*‡	68†	68‡	75$	108+	–
BARNES	75†	–	–	–	–	–	–	–	–	–	–	–	–
BEARDSLEY	–	–	–	65†	–	–	–	72‡	–	–	–	–	–
BOULD	–	–	–	–	–	–	–	–	–	–	–	–	–
CAMPBELL	–	–	–	–	–	–	65/	–	–	85/	–	–	–
COLLYMORE	–	–	–	–	–	–	–	–	–	–	–	–	–
EHIOGU	–	–	–	–	–	–	–	76+	–	–	–	–	–
FERDINAND	–	–	–	*†	*†	–	*+	–	–	–	–	–	–
FLOWERS	–	–	–	–	–	–	–	*†	–	–	–	–	–
FOWLER	–	–	–	–	76†	*	–	72/	–	–	75$	108$	–
GASCOIGNE	*†	–	*	*	*+	*	–	*	*‡	*	*	*	*
HOWEY	*	–	–	*	*	–	–	–	–	–	–	–	–
INCE	–	–	–	*	*	*	*/	–	*	*+	*†	–	*
JONES	–	–	–	–	–	–	–	–	–	–	–	–	–
LE SAUX	*	–	–	79‡	–	–	–	–	–	–	–	–	–
LEE	75†	*	*	–	76‡	–	*	–	–	–	–	–	–
McMANAMAN	*	*	*	79+	*	*	–	*$	*	*	*	*‡	*
NEVILLE, G.	*	*	*	*	*	*	*	*	*	*	*	*	–
NEVILLE, P.	–	–	–	–	–	–	–	*	–	–	–	–	–
PALLISTER	–	*	*	–	–	–	–	–	–	–	–	–	–
PEARCE	–	*	*	*‡	*	*	*	–	*	*†	*	*	*
PLATT	–	–	–	–	76+	*	*$	–	75‡	–	67†	–	–
REDKNAPP	*+	*	*†	–	–	–	–	*	–	45†/	–	–	–
RUDDOCK	–	–	–	–	–	–	–	–	–	–	–	–	–
SEAMAN	*	*	*	*	*	*	*†	–	*	*	*	*	*
SHEARER	*	*	*	*	–	–	76+	*/	*	*	*‡	*	*
SHERINGHAM	–	68†	*	–	*‡	*	*	–	*/	*‡	*$	*$	*
SOUTHGATE	–	–	–	79$	*	–	11‡	*	*	*	*	*	*
STONE	–	68+	5†	*	*	*	–	80$	68/	77+	–	108‡	
WALKER	–	–	–	–	–	65†	65†	–	–	–	–	–	–
WILCOX	–	–	–	–	–	–	*	–	–	–	–	–	–
WISE	*	*+	–	*$	–	–	65$	–	–	–	–	–	–

• Started match. – No appearance. A number indicates an appearance as substitute, the number relating the minute the player entered the match.

	Player	Club	Tot	St	Sub	SNU	PS
Tony	ADAMS	Arsenal	10	10	0	0	1
Darren	ANDERTON	Tottenham	7	7	0	1	2
Nick	BARMBY	Middlesbrough	8	4	4	2	3
John	BARNES	Liverpool	1	0	1	0	0
Peter	BEARDSLEY	Newcastle Utd	2	0	2	2	0
Steve	BOULD	Arsenal	0	0	0	1	0
Sol	CAMPBELL	Tottenham	2	0	2	5	0
Stan	COLLYMORE	Liverpool	0	0	0	1	0
Ugo	EHIOGU	Aston Villa	1	0	1	1	0
Les	FERDINAND	Newcastle Utd	3	3	0	6	3
Tim	FLOWERS	Blackburn Rvrs	1	1	0	9	1
Robbie	FOWLER	Liverpool	5	1	4	3	0
Paul	GASCOIGNE	Rangers	11	11	0	0	3
Steve	HOWEY	Newcastle Utd	3	3	0	2	0
Paul	INCE	Internazionale	7	7	0	0	3
Rob	JONES	Liverpool	0	0	0	1	0
Graeme	LE SAUX	Blackburn Rvrs	2	1	1	0	0
Robert	LEE	Newcastle United	5	3	2	0	0
Steve	McMANAMAN	Liverpool	12	11	1	0	2
Gary	NEVILLE	Manchester Utd	12	12	0	0	0
Phil	NEVILLE	Manchester Utd	1	1	0	5	0
Gary	PALLISTER	Manchester Utd	2	2	0	0	0
Stuart	PEARCE	N. Forest	11	11	0	0	3
David	PLATT	Arsenal	7	4	3	1	2
Jamie	REDKNAPP	Liverpool	5	4	1	1	3
Neil	RUDDOCK	Liverpool	0	0	0	1	0
David	SEAMAN	Arsenal	12	12	0	0	0
Alan	SHEARER	Blackburn Rvrs	11	10	1	0	2
Teddy	SHERINGHAM	Tottenham	10	9	1	1	5
Darren	SOUTHGATE	Aston Villa	9	7	2	0	0
Steve	STONE	N. Forest	9	3	6	2	0
Ian	WALKER	Tottenham	2	0	2	7	0
Jason	WILCOX	Blackburn	1	1	0	0	0
Denis	WISE	Chelsea	4	3	1	1	2
Mark	WRIGHT	Liverpool	2	2	0	1	1

EURO '96

Group A

Final Table

	P	W	D	L	F	A	Pts
England	3	2	1	0	7	2	7
Holland	3	1	1	1	3	4	4
Scotland	3	1	1	1	2	4	4
Switzerland	3	0	1	2	1	4	1

England v Switzerland 1-1
Holland v Scotland 0-0
England v Scotland 2-0
Holland v Switzerland 2-0
England v Holland 4-1
Scotland v Switzerland 1-0

Group B

Final Table

	P	W	D	L	F	A	Pts
France	3	2	1	0	5	2	7
Spain	3	1	2	0	4	3	5
Bulgaria	3	1	1	1	3	4	4
Romania	3	0	0	3	1	4	0

Spain v Bulgaria 1-1
Romania v France 0-1
Bulgaria v Romania 1-0
France v Spain 1-1
France v Bulgaria 3-1
Romania v Spain... 1-2

Group C

Final Table

	P	W	D	L	F	A	Pts
Germany	3	2	1	0	5	0	7
Czech Rep.	3	1	1	1	5	6	4
Italy	3	1	1	1	3	3	4
Russia	3	0	1	2	4	8	1

Germany v Czech Republic ... 2-0
Italy v Russia 2-1
Czech Republic v Italy 2-1
Russia v Germany 0-3
Russia v Czech Republic 3-3
Italy v Germany 0-0

Group D

Final Table

	P	W	D	L	F	A	Pts
Portugal	3	2	1	0	5	1	7
Croatia	3	2	0	1	4	3	6
Denmark	3	1	1	1	4	4	4
Portugal	3	0	0	3	0	5	0

Denmark v Portugal... 1-1
Turkey v Croatia 0-1
Portugal v Turkey 1-0
Croatia v Denmark 3-0
Croatia v Portugal 0-3
Turkey v Denmark 0-3

Quarter Finals

England	v	Spain	0-0	75,440	aet 4-2 on pens
France	v	Holland	0-0	37,465	aet 5-4 on pens
Germany	v	Croatia	2-1	43,412	
Portugal	v	Czech Republic	0-1	26,832	

Semi Finals

England	v	Germany	1-1	75,862	aet 5-6 on pens
France	v	Czech Republic	0-0	43,877	aet 5-6 on pens

Final

Germany	v	Czech Republic	2-1	73,611	golden goal win

CLUB DIRECTORY
1996-97

Arsenal

Formed as Dial Square, a workshop in Woolwich Arsenal with a sundial over the entrance, in October 1886, becoming Royal Arsenal, the 'Royal' possibly from a local public house, later the same year. Turned professional and became Woolwich Arsenal in 1891. Selected for an expanded Football League Division Two in 1893, the first southern team to join.

Moved from the Manor Ground, Plumstead south-east London, to Highbury, north London, in 1913 changing name again at the same time. Elected from fifth in Division Two to the expanded First Division for the 1919-20 season and never relegated. Premier League founder members 1992.

Ground: Arsenal Stadium, Highbury, London N5 1BU
Phone Club: 0171-704-4000   **Match Info:** 0171-704-4242
Box Office: 0171-704-4040   **News:** 0891 20 20 20
Capacity: 39,497   **Pitch size:** 110 yds x 71 yds
Colours: Red/White sleeves, White, Red   **Nickname:** Gunners

Chairman: P.D. Hill-Wood   **Vice-Chairman:** David Dein
MD/Secretary: Ken Friar
Manager: Bruce Rioch   **Assistant/Coach:** Stuart Houston
Physio: Gary Lewin MCSP SRP

League History: 1893 Elected to Division 2; 1904-13 Division 1; 1913-19 Division 2; 1919-92 Division 1; 1992-93 – FA Premier League.

Honours: *Football League: Division 1 – Champions:* 1930-31, 1932-33, 1933-34, 1934-35, 1937-38, 1947-48, 1952-53, 1970-71, 1988-89, 1990-91; *Runners-up:* 1925-26, 1931-32, 1972-73; *Division 2 – Runners-up:* 1903-04. *FA Cup: Winners:* 1929-30, 1935-36, 1949-50, 1970-71, 1978-79, 1992-93; *Runners-up:* 1926-27, 1931-32, 1951-52, 1971-72, 1977-78, 1979-80. *Football League Cup: Winners:* 1986-87, 1992-93; *Runners-up:* 1967-68, 1968-69, 1987-88. *League-Cup Double Performed:* 1970-71. *Cup-Cup Double Performed:* 1992-93; *Cup-Winners' Cup Winners:* 1993-94 (winners), *Runners-up:* 1979-80, 1994-95; *Fairs Cup Winners:* 1969-70. *European Super Cup Runners-up:* 1994-95.

European Record: Champions' Cup (2): 71-72 (QF), 91-92 (2); Cup-Winners' Cup (3): 79-80 (F), 93-94 (W), 94-95 (F); UEFA Cup (6): 63-64 (2), 69-70 (W), 71-70 (Q), 78-79 (3), 81-82 (2), 82-83 (1)

Managers: Sam Hollis 1894-97; Tom Mitchell 1897-98; George Elcoat 1898-99; Harry Bradshaw 1899-1904; Phil Kelso 1904-08; George Morrell

1908-15; Leslie Knighton 1919-25; Herbert Chapman 1925-34; George Allison 1934-47; Tom Whittaker 1947-56; Jack Crayston 1956-58; George Swindin 1958-62; Billy Wright 1962-66; Bertie Mee 1966-76; Terry Neill 1976-83; Don Howe 1984-86; *(FAPL)* George Graham May 1986-Feb 1995; Stewart Houston (caretaker) Feb-1995-May 1995; Bruce Rioch May 1995–

Season 1995-96

Biggest Home Win:	4-2 v Southampton, 23/9/95; Sheff. Wed, 21/11/95
Biggest Home Defeat:	1-3 v Wimbledon, 30/19/95
Biggest Away Win:	3-0 v Leeds Utd, 14/10/95 and Wimbledon, 16/3/96
Biggest Away Defeat:	1-3 v Liverpool 23/1/95
Biggest Home Att:	38,317 v Manchester United, 4/11/95
Smallest Home Att:	34,519 v Manchester City, 5/3/96
Average Attendance:	37,568 (3rd highest)
Leading Scorers:	15 – Ian Wright. 11– Dennis Bergkamp

Last Season: *FAPL:* 5 (UEFA) *FA Cup:* 3 *Coca-Cola Cup:* SF

All-Time Records

Record FAPL Win:	5-1 v Ipswich Town, 5/02/94 & Norwich City 1/4/95
Record FAPL Defeat:	0-3 v Leeds Utd, 21/11/92; Coventry City 14/8/93; Liverpool 28/8/94; Man. United 22/3/95
Record FL Win:	12-0 v Loughborough Town, Division 2, 12/3/1900
Record FL Defeat:	0-8 v Loughborough Town, Division 2, 12/12/1896
Record Cup Win:	11-1 v Darwen, FA Cup R3, 9/1/32
Record Fee Received:	£2m David Rocastle, Leeds United, 7/92
Record Fee Paid:	£7.5m Dennis Bergkamp, Internazionale, 6/95
Most FL Apps:	547 – David O'Leary, 1975-92
Most FAPL Apps:	147 – David Seaman
Most FAPL Goals:	71 – Ian Wright

Highest Scorer in FAPL Season: Ian Wright, 30, 1992-93
Record Attendance (all-time): 73,295 v Sunderland, Division 1, 9/3/35
Record Attendance (FAPL): 38,377 v Tottenham Hotspur 29/4/95
Most FAPL Goals in Season: 53, 1993-94 – 42 games
Most FAPL Points in Season: 71, 1993-94 – 42 games

5-Year Record

	Div.	P	W	D	L	F	A	Pts	Pos	FAC	FLC
91-92	1	42	19	15	8	81	46	72	4	3	3
92-93	PL	42	15	11	16	40	38	56	10	W	W
93-94	PL	42	18	17	7	53	28	71	4	4	4
94-95	PL	42	13	12	17	52	49	51	12	3	5
95-96	PL	38	17	12	9	49	32	63	5	3	SF

Summary 1995-96

Player	Tot	St	Sb	Snu	PS	Gls	Y	R	Fa	La	Fg	Lg
ADAMS	21	21	0	0	0	1	4	1	2	5	0	2
BARTRAM	0	0	0	15	0	0	0	0	0	0	0	0
BERGKAMP	33	33	0	0	1	11	5	0	1	7	0	5
BOULD	19	19	0	0	2	0	7	1	0	5	0	1
CLARKE	6	4	2	2	2	0	0	0	2	0	0	0
DICKOV	7	1	6	3	0	1	0	0	0	0	0	0
DIXON	38	38	0	0	1	2	2	0	2	7	0	0
HARTSON	19	15	4	10	4	4	3	0	1	3	0	1
HELDER	24	15	9	5	5	1	0	0	2	6	0	0
HILLIER	5	3	2	7	1	0	0	0	0	2	0	0
HUGHES	1	0	1	4	0	0	0	0	0	1	0	0
JENSEN	15	13	2	8	4	0	4	0	2	6	0	0
KEOWN	34	34	0	0	3	0	6	0	2	5	0	1
LINIGHAN	18	17	1	4	1	0	0	0	1	2	0	0
MARSHALL	11	10	1	2	1	1	4	0	0	0	0	0
McGOLDRICK	1	0	1	0	0	0	0	0	0	0	0	0
McGOWAN	1	1	0	0	0	0	0	0	1	0	0	0
MERSON	38	38	0	0	2	5	2	0	2	7	0	0
MORROW	4	3	1	5	2	0	0	0	0	1	0	0
PARLOUR	22	20	2	0	6	0	7	0	0	4	0	0
PLATT	29	27	2	0	0	6	3	0	1	3	0	0
ROSE	4	1	3	7	0	0	0	0	0	0	0	0
SEAMAN	38	38	0	0	0	0	0	0	2	7	0	0
SHAW	3	0	3	2	0	0	0	0	0	0	0	0
WINTERBURN	36	36	0	0	1	2	6	0	1	7	0	0
WRIGHT	31	31	0	0	4	15	8	0	2	7	1	7

Passing Times

After a turbulent and fruitless final season under the successful but ultimately controversial leadership of George Graham, Arsenal made a return to the higher echelons of the Premier League during Bruce Rioch's first year at the helm. Although the Gunners were never serious title contenders, they reclaimed the mantle of London's top club with victory over Bolton Wanderers on the final day of the season – a win that clinched sixth position and a UEFA Cup place.

Rioch's major task has been to remodel the direct style of Graham into a more attractive passing game. The re-structuring of the team didn't always go down well with all players and for a while there was even serious talk of perennial top scorer Ian Wright leaving the club following a late transfer request.

Three draws and a win at Goodison Park signalled a solid if unspectacular start to the season while a run of five wins in six games took the Gunners to third place towards the end of September but a 1-0 defeat at relegation bound Bolton heralded the beginning of a six match winless away run. Arsenal's home form remained good during this spell with eventual champions Manchester United going down 1-0 at Highbury. Long time leaders Newcastle United were twice defeated 2-0 in north London, the first occasion being a stormy Coca Cola Cup tie. Indeed as Arsenal's league form slipped during December and January it was the Coca Cola Cup which kept the Gunners' season alive. Endsleigh League sides Hartlepool and Barnsley were dismissed without troubling England's number one 'keeper David Seaman while Premiership rivals Sheffield Wednesday and Newcastle both succumbed at Highbury. The victory over Newcastle came four days after an embarrassing home draw with Sheffield United in the FA Cup 3rd Round and in mid January the Yorkshire club saw off their more illustrious opponents in the replay.

Arsenal's hopes of reaching their fifth cup final in four seasons looked bright in the first leg as Dennis Bergkamp struck twice to give them an early lead in their Coca-Cola Cup semi final against Aston Villa. But surprising defensive lapses allowed the Midlanders to draw level and they eventually went through on the away goals rule after a scoreless second leg.

Although cup success proved to be beyond Rioch first time round the supporters relished the new style and the new signings and 15 of the Gunners 18 home Premiership matches attracted gates of between 37,000 and 39,000.

Arsenal's bold preseason £7.5m signing of Bergkamp took time to reap rewards with his first goal not arriving until the clubs seventh game of the season. The Dutch master went on to score 11 times in the Premiership and with Ian Wright (15 league goals) formed a formidable partnership.

Another plus point for the Gunners was Paul Merson who emerged from his personal nightmare as a self-confessed alcoholic and drug addict with flying colours. But the season was not without its problems. For much of it Arsenal had to do without their centre-backs Adams and Bould, yet they still maintained the best defensive record in the Premiership. England skipper David Platt also missed a large part of the year following two knee operations and never really had a chance to show the Highbury faithful what he can do.

Rioch has openly stated his intent to buy at least three more international class players and, should they arrive, it would be a major surprise if the Gunners were not to mount a title and cup challenge in 1996-97. ∎

Results 1995-96

FA Carling Premiership

Date	Opponents	Ven	Res	Pos	Atten	Scorers
20-Aug	Middlesbro'	H	1-1	–	37,308	Wright (36)
23-Aug	Everton	A	2-0	–	35,775	Platt (69); Wright (86)
26-Aug	Coventry C.	A	0-0	7	20,065	
29-Aug	N. Forest	H	1-1	7	38,248	Platt (41)
10-Sep	Man. City	A	1-0	6	23,994	Wright (90)
16-Sep	West Ham	H	1-0	5	38,065	Wright (75 pen)
23-Sep	Southampton	H	4-2	5	38,136	Bergkamp (17, 68); Adams (23); Wright (73)
30-Sep	Chelsea	A	0-1	6	31,048	
14-Oct	Leeds United	A	3-0	3	38,552	Merson (43); Bergkamp (56); Wright (86)
21-Oct	Aston Villa	H	2-0	3	38,271	Merson (47); Wright (78)
30-Oct	Bolton Wan.	A	0-1	4	18,682	
04-Nov	Man. United	H	1-0	3	38,317	Bergkamp (14)
18-Nov	Tottenham	A	1-2	3	32,894	Bergkamp (14)
21-Nov	Sheff. Wed.	H	4-2	3	34,556	Bergkamp (3); Winterburn (53); Dickov (64); Hartson (86)
26-Nov	Blackburn R.	H	0-0	3	37,695	
02-Dec	Aston Villa	A	1-1	3	37,770	Platt (60)
09-Dec	Southampton	A	0-0	3	15,238	
16-Dec	Chelsea	H	1-1	5	38,295	Dixon (88)
23-Dec	Liverpool	A	1-3	7	39,806	Wright (8 pen)
26-Dec	QPR	H	3-0	5	38,259	Wright (44); Merson (81, 83)
30-Dec	Wimbledon	H	1-3	6	37,640	Wright (27)
02-Jan	Newcastle U.	A	0-2	5	26,530	
13-Jan	Middlesbro'	A	3-2	5	29,359	Merson (6); Platt (59); Helder (62)
20-Jan	Everton	H	1-2	7	38,275	Wright (38)
03-Feb	Coventry C.	H	1-1	8	35,623	Bergkamp (24)
10-Feb	N. Forest	A	1-0	5	27,222	Bergkamp (59)
24-Feb	West Ham	A	1-0	6	24,217	Hartson (1)
02-Mar	QPR	A	1-1	7	17,970	Bergkamp (50)
05-Mar	Man. City	H	3-1	5	34,519	Hartson (29, 55); Dixon (41)
16-Mar	Wimbledon	A	3-0	5	18,335	Winterburn (61); Platt (65); Bergkamp (83)
20-Mar	Man. United	A	0-1	5	50,028	
23-Mar	Newcastle U.	H	2-0	5	38,271	Marshall (3); Wright (17)
06-Apr	Leeds United	H	2-1	5	37,619	Wright (44, 90)
08-Apr	Sheff. Wed.	A	0-1	5	24,349	
15-Apr	Tottenham	H	0-0	5	38,273	

27-Apr	Blackburn R.	A	1-1	5	29,834	Wright (75 pen)
01-May	Liverpool	H	0-0	5	38,323	
05-May	Bolton Wan.	H	2-1	5	38,104	Platt (82); Bergkamp (84)

FA Challenge Cup

Date	Opponents	Vn	Rnd	Res	Atten	Scorers
06-Jan	Sheff. United	H	3R	1-1	33,453	Wright (70)
17-Jan	Sheff. United	A	3RR	0-1	22,255	

Coca-Cola League Cup

Date	Opponents	Vn	Rnd	Res	Atten	Scorers
19-Sep	Hartlepool	A	2R1L	3-0	4,945	Adams (10, 85); Wright (40)
03-Oct	Hartlepool	H	2R2L	5-0	27,194	Bergkamp (29, 49); Wright (33, 58, 87)
24-Oct	Barnsley	A	3R	3-0	18,429	Bould (38); Bergkamp (42); Keown (76)
29-Nov	Sheff. Wed.	H	4R	2-1	35,361	Wright (39 pen); Hartson (64)
10-Jan	Newcastle U.	H	QF	2-0	37,857	Wright (44, 89)
14-Feb	Aston Villa	H	SF1L	2-2	37,562	Bergkamp (26, 32)
21-Feb	Aston Villa	A	SF2L	0-0	39,334	

After extra time. Villa win on away goals rule

Arsenal – Premiership Fact File

- Arsenal have changed their club phone numbers during the close season. Gooner fans should make sure they update their dairies.
- Lee Dixon, Paul Merson and David Seaman were the only players to feature in all 38 of Arsenal's Premiership games last season.
- Despite long term injuries to skipper Tony Adams and defensive lynchpin Steve Bould, Arsenal had the best defensive record in the Premiership – they conceded just 32 goals during the season.
- While the early season talk was of the wait for Dennis Bergkamp's first goal which came in his seventh Gunners match against Southampton, fellow Dutchman Glen Helder had to wait until the 13th January 1996 to get his name on the Premiership scoresheet at Middlesbrough – it was his 30th game!
- Should Steve Bould make an apperance in the Premiership this season (and I fully expect him to) it will be his 100th in the top flight league.
- During the 1995-96 season three Arsenal players joined the Premier Century Club – Paul Merson (128), Martin Keown (127) and Tony Adams (118).

Aston Villa

Founded in 1874 by cricketers from the Aston Wesleyan Chapel, Lozells, who played on Aston Park, moving to a field in Wellington Road, Perry Barr in 1876. Prominent nationally, the club was a founder member of the Football League in 1888.

The landlord at Perry Barr made such demands that the club sought its own ground and eventually moved back to Aston occupying the Aston Lower Grounds, which had already been used for some big games. Not known as Villa Park until some time later, the ground first saw League football in 1897. Premier League founder members 1992.

Ground: Villa Park, Trinity Rd, Birmingham, B6 6HE
Phone Club: 0121-327 2299   **News:** 0891 12 11 48
Box Office: 0121-327 5353   **Ticket:** 0891 12 18 48
Capacity: 40,530   **Pitch:** 115 yds x 75 yds
Colours: Claret/Blue, White, Blue/Claret   **Nickname:** The Villains

President: Harold Musgrove   **Chairman:** Doug Ellis
Secretary: Steven Stride
Manager: Brian Little   **Assistant:** Allan Evans
First Team Coach: John Gregory   **Physio:** Jim Walker

League History: 1888 Founder Member of the League; 1936-38 Division 2; 1938-59 Division 1; 1959-60 Division 2; 1960-67 Division 1; 1967-70 Division 2; 1970-72 Division 3; 1972-75 Division 2; 1975-87 Division 1; 1987-88 Division 2; 1988-92 Division 1; 1992- FA Premier League.

Honours: *FA Premier League – Runners*-up 1992-93; *Football League: Division 1 – Champions* 1893-94, 1895-96, 1896-97, 1898-99, 1899-1900, 1909-10, 1980-81; *Runners-up* 1888-89, 1902-03, 1907-08, 1910-11, 1912-13, 1913-14, 1930-31, 1932-33, 1989-90; *Division 2 – Champions* 1937-38, 1959-60; *Runners-up* 1974-75, 1987-88; *Division 3 – Champions* 1971-72. *FA Cup: Winners* 1887, 1895, 1897, 1905, 1913, 1920, 1957; *Runners-up* 1892, 1924. *League-Cup Double Performed:* 1896-97. *Football League Cup: Winners* 1961, 1975, 1977, 1994, 1996; *Runners-up* 1963, 1971. *Champions' Cup Winners –* 1981-82; *European Super Cup Winners:* 1982-83; *World Club Championship Runners-up:* 1982-83.

European Record: CC (2): 81-82 (W), 82-83 (QF); CWC (0); UEFA (6): 75-76 (1), 77-78 (Q), 83-84 (2), 90-91 (2), 93-94 (2), 94-95 (2).

Managers: George Ramsay 1884-1926; W.J. Smith 1926-34; Jimmy McMullan 1934-35; Jimmy Hogan 1936-44; Alex Massie 1945-50; George Martin 1950-53; Eric Houghton 1953-58; Joe Mercer 1958-64; Dick Taylor 1965-67; Tommy Cummings 1967-68; Tommy Docherty 1968-70; Vic Crowe 1970-74; Ron Saunders 1974-82; Tony Barton 1982-84; Graham Turner 1984-86; Billy McNeill 1986-87; Graham Taylor 1987-91; Dr Jozef Venglos 1990-91; (FAPL) Ron Atkinson June 1991-Nov 1994; Brian Little Nov 1994-

Season 1995-96

Biggest Home Win: 4-1 v Coventry City, 16/12/95
Biggest Home Defeat: 0-2 v Liverpool, 31/12/95
Biggest Away Win: 4-1 v West Ham United, 4/11/95
Biggest Away Defeat: 0-3 v Liverpool, 3/3/96
Biggest Home Att: 39,336 v Manchester City, 27/4/96
Smallest Home Att: 23,933 v Middlesbrough, 19/3/96
Average Attendance: 32,613 (7th largest)
Leading Scorers: 17 – Dwight Yorke, 12 – Salvo Milosevic
Last Season: *FAPL:* 4 (UEFA) *FA Cup:* SF *Coca-Cola Cup:* Winners

All-Time Records

Record FAPL Win: 7-1 v Wimbledon, 11/2/95
Record FAPL Defeat: 1-5 v Newcastle United, 27/4/94
Record FL Win: 12-2 v Accrington S, Division 1, 12/3/1892
Record FL Defeat: 1-8 v Blackburn R, FA Cup R3, 16/2/1889
Record Cup Win: 13-0 v Wednesbury Old Ath, FA Cup R1, 30/10/1886
Record Fee Received: £5.5m from Bari for David Platt, 8/1991
Record Fee Paid: £3.5m to Partizan Belgrade for Savo Milsosevic
Most FL Apps: Charlie Aitken, 561, 1961-76
Most FAPL Apps: 142 – Paul McGrath
Most FAPL Goals: 38 – Dean Saunders
Highest Scorer in FAPL season: Dean Saunders, 17, 1992-93; Dwight Yorke, 17, 1995-96
Record Attendance (all-time): 76,588 v Derby Co, FA Cup R6, 2/2/1946
Record Attendance (FAPL): 45,347 v Liverpool, 7/5/94
Most FAPL Goals in Season: 57, 1992-93 – 42 games
Most FAPL Points in Season: 74, 1992-93 – 42 games

	Div.	P	W	D	L	F	A	Pts	Pos	FAC	FLC
91-92	1	42	17	9	16	48	44	60	7	2	6
92-93	PL	42	21	11	10	57	40	74	2	4	4
93-94	PL	42	15	12	15	46	50	57	10	5	W
94-95	PL	42	11	15	16	51	56	48	18	4	4
95-96	PL	38	18	9	11	52	35	63	4	SF	W

Summary 1995-96

Player	Tot	St	Sb	Snu	PS	Gls	Y	R	Fa	La	Fg	Lg
BOSNICH	38	38	0	0	1	0	1	0	5	8	0	0
BROWNE	2	2	0	0	0	0	2	0	1	0	0	0
CARR	2	1	1	4	0	0	1	0	1	0	1	0
CHARLES	34	34	0	0	1	1	1	0	5	8	0	0
DAVIS	2	0	2	0	0	0	0	0	1	0	0	0
DRAPER	36	36	0	0	3	2	1	0	5	8	2	1
EHIOGU	36	36	0	0	0	1	7	0	5	8	0	1
FARRELLY	4	1	3	6	0	0	0	0	0	1	0	0
FENTON	3	0	3	5	0	0	0	0	0	2	0	0
HENDRIE	3	2	1	5	0	0	1	1	0	0	0	0
JOACHIM	11	4	7	1	3	1	0	0	0	0	0	0
JOHNSON	25	19	6	5	4	5	5	0	4	4	1	2
McGRATH	30	29	1	0	5	2	3	0	4	6	0	0
MILOSEVIC	37	36	1	0	5	12	6	0	5	7	1	1
MURRAY	3	3	0	0	1	0	0	0	0	0	0	0
OAKES	0	0	0	16	0	0	0	0	0	0	0	0
SCIMECA	17	7	10	7	2	0	1	0	2	3	0	0
SOUTHGATE	31	31	0	0	1	1	1	0	4	8	0	1
SPINK	2	0	2	19	0	0	0	0	0	0	0	0
STAUNTON	13	11	2	3	4	0	0	0	2	4	0	1
TAYLOR	25	24	1	2	2	3	5	0	3	6	1	1
TILER	1	1	0	0	1	0	0	0	0	0	0	0
TOWNSEND	31	30	1	0	3	2	9	1	4	8	0	1
WRIGHT	38	38	0	0	0	2	2	0	5	8	0	0
YORKE	35	35	0	0	5	17	0	0	5	8	2	6

OGs 3

Little More than Enough!

As a player with Aston Villa, Brian Little picked up two League Cup winners medals during the 1970s and it was in the same competition two decades later that he led the club, as manager, to its first silverware under his leadership. Such reward seemed unlikely as Little set about rebuilding the side during the second half of the 1994-95 season but with three big money summer signings Villa's squad took shape. Little strengthened the side in every department, Crystal Palace defender Gareth Southgate signed at a cost of £2.5m, midfielder Mark Draper made the short journey from Little's previous club, Leicester City, for over £3m while a further £3.5m was spent on Partizan Belgrade striker Savo Milosevic. Towards the end of the season Villa splashed out another £3m to bring the Leicester duo of Liam Daish and Julian Joachim to Villa Park. Southgate comfortably justified his fee and by the end of the season had forced his way into England's Euro 96 squad.

Draper was quick to make his mark when scoring during an opening day 3-1 win over Manchester United at Villa Park. Victory at Tottenham confirmed Villa's bright start and with just one defeat from their opening eight games the club was in second place come the end of September. Second was the highest position Villa reached and they finally came to rest in fourth place where they had been since early February – a vast improvement on their fortunes for the previous two seasons.

But it was in the cups that Little's side really caught the imagination as they closed in on a Wembley double in the domestic competitions. In the Coca Cola Cup, Endsleigh League sides Peterborough United and Stockport County were dispatched with ease before an Andy Townsend goal accounted for QPR at Villa park. A quarter final Midlands showdown with Wolverhampton Wanderers ended with victory thanks to Tommy Johnson's last goal of the season while things looked bleak during the semi final 1st Leg tie at Highbury as Villa trailed by two goals despite playing well. Dwight Yorke's fourth brace of the season ensured equality for the return match and in front of their second highest gate of the season, 39,334 (two less than for the league match with Manchester City), a goalless draw took Villa to Wembley. Milosevic crowned his first season in England with the opening goal as Villa crushed Leeds United 3-0 in the final. Ian Taylor scored the second and it was fitting that Yorke should get the third as his magnificent smile had become one of the most engaging features of a thrilling season.

Villa's Coca Cola Cup run had seen the club enjoy favourable home draws on the road to Wembley but the same could not be said of the FA Cup although a 3rd Round tie at Gravesend & Northfleet was switched to the Midlands. Once the Beazer Homes League side had been seen off Villa notched up some very creditable victories at Sheffield United and Ipswich Town to set up a quarter final tie at Nottingham Forest. Franz Carr celebrated his return to the side after a year out through injury by scoring the deciding goal against his former club. The semi final, though, was a big disappointment for Villa. An early injury to Southgate disrupted the defence which Liverpool exploited to the full, although two late goals gave the final score of 3-0 an untrue reflection on the game.

Overall it was a season of great excitement for Villa as Yorke's potential was fully realised, Milosevic displayed tremendous ability and scored 14 times despite some occasional erratic finishing while in midfield Taylor and Townsend were an inspiration. A touch more consistency could turn Villa into title contenders. ∎

Results 1995-96

FA Carling Premiership

Date	Opponents	Ven	Res	Pos	Atten	Scorers
19-Aug	Man. United	H	3-1	–	34,655	Taylor (14); Draper (27); Yorke (36 pen)
23-Aug	Tottenham	A	1-0	–	26,726	Ehiogu (69)
26-Aug	Leeds United	A	0-2	6	35,086	
30-Aug	Bolton Wan.	H	1-0	5	31,770	Yorke (75)
09-Sep	Blackburn R.	A	1-1	5	27,084	Milosevic (33)
16-Sep	Wimbledon	H	2-0	3	26,928	Draper (7); Taylor (47)
23-Sep	N. Forest	H	1-1	5	33,972	Townsend (67
30-Sep	Coventry C.	A	3-0	2	20,987	Yorke (1); Milosevic (84, 87)
14-Oct	Chelsea	H	0-1	6	34,922	
21-Oct	Arsenal	A	0-2	7	38,271	
28-Oct	Everton	H	1-0		32,792	Yorke (76)
04-Nov	West Ham	A	4-1	6	23,637	Milosevic (33, 89); Johnson (49); Yorke (54)
18-Nov	Newcastle U.	H	1-1	4	39,167	Johnson (22)
20-Nov	Southampton	A	1-0	3	13,582	Johnson (3)
25-Nov	Man. City	A	0-1	4	28,027	
02-Dec	Arsenal	H	1-1	4	37,770	Yorke (65)
10-Dec	N. Forest	A	1-1	6	25,790	Yorke (47)
16-Dec	Coventry C.	H	4-1	4	28,476	Johnson (12); Milosevic (48, 64, 80)
23-Dec	QPR	A	0-1	6	14,778	
01-Jan	Middlesbro'	A	2-0	5	28,535	Wright (21); Johnson (40)
13-Jan	Man. United	A	0-0	7	42,667	
21-Jan	Tottenham	H	2-1	5	35,666	McGrath (23); Yorke (79)
31-Jan	Liverpool	H	0-2	6	39,332	
03-Feb	Leeds United	H	3-0	4	35,982	Yorke (11, 23); Wright (61)
10-Feb	Bolton Wan.	A	2-0	4	18,099	Yorke (40, 53)
24-Feb	Wimbledon	A	3-3	4	12,193	OG (Reeves 33); Yorke (49 pen); OG (Cunningham 58)
28-Feb	Blackburn R.	H	2-0	4	28,008	Joachim (55); Southgate (71)
03-Mar	Liverpool	A	0-3	4	39,508	
06-Mar	Sheff. Wed.	H	3-2	4	27,893	Milosevic (61, 62); Townsend (75)
09-Mar	QPR	H	4-2	4	28,221	Milosevic (18); Yorke (65, 80); OG (Yates 82)
16-Mar	Sheff. Wed.	A	0-2	4	22,964	
19-Mar	Middlesbro'	H	0-0	4	23,933	
06-Apr	Chelsea	A	2-1	4	23,530	Milosevic (40); Yorke (59)

08-Apr	Southampton	H	3-0	4	34,059	Taylor (64)
14-Apr	Newcastle U.	A	0-1	4	36,510	
17-Apr	West Ham	H	1-1	4	26,768	McGrath (27)
27-Apr	Man. City	H	0-1	4	39,336	
05-May	Everton	A	0-1	4	40,127	

FA Challenge Cup

Date	Opponents	Vn	Rnd	Res	Atten	Scorers
06-Jan	Gravesend N.	A†	3R	3-0	26,021	Draper (2); Milosevic (47); Johnson (72)
	† Played at Villa Park					
28-Jan	Sheff. Utd	A	4R	1-0	18,749	Yorke (63 pen)
17-Feb	Ipswich Tn	A	5R	3-1	20,748	Draper (10); Yorke (19); Taylor (55)
13-Mar	N. Forest	A	QF	1-0	21,067	Carr (26)
31-Mar	Liverpool	N	SF	0-3	39,072	
	Played at Old Trafford					

Coca-Cola League Cup

Date	Opponents	Vn	Rnd	Res	Atten	Scorers
20-Sep	Peterborough	H	2R1L	6-0	19,602	Draper (12); Yorke (15, 24); Johnson (69), Own goal (Heald 79), Southgate (89)
04-Oct	Peterborough	A	2R2L	1-0	5,745	Staunton (87)
25-Oct	Stockport Cty	H	3R	2-0	17,679	Ehiogu (57); Yorke (65)
29-Nov	QPR	H	4R	1-0	24,951	Townsend (60)
10-Jan	Wolves	H	QF	1-0	39,277	Johnson (67)
14-Feb	Arsenal	A	SF1L	2-2	37,562	Yorke (39, 72)
21-Feb	Arsenal	H	SF2L	0-0	39,334	
	After extra time. Villa win on away goals rule					
24-Mar	Leeds United	W	Final	3-0	77,065	Milosevic (20); Taylor (54); Yorke (89)

Villa – Premiership Fact File

- Mark Draper scored on his debut for Villa during the opening day 3-1 win over Manchester United.
- Villa's three wins in their opening four games was their best start to a league campaign since 1980.
- Dwight Yorke notched his 50th goal for Villa in all competitions when he scored in the 3-0 home win over Leeds United on 3rd February.
- Mark Bosnich and Dwight Yorke both moved past the 100 Premiership appearance point during last season. They should be joined by Ugo Ehiogu and Mark Draper this season who have 96 and 75 appearances respectively.

Blackburn Rovers

Founded in 1875 by local school-leavers. Used several pitches, including Alexander Meadows, the East Lancashire Cricket Club ground, and became known nationally for their FA Cup exploits, eclipsing the record of Blackburn Olympic, the first club to take the trophy away from London. Three consecutive wins in the 1880s, when in the finals Queen's Park (twice) and West Bromwich Albion were beaten, brought recognition by way of a special shield awarded by the FA to commemorate the achievement.

Founder member of the Football League in 1888, the club settled at Ewood Park in 1890, purchasing the ground outright in 1893-94. Premier League founder member 1992 and champions in 1994-95.

Ground: Ewood Park, Blackburn, BB2 4JF
Phone: 01254-698888   **Info:** 0891-12 11 79
Ticket: 0891-12 10 14
Capacity: 30,591   **Pitch:** 115yds x 76yds
Colours: Blue/White, White, Blue **Nickname:** Blue and Whites

Club President: W.H. Bancroft   **Snr-Vice President:** J. Walker
Chairman: R.D. Coar BSC   **Vice-Chairman:** R.L. Matthewman
Secretary: tba (John Howarth resigned after 25 years with Rovers)
Director of Football: Kenny Dalglish MBE
Manager: Ray Harford   **Coach:** Tony Parkes
Physio: M. Pettigrew

League History: 1888 Founder member of the League; 1936-39 Division 2; 1946-48 Division 1; 1948-58 Division 2; 1958-66 Division 1; 1966-71 Division 2; 1971-75 Division 3; 1975-79 Division 2; 1979-80 Division 3; 1980-92 Division 2; 1992 – FA Premier League.

Honours: *FA Premier League: Champions* 1994-95; *Runners up* 1993-94; *Football League: Division 1 – Champions* 1911-12, 1913-14; *Division 2 – Champions* 1938-39; *Runners-up* 1957-58; *Division 3 – Champions* 1974-75; Runners-up 1979-1980. *FA Cup: Winners* 1884, 1885, 1886, 1890, 1891, 1928; *Runners-up* 1882, 1960. *Full Members' Cup: Winners* 1986-87.

European Record: CC (1): 95-96; CWC (0): UEFA (1) : 94-95 (1).

Managers: Thomas Mitchell 1884-96; J. Walmsley 1896-1903; R.B. Middleton 1903-25; Jack Carr 1922-26 (TM under Middleton to 1925); Bob Crompton 1926-31 (Hon. TM); Arthur Barritt 1931-36 (had been Secretary from 1927); Reg Taylor 1936-38; Bob Crompton 1938-41; Eddie Hapgood

1944-47; Will Scott 1947; Jack Burton 1947-49; Jackie Bestall 1949-53; Johnny Carey 1953-58; Dally Duncan 1958-60; Jack Marshall 1960-67; Eddie Quigley 1967-70; Johnny Carey 1970-71; Ken Furphy 1971-73; Gordon Lee 1974-75; Jim Smith 1975-78; Jim Iley 1978; John Pickering 1978-79; Howard Kendall 1979-81; Bobby Saxton 1981-86; Don Mackay 1987-91; *(FAPL)* Kenny Dalglish October 1991-May 1995; Ray Harford May 1995-

Season 1995-96

Biggest Home Win: 7-0 v Nottingham Forest, 18/11/95
Biggest Home Defeat: 0-3 v Everton, 30/3/96
Biggest Away Win: 5-1 v Nottingham Forest, 13/4/96
Biggest Away Defeat: 0-5 v Coventry City, 9/12/95
Biggest Home Att: 30,895 v Liverpool, 24/2/96
Smallest Home Att: 24,174 v Wimbledon, 17/4/96
Average Attendance: 27,714 (11th highest)
Leading Scorers: 31 – Alan Shearer, 6 – Graham Fenton
Last Season: *FAPL:* 7 *FA Cup:* 3 *Coca-Cola Cup:* 4

All-Time Records

Record FAPL Win: 7-0 v Nottingam Forest 18/11/95,
                               7-1 v Norwich City, 3/10/92
Record FAPL Defeat: 0-5 v Coventry City, 9/1/95
Record FL Win: 9-0 v Middlesbrough, Division 2, 6/11/1954
Record FL Defeat: 0-8 v Arsenal, Division 1, 25/2/1933
Record Cup Win: 11-0 v Rossendale, FA Cup R1, 13/10/1884
Record Fee Received: £3.75m from Newcastle United for David Batty, 2/96
Record Fee Paid: £5m to Norwich City for Chris Sutton, 7/94
Most FL Apps: Derek Fazackerley, 596, 1970-86
Most FAPL Apps: 149 – Tim Sherwood
Most FAPL Goals: 112 – Alan Shearer
Highest Scorer in FAPL Season: Alan Shearer, 34, 1994-95
Record Attendance (all-time): 61,783 v Bolton W, FA Cup R6, 2/3/1929
Record Attendance (FAPL): 30,895 v Liverpool, 24/2/96
Most FAPL Goals in Season: 80, 1994-95 – 42 games
Most FAPL Points in Season: 89, 1994-95 – 42 games

5-Year Record

	Div.	P	W	D	L	F	A	Pts	Pos	FAC	FLC
91-92	2	46	21	11	14	70	53	74	6	4	1
92-93	PL	42	20	11	11	68	46	71	4	6	SF
93-94	PL	42	25	9	8	63	36	84	2	4	4
94-95	PL	42	27	8	7	80	39	89	1	3	4
95-96	PL	38	18	7	13	61	47	61	7	3	4

Summary 1995-96

Player	Tot	St	Sb	Snu	PS	Gls	Y	R	Fa	La	Fg	Lg
ATKINS	4	0	4	0	0	0	0	1	0	0	0	0
BATTY	23	23	0	0	1	1	5	0	1	4	0	0
BERG	38	38	0	0	0	0	5	1	2	4	0	0
BOHINEN	20	18	2	0	1	4	3	0	1	0	0	0
COLEMAN	20	19	1	0	1	0	2	0	2	0	0	0
CROFT	0	0	0	4	0	0	0	0	0	0	0	0
FENTON	14	4	10	2	4	6	2	0	0	0	0	0
FLITCROFT	3	3	0	1	0	0	1	1	0	0	0	0
FLOWERS	37	37	0	0	0	0	3	1	2	3	0	0
GALLACHER	14	2	2	2	3	2	1	0	2	0	0	0
GIVEN	0	0	0	1	0	0	0	0	0	0	0	0
GUDMUNDSSON	4	1	3	4	1	0	0	0	0	0	0	0
HENDRY	33	33	0	0	1	1	9	0	2	4	0	0
HOLMES	8	7	1	1	3	1	1	0	0	0	0	0
KENNA	32	32	0	0	1	0	2	0	2	4	0	0
Le SAUX	15	14	1	0	2	1	2	0	0	2	0	0
MAKEL	3	0	3	1	0	0	0	0	0	0	0	0
MARKER	9	8	1	3	2	1	0	0	0	0	0	0
McKINLAY	19	13	6	3	2	2	5	1	2	1	0	0
MIMMS	2	1	1	25	0	0	0	0	0	1	0	0
NEWELL	30	26	4	2	9	3	7	0	2	4	0	1
PEARCE	12	12	0	0	1	1	1	0	0	3	0	0
RIPLEY	27	27	0	1	10	0	1	0	2	3	0	0
SHEARER	35	35	0	0	0	31	4	0	2	4	0	5
SHERWOOD	33	33	0	1	2	4	8	0	2	4	0	0
SUTTON	13	9	4	4	4	0	3	0	0	3	0	1
WARHURST	10	1	9	7	2	0	0	0	0	3	0	0
WILCOX	10	10	0	0	2	3	0	0	0	0	0	0

Away Day Troubles

Despite finishing sixth in the Premiership, Blackburn Rovers picked up the award of under achievers thanks in the main to a pretty dire away record. The reigning champions, now under the leadership of Ray Harford with Kenny Dalglish working behind the scenes as the Director of Football, received their first setback a week before the start of the league season with a defeat at Wembley in the FA Charity Shield. The league campaign kicked off with an Alan Shearer penalty taking all three points off QPR but Rovers then lost four and drew one of their next five games to slip down to 17th position. A 3-0 defeat at Liverpool was offset by a 5-1 thrashing of Coventry which saw Shearer score the first of his five hat tricks during the season. A run of ten consecutive wins at Ewood Park raised expectations but it was not until mid January that an away victory was achieved, during which time the side suffered a 5-0 reversal in the return match with Coventry. By the end of the season only the top two sides had won more home matches and only Liverpool had scored more goals away from home had it not been for their five goals at the City Ground only Middlesbrough would have found the back of the net less times. Rovers demonstrated their ability to still live with the best when beating Newcastle with two late goals, ironically from Geordie Graham Fenton, while the two games with Nottingham Forest saw amazing 7-0 and 5-1 victories for the Lancastrians. The home victory was Blackburn's highest for 41 years and ended Forest's 25 match unbeaten run in the Premiership.

Rovers' frustrating league form would have been happily accepted had they found glory in their first season in the Champions' League. Instead of being another avenue to fund further expenditure at Ewood Park, Rovers' European adventure was a nightmare as defeats in the first three games against Spartak Moscow, Rosenborg and Legia Warsaw edged the club towards the exit. England's champions were finally removed from the competition with a 3-0 defeat in Moscow on a night which saw the Newcastle bound David Batty and Graeme Le Saux come to blows. A 4-1 win over Rosenborg in the final group match saw Mike Newell score a hat trick but it was far too late to salvage a place in Europe.

The domestic cup competitions did little to appease the fans as Division One side Ipswich Town put Rovers out of the FA Cup at the first hurdle while Shearer scored four of the five goals which put Swindon two out of the Coca Cola Cup in the 2nd Round. Blackburn recovered from a goal down to beat Watford in Round Three but there was no way back at Leeds as Rovers went out 2-1.

Standing head and shoulders above all others during the season was Shearer. He may have gone the best part of two years without a goal for his country but he became the first player to score thirty or more league goals in the top flight in three consecutive seasons and scored his 100th league goal in just 124 games with a stunning effort against Spurs.

The famed Blackburn cheque book was again in frequent use with ten signings being made during the season, five of which were in excess of seven figures. Chris Coleman joined from Crystal Palace for £2.8m but the most expensive capture was Garry Flitcroft from Manchester City at £3.2m just prior to the transfer deadline. Flitcroft lasted just two minutes of his debut before being dismissed for use of an elbow. One of the most controversial signings was that of Lars Bohinen from Nottingham Forest. The Norwegian brushed aside off the field acrimony about his move to score twice against his former club during the 7-0 win. ∎

Results 1995-96

FA Carling Premiership

Date	Opponents	Ven	Res	Pos	Atten	Scorers
19-Aug	QPR	H	1-0		25,932	Shearer (6 pen)
23-Aug	Sheff. Wed.	A	1-2		25,544	Shearer (60)
26-Aug	Bolton Wan.	A	1-2	12	20,253	Holmes (61)
28-Aug	Man. United	A	1-2	13	29,843	Shearer (59)
09-Sep	Aston Villa	H	1-1	15	27,084	Shearer (82)
16-Sep	Liverpool	A	0-3	17	39,502	
23-Sep	Coventry C.	H	5-1	13	24,382	Shearer (8, 60, 67); Hendry (23); Pearce (75)
30-Sep	Middlesbro'	A	0-2	13	29,462	
14-Oct	Southampton	H	2-1	14	26,780	Bohinen (16); Shearer (77)
21-Oct	West Ham	A	1-1	11	21,776	Shearer (89)
28-Oct	Chelsea	H	3-0	11	27,733	Sherwood (39); Shearer (49); Newell (57)
05-Nov	Everton	A	0-1	11	30,097	
08-Nov	Newcastle U.	A	0-1	11	36,473	
18-Nov	N. Forest	H	7-0	10	27,660	Shearer (20, 58, 68); Bohinen (28, 76); Newell (82); Le Saux (90)
26-Nov	Arsenal	A	0-0	13	37,695	
02-Dec	West Ham	H	4-2	10	26,638	Shearer (3, 17, 65 pen); Newell (32)
09-Dec	Coventry City	A	0-5	12	13,376	
16-Dec	Middlesbrough	H	1-0	11	27,996	Shearer (42)
23-Dec	Wimbledon	H	1-1	11	7,105	Sherwood (27)
26-Dec	Man. City	H	2-0	10	28,915	Shearer (11); Batty (50)
30-Dec	Tottenham	H	2-1	9	30,004	Marker (31); Shearer (41)
01-Jan	Leeds Utd	A	0-0	10	31,285	
13-Jan	QPR	A	1-0	8	13,957	Shearer (77)
20-Jan	Sheff. Wed.	H	3-0	6	24,732	Shearer (28); Bohinen (31); Gallacher (84)
03-Feb	Bolton Wan.	H	3-1	6	30,419	Shearer (12, 83, 90)
10-Feb	Man. United	A	0-1	6	42,681	
24-Feb	Liverpool	H	2-3	9	30,895	Wilcox (25); Sherwood (84)
28-Feb	Aston Villa	A	0-2	9	28,008	
02-Mar	Man. City	A	1-1	10	29,078	Shearer (57)
13-Mar	Leeds Utd	H	1-0	8	23,358	Fenton (47)
16-Mar	Tottenham	A	3-2	7	32,287	Shearer (7 pen, 34, 90)
30-Mar	Everton	H	0-3	8	29,468	
06-Apr	Southampton	A	0-1	9	14,793	
08-Apr	Newcastle U.	H	2-1	9	30,717	Fenton (86, 90)

13-Apr	N. Forest	A	5-1	8	25,273	Shearer (27); McKinlay (30); Wilcox (45, 69); Fenton (86)
17-Apr	Wimbledon	H	3-2	6	24,174	Shearer (13, 46); Fenton (58)
27-Apr	Arsenal	H	1-1	6	29,834	Gallacher (12)
05-May	Chelsea	A	3-2	6	28,436	Sherwood (37); McKinlay (48); Fenton (59)

UEFA Champions' League

Date	Opponents	Vn	Rnd	Res	Atten	Scorers
13-Sep	Spartak Moscow	H	B	0-1	20,940	
27-Sep	Rosenborg	A	B	1-2	12,210	Newell (62)
18-Oct	Legia Warsaw	A	B	0-1	15,000	
01-Nov	Legia Warsaw	H	B	0-0	20,897	
22-Nov	Spartak Moscow	A	B	0-3	35,000	
06-Dec	Rosenborg	H	B	4-1	20,677	Shearer (16 pen); Newell (31, 38, 41)

FA Challenge Cup

Date	Opponents	Vn	Rnd	Res	Atten	Scorers
06-Jan	Ipswich Tn	A	3R	0-0	21,236	
16-Jan	Ipswich Tn	H	3RR	0-1	19,606	after extra time

Coca-Cola League Cup

Date	Opponents	Vn	Rnd	Res	Atten	Scorers
20-Sep	Swindon Tn	A	2R1L	3-2	14,740	Sutton (28); Shearer (42, 84)
04-Oct	Swindon Tn	H	2R2L	2-0	16,924	Shearer (37, 83)
24-Oct	Watford	A	3R	2-1	17,035	Shearer (58); Newell (79)
29-Nov	Leeds United	A	4R	1-2	26,006	Own Goal (Kelly 51)

FA Charity Shield

Date	Opponents	Vn	Res	Atten	Scorers
13-Aug	Everton	Wembley	0-1	40,149	

Rovers – Premiership Fact File

- Alan Shearer's 41st minute goal against Tottenham at Ewood Park on the last day of 1995 was his 100th in the Premiership. He is the first player to reach 100 Premier League goals. He also set a new record with five hat-tricks.
- A 5-1 win over Coventry City on 23rd September marked the start of a run of 10 consecutive Premiership wins. Alan Shearer scored in every match. The run came to an end when Liverpool won 3-2 at Ewood. Shearer failed to score!
- Rovers did not record their first away win until mid-January when they won 1-0 at QPR on the 13th.

Chelsea

Founded in 1905. The Mears brothers developed Stamford Bridge Athletic Ground, which they owned, into a football stadium for use for prestigious matches and, prospectively, nearby Fulham FC. But Fulham did not take up the chance so the Mears brothers established their own club, rejecting possible names such as 'London' and 'Kensington' in favour, eventually, of Chelsea.

Judging that the club would not be accepted into the Southern League, it sought membership of the Football League. This was gained at the first attempt and it started the 1906-07 season in Division Two. Premier League founder members 1992.

Ground: Stamford Bridge, London SW6 1HS
Phone: 0171-385 5545   **News:** 0891 12 11 59
Ticket News: 0891-12 10 11   **Booking:** 0171-386 7799
Capacity: 31,791 (>41,000)   **Pitch:** 110 yds x 72 yds
Colours: Royal Blue, Royal Blue, White   **Nickname:** The Blues

President: G.M. Thomson   **Chairman:** Ken W. Bates
MD: Colin Hutchinson
Match Secretary: Keith Lacy   **Company Secretary:** Alan Shaw
Manager: Ruud Gullit   **Assistant:** Peter Shreeves
Coach: Graham Rix   **Physio:** Bob Ward

League History: 1905 Elected to Division 2; 1907-10 Division 1; 1910-12 Division 2; 1912-24 Division 1; 1924-30 Division 2; 1930-62 Division 1; 1962-63 Division 2; 1963-75 Division 1; 1975-77 Division 2; 1977-79 Division 1; 1979-84 Division 2; 1984-88 Division 1; 1988-89 Division 2; 1989-92 Division 1; 1992- FA Premier League.

Honours: *Football League: Division 1 Champions:* 1954-55; *Division 2 Champions:* 1983-84, 1988-89; *Runners-up:* 1906-7, 1911-12, 1929-30,1962-63, 1976-77. *FA Cup: Winners:* 1970; *Runners-up:* 1914-15, 1966-67, 1993-94. *Football League Cup: Winners:* 1964-65; *Runners-up:* 1971-72; *Full Members' Cup Winners:* 1985-86. *Zenith Data Systems Cup Winners:* 1989-90.

European Record: CC (0) – ; CWC (3): 70-71 (W), 71-72 (2), 94-95 (SF); UEFA (2): 65-66 (SF), 68-69 (2).

Managers: John Tait Robertson 1905-07; David Calderhead 1907-33; A. Leslie Knighton 1933-39; Billy Birrell 1939-52; Ted Drake 1952-61; Tommy Docherty 1962-67; Dave Sexton 1967-74; Ron Stuart 1974-75; Eddie McCreadie 1975-77; Ken Shellito 1977-78; Danny Blanchflower 1978-79; Geoff Hurst 1979-81; John Neal 1981-85 (Director to 1986); John Hollins 1985-88; Bobby Campbell 1988-91; *(FAPL)* Ian Porterfield June 1991-1993; Dave Webb 1993; Glenn Hoddle July 1993-June 1996; Ruud Gullit June 1996-

Season 1995-96

Biggest Home Win:	5-0 v Middlesbrough, 4/2/96
Biggest Home Defeat:	1-4 v Manchester United, 21/10/95
Biggest Away Win:	3-1 v West Ham United, 11/9/95
Biggest Away Defeat:	0-3 v Blackburn Rovers, 28/10/95
Biggest Home Att:	31,137 v Liverpool, 30/12/95
Smallest Home Att:	17,078 v Manchester City, 12/3/96
Average Attendance:	25,598 (13th highest)
Leading Scorers:	13 – John Spencer, 8 – Mark Hughes

Last Season: *FAPL:* 11 *FA Cup:* SF *Coca-Cola Cup:* 2

All-Time Records

Record FAPL Win:	5-0 v Middlesbrough, 4/2/96
Record FAPL Defeat:	1-4 v Leeds United, 6/11/93,
	1-4 v Manchester United, 21/10/95
Record FL Win:	9-2 v Glossop N E, Division 2, 1/9/1906
Record FL Defeat:	1-8 v Wolverhampton W, Division 1, 26/9/1953
Record Cup Win:	13-0 v Jeunesse Hautcharage, CWC, 1R2L,
	29/9/1971

Record Fee Received: £2.2m from Tottenham H for Gordon Durie, 7/1991
Record Fee Paid: £4.9m to Lazio for Roberto Di Matteo, 7/96

Most FL Apps:	Ron Harris, 655, 1962-80
Most FAPL Apps:	103 – Gavin Peacock
Most FAPL Goals:	36 – John Spencer

Highest Scorer in FAPL Season: 13: Mark Stein (93/4), John Spencer (95/6)
Record Attendance (all-time): 82,905 v Arsenal, Div 1, 12/10/1935
Record Attendance (FAPL): 37,064 v Manchester United, 11/9/93
Most FAPL Goals in Season: 51, 1992-93 – 42 games
Most FAPL Points in Season: 56, 1992-93 – 42 games

5-Year Record

	Div.	P	W	D	L	F	A	Pts	Pos	FAC	FLC
91-92	1	42	13	14	15	50	60	53	14	6	2
92-93	PL	42	14	14	14	51	54	56	11	3	4
93-94	PL	42	13	12	17	49	53	51	14	F	3
94-95	PL	42	13	15	14	50	55	54	11	4	3
95-96	PL	38	12	14	12	46	44	50	11	SF	2

Summary 1995-96

Player	Tot	St	Sb	Snu	PS	Gls	Y	R	Fa	La	Fg	Lg
BARNESS	0	0	0	1	0	0	0	0	0	1	0	0
BURLEY	22	16	6	1	5	0	1	0	2	2	0	0
CLARKE	22	21	1	1	0	0	2	0	8	1	0	0
COLGAN	0	0	0	1	0	0	0	0	0	0	0	0
DOW	1	1	0	1	0	0	0	0	0	0	0	0
DUBERRY	22	22	0	0	2	0	3	0	8	0	2	0
FURLONG	28	14	14	4	2	3	3	0	8	2	1	0
GULLIT	31	31	0	0	2	3	2	0	7	2	3	0
HALL	5	5	0	2	0	1	1	0	0	0	0	0
HITCHCOCK	12	12	0	23	0	0	0	0	7	0	0	0
HUGHES	31	31	0	0	3	8	12	1	6	2	4	0
IZZET	0	0	0	1	0	0	0	0	0	0	0	0
JOHNSEN	22	18	4	1	2	0	6	0	2	2	0	0
KHARINE	26	26	0	7	0	0	1	0	1	2	0	0
KJELDBJERG	0	0	0	0	0	0	0	0	0	0	0	0
LEE	31	29	2	0	2	1	3	0	7	1	0	0
MINTO	10	10	0	0	2	0	1	0	0	1	0	0
MORRIS	1	0	1	0	0	0	0	0	0	0	0	0
MYERS	20	20	0	1	0	0	2	0	3	0	0	0
NEWTON	24	21	3	0	1	1	2	0	3	1	0	0
PEACOCK	28	17	11	1	8	5	1	0	7	1	2	0
PETRESCU	24	22	2	0	1	2	3	0	7	0	1	0
PHELAN	12	12	0	0	1	0	1	0	8	0	0	0
ROCASTLE	1	1	0	0	0	0	0	0	0	0	0	0
SINCLAIR	13	12	1	1	3	1	5	1	0	2	0	0
SPACKMAN	16	13	3	7	3	0	0	1	3	1	0	0
SPENCER	28	23	5	2	9	13	6	0	8	1	1	0
STEIN	8	7	1	4	5	0	1	0	0	1	0	0
WISE	35	34	1	0	4	7	10	0	7	2	1	0
					OG	1						

One Master for Another

The days when the Kings Road was a fashion leader may have long gone but just up the road at Stamford Bridge Chelsea became one of the fashionable clubs once again after a break of almost a generation. Manager Glenn Hoddle pulled off a thrilling double coup during the close season with the signing of Ruud Gullit and Mark Hughes. Gullit had no trouble in winning over the Chelsea fans on the pitch and, just like Jurgen Klinsmann at Tottenham a year earlier, his exemplary behaviour and courtesy away from the ground earned him respect from a much wider audience. The suspicion that Manchester United had parted with Hughes before his sell by date was supported by his dozen goals.

Chelsea's league form was patchy throughout the season but with Gullit and Dennis Wise on song they were one of the most entertaining sides around. Surprisingly, it took the Blues 276 minutes to score their first league goal of the season, a Wise penalty against Coventry, and although that match only ended as a draw, Chelsea were on their way and roared to four wins in the next five outings.

Manchester United ended the run with a 4-1 thrashing at Stamford Bridge which was quickly followed by a 3-0 defeat at Blackburn. From then on Chelsea's form in the league went in fits and starts and once again draws (14) featured high in the final analysis. A run of just one defeat in 12 games nudged the side into the top ten but five draws during that spell denied Chelsea a positive surge up the table. The run ended, ironically, with perhaps their finest performance of the season as Gavin Peacock scored a hat trick during a 5-0 win over Middlesbrough. After that the Blues won just two of the remaining 13 leagues.

The make up of the squad suggested that Hoddle's best hopes for glory would probably come in one of the cup competitions but Chelsea's Coca Cola Cup dreams quickly lost their fizz as Stoke City moved through to the 3rd Round by virtue of being the first visiting side to win at the Bridge.

The FA Cup campaign got off to an absorbing start, a Hughes goal was wiped out deep into injury time at home to Newcastle in the 3rd Round but justice was done when Gullit took the replay into extra time with a late equaliser, Chelsea clinched a place in Round Four with a penalty shoot out victory. Neighbours QPR were seen off after an exciting tussle at Loftus Road with replays were required to move past Grimsby Town and the ever difficult Wimbledon to set up a semi final with Manchester United at Villa Park. A goal by Gullit gave Chelsea a deserved lead but the Blues were already without the injured Dan Petrescu and had lost Steve Clarke through injury when Terry Phelan strained a thigh muscle. As Chelsea dithered over the substitution United seized the initiative and struck twice in five minutes to effectively end Chelsea's season.

No honours maybe, but it was undoubtedly a season of great encouragement although boardroom battles continued as in days of yore. John Spencer had a marvellous season with 14 goals while at the back 20-year old Michael Duberry was a revelation. One setback though was a broken leg sustained by Eddie Newton.

Just two days before the league season came to its conclusion Chelsea lost the services of Hoddle, who answered the call of his country to take over as England coach at the end of Euro 96. Chelsea reacted positively to the loss of their popular manager and presented Gullit with his first managerial appointment. The legendary Dutchman quickly revealed his intentions for the 96-97 season with the imaginative signing of Italian striker Gianluca Vialli. ■

Results 1995-96

FA Carling Premiership

Date	Opponents	Ven	Res	Pos	Atten	Scorers
19-Aug	Everton	H	0-0	–	30,189	
23-Aug	N. Forest	A	0-0	–	27,007	
26-Aug	Middlesbro'	A	0-2	16	28,286	
30-Aug	Coventry C.	H	2-2	14	24,398	Wise (6 pen); Hughes (10)
11-Sep	West Ham	A	3-1	11	19,228	Wise (31); Spencer (33, 89)
16-Sep	Southampton	H	3-0	8	26,237	Sinclair (74); Gullit (86); Hughes (90)
24-Sep	Newcastle U.	A	0-2	10	36,225	
30-Sep	Arsenal	H	1-0	10	31,048	Hughes (51)
14-Oct	Aston Villa	A	1-0	9	34,922	Wise (72)
21-Oct	Man. United	H	1-4	9	31,019	Hughes (76)
28-Oct	Blackburn R.	A	0-3	10	27,733	
04-Nov	Sheff. Wed.	H	0-0	20	23,216	
18-Nov	Leeds United	A	0-1	12	36,209	
22-Nov	Bolton Wan.	H	3-2	10	17,495	Lee (17); Hall (59); Newton (85)
25-Nov	Tottenham	H	0-0	11	31,059	
02-Dec	Man. United	A	1-1	11	42,019	Wise (53)
09-Dec	Newcastle U.	H	1-0	10	31,098	Petrescu (43)
16-Dec	Arsenal	A	1-1	10	38,295	Spencer (25)
23-Dec	Man. City	H	1-0	9	28,668	Peacock (76)
26-Dec	Wimbledon	H	1-2	11	21,906	Petrescu (12)
30-Dec	Liverpool	H	2-2	12	31,137	Spencer (9, 44)
02-Jan	QPR	A	2-1	12	14,904	OG (Brazier 78); Furlong (90)
13-Jan	Everton	A	1-1	12	34,968	Spencer (20)
20-Jan	N. Forest	H	1-0	10	24,482	Spencer (55)
04-Feb	Middlesbro'	H	5-0	8	21,060	Peacock (28, 38, 55); Spencer (31), Furlong (52)
10-Feb	Coventry C.	A	0-1	10	20,639	
17-Feb	West Ham	H	1-2	10	25,252	Peacock (13)
24-Feb	Southampton	A	3-2	8	15,226	Wise (20, 26 pen); Gullit (53)
02-Mar	Wimbledon	A	1-1	8	17,048	Furlong (35)
12-Mar	Man. City	H	1-1	8	17,078	Gullit (25)
16-Mar	Liverpool	A	0-2	9	40,820	
23-Mar	QPR	H	1-1	10	25,590	Spencer (9)
06-Apr	Aston Villa	H	1-2	11	23,530	Spencer (8)
08-Apr	Bolton Wan.	A	1-2	11	18,021	Spencer (13)
13-Apr	Leeds United	H	4-1	11	22,131	Hughes (18, 35, 48 pen); Spencer (19)
17-Apr	Sheff. Wed.	A	0-0	11	25,094	
27-Apr	Tottenham	A	1-1	10	32,918	Hughes (35)
05-May	Blackburn R.	H	2-3	11	28,436	Wise (35); Spencer (88)

FA Challenge Cup

Date	Opponents	Vn	Rnd	Res	Atten	Scorers
07-Jan	Newcastle U.	H	3R	1-1	25,151	Hughes (35)
17-Jan	Newcastle U.	A	3RR	2-2	36,535	Wise (61 pen); Gullit (88)
	aet, Chelsea won 4-2 on pens.					
29-Jan	QPR	A	4R	2-1	18,542	Peacock (19); Furlong (45)
21-Feb	Grimsby Tn	H	5R	0-0	9,648	
28-Feb	Grimsby Tn	H	5RR	4-1	28,545	Duberry (21); Hughes (54); Spencer (56); Peacock (58)
09-Mar	Wimbledon	H	QF	2-2	30,805	Hughes (70); Gullit (80)
20-Mar	Wimbledon	A	QFR	3-1	21,380	Petrescu (20); Duberry (79); Hughes (84)
31-Mar	Man. United	N	SF	1-2	38,421	Gullit (35)
	Played at Villa Park					

Coca-Cola League Cup

Date	Opponents	Vn	Rnd	Res	Atten	Scorers
20-Sep	Stoke City	A	2R1L	0-0	15,574	
04-Oct	Stoke City	H	2R2L	0-1	16,272	
	Stoke City won 1-0 on aggregate.					

Chelsea – Premiership Fact File

- No player completed all 38 of Chelsea's Premiership games last season. Mark Hughes, David Lee and new manager Ruud Gullit weighed in with the most games appearing in 31 of their encounters.
- Chelsea fans had to wait 276 minutes for them to score their first Premiership goal of the season – Dennis Wise blasting home a sixth minute penalty against Coventry City.
- Mark Hughes managed to score against his former Manchester United team mates. It was scant consolation though as the Blues lost the game 4-1 at Stamford Bridge.
- Gavin Peacock made his 100th Premiership appearance for Chelsea during the 1995-96 season bringing his Chelsea total to 103 and all-time Premiership total to 135 (includes 35 for Newcastle United).
- Other players to have passed the century appearance mark during last season were Phelan (115), Sinclair (115), Wise (110), Clarke (110) and Kharine (102). John Spencer (99) and Erland Johnsen (96) look set to break the 100 barrier in 1996-97.

Coventry City

Founded as Singer's FC, cycle manufacturers, in 1883. Joined the Birmingham and District League in 1894; in 1898 changed name to Coventry City; and in 1905 moved to the Athletic Ground, Highfield Road. Elected to Division One of the Southern League in 1908, but relegated to the Second in 1914.

Joined the Wartime Midland Section of the Football League in 1918 and elected to an expanded Second Division of the Football League for 1919-20. Founder members of the Fourth Division in 1958. Promoted to Division One for the first time in 1967 and never relegated. Premier League founder members 1992.

Ground: Highfield Road Stadium, King Richard St, Coventry, CV2 4FW
Phone: 01203-234000   **News:** 0891 12 11 66
Box Office: 01203-234020
Capacity: 24,021   **Pitch:** 110 yds x 75 yds
Colours: All Sky Blue   **Nickname:** Sky Blues

Life President: Derrick H. Robbins   **Chairman:** Bryan Richardson
Deputy-Chairman: Mike McGinnity **Secretary:** Graham Hover
Manager: Ron Atkinson
Assistants: Mick Brown & Gordon Strachan   **Physio:** George Dalton

League History: 1919 Elected to Division 2; 1925-26 Division 3 (N); 1926-36 Division 3 (S); 1936-52 Division 2; 1952-58 Division 3 (S); 1958-59 Division 4; 1959-64 Division 3; 1964-67 Division 2; 1967-92 Division 1; 1992 – FA Premier League.

Honours: *Football League Division 2 Champions:* 1966-67; *Division 3 Champions:* 1963-64; *Division 3 (S) Champions:* 1935-36; *Runners-up:* 1933-34; *Division 4 Runners-up:* 1958-59; *FA Cup Winners:* 1986-87.

European Record: CC (0): – ; CWC (0) – ; UEFA (1): 70-71 (2)

Managers: H.R. Buckle 1909-10; Robert Wallace 1910-13; Frank Scott-Walford 1913-15; William Clayton 1917-19; H. Pollitt 1919-20; Albert Evans 1920-24; Jimmy Ker 1924-28; James McIntyre 1928-31; Harry Storer 1931-45; Dick Bayliss 1945-47; Billy Frith 1947-48; Harry Storer 1948-53; Jack Fairbrother 1953-54; Charlie Elliott 1954-55; Jesse Carver 1955-56; Harry Warren 1956-57; Billy Firth 1957-61; Jimmy Hill 1961-67; Noel Cantwell 1967-72; Bob Dennison 1972; Joe Mercer 1972-75; Gordon Milne 1972-81; Dave Sexton 1981-83; Bobby Gould 1983-84; Don Mackay 1985-86; George

Curtis 1986-87 (became MD); John Sillett 1987-90; Terry Butcher 1990-92; Don Howe 1992; *(FAPL)* Bobby Gould July 1992-93; Phil Neal Nov 1993-Feb 1995; Ron Atkinson Feb 1995-

Season 1995-96

Biggest Home Win:	5-0 v Blackburn Rovers, 9/12/95
Biggest Home Defeat:	0-4 v Manchester United, 22/11/95
Biggest Away Win:	2-0 v Wimbledon, 27/4/96
Biggest Away Defeat:	1-5 v Blackburn Rovers, 23/9/95
Biggest Home Att:	23,344 v Manchester United, 22/11/95
Smallest Home Att:	12,496 v Wimbledon, 25/11/95
Average Attendance:	18,508 (17th highest)
Leading Scorers:	14 – Dion Dublin, 8 – Noel Whelan

Last Season: *FAPL:* 16 *FA Cup:* 4 *Coca-Cola Cup:* 4

All-Time Records

Record FAPL Win:	5-0 v Blackburn Rovers, 9/12/95
	5-1 v Liverpool, 19/12/92
Record FAPL Defeat:	0-5 v Manchester United, 28/12/92
Record FL Win:	9-0 v Bristol C, Division 3 (S), 28/4/1934
Record FL Defeat:	2-10 v Norwich C, Division 3 (S), 15/3/1930
Record Cup Win:	7-0 v Scunthorpe U, FA Cup R1, 24/11/1934
Record Fee Received:	£3.6m from Liverpool for Phil Babb, 9/94
Record Fee Paid:	£3m to Leeds United for Gary McAllister, 7/96
Most FL Apps:	George Curtis, 486, 1956-70
Most FAPL Apps:	134 – Peter Ndlovu
Most FAPL Goals:	34 – Peter Ndlovu

Highest Scorer in FAPL Season: Mick Quinn, 17, 1992-93
Record Attendance (all-time): 51,455 v Wolves, Division 2, 29/4/67
Record Attendance (FAPL): 24,410 v Manchester United 12/04/93
Most FAPL Goals in Season: 62, 1992-93 – 42 games
Most FAPL Points in Season: 56, 1993-94 – 42 games

5-Year Record

	Div.	P	W	D	L	F	A	Pts	Pos	FAC	FLC
91-92	1	42	11	11	20	35	44	44	19	3	4
92-93	PL	42	13	13	16	52	57	52	15	3	2
93-94	PL	42	14	14	14	43	45	56	11	3	3
94-95	PL	42	12	14	16	44	62	50	16	4	3
95-96	PL	38	8	14	16	42	60	38	16	4	4

Summary 1995-96

Player	Tot	St	Sb	Snu	PS	Gls	Y	R	Fa	La	Fg	Lg
BARNWELL	1	0	1	0	0	0	1	0	0	0	0	0
BOLAND	3	2	1	5	0	0	0	0	0	0	0	0
BORROWS	19	19	0	1	2	0	6	0	1	3	0	0
BURROWS	13	13	0	0	2	0	4	0	1	0	0	0
BUSST	17	16	1	0	1	2	2	0	3	2	0	1
CHRISTIE	1	0	1	5	0	0	0	0	0	1	0	0
COOK	3	2	1	0	2	0	0	0	0	0	0	0
DAISH	11	11	0	0	0	1	2	0	0	0	0	0
DARBY	0	0	0	4	0	0	0	0	0	0	0	0
DUBLIN	34	34	0	0	1	14	3	0	3	2	2	0
FILAN	13	13	0	24	0	0	0	0	0	2	0	0
GILLESPIE	0	0	0	1	0	0	0	0	0	0	0	0
GOULD	0	0	0	12	0	0	0	0	0	2	0	0
HALL	25	24	1	3	1	0	1	0	2	4	0	0
ISAIAS	11	9	2	2	1	2	1	0	0	2	0	0
JESS	12	9	3	0	1	1	0	0	0	0	0	0
LAMPTEY	6	3	3	3	2	0	0	0	1	4	0	2
NDLOVU	32	27	5	0	5	5	2	0	1	4	0	1
OGRIZOVIC	25	25	0	0	0	0	0	0	3	1	0	0
PICKERING	29	26	3	4	3	0	4	0	2	3	1	0
RENNIE	11	9	2	1	2	2	3	0	0	1	0	0
RICHARDSON	33	33	0	0	1	0	6	1	3	4	0	1
SALAKO	37	34	3	1	2	3	3	0	3	3	1	1
SHAW	21	21	0	1	0	0	2	1	3	0	0	0
SHILTON	0	0	0	3	0	0	0	0	0	0	0	0
STRACHAN	12	5	7	3	2	0	1	0	2	3	0	0
TELFER	31	31	0	3	6	1	4	0	3	4	1	0
WHELAN	21	21	0	0	1	8	3	0	3	0	1	0
WHYTE	1	1	0	0	0	0	0	0	0	0	0	0
WILLIAMS J.	0	0	0	1	0	0	0	0	0	0	0	0
WILLIAMS P.	32	30	2	1	1	2	9	1	1	4	0	1

OGs 1

Potential Never Realised

Being involved in a relegation battle is nothing new to Coventry City but leaving survival until the final day of the season is late even by their standards. Premiership salvation was guaranteed courtesy of a goalless home draw with Leeds United and it was the Sky Blues' defence which came up trumps at just the right time by going through their final four games without conceding a goal.

Two topics surrounded Coventry that will have surprised few people. Firstly, that they were at the wrong end of the table for much of the season and, secondly, that manager Ron Atkinson was dabbling in the transfer market. Big Ron strove to make his side fashionable and went some way towards achieving this with the signing of Brazilians Carlos Batista and Marques Isaias although the combined fee of £650,000 was little more than pocket money by the Coventry manager's standards. Having finished just five points clear of the drop the previous season Atkinson sought to further strengthen the side by taking Paul Telfer, John Salako, Paul Williams, Nil Lamptey, Richard Shaw, Noel Whelan, Liam Daish and Eoin Jess to Highfield Road during the season.

The new look Coventry hardly made the desired start with just one of the opening 16 league games being won. Goal scoring was a problem with just 11 being scored in 14 games and when a 4-0 defeat at home to Manchester United sent Coventry to the foot of the table, pressure was mounting on the Sky Blues. They responded with a 3-3 draw at home to Wimbledon and then a remarkable 4-3 defeat at Sheffield Wednesday at the start of December which included a hat trick for luckless top scorer Dion Dublin. A week later champions Blackburn Rovers were humbled 5-0 at Highfield Road and with two more wins from the next three outings Coventry climbed out of the relegation places for the first time in two months. With £2m signing Whelan scoring at a good rate following his pre-Christmas moves Coventry looked set to move clear of danger only to embark on another dismal run of one win in 12 games.

Defeats against fellow strugglers Bolton and Southampton, and then at Spurs plunged City to just one place off the bottom with six games remaining. Whelan's ninth goal of the season started a recovery as Liverpool were surprisingly overcome at Highfield Road but the club suffered a double blow at Old Trafford on Easter Monday when David Busst suffered a horrendous broken leg and City lost 1-0. It was to be the last goal Coventry conceded as draws with Forest and Leeds and wins over QPR and Wimbledon extended Coventry's stay in the top flight into a 30th season.

The Coca Cola Cup provided one of the high points of Coventry's season for, after seeing off Hull City; the Sky Blues came back from two down to defeat Spurs at Highfield Road only to lose 2-1 to Wolverhampton Wanderers in Round Four.

A fine second half display at Plymouth Argyle took Coventry through to the 4th Round of the FA Cup but a 2-1 replay defeat away to Manchester City left the club with nothing more to concentrate on than Premiership survival.

Big Ron is unlikely to settle for another poor showing in the cups and one more struggle against relegation as he looks forward to his second full season in charge of the club and the £3.5m spent on Daish and Jess late in the season demonstrates that Coventry are determined to bring success to Highfield Road. ∎

Results 1995-96

Date	Opponents	Ven	Res	Pos	Atten	Scorers
19-Aug	Newcastle U.	A	0-3	–	36,485	
23-Aug	Man. City	H	2-1	–	16,568	Telfer (12); Dublin (86)
26-Aug	Arsenal	H	0-0	11	20,081	
30-Aug	Chelsea	A	2-2	10	24,398	Isaias (40); Ndlovu (54)
09-Sep	N. Forest	H	1-1	11	17,238	Dublin (12)
16-Sep	Middlesbro'	A	1-2	14	27,882	Isaias (47)
23-Sep	Blackburn R.	A	1-5	16	24,382	Ndlovu (34)
30-Sep	Aston Villa	H	0-3	18	21,004	
14-Oct	Liverpool	A	0-0	17	39,079	
21-Oct	Sheff. Wed.	H	0-1	17	14,002	
28-Oct	Leeds United	A	1-3	18	30,161	Dublin (12)
04-Nov	Tottenham	H	2-3	18	17,545	Dublin (9); Williams P. (48)
19-Nov	QPR	A	1-1	18	11,189	Dublin (75)
22-Nov	Man. United	H	0-4	20	23,344	
25-Nov	Wimbledon	H	3-3	19	12,496	OG (Heald 34); Dublin (67); Rennie (83)
03-Dec	Sheff. Wed.	A	3-4	20	16,229	Dublin (18, 37, 55)
09-Dec	Blackburn R.	H	5-0	19	13,409	Busst (40); Dublin (60); Rennie (64); Ndlovu (74); Salako (88)
16-Dec	Aston Villa	A	1-4	19	28,486	Dublin (59)
23-Dec	Everton	H	2-1	19	16,638	Busst (48); Whelan (84)
30-Dec	Bolton Wan.	A	2-1	17	16,678	Whelan (44); Salako (90 pen)
01-Jan	Southampton	H	1-1	17	16,822	Whelan (83)
14-Jan	Newcastle U.	H	0-1	17	20,553	
20-Jan	Man. City	A	1-1	17	25,710	Dublin (66)
31-Jan	West Ham	A	2-3	18	18,884	Dublin (62); Whelan (82)
03-Feb	Arsenal	A	1-1	18	35,623	Whelan (23)
10-Feb	Chelsea	H	1-0	17	20,629	Whelan (43)
24-Feb	Middlesbro'	H	0-0	17	17,979	
02-Mar	West Ham	H	2-2	16	17,448	Salako (7); Whelan (15)
09-Mar	Everton	A	2-2	15	34,517	Daish (38); Williams P. (85)
16-Mar	Bolton Wan.	H	0-2	16	17,168	
25-Mar	Southampton	A	0-1	16	14,461	
30-Mar	Tottenham	A	1-3	19	26,808	Dublin (20)
06-Apr	Liverpool	H	1-0	18	23,037	Whelan (18)
08-Apr	Man. United	A	0-1	19	50,332	
13-Apr	QPR	H	1-0	18	22,916	Jess (70)
17-Apr	N. Forest	A	0-0	17	24,629	
27-Apr	Wimbledon	A	2-0	16	15,790	Ndlovu (52, 89)
05-May	Leeds United	H	0-0	16	22,769	

FA Challenge Cup

Date	Opponents	Vn	Rnd	Res	Atten	Scorers
06-Jan	Plymouth A.	A	3R	3-1	17,721	Pickering (53); Salako (55); Telfer (58)
07-Feb	Man. City	H	4R	2-2	18,775	Whelan (2); Dublin (90)
14-Feb	Man. City	A	4RR	1-2	22,419	Dublin (85)

Coca-Cola League Cup

Date	Opponents	Vn	Rnd	Res	Atten	Scorers
20-Sep	Hull City	H	2R1L	2-0	8,915	Richardson (25); Lamptey (36)
04-Oct	Hull City	A	2R2L	1-0	9,609	Lamptey (10)
	Coventry City won 3-0 on aggregate.					
25-Oct	Tottenham	H	3R	3-2	18,267	Ndlovu (35 pen); Busst (61); Salako (76)
29-Nov	Wolves	A	4R	1-2	24,628	Williams P. (67)

Coventry City – Premiership Fact File

- City have changed their phone numbers at Highfield Road since 1st June 1996. Sky Blue fans should update their diaries.
- If you're a footballer and you're name is Paul Williams then you have a good chance of playing for the Sky Blues – they've had three first teamers by thantname in the past two seasons which makes record keeping difficult! The current Paul Williams joined from Derby County at the start of last season and was voted the club's Player of the Year for 1995-96!
- With 37 appearances John Salako appeared in the most Premiership matches for Coventry City last season.
- Gates at the Highfield Road Stadium were up by over 4,000 per game on the 1994-95 season.
- City will hope for better things in cup competitions this season – in the past five seasons they have failed to progress past the 4th round.
- Coventry recorded just one win out of their first 16 Premiership encounters. They broke their duck in convincing style though with a 5-0 thrashing of the then reigning champions Blackburn Rovers!
- Coventry will be competing for a successive 30th season in the top flight of English football.
- Players to pass the 100 Premiership appearance mark during last season included Steve Ogrizovic (123), David Borrows (121) and David Burrows (102). John Salako with 89 could pass the mark during 1996-97 but will Gordon Strachan reach his century? He currently has 87 appearances.

Derby County

In 1884 members of the Derbyshire County Cricket team formed the football club as a way of boosting finances in the cricket close season. They played their first season at the Racecourse ground and entered the FA Cup. A year later the club moved to the Baseball Ground where they have remained ever since. In 1888 they became founder members of the Football League. Since their formation they have fluctuated through the top divisions, but enjoyed a sparkling spell during the 1970s.

Ground: The Baseball Ground, Shaftesbury Crescent, Derby, DE23 8NB
Phone: 01332-340105   **News:** 0891-12 11 87
Capacity: 19,500 (15,000 seated)   **Pitch:** 110 yds x 71 yds
Colours: White & Black, Black, White & Black
Nickname: The Rams

Chairman: Lionel Pickering   **Vice-Chairman:** Peter Gadsby
CEO: Keith Loring   **Secretary:** Keith Pearson
Manager: Jim Smith   **Coach:** Billy McEwan
Physio: Gordon Guthrie

League History: 1888 Founder members of Football League; 107-12 Division 1; 1912-14 Division 2; 1914-15 Division 1; 1915-21 Division 1; 1921-26 Division 2; 1926-53 Division 1; 1953-55 Division 2; 1955-57 Division 3N; 1957-69 Division 2; 1969-80 Division 1; 1980-84 Division 2; 1984-86 Division 3; 1986-87 Division 2; 1987-91 Division 1; 1991-92 Division 2; 1992-96 Division 1; 1996- FA Premier League.

Honours: *Football League Division 1 Champions:* 1971-72, 1974-75; *Runners-up:* 1895-96, 1929-30, 1935-36, 1995-96; *Division2 Champions:* 1911-12, 1914-15, 1968-69, 1986-87; *Runners-up:* 1925-26; *Division 3N Champions:* 1956-57; *Runners-up:* 1955-56; *FA Cup Winners:* 1945-46; *Runners-up:* 1897-98, 1888-89, 1902-03; *Anglo Italian Cup Runners-up:* 1992-93.

European Record: CC (2): 1972-73(SF), 1975-76(2); CWC (0) – ; UEFA (2): 1974-75(3), 1976-77(2)

Managers: Harry Bradshaw 1904-09; Jimmy Methven 1906-22; Cecil Potter 1922-25; George Jobey 1925-41; Ted Manger 1944-46; Stuart McMillan 1946-53; Jack Barker 1953-55; Harry Storer 1955-62; Tim Ward 1962-67; Brian Clough 1967-73; Dave Mackay 1973-76; Colin Murphy 1977; Tommy Docherty 1977-79; Colin Addison 1979-82; Johnny Newman 1982; Peter

Taylor 1982-84; Roy McFarland 1984, Arthur Cox 1984-93; Roy McFarland 1993-95; Jim Smith June 1995-.

Season 1995-96

Biggest Home Win: 6-2 v Tranmere Rovers, 8/4/96
Biggest Home Defeat: 0-1 v Leicester City, 10/9/95
Biggest Away Win: 4-1 v Birmingham City, 21/11/95
Biggest Away Defeat: 1-5 v Tranmere Rovers, 4/11/95
Biggest Home Att: 17,460 v Wolverhampton Wdrs, 10/2/96
Smallest Home Att: 9,590 v Millwall, 1/10/95
Average Attendance: 14,558
Leading Scorers: 20 – Dean Sturridge, 11 – Gabbiadini, Willems
Last Season: *Division 1:* 2 *FA Cup:* 3 *Coca-Cola Cup:* 3

All-Time Records

Record FAPL Win: –
Record FAPL Defeat: –
Record FL Win: 9-0 v Wolverhampton Wanderers, Div.1 10/1/1891
Record FL Defeat:
Record Cup Win: 12-0 v Finn Harps, UEFA Cup 1R1L, 15/9/76
Record Fee Received: £2.9m from Liverpool for Dean Saunders, 7/91
Record Fee Paid: £2.5m to Notts County for Craig Short, 9/92
Most FL Apps: Kevin Hector, 486, 1966-78, 1980-82
Most FAPL Apps: –
Most FAPL Goals: –
Highest Scorer in FAPL season: –
Record Attendance (all-time): –
Record Attendance (FAPL): –
Most FAPL Goals in Season: –
Most FAPL Points in Season: –

5-Year Record

	Div.	P	W	D	L	F	A	Pts	Pos	FAC	FLC
91-92	2	46	23	9	14	69	51	78	3	4	3
92-93	1	46	19	9	18	68	57	66	8	6	3
93-94	1	46	20	11	15	73	68	71	6	3	3
94-95	1	46	18	12	16	66	51	66	9	3	4
95-96	1	46	21	16	9	71	51	79	2	3	3

Summary 1995-96

Player	Tot	St	Sb	Snu	PS	Gls	Fa	La	Fg	Lg
BODEN	4	4	0	0	1	0	0	0	0	0
CARBON	5	2	3	1	0	0	0	0	0	0
CARSLEY	35	31	4	3	9	1	0	2	0	0
COOPER	2	0	2	0	0	0	0	0	0	0
FLYNN	42	29	13	3	4	2	1	3	0	0
GABBIADINI	39	33	6	1	14	11	1	3	1	1
HARKES	8	7	1	0	2	0	0	0	0	0
HODGES	8	1	7	2	0	0	0	0	0	0
HOULT	41	40	1	3	0	0	1	2	0	0
KAVANAGH	9	8	1	3	0	0	1	1	0	0
NICHOLSON	20	19	1	0	2	0	1	3	0	0
POWELL, Chris	19	19	0	0	6	0	0	0	0	0
POWELL, Darryl	37	37	0	0	8	5	0	2	0	0
PREECE	13	10	3	0	1	1	0	2	0	0
QUY	0	0	0	1	0	0	0	0	0	0
ROWLETT	35	34	1	0	2	0	1	2	0	0
SIMPSON	39	21	18	5	8	10	1	2	1	1
STALLARD	3	3	0	2	3	0	0	1	0	1
STIMAC	27	27	0	0	2	1	1	0	0	0
STURRIDGE	39	33	6	0	2	20	0	2	0	0
SUTTON, Steve	6	6	0	8	1	0	0	1	0	0
SUTTON, Wayne	1	1	0	0	0	0	0	0	0	0
TROLLOPE	17	7	10	10	2	0	1	2	0	0
VAN DER LAAN	39	39	0	1	10	6	1	3	0	0
WARD	7	5	2	0	2	1	0	0	0	0
WASSALL	17	16	1	2	1	0	0	2	0	0
WEBSTER	3	3	0	0	1	0	0	0	0	0
WILLEMS	33	31	2	0	6	11	1	2	0	1
WRACK	11	2	9	1	2	0	1	3	0	0
WRIGHT	0	0	0	1	0	0	0	0	0	0
YATES	38	38	0	0	2	2	1	3	0	0

Smith's Crisp Promotion

As Derby County contemplated a fifth season in Division One, the club turned to a manager with vast experience, in the form of Jim Smith, to guide them into the Premiership. The early signs were not encouraging; with four games played Derby were just one place off the foot of the table. Wins at Luton and Southend nudged the side in the right direction but it was not until the final weekend of October that the Rams recorded a victory at the Baseball Ground. That game, a 2-1 win over Oldham, was Derby's 14th Endsleigh League match of the season and despite their poor record County were still only ten points off the pace set by Millwall.

Smith made his first seven figure signing as Derby manager with the transfer of Igor Stimac from Hadjuk Split for £1.5m – 16 years earlier Smith had been the first manager to sell a player for a million pounds. Stimac opened his account on the day of Bonfire Night but the fireworks were all in the Derby goalmouth as Tranmere stormed a 5-1 win, sending the Rams back down to 17th. The reversal at Prenton Park was Derby's first in six outings and more significantly they would not lose any of the next 20 games. A 3-0 triumph over West Brom at the Baseball Ground was the first of ten wins in 11 games as the leap from 17th to top was completed quite amazingly in under six weeks.

Other promotion chasers were blown away as Derby opened up an eight point lead by the middle of January. Birmingham were crushed 4-1 at St Andrews, Millwall went down at the New Den, Sunderland lost 3-1 at the Baseball Ground while Leicester were held at Filbert Street. The title surge was slowed on 20 January when Port Vale held out for a point at Vale Park, five of the next eight games were drawn and worse was to come when Sunderland gained revenge with a 3-0 win at Roker Park. A disappointing home draw with struggling Watford and defeat at Norwich followed. One day after the Watford match top place was surrendered to Sunderland.

A number of sides had succumbed to the pressure of being top of the Endsleigh League, were Derby the next in line? The response was impressive with Stoke's promotion surge slowed by a 3-1 defeat at the Baseball Ground but a 1-0 setback at Ipswich, Derby's fifth away match without a win, kept the promotion party on hold. A single goal victory at lowly Oldham allowed the Rams to move five points clear of third placed Palace and on Easter Monday Paul Simpson hit Derby's only hat trick as the side revenged their earlier defeat at Tranmere with a 6-2 home thrashing. Derby edged closer to automatic promotion with a point off both Charlton and Birmingham and the confirmation of Premiership football was received by virtue of a 2-1 victory over Palace with skipper Robin Van der Laan scoring the promotion clinching goal.

Derby's cup fortunes can be summed up in two words – Leeds United. It was Leeds who removed the Rams from the Coca Cola Cup with a 3rd Round victory at the Baseball Ground after Shrewsbury Town had been seen off in the previous round. Derby looked to be having no such problems in the FA Cup as they went into a two goal league against their Premiership visitors despite having lost the injured Stimac and seen defender Gary Rowett dismissed. But there was to be no giant killing for the side then seven points clear at the summit of the Endsleigh League as Leeds staged a remarkable comeback to go through 4-2.

During the season Jim Smith passed the 1000th game in charge mark – a fact noted when he received an LMA Special Award during the close season. ∎

Results 1995-96

Date	Opponents	Ven	Res	Pos	Atten	Scorers
13-Aug	Port Vale	H	0-0	–	10,869	
19-Aug	Reading	A	2-3	–	9,280	Sturridge (62); Preece (83)
26-Aug	Grimsby	H	1-1	–	10,564	Sturridge (58)
30-Aug	Wolves	A	0-3	23	26,053	
02-Sep	Luton Tn	A	2-1	16	6,427	Sturridge (15, 63)
10-Sep	Leicester C.	H	0-1	19	11,767	
13-Sep	Southend U.	A	1-0	17	9,242	Sturridge
16-Sep	Portsmouth	A	2-2	20	14,434	Van der Laan (32); Flynn (59)
23-Sep	Barnsley	A	0-2	21	8,929	
01-Oct	Millwall	H	2-2	20	9,590	Van der Laan, Willems
07-Oct	Sheffield U.	A	2-0	16	12,721	Gabbiadini (29); Willems (46)
14-Oct	Ipswich Tn	H	1-1	17	13,034	Gabbiadini (27)
22-Oct	Stoke City	A	1-1	17	9,435	Van der Laan (89)
28-Oct	Oldham Ath.	H	2-1	14	11,545	Van der Laan (33); Simpson (49)
04-Nov	Tranmere R.	A	1-5	17	8,565	Stimac (52)
11-Nov	WBA	H	3-0	14	13,765	Gabbiadini (16, 61); Sturridge (27)
18-Nov	Charlton Ath.	H	2-0	10	12,963	Willems (43); Gabbiadini (62)
21-Nov	Birmingham	A	4-1	8	19,417	Sturridge (5); Willems (39); Gabbiadini (46); Powell (73)
25-Nov	Crystal P.	A	0-0	10	13,506	
02-Dec	Sheffield U.	H	4-2	7	13,841	Sturridge (29); Willems (65, 66); Gabbiadini (74)
09-Dec	Barnsley	H	4-1	2	14,415	Carsley (2); Gabbiadini (52); Sturridge (63); Willems (80)
16-Dec	Millwall	A	1-0	2	7,694	Sturridge (43)
23-Dec	Sunderland	H	3-1	1	16,882	Gabbiadini (36); Sturridge (84); Willems (65)
26-Dec	Huddersfield	A	1-0	1	18,495	Willems (77)
01-Jan	Norwich City	H	2-1	1	16,714	Willems (37); Gabbiadini (90)
13-Jan	Reading	H	3-0	1	15,123	Sturridge (48, 66); Flynn (82)
20-Jan	Port Vale	A	1-1	1	11,974	Sturridge (44)
03-Feb	Grimsby Tn	A	1-1	1	7,818	Powell (49)
10-Feb	Wolves	H	0-0	1	17,460	
17-Feb	Southend U.	A	2-1	1	8,331	Simpson (54); Willems (86)
21-Feb	Luton Tn	H	1-1	1	14,825	Powell

24-Feb	Portsmouth	H	3-2	1	16,120	Yates (71); Sturridge (76); Gabbiadini (84)
28-Feb	Leicester C.	A	0-0	1	20,911	
02-Mar	Huddersfield	H	3-2	1	17,097	Simpson (12, 75); Van der Laan (21)
05-Mar	Watford	A	0-0	1	8,306	
09-Mar	Sunderland	A	0-3	1	21,644	
16-Mar	Watford	H	1-1	1	15,939	Simpson (84 pen)
23-Mar	Norwich C.	A	0-1	2	15,349	
30-Mar	Stoke City	H	3-1	2	17,245	Sturridge (53, 79); Powell (58)
02-Apr	Ipswich Tn	A	0-1	2	16,210	
06-Apr	Oldham Ath.	A	1-0	2	8,119	Simpson (58 pen)
08-Apr	Tranmere R.	H	6-2	2	16,723	Powell (38); Yates (50); Simpson (54, 57, 69); Sturridge (67);
14-Apr	Charlton Ath.	A	0-0	2	11,334	
20-Apr	Birmingham	H	1-1	2	16,757	Simpson (55)
28-Apr	Crystal P.	H	2-1	2	17,041	Sturridge (3); Van der Laan (65)
05-May	WBA	A	2-3	2	23,858	Sturridge (15), Ward (88)

FA Challenge Cup

Date	Opponents	Vn	Rnd	Res	Atten	Scorers
07-Jan	Leeds United	H	3R	2-4	16,155	Gabbiadini (49); Simpson (50)

Coca-Cola League Cup

Date	Opponents	Vn	Rnd	Res	Atten	Scorers
19-Sep	Shrewsbury	A	2R1L	3-1	3,170	Simpson (29); Stallard (33); Gabbiadini (68)
04-Oct	Shrewsbury	H	2R2L	1-1	8,825	Willems (30)
25-Oct	Leeds United	H	3R	0-1	16,030	

Everton

The cricket team of St. Domingo's Church turned to football around 1878. Playing in Stanley Park, in late 1879 changed name to Everton FC, the name of the district to the west of the park.

Moved to a field at Priory Road in 1882 and then, in 1884, moved to a site in Anfield Road. As one of the country's leading teams, became founder members of the Football League in 1888. Moved to Goodison Park, a field on the north side of Stanley Park, in 1892 following a dispute with the ground's landlord. Premier League founder members 1992.

Ground: Goodison Park, Liverpool, L4 4EL
Phone: 0151 521 2020   **Box Office:** 0151 523 6666
Dial-a-Seat: 0151 525 1231   **Info:** 0891 12 11 99
Colours: Royal Blue, White, Blue   **Nickname:** The Toffees
Capacity: 40,160   **Pitch:** 112 yds x 78 yds
Radio Everton: 1602AM

Chairman: Peter Johnson   **Secretary:** Michael Dunford
Manager: Joe Royle   **Assistant:** Willie Donachie
Coach: Jimmy Gabriel   **Physio:** Les Helm

League History: 1888 Founder Member of the Football League; 1930-31 Division 2; 1931-51 Division 1; 1951-54 Division 2; 1954-92 Division 1; 1992-FA Premier League.

Honours: *Football League Division 1 Champions:* 1890-91, 1914-15, 1927-28, 1931-32, 1938-39, 1962-63, 1969-70, 1984-85, 1986-87; *Runners-up:* 1889-90, 1894-95, 1901-02, 1904-05, 1908-09, 1911-12, 1985-86; *Division 2 Champions:* 1930-31; *Runners-up:* 1953-54. *FA Cup Winners:* 1906, 1933, 1966, 1984, 1995; *Runners-up:* 1893, 1897, 1907, 1968, 1985, 1986, 1989. *Football League Cup Runners-up:* 1976-77, 1983-84. *League Super Cup Runners-up:* 1986. *Cup-Winners' Cup Winners:* 1984-85; *Simod Cup Runners-up:* 1989. *Zenith Data Systems Cup Runners-up:* 1991.

European Record: CC (2): 63-64(1), 70-71(QF); CWC (3): 66-67(2), 84-85(W), 95-96(2). UEFA (6): 62-63(1), 64-65(3), 65-66(2), 75-76(1), 78-79(2), 79-80(1).

Managers: W.E. Barclay 1888-89; Dick Molyneux 1889-1901; William C. Cuff 1901-18; W.J. Sawyer 1918-19; Thomas H. McIntosh 1919-35; Theo Kelly 1936-48; Cliff Britton 1948-56; Ian Buchan 1956-58; Johnny Carey

1958-61; Harry Catterick 1961-73; Billy Bingham 1973-77; Gordon Lee 1977-81; Howard Kendall 1981-87; Colin Harvey 1987-90; (FAPL) Howard Kendall Nov 1990-93; Mike Walker Jan 1993-Nov 1994; Joe Royle Nov 1994-

Season 1995-96

Biggest Home Win: 4-0 v Middlesbrough, 26/12/95
Biggest Home Defeat: 2-4 v Wimbledon, 23/3/96
Biggest Away Win: 5-2 v Sheffield Wednesday, 27/4/96
Biggest Away Defeat: 1-3 v QPR, 8/4/96
Biggest Home Att: 40,127 v Aston Villa, 5/5/96
Smallest Home Att: 30,009 v QPR, 22/11/95
Average Attendance: 35,442 (5th highest)
Leading Scorers: 16 – Andrei Kanchelskis, 9 – Graham Stuart
Last Season: *FAPL: 6 FA Cup: 4 Coca-Cola Cup: 2*

All-Time Records

Record FAPL Win: 6-2 v Swindon Town, 15/1/94
Record FAPL Defeat: 1-5 v Norwich City 25/9/93; Sheffield Wnd 2/4/94
Record FL Win: 9-1 v Manchester City, Division 1, 3/9/1906;
                          Plymouth Argyle, Division 2, 27/12/1930
Record FL Defeat: 4-10 v Tottenham H, Division 1, 11/10/1958
Record Cup Win: 11-2 v Derby County, FA Cup R1, 18/1/1890
Record Fee Received: £2.75m from Barcelona for Gary Lineker, 7/86
Record Fee Paid: £5m to Man. United for Andrei Kanchelskis 7/95
Most FL Apps: Ted Sagar, 465, 1929-53
Most FAPL Apps: 161 – Neville Southall
Most FAPL Goals: 29 – Paul Rideout
Highest Scorer in FAPL season: 16 – Tony Cottee, 93-94
                          and Andrei Kanchelskis 95-96
Record Attendance (all-time): 78,299 v Liverpool, Division 1, 18/9/1948
Record Attendance (FAPL): 40,011 v Manchester United, 25/2/95
Most FAPL Goals in Season: 64, 1995-96 – 38 games
Most FAPL Points in Season: 61, 1995-96 – 38 games

	Div.	P	W	D	L	F	A	Pts	Pos	FAC	FLC
91-92	1	42	13	14	15	52	51	53	12	4	4
92-93	PL	42	15	8	19	53	55	53	13	3	4
93-94	PL	42	12	8	22	42	63	44	17	3	4
94-95	PL	42	11	17	14	44	51	50	15	W	2
95-96	PL	38	17	10	11	64	44	61	6	4	2

Summary 1995-96

Player	Tot	St	Sb	Snu	PS	Gls	Y	R	Fa	La	Fg	Lg
ABLETT	13	13	0	0	3	0	3	0	3	1	1	0
ALLEN, Graham	0	0	0	2	0	0	0	0	0	0	0	0
AMOKACHI	25	17	8	6	4	6	1	0	3	1	1	0
BARLOW	3	0	3	3	0	0	0	0	0	1	0	0
BARRETT	8	8	0	0	0	0	1	0	2	0	0	0
BRANCH	3	1	2	0	1	0	0	0	0	0	0	0
EBBRELL	25	24	1	2	1	4	5	0	4	0	1	0
FERGUSON	18	16	2	0	2	5	4	0	2	0	2	0
GRANT	13	11	2	5	4	1	1	0	1	2	0	0
HINCHCLIFFE	28	23	5	2	4	2	4	0	3	2	0	1
HOLMES	1	1	0	0	0	0	0	0	0	0	0	0
HORNE	26	25	1	5	1	1	9	1	4	2	0	0
HOTTIGER	9	9	0	0	1	0	0	0	0	0	0	0
JACKSON	14	14	0	1	1	0	2	0	2	1	0	0
KANCHELSKIS	32	32	0	0	3	16	2	0	4	0	0	0
KEARTON	0	0	0	25	0		0	0	0	0	0	0
LIMPAR	28	22	6	5	9	3	5	0	4	1	0	0
O'CONNOR	4	3	1	2	0	0	2	0	0	0	0	0
PARKINSON	28	28	0	0	3	3	9	0	2	1	0	0
RIDEOUT	25	19	6	1	3	6	2	0	2	2	0	0
SAMWAYS	4	3	1	0	0	1	0	0	0	1	0	0
SHORT	23	22	1	5	2	2	6	0	3	2	0	0
SOUTHALL	38	38	0	0	0	0	0	0	4	3	0	0
SPEARE	0	0	0	3	0	0	0	0	0	0	0	0
STUART	29	27	2	0	2	9	3	0	4	1	3	1
UNSWORTH	31	28	3	3	1	2	3	1	2	1	0	0
WATSON	34	34	0	0	0	1	6	1	4	1	0	0
OG						1						

Royle Shield

After the excitement generated by their FA Cup victory the previous season following the appointment of Joe Royle as manager, Everton held high hopes that 1995-96 would be their year. To a degree those expectations were met as Everton attained their highest league position for six years and their best points total for eight years but a failure to progress further than one round in any of the various cup competitions did dampen a lot of the satisfaction of those achievements.

Royle was conspicuous by his absence in the transfer market during the close season but the one major signing he did complete, the £5m transfer of Andrei Kanchelskis from Manchester United after a prolonged delay, was one of the major coups of the season. Kanchelskis scored 16 times in the Premiership which included Everton's only hat trick for the season, despite missing five weeks with a shoulder injury. Just one other major signing was made during the season and that saw Marc Hottiger move from Newcastle for £700,000. The highly vaunted return of Duncan Ferguson, following his spell in a Scottish prison, attracted over ten thousand spectators to watch a Reserve team fixture but once back in the First team he found the back of the net just five times in the league.

Everton were goalless in their opening two league matches before scoring twice in each of the next four games but it was a generally low key first nine weeks to the campaign with just two games being won which left the Toffeemen down in 16th place. Everton's season took off during November when wins over Blackburn, arch rivals Liverpool and QPR lifted Royle's side five places and three more consecutive victories over the festive period took the Blues into the top ten for the first time since August. Everton stayed in the top ten for the remainder of the season and a fine final flourish of four wins, one draw and just one defeat in their last six games would have secured a place in the UEFA Cup had Arsenal not scored a couple of late goals against Bolton on the last day of the season.

Everton's first appearance in European football for eleven years saw Icelandic side Reykjavik overcome, after a struggle, in the 1st Round. Feyenoord gained a goalless draw at Goodison in Round Two before completing the task in Holland. The Dutch side also put Everton out of Europe when they last met during the 1979-80 season.

Domestic competitions were not much more to Everton's liking although a second half goal by Vinny Samways against Blackburn Rovers at Wembley took the Charity Shield to Merseyside before the start of the league campaign. The Blues were out of the Coca Cola Cup by the first week of October when Millwall, after being held at home, won 4-2 at Goodison Park. Everton's grip on the FA Cup was shaky from the start with Endsleigh League side Stockport County falling to a last minute John Ebbrell goal in a replay while in the 4th Round it was Port Vale's turn to score a last minute goal to force a replay which the struggling Endsleigh Division One side won at Vale Park.

Nigerian Daniel Amokachi did not quite match the impact made towards the end of the previous season but Graham Stuart had a very productive campaign with his 14 goals making him the second highest scorer, in fact Everton did not lose in any of the eight league matches in which he scored. ■

Results 1995-96

FA Carling Premiership

Date	Opponents	Ven	Res	Pos	Atten	Scorers
19-Aug	Chelsea	A	0-0	–	29,858	
23-Aug	Arsenal	H	0-2	–	36,047	
26-Aug	Southampton	H	2-0	10	33,668	Limpar (34); Amokachi (42)
30-Aug	Man. City	A	2-0	7	28,432	Parkinson (58); Amokachi (75)
09-Sep	Man. United	H	2-3	9	39,496	Limpar (27); Rideout (55)
17-Sep	N. Forest	A	2-3	12	24,786	Rideout (62, 81)
23-Sep	West Ham	A	1-2	14	21,085	Samways (40)
01-Oct	Newcastle U.	H	1-3	14	33,080	Limpar (81)
14-Oct	Bolton Wan.	A	1-1	14	20,427	Rideout (85)
22-Oct	Tottenham	H	1-1	15	33,629	Stuart (12)
28-Oct	Aston Villa	A	0-1	16	32,792	
05-Nov	Blackburn R.	H	1-0	13	30,097	Stuart (23)
18-Nov	Liverpool	A	2-1	13	40,818	Kanchelskis (53, 68)
22-Nov	QPR	H	2-0	11	30,009	Stuart (18); Rideout (36)
22-Nov	Sheff. Wed.	H	2-2	12	35,898	Kanchelskis (45); Amokachi (53)
02-Dec	Tottenham	A	0-0	12	32,894	
11-Dec	West Ham	H	3-0	11	31,778	Stuart (33); Unsworth (43 pen); Ebbrell (68)
16-Dec	Newcastle U.	A	0-1	12	36,557	
23-Dec	Coventry C.	A	1-2	12	16,639	Rideout (67)
26-Dec	Middlesbro'	H	4-0	12	40,091	Short (10); Stuart (45, 59); Kanchelskis (67)
30-Dec	Leeds United	H	2-0	11	40,009	OG (Wetherall 5); Kanchelskis (51)
01-Jan	Wimbledon	A	3-2	9	11,121	Ebbrell (1); Ferguson (23,25)
13-Jan	Chelsea	H	1-1	10	34,968	Unsworth (35 pen)
20-Jan	Arsenal	A	2-1	9	38,275	Stuart (50); Kanchelskis (84)
03-Feb	Southampton	A	2-2	9	15,136	Stuart (53); Horne (57)
10-Feb	Man. City	H	2-0	8	37,354	Parkinson (37); Hinchcliffe (47 pen)
21-Feb	Man. United	A	0-2		42,459	
24-Feb	N. Forest	H	3-0	7	33,163	Kanchelskis (52); Watson (56); Ferguson (60)
02-Mar	Middlesbro'	A	2-0	6	29,407	Grant (28); Hinchcliffe (44 pen)
09-Mar	Coventry C.	H	2-2	7	34,517	Ferguson (17, 25)
17-Mar	Leeds United	A	2-2	6	29,425	Stuart (28); Kanchelskis (50)
23-Mar	Wimbledon	H	2-4	7	31,382	Short (21); Kanchelskis (61)

126

30-Mar	Blackburn R.	A	3-0	7	29,468	Amokachi (71);
						Kanchelskis (77, 90)
06-Apr	Bolton Wan.	H	3-0	6	37,974	Hottiger (21);
						Kanchelskis (86);
						Amokachi (90)
08-Apr	QPR	A	1-3	7	18,349	Ebbrell (80)
16-Apr	Liverpool	H	1-1	7	40,120	Kanchelskis (19)
27-Apr	Sheff.Wed.	A	5-2	6	32,724	Amokachi (4); Ebbrell (10);
						Kanchelskis (21, 54, 65)
05-May	Aston Villa	H	1-0	6	40,127	Parkinson (78)

Cup-Winners' Cup

Date	Opponents	Vn	Rnd	Res	Atten	Scorers
14-Sep	FC Reykjavik	A	1R1L	3-2	6,000	Ebbrell (22);
						Unsworth (57 pen);
						Amokachi (88)
28-Sep	FC Reykjavik	H	1R2L	3-1	18,422	Stuart (56); Grant (65);
	Everton won 6-3 on aggregate					Rideout (87).
19-Oct	Feyenoord	H	2R1L	0-0	27,526	
02-Nov	Feyenoord	A	2R2L	0-1	40,000	
	Feyenoord won 1-0 on aggregate					

FA Challenge Cup

Date	Opponents	Vn	Rnd	Res	Atten	Scorers
07-Jan	Stockport C.	H	3R	2-2	28,921	Stuart (7); Ablett (44)
17-Jan	Stockport C.	A	3RR	3-2	11,283	Ferguson (71); Stuart (73);
	Everton won 5-4 on aggregate					Ebbrell (89)
27-Jan	Port Vale	H	4R	2-2	33,168	Amokachi (39); Ferguson (88)
14-Feb	Port Vale	A	4RR	1-2	19,197	Stuart (32)

Coca-Cola League Cup

Date	Opponents	Vn	Rnd	Res	Atten	Scorers
20-Sep	Millwall	A	2R1L	0-0	12,053	
04-Oct	Millwall	H	2R2L	2-4	14,891	Hinchcliffe (47 pen);
	Millwall won 4-2 on aggregate					Stuart (55).

FA Charity Shield

Date	Opponents	Vn	Res	Atten	Scorers
13-Aug	Blackburn R.	W	1-0	40,149	Samways (57)

Leeds United

Leeds City, founded in 1904, took over the Elland Road ground of the defunct Holbeck Club and in 1905 gained a Football League Division Two place. The club was, however, expelled in 1919 for disciplinary reasons associated with payments to players during the War. The club closed down.

Leeds United FC, a new professional club, emerged the same year and competed in the Midland League. The club was elected to Football League Division Two for season 1920-21. The club has subsequently never been out of the top two divisions. Premier League founder member 1992.

Ground: Elland Road, Leeds, LS11 0ES
Phone: 0113 271 6037 **Nickname:** United
Colours: All White
Capacity: 39,704 **Pitch:** 117 yds x 76 yds

President: The Right Hon. The Earl of Harewood LLD
Chairman: Leslie Silver OBE **Vice-Chairman:** Peter Gilman
MD: Bill Fotherby **Secretary:** Nigel Pleasants
Manager: Howard Wilkinson
First Team Coaches: Peter Gunby, Paul Hart, Mike Hennigan
Physios: Alan Sutton, Geoff Ladley
At the time of going to press a number of boardroom changes were pending as such the above information may have changed by publication.

League History: 1920 Elected to Division 2; 1924-27 Division 1; 1927-28 Division 2; 1928-31 Division 1; 1931-32 Division 2; 1932-47 Division 1; 1947-56 Division 2; 1956-60 Division 1; 1960-64 Division 2; 1964-82 Division 1; 1982-90 Division 2; 1990-92 Division 1; 1992- FA Premier League.

Honours: *Football League Division 1 Champions:* 1968-69, 1973-74, 1991-92; *Runners-up:* 1964-65, 1965-66, 1969-70, 1970-71, 1971-72; *Division 2 Champions:* 1923-24, 1963-64, 1989-90; *Runners-up:* 1927-28, 1931-32, 1955-56. *FA Cup Winners:* 1971-72; *Runners-up:* 1964-65, 1969-70, 1972-73. *Football League Cup Winners:* 1967-68. *Runners-up:* 1995-96 *Champions' Cup Runners-up:* 1974-75; *Cup-Winners' Cup Runners-up:* 1972-73; *UEFA Cup Winners:* 1967-68, 1970-71; *Runners-up:* 1966-67.

European Record: CC (3): 69-70(SF), 74-75(F), 92-93(2). CWC (1): 72-73 (F); UEFA (9): 65-66(SF), 66-67(F), 67-68(W), 68-69(QF), 70-71(W), 71-72(1), 73-74(3), 79-80(2), 95-96(2).

Managers: Dick Ray 1919-20; Arthur Fairclough 1920-27; Dick Ray 1927-35; Bill Hampson 1935-47; Willis Edwards 1947-48; Major Frank Buckley 1948-53; Raich Carter 1953-58; Bill Lambton 1958-59; Jack Taylor 1959-61; Don Revie 1961-74; Brian Clough 1974; Jimmy Armfield 1974-78; Jock Stein 1978; Jimmy Adamson 1978-80; Allan Clarke 1980-82; Eddie Gray 1982-85; Billy Bremner 1985-88; *(FAPL)* Howard Wilkinson October 1988 -.

Season 1995-96

Biggest Home Win: 3-1 v Coventry City, 28/10/95
Biggest Home Defeat: 0-3 v Arsenal, 14/10/95
Biggest Away Win: 4-2 v Wimbledon, 23/9/95
Biggest Away Defeat: 2-6 v Sheffield Wednesday, 16/12/95
Biggest Home Att: 38,901 v Manchester United, 24/12/95
Smallest Home Att: 27,984 v Wimbledon, 9/12/95
Average Attendance: 32,629 (6th highest)
Leading Scorers: 12 – Tony Yeboah, 7 – Brian Deane
Last Season: *FAPL:* 13 *FA Cup:* QF *Coca-Cola Cup:* Final

All-Time Records

Record FAPL Win: 5-0 v Tottenham H, 25/8/92; Swindon Tn, 7/5/94
Record FAPL Defeat: 2-6 v Sheffield Wednesday (A), 16/12/95
Record FL Win: 8-0 v Leicester City, Division 1, 7/4/1934
Record FL Defeat: 1-8 v Stoke City, Division 1, 27/8/1934
Record Cup Win: 10-0 v Lyn (Oslo), European Cup, 1R1L, 17/9/69
Record Fee Received: £2.75 from Blackburn R. for David Batty, 10/1993
Record Fee Paid: £4.5m to Parma for Tomas Brolin, 11/95
Most FL Apps: Jack Charlton, 629, 1953-73
Most FAPL Apps: 151 – Gary McAllister
Most FAPL Goals: 29 – Rod Wallace
Highest Scorer in FAPL Season: Rod Wallace, 17, 1993-94
Record Attendance (all-time): 57,892 v Sunderland, FA Cup 5R replay, 15/3/67
Record Attendance (FAPL): 41,125 v Manchester United, 27/4/94
Most FAPL Goals in Season: 65, 1993-94
Most FAPL Points in Season: 73, 1994-95

	Div.	P	W	D	L	F	A	Pts	Pos	FAC	FLC
91-92	1	42	21	16	4	74	37	82	1	3	5
92-93	PL	42	12	15	15	57	62	51	17	4	3
93-94	PL	42	18	16	8	65	39	70	5	4	2
94-95	PL	42	20	13	9	59	38	73	5	5	2
95-96	PL	38	12	7	19	40	57	43	13	QF	F

Summary 1995-96

Player	Tot	St	Sb	Snu	PS	Gls	Y	R	Fa	La	Fg	Lg
BEENEY	10	10	0	6	0	0	0	1	1	1	0	0
BEESLEY	10	8	2	9	1	0	2	0	4	5	0	0
BLUNT	3	2	1	0	1	0	0	0	0	0	0	0
BOWMAN	3	1	2	3	0	0	0	0	0	1	0	0
BROLIN	19	17	2	0	9	4	4	0	2	4	0	0
CHAPMAN	2	2	0	0	1	0	0	1	0	0	0	0
COUZENS	14	8	6	4	4	0	1	0	0	2	0	1
DEANE	34	30	4	0	3	7	5	0	6	7	1	2
DORIGO	17	17	0	0	5	1	2	0	3	4	0	0
FORD	11	11	0	3	5	0	3	0	5	4	0	0
GRAY	15	12	3	1	2	0	0	0	2	2	0	0
HARTE	4	2	2	0	0	0	1	0	0	1	0	0
JACKSON	1	0	1	0	0	0	0	0	0	0	0	0
JOBSON	12	12	0	0	0	1	2	0	1	0	0	0
KELLY	34	34	0	0	1	0	4	1	5	8	0	0
KEWELL	2	2	0	0	2	0	0	0	0	0	0	0
LUKIC	28	28	0	0	1	0	0	0	5	7	0	0
MASINGA	9	5	4	2	3	0	1	0	4	2	0	2
MAYBURY	1	1	0	0	1	0	0	0	0	0	0	0
McALLISTER	36	36	0	0	0	5	1	0	6	8	3	1
PALMER	35	35	0	0	1	2	8	0	6	8	0	0
PEMBERTON	17	16	1	3	3	0	8	1	2	3	0	0
PETTINGER	0	0	0	2	0	0	0	0	0	0	0	0
RADEBE	13	10	3	3	2	0	2	0	4	3	0	0
SHARP	1	0	1	0	0	0	0	0	0	0	0	0
SPEED	29	29	0	0	1	2	2	0	1	7	1	3
TINKLER	9	5	4	5	0	0	2	0	0	1	0	0
WALLACE	24	12	12	3	6	1	1	0	4	4	1	0
WETHERALL	34	34	0	1	0	4	5	0	5	8	0	0
WHELAN	8	3	5	2	2	0	0	0	0	2	0	0
WHITE	4	1	3	0	1	1	0	0	0	1	0	0
WORTHINGTON	16	12	4	7	2	0	4	0	3	3	0	0
YEBOAH	23	23	0	0	3	12	1	0	6	7	1	3

Explosive Fizzle...

Leeds United kicked off the season in explosive form, or more to the point one player in particular did as Tony Yeboah staged his personal goal of the season extravaganza. He scored stunning goals almost at will and by the end of September he had a goal a game record from eight Premiership matches, not to mention hat-tricks against Monaco and Wimbledon.

Boosted by Yeboah's goals, Leeds topped the table at the end of the first month of the season having taken maximum points off West Ham, Liverpool and Aston Villa, but with a draw at Southampton pole position was surrendered. After that Leeds decline was swift with Spurs handing Leeds their first defeat. But just as Leeds looked set to drop out of the top half in December for the first time, they beat Manchester United 3-1 at Elland Road and followed it with a 2-0 win at Bolton. It was to be the last time Leeds won two consecutive league games.

The loss of Yeboah for six weeks to play in the African Nations Cup Finals did little to help Leeds' cause but even he had lost his goal touch by the time Leeds splashed out a club record £4.5m in November on Tomas Brolin. The Swedish international joined from Parma with a clause in his contract whereby he could leave at the end of the season if he did not settle and after numerous appearances on the subs bench that early exit became accepted as inevitable. Another disappointment was the lack of goals from Brian Deane whose first goal did not arrive until Leeds 18th match of the season.

After the win over Bolton, Leeds won just three more Premiership matches and lost eight out of ten away games. The team were criticised for an alleged lack of commitment but fought hard, although unsuccessfully, to slow the championship charges of both Manchester United and Newcastle towards the end of April. The season ended with United down in 13th position and with their lowest points per game total since the formation of the Premiership.

Making their first appearance in the UEFA Cup for 16 years, Leeds made a magnificent start, a Yeboah hat-trick paving the way for a very impressive victory over Monaco in the principality. It was to be United's only win in Europe as Monaco won the return match at Elland Road and PSV Eindhoven did likewise in the 2nd Round as they won an absorbing contest 5-3. But as had been suggested in the first meeting, Leeds were living on borrowed time and went down to an aggregate 8-3 defeat, their heaviest reversal in Europe.

On the home front Leeds fared admirably in the cups due in no small part to several late comebacks. In the 3rd Round of the FA Cup Leeds trailed by two goals at Derby but stormed back to win 4-2. Leeds had already put Derby out of the Coca Cola Cup with victory at the Baseball Ground. Bolton were despatched by a first minute Rod Wallace goal while a second half brace from the ever reliable Gary McAllister saw off luckless Port Vale in a replay at Vale Park. The run ended at Anfield with a comprehensive 3-0 defeat following a drab meeting at Elland Road.

Hopes of lifting their first silverware since winning the league in 1992 looked good in the Coca Cola Cup although the team went through a series of close encounters in easing their way past Notts County, Derby, Blackburn and Reading. Leeds had a favourable draw in the semi-final which they took full advantage of by disposing of Birmingham City 5-1 on aggregate. By the time of the final, though, Leeds had lost any sort of form and, four days after going out of the FA Cup, were soundly beaten 3-0 at Wembley by Aston Villa. ∎

131

Results 1995-96

Date	Opponents	Ven	Res	Pos	Atten	Scorers
19-Aug	West Ham	A	2-1	–	22,901	Yeboah (48, 57)
21-Aug	Liverpool	H	1-0	–	35,852	Yeboah (51)
26-Aug	Aston Villa	H	2-0	1	35,086	Speed (4); White (87)
30-Aug	Southampton	A	1-1	2	15,212	Dorigo (70)
09-Sep	Tottenham	A	1-2	4	30,034	Yeboah (51)
16-Sep	QPR	H	1-3	7	31,504	Wetherall (87)
23-Sep	Wimbledon	A	4-2	6	13,307	Palmer (32); Yeboah (42, 44, 74)
30-Sep	Sheff. Wed.	H	2-0	5	34,076	Yeboah (33); Speed (59)
14-Oct	Arsenal	H	0-3	7	38,552	
21-Oct	Man. City	A	0-0	8	26,390	
28-Oct	Coventry C.	H	3-1	8	30,161	McAllister (40, 44, 89 pen)
04-Nov	Middlesbro'	A	1-1	8	29,467	Deane (44)
18-Nov	Chelsea	H	1-0	5	36,209	Yeboah (80)
25-Nov	Newcastle U.	A	1-2	8	26,572	Deane (30)
02-Dec	Man. City	H	0-1	9	33,249	
09-Dec	Wimbledon	H	1-1	9	27,984	Jobson (75)
16-Dec	Sheff. Wed.	A	2-6	9	24,573	Brolin (28); Wallace (84)
24-Dec	Man. United	H	3-1	9	39,801	McAllister (6 pen); Yeboah (35); Deane (72)
27-Dec	Bolton Wan.	A	2-0	8	18,414	Brolin (39); Wetherall (63)
30-Dec	Everton	A	0-2	10	40,009	
01-Jan	Blackburn R.	H	0-0	11	31,285	
13-Jan	West Ham	A	2-0	9	30,658	Brolin (25, 62)
20-Jan	Liverpool	A	0-5	11	40,254	
31-Jan	N. Forest	A	1-2	11	24,465	Palmer (54)
03-Feb	Aston Villa	A	0-3	11	35,982	
02-Mar	Bolton Wan.	H	0-1	12	30,106	
06-Mar	QPR	A	2-1	12	13,991	Yeboah (10, 25)
13-Mar	Blackburn R.	A	0-1	12	23,358	
17-Mar	Everton	H	2-2	12	29,425	Deane (6, 45)
30-Mar	Middlesbro'	H	0-1	12	31,778	Deane (53)
03-Apr	Southampton	H	1-0	12	26,077	Deane (73)
06-Apr	Arsenal	A	1-2	12	37,619	
08-Apr	N. Forest	H	1-3	13	29,220	Wetherall (9)
13-Apr	Chelsea	A	1-4	13	22,131	McAllister (65)
17-Apr	Man. United	A	0-1	13	48,382	
29-Apr	Newcastle U.	H	0-1	13	38,862	
02-May	Tottenham	H	1-3	13	30,061	Wetherall (13)
05-May	Coventry C.	A	0-0	13	22,769	

FA Challenge Cup

Date	Opponents	Vn	Rnd	Res	Atten	Scorers
07-Jan	Derby Cty	A	3R	4-2	16,155	Speed (57); Deane (58); McAllister (90); Yeboah (90)
14-Feb	Bolton Wan.	A	4R	1-0	16,694	Wallace (1)
21-Feb	Port Vale	H	5R	0-0	18,607	
27-Feb	Port Vale	A	5RR	2-1	14,023	McAllister (64, 89)
10-Mar	Liverpool	H	QF	0-0	24,632	
20-Mar	Liverpool	A	QFR	0-3	30,812	

Coca-Cola League Cup

Date	Opponents	Vn	Rnd	Res	Atten	Scorers
19-Sep	Notts County	H	2R1L	0-0	12,384	
03-Oct	Notts County	A	2R2L	3-2	12,477	McAllister (19); Couzens (73); Speed (90)
	Leeds win 3-2 on aggregate					
25-Oct	Derby Cty	A	3R	1-0	16,030	Speed (72)
29-Nov	Blackburn R.	H	4R	2-1	26,006	Deane (21); Yeboah (29)
10-Jan	Reading	H	QF	2-1	14,023	Masinga (35); Speed (44)
11-Feb	Birmingham	A	SF1L	2-1	24,781	Yeboah (54); OG (Whyte 72)
25-Feb	Birmingham	H	SF2L	3-0	35,435	Masinga (54); Yeboah (56); Deane (86)
	Leeds win 5-1 on aggregate					
24-Mar	Aston Villa	W	Final	0-3	77,056	

UEFA Cup

Date	Opponents	Vn	Rnd	Res	Atten	Scorers
12-Sep	Monaco	A	1R1L	3-0	12,486	Yeboah (2,65, 81)
26-Sep	Monaco	H	1R2L	0-1	24,501	
	Leeds win 3-1 on aggregate					
17-Oct	PSV	H	2R1L	3-5	24,846	Speed (6); Palmer (48); McAllister (72)
31-Oct	PSV	A	2R2L	0-3	25,750	
	PSV win 3-8 on aggregate					

Leeds United – Premiership Fact File

- Leeds scored in their first eight matches and their early season form saw them top the Premiership in August.
- He may have departed to Coventry City now but Gary McAllister's goal for Leeds at Manchester United on Christmas Eve was his 100th in first team football club spread across Scotland and England. His century of strikes included 24 penalties.
- Leeds' 8-3 aggregate defeat against PSV in the UEFA Cup was their heaviest in European competition.

Leicester City

Founded in 1884 as Leicester Fosse by former pupils of the Wyggeston School from the western part of the city near the old Roman Fosse Way. Moved to their present ground in 1891 and, from the Midland League joined Division Two of the Football League in 1894. Promoted for the first time in 1908, they have been relegated seven times from the top flight.

FA Cup runners-up four times, they gained European Cup-Winners' Cup experience in 1961-62. Members of the new Division One in its first season, 1992-93, and promoted to the Premier League following play-off success in 1994.Relegated straight back but re-promoted, again via the play-offs at the end of the 1995-96 season.

Ground: City Stadium, Filbert Street, Leicester LE2 7FL
Phone: 0116 255 5000   **Info:** 0891-12 11 85
Tickets: 0116 291 5253   **Colours:** All Blue
Capacity: 22,517   **Pitch:** 112 x 75 yds
Club Nickname: Filberts or Foxes

President: Ken Brigstock   **Chairman:** Martin George
CEO: Barrie Pierpoint   **Secretary:** Ian Silvester
Manager: Martin O'Neill
Coaches: Paul Franklin, Steve Walford
Physios: Alan Smith, Mick Yeoman

League History: 1894 Elected to Division 2; 1908-09 Division 1; 1009-25 Division 2; 1925-35 Division 1; 1935-37 Division 2; 1937-39 Division 1; 1946-54 Division 2; 1954-55 Division 1; 1955-57 Division 2; 1957-69 Division 1; 1969-71 Division 2; 1971-78 Division 1; 1978-80 Division 2; 1980-81 Division 1; 1981-83 Division 2; 1983-87 Division 1; 1987-92 Division 2; 1992-94 Division 1; 1994-95 FA Premier League. 1995-96 Division 1. 1996- FA Premier League

Honours: *Football League:* Division 1 – Runners-up 1928-29; Division 2 – Champions 1924-25, 1936-37, 1953-54, 1956-57, 1970-71, 1979-80; Runners-up 1907-08. *FA Cup:* Runners-up 1949, 1961, 1963, 1969. *Football League Cup:* Winners 1964; Runners-up 1965.

European Competitions: CC (0) – ; CWC (1): 61-62(2); UEFA (0) –

Managers (and Secretary-managers): William Clarke 1896-97, George

Johnson 1898-1907, James Blessington 1907-09, Andy Aitkin 1909-11, J.W. Bartlett 1912-14, Peter Hodge 1919-26, William Orr 1926-32, Peter Hodge 1932-34, Andy Lochead 1934-36, Frank Womack 1936-39, Tom Bromilow 1939-45, Tom Mather 1945-46, Johnny Duncan 1946-49, Norman Bullock 1949-55, David Halliday 1955-58, Matt Gillies 1959-68, Frank O'Farrell 1968-71, Jimmy Bloomfield 1971-77, Frank McLintock 1977-78, Jock Wallace 1978-82, Gordon Milne 1982-86, Bryan Hamilton 1986-87, David Pleat 1987-91, Brian Little May 1991-Nov 94; Mark McGhee Dec 94-Dec 95, Martin O'Neill Dec 95-.

Season 1995-96

Biggest Home Win: 4-2 v Portsmouth, 30/8/95
Biggest Home Defeat: 1-3 v Southend United, 23/9/95
Biggest Away Win: 3-1 v Sheffield United, 21/10/95
Biggest Away Defeat: 2-4 v Ipswich Town, 3/3/96
Biggest Home Attendance: 20,911 v Derby County, 28/2/96
Smallest Home Attendance: 12,543 v Millwall, 23/3/96
Average Attendance: 16,198
Leading Scorer: 19 – Iwan Roberts, 7 – Emile Heskey

All-Time Records

Record FAPL Win: 4-3 v Southampton, 15/10/94
Record FAPL Defeat: 0-4 v Manchester United, 15/4/95
Record FL Win: 10-0 v Portsmouth, Division 1, 20/10/28
Record FL Defeat: 0-12 v Nottingham Forest, Division 1, 21/4/09
Record Cup Win: 8-1 v Coventry City (away), LC R5, 1/12/64
Record Fee Received: £3.5m from Aston Villa for Mark Draper, 7/95
Record Fee Paid: £1.25m to Notts County for Mark Draper, 8/94
Most FL Apps: Adam Black, 528, 1920-35
Most FAPL Apps: Mark Draper, 39, 1994-95
Most FAPL Goals: Iwan Roberts, 9, 1994-95
Highest Scorer in FAPL season: 9 – Iwan Roberts, 1994-95
Record Attendance (all-time): 47,298 v Tottenham H, FAC Rd5, 18/2/28
Record Attendance (FAPL): 21,393 v Liverpool, 26/12/94
Most FAPL Goals in Season: 49, 1994-95 – 42 games
Most FAPL Points in Season: 29, 1994-95 – 42 games

5-Year League Record

	Div.	P	W	D	L	F	A	Pts	Pos	FAC	FLC
91-92	2	46	23	8	15	62	55	77	4	4	2
92-93	1	46	22	10	14	71	64	76	6	3	3
93-94	1	46	19	16	11	72	59	73	4	3	3
94-95	PL	42	6	11	25	45	80	29	21	5	2
95-96	1	46	19	14	13	66	60	71	5	3	3

Summary 1995-96

Player	Tot	St	Sb	Snu	PS	Gls	Fa	La	Fg	Lg
BLAKE	8	6	2	6	4	0	0	2	0	0
CAREY	19	16	3	11	1	1	0	2	0	0
CLARIDGE	14	14	0	0	1	5	0	0	0	0
CORICA	16	16	0	0	4	2	2	0	0	0
GEE	2	1	1	1	1	0	0	0	0	0
GRAYSON	41	39	2	1	3	2	2	4	0	0
HESKEY	30	20	10	1	3	7	0	2	0	0
HILL	27	24	3	5	4	0	2	4	0	0
IZZET	9	8	1	0	0	1	0	0	0	0
JOACHIM	22	14	8	2	8	1	2	3	0	1
KALAC	1	1	0	0	0	0	0	1	0	0
KAAMARK	1	1	0	0	0	0	0	1	0	0
LAWRENCE	15	10	5	4	7	0	0	0	0	0
LENNON	15	14	1	0	0	1	0	0	0	0
LEWIS	14	10	4	6	5	1	0	1	0	0
LOWE	28	21	7	3	4	3	1	4	0	0
MCMAHON	3	1	2	1	1	1	0	1	0	0
PARKER	40	36	4	2	0	3	2	4	0	0
PHILPOTT	6	1	5	1	1	0	2	0	0	0
POOLE	45	45	0	0	0	0	2	3	0	0
ROBERTS	37	34	3	0	2	19	2	3	0	1
ROBINS	31	19	12	11	10	6	2	3	0	4
ROLLING	17	17	0	2	3	0	1	3	0	0
SMITH	1	1	0	3	1	0	1	0	0	0
TAYLOR	39	39	0	0	9	6	1	3	0	0
WALSH	37	37	0	0	0	4	2	2	0	0
WATTS	9	9	0	0	0	0	0	0	0	0
WHITLOW	42	41	1	0	0	3	1	4	0	0
WILLIS	12	11	1	3	3	0	0	2	0	0

Play-off Experts Reign Again

Whilst the play-off system may still cause some mutterings of discontent in certain quarters there are no such complaints at Filbert Street as Leicester City clambered into the Premiership with victory at Wembley in the play-off final for the second time in three seasons. The onus now is for Leicester to prove that they can bridge the gap between the top two Divisions and survive for more than one season in the top flight, something that they failed to accomplish last time around.

Following their relegation at the end of the previous season Leicester were keen to make an instant impression in the Endsleigh League and a 2-1 win at Sunderland was the perfect start. Defeat at home to Stoke in the opening home game was no more than a minor setback as a draw at Luton was followed by maximum points from four games which included impressive wins over Wolves and Derby and carried the Foxes to the top of the table – Iwan Roberts scored a hat trick during a 4-2 win over Portsmouth. It would be another seven months until Leicester next won three or more games consecutively and they were toppled from the top at the end of October when Crystal Palace won 3-2 at Filbert Street as Leicester battled back from three down. Wins at West Brom and Watford helped retain second place but with a dreadful run of just one win in 13 games Leicester dipped to tenth place but were still only three points from the play-off places. By now Leicester were under new management; Mark McGhee had packed his bags in December and headed for Wolves while Martin O'Neill moved across from Norwich.

O'Neill's early days were hardly likely to convince Leicester fans that the good times were back as only one of his first ten matches ended in victory. The one bright spot was at Molineux on 21 February where City won 3-2 but with just two wins during March the promotion hopes were fading. Two profitable trips to south London, at Charlton and Palace, offered new hope but a home defeat by West Brom and a draw at Tranmere looked to have finally finished off the dream. Only 12 points from their last four games would get City into a play-off position, Steve Claridge, signed just before the deadline from Birmingham for £1.2m, scored twice as Oldham were defeated and Claridge joined Steve Walsh on the scoresheet as Huddersfield were overcome and Leicester moved into the vital sixth position.

Claridge scored for a third successive game as local youngster Emile Heskey and Neil Lennon, a £750,000 signing from Crewe in February, added to Birmingham's misery during a 3-0 win at Filbert Street. A goal by Mustafa Izzet at Vicarage Road finally clinched sixth place and condemned Graham Taylor's Watford to relegation. City faced Stoke in the play-off and having lost both meetings in the league got off to a bad start with a goalless draw at Filbert Street, but with a Garry Parker strike at the Victoria Ground won through to Wembley. It was Parker who pulled Leicester level from one down at Wembley against Palace to set up Claridge for a dramatic winner seconds from the end of extra time.

Leicester may have taken to the play-offs but cup football was not to their liking as a 5-0 FA Cup 3rd Round replay defeat was received at Manchester City while, after a comfortable two legged victory over Burnley in the Coca Cola Cup, the Foxes went out at home to relegation bound Bolton. ∎

Results 1995-96

Date	Opponents	Ven	Res	Pos	Atten	Scorers
12-Aug	Sunderland	A	2-1		18,593	Robins, Corica
19-Aug	Stoke City	H	2-3		17,719	Walsh (72); Parker (75 pen)
26-Aug	Luton Town	A	1-1	9	7,612	Parker (64)
30-Aug	Portsmouth	H	4-2	3	15,170	Roberts (15, 38, 44); Parker (45)
02-Sep	Wolves	H	1-0	2	18,441	Whitlow (27)
10-Sep	Derby County	A	1-1	1	11,767	Joachim (32)
12-Sep	Port Vale	A	2-0	1	8,814	McMahon (44); Roberts (80)
16-Sep	Reading	H	1-1	1	19,103	Roberts (80)
23-Sep	Southend U.	H	1-3	1	15,276	Lowe (12)
30-Sep	Norwich City	A	1-0	1	18,435	Heskey (87)
07-Oct	Barnsley	A	2-2	1	13,669	Walsh (11); Robins (83)
14-Oct	Charlton Ath	H	1-1	1	16,771	Lowe (26)
21-Oct	Sheffield Utd	A	3-1	1	13,100	Taylor (5); Lowe (70); Roberts (79)
28-Oct	C.Palace	H	2-3	2	18,376	Taylor (76); Robins (80)
05-Nov	WBA	A	3-2	2	16,071	Taylor (15, 44); Roberts (30)
11-Nov	Watford	H	1-0	2	16,230	Roberts (15)
19-Nov	Tranmere R.	H	0-1	2	13,125	
21-Nov	Huddersfield	A	1-3	2	14,300	Robins (45)
26-Nov	Birmingham	A	2-2	4	17,350	Roberts (9); Grayson (16)
02-Dec	Barnsley	H	2-2	2	15,125	Roberts (14); Grayson (89)
09-Dec	Southend U.	A	1-2	8	5,835	Roberts (38)
17-Dec	Norwich City	H	3-2	3	14,251	Whitlow (36); Roberts (67); Heskey (79)
23-Dec	Grimsby Tn	A	2-2	3	7,713	Roberts (73); Walsh (90)
01-Jan	Millwall	A	1-1	3	9,953	Corcia (45)
13-Jan	Stoke City	A	0-1	5	13,669	
21-Jan	Sunderland	H	0-0	5	16,130	
03-Feb	Luton Town	H	1-1	7	14,821	Roberts (60)
10-Feb	Portsmouth	A	1-2	10	9,003	Roberts (28)
17-Feb	Port Vale	H	1-1	8	13,758	Taylor (14)
21-Feb	Wolves	A	3-2	6	27,381	Roberts (38); Heskey (60, 80)
24-Feb	Reading	A	1-1	6	9,817	Lewis (72)
28-Feb	Derby County	H	0-0	7	20,911	
03-Mar	Ipswich Tn	A	2-4	8	9,817	Roberts (55, 75)
09-Mar	Grimsby Tn	H	2-1	7	13,784	Heskey (44, 86)
13-Mar	Ipswich Tn	H	0-2	8	17,783	
16-Mar	Oldham Ath	A	1-3	8	5,582	Whitlow (70)
23-Mar	Millwall	H	2-1	8	12,543	Carey (1), Taylor (57)

30-Mar	Sheffield U.	H	0-2	9	15,230	
02-Apr	Charlton Ath	A	1-0	7	11,287	Claridge (32)
06-Apr	C.Palace	A	1-0	7	17,331	Roberts (27)
09-Apr	WBA	H	1-2	8	17,889	Robins (56)
13-Apr	Tranmere R.	A	1-1	8	8,882	Robins (16)
17-Apr	Oldham Ath	H	2-0	7	12,790	Claridge (58, 78)
20-Apr	Huddersfield	H	2-1	6	17,619	Walsh (40); Claridge (62)
27-Apr	Birmingham C.H	3-0	6	19,702	Claridge (32); Heskey (39); Lennon (89)
05-May	Watford	A	1-0	6	20,089	Izzett (59)

Promotion Play-offs

Date	Opponents	Vn	Res	Rd	Atten	Scorers
12-May	Stoke City	H	1-0	1L	20,325	
15-May	Stoke City	A	1-0	2L	21,037	Parker
	Leicester City won 1-0 on aggregate.					
27-May	C. Palace	W	2-1	F	73,573	Parker (76 pen); Claridge (120)
	After extra time					

FA Challenge Cup

Date	Opponents	Vn	Rnd	Res	Atten	Scorers
06-Jan	Man. City	H	3R	0-0	20,640	
17-Jan	Man. City	A	3RR	0-5	19,980	

Coca-Cola League Cup

Date	Opponents	Vn	Rnd	Res	Atten	Scorers
20-Sep	Burnley	H	2R1L	2-0	11,142	Robins (27); Joachim (56)
03-Oct	Burnley	A	2R2L	2-0	4,553	Robins (79, 87)
	Leicester City won 2-0 on aggregate.					
24-Oct	Bolton Wand.	A	3R	0-0	9,166	
08-Nov	Bolton Wand.	H	3RR	2-3	14,884	Robins (50); Roberts (66)

Liverpool

Following a dispute between Everton and its Anfield landlord a new club, Liverpool AFC, was formed in 1892 by the landlord, former Everton committee-man John Houlding, with its headquarters at Anfield. An application for Football League membership was rejected without being put to the vote. Instead the team joined the Lancashire League and immediately won the championship.

After that one campaign, when the Liverpool Cup was won but there was early FA Cup elimination, Liverpool was selected to fill one of two vacancies in an expanded Football League Second Division in 1893. Premier League founder members 1992.

Ground: Anfield Road, Liverpool L4 0TH
Phone: 0151-263 2361   **Match Info:** 0151-260 9999 (24 hrs)
News: 0891- 12 11 84   **Box Office:** 0151-263 5727
Capacity: 41,000   **Pitch:** 110 yds x 75 yds
Colours: All Red/White Trim   **Nickname:** Reds or Pool

Chairman: D.R. Moores
CEO/General Secretary: Peter Robinson
Manager: Roy Evans   **Coach:** Ronny Moran

League History: 1893 Elected to Division 2; 1894-95 Division 1; 1895-96 Division 2; 1896-1904 Division 1; 1904-05 Division 2; 1905-54 Division 1; 1954-62 Division 2; 1962-92 Division 1; 1992- FA Premier League.

Honours: *Football League Division 1 Champions:* 1900-01, 1905-06, 1921-22, 1922-23, 1946-47, 1963-64, 1965-66, 1972-73, 1975-76, 1976-77, 1978-79, 1979-80, 1981-82, 1982-83, 1983-84, 1985-86, 1987-88, 1989-90; *Runners-up:* 1898-99, 1909-10, 1968-69, 1973-74, 1974-75, 1977-78, 1984-85, 1986-87, 1988-89, 1990-91; *Division 2 Champions:* 1893-94, 1895-96, 1904-05, 1961-62. *FA Cup Winners:* 1964-65, 1973-74, 1985-86, 1988-89, 1991-92; *Runners-up:* 1913-14, 1949-50, 1970-71, 1976-77, 1987-88, 1995-96; *Football League Cup Winners:* 1980-81, 1981-82, 1982-83, 1983-84, 1994-95; *Runners-up:* 1977-78, 1986-87, 1995-96; *League Super Cup Winners:* 1985-86; *Champions' Cup Winners:* 1976-77; 1977-78, 1980-81; 1983-84; *Runners-up:* 1984-85; *Cup-Winners' Cup Runners-up:* 1965-66; *UEFA Cup Winners:* 1972-73, 1975-76; *European Super Cup Winners:* 1977; *Runners-up:* 1984; *World Club Championship Runners-up:* 1981, 1984.

European Record: CC (12): 64-65(SF), 66-67(2), 73-74(2), 76-77(W), 77-78(W), 78-79(1), 79-80(1), 80-81(W), 81-82(QF), 82-83(QF), 83-84(W), 84-85(F); CWC (4): 65-66(F), 71-72(2), 74-75(2), 92-93(2); UEFA (8) 67-68(3), 68-69(1), 69-70(2), 70-71(SF), 72-73(W), 75-76(W), 91-92(QF), 94-95(2).

Managers: W.E. Barclay 1892-96; Tom Watson 1896-1915; David Ashworth 1920-22; Matt McQueen 1923-28; George Patterson 1928-36 (continued as secretary); George Kay 1936-51; Don Welsh 1951-56; Phil Taylor 1956-59; Bill Shankly 1959-74; Bob Paisley 1974-83; Joe Fagan 1983-85; Kenny Dalglish 1985-91; *(FAPL)* Graeme Souness 1991-94; Roy Evans January 1994-

Season 1995-96

Biggest Home Win:	6-0 v Manchester City, 28/10/95
Biggest Home Defeat:	1-2 v Everton, 18/11/94
Biggest Away Win:	3-1 v Tottenham 26/8/95 & Southampton 22/10/95
Biggest Away Defeat:	2-1 v Newcastle United 4/11/95 & Middlesbrough 25/11/95
Biggest Home Att:	40,820 v Chelsea, 16/3/96
Smallest Home Att:	34,063 v Wimbledon
Average Attendance:	39,553 (2nd highest)
Leading Scorer:	28 – Robbie Fowler, 14 – Stan Collymore

Last Season: *FAPL:* 3rd *FA Cup:* Final *Coca-Cola Cup:* 4

All-Time Records

Record FAPL Win:	6-0 v Manchester City, home, 28/10/95
Record FAPL Defeat:	1-5 v Coventry City, away, 19/12/92
Record FL Win:	10-1 v Rotherham Town, Division 2, 18/2/1896 *and* 9-0 v Crystal Palace, Division 1, 12/9/89
Record FL Defeat:	1-9 v Birmingham City, Division 2, 11/12/54
Record Cup Win:	11-0 v Stromsgodset Drammen, CWC 1R1L, 17/9/74
Record Fee Received:	£3.2m from Juventus for Ian Rush, 6/1986
Record Fee Paid:	£8.5m to N. Forest for Stan Collymore, 6/95
Most FL Apps:	Ian Callaghan, 640, 1960-78
Most FAPL Apps:	127 – John Barnes
Most FAPL Goals:	65 – Robbie Fowler

Highest Scorer in FAPL Season: Robbie Fowler, 28 1995-96
Record Attendance (all-time): 61,905 v Wolves, FA Cup R4, 2/2/1952
Record Attendance (FAPL): 44,619 v Everton, 20/3/93
Most FAPL Goals in Season: 65, 1994-95 – 42 games
Most FAPL Points in Season: 74, 1994-95 – 42 games

5-Year Record

	Div.	P	W	D	L	F	A	Pts	Pos	FAC	FLC
91-92	1	42	16	16	10	47	40	64	6	W	4
92-93	PL	42	16	11	15	62	55	59	6	3	4
93-94	PL	42	17	9	16	59	55	60	8	3	4
94-95	PL	42	21	11	10	65	37	74	4	QF	W
95-96	PL	38	20	11	7	70	34	71	3	F	4

Summary 1995-96

Player	Tot	St	Sb	Snu	PS	Gls	Y	R	Fa	La	Fg	Lg
BABB	28	28	0	0	1	0	2	0	4	4	0	0
BARNES	36	36	0	0	2	3	0	0	7	3	0	0
BJORNEBYE	2	2	0	0	0	0	0	0	0	0	0	0
CHARNOCK	0	0	0	1	0	0	0	0	0	0	0	0
CLOUGH	3	2	1	3	0	0	1	0	0	0	0	0
COLLYMORE	30	29	1	2	6	14	2	0	7	4	5	0
FOWLER	38	36	2	0	2	28	3	0	7	4	6	1
HARKNESS	24	23	1	1	3	1	4	0	2	4	0	1
JAMES	38	38	0	0	0	0	1	0	7	4	0	0
JONES	33	33	0	0	8	0	2	0	7	3	0	0
KENNEDY	4	1	3	10	0	0	0	0	0	1	0	0
MATTEO	5	5	0	8	2	0	0	0	0	0	0	0
McATEER	29	27	2	2	0	4	4	0	7	4	3	0
McMANAMAN	38	38	0	0	1	6	1	0	7	4	2	1
PEARS	0	0	0	4	0	0	0	0	0	0	0	0
REDKNAPP	23	19	4	2	3	3	1	0	2	3	0	1
RUDDOCK	20	18	2	1	1	5	7	0	0	4	0	0
RUSH	20	10	10	8	2	5	0	0	4	2	1	1
SCALES	27	27	0	0	1	0	3	0	7	2	0	1
THOMAS	27	18	9	3	1	1	3	0	7	1	0	1
WARNER	0	0	0	33	0	0	0	0	0	0	0	0
WRIGHT	28	28	0	1	2	2	7	0	7	3	0	0
					OG	2						

142

Kop Back on Course

Liverpool's re-emergence as the major force in English football continued to gather momentum during 95-96 and that the double again went to Old Trafford will only add to Roy Evans' determination to succeed.

Liverpool made their most serious championship challenge for five years although they always trailed the leaders by some distance before claiming their highest league position, third, since 1991. Stan Collymore, Britain's most expensive signing at £8.5m, marked his debut with a superb goal against Sheffield Wednesday on the opening day but he soon lost his place and was fined for criticising the club in a magazine article. Liverpool were in third place by the end of September having already crushed Blackburn 3-0 and seen Robbie Fowler score four times during a 5-2 win over Bolton. He later added another hat trick against Arsenal. The momentum was maintained during October with Manchester City coming in for particular punishment as Liverpool thrashed the Mancunians 4-0 and 6-0 in the Coca Cola Cup and Premiership within the space of four days. But just when it seemed as though Liverpool were poised to close the gap on leaders Newcastle, the Reds slipped to an unfortunate 2-1 defeat at St James' Park and followed it with their only home league defeat of the season, agonisingly inflicted by Stanley Park neighbours Everton. Wins were hard to come by and the club slipped to eighth position. Liverpool then began a run of 15 games without defeat which kept Evans' side snapping at the heels of the top two clubs only for a final indifferent spell to restrict them to the third position occupied since the turn of the year.

In Europe the club fell short of expectations. Goals by the very influential England pairing of Steve McManaman and Jamie Redknapp gave the Reds a 2-1 UEFA Cup 1st Round victory away to Spartak Vladikavkaz but they turned out to be Liverpool's last European goals of the season. A goalless draw in the return set up a 2nd Round tie at Brondby and with another blank scoreline the sides went to Anfield where the Danish side received a standing ovation from home supporters after a late goal condemned the Merseysiders to a surprise defeat.

Liverpool made impressive inroads in the Coca Cola Cup with Sunderland and Manchester City being disposed of without a goal conceded but in front of one of eleven gates in excess of 40,000 at Anfield, Liverpool were defeated by Newcastle United in the 4th Round.

It was in the FA Cup where Liverpool enjoyed most success. In the 3rd Round Ian Rush, in the week he received the MBE, set a new post war record of 42 FA Cup goals during a 7-0 rout of Rochdale. Collymore scored a hat trick that day and was also on the scoresheet as Shrewsbury Town and Charlton Athletic were ousted. In the quarter final a McManaman brace helped to account for Leeds in a replay at Anfield and in the semi-final Aston Villa went down by the same score, 3-0, this time it was Fowler who scored twice. What should have been a classic Cup Final with Manchester United turned out to be a damp squib with Liverpool criticised for defensive tactics which ultimately failed as United won with a late goal.

Liverpool were relatively restrained in the transfer market with Jason McAteer being their only major signing during the season at a cost of £4.5m. Moving in the opposite direction was an array of big names. Nigel Clough joined Manchester City for £1.5m while Mark Walters, Jan Molby and Paul Stewart all left on free transfers as did Rush who joined Leeds at the end of the season after 16 years at Anfield. Bob Paisley, Liverpool's most successful manager, died in February. ∎

Results 1995-96

Date	Opponents	Ven	Res	Pos	Atten	Scorers
19-Aug	Sheff. Wed.	H	1-0	–	40,535	Collymore (60)
21-Aug	Leeds United	A	0-1	–	35,852	
26-Aug	Tottenham	A	3-1	7	31,254	Barnes (7, 42); Fowler (55)
30-Aug	QPR	H	1-0	3	37,548	Ruddock (30)
09-Sep	Wimbledon	A	0-1	5	19,530	
16-Sep	Blackburn R.	H	3-0	4	39,502	Redknapp (12); Fowler (22); Collymore (29)
23-Sep	Bolton Wan.	H	5-2	3	40,104	Fowler (12, 30, 47, 65); Harkness (84)
01-Oct	Man. United	A	2-2	4	34,934	Fowler (32, 53)
14-Oct	Coventry C.	H	0-0	5	39,079	
22-Oct	Southampton	A	3-1	5	15,245	McManaman (23, 55); Redknapp (73)
28-Oct	Man. City	H	6-0	3	39,267	Rush (3, 64); Redknapp (6); Fowler (47, 60); Ruddock (53)
04-Nov	Newcastle U.	A	1-2	5	36,547	Rush (11)
18-Nov	Everton	A	1-2	7	40,818	Fowler (88)
22-Nov	West Ham	A	0-0	6	24,324	
25-Nov	Middlesbro'	A	1-2	8	29,390	Ruddock (63)
02-Dec	Southampton	H	1-1	8	38,007	Collymore (67)
09-Dec	Bolton Wan.	A	1-0	7	21,042	Collymore (61)
17-Dec	Man. United	H	2-0	5	40,546	Fowler (44, 87)
23-Dec	Arsenal	H	3-1	4	39,806	Fowler (40, 59, 78)
30-Dec	Chelsea	A	2-2	3	31,137	McManaman (34, 76)
01-Jan	N. Forest	H	4-2	3	39,206	Fowler (31,42); Collymore (62); OG (Cooper 86)
13-Jan	Sheff. Wed.	A	1-1	4	32,747	Rush (87)
20-Jan	Leeds United	H	5-0	3	40,254	Ruddock (25, 90); Fowler (60 pen, 67); Collymore (88)
31-Jan	Aston Villa	A	2-0	2	39,332	Collymore (62); Fowler (65)
03-Feb	Tottenham	H	0-0	3	40,628	
11-Feb	QPR	A	2-1	3	18,405	Wright (15); Fowler (30)
24-Feb	Blackburn R.	A	3-2	3	33,163	Collymore (11, 21); Thomas (70)
03-Mar	Aston Villa	H	3-0	3	39,508	McManaman (1); Fowler (5, 8)
13-Mar	Wimbledon	H	2-2	3	34,063	McManaman (35); Collymore (68)

16-Mar	Chelsea	H	2-0	3	40,820	Wright (2); Fowler (62)
23-Mar	N. Forest	A	0-1	3	29,058	
03-Apr	Newcastle U.	H	4-3	3	40,702	Fowler (2, 57); Collymore (63, 90)
06-Apr	Coventry C.	A	0-1	3	23,137	
08-Apr	West Ham	H	2-0	3	40,326	Collymore (22); Barnes (38)
16-Apr	Everton	A	1-1	3	39,022	Fowler (87)
27-Apr	Middlesbro'	H	1-0	3	40,782	Collymore (70)
01-May	Arsenal	A	0-0	3	38,323	
05-May	Man. City	A	2-2	3	31,436	OG (Lomas 6); Rush (41)

UEFA Cup

Date	Opponents	Vn	Rnd	Res	Atten	Scorers
12-Sep	Spartak Vlad.	A	1R1L	2-1	43,000	McManaman(32); Redknapp (53)
26-Sep	Spartak Vlad.	H	1R2L	0-0	35,042	*Liverpool won 2-1 on agg.*
17-Oct	Brondby	A	2R1L	0-0	37,648	
31-Oct	Brondby	H	2R2L	0-1	35,878	*Brondby won 1-0 on agg.*

FA Challenge Cup

Date	Opponents	Vn	Rnd	Res	Atten	Scorers
06-Jan	Rochdale	H	3R	7-0	28,126	Fowler (21); Collymore (43, 44, 70); OG (Valentine 48); Rush (62); McAteer (86)
18-Feb	Shrewsbury	A	4R	4-0	7,752	Collymore (8); OG(69); Fowler (75); McAteer (84)
28-Feb	Charlton Ath.	H	5R	2-1	36,818	Fowler (12); Collymore (58)
10-Mar	Leeds United	A	QF	0-0	34,632	
20-Mar	Leeds United	H	QFR	3-0	30,812	McManaman (57, 73); Fowler (81)
31-Mar	Aston Villa	N	SF	3-0	39,072	Fowler (16, 85); McAteer (90)
	Played at Old Trafford					
11-May	Man. United	W	FIN	0-1	79,007	

Coca-Cola League Cup

Date	Opponents	Vn	Rnd	Res	Atten	Scorers
20-Sep	Sunderland	H	2R1L	2-0	25,579	McManaman (9); Thomas (73)
04-Oct	Sunderland	A	2R2L	1-0	20,560	Fowler (39)
	Liverpool won 3-0 on aggregate					
25-Oct	Man. City	H	3R	4-0	29,394	Scales (9); Fowler (74); Rush (79); Harkness (82)
29-Nov	Newcastle U.	H	4R	0-1	40,077	

Manchester United

Came into being in 1902 upon the bankruptcy of Newton Heath. Predecessors appear to have been formed in 1878 as Newton Heath (LYR) when workers at the Carriage and Wagon Department at the Lancashire and Yorkshire Railway formed a club. This soon outgrew railway competition.

Turned professional in 1885 and founder member of Football Alliance in 1889. In 1892 Alliance runners-up Newton Heath was elected to an enlarged Division One of the Football League. In 1902 the club became Manchester United and, in February 1910, moved from Bank Street, Clayton, to Old Trafford. Premier League founder member 1992. Three times Premiership champions and the only side to have completed the Double twice.

Ground: Old Trafford, Manchester, M16 0RA
Phone: 0161-872 1661   **Info:** 0891 12 11 61
Capacity: 44,622   **Pitch:** 116yds x 76yds
Colours: Red, White, Black   **Nickname:** Red Devils
Manchester United Radio: 1413AM

Chairman/Chief Executive: Martin Edwards
Secretary: Kenneth Merrett
Manager: Alex Ferguson   **Assistant:** Brian Kidd

League History: 1892 Newton Heath elected to Division 1; 1894-1906 Division 2; 1906-22 Division 1; 1922-25 Division 2; 1925-31 Division 1; 1931-36 Division 2; 1936-37 Division 1; 1937-38 Division 2; 1938-74 Division 1; 1974-75 Division 2; 1975-92 Division 1; 1992 – FA Premier League.

Honours: *FA Premier League Champions:* 1992-93, 1993-94, 1995-96; *Runners-up:* 1994-95; *Football League: Division 1 Champions:* 1907-8, 1910-11, 1951-52, 1955-56, 1956-57, 1964-65, 1966-67; *Runners-up:* 1946-47, 1947-48, 1948-49, 1950-51, 1958-59, 1963-64, 1967-68, 1979-80, 1987-88, 1991-92. *Division 2 Champions:* 1935-36, 1974-75; *Runners-up:* 1896-97, 1905-06, 1924-25, 1937-38. *FA Cup Winners:* 1908-09, 1947-48, 1962-63, 1976-77, 1982-83, 1984-85, 1989-90, 1993-94, 1995-96; *Runners-up:* 1957, 1958, 1976, 1979, 1995; *Football League Cup Winners:* 1991-92; *Runners-up:* 1982-83, 1990-91, 1993-94. *Champions' Cup Winners:* 1967-68; *Cup-Winners' Cup Winners:* 1990-91. *League/Cup Double Performed:* 1993-94, 1995-96.

European Record: CC (7): 56-57(SF), 57-58(SF), 65-66(SF), 67-68(W), 68-69(SF), 93-94(SF), 94-95(CL): CWC (5): 63-64(QF), 77-78(2), 83-84(SF),

90-91(W), 91-92(2). UEFA (7): 64-65(SF), 76-77(2), 80-81(1), 82-83(1), 84-85(QF), 92-93(1), 95-96(1).

Managers: Ernest Magnall 1900-12; John Robson 1914-21; John Chapman 1921-26; Clarence Hildrith 1926-27; Herbert Bamlett 1927-31; Walter Crickman 1931-32; Scott Duncan 1932-37; Jimmy Porter 1938-44; Walter Crickmer 1944-45; Matt Busby 1945-69 (continued as GM then Director); Wilf McGuinness 1969-70; Frank O'Farrell 1971-72; Tommy Docherty 1972-77; Dave Sexton 1977-81; Ron Atkinson 1981-86; *(FAPL)* Alex Ferguson Nov 1986-

Season 1995-96

Biggest Home Win:	5-0 v Nottingam Forest, 28/4/96
Biggest Home Defeat:	none
Biggest Away Win:	6-0 v Bolton Wanderers, 25/2/96
Biggest Away Defeat:	1-4 v Tottenham Hotspur, 1/1/96
Biggest Home Att:	53,926 v Nottingham Forest, 28/4/96
Smallest Home Att:	31,966 v West Ham United, 23/8/95
Average Attendance:	41,681 – (1st highest)
Leading Scorer:	14 – Eric Cantona, 11 – Andy Cole, Ryan Giggs
Last Season:	*FAPL:* 1 – Champions *FA Cup:* Winners *Coca-Cola Cup:* 2

All-Time Records

Record FAPL Win:	9-0 v Ipswich Town, 4/3/95
Record FAPL Defeat:	1-4 v Tottenham Hotspur, 1/1/96
Record FL Win:	10-1 v Wolverhampton W, Division 2, 15/10/1892
Record FL Defeat:	0-7 v Blackburn R, Div. 1, 10/4/26; Aston Villa, Div. 1, 27/12/30; Wolves, Div. 2, 26/12/31

Record Cup Win: 10-0 v RSC Anderlecht, Champions Cup, Pr2L, 26/9/56

Record Fee Received:	£7m from Internazionale (Italy) for Paul Ince 6/95
Record Fee Paid:	£7m to Newcastle United for Andy Cole 1/95 (inc. part exchange of Keith Gillespie – £1m).
Most FL Apps:	Bobby Charlton, 606, 1956-73
Most FAPL Apps:	153 – Denis Irwin
Most FAPL Goals:	53 – Eric Cantona

Highest Scorer in FAPL Season: Cantona, 18, 1993-94

Record Attendance (all-time): 70,504 v Aston Villa, Division 1, 27/12/1920

Record Attendance (FAPL): 53,926 v Nottingham Forest, 28/4/9

Most FAPL Goals in Season: 80, 1993-94 – 42 games

Most FAPL Points in Season: 92, 1993-94 – 42 games

5-Year Record

	Div.	P	W	D	L	F	A	Pts	Pos	FAC	FLC
91-92	1	42	21	15	6	63	33	78	2	4	W
92-93	PL	42	24	12	6	67	31	84	1	5	3
93-94	PL	42	27	11	4	80	38	92	1	W	F
94-95	PL	42	26	10	6	77	28	88	2	F	3
95-96	PL	38	25	7	6	73	35	82	1	W	2

Summary 1995-96

Player	Tot	St	Sb	Snu	PS	Gls	Y	R	Fa	La	Fg	Lg
BECKHAM	33	26	7	4	5	7	5	0	3	2	1	0
BRUCE	30	30	0	2	5	1	4	0	5	2	0	0
BUTT	32	31	1	0	4	2	7	1	7	0	1	0
CANTONA	30	30	0	0	1	14	1	0	7	1	5	0
CASPER	0	0	0	1	0	0	0	0	0	0	0	0
COLE	34	32	2	1	10	11	4	0	7	1	2	0
COOKE	4	1	3	0	1	0	0	0	0	2	0	0
COTON	0	0	0	2	0	0	0	0	0	0	0	0
DAVIES	6	1	5	2	1	0	0	0	0	1	0	0
GIGGS	33	30	3	0	2	11	0	0	7	2	1	0
IRWIN	31	31	0	0	2	1	4	0	6	1	0	0
KEANE	29	29	0	0	2	6	7	2	7	1	0	0
MAY	16	11	5	1	2	1	1	0	2	0	0	0
McCLAIR	22	12	10	4	4	3	1	0	0	1	0	0
McGIBBON	0	0	0	3	0	0	0	0	0	1	0	0
NEVILLE, Gary	31	30	1	3	1	0	7	0	6	1	0	0
NEVILLE, Phil	24	21	3	3	6	0	2	0	7	2	0	0
O'KANE	1	0	1	0	0	0	0	0	0	0	0	0
PALLISTER	21	21	0	0	1	1	3	0	3	2	0	0
PARKER	6	5	1	10	1	0	0	0	2	1	0	0
PILKINGTON	3	2	1	3	0	0	0	0	1	1	0	0
PRUNIER	2	2	0	0	0	0	0	0	0	0	0	0
SCHMEICHEL	36	36	0	0	1	0	1	0	6	1	0	0
SCHOLES	26	16	10	9	11	10	2	0	2	1	1	2
SHARPE	31	21	10	2	4	4	3	0	6	2	2	0
THORNLEY	1	0	1	0	0	0	0	0	0	0	0	0
					OG	1						

Second Double Deserved

For a manager that had guided Manchester United to a period of sustained success over the previous five years, Alex Ferguson had to withstand a fair amount of criticism and questioning of his wisdom in allowing Paul Ince, Andrei Kanchelskis and Mark Hughes to be sold for a combined fee of £13.5m just after United had surrendered the championship to Blackburn. The club was also conspicuous by its absence in the transfer market in the opposite direction as just Mick Culkin, £200,000 from York, and Tony Coton in January from Manchester City for £500,000 were their sole purchases. But what United had that no other club did was Eric Cantona. Although banned until the start of October and overlooked by his national side for Euro 96, the Frenchman was to have a staggering influence on United's season and the destination of the league and cup double.

United, sporting a good number of youngsters in their side which suggests that their dominance of the English game is far from over, got off to a disappointing start with a 3-1 defeat at Aston Villa but with a fine ten match unbeaten run the Reds were soon closing in on leaders Newcastle. United briefly topped the table with a draw at Sheffield Wednesday but by the time Cantona made his goalscoring return, from the penalty spot during a 2-2 draw with Liverpool, they had been replaced at the summit. The team faltered with a run of five games without a win, which included defeats at Liverpool and Leeds on Boxing Day. A win over Newcastle got things back on track. A fortuitous victory over QPR kept the momentum going but a 4-1 defeat at White Hart Lane on New Years Day, their heaviest for four years, again cast doubts on United's title aspirations. A goalless draw left United eight points adrift of Newcastle and before January was out the gap had risen to a mighty twelve points. United's response was magnificent with 31 of the next available 33 points coming their way, including a vital and enthralling 1-0 victory at St James' Park which saw great Dane Peter Schmeichel give a stunning solo performance. Cantona scored the winner at Newcastle and followed it up with vital strikes in the next three games against QPR (an injury time equaliser), Arsenal (in front of their first 50,000 gate of the season) and Spurs – a goal which took United into pole position as Newcastle faltered. Cantona again scored in a 3-2 win at Maine Road and made it six in six games with the deciding strike at home to Coventry. Defeat at Southampton – caused according to Ferguson by United's grey shirts – slowed the charge but a last day of the season 3-0 triumph at Middlesbrough confirmed United's third title in four years.

Manchester United's less than perfect start to their league campaign was mirrored in the cups. In the Coca Cola Cup a makeshift side never recovered from a a 3-0 defeat at old Trafford to Division Two side York City and Rotor Volgograd disposed of United in the first round of the UEFA Cup and only a last minute goal by 'keeper Schmeichel preserved United's unbeaten home record in Europe!

The FA Cup was the second half of the double and after a fortunate win over Sunderland in the 3rd Round, Reading, rivals Manchester City and Southampton were put paid to, which set up a semi final with Chelsea. Goals by Cole and Beckham carried the Reds through to become the sixth club to reach the FA Cup Final in three consecutive seasons. The final itself was a dismal affair decided, almost fittingly and in accordance with the script, by Footballer of the Year Cantona as United became the first side to complete the double twice. ■

Results 1995-96

FA Carling Premiership

Date	Opponents	Ven	Res	Pos	Atten	Scorers
19-Aug	Aston Villa	A	1-3		34,655	Beckham (82)
23-Aug	West Ham	H	2-1		31,966	Scholes (50); Keane (68)
26-Aug	Wimbledon	H	3-1	5	32,226	Keane (27, 79); Cole (59);
28-Aug	Blackburn R.	A	2-1	4	29,843	Sharpe (46); Beckham (68)
09-Sep	Everton	A	3-2	2	39,496	Sharpe (3, 49); Giggs (73)
16-Sep	Bolton Wan.	H	3-0	2	32,812	Scholes (17, 85); Giggs (33)
23-Sep	Sheff. Wed.	A	0-0	1	34,101	
01-Oct	Liverpool	H	2-2	3	34,934	Butt (1); Cantona (70 pen)
14-Oct	Man. City	H	1-0	2	35,707	Scholes (4)
21-Oct	Chelsea	A	4-1	2	31,019	Scholes (3, 10); Giggs (79); McClair (88)
28-Oct	Middlesbro	H	2-0	2	36,580	Pallister (43); Cole (87)
04-Nov	Arsenal	A	0-1	2	38,317	
18-Nov	Southampton	H	4-1	2	39,301	Giggs (1, 4); Scholes (8); Cole (69)
22-Nov	Coventry C.	A	4-0	2	23,400	Irwin (28); McClair (47, 76); Beckham (57)
27-Nov	N. Forest	A	1-1	2	29,263	Cantona (66 pen)
02-Dec	Chelsea	H	1-1	2	42,019	Beckham (60)
09-Dec	Sheff. Wed.	H	2-2	2	41,849	Cantona (17, 84)
17-Dec	Liverpool	A	0-2	2	40,546	
24-Dec	Leeds United	A	1-3	2	39,801	Cole (33)
27-Dec	Newcastle U.	H	2-0	2	42,024	Cole (5); Keane (53)
30-Dec	QPR	H	2-1	2	41,890	Cole (44); Giggs (52)
01-Jan	Tottenham	A	1-4	2	32,852	Cole (36)
13-Jan	Aston Villa	H	0-0	2	42,667	
22-Jan	West Ham	A	1-0	2	24,197	Cantona (8)
03-Feb	Wimbledon	A	4-2	2	25,380	Cole (42); OG (Perry 45); Cantona (70, 80 pen)
10-Feb	Blackburn R.	H	1-0	2	42,681	Sharpe (14)
21-Feb	Everton	H	2-0	2	42,459	Keane (30); Giggs (82)
25-Feb	Bolton Wan.	A	6-0	2	21,381	Beckham (5); Bruce (15); Cole (70); Scholes (76, 79); Butt (90)
04-Mar	Newcastle U.	A	1-0	2	36,584	Cantona (51)
16-Mar	QPR	A	1-1	1	18,817	Cantona (90)
20-Mar	Arsenal	H	1-0	1	50,028	Cantona (66)
24-Mar	Tottenham	H	1-0	1	50,157	Cantona (50)
06-Apr	Man. City	A	3-2	1	29,688	Cantona (7 pen); Cole (41); Giggs (77)
08-Apr	Coventry C.	H	1-0	1	50,332	Cantona (47)

13-Apr	Southampton	A	1-3	1	15,262	Giggs (89)
17-Apr	Leeds United	H	1-0	1	48,382	Keane (72)
28-Apr	N. Forest	H	5-0	1	53,926	Scholes (41); Beckham (44, 54); Giggs (69); Cantona (89)
05-May	Middlesbro'	A	3-0	1	29,921	May (15); Cole (54); Giggs (80)

UEFA Cup

Date	Opponents	Vn	Rnd	Res	Atten	Scorers
12-Sep	Rotor V'gd	A	1R1L	0-0	40,000	
26-Sep	Rotor V'gd	H	1R2L	2-2	29,724	Scholes (59); Schmeichel (89)

Rotor Volgograd won on away goals rule. 2-2 on aggregate

FA Challenge Cup

Date	Opponents	Vn	Rnd	Res	Atten	Scorers
06-Jan	Sunderland	H	3R	2-2	41,563	Butt (12); Cantona (79)
16-Jan	Sunderland	A	3RR	2-1	21,378	Scholes (70); Cole (89)
27-Jan	Reading	A	4R	3-0	14,780	Giggs (36); Parker (56); Cantona (89)
18-Feb	Man. City	H	5R	2-1	42,693	Cantona (39 pen); Sharpe (77)
11-Mar	Southampton	H	QF	2-0	45,446	Cantona (49); Sharpe (90)
31-Mar	Chelsea	N	SF	2-1	38,421	Cole (56); Beckham (59)
	Played at Villa Park					
11-May	Man. United	W	FIN	1-0	79,007	Cantona (85)

Coca-Cola League Cup

Date	Opponents	Vn	Rnd	Res	Atten	Scorers
20-Sep	York City	H	2R1L	0-3	29,049	
03-Oct	York City	A	2R2L	3-1	9,386	Scholes (6, 80); Cooke (13)

York City won 4-3 on aggregate

Manchester United – Premiership Fact File

- United became the first side ever to complete the League and Cup double twice.
- Amazingly United scored in 34 of their 38 Premiership games. Only Sheffield Wednesday, Arsenal, Liverpool and Aston Villa managed shut-outs.
- David May scored his first Premiership goal for United in the title clincher at Middlesbrough on the last day of the season.
- Goalkeeper Peter Schmeichel scored for United during their UEFA Cup match at Old Trafford against Rotor Volgograd. It was a last minute headed equaliser that preserved United's unbeaten home record in Europe.

Middlesbrough

Formed in 1876 and played first game in 1877. Turned professional in 1889, but reverted to amateur status shortly afterwards, being early winners of the FA Amateur Cup. League football was first played in Middlesbrough by the Ironpolis side for one season, 1893-94. Middlesbrough turned professional again, were elected to Division Two in 1899, and moved to Ayresome Park in 1903. They were founder members of the Premier League in 1993 but were relegated in their first season. Moved to purpose built stadium in 1995 coinciding with return to Premiership.

Ground: The Cellnet Riverside Stadium, Middlesbrough, TS3 6RS
Phone: 01642 227227   **Info:** 0891 42 42 00
Tickets: 01642 207014   **Club Shop:** 01642 207005
Nickname: The Boro
Colours: Red with Black, White with Black, Red with Black.
Capacity: 31,000

Chairman: Steve Gibson   **CEO:** Keith Lamb
Secretary: Karen Nelson
Manager: Bryan Robson   **Assistant:** Viv Anderson
First Team Coach: John Pickering   **Physios:** Bob Ward, Tommy Johnson

League History: 1899 Elected to Division 2; 1902-24 Division 1; 1924-27 Division 2; 1927-28 Division 1; 1928-29 Division 2; 1929-54 Division 1; 1954-66 Division 2; 1966-67 Division 3; 1967-74 Division 2; 1974-82 Division 2; 1982-86 Division 2; 1986-87 Division 3; 1988-89 Division 1; 1989-92 Division 2; 1992-93 FAPL; 1993-95 Division 1; 1995- FAPL.

Honours: *Division 1 (new) Champions:* 1994-95; *Division 2 Champions* 1926-27, 1928-29, 1973-74; *Runners-up:* 1901-02, 1991-92; *Division 3 Runners up:* 1966-67, 1986-87; *FA Amateur Cup Winners:* 1895, 1898; *Anglo-Scottish Cup Winners:* 1975-76.

European Record: Never qualified

Managers: John Robson 1899-05; Alex Massie 1905-06; Andy Atkin 1906-09; J.Gunter 1908-10; Andy Walker 1910-11; Tom McIntosh 1911-19; James Howie 1920-23; Herbert Bamlett 1923-26; Peter McWilliam 1927-34; Wilf Gillow 1933-44; David Jack 1944-52; Walter Rowley 1952-54; Bob Dennison 1954-63; Raich Carter 1963-66; Stan Anderson 1966-73; Jack Charlton 1973-77; John Neal 1977-81; Bobby Murdoch 1981-82; Malcolm

Allison 1982-84; Willie Maddren 1984-86; Bruce Rioch 1986-90; Colin Todd 1990-91; Lennie Lawrence 1991-94; *(FAPL)*: Bryan Robson May 1994-

Season 1995-96

Biggest Home Win:	4-1 v Manchester City, 9/12/95
Biggest Home Defeat:	1-4 v Bolton Wanderers, 17/2/96
Biggest Away Win:	1-0 v Leeds Utd, Man. City and Sheff.Wednesday
Biggest Away Defeat:	0-5 v Chelsea, 04/2/96
Biggest Home Att:	30,011 v Newcastle United, 10/2/96
Smallest Home Att:	23,392 v Nottingam Forest, 16/3/96
Average Attendance:	28,920 (9th highest)
Leading Scorer:	7 – Nick Barmby, 6 – Jan Fjortoft

Last Season: *FAPL: 12th FA Cup: 4 Coca-Cola Cup: 4*

All-Time Records

Record FAPL Win:	4-1 v Leeds United, 22/8/92 and
	4-1 v Manchester City, 9/12/95
Record FAPL Defeat:	0-5 v Chelsea (away), 04/2/96;
	1-5 v Aston Villa, 17/1/93
Record FL Win:	9-0 v Brighton &HA, D2 23/8/58
Record FL Defeat:	0-9 v Blackburn Rovers, D2 6/11/54
Record Cup Win:	9-3 v Goole Town, FAC1, 9/1/15
Record Fee Received:	£2.3m, Gary Pallister to Manchester Utd, 8/89
Record Fee Paid:	£5.25m to Tottenham for Nicky Barmby, 8/95

Record Attendance (all-time): 53,596 v Newcastle Utd, D1 27/12/49
                              at Ayresome Park
Record Attendance (FAPL): 30,011 v Newcastle United, 10/2/96
                              at Cellnet Stadium – also record

Most FL Apps:	Tim Williamson, 563, 1902-23
Most FAPL Apps:	60 – Derek Whyte
Most FAPL Goals:	27 – Chris Morris

Highest Scorer in FAPL Season: Paul Wilkinson 15, 1992-93
Most FAPL Goals in Season: 54, 1992-93 – 42 games
Most FAPL Points in Season: 44, 1992-93 – 42 games

5-Year Record

	Div.	P	W	D	L	F	A	Pts	Pos	FAC	FLC
91-92	2	46	23	11	12	58	41	80	2	5	SF
92-93	PL	42	11	11	20	54	75	44	21	4	2
93-94	1	46	18	13	15	66	54	67	9	3	3
94-95	1	46	23	13	10	67	40	82	1	3	3
95-96	PL	38	11	10	17	35	50	43	12	4	4

Summary 1995-96

Player	Tot	St	Sb	Snu	PS	Gls	Y	R	Fa	La	Fg	Lg
BARMBY	32	32	0	0	0	7	4	0	3	4	1	1
BARRON	1	1	0	2	0	0	0	0	0	0	0	0
BLACKMORE	5	4	1	3	0	0	0	0	0	1	0	0
BRANCO	7	5	2	3	2	0	1	0	0	0	0	0
CAMPBELL	2	1	1	2	1	0	0	0	0	0	0	0
COX	35	35	0	0	0	2	7	0	2	5	0	0
FJORTOFT	28	27	1	5	6	6	3	0	0	6	0	2
FLEMING	14	14	0	0	1	1	2	0	2	1	0	0
FREESTONE	3	2	1	0	1	1	0	0	1	0	0	0
HENDRIE	13	7	6	4	1	1	1	0	0	3	0	0
HIGNETT	22	17	5	4	4	5	5	0	1	4	0	2
JUNINHO	21	20	1	1	5	2	2	0	3	2	0	0
KAVANAGH	7	6	1	3	3	1	1	0	0	0	0	0
LIDDLE	13	13	0	3	0	0	3	0	1	3	0	0
MILLER	6	6	0	2	0	0	0	0	0	0	0	0
MOORE	12	5	7	11	1	0	0	1	0	3	0	0
MORENO	7	2	5	13	0	0	0	0	1	2	0	0
MORRIS	23	22	1	0	2	2	9	0	2	4	0	0
MUSTOE	21	21	0	0	2	1	3	0	0	3	0	1
O'HALLORAN	3	2	1	0	1	0	1	0	2	0	0	0
PEARSON	36	36	0	0	3	0	6	0	3	5	0	0
POLLOCK	31	31	0	0	4	1	10	0	3	6	1	0
ROBERTS	0	0	0	1	0	0	0	0	0	0	0	0
ROBSON	2	1	1	1	0	0	0	0	1	1	0	0
STAMP	12	11	1	0	2	2	0	0	1	2	0	0
SUMMERBELL	1	0	1	0	0	0	1	0	0	0	0	0
VICKERS	32	32	0	0	0	1	1	0	3	6	0	1
WALSH	31	31	0	1	0	0	1	0	3	6	0	0
WHELAN	13	9	4	10	1	1	4	1	3	3	0	0
WHYTE	25	24	1	0	2	0	8	1	0	3	0	0
WILKINSON	2	1	1	2	0	0	0	0	3	0	0	0

OG 1

Samba Fades to Latin Flavour

Middlesbrough crowned their return to the Premiership after a gap of just two years with a move into the magnificent Riverside Stadium and the £5.25m signing of homesick England star Nicky Barmby from Tottenham. Just prior to the start of the season Boro manager Bryan Robson, having gained promotion at the end of his first season as a manager, further strengthened his side with the £1m signing of Croatian Igor Cvitanovic and former Manchester United 'keeper Gary Walsh for £250,000.

Barmby wasted little time in starting to pay off his fee by opening the scoring during the first Sunday match of the season, a 1-1 draw at Arsenal. Barmby's excellent early season form was matched by Craig Hignett who scored during a 2-0 win over Chelsea, Boro's first win of the season. Without a win from the next three games Boro slipped to 11th but a run of five consecutive victories, including four straight clean sheets, lifted the side into fourth place. The success ended with Robson's first return to Manchester United since leaving in 1994. Sentiment was pushed to one side as United won 2-0. Robson made his most audacious move yet in the transfer market during October with the capture of Juninho from Sao Paulo for £4.75m but the Brazilian Player of the Year, despite thrilling crowds with his dynamic close skills, had to wait until the end of November for his first taste of success when Boro defeated Liverpool at the Riverside. That win sparked a revival in Middlesbrough's fortunes with four goals being put past both Manchester City and West Ham. Sandwiched in between was a 1-0 defeat at Blackburn.

Boro headed into Christmas in fifth place with optimism high but their away form, only one goal from the previous four games, giving concern. Everton heightened those concerns with a 4-0 thrashing at Goodison on Boxing Day and that reversal set the Teeside club on a downward spiral. Eight successive Premiership defeats were suffered including a 5-0 hammering at Chelsea and an embarrassing 4-1 home defeat against bottom side Bolton; it equalled the worst run in Boro's history. Two defeats and three draws, the last of which was at Villa Park, extended the winless run to 13 games before Graham Kavanagh's first goal since December 1993 clinched victory at Leeds. A brace from Jan Aage Fjortoft and Chris Freestone's first Premiership goal saw Boro to victory over Sheffield Wednesday on Good Friday but it was to be their last success of the season which ended with a 3-0 defeat at home to Manchester United.

Boro's declining league form was carried into the FA Cup in the New Year. After seeing off Notts County in the 3rd round they were held at home by Wimbledon in front of 29,192 spectators but lost the replay in south London in front of a crowd of little more than five thousand. Boro played in three rounds of the Coca Cola Cup, beating Endsleigh League sides Rotherham United, 3-1 on aggregate, and Crystal Palace 2-0 after a replay only to lose in a replay at St Andrews to eventual semi finalists Birmingham.

Overall the season will be seen as one of consolidation for Robson's team but the expectations for 96/97 will be a deal higher. During the spring Robson signed Brazilian defender Branco and needs to nurture his talents and those of Juninho into the team far better than was seen during the second half of this season if his side are to be successful. Another worry for the Boro boss was their lack of goals. Top scorer in the league was Barmby with just seven while the side failed to score in ten of the final 19 matches and only twice scored more than one goal in that time. This may be solved by the audacious pre-season capture of £7m Fabio Ravanelli. ∎

Results 1995-96

Date	Opponents	Ven	Res	Pos	Atten	Scorers
20-Aug	Arsenal	A	1-1	–	37,308	Barmby (31)
26-Aug	Chelsea	H	2-0	–	28,286	Hignett (39); Fjortoft (76)
30-Aug	Newcastle U.	A	0-1	11	36,483	
09-Sep	Bolton Wan.	A	1-1	12	18,376	Hignett (77)
12-Sep	Southampton	H	0-0	11	29,188	
16-Sep	Coventry C.	H	2-1	9	27,882	Vicers (57); Fjortoft (78)
23-Sep	Man. City	A	1-0	7	25,865	Barmby (16)
30-Sep	Blackburn R.	A	2-0	7	29,462	Barmby (44); Hignett (72)
15-Oct	Sheff. Wed.	A	1-0	4	21,177	Hignett (68 pen)
21-Oct	QPR	H	1-0	4	29,293	Hignett (15 pen)
28-Oct	Man. United	A	0-2	6	36,580	
04-Nov	Leeds United	H	1-1	6	29,467	Fjortoft (9)
18-Nov	Wimbledon	A	0-0	7	13,780	
21-Nov	Tottenham	H	0-1	9	29,487	
25-Nov	Liverpool	H	2-1	6	29,390	Cox (2); Barmby (64)
02-Dec	QPR	A	1-1	6	17,546	Morris (8)
09-Dec	Man. City	H	4-1	4	29,469	Barmby (33, 54); Stamp (53); Juninho (74)
16-Dec	Blackburn R.	A	0-1	6	27,996	
23-Dec	West Ham	H	4-2	5	28,640	Fjortoft (20); Cox (21); Morris (28); Hendrie (82)
26-Dec	Everton	A	0-4	6	40,091	
30-Dec	N. Forest	A	0-1	7	27,027	
01-Jan	Aston Villa	H	0-2	9	28,535	
13-Jan	Arsenal	H	2-3	11	29,359	Juninho (38); Stamp (55)
20-Jan	Southampton	A	1-2	12	15,151	Barmby (44)
04-Feb	Chelsea	A	0-5	12	21,060	
10-Feb	Newcastle U.	H	1-2	12	30,011	OG (Beresford 37)
17-Feb	Bolton Wan.	H	1-4	13	29,354	Pollock (36)
24-Feb	Coventry C.	A	0-0	13	18,810	
02-Mar	Everton	H	0-2	13	29,407	
09-Mar	West Ham	A	0-2	13	23,850	
16-Mar	N. Forest	H	1-1	13	23,392	Mustoe (57)
19-Mar	Aston Villa	A	0-0	13	23,933	
30-Mar	Leeds United	A	1-0	13	31,778	Kavanagh (4)
05-Apr	Sheff. Wed.	H	3-1	13	29,751	Fjortoft (53, 66); Freestone (71)
8-Apr	Tottenham	A	1-1	12	32,036	Whelan (85)
13-Apr	Wimbledon	H	1-2	12	29,192	Fleming (23)
27-Apr	Liverpool	A	0-1	12	40,782	
05-May	Man. United	H	0-3	13	29,921	

FA Challenge Cup

Date	Opponents	Vn	Rnd	Res	Atten	Scorers
06-Jan	Notts County	A	3R	2-1	12,621	Pollock (46); Barmby (48)
07-Feb	Wimbledon	H	4R	0-0	28,915	
13-Feb	Wimbledon	A	4RR	0-1	5,220	

Coca-Cola League Cup

Date	Opponents	Vn	Rnd	Res	Atten	Scorers
20-Sep	Rotherham	H	2R1L	2-1	13,280	Mustoe (20), Fjortoft (41)
03-Oct	Rotherham	A	2R2L	1-0	6,867	Vickers (50
	Middlesbrough won 3-1 on aggregate					
25-Oct	C. Palace	A	3R	2-2	11,873	Barmby (14); Hignett (20)
08-Nov	C. Palace	H	3RR	2-0	16,150	Hignett (8); Fjortoft (76)
29-Nov	Birmingham	H	4R	0-0	28,031	
20-Dec	Birmingham	A	4RR	0-2	19,878	

Boro – Premiership Fact File

- Middlesbrough became the first club to field two Brazilians in a Premiership match when Juninho and Branco turned out against Sheffield Wednesday at the Riverside on 5th April. Boro won 3-1.
- The new link road connecting Middlesbrough's Riverside Stadium to the A66 Middlesbrough By Pass should be completed by the start of the 1996-97 season. The £6million it cost is a little less than half the cost of the stadium itself.
- Middlesbrough will be closing in the two open corners of the Riverside Stadium to increase the capacity to 34,000. Work should start during the season.
- Boro were able to break the 30,000 attendance mark for the first time in their derby match with Newcastle on 10th February. It was made possible following the installation of 330 extra seats in the East Stand!
- The close season signing of Fabrizio Ravanelli brought Bryan Robson's spending to some £24 million – nearly twice the cost of Boro's stadium!
- Middlesbrough Reserves played their first ever match at the Riverside Stadium when Aston Villa were the opponents on 19th February. Boro Reserves normally play at Hartlepool's Victoria Park ground.

Newcastle United

Formed 1882 as Newcastle East End on the amalgamation of Stanley and Rosewood. Founder members, as a professional club, of the Northern League in 1889. Moved from Chillington Road, Heaton in 1892 to take over the home of the defunct Newcastle West End, with several of those associated with the West End side joining the newcomers.

Applied for Football League Division One membership in 1892, failed and decided against a place in the new Second Division, staying in the Northern League. Later in 1892 changed name to Newcastle United. Elected to an expanded Football League Division Two in 1893.

Ground: St James' Park, Newcastle-upon-Tyne, NE1 4ST
Phone: 0191-232 8361   **Info:** 0891 12 11 90
Colours: Black/White, Black, Black   **Nickname:** Magpies
Capacity: 36,401   **Pitch:** 115 yds x 75 yds

President: Trevor Bennett   **Chairman:** Sir John Hall
General Manager/Secretary: Russell Cushing
Manager: Kevin Keegan   **Assistant:** Terry McDermott
Coaches: Chris McMenemy, Arthur Cox   **Physio:** Derek Wright

League History: 1893 Elected to Division 2; 1898-1934 Division 1; 1934-48 Division 2; 1948-61 Division 1; 1961-65 Division 2; 1965-78 Division 1; 1978-84 Division 2; 1984-89 Division 1; 1989-92 Division 2; 1992-1993 Division 1; 1993- FA Premier League.

Honours: *Football League: Division 1 Champions:* 1904-05, 1906-07, 1908-09, 1926-27, 1992-93; *FA Premier League Runners-up:* 1995-96;*Division 2 Champions:* 1964-65; *Runners-up:* 1897-98, 1947-48. *FA Cup Winners:* 1910, 1924, 1932, 1951, 1952, 1955; *Runners-up:* 1905, 1906, 1908, 1911, 1974; *Football League Cup Runners-up:* 1975-76; *Texaco Cup Winners:* 1973-74, 1974-75. *UEFA Cup Winners:* 1968-69.

European Record: CC (0): –; CWC (0): – ; UEFA (5): 68-69(W), 69-70(QF), 70-71(2), 77-78(2), 94-95(2).
Managers: Frank Watt 1895-1932 (secretary until 1932); Andy Cunningham 1930-35; Tom Mather 1935-39; Stan Seymour 1939-47 (hon manager); George Martin 1947-50; Stan Seymour 1950-54 (hon manager); Duggie Livingstone; 1954-56, Stan Seymour (Non manager) 1956-58; Charlie Mitten 1958-61; Norman Smith 1961-62; Joe Harvey 1962-75; Gordon Lee 1975-77; Richard Dinnis 1977; Bill McGarry 1977-80; Arthur Cox 1980-84; Jack

158

Charlton 1984; Willie McFaul 1985-88; Jim Smith 1988-91; Ossie Ardiles 1991-92; *(FAPL)* Kevin Keegan Feb. 1992-

Season 1995-96

Biggest Home Win: 6-1 v Wimbledon, 21/10/95
Biggest Home Defeat: 0-1 v Manchester United, 4/3/96
Biggest Away Win: 3-1 v Bolton Wdrs, 22/8/95 and Everton 1/10/95
Biggest Away Defeat: 3-4 v Liverpool, 3/4/96
Biggest Home Att: 36,589 v Tottenham Hotspur, 5/5/96
Smallest Home Att: 36,225 v Chelsea, 24/9/95
Average Attendance: 36,504 (4th highest)
Leading Scorer: 25 – Les Ferdinand, 8 – Peter Beardsley, Robert Lee
Last Season: *FAPL:* 2nd *FA Cup:* 3 *Coca-Cola Cup:* QF

All-Time Records

Record FAPL Win: 7-1 v Swindon Town, 12/3/94
Record FAPL Defeat: 0-3 v Queens Park Rangers, 4/2/95
Record FL Win: 13-0 v Newport County, Division 2, 5/10/1946
Record FL Defeat: 0-9 v Burton Wanderers, Division 2, 15/4/1895
Record Cup Win: 9-0 v Southport (at Hillsborough), FA Cup R4, 1/2/1932
Record Fee Received: £7m from Manchester United for Andy Cole,
                           1/1995 (inc part exchange)
Record Fee Paid: £6m to QPR for Les Ferdinand, 6/95
Most FL Apps: Jim Lawrence, 432, 1904-22
Most FAPL Apps: 104 – Peter Beardsley
Most FAPL Goals: 55 – Andy Cole
Highest Scorer in FAPL Season: Andy Cole, 34, 1993-94
Record Attendance (all-time): 68,386 v Chelsea, Division 1, 3/9/1930
Record Attendance (FAPL): 36,589 v Tottenham Hotspur, 5/5/96
Most FAPL Goals in Season: 82, 1993-94 – 42 games
Most FAPL Points in Season: 78, 1995-96 – 38 games

5-Year Record

	Div.	P	W	D	L	F	A	Pts	Pos	FAC	FLC
91-92	2	46	13	13	20	66	84	52	20	3	3
92-93	1	46	29	4	8	85	37	93	1	5	3
93-94	PL	42	23	8	11	82	41	77	3	4	3
94-95	PL	42	20	12	10	67	47	72	6	QF	4
95-96	PL	38	24	6	8	66	37	78	2	3	QF

Summary 1995-96

Player	Tot	St	Sb	Snu	PS	Gls	Y	R	Fa	La	Fg	Lg
ALBERT	23	19	4	5	1	4	5	0	2	3	1	1
ASPRILLA	14	11	3	0	3	3	2	0	0	0	0	0
BARTON	31	30	1	4	4	0	3	0	2	5	0	1
BATTY	11	11	0	0	0	1	2	0	0	0	0	0
BEARDSLEY	35	35	0	0	2	8	6	0	2	3	1	2
BERESFORD	33	32	1	1	2	0	6	1	1	2	0	0
BRAYSON	0	0	0	1	0	0	0	0	0	1	0	0
CLARK	28	22	6	4	2	2	1	0	2	3	0	0
CRAWFORD	0	0	0	0	0	0	0	0	0	1	0	0
ELLIOTT	6	5	1	13	0	0	2	0	2	2	0	0
FERDINAND	37	37	0	0	1	25	4	0	2	5	1	3
FOX	4	2	2	2	1	0	0	0	0	1	0	0
GILLESPIE	28	26	2	5	11	4	3	0	0	4	0	1
GINOLA	34	34	0	0	5	5	5	0	2	4	0	0
HISLOP	24	24	0	2	1	0	0	0	0	4	0	0
HOLLAND	0	0	0	2	0	0	0	0	0	1	0	0
HOTTIGER	1	0	1	2	0	0	0	0	0	2	0	0
HOWEY	28	28	0	0	2	1	2	0	1	3	0	0
HUCKERBY	1	0	1	1	0	0	0	0	1	0	0	0
KITSON	7	2	5	5	2	2	1	0	2	0	0	0
LEE	36	36	0	0	3	8	3	0	1	4	0	1
PEACOCK	34	33	1	2	0	0	3	0	1	5	0	2
SELLARS	6	2	4	2	0	0	0	0	0	2	0	1
SRNICEK	15	14	1	12	0	0	0	0	2	2	0	0
WATSON	23	15	8	10	1	3	0	0	0	5	0	1

Heavy Spending Not Repaid

Newcastle may not have matched their record of six successive victories at the start of the 94-95 season but with nine wins in ten games by 21 October and just one defeat suffered by 3 December it did appear that Kevin Keegan was to have the honour of being the first manager to guide the Geordies to the championship since 1927. Leading the charge were two of Keegan's new multi-million pound signings Les Ferdinand and David Ginola. After 14 Premiership games Ferdinand was going along at a goal a game and receiving excellent support from the evergreen Peter Beardsley and England new boy Rob Lee. In goal, Shaka Hislop, a £1,575,000 signing from Reading, kept three clean sheets in his first four games.

After four straight wins the first points were dropped in a surprise defeat at Southampton but five more victories, including a 6-1 win over Wimbledon who finished the day with Vinney Jones in goal, left the side four points clear at the top of the table. After a scintillating draw at Tottenham it was back to winning ways with home wins over Liverpool and Blackburn, the first one somewhat fortuitously. Although Newcastle's form at St James' Park remained impressive the draw at Spurs started a run of five away games without a win; indeed of their last 14 away Premiership matches just three were won. The Magpies' quite magnificent home record stayed intact until the arrival of Manchester United for a potential showdown on 4 March. With the Reds having won the earlier encounter at Old Trafford the Magpies needed a win to ensure supremacy at the top of the table. The match was also of great significance psychologically, a 2-1 win over Bolton on 21 January put Newcastle 12 points clear but by the time of the Reds' visit the lead was down to four points. Newcastle launched an amazing first half assault on the visitors' goal but managed to lose 1-0 and with that defeat the Magpies' title aspirations dropped significantly. West Ham were completely swept aside during Newcastle's next match but defeat at Arsenal, that allowed Manchester United to go top on goal difference, was followed by an extraordinary match at Anfield which eventually saw Newcastle lose 4-3 during injury time. Two late goals also overturned a lead at Blackburn. Successive single goal victories over Villa, Southampton and Leeds kept Newcastle in with a shout as the season went into its final week but draws with Forest and Spurs confirmed that this was not to be Newcastle's season.

Newcastle actually tasted defeat at home for the first time during the season when Chelsea, after being held by a late Ferdinand goal at Stamford Bridge, won a penalty shoot-out at St James' Park in the 3rd Round of the FA Cup. The Coca Cola Cup looked destined for the north-east as Newcastle thrashed Bristol City and Stoke City while a clever Steve Watson goal at Liverpool took the Magpies through to a quarter final tie at Highbury. It was here that the Wembley dream ended as Arsenal, on a night which saw brilliant Frenchman Ginola dismissed, won 2-0.

Keegan may have spent heavily during the close season but it did not hinder his purchasing powers during the season with over £10m being spent in February on taking Colombian Faustino Asprilla and England midfielder David Batty to St James' Park. The United manager was frequently questioned as to whether the arrival of the independent and unpredictable Asprilla had cost Newcastle the title as their style and cohesion of earlier in the season disappeared. Keegan, however, who was praised by a top FIFA official for the way he conducted himself after the defeat at Liverpool, later that month launched an astonishing public attack on the Manchester United manager live on television. ∎

Results 1995-96

FA Carling Premiership

Date	Opponents	Ven	Res	Pos	Atten	Scorers
19-Aug	Coventry C.	H	3-0	–	36,485	Lee (7); Beardsley (82 pen); Ferdinand (83)
22-Aug	Bolton Wan.	A	3-1	–	20,243	Ferdinand (17, 84); Lee (77)
27-Aug	Sheff. Wed.	A	2-0	1	24,815	Ginola (53); Beardsley (75)
30-Aug	Middlesbro'	H	1-0	1	36,483	Ferdinand (67)
09-Sep	Southampton	A	0-1	1	15,237	
16-Sep	Man. City	H	3-1	1	36,501	Beardsley (18 pen); Lee (38); Ferdinand (59)
24-Sep	Chelsea	H	2-0	1	36,225	Ferdinand (41, 57)
01-Oct	Everton	A	3-1	1	33,080	Ferdinand (20); Lee (59); Kitson (65)
14-Oct	QPR	A	3-2	1	18,254	Gillespie (48, 72); Ferdinand (57)
21-Oct	Wimbledon	H	6-1	1	36,434	Howey (31); Ferdinand (35, 41, 63); Clark (5); Albert (84)
29-Oct	Tottenham	A	1-1	1	32,279	Ginola (47)
04-Nov	Liverpool	H	2-1	1	36,547	Ferdinand (3); Watson (89)
08-Nov	Blackburn R.	H	1-0	1	36,463	Lee (13)
18-Nov	Aston Villa	A	1-1	1	39,167	Ferdinand (58)
25-Nov	Leeds United	H	2-1	1	36,572	Lee (70); Beardsley (72)
03-Dec	Wimbledon	A	3-3	1	18,002	Ferdinand (8, 29); Gillespie (35)
09-Dec	Chelsea	A	0-1	1	31,098	
16-Dec	Everton	H	1-0	1	36,557	Ferdinand (17)
23-Dec	N. Forest	H	3-1	1	36,531	Lee (12, 74); Ginola (25)
27-Dec	Man. United	A	0-2	1	42,024	
02-Jan	Arsenal	H	2-0	1	36,530	Ginola (1); Ferdinand (47)
14-Jan	Coventry C.	A	1-0	1	20,547	Watson (44)
20-Jan	Bolton Wan.	H	2-1	1	36,534	Kitson (9); Beardsley (37)
03-Feb	Sheff. Wed.	H	2-0	1	36,567	Ferdinand (54); Clark (90)
10-Feb	Middlesbro'	A	2-1	1	30,011	Watson (73); Ferdinand (78)
21-Feb	West Ham	H	0-2	1	23,843	
24-Feb	Man. City	A	3-3	1	31,115	Albert (44, 81); Asprilla (71)
04-Mar	Man. United	H	0-1	1	36,584	
18-Mar	West Ham	A	3-0	1	36,331	Albert (21); Asprilla (55); Ferdinand (65)
23-Mar	Arsenal	A	0-2	2	38,271	
03-Apr	Liverpool	A	3-4	2	40,702	Ferdinand (10); Ginola (14); Asprilla (60)
06-Apr	QPR	H	2-1	2	36,583	Beardsley (77, 81)

162

08-Apr	Blackburn R.	A	1-2	2	30,717	Batty (76)
14-Apr	Aston Villa	H	1-0	2	36,510	Ferdinand (64)
17-Apr	Southampton	H	1-0	2	36,554	Lee (10)
29-Apr	Leeds United	A	1-0	2	38,862	Gillespie (17)
02-May	N. Forest	A	1-1	2	28,280	Beardsley (32)
05-May	Tottenham	H	1-1	2	36,589	Ferdinand (71)

FA Challenge Cup

Date	Opponents	Vn	Rnd	Res	Atten	Scorers
07-Jan	Chelsea	A	3R	1-1	25,151	Ferdinand (90)
17-Jan	Chelsea	H	3RR	2-2	36,535	Albert (43); Beardsley (64 pen)

After extra time. Chelsea won 4-2 on penalties

Coca-Cola League Cup

Date	Opponents	Vn	Rnd	Res	Atten	Scorers
19-Sep	Bristol City	A	2R1L	5-0	15,952	Peacock (8); Sellars (22); Ferdinand (30); Gillespie (46); Lee (85)
04-Oct	Bristol City	H	2R2L	3-1	36,357	Barton (48); Albert (55); Ferdinand (65)
25-Oct	Stoke City	A	3R	4-0	23,000	Beardsley (30, 39); Ferdinand (52); Peacock (73)
29-Nov	Liverpool	A	4R	1-0	40,077	Watson (77)
10-Jan	Arsenal	A	QF	0-2	37,857	

Magpies – Premiership Fact File

- Newcastle United won nine of their first ten Premiership games last season having started the season with six successive victories.
- United won just three of their last 14 Premiership games.
- St James Park saw Newcastle win 17 of the 19 Premiership games staged there. Only Manchester United and Tottenham Hotspur denied the Magpies victories.
- The match at Liverpool ending in a 4-3 defeat has been hailed as the greatest league game ever played. Few who saw it would disagree.
- Peter Beardsley scored his 100th goal in Newcastle United colours last season. It proved to be the winner in a 2-1 victory over Bolton Wanderers at St James Park on 21st January. Beardsley scored 62 goals for United during his first spell at the club.
- Les Ferdinand requires 15 goals to match Alan Shearer's century of Premiership strikes.

Nottingham Forest

Founded in 1865 by players of a hockey-like game, shinney, who played at the Forest Recreation Ground. They played their first game in 1866. Had several early homes, including a former Notts County ground, The Meadows, and Trent Bridge Cricket Ground.

Founder members of the Football Alliance in 1889 and champions in 1892 when elected to an extended Football League top division. In 1898 moved from the Town Ground to the City Ground at West Bridgford. Run by a Committee until 1982, the last League club to become a limited company. Premier League founder members 1992. Relegated after one season, but promoted back at the first attempt.

Ground: City Ground, Nottingham NG2 5FJ
Phone: 0115-952 6000   **News:** 0891 12 11 74
Box Office: 0115-952-6002   **Info:** 0115-952 6016 (24 hrs)
Capacity: 30,539   **Pitch:** 115yds x78 yds
Colours: Red, White, Red   **Nickname:** Reds

Chairman: Fred Reacher   **Vice-Chairman:** Irving Korn
Secretary: Paul White
Manager: Frank Clark   **Assistant Manager:** Alan Hill
First Team Coach: Liam O'Kane   **Physio:** John Haselden

League History: 1892 elected to Division 1; 1906-07 Division 2; 1907-11 Division 1; 1911-22 Division 2; 1922-25 Division 1; 1925-49 Division 2; 1949-51 Division 3(S); 1951-57 Division 2; 1957-72 Division 1; 1972-77 Division 2; 1977-92 Division 1; 1992-93 FA Premier League; 1993-94 Division 1; 1994- FA Premier League.

Honours: *Football League Division 1 Champions:* 1977-78; *Runners-up:* 1966-67, 1978-79; *Division 2 Champions:* 1906-07, 1921-22; *Runners-up:* 1956-57; *Division 3(S) Champions:* 1950-51. *FA Cup Winners:* 1898, 1959; *Runners-up:* 1991. *Anglo-Scottish Cup Winners:* 1976-77. *Football League Cup Winners:* 1977-78, 1978-79, 1988-89, 1989-90; *Runners-up:* 1979-80, 1991-92; *Simod Cup Winners:* 1989; *Zenith Data Systems Cup Winners:* 1991-92; *Champions' Cup Winners:* 1978-79, 1979-80; *European Super Cup Winners:* 1979-80; *Runners-up:* 1980-81. *World Club Championship Runners-up:* 1980-81.

European Record: CC (3): 78-79(W), 79-80(W), 80-81(1); CWC(0): –; UEFA (5): 61-62(1), 67-68(2), 83-84(3), 84-85(1), 95-96(QF).

Managers: Harry Radford 1889-97; Harry Haslam 1897-09; Fred Earp 1909-12; Bob Masters 1912-25; Jack Baynes 1925-29; Stan Hardy 1930-31; Noel Watson 1931-36; Harold Wightman 1936-39; Billy Walker 1939-60; Andy Beattie 1960-63; John Carey 1963-68; Matt Gillies 1969-72; Dave Mackay 1972-73; Allan Brown 1973-75; *(FAPL)* Brian Clough 1975-93; Frank Clark June 1993-

Season 1995-96

Biggest Home Win: 4-1 v Wimbledon, 6/11/95
Biggest Home Defeat: 1-5 v Blackburn Rovers, 13/4/96
Biggest Away Win: 4-3 v Southampton, 19/8/95
Biggest Away Defeat: 0-7 v Blackburn Rovers, 18/11/95
Biggest Home Att: 29,263 v Manchester United, 27/11/95
Smallest Home Att: 20,810 v Wimbledon, 6/11/95
Average Attendance: 25,916 (12th highest)
Leading Scorer: 8 – Jason Lee, Brian Roy, Ian Woan
Last Season: *FAPL:* 9th *FA Cup:* QF *Coca-Cola Cup:* 2

All-Time Records

Record FAPL Win: 7-1 v Sheffield Wednesday, 1/4/95
Record FAPL Defeat: 0-7 v Blackburn Rovers (away), 18/11/95
Record FL Win: 12-0 v Leicester Fosse, Division 1, 12/4/09
Record FL Defeat: 1-9 v Blackburn R, Division 2, 10/4/37
Record Cup Win: 14-0 v Clapton (away), FA Cup R1, 17/1/1891
Record Fee Received: £8.5m from Liverpool for Stan Collymore, 6/95
Record Fee Paid: £2.9m to Foggia for Bryan Roy, 7/94
Most FL Apps: Bob McKinlay, 614, 1951-70
Most FAPL Apps: 117 – Mark Crossley
Most FAPL Goals: 23 – Stan Collymore
Record Attendance (all-time): 49,945 v Manchester Utd, Div 1 28/10/67
Record Attendance (FAPL): 29,263 v Manchester United, 27/11/95
Highest Scorer in FAPL Season: Stan Collymore, 23, 1994-95
Most FAPL Goals in Season: 72, 1994-95 – 42 games
Most FAPL Points in Season: 77, 1994-95 – 42 games

5-Year Record

	Div.	P	W	D	L	F	A	Pts	Pos	FAC	FLC
91-92	1	42	16	11	15	60	58	59	8	6	F
92-93	PL	42	10	10	22	41	62	40	22	5	5
93/94	1	46	23	14	9	74	49	83	2	3	5
94-95	PL	42	22	11	9	72	43	77	3	4	4
95-96	PL	38	15	13	10	50	54	58	9	QF	2

Summary 1995-96

Player	Tot	St	Sb	Snu	PS	Gls	Y	R	Fa	La	Fg	Lg
ALLEN	3	1	2	1	0	1	1	0	0	0	0	0
ARMSTRONG	0	0	0	1	0	0	0	0	0	0	0	0
BART-WILLIAMS	33	33	0	2	1	0	2	0	7	2	0	0
BLACK	2	1	1	0	1	0	0	0	0	0	0	0
BOHINEN	7	7	0	0	3	0	1	0	0	1	0	2
CAMPBELL	21	21	0	1	7	3	2	0	7	0	3	0
CHETTLE	37	37	0	0	0	0	4	1	7	2	0	0
COOPER	37	37	0	0	1	5	7	0	5	2	0	0
CROSSLEY	38	38	0	0	0	0	0	0	7	2	0	0
FETTIS	0	0	0	1	0	0	0	0	0	0	0	0
GEMMILL	31	26	5	3	7	1	4	0	7	1	0	0
GUINAN	2	1	1	0	1	0	0	0	0	0	0	0
HAALAND	17	12	5	12	1	0	4	0	2	0	0	0
HOWE	9	4	5	10	3	2	1	0	0	0	0	0
IRVING	1	0	1	2	0	0	0	0	0	0	0	0
LEE	28	21	7	2	3	8	5	1	4	2	0	0
LYTTLE	33	32	1	3	3	1	0	0	7	2	0	0
McGREGOR	14	7	7	7	5	2	0	0	2	0	0	0
PEARCE	31	31	0	0	0	3	3	0	4	1	2	1
PHILLIPS	18	14	4	9	1	0	1	0	6	1	0	0
ROY	28	25	3	0	9	8	3	0	6	1	1	0
SILENZI	10	3	7	6	1	0	1	0	3	1	1	1
STONE	34	34	0	0	1	7	3	0	6	2	0	0
TRACEY	0	0	0	3	0	0	0	0	0	0	0	0
WOAN	33	33	0	0	1	8	5	0	7	2	3	0

OGs 1

Record Set

Following the transfer of their top scorer for the past two seasons, Stan Collymore, Nottingham Forest manager Frank Clark had £8.5m at his disposal and sought to restructure the side with three costly signings, Chris Bart-Williams, Andy Silenzi and Kevin Campbell. Although Clark admitted fitting the new players into the side was a problem, Forest still managed to extend an unbeaten run begun towards the end of the previous season into a Premiership record of 25 games. The 12 match unbeaten run at the start of the season included three goal victories over Manchester City and Wimbledon while the most impressive win was a 1-0 triumph at Tottenham where Steve Stone, who was to become an England regular by the end of the season, scored.

Six draws during the opening dozen games denied Forest the opportunity to rise any higher than fifth and on 18 November the run came to a shattering end when reigning champions Blackburn Rovers ran seven goals past the ever present Mark Crossley without reply. Forest responded with a run of four consecutive 1-1 draws before going down at Newcastle; by now they were down in eighth position. Although Forest went onto lose the next four away games some respite was achieved at home where six wins in seven outings ensured that they slipped to no lower than tenth. With good progress being made in Europe and the FA Cup, Forest's league form became almost incidental but nonetheless defeats of 5-1 at home to Blackburn – giving the Lancashire club a remarkable 12-1 aggregate – and 5-0 at Old Trafford during the run-in suggested that more rebuilding will be required for next season. One of Forest's biggest failures was to find a suitable replacement for Collymore; Lee, Ian Woan and Bryan Roy all chipped in with eight league goals but not one player managed to get into double figures.

Searching for their first FA Cup success since 1959, Forest made a good start with a late Stuart Pearce goal salvaging a draw at Stoke City before Campbell and Pearce set up a 4th Round tie at home to Oxford United in the replay. Again Forest struggled in the first meeting but strolled through 3-0 in the replay. A 5th Round clash with Spurs was abandoned due to a snow storm then a brace of stupendous strikes from Woan ensured that another replay was required as the sides drew 2-2 at the City Ground. Still not separated after extra time Forest won on penalties but were then put out by old boy Franz Carr at home to Villa in the quarter final.

With the Coca Cola Cup, perhaps, interfering with the UEFA Cup it was not such a surprise to see Forest fall at the first hurdle with Bradford City holding out for a 2-2 draw in Nottingham having won the 1st Leg 3-2 at the Pulse Stadium. Clark's side, inexperienced in European football, made solid if unspectacular progress in the UEFA Cup. Malmo were unlucky not to win by more than 2-1 in their 1st Round, 1st Leg, fixture in Sweden. Woan's goal proved decisive as Roy's strike in the return took Forest through on the away goals. Stone struck the winner in Auxerre in Round Two and a shut-out in Nottingham again squeezed the English side through. Lyon went the same way as their compatriots as a Paul McGregor goal settled their Third Round encounter but in the quarter final Forest met their match. Chettle gave hope of a recovery when scoring during a 2-1 defeat away to Bayern Munich but in the return Klinsmann struck twice as Bayern hammered Forest 5-1. ∎

Results 1995-96

FA Carling Premiership

Date	Opponents	Ven	Res	Pos	Atten	Scorers
19-Aug	Southampton	A	4-3	–	15,164	Cooper(8); Woan (36); Roy (41, 79)
23-Aug	Chelsea	H	0-0	–	27,007	
26-Aug	West Ham	H	1-1	8	26,645	Pearce (35 pen)
29-Aug	Arsenal	A	1-1	9	38,248	Campbell (61)
09-Sep	Coventry C.	A	1-1	7	17,219	Roy (23)
17-Sep	Everton	H	3-2	6	24,786	OG (Watson 17); Lee (20); Woan (64)
23-Sep	Aston Villa	A	1-1	8	33,972	Lyttle (87)
30-Sep	Man. City	H	3-0	8	25,620	Lee (10, 46); Stone (82)
14-Oct	Tottenham	A	1-0	5	32,876	Stone(63)
21-Oct	Bolton Wan.	H	3-2	5	25,426	Roy (27); Lee (68); Cooper (90)
28-Oct	QPR	A	1-1	5	17,549	Lee (47)
06-Nov	Wimbledon	H	4-1	5	20,810	Roy (8); Pearce (31); Lee (47); Gemmill (87)
18-Nov	Blackburn R.	A	0-7	6	27,660	
27-Nov	Man. United	H	1-1	6	29,263	McGregor (19)
02-Dec	Bolton Wan.	A	1-1	7	17,342	Cooper (90)
10-Dec	Aston Villa	H	1-1	8	25,790	Stone (82)
18-Dec	Man. City	A	1-1	8	25,660	Campbell (69)
23-Dec	Newcastle U.	A	1-3	8	36,531	Woan (14)
26-Dec	Sheff. Wed.	H	1-0	8	27,810	Lee (7)
30-Dec	Middlesbro'	H	1-0	6	27,027	Pearce (8 pen)
01-Jan	Liverpool	A	2-4	7	39,206	Stone (13); Woan (18)
13-Jan	Southampton	H	1-0	6	23,321	Cooper (44)
20-Jan	Chelsea	A	0-1	7	24,482	
31-Jan	Leeds United	A	2-1	7	24,465	Campbell (39); Roy (57 pen)
03-Feb	West Ham	A	0-1	7	21,257	
10-Feb	Arsenal	H	0-1	9	27,222	
24-Feb	Everton	A	0-3	10	33,163	
02-Mar	Sheff. Wed.	H	3-1	9	21,930	Howe (10); McGregor (46); Roy (80)
16-Mar	Middlesbro'	A	1-1	10	29,392	Allen (56)
23-Mar	Liverpool	H	1-0	9	29,058	Stone (43)
30-Mar	Wimbledon	A	0-1	9	9,807	
06-Apr	Tottenham	H	2-1	8	27,053	Stone (40); Woan (61)
08-Sep	Leeds United	A	3-1	8	29,220	Cooper (18); Lee (30); Woan (66)
13-Apr	Blackburn R.	H	1-5	9	25,273	Woan (40)
17-Apr	Coventry C.	H	0-0	9	24,629	

28-Apr	Man. United	A	0-5	9	53,926	
02-May	Newcastle U.	H	1-1	9	28,280	Woan (75)
05-May	QPR	H	3-0	9	22,910	Stone (44); Roy (63); Howe (77)

UEFA Cup

Date	Opponents	Vn	Rnd	Res	Atten	Scorers
12-Sep	Malmo	A	1R1L	1-2	12,489	Woan (38)
26-Sep	Malmo	H	1R2L	1-0	23,817	Roy (69)
						2-2 on aggregate. Nottingham Forest won on away goals rule
17-Oct	Auxerre	A	2R1L	1-0	18,000	Stone (23)
31-Oct	Auxerre	H	2R2L	0-0	28,064	
						Nottingham Forest won 1-0 on aggregate
21-Nov	Lyon	H	3R1L	1-0	22,141	McGregor (84)
05-Dec	Lyon	A	3R2L	0-0	37,000	
						Nottingham Forest won 1-0 on aggregate
05-Mar	B. Munich	A	QF1L	1-2	38,000	Chettle (17)
19-Mar	B. Munich	H	QF2L	1-5	28,844	Stone (82)
						Bayern Munich won 7-2 on aggregate

FA Challenge Cup

Date	Opponents	Vn	Rnd	Res	Atten	Scorers
06-Jan	Stoke City	A	3R	1-1	18,000	Pearce (82)
17-Jan	Stoke City	H	3RR	2-0	17,372	Campbell (16); Pearce (55 pen)
07-Feb	Oxford Utd	H	4R	1-1	15,050	Campbell (54)
13-Feb	Oxford Utd	A	4RR	3-0	8,022	Campbell (40); Woan (82 pen); Silenzi (85)
19-Feb	*Tottenham*	*H*	*5R*	*–*	*17,000*	
						Match abandoned after 15 minutes due to snow
28-Feb	Tottenham	H	5R	2-2	18,600	Woan (4, 72)
09-Mar	Tottenham	A	5RR	1-1	31,055	Roy (9)
						Nottingham Forest won 3-1 on penalties
13-Mar	Aston Villa	H	QF	0-1	21,067	

Coca-Cola League Cup

Date	Opponents	Vn	Rnd	Res	Atten	Scorers
19-Sep	Bradford C.	A	2R1L	2-3	9,288	Bohinen (18, 90)
04-Oct	Bradford C.	H	2R2L	2-2	15,321	Pearce (19); Silenzi (63)
						Bradford City won 5-4 on aggregate

Sheffield Wednesday

Founded in 1867 by members of the Wednesday Cricket Club and played at Highfield before moving to Myrtle Road. Were first holders of the Sheffield FA Cup. The club played at Sheaf House then Endcliff and became professionals in 1886. In 1887 moved to Olive Grove.

Refused admission to the Football League, the club was founder member, and first champions, of the Football Alliance in 1889. In 1892 most Alliance clubs became founder members of Football League Division Two, but Wednesday were elected to an enlarged top division. The club moved to Hillsborough in 1899. Founder member of the Premier League 1992.

Ground: Hillsborough, Sheffield, S6 1SW
Phone: 0114-234 3122 **News:** 0891 12 11 86
Box Office: 0114-234 7233
Capacity: 36,020 **Pitch:** 115 yds x 77 yds
Colours: Blue/White, Blue, Blue **Nickname:** The Owls

Chairman: D.G. Richards **Vice-Chairman:** K.T. Addy
Secretary: G.H. Mackrell FCCA
Manager: David Pleat **Assistant:** Danny Bergara
Physio: D. Galley

League History: 1892 Elected to Division 1; 1899-1900 Division 2; 1900-20 Division 1; 1920-26 Division 2; 1926-37 Division 1; 1937-50 Division 2; 1950-51 Division 1; 1951-52 Division 2; 1952-55 Division 1; 1955-56 Division 2; 1956-58 Division 1; 1958-59 Division 2; 1959-70 Division 1; 1970-75 Division 2; 1975-80 Division 3; 1980-84 Division 2; 1984-90 Division 1; 1990-91 Division 2; 1991-92 Division 1; 1992- FA Premier League.

Honours: *Football League: Division 1 Champions:* 1902-03, 1903-04, 1928-29, 1929-30; *Runners-up:* 1960-61; *Division 2 Champions:* 1899-1900, 1925-26, 1951-52, 1955-56, 1958-59; *Runners-up:* 1949-50, 1983-84. *FA Cup Winners:* 1895-96, 1906-07, 1934-35; *Runners-up:* 1889-90, 1965-66, 1992-93; *Football League Cup Winners:* 1990-91; *Runners-up:* 1992-93.

European Record: CC (0): –; CWC (0): – ; UEFA (3): 61-62(QF), 63-64(2), 92-93(2).

Managers: Arthur Dickinson 1891-1920; Robert Brown 1920-33; Billy Walker 1933-37; Jimmy McMullan 1937-42; Eric Taylor 1942-58 (continued as GM to 1974); Harry Catterick 1958-61; Vic Buckingham 1961-64; Alan

170

Brown 1964-68; Jack Marshall 1968-69; Danny Williams 1969-71; Derek Dooley 1971-73; Steve Burtenshaw 1974-75; Len Ashurst 1975-77; Jackie Charlton 1977-83; Howard Wilkinson 1983-88; Peter Eustace 1988-89; Ron Atkinson 1989-91; *(FAPL)* Trevor Francis June 1991-May 1995; David Pleat July 1995-

Season 1995-96

Biggest Home Win:	6-2 v Leeds United, 16/12/95
Biggest Home Defeat:	2-5 v Everton, 27/4/96
Biggest Away Win:	3-0 v QPR, 9/9/95
Biggest Away Defeat:	2-4 v Arsenal, 21/11/95
Biggest Home Att:	33,101 v Manchester United, 23/9/95
Smallest Home Att:	16,229 v Coventry City, 3/12/95
Average Attendance:	24,877 (14th highest)
Leading Scorer:	13 – David Hirst, 8 – Marc Degryse

Last Season: *FAPL:* 15 *FA Cup:* 3 *Coca-Cola Cup:* 4

All-Time Records

Record FAPL Win:	6-2 v Leeds United, 16/12/95
Record FAPL Defeat:	1-7 v Nottingham Forest, 1/4/95
Record FL Win:	9-1 v Birmingham, Division 1, 13/12/1930
Record FL Defeat:	0-10 v Aston Villa, Division 1, 5/10/1912
Record Cup Win:	12-0 v Halliwell, FA Cup R1, 17/1/1891
Record Fee Received:	£2.7m from Blackburn R. for Paul Warhurst, 9/1993
Record Fee Paid:	£2.7m to Sampdoria for Des Walker, 7/1993 *and* £2.7m to QPR for Andy Sinton, 8/1993
Most FL Apps:	Andy Wilson, 502, 1900-20
Most FAPL Apps:	155 – Peter Atherton
Most FAPL Goals:	48 – Mark Bright

Highest Scorer in FAPL Season: Bright, 19, 1993-94

Record Attendance (all-time): 72,841 v Man City, FA Cup R5, 17/2/1934

Record Attendance (FAPL): 37,708 v Manchester United, 26/12/92

Most FAPL Goals in Season: 76, 1993-94 – 42 games

Most FAPL Points in Season: 64, 1993-94 – 42 games

5-Year Record

	Div.	P	W	D	L	F	A	Pts	Pos	FAC	FLC
91-92	1	42	21	12	9	62	49	75	3	4	3
92-93	PL	42	15	14	13	55	51	59	7	F	F
93-94	PL	42	16	16	10	76	54	64	7	4	SF
94-95	PL	42	13	12	17	49	57	51	13	4	4
95-96	PL	38	10	10	18	48	61	40	15	3	4

Summary 1995-96

Player	Tot	St	Sb	Snu	PS	Gls	Y	R	Fa	La	Fg	Lg
ATHERTON	35	35	0	1	0	0	6	0	1	4	0	0
BLINKER	9	9	0	0	4	2	1	0	0	0	0	0
BRIGHT	25	15	10	0	1	7	2	0	0	4	0	3
BRISCOE	25	22	3	2	4	0	1	0	0	1	0	0
DEGRYSE	34	30	4	1	9	8	0	0	1	3	0	4
DONALDSON	3	1	2	1	1	1	0	0	0	0	0	0
HIRST	30	29	1	0	9	13	1	1	1	3	0	1
HUMPHRIES	5	1	4	0	1	0	0	0	0	0	0	0
HYDE	26	14	12	5	4	1	2	0	0	3	0	0
INGESSON	5	3	2	1	0	0	0	0	0	2	0	0
KOVACEVIC	16	8	8	0	5	4	1	0	1	0	0	0
NEWSOME	8	8	0	0	0	1	1	0	0	0	0	0
NICOL	19	18	1	3	2	0	1	0	0	0	0	0
NOLAN	29	29	0	0	3	0	1	0	1	4	0	0
PEARCE	3	3	0	1	0	0	1	0	0	1	0	0
PEMBRIDGE	25	24	1	0	7	2	0	0	0	3	0	1
PETRESCU	8	8	0	0	1	0	2	0	0	0	0	0
PLATTS	2	0	2	2	0	0	0	0	0	0	0	0
PORIC	1	1	0	0	0	0	0	0	0	0	0	0
PRESSMAN	30	30	0	0	1	0	0	0	1	4	0	0
SHERIDAN	17	13	4	2	6	0	4	0	0	0	0	0
SINTON	10	7	3	3	0	0	1	0	1	3	0	0
STEFANOVIC	6	5	1	2	3	0	0	0	1	0	0	0
WADDLE	32	23	9	0	7	2	1	0	1	4	0	0
WALKER	36	36	0	0	0	0	2	0	1	4	0	0
WATTS	11	9	2	6	1	1	3	0	0	1	0	0
WHITTINGHAM	29	27	2	2	2	6	4	0	1	4	0	1
WILLIAMS	5	2	3	3	2	0	2	0	0	2	0	0
WOODS	8	8	0	3	1	0	0	0	0	0	0	0

Foreign Legion

A slump in league and cup fortunes the previous season ended with Trevor Francis dismissed as manager and David Pleat assuming the hot seat at Hillsborough. Pleat made one major addition to Francis' squad during the close season with the £1.5m signing of Belgian captain Marc Degryse and in October, after an indifferent start, he moved into the transfer market in a big way. Wednesday began the season reasonably enough with a single goal defeat being followed by handing Blackburn their first defeat since winning the championship. But with just two wins from the next 13 games, away to strugglers QPR and Coventry, Wednesday slipped to 15th in the Premiership. Pleat attempted to arrest the slide by investing £4m on Red Star Belgrade duo Darko Kovacevic and Dejan Stefanovic but neither was seen in action until Christmas. Pleat also added Steve Nicol to his squad on a free transfer from Notts County.

Wednesday had little trouble in recouping their money with Dan Petrescu, Klas Ingesson, Andy Preece and Andy Sinton all departing for a combined fee which matched that of the new arrivals. The most bitter exit was made by Petrescu who, despite being ever present, made disparaging comments about the club in newspaper articles.

Just prior to the arrival of the Yugoslavs, Wednesday hit a rich vein of scoring with 18 goals in six Premiership matches but with 15 goals conceded during the same period just two matches were won, most memorable of which was a 6-2 thrashing of county neighbours Leeds. The run also included Wednesday's second win of the season over Coventry, something that was achieved the hard way with the lead being lost three times before Mark Bright clinched a 4-3 win. Striker Kovacevic made his presence felt on New Years Day when scoring a brace during a 4-2 victory over Bolton and was on target the next game as Liverpool were held at Hillsborough but from then on goals were hard to come by for the Owls. Defeats in six of the next seven games only cost Wednesday one place in the table but with three goals conceded in four of those games they were clearly on the slide. Following the last of those defeats, at Aston Villa, Jon Newsome, who began his career with the Owls, was taken to Hillsborough from Norwich for £1.6m to bolster the leaky defence. He was in the side for a swift 2-0 revenge victory over Villa and a 1-0 win over Southampton but with just one victory from the final seven games – 1-0 against Arsenal – Pleat's side came perilously close to the drop. It was finally avoided with a point taken off West Ham on the final day of the season courtesy of Newsome's 89th minute equaliser at Upton Park.

Between the 1990-91 and 93-94 seasons Sheffield Wednesday featured in three cup finals and one semi final but as with the 94-95 season this campaign was a big disappointment to the Hillsborough fans. Wednesday had the dubious distinction of being the first Premiership club to be knocked out of the FA Cup when going down 2-0 to Endsleigh League Division One side Charlton Athletic at the Valley. Their Coca Cola Cup fortunes were a touch better; after drawing 2-2 at Crewe Alexandra, Wednesday won the 2nd Leg 5-2 with Bright scoring their only hat trick of the season. A potentially tricky tie at Millwall in Round Three was successfully negotiated with goals from Mark Pembridge and Guy Whittingham setting up a 4th Round tie with Arsenal at Hillsborough which was lost despite Degryse scoring his fourth Coca Cola Cup goal of the season. ∎

Results 1995-96

Date	Opponents	Ven	Res	Pos	Atten	Scorers
19-Aug	Liverpool	A	0-1	–	40,535	
23-Aug	Blackburn R.	H	2-1	–	25,544	Waddle (18); Pembridge (83)
27-Aug	Newcastle U.	A	0-2	13	24,815	
30-Aug	Wimbledon	A	2-2	12	6,352	Degryse (10); Hirst (46)
09-Sep	QPR	A	3-0	8	12,459	Bright (56, 60); Donaldson (78)
16-Sep	Tottenham	H	1-3	13	26,565	Hirst (8)
23-Sep	Man. United	H	0-0	12	34,101	
30-Sep	Leeds United	A	0-2	13	34,076	
15-Oct	Middlesbro'	H	0-1	15	21,177	
21-Oct	Coventry C.	A	1-0	12	13,998	Whittingham (16)
28-Oct	West Ham	H	0-1	13	23,917	
04-Nov	Chelsea	A	0-0	13	23,216	
18-Nov	Man. City	H	1-1	14	24,422	Hirst (14 pen)
21-Nov	Arsenal	A	2-4	14	34,556	Hirst (9); Waddle (20)
22-Nov	Everton	A	2-2	15	35,898	Bright (2, 35)
03-Dec	Coventry C.	H	4-3	14	16,229	Whittingham (25); Hirst (39); Degryse (60); Bright (73)
09-Dec	Man. United	A	2-2	14	41,849	Bright (59); Whittingham (78)
16-Dec	Leeds United	H	6-2	14	24,573	Degryse (5, 25); Whittingham (18); Bright (67); Hirst (72, 86)
23-Dec	Southampton	H	2-2	14	25,115	Hirst (14 pen, 50 pen)
26-Dec	N. Forest	A	0-1	14	27,810	
01-Jan	Bolton Wan.	H	4-2	13	24,872	Kovacevic (22, 45); Hirst (54 pen, 60)
13-Jan	Liverpool	H	1-1	13	32,747	Kovacevic (7)
20-Jan	Blackburn R.	A	0-3	13	24,732	
03-Feb	Newcastle U.	A	0-2	14	36,567	
10-Feb	Wimbledon	H	2-1	13	19,085	Degryse (55); Watts (85)
17-Feb	QPR	H	1-3	14	22,442	Hyde (22)
24-Feb	Tottenham	A	0-1	14	32,047	
02-Mar	N. Forest	H	1-3	14	21,930	Kovacevic
06-Mar	Aston Villa	A	2-3	14	27,893	Blinker (8, 63)
16-Mar	Aston Villa	H	2-0	14	22,964	Whittingham (58); Hirst (87)
20-Mar	Southampton	A	1-0	14	13,216	Degryse (1)
23-Mar	Bolton Wan.	A	1-2	14	18,368	Whittingham (37)
05-Apr	Middlesbro'	A	1-3	14	29,751	Pembridge (54)
08-Apr	Arsenal	H	1-0	14	24,349	Degryse (61)

13-Apr	Man. City	A	0-1	15	30,898	
17-Apr	Chelsea	H	0-0	15	25,094	
27-Apr	Everton	H	2-5	15	32,724	Hirst (9); Degryse (64)
05-May	West Ham	A	1-1	15	23,790	Newsome (89)

FA Challenge Cup

Date	Opponents	Vn	Rnd	Res	Atten	Scorers
06-Jan	Charlton Ath	A	3R	0-2	13,815	

Coca-Cola League Cup

Date	Opponents	Vn	Rnd	Res	Atten	Scorers
19-Sep	Crewe Alex.	A	2R1L	2-2	5,702	Degryse (2, 34)
04-Oct	Crewe Alex.	H	2R2L	5-2	12,039	Degryse (2); Hirst (16); Bright (45,63,77)
	Sheffield Wednesday won 7-4 on aggregate					
25-Oct	Millwall	A	3R	2-0	12,882	Pembridge (15); Whittingham (64)
29-Nov	Arsenal	H	4R	1-2	35,361	Degryse (16)

Wednesday – Premiership Fact File

- Wednesday's 6-2 defeat of Leeds United at Hillsborough on 16th December 1995 was their best ever in the Premiership.
- Peter Atherton has recorded the most appearances for Wednesday in the Premiership. He has missed just nine of the 164 games possible.
- Having beaten Blackburn Rovers 2-1 in their first home game of the season, Wednesday had to wait until the 4th December to record their next home win in the Premiership. Coventry City were defeated 4-3 on that day. The home goals flowed for the next three matches with 6-2, 2-2 and 4-2 results.
- Mark Bright requires two more goals in the Premiership to reach his half century.

Southampton

Formed 1885 by members of the St Mary's Young Men's Association, St Mary's FC. The church link was dropped, though the name retained, in 1893. In 1895 applied for a Southern League place, but was refused only to be invited to fill a subsequent vacancy. 'St. Mary's' was dropped after two seasons. Moved from the County Cricket Ground to the Dell in 1898.

Six times Southern League champions, Southampton were founder members of Football League Division Three in 1920 (this becoming Division Three (South) the following season); of Division Three at the end of regionalisation in 1958; and of the Premier League, 1992.

Ground: The Dell, Milton Road, Southampton, SO9 4XX
Phone: 01703-220505   **News:** 0891 12 15 93
Box Office: 01703-228575
Capacity: 15,288
Colours: Red/White, Black, Black   **Pitch:** 110 yds x 72 yds
    Nickname: The Saints

President: J. Corbett   **Chairman:** F.G. Askham FCA
Vice-Chairman: K. St. J. Wiseman   **Secretary:** Brian Truscott
Director of Football: Lawrie McMenemy
Manager: Graeme Souness   **Assistant:** Phil Boersma
Physio: Don Taylor

League History: 1920 Original Member of Division 3; 1921 Division 3 (S); 1922-53 Division 2; 1953-58 Division 3 (S); 1958-60 Division 3; 1960-66 Division 2; 1966-74 Division 1; 1974-78 Division 2; 1978-92 Division 1; 1992 – FA Premier League.

Honours: *Football League: Division 1 Runners-up:* 1983-84; *Division 2 Runners-up:* 1965-66, 1977-78; *Division 3 (S) Champions:* 1921-22; *Runners-up:* 1920-21; *Division 3 Champions:* 1959-60. *FA Cup Winners:* 1975-76; *Runners-up:* 1900, 1902. *Football League Cup Runners-up:* 1978-79. *Zenith Data Systems Cup Runners-up:* 1991-92.

European Record: CWC (1): 76-77(QF). UEFA (5): 69-70(3), 71-72(1), 81-82(2), 82-83(1), 84-85(1).

Managers: Cecil Knight 1894-95; Charles Robson 1895-97; E. Arnfield 1897-1911 (continued as secretary); George Swift 1911-12; E. Arnfield 1912-19; Jimmy McIntyre 1919-24; Arthur Chadwick 1925-31; George Kay 1931-36; George Cross 1936-37; Tom Parker 1937-43; J.R. Sarjantson stepped down from the board to act as secretary-manager 1943-47 with the next two listed being team managers during this period); Arthur Dominy 1943-46; Bill Dodgin Snr 1946-49; Sid Cann 1949-51; George Roughton 1952-55; Ted Bates 1955-73; Lawrie McMenemy 1973-85; Chris Nicholl 1985-91; *(FAPL)* Ian Branfoot 1991-94; Alan Ball Jan 1994-July 1995; Dave Merrington July 1995-June 1996; Graeme Souness July 1996-

Season 1995-96

Biggest Home Win: 3-1 v Manchester United, 13/4/96
Biggest Home Defeat: 3-4 v Nottingham Forest, 19/8/95
Biggest Away Win: 2-1 v Wimbledon, 28/10/95
Biggest Away Defeat: 1-4 v Manchester United, 18/11/95
Biggest Home Att: 15,262 v Manchester United, 13/4/96
Smallest Home Att: 13,216 v Sheffield Wednesday
Average Attendance: 14,822 (19th/20)
Leading Scorer: 8 – Neil Shipperley, 7 – Matt Le Tissier
Last Season: *FAPL:* 17 *FA Cup:* QF *Coca-Cola Cup:* 4

All-Time Records

Record FAPL Win: 5-1 v Swindon Town, 25/8/93
Record FAPL Defeat: 1-5 v Newcastle United, 27/8/94
Record FL Win: 9-3 v Wolverhampton Wds, Division 2, 18/9/1965
Record FL Defeat: 0-8 v Tottenham Hotspur, Division 2, 28/3/1936;
                            Everton, Division 1, 20/11/1971
Record Cup Win: 7-1 v Ipswich Town, FA Cup R3, 7/1/1961
Record Fee Received: £3.3m from Blackburn R. for Alan Shearer, 7/1992
Record Fee Paid: £1.2m to Chelsea for Neil Shipperley, 1/1995
Most FL Apps: Terry Payne, 713, 1956-74
Most FAPL Apps: 153 Matthew Le Tissier
Most FAPL Goals: 67 Matthew Le Tissier
Highest Scorer in FAPL Season: 25, Matthew Le Tissier, 1993-94
Record Attendance (all-time): 31,044 v Man United, Division 1, 8/10/1969
Record Attendance (FAPL): 19,654 v Tottenham Hotspur, 15/8/92
Most FAPL Goals in Season: 61, 1994-95 – 42 games
Most FAPL Points in Season: 54, 1994-95 – 42 games

5-Year Record

	Div.	P	W	D	L	F	A	Pts	Pos	FAC	FLC
91-92	1	42	14	10	18	39	55	52	16	6	4
92-93	PL	42	13	11	18	54	61	50	18	3	3
93-94	PL	42	12	7	23	49	66	43	18	3	2
94-95	PL	42	12	18	12	61	63	54	10	5	3
95-96	PL	38	9	11	18	34	52	38	17	QF	4

Summary 1995-96

Player	Tot	St	Sb	Snu	PS	Gls	Y	R	Fa	La	Fg	Lg
BEASANT	36	36	0	1	0	0	0	0	6	4	0	0
BENALI	30	29	1	0	3	0	6	0	1	4	0	0
BENNETT	11	5	6	4	5	0	0	0	0	1	0	0
CHARLTON	26	24	2	1	6	0	4	0	6	1	0	0
DODD	36	36	0	0	0	2	4	0	5	4	1	0
GROBBELAAR	2	2	0	25	0	0	0	0	0	0	0	0
HALL	30	30	0	0	1	1	6	0	5	4	1	1
HEANEY	17	15	2	0	7	2	5	0	1	3	0	0
HUGHES	11	6	5	3	0	1	1	0	1	2	0	0
Le TISSIER	34	34	0	0	1	7	11	1	5	4	1	2
McDONALD	1	0	1	1	0	0	0	0	1	0	0	0
MADDISON	15	13	2	6	3	1	1	0	2	3	0	0
MAGILTON	31	31	0	1	2	3	2	0	6	3	2	0
MASKELL	1	0	1	0	0	0	0	0	1	0	0	0
MONKOU	32	31	1	0	2	2	7	0	6	4	0	1
NEILSON	18	15	3	1	3	0	3	0	2	0	0	0
OAKLEY	10	5	5	0	3	0	0	0	3	0	1	0
ROBINSON	6	0	6	5	0	0	0	0	2	0	0	0
SHEERIN	0	0	0	1	0	0	0	0	0	0	0	0
SHIPPERLEY	37	37	0	0	4	8	1	0	6	4	3	2
TISDALE	9	5	4	3	0	1	0	0	0	0	0	0
VENISON	22	21	1	0	1	0	6	0	3	2	0	0
WALTERS	4	4	0	1	3	0	2	0	4	0	0	0
WARREN	7	1	6	1	0	0	0	0	0	1	0	0
WATSON	25	18	7	3	7	3	1	1	5	3	1	2
WIDDRINGTON	21	20	1	3	3	2	2	0	4	2	0	0

OGs 1

Manager Go-Round Continues

Following the loss of manager Alan Ball to Manchester City during the close season, Southampton looked to promote from within for his replacement and presented the task of further improving upon the previous season's tenth position to Dave Merrington. The new Saints boss had the bonus of Matt Le Tissier once again ignoring all the overtures heading his way during the close season from rival clubs eager for his signature. On the opening day of the campaign Le Tissier added fuel to the 'Le Tiss for England' lobby with a hat trick, including two penalties against Nottingham Forest, but it was not a treble that he will remember with much affection given that Forest won 4-3 – it was also one of only two occasions when the Saints scored more than twice in a league game. After a defeat at Everton and a draw with Leeds, Southampton clinched their first win of the season by ending Newcastle's 100% record with a Jim Magilton goal at the Dell.

A goalless draw at Middlesbrough took the Saints up to 14th position but with seven goals conceded in two games at Chelsea and Arsenal they encountered their first flirtation in the relegation zone. A point was taken off another London side, West Ham, only for Blackburn and Liverpool to add to the gloom descending on the Dell. Hopes of climbing to a more respectable position in the Premiership increased with successive victories over Wimbledon and QPR but it was to be the only time all season when two consecutive matches were won. Manchester United ended the revival with a crushing 4-1 result at Old Trafford and with just two wins from their next 16 Premiership matches it seemed as though Southampton were on the verge of the drop after 18 years in the top flight.

A run of just five points from four consecutive home games, followed by four consecutive defeats, saw the Saints drop three places back into the relegation zone. Once again Southampton hauled themselves clear when an early goal by the long serving Jason Dodd saw off Coventry at the Dell, it was the start of three successive home wins but with four defeats mixed in with those results the Saints' future still hung in the balance. The Saints not only helped their own survival chances on 13 April but also threw the title race wide open when storming to a three goal lead over Manchester United at the Dell. United put the eventual 3-1 defeat down to the grey shirts worn during the first half. After a reversal at Newcastle they were gifted a goal at Bolton, and needed just a point at home to Wimbledon on the final day of the season to stay up; the required result was duly achieved.

In the FA Cup 3rd Round south coast neighbours Portsmouth were trounced 3-0 while, after trailing to Crewe Alexandra for almost an hour in the 4th Round, the Saints forced a replay at Gresty Road where they surged into an early three goal lead but were thankful to hold onto for a slender 3-2 win. Swindon Town proved equally difficult in the 5th Round before replay goals by Matthew Oakley, his first for the club, and Neil Shipperley set up a quarter final tie with Manchester United at Old Trafford which saw the Saints put in a fine performance despite going down by 2-0. In the Coca Cola Cup, Cardiff City were beaten in both legs of the 2nd Round tie while West Ham were disposed of by a late Shipperley goal in Round Three. But hopes of an extended run in the competition were short lived as Reading put them out in the 4th Round at Elm Park. The season ended as it had begun when, in a surprise move, manager Dave Merrington was sacked and former Liverpool and Rangers manager Graeme Souness installed as the new Saints manager. ■

179

Results 1995-96

Date	Opponents	Ven	Res	Pos	Atten	Scorers
19-Aug	N. Forest	H	3-4	–	15,165	Le Tissier (10 pen, 68 pen, 81)
26-Aug	Everton	A	0-2	–	33,668	
30-Aug	Leeds United	H	1-1	19	15,212	Widdrington (81)
09-Sep	Newcastle U.	H	1-0	15	15,237	Magilton (65)
11-Sep	Middlesbro'	A	0-0	14	29,181	
16-Sep	Chelsea	A	0-3	16	26,237	
23-Sep	Arsenal	A	2-4	18	38,136	Watson (24); Monkou (45)
02-Oct	West Ham	H	0-0	17	13,568	
14-Oct	Blackburn R.	A	1-2	18	26,780	Maddison (90)
22-Oct	Liverpool	H	1-3	18	15,245	Watson (3)
28-Oct	Wimbledon	A	2-1	17	7,982	Shipperley (9, 75)
04-Nov	QPR	H	2-0	15	15,137	Dodd (2); Le Tissier (76)
18-Nov	Man. United	A	1-4	15	39,301	Shipperley (85)
20-Nov	Aston Villa	H	0-1	15	13,582	
25-Nov	Bolton Wan.	H	1-0	14	14,404	Hughes (74)
02-Dec	Liverpool	A	1-1	14	38,007	Shipperley (60)
09-Dec	Arsenal	H	0-0	15	15,238	
16-Dec	West Ham	A	1-2	15	18,501	OG (Bishop 22)
23-Dec	Sheff. Wed.	A	2-2	15	25,115	Heaney (7); Magilton (80 pen)
26-Dec	Tottenham	H	0-0	15	15,238	
01-Jan	Coventry C.	A	1-1	16	16,818	
13-Jan	N. Forest	A	0-1	16	23,321	
20-Jan	Middlesbro'	H	2-1	16	15,151	Shipperley (64); Hall (71)
31-Jan	Man. City	A	1-1	15	15,172	Shipperley (66)
03-Feb	Everton	H	2-2	15	15,136	Watson (46); Magilton (77)
24-Feb	Chelsea	H	2-3	15	15,226	Widdrington (60); Shipperley (38)
02-Mar	Tottenham	A	0-1	18	26,320	
16-Mar	Man. City	H	1-2	18	29,550	Tisdale (64)
20-Mar	Sheff. Wed.	H	0-1	18	13,216	
25-Mar	Coventry C.	H	1-0	17	14,461	Dodd (2)
30-Mar	QPR	A	0-3	17	17,615	
03-Apr	Leeds United	A	0-1	17	26,077	
06-Apr	Blackburn R.	H	1-0	16	14,793	Le Tissier (80)
08-Apr	Aston Villa	A	0-3	16	34,059	
13-Apr	Man. United	H	3-1	16	15,262	Monkou (11); Shipperley (23); Le Tissier (43)
17-Apr	Newcastle U.	A	0-1	16	36,554	

| 27-Apr | Bolton Wan. | A | 1-0 | 17 | 18,795 | Le Tissier (26) |
| 05-May | Wimbledon | H | 0-0 | 17 | 15,172 | |

FA Challenge Cup

Date	Opponents	Vn	Rnd	Res	Atten	Scorers
07-Jan	Portsmouth	H	3R	3-0	15,236	Magilton (13, 46); Shipperley (80)
07-Feb	Crewe Alex.	H	4R	1-1	13,736	Le Tissier (63)
13-Feb	Crewe Alex.	A	4RR	3-2	5,579	Shipperley (9); Hall (20); Dodd (26)
17-Feb	Swindon Tn	A	5R	1-1	15,035	Watson (76)
28-Feb	Swindon Tn	H	5RR	2-0	13,962	Oakley (63); Shipperley (76)
11-Mar	Man. United	A	QF	0-2	45,446	

Coca-Cola League Cup

Date	Opponents	Vn	Rnd	Res	Atten	Scorers
19-Sep	Cardiff City	A	2R1L	3-0	9,041	Le Tissier (27,47); Shipperley (51)
04-Oct	Cardiff City	H	2R2L	2-1	12,709	Watson (52); Hall (82)
	Southampton won 5-1 on aggregate					
25-Oct	West Ham	H	3R	2-1	11,059	Watson (4); Shipperley (79)
28-Nov	Reading	A	4R	1-2	13,742	Monkou (44)

Saints – Premiership Fact File

- Francis Benali made his 200th league appearance for Southampton in the match with Newcastle at the Dell on 16th April. In the same game Ken Monkou completed his 150th full Saints appearance.
- Matt Le Tissier with 153 Premiership appearances and 67 Premiership goals is third in the all time combined list. His total of 220 is behind that of Alan Shearer (250) and Les Ferdinand (232).
- Ken Monkou broke into the Premiership 100 appearance club last season finishing with 131 matches. Gordon Watson (94), Neil Shipperley (93) and Dave Beasant (91) could all complete their century during the coming season.

Sunderland

Formed in 1879 as The Sunderland and District Teachers' Association FC by James Allan, a Scottish school teacher. Originally membership was restricted to teachers only, but this requirement was soon removed. Became Sunderland AFC in 1880 and had their first ground at the Blue House pub. Played at a number of grounds until they moved to their current Roker Park site in 1898. Elected to Division 2 of the Football League in 1890 and best remembered for their famous FA Cup win over Leeds United in 1973.

Ground: Roker Park, Sunderland, SR6 9SW
Phone: 0191-514-0332   **News:** 0891 12 11 40
Capacity: 22,657   **Pitch:** 113 x 74 yds
Colours: Red & White stripes, Black, Red with White trim
Nickname: The Rokermen

Chairman: JR Featherstone   **CEO:** JM Ficking
Deputy Chairman: GS Wood   **Secretary:** G
Manager: Peter Reid   **Assistant:** Paul Bracewell
Head Coach: Bobby Saxton   **Physio:** Steve Smelt

League History: 1890 Elected to Division 1; 1958-64 Division 2; 1964-70 Division 1; 1970-76 Division 2; 1976-77 Division 1; 1977-80 Division 2; 1980-85 Division 1; 1985-87 Division 2; 1987-88 Division 3; 1988-90 Division 2; 1990-91 Division 1; 1991-92 Division 2; 1992-96 Division 1; 1996- FAPL.

Honours: *Football League Division 1 Champions:* 1891-92, 1892-93, 1894-95, 1901-02, 1912-13, 1935-36, 1995-96; *Runners-up:* 1893-94, 1897-88; 1900-01, 1922-23, 1934-35; *Division 2 Champions:* 1975-76; *Runners-up:* 1963-64, 1979-80; *Division 3 Champions:* 1987-88; *FA Cup Winners:* 1936-37, 1972-73; *Runners-up:* 1912-13, 1991-92. *Football League Cup Runners-up:* 1984-85.

European Record: CC (0): – ; CWC (1) 1973-74(2) ; UEFA (0): –

Managers: Tom Watson 1888-96, Bob Campbell 1896-99, Alex Mackie 1899-1905, Bob Kyle 1905-28, Johnny Cochrane 1928-39, Bill Murray 1939-57, Alan Brown 1957-64, George Hardwick 1964-65, Ian McColl 1965-68, Alan Brown 1968-72, Bob Stokoe 1972-76, Jimmy Adamson 1976-78, Ken Knighton 1979-81, Alan Durban 1981-84, Len Ashurst 1984-85, Lawrie McMenemy 1985-87, Denis Smith 1987-91, Malcolm Crosby 1992-93, Terry

Butcher 1993, Mick Buxton 1993-94, Lou Macari 1994-1995, Peter Reid 1995-.

Season 1995-96

Biggest Home Win:	6-0 v Millwall, 9/12/95
Biggest Home Defeat:	1-2 v Leicester City, 12/8/95
Biggest Away Win:	4-0 v Grimsby Town, 3/3/96
Biggest Away Defeat:	0-3 v Ipswich Town, 2/9/95 *and*
	0-3 v Wolverhampton Wdrs, 3/2/96
Biggest Home Att:	22,027 v WBA, 27/4/96
Smallest Home Att:	12,282 v Portsmouth, 12/9/95
Average Attendance:	17,512
Leading Scorer:	13 – Craig Russell, 8 – Phil Gray

Last Season: *FL:* Champions *FA Cup:* 3 *Coca-Cola Cup:* 2

All-Time Records

Record FAPL Win:	–
Record FAPL Defeat:	–
Record FL Win:	9-1 v Newcastle United (away), Div 1,. 5/12/08
Record FL Defeat:	0-8 v West Ham United, Div 1, 19/10/68 *and*
	0-8 v Watford Div 1, 25/9/82
Record Cup Win:	11-1 v Fairfield, FA Cup 1st Rd, 2/2/1895
Record Fee Received:	£1.5m from C. Palace for Marco Gabbiadini, 9/91
Record Fee Paid:	£
Most FL Apps:	Jim Montgomery, 537, 1966-77
Most FAPL Apps:	–
Most FAPL Goals:	–
Highest Scorer in FAPL Season:	–
Record Attendance (all-time):	75,118 v Derby County, FA Cup 6RR, 8/3/33
Record Attendance (FAPL):	–
Most FAPL Goals in Season:	–
Most FAPL Points in Season:	–

	Div.	P	W	D	L	F	A	Pts	Pos	FAC	FLC
91-92	1	46	14	11	21	61	65	53	18	6	2
92-93	1	46	13	11	22	50	64	50	21	4	1
93-94	1	46	19	8	19	54	57	65	12	4	3
94-95	1	46	12	18	16	41	45	54	20	4	2
95-96	1	46	22	17	7	59	33	83	1	3	2

Summary 1995-96

Player	Tot	St	Sb	Snu	PS	Gls	Fa	La	Fg	Lg
AGNEW	28	25	3	3	7	5	2	1	1	0
AISTON	14	4	10	4	4	0	0	1	0	0
ANGELL	2	2	0	0	2	0	0	1	0	1
ARMSTRONG	1	0	1	3	0	0	0	1	0	0
AITKINSON	7	5	2	2	2	0	0	3	0	0
BALL	36	35	1	0	1	4	1	4	0	0
BRACEWELL	38	38	0	0	3	0	2	4	0	0
BRIDGES	16	2	14	6	4	4	0	0	0	0
CHAMBERLAIN	29	29	0	0	0	0	2	4	0	0
COOKE	6	6	0	0	1	0	0	0	0	0
GIVEN	17	17	0	0	0	0	0	0	0	0
GRAY, P	32	28	4	2	4	8	2	4	1	0
GRAY, Martin	7	4	3	5	1	0	1	2	0	0
GRAY, Michael	46	46	0	0	7	4	2	4	0	0
HALL	14	8	6	10	0	0	0	0	0	0
HOLLOWAY	0	0	0	2	0	0	0	0	0	0
HOWEY	27	17	10	13	6	3	2	1	0	2
KELLY	10	9	1	1	3	2	1	1	0	0
KUBICKI	46	46	0	0	1	0	2	4	0	0
MELVILLE	40	40	0	1	0	4	2	3	0	0
MULLIN	10	5	5	3	4	1	1	1	0	0
ORD	42	41	1	0	1	1	2	3	0	0
RUSSELL	41	35	6	2	19	13	2	4	1	0
SCOTT	43	43	0	0	0	6	2	3	0	0
SMITH, M	22	10	12	2	6	2	2	4	0	0
STEWART	12	11	1	0	4	1	0	0	0	0
					OG	1				

Reid Roar

Having survived just one season the last time they made it to the top flight of English football, Sunderland will be looking to Peter Reid to prove that the gap between the Endsleigh League and Premiership is not an unscalable chasm. North-east rivals Middlesbrough successfully made the transition a year earlier but Reid is unlikely to have the financial backing that aided his counterpart at the Riverside Stadium. Reid went into the campaign with just one major signing when he forked out £900,000 on Wolves striker David Kelly. Later in the season a further £300,000 was invested in Chelsea defender Gareth Hall.

The previous season saw Sunderland finish just one place clear of relegation and an ominous start was made with a 2-1 reversal at home to Leicester and with just one win from their first five matches the Rokermen were down in 17th position. That win came at home to Wolves, a match which saw the previous season's top scorer, Phil Gray, open his account and it sparked a nine match unbeaten run on Wearside. A 3-0 defeat at Ipswich on 2 September was the last suffered for almost three months but the eleven games without defeat included five draws. Sunderland moved into an automatic promotion place for the first time on 3 December when Martin Scott's second successful penalty of the season earned a 1-0 home win over Crystal Palace. Full of confidence Sunderland then set about leaders Millwall in grand style with a six goal destruction that sent the Lions spinning from first to seventh. Star of the show for Sunderland was Craig Russell, given his chance by injury to Kelly. He struck four times with the Wearsiders' only hat trick of the season.

But their reign at the top was short as a draw and two defeats sent them plummeting to eighth, and a solitary goal victory over Grimsby was only a temporary reprieve as the next four games yielded just three points. When Ipswich headed for Roker Park on 20 February, Sunderland were ten points adrift of leaders Derby with just one game in hand and 17 to play. A goal by Russell, only their fourth in eight games, clinched the points and with the benefit of an own goal against Luton the final ascent had begun. Sunderland moved back into the promotion slots with a 2-0 win at Southend and with a 4-0 thrashing of Grimsby slipped into top gear to crush Derby 3-0 at Roker Park. Oldham, twice, and Birmingham were swept away as nine straight wins saw Sunderland assume control of Division One.

The victory march was surprisingly halted by a rejuvenated Watford as the sides fought out a thrilling 3-3 draw at Vicarage Road. Those were the final goals conceded until the last day of the season as six consecutive clean sheets were recorded. Tranmere spoilt the party with a 2-0 win on that final day but it mattered not a jot as promotion had been secured with a club record 18 match unbeaten run and the championship wrapped up during a goalless draw with West Brom. Sunderland ended the season with another club record of 26 clean sheets, 20 of which had come during the last 29 games.

Little progress was made in the cup competitions despite some sterling performances. Manchester United were fortunate to escape from Old Trafford with a draw in the 3rd Round of the FA Cup but an 89th minute goal from Andy Cole ended Sunderland's dream in the replay. The Coca Cola Cup kicked off with a slender 4-3 aggregate victory over Preston North End but Liverpool removed the Wearsiders with wins in both legs of their 2nd Round tie.

In the close season manager Peter Reid was awarded the LMA Managers' Manager of the Year award. ∎

Results 1995-96

Date	Opponents	Ven	Res	Pos	Atten	Scorers
12-Aug	Leicester City	H	1-2		18,593	Agnew
19-Aug	Norwich City	A	0-0	21	16,700	
26-Aug	Wolves	H	2-0	12	16,816	Melville (8); Gray, P (28)
30-Aug	Port Vale	A	1-1	14	7,693	Gray, P (51)
02-Sep	Ipswich Tn	A	0-3	17	12,390	
09-Sep	Southend U.	H	1-0	15	13,805	Russell (40)
12-Sep	Portsmouth	H	1-1	15	12,282	Melville (6)
16-Sep	Luton Town	A	2-0	9	6,955	Mullin (51); Gray, P (81)
23-Sep	Millwall	A	2-1	7	8,691	Scott (44 pen); Smith (79)
30-Sep	Reading	H	2-2	6	17,503	Kelly (75); Melville (89)
07-Oct	C. Palace	A	1-0	3	13,754	Kelly (75)
14-Oct	Watford	H	1-1	4	17,970	Scott (72)
21-Oct	Huddersfield	A	1-1	5	16,054	Gray, P (83)
28-Oct	Barnsley	H	2-1	4	17,024	Russell (20); Howey (62)
05-Nov	Charlton Ath	A	1-1	4	11,626	Gray, M (18)
18-Nov	Sheffield U.	H	2-0	4	16,640	Gray, P (67, 72)
22-Nov	Stoke City	A	0-1	7	11,754	
25-Nov	WBA	A	1-0	4	15,931	Howey (10)
03-Dec	C. Palace	H	1-0	2	12,777	Scott (39 pen)
09-Dec	Millwall	H	6-0	1	18,951	Scott (15 pen); Russell (32, 58, 72, 90); Gray, P (51)
16-Dec	Reading	A	1-1	1	9,431	Smith (12)
23-Dec	Derby Cty	A	1-3	2	16,882	Gray, M (25)
14-Jan	Norwich City	H	0-1	8	14,983	
21-Jan	Leicester City	A	0-0	7	16,130	
24-Jan	Grimsby Tn	H	1-0	4	14,656	Ord (64)
30-Jan	Tranmere R.	H	0-0	3	17,616	
03-Feb	Wolves	A	0-3	5	26,537	
10-Feb	Port Vale	H	0-0	5	15,954	
17-Feb	Portsmouth	A	2-2	5	12,241	Howey (8); Agnew (89)
20-Feb	Ipswich Tn	A	1-0	3	14,052	Russell (38)
24-Feb	Luton Town	H	1-0	3	16,693	OG (James 38)
27-Feb	Southend U.	A	2-0	2	5,786	Scott (53 pen); Bridges (80)
03-Mar	Grimsby Tn	A	4-0	2	5,318	Ball (34); Russell (73); Gray, P (89); Bridges (90)
09-Mar	Derby Cty	H	3-0	2	21,644	Russell (8, 67); Agnew (32)
12-Mar	Oldham Ath	A	2-1	2	7,149	Gray, M (11); Ball (86)
17-Mar	Birmingham	A	2-0	1	23,250	Agnew (16); Melville (63)
23-Mar	Oldham Ath	H	1-0	1	20,631	Scott (82)
30-Mar	Huddersfield	H	3-2	1	20,131	Ball (24); Bridges (83, 87)

02-Apr	Watford	A	3-3	1	11,195	Agnew (16); Ball (18); Russell (41)
06-Apr	Barnsley	A	1-0	1	13,189	Russell (24)
08-Apr	Charlton Ath	H	0-0	1	20,914	
13-Apr	Sheffield U.	A	0-0	1	20,050	
16-Apr	Birmingham	H	3-0	1	19,831	Gray, M (18); Stewart (21); Russell (62)
21-Apr	Stoke City	H	0-0	1	21,276	
27-Apr	WBA	H	0-0	1	22,027	
05-May	Tranmere R.	A	0-2	1	16,193	

FA Challenge Cup

Date	Opponents	Vn	Rnd	Res	Atten	Scorers
06-Jan	Man. United	A	3R	2-2	41,563	Agnew (61); Russell (64)
16-Jan	Man. United	H	3RR	1-2	21,378	Gray, P (24)

Coca-Cola League Cup

Date	Opponents	Vn	Rnd	Res	Atten	Scorers
15-Aug	Preston NE	A	1R1L	1-1	6,323	Angell (50)
23-Aug	Preston NE	H	1R2L	3-2	7,404	Howey (47, 85); OG (Kidd 48)
	Sunderland win 4-3 on aggregate					
20-Sep	Liverpool	A	2R1L	0-2	25,579	
04-Oct	Liverpool	H	2R2L	0-1	20,560	
	Liverpool win 3-0 on aggregate					

Tottenham Hotspur

Formed in 1882 by members of the schoolboys' Hotspur CC as Hotspur FC and had early Church connections. Added 'Tottenham' in 1884 to distinguish club from London Hotspur FC. Turned professional in 1895 and elected to the Southern League in 1896 having been rebuffed by the Football League.

Played at two grounds (Tottenham Marshes and Northumberland Park) before moving to the site which became known as White Hart Lane in 1899. Joined the Football League Second Division 1908. Having failed to gain a place in the re-election voting, it secured a vacancy caused by a late resignation. Premier League founder members 1992.

Ground: 748 High Road, Tottenham, London, N17 0AP
Phone: 0181-365 5000   **News:** 0891-100 500
Box Office: 0181-365 5050
Capacity: 30,246   **Pitch:** 110 yds x 73 yds
Colours: White, Navy Blue, White   **Nickname:** Spurs

Chairman: Alan Sugar   **President:** W.E. Nicholson OBE
Chief Executive: Claude Littner   **Secretary:** Peter Barnes
Manager: Gerry Francis   **Physio:** Tony Lenaghan

League History: 1908 Elected to Division 2; 1909-15 Division 1; 1919-20 Division 2; 1920-28 Division 1; 1928-33 Division 2; 1933-35 Division 1; 1935-50 Division 2; 1950-77 Division 1; 1977-78 Division 2; 1978-92 Division 1; 1992- FA Premier League.

Honours: *Football League: Division 1 Champions:* 1950-51, 1960-61; *Runners-up:* 1921-22, 1951-52, 1956-57, 1962-63; *Division 2 Champions:* 1919-20, 1949-50; *Runners-up:* 1908-09, 1932-33; *FA Cup Winners:* 1900-01, 1920-21, 1960-61, 1961-62, 1966-67, 1980-81, 1981-82, 1990-91; *Runners-up:* 1986-87; *Football League Cup Winners:* 1970-71, 1972-73; *Runners-up:* 1981-82; *Cup-Winners' Cup Winners:* 1962-63; *Runners-up:* 1981-82; *UEFA Cup Winners:* 1971-72, 1983-84; *Runners-up:* 1973-74.

European Record: CC (1): 61-62(SF); CWC (6): 62-63(W), 63-64(2), 67-68(2), 81-82(SF), 82-83(2), 91-92(QF). UEFA (5): 71-72(W), 72-73(SF), 73-74(F), 83-84(W), 84-85(QF).

Managers: Frank Brettell 1898-99; John Cameron 1899-1907; Fred Kirkham 1907-08; Peter McWilliam 1912-27; Billy Minter 1927-29; Percy Smith 1930-35; Jack Tresadern 1935-38; Peter McWilliam 1938-42; Arthur Turner 1942-46; Joe Hulme 1946-49; Arthur Rowe 1949-55; Jimmy Anderson 1955-

58; Bill Nicholson 1958-74; Terry Neill 1974-76; Keith Burkinshaw 1976-84; Peter Shreeves 1984-86; David Pleat 1986-87; Terry Venables 1987-91; Peter Shreeves 1991-92; Doug Livermore 1992-June 1993; Ossie Ardiles June 1993-Nov 1994; Gerry Francis Nov 1994-.

Season 1995-96

Biggest Home Win:	4-1 v Manchester United, 1/1/96
Biggest Home Defeat:	2-3 v Blackburn Rovers, 16/3/96
Biggest Away Win:	3-1 v Leeds Utd and Sheff.Wednesday
Biggest Away Defeat:	1-2 v Aston Villa, Blackburn Rvrs and N.Forest
Biggest Home Att:	32,918 v Chelsea, 27/4/96
Smallest Home Att:	25,321 v Wimbledon 30/9/95
Average Attendance:	30,931 (8th/20)
Leading Scorer:	16 – Teddy Sheringham, 15 – Chris Armstrong

Last Season: *FAPL: 8 FA Cup: 5 Coca-Cola Cup: 3*

All-Time Records

Record FAPL Win:	5-0 v Oldham Athletic, 18/9/93
Record FAPL Defeat:	0-6 v Sheffield United, 2/3/93
Record FL Win:	9-0 v Bristol Rovers, Division 2, 22/10/77
Record FL Defeat:	0-7 v Liverpool, Division 1, 2/9/1978
Record Cup Win:	13-2 v Crewe Alex, FA Cup, R4 replay, 3/2/60
Record Fee Received:	£5.5m from Lazio for Paul Gascoigne, 5/92
Record Fee Paid:	£4.5m to Crystal Palace for Chris Armstrong, 6/95
Most FL Apps:	Steve Perryman, 655, 1969-86
Most FAPL Apps:	140 – Teddy Sheringham
Most FAPL Goals:	69 – Teddy Sheringham

Highest Scorer in FAPL Season: Jurgen Klinsmann, 24, 1994-95
Record Attendance (all-time): 75,038 v Sunderland, FA Cup R6, 5/3/38
Record Attendance (FAPL): 33,709 v Arsenal, 12/12/92
Most FAPL Goals in Season: 66, 1994-95 – 42 games
Most FAPL Points in Season: 62, 1994-95 – 42 games

	Div.	P	W	D	L	F	A	Pts	Pos	FAC	FLC
91-92	1	42	15	7	20	58	63	52	15	3	SF
92-93	PL	42	16	11	15	60	66	59	8	SF	4
93-94	PL	42	11	12	19	54	59	45	15	4	5
94-95	PL	42	16	14	12	66	58	62	7	SF	3
95-96	PL	38	16	13	9	50	38	61	8	5	3

Summary 1995-96

Player	Tot	St	Sb	Snu	PS	Gls	Y	R	Fa	La	Fg	Lg
ANDERTON	8	6	2	0	1	2	0	0	0	0	0	0
ARMSTRONG	36	36	0	0	1	15	5	0	6	3	4	3
AUSTIN	28	28	0	0	0	0	8	0	4	3	0	0
CALDERWOOD	29	26	3	2	2	0	6	0	4	3	0	0
CAMPBELL	31	31	0	1	10	1	2	0	6	1	0	0
CASKEY	3	3	0	2	0	0	0	0	3	0	0	0
CUNDY	1	0	1	0	0	0	1	0	0	0	0	0
DAY	0	0	0	22	0	0	0	0	0	0	0	0
DOZZELL	28	24	4	1	2	3	7	0	3	2	0	0
DUMITRESCU	5	5	0	0	1	1	0	0	0	0	0	0
EDINBURGH	22	15	7	8	1	0	5	0	4	2	0	0
FOX	26	26	0	0	3	6	1	0	6	0	0	0
HOWELLS	29	29	0	0	5	3	6	0	2	2	0	1
KERSLAKE	2	2	0	0	1	0	0	0	0	0	0	0
MABBUTT	32	32	0	0	1	0	4	0	5	3	0	0
McMAHON	14	7	7	4	0	0	0	0	1	3	0	0
NETHERCOTT	13	9	4	5	0	0	2	0	3	0	0	0
ROSENTHAL	33	26	7	2	5	1	2	0	5	2	2	1
SCOTT	2	0	2	2	0	0	0	0	0	1	0	0
SHERINGHAM	38	38	0	0	1	16	2	0	6	3	5	3
SINTON	9	8	1	0	3	0	1	0	0	0	0	0
SLADE	5	1	4	5	1	0	0	0	2	1	0	0
THORSTVEDT	0	0	0	16	0	0	0	0	0	0	0	0
WALKER	38	38	0	0	0	0	1	0	6	3	0	0
WILSON	28	28	0	2	0	0	1	0	5	2	1	0
					OG	2						

Promise Still Not Fulfiled

The calibre of player departing from White Hart Lane during the close season suggested that manager Gerry Francis was facing a tough task in bettering Tottenham Hotspur's seventh placing in 1994-95, their best season for five years. Jurgen Klinsmann joined Bayern Munich for £2m, Gica Popescu went to Barcelona for £3.5m and on the eve of the season Nick Barmby headed back north to Middlesbrough for a record Spurs' sale of £5.25m. Further income was received during the season when Darren Caskey and Ilie Dumitrescu joined Reading and West Ham respectively for almost £2.5m. The capital did not stay in Spurs' account for long though as Chris Armstrong from Crystal Palace and Ruel Fox from Newcastle moved to White Hart Lane for a combined fee of close on £9m.

The personnel changes go some way towards explaining the poor start Spurs made to the season, with three games played they were just one off the foot of the table. The recovery, however, was not long in coming and with four straight wins Spurs were up to ninth. The run ended at home to Nottingham Forest but it was the only blip in 17 Premiership matches. After a slow start the Teddy Sheringham and Armstrong double act clicked and for a while was the most productive partnership in the top flight. Armstrong had to wait until 22 October for his first goal when he clipped home an excellent effort at Everton; his quiet start was forgiven by the fans though when he came up with the winner against Arsenal. Tottenham became the first visiting side to win at Middlesbrough a week later (Armstrong) and moved into the top five. It was the first of five consecutive clean sheets but the shut-outs were ended somewhat surprisingly by Bolton on two days before Christmas who picked up their first away point of the season with two late goals. That setback instigated a spell of just two wins in eight games, ironically both wins were over the Manchester clubs including a thumping 4-1 triumph over United while the win over City lifted Spurs to third.

Having suffered their first away defeat of the season on the final day of 1995, at Blackburn, Spurs then struggled to repeat their awayday success of earlier in the season and won just two of the last nine away Premiership games. An inconsistent spell during early spring looked to have cost Tottenham any chance of a place in the UEFA Cup but a 3-1 win at Leeds on the last Thursday of the season took the club back into sixth place. A good point at Newcastle, though, on the final day was not sufficient to hold onto that slot as Arsenal, Blackburn and Everton all won to deny Francis his first taste of European action.

Spurs' tradition of being a cup fighting outfit was dented in the Coca Cola Cup where an easy 2nd Round victory over Chester City was banished from the memory when a two goal lead was overturned by Coventry City at Highfield Road. In the FA Cup a none too impressive performance dragged Hereford United, minus their Bull, back to White Hart Lane for a replay in Round Three. Sheringham scored a hat trick as Spurs moved through to face Wolverhampton Wanderers and after being held at home Spurs were good value for a 2-0 success. A snowstorm led to an abandonment with Nottingham Forest at the City Ground in the 5th Round and following a 2-2 draw a replay was held at White Hart Lane. For once Stuart Pearce was on the winning side from a penalty shoot-out as Spurs went down 3-1 after the sides were level at the end of extra time. ■

Results 1995-96

FA Carling Premiership

Date	Opponents	Ven	Res	Pos	Atten	Scorers
19-Aug	Man. City	A	1-1	–	30,827	Sheringham (33)
23-Aug	Aston Villa	H	0-1	–	26,726	
26-Aug	Liverpool	H	1-3	19	31,254	Dumitrescu (87)
30-Aug	West Ham	A	1-1	18	23,516	Rosenthal (54)
09-Sep	Leeds United	H	2-1	13	30,034	Howells (27); Sheringham (66)
16-Sep	Sheff. Wed.	A	3-1	10	26,565	Sheringham (32, 65 pen); OG (Walker 6)
25-Sep	QPR	A	3-2	9	15,659	Sheringham (48 pen, 75); Dozzell (73)
30-Sep	Wimbledon	H	3-1	9	25,321	Sheringham (7, 32); OG (Elkins 63)
14-Oct	N. Forest	H	0-1	10	32,876	
22-Oct	Everton	A	1-1	9	33,629	Armstrong (37)
29-Oct	Newcastle U.	H	1-1	9	32,279	Armstrong (21)
04-Nov	Coventry C.	A	3-2	9	17,545	Fox (20); Sheringham (25); Howells (46)
18-Nov	Arsenal	H	2-1	9	32,894	Sheringham (29); Armstrong (54)
21-Nov	Middlesbro'	A	1-0	5	29,487	Armstrong (71)
25-Nov	Chelsea	A	0-0	5	31,059	
02-Dec	Everton	H	0-0	5	32,894	
09-Dec	QPR	H	1-0	5	28,851	Sheringham (3)
16-Dec	Wimbledon	A	1-0	3	16,193	Fox (85)
23-Dec	Bolton Wan.	H	2-2	4	30,702	Sheringham (53); Armstrong (71)
26-Dec	Southampton	A	0-0	3	15,238	
30-Dec	Blackburn R.	A	1-2	4	30,004	Sheringham (53)
01-Jan	Man. United	H	4-1	4	32,852	Sheringham (35); Campbell (45); Armstrong (48, 66)
13-Jan	Man. City	H	1-0	3	31,438	Armstrong (65)
21-Jan	Aston Villa	A	1-2	4	35,666	Fox (26)
03-Feb	Liverpool	A	0-0	5	40,628	
12-Feb	West Ham	H	0-1	5	29,781	
24-Feb	Sheff. Wed.	H	1-0	5	32,047	Armstrong (31)
02-Mar	Southampton	H	1-0	5	26,320	Dozzell (63)
16-Mar	Blackburn R.	H	2-3	8	31,803	Sheringham (61); Armstrong (80)
20-Mar	Bolton Wan.	A	3-2	6	17,829	Howells (17); Fox (54); Armstrong (60)

24-Mar	Man. United	A	0-1	6	50,157	
30-Mar	Coventry C.	H	3-1	6	26,808	Sheringham (50); Fox (51, 64)
06-Apr	N. Forest	A	1-2	7	27,053	Armstrong (80)
08-Apr	Middlesbro'	H	1-1	6	32,036	Armstrong (84)
15-Apr	Arsenal	A	0-0	6	38,273	
27-Apr	Chelsea	H	1-1	6	32,918	Armstrong (73)
02-May	Leeds United	A	3-1	6	30,061	Armstrong (18); Anderton (24, 66)
05-May	Newcastle U.	A	1-1	8	36,589	Dozzell (57)

FA Challenge Cup

Date	Opponents	Vn	Rnd	Res	Atten	Scorers
06-Jan	Hereford	A	3R	1-1	8,806	Rosenthal (31)
17-Jan	Hereford	H	3RR	5-1	31,534	Sheringham (23, 54, 80); Armstrong (29, 58)
27-Jan	Wolves	H	4R	1-1	32,812	Wilson (12)
07-Feb	Wolves	A	4RR	2-0	27,846	Rosenthal (7); Sheringham (9)
28-Feb	N. Forest	A	5R	2-2	18,600	Armstrong (9, 28)
09-Mar	N. Forest	H	5RR	1-1	31,055	Sheringham (32)

After extra time. Nottingham Forest won 3-1 on penalties

Coca-Cola League Cup

Date	Opponents	Vn	Rnd	Res	Atten	Scorers
20-Sep	Chester City	H	2R1L	4-0	17,645	Armstrong (20, 30); Sheringham (43); Rosenthal (90)
04-Oct	Chester City	A	2R2L	3-1	5,372	Sheringham (36, 68); Howells (45)
	Tottenham Hotspur won 7-1 on aggregate					
25-Oct	Coventry C.	A	3R	2-3	18,227	Armstrong (2); OG (Busst 20)

Spurs – Premiership Fact File

- Teddy Sheringham completed all 38 of Spurs Premiership games – the only Tottenham player to do so. It brought his all-time Premiership total to 140. His total of 69 goals puts him fourth in the all-time Premiership list.
- Gerry Francis signed a two year contract with Spurs during the close season. Francis had previously always worked without a contract.
- Spurs only failed to score in two of their first 14 games and only nine times in the full 38 game schedule.
- Teddy Sheringham and Chris Armstrong scored 31 of Spurs 50 Premiership goals last season.

West Ham United

Thames Ironworks founded 1895, to give recreation for the shipyard workers. Several different grounds were used as the club entered the London League (1896) and won the championship (1898). In 1899, having become professional, won the Southern League Second Division (London) and moved into Division One.

On becoming a limited liability company the name was changed to West Ham United. Moved from the Memorial Ground to a pitch in the Upton Park area, known originally as 'The Castle', in 1904. Elected to an expanded Football League Division Two for the 1919-20 season and never subsequently out of the top two divisions.

Ground: Boleyn Ground, Green Street, Upton Park, London E13 9AZ
Phone: 0181-548-2748   **News:** 0891 12 11 65
Capacity: 24,500   **Pitch:** 112 yds x 72 yds
Colours: Claret, White, White   **Nickname:** The Hammers

Chairman: T.Brown   **Vice-Chairman:** Martin Cearns
Managing Director: Peter Storrie   **Secretary:** Richard Skirrow
Manager: Harry Redknapp   **Assistant:** Frank Lampard
First Team Coaches: Paul Hilton, Tony Carr
Physio: John Green

League History: 1919 Elected to Division 2; 1923-32 Division 1; 1932-58 Division 2; 1958-78 Division 1; 1978-81 Division 2; 1981-89 Division 1; 1989-91 Division 2; 1991-1993 Division 1; 1993- FA Premier League.

Honours: *Football League: Division 1 Runners-up:* 1992-93; *Division 2 Champions:* 1957-58, 1980-81; *Runners-up:* 1922-23, 1990-91. *FA Cup Winners:* 1964, 1975, 1980; *Runners-up:* 1922-23. *Football League Cup Runners-up:* 1966, 1981. *Cup-Winners' Cup Winners:* 1964-65; *Runners-up:* 1975-76.

European Record: CC (0): –; CWC (4): 64-65(W), 65-66(SF), 75-76(F), 80-81(QF); UEFA (0): –.

Managers: Syd King 1902-32; Charlie Paynter 1932-50; Ted Fenton 1950-61; Ron Greenwood 1961-74 (continued as GM to 1977); John Lyall 1974-89; Lou Macari 1989-90; *(FAPL)* Billy Bonds Feb 1990-Aug 1994; Harry Redknapp Aug 1994-.

Season 1995-96

Biggest Home Win:	4-2 v Manchester City, 23/3/96
Biggest Home Defeat:	1-4 v Aston Villa, 4/11/95
Biggest Away Win:	3-0 v Bolton Wanderers, 18/11/95
Biggest Away Defeat:	2-4 v Blackburn Rvrs 2/12/95
	and Middlesbrough 23/12/95
Biggest Home Att:	24,324 v Liverpool, 22/11/95
Smallest Home Att:	18,501 v Southampton, 16/12/95
Average Attendance:	22,317 (15th/20)
Leading Scorer:	10 – Tony Cottee, Julian Dicks

Last Season: *FAPL:* 10 *FA Cup:* 4 *Coca-Cola Cup:* 3

All-Time Records

Record FAPL Win:	4-1 v Tottenham Hotspur, 4/4/94
Record FAPL Defeat:	0-5 v Sheffield Wednesday, 18/12/93
Record FL Win:	8-0 v Rotherham United, Division 2, 8/3/58;
	Sunderland, Division 1, 19/10/68
Record FL Defeat:	2-8 v Blackburn Rovers, Division 1, 26/12/63
Record Cup Win:	10-0 v Bury, League Cup, R2 2nd leg, 25/10/83
Record Fee Received:	£2m from Everton for Tony Cottee, 7/1988
Record Fee Paid:	£2.4m to Espanyol for Florin Raducioiu, 7/96
Most FL Apps:	Billy Bonds, 663, 1967-88
Most FAPL Apps:	120 – Ludek Miklosko
Most FAPL Goals:	23 – Cottee

Highest Scorer in FAPL Season: 13 – Trevor Morley, 1993-94;
Tony Cottee 1994-95

Record Attendance (all-time): 42,322 v Tottenham H, Div 1, 17/10/1970
Record Attendance (FAPL): 28,832 v Manchester United, 26/2/94
Most FAPL Goals in Season: 47, 1993-94 – 42 games
Most FAPL Points in Season: 52, 1993-94 – 42 games

5-Year Record

	Div.	P	W	D	L	F	A	Pts	Pos	FAC	FLC
91-92	1	42	9	11	22	37	59	38	22	5	4
92-93	1	46	26	10	10	81	41	88	2	4	2
93-94	PL	42	13	13	16	47	58	52	13	6	3
94-95	PL	42	13	11	18	44	48	50	14	4	4
95-96	PL	38	14	9	15	43	52	51	10	4	3

Summary 1995-96

Player	Tot	St	Sb	Snu	PS	Gls	Y	R	Fa	La	Fg	Lg
ALLEN	3	3	0	0	0	1	1	0	0	0	0	0
BILLIC	13	13	0	0	1	0	1	0	0	0	0	0
BISHOP	35	35	0	0	3	1	3	0	3	3	0	1
BOERE	1	0	1	0	0	0	0	0	0	0	0	0
BOOGERS	4	0	4	3	0	0	0	1	0	0	0	0
BREACKER	22	19	3	2	0	0	6	0	0	2	0	0
BROWN	3	3	0	0	0	0	0	0	0	0	0	0
COTTEE	33	30	3	1	11	10	1	0	3	3	0	2
DANI	10	3	7	1	2	2	0	0	0	0	0	0
DICKS	34	34	0	0	0	10	5	1	3	3	0	1
DOWIE	33	33	0	0	1	8	6	0	3	3	1	0
DUMITRESCU	3	2	1	0	2	0	0	0	0	0	0	0
FERDINAND	1	0	1	0	0	0	0	0	0	0	0	0
FINN	1	1	0	0	0	0	0	0	0	0	0	0
GORDON	1	0	1	0	0	0	0	0	1	0	0	0
HARKES	10	6	4	3	3	0	1	0	2	0	0	0
HUGHES	28	28	0	0	4	0	1	0	3	2	1	0
HUTCHISON	12	8	4	1	3	2	3	0	0	0	0	0
LAMPARD	2	0	2	0	0	0	0	0	0	0	0	0
LAZARIDIS	4	2	2	0	1	0	0	0	1	1	0	0
MARTIN	14	10	4	7	1	0	0	0	1	2	0	0
MIKLOSKO	36	36	0	0	0	0	1	1	3	3	0	0
MONCUR	20	19	1	0	5	0	4	0	1	3	1	1
POTTS	34	34	0	2	2	0	3	0	3	3	0	0
RIEPER	36	35	1	1	0	2	2	0	3	3	0	0
ROWLAND	23	19	4	4	5	0	4	0	2	0	0	0
SEALEY	2	1	1	27	0	0	0	0	0	0	0	0
SHILTON	0	0	0	3	0	0	0	0	0	0	0	0
SLATER	22	16	6	2	7	2	1	0	1	2	0	0
WATSON	1	0	1	0	0	0	0	0	0	0	0	0
WHITBREAD	2	0	2	1	0	0	0	0	1	0	0	0
WHYTE	0	0	0	2	0	0	0	0	0	0	0	0
WILLIAMSON	29	28	1	0	3	4	5	0	3	1	0	0
					OG	1						

Ironing Out Problems

Harry Redknapp, beginning his second season as manager at Upton Park, swooped in the transfer market during the close season to sign Robbie Slater from Blackburn Rovers for £600,000 while Matt Holmes and Matt Rush departed for a combined fee of around £1m and later in the season Jeroen Boere, Ian Feuer and Martin Allen also left, the latter after six years with the Hammers. Replacing Boere was Northern Ireland international Iain Dowie who, in an exchange deal with Crystal Palace, arrived for his second spell with the club. Early in the season Michael Hughes returned to the club on loan from Strasbourg.

The season, West Ham's third in the Premiership, began very poorly and with just two points from the opening six fixtures they found only Manchester City below them. Julian Dicks, whose consistency during the season had no lack of backers wanting the 'bad boy' of football to be called up into the England squad, scored twice against Everton on 23 September to clinch the Hammers' first win of the season. With a run of just one defeat from the next nine games Redknapp's side climbed to tenth in the table but just as quickly as West Ham rose up the table so they fell as six games in seven were lost.

The festive period brought little respite and it took until the final day of January before a welcome victory was secured, Coventry the victims. By now Redknapp had reinforced his side with the signing of Romanian international Ilie Dumitrescu from Spurs for £1.65m, a deal that was protracted due to work permit problems, and Portuguese pin-up Dani on loan from Sporting Lisbon until the end of the season at a cost of £130,000. The success over Coventry, with goals from Marc Rieper, the reliable Tony Cottee and Dowie, directed the Hammers on a trail of success that was to culminate in their highest position for a decade.

There were some notable scalps during that five match winning run including derby victories over Spurs and Chelsea. On the day West Ham ended Spurs' four month unbeaten home record Dani opened his account and Slaven Bilic (who joined Rieper at the Euro 96 Championships playing for Croatia and Denmark respectively), a £1.3m signing, made his full debut. After the win at Chelsea, during which West Ham trailed at the interval, goals by Danny Williamson and Cottee further hindered Newcastle's title aspirations. The Magpies took revenge four games later with a 3-0 win that flattered the Hammers.

It was Arsenal who had ended the winning streak but West Ham maintained 11th place and, surprisingly, after an inconsistent spell rose to 10th on the back of a 1-1 draw with Wimbledon. Just one of the final six games were won but West Ham's future in the Premiership had long since been secured.

The FA Cup was kind to West Ham in that it gave them home draws against Endsleigh League opposition but after seeing off Southend United at Upton Park, with Jon Moncur's only home goal of the season and Hughes' solitary goal in any competition, they crashed 3-0 in a replay away to Grimsby Town just two days after a league game with Spurs.

The Coca Cola Cup also failed to bring much joy to East London as a 2nd Round triumph in both legs against Bristol Rovers was soon forgotten as the Hammers went down to Southampton at the Dell in Round Three.

The run-up to the 1996-97 season proved to be equally as busy as it was in 95-96 with several big name signings arriving at the Boleyn Ground, most significant amongst them the record signing of Romanian Florin Raducioiu. ■

Results 1995-96

FA Carling Premiership

Date	Opponents	Ven	Res	Pos	Atten	Scorers
19-Aug	Leeds United	H	1-2	–	22,901	Williamson (5)
23-Aug	Man. United	A	1-2	–	31,966	OG (Bruce 56)
26-Aug	N. Forest	A	1-1	17	26,645	Allen (14)
30-Aug	Tottenham	H	1-1	17	23,516	Hutchison (24)
11-Sep	Chelsea	H	1-3	19	19,228	Hutchison (73)
16-Sep	Arsenal	A	0-1	19	38,065	
23-Sep	Everton	H	2-1	17	21,085	Dicks (7 pen, 41 pen)
02-Oct	Southampton	A	0-0	16	13,568	
16-Oct	Wimbledon	A	1-0	13	9,411	Cottee (18)
21-Oct	Blackburn R.	H	1-1	13	21,776	Dowie (25)
28-Oct	Sheff. Wed.	A	0-1	12	23,917	Dowie (40)
04-Nov	Aston Villa	H	1-4	12	23,637	Dicks (85 pen)
18-Nov	Bolton Wan.	A	3-0	11	19,047	Bishop (46); Cottee (68); Williamson (89)
22-Nov	Liverpool	H	0-0	13	24,324	
25-Nov	QPR	H	1-0	10	21,504	Cottee (84)
02-Dec	Blackburn R.	A	2-4	13	26,638	Dicks (75 pen); Slater (86)
11-Dec	Everton	A	0-3	13	31,778	
16-Dec	Southampton	H	2-1	13	18,501	Cottee (80); Dowie (82)
23-Dec	Middlesbro'	A	2-4	13	28,640	Cottee (80); Dicks (86)
01-Jan	Man. City	A	1-2	14	26,024	
13-Jan	Leeds United	A	0-2	14	30,658	
22-Jan	Man. United	H	0-1	16	24,197	
31-Jan	Coventry C.	H	3-2	14	18,884	Rieper (46); Cottee (59); Dowie (85)
03-Feb	N. Forest	H	1-0	13	21,257	Slater (19)
12-Feb	Tottenham	A	1-0	13	29,781	Dani (4)
17-Feb	Chelsea	A	2-1	12	25,252	Dicks (62); Williamson (72)
21-Feb	Newcastle U.	H	2-0	11	23,843	
24-Feb	Arsenal	H	0-1	11	24,217	
02-Mar	Coventry C.	A	2-2	11	17,459	Cottee (2); Rieper (22)
09-Mar	Middlesbro'	H	2-0	11	23,850	Dowie (1); Dicks (62 pen)
18-Mar	Newcastle U.	A	0-3	11	36,331	
23-Mar	Man. City	H	4-2	11	24,017	Dowie (21, 53); Dicks (83); Dani (84)
06-Apr	Wimbledon	H	1-1	10	20,402	Dicks (6)
08-Apr	Liverpool	A	0-2	10	40,326	
13-Apr	Bolton Wan.	H	1-0	10	23,086	Cottee (28)
17-Apr	Aston Villa	H	1-1	10	26,768	Cottee (84)
27-Apr	QPR	A	0-3	11	18,828	
05-May	Sheff. Wed.	H	1-1	11	23,790	Dicks (72)

FA Challenge Cup

Date	Opponents	Vn	Rnd	Res	Atten	Scorers
06-Jan	Southend U.	H	3R	2-0	23,284	Moncur (58); Hughes (87)
07-Feb	Grimsby Tn	H	4R	1-1	22,030	Dowie (35)
14-Feb	Grimsby Tn	A	4RR	0-3	8,382	

Coca-Cola League Cup

Date	Opponents	Vn	Rnd	Res	Atten	Scorers
20-Sep	Bristol R.	A	2R1L	1-0	7,103	Moncur (34)
04-Oct	Bristol R.	H	2R2L	3-0	15,375	Dicks (37 pen); Bishop (49); Cottee (75)
	West Ham United won 4-0 on aggregate					
25-Oct	Southampton	A	1-2	3R	11,059	Cottee (33)

Hammers – Premiership Fact File

- United achieved their highest ever position in the Premiership – 10th – on 25th November 1995 when they beat QPR 1-0. Although they matched that later in the season, the Hammers finally finished 11th.
- Marco Boogers came on as a sub in the second game of the season in the 73rd minute. His appearance against Manchester United didn't last too long though as he was red carded in the 88th minute.
- The Hammers used 31 players in their 38 Premiership games last season, plus an additional two players who made it to the bench but no further.
- Two penalties by Julian Dicks secured West Ham their first Premiership win of the season after seven games with a 2-1 win over Everton.
- Famous names appeared on the West Ham team sheet last season. Rio Ferdinand is cousin of Newcastle United hotshot Les Ferdinand, while the current Frank Lampard is the son of long serving veteran – Frank Lampard! Frank Lampard Jnr was also voted Young Hammer of the Year while both players are part of the England Youth team.

Wimbledon

Founded 1889 as Wimbledon Old Centrals, an old boys' side of the Central School playing on Wimbledon Common. Member of the Southern Suburban League, the name was changed to Wimbledon in 1905. Moved to Plough Lane in 1912. Athenian League member for two seasons before joining the Isthmian League in 1921.

FA Amateur Cup winners 1963 and seven times Isthmian League champions. Turned professional in 1965 joining the Southern League of which they were champions three times before being elected to Football League Division Four in 1977. Started ground sharing at Selhurst Park in 1991 and founder member of the Premier League 1992.

Ground: Selhurst Park, South Norwood, London SE25 6PY
Phone: 0181-771 2233   **News:** 0891 12 11 75
Box Office: 0181-771 8841
Colours: All Blue with Yellow trim   **Nickname:** The Dons
Capacity: 26,995   **Pitch:** 110 yds x 74 yds

Chairman: S.G.Reed   **Vice-Chairman:** J. Lelliott
Owner: Sam Hamman   **Chief Executive:** David Barnard
Secretary: Steve Rooke   **Manager:** Joe Kinnear
Assistant: Terry Burton   **Physio:** Steve Allen

League History: 1977 Elected to Division 4; 1979-80 Division 3; 1980-81 Division 4; 1981-82 Division 3; 1982-83 Division 4; 1983-84 Division 3; 1984-86 Division 2; 1986-92 Division 1; 1992- FA Premier League.

Honours: *Football League Division 3 Runners-up:* 1983-84; *Division 4 Champions:* 1982-83. *FA Cup Winners:* 1987-88. *FA Amateur Cup Winners:* 1963.

European Record: Never qualified. InterToto Cup (1995).

Managers: Les Henley 1955-71; Mike Everitt 1971-73; Dick Graham 1973-74; Allen Batsford 1974-78; Dario Gradi 1978-81; Dave Bassett 1981-87; Bobby Gould 1987-90; Ray Harford 1990-91; Peter Withe 1991; *(FAPL)* Joe Kinnear January 1992-

Season 1995-96

Biggest Home Win: 3-0 v Manchester City, 8/4/96
Biggest Home Defeat: 2-4 v Leeds Utd 23/9/95 and Manchester Utd 3/2/96
Biggest Away Win: 4-2 v Everton, 23/3/96
Biggest Away Defeat: 1-6 v Newcastle United, 21/10/95
Biggest Home Att: 24,432 v Manchester United, 3/2/96
Smallest Home Att: 6,352 v Sheffield Wednesday, 30/8/95
Average Attendance: 13,180 (20th/20)
Leading Scorer: 11 – Robbie Earle, 10 – Dean Holdsworth
Last Season: *FAPL:* 14th *FA Cup:* QF *Coca-Cola Cup:* 2

All-Time Records

Record FAPL Win: 4-0 v Crystal Palace, 9/4/1993
Record FAPL Defeat: 1-7 v Aston Villa, 11/2/1995
Record FL Win: 6-0 v Newport County, Division 3, 3/9/1983
Record FL Defeat: 0-8 v Everton, League Cup R2, 29/8/1978
Record Cup Win: 7-2 v Windsor & Eton, FA Cup R1, 22/11/1980
Record Fee Received: £4.5m from Newcastle for Warren Barton, 6/95
Record Fee Paid: £2m to Millwall for Ben Thatcher, 7/96
Most FL Apps: Alan Cork, 430, 1977-92
Most FAPL Apps: 139 – Dean Holdsworth
Most FAPL Goals: 53 – Dean Holdsworth
Record Scorer in FAPL Season: Holdsworth, 19, 1992-93
Record Attendance (all-time): 30,115 v Manchester United, 8/5/93
Record Attendance (FAPL): 30,115 v Manchester United, 8/5/93
Most FAPL Goals in Season: 56, 1992-93 *and* 56, 1993-94 – 42 games
Most FAPL Points in Season: 65, 1993-94 – 42 games

5-Year Record

	Div.	P	W	D	L	F	A	Pts	Pos	FAC	FLC
91-92	1	42	14	13	15	53	53	53	13	3	2
92-93	PL	42	14	12	16	56	55	54	12	5	3
93-94	PL	42	18	11	13	56	53	65	6	5	5
94-95	PL	42	15	11	16	48	65	56	9	5	3
95-96	PL	38	10	11	17	55	70	41	14	QF	2

Summary 1995-96

Player	Tot	St	Sb	Snu	PS	Gls	Y	R	Fa	La	Fg	Lg
ARDLEY	6	4	2	2	1	0	1	0	2	1	0	0
BLACKWELL	8	8	0	0	0	0	0	0	2	0	0	0
BLISSETT	4	0	4	0	0	0	0	0	0	0	0	0
CASTLEDINE	4	2	2	0	1	1	0	0	2	0	0	0
CLARKE	18	9	9	0	4	2	0	0	4	2	1	1
CUNNINGHAM	33	32	1	0	3	0	5	0	7	2	0	0
EARLE	37	37	0	0	2	11	2	1	7	2	1	2
EKOKU	31	28	3	0	15	7	5	0	7	1	3	0
ELKINS	10	7	3	0	1	0	3	0	0	1	0	0
EUELL	9	4	5	2	0	2	1	0	6	0	0	0
FEAR	4	4	0	0	3	0	1	0	1	0	0	0
FITZGERALD	4	2	2	1	0	0	1	1	0	0	0	0
GAYLE	34	21	13	0	11	5	0	0	8	2	0	0
GOODMAN	27	9	18	3	5	6	0	0	3	1	3	0
HARFORD	21	17	4	2	10	2	6	0	7	1	0	0
HEALD	18	18	0	0	1	0	1	1	0	2	0	0
HOLDSWORTH	33	31	2	0	11	10	7	1	5	2	2	4
JONES	31	27	4	0	1	3	7	2	3	2	0	0
KIMBLE	31	31	0	0	1	0	2	0	8	1	0	0
LEONHARDSEN	29	28	1	0	6	4	6	0	7	2	1	0
McALLISTER	2	2	0	0	1	0	0	0	0	0	0	0
PEARCE	7	6	1	7	2	0	1	0	2	0	0	0
PERRY	36	35	1	0	1	0	8	0	7	1	0	0
REEVES	25	21	4	2	0	1	1	0	6	0	0	0
SEGERS	4	3	1	2	0	0	0	0	0	0	0	0
SKINNER	1	1	0	0	1	0	0	0	0	0	0	0
SULLIVAN	16	16	0	0	0	0	0	0	8	0	0	0
TALBOYS	5	3	2	1	1	0	1	0	1	1	0	0
THORN	14	11	3	6	3	0	2	0	0	2	0	0
TRACEY	1	1	0	0	0	0	0	0	0	0	0	0
						OG	1					

Ding, Don Season Again

Wimbledon have been in the top flight since 1986 and that they are now entering their tenth season as a Premiership club on such a small budget is a tribute to the organisation of the club in general and the managerial skills of Joe Kinnear in particular. The close season had a familiar ring to it as Warren Barton was sold to Newcastle for £4m while just £600,000 was spent on Andy Pearce in November.

The Dons got off to a terrific start with six points and six goals collected from the opening two fixtures but, as time was to prove, it was a flattering beginning as their victims, Bolton and QPR, ended up as relegation fodder. Manchester United put matters into perspective with a 3-1 win at Old Trafford but Wimbledon moved into third place when a draw with Sheffield Wednesday was followed by a winning Mick Harford goal against Liverpool. That, though, was as good as it got for the Dons as the next seven games were lost and goals conceded at an alarming rate. Leeds and Forest claimed four goals apiece while Newcastle, complete with Barton, won 6-1 at St James' Park. Wimbledon owner Sam Hamman wasn't pleased with the referee Graham Poll who dismissed 'keeper Paul Heald. Hamman said that it was the fourth time that Poll had been in charge of a Wimbledon match this season and in addition to sending off four of his players, had cautioned 22.

The procession of defeats ended with a draw at home to Middlesbrough but it was another six winless matches before their fortunes improved. A 3-1 lead was squandered at Coventry on 25 November despite the home side going down to nine men and a week later the Dons again drew 3-3, this time with Newcastle in a classic encounter. A third successive draw was followed by defeat at home to Spurs as Wimbledon slipped into the relegation places for the first time. A late goal by Robbie Earle took a point off Blackburn and on Boxing Day Earle was joined on the scoresheet by Efan Ekoku as the Dons moved out of the bottom three with a 2-1 win at Chelsea. The win, however, was soured by Vinny Jones' third dismissal of the season. Earle became the first Wimbledon player to score in three successive league matches for two seasons when he notched two during a 3-1 victory at Highbury as the year ended in style. The new year began disappointingly with defeats by Everton and Bolton but a second win over QPR took the Dons to 14th, their highest placing for three months. Another mini slump, sparked by a 4-2 home reversal against Manchester United, left Kinnear's Crazy Gang just one place above the relegation trap door but 13 points from five games ensured that Selhurst Park, despite talk of a possible move for the club to either Wales or Dublin, would see Premiership football for another season.

Wimbledon's fluctuating fortunes in the league may have made for a fascinating campaign but it was nothing compared to their two matches with Charlton Athletic in the Coca Cola Cup. After going down 5-4 at home in their 2nd Round 1st Leg tie the Dons drew 3-3 at the Valley and went out by an extraordinary 8-7 aggregate. The FA Cup was a more mundane affair with an Andy Clarke goal accounting for Watford in a 3rd Round replay. Indeed the Dons had replays in all four rounds of the competition in which they were involved. Middlesbrough went down to a Dean Holdsworth replay goal while a brace from Jon Goodman brought about Huddersfield Town's downfall in a second meeting. Wimbledon maintained the sequence of gaining an away draw when holding Chelsea in a controversial quarter final tie but it was Wimbledon who had the Blues after their neighbours won the replay at Selhurst Park. ∎

Results 1995-96

FA Carling Premiership

Date	Opponents	Ven	Res	Pos	Atten	Scorers
19-Aug	Bolton Wan.	H	3-2	–	9,317	Ekoku (5); Earle (23); Holdsworth (55)
23-Aug	QPR	A	3-0	–	11,837	Leonhardson (30); Holdsworth (56); Goodman (83)
26-Aug	Man. United	A	1-3	3	32,226	Earle (64)
30-Aug	Sheff. Wed.	H	2-2	6	6,352	Goodman (17); Holdsworth (84 pen)
09-Sep	Liverpool	H	1-0	3	19,530	Harford (28)
16-Sep	Aston Villa	A	0-2	6	26,928	
23-Sep	Leeds United	H	2-4	9	13,307	Holdsworth (43); Reeves (59)
30-Sep	Tottenham	A	1-3	11	25,321	Earle (39)
16-Oct	West Ham	H	0-1	12	9,411	
21-Oct	Newcastle U.	A	1-6	14	36,434	Gayle (6)
28-Oct	Southampton	H	1-2	15	7,982	Ewell (64)
06-Nov	N. Forest	A	1-4	16	20,810	Jones (11)
18-Nov	Middlesbro'	H	0-0	16	13,780	
22-Nov	Man. City	A	0-1	17	23,617	
25-Nov	Coventry C.	A	3-3	16	12,523	Jones (28 pen); Goodman (43); Leonhardsen (58)
03-Dec	Newcastle U.	H	3-3	17	18,002	Holdsworth (19, 65); Ekoku (21)
09-Dec	Leeds United	A	1-1	17	27,984	Leonhardsen (4)
16-Dec	Tottenham	H	0-1	18	16,193	
23-Dec	Blackburn R.	H	1-1	18	7,105	Earle (82)
26-Dec	Chelsea	A	2-1	16	21,906	Earle (35); Ekoku (39)
30-Dec	Arsenal	A	3-1	15	37,640	Earle (38, 67); Holdsworth (50)
01-Jan	Everton	H	2-3	15	11,121	Holdsworth (54); Ekoku (72)
13-Jan	Bolton Wan.	A	0-1	15	16,216	
20-Jan	QPR	H	2-1	14	9,123	Leonhardsen (40); Clarke (74)
03-Feb	Man. United	H	2-4	16	24,432	Gayle (68); Ewell (76)
10-Feb	Sheff. Wed.	A	1-2	16	19,085	Gayle (60)
24-Feb	Aston Villa	H	3-3	16	12,193	Goodman (10, 48); Harford (90)
02-Mar	Chelsea	H	1-1	15	17,048	OG (Clarke 38)
13-Mar	Liverpool	A	2-2	15	34,063	Ekoku (54); Holdsworth (60)
16-Mar	Arsenal	H	0-3	17	18,335	

23-Mar	Everton	A	4-2	15	31,382	Gayle (12); Castledine (65); Clarke (85); Goodman (88)
30-Mar	N. Forest	H	1-0	15	9,807	Holdsworth (81)
06-Apr	West Ham	A	1-1	15	20,462	Jones (9)
08-Apr	Man. City	H	3-0	15	11,844	Earle (40, 47); Ekoku (52)
13-Apr	Middlesbro'	A	2-1	14	29,192	Earle (12); Ekoku (64)
17-Apr	Blackburn R.	A	2-3	14	24,174	Earle (22); Gayle (48)
27-Apr	Coventry C.	H	0-2	14	15,540	
05-May	Southampton	A	0-0	14	15,172	

FA Challenge Cup

Date	Opponents	Vn	Rnd	Res	Atten	Scorers
06-Jan	Watford	A	3R	1-1	11,187	Mooney (36)
17-Jan	Watford	H	3RR	1-0	5,142	Clarke (78)
07-Feb	Middlesbro'	A	4R	0-0	28,915	
13-Feb	Middlesbro'	H	4RR	1-0	5,220	Holdsworth (73)
17-Feb	Huddersfield	A	5R	2-2	17,307	Ekoku (66, 90)
28-Feb	Huddersfield	H	5RR	3-1	7,015	Ekoku (9); Goodman (42, 85)
09-Mar	Chelsea	A	QF	2-2	30,805	Earle (54); Holdsworth (81)
20-Mar	Chelsea	H	QFR	1-3	21,380	Goodman (39)

Coca-Cola League Cup

Date	Opponents	Vn	Rnd	Res	Atten	Scorers
20-Sep	Charlton Ath.	H	2R1L	4-5	3,717	Holdsworth (12, 71); Clarke (88)
03-Oct	Charlton Ath.	A	2R2L	3-3	9,823	Holdsworth(31, 81 pen); Earle (46)

Charlton Athletic won 8-7 on aggregate

Dons – Premiership Fact File

- Andy Clarke – the striker Wimbledon brought from Barnet when they were still a Non-League side – has an interesting Premiership record. He is only one appearance short of making his 100th appearance – but 50 of them were made as a substitute, more than any other player!
- Referee Graham Poll took charge of four Wimbledon matches last season during which he red carded four Dons players and cautioned 22!
- Robbie Earle became the first Wimbledon player to score in three successive matches in two seasons when he scored twice in the 3-1 win at Arsenal at the end of the year. He managed another three successive matches with goals in April.
- Since entering the top flight of English football in 1986 Wimbledon's lowest final league position is bettered only by those of Arsenal and Liverpool.

D1: Bolton Wanderers

Formed in 1874 as a Sunday School side, Christ Church. This connection ended in 1877 when they adopted their present name. Turned professional in 1895 and were Football League founder members. Moved from Pikes Lane to present ground in 1895. Members of the reorganised Division One on formation of the Premier League, they were last in the top flight in season 1979-80.

Ground: Burnden Park, Bolton.
Phone: 01204-389200   **Box Office:** 01204-521101
Info: 0891-12 11 64
Capacity: 22,500   **Pitch:** 113 yds x 76 yds
Colours: White, Navy Blue,Navy Blue   **Nickname:** The Trotters

President: Nat Lofthouse   **Chairman:** G. Hargreaves
Secretary: Des McBain
Manager: Colin Todd   **Coach:** Ian Porterfield
Physio: E. Simpson

League History: 1892 Founder members of League; 1899-00 Division 2; 1900-03 Division 1; 1903-05 Division 2; 1905-08 Division 1; 1900-09 Division 2; 1909-10 Division 1; 1910-11 Division 2; 1911-33 Division 1; 1933-35 Division 2; 1935-64 Division 1; 1964-71 Division 2; 1971-73 Division 3; 1973-78 Division 2; 1978-80 Division 1; 1983-87 Division 3; 1987-88 Division 4; 1988-92 Division 3; 1992-93 Division 2; 1993-94 Division 1; FAPL 1994-96; Division 1 1996-

Honours: *FA Cup Winners:* 1922-23, 1925-26, 1928-29, 1957-58; *Runners-up:* 1883-84, 1903-04, 1952-53; *League Cup Runners-up:* 1994-95; *Division Two Champions:* 1908-09, 1977-78; *Division Three Champions:* 1972-73; *FA Charity Shield Winners:* 1958; *Sherpa Van Trophy Winners:* 1988-89; *Freight Rover Trophy Runners-up:* 1985-86.

European Record: Never qualified.

Managers: Tom Rawthorne 1874-85; JJ Bentley 1885-86; WG Struthers 1886-87; Fitzroy Norris 1887; JJ Bentley 1887-95; Harry Downs 1895-96; Frank Brettell 1896-98; John Somerville 1889-1910; Will Settle 1910-15; Tom Mather 1915-19; Charles Foweraker 1991-44; Walter Rowley 1944-50; Bill Ridding 1951-68; Nat Lofthouse 1968-70; Jimmy McIlroy 1971; Jimmy Meadows 1971; Nat Lofthouse 1971; Jimmy Armfield 1971-74; Ian Greaves 1974-80; Stan Anderson 1980-81; George Mulhall 1981-82; John McGovern

206

1982-85; Charlie Wright 1985; Phil Neal 1995-92; Bruce Rioch 1992-1995; *(FAPL)* Roy McFarland/Colin Todd June 1995-Jan 1996; Colin Todd Jan 1996-

Season 1995-96

Biggest Home Win:	2-1 v Blackburn Rvrs, Chelsea and Sheff.Weds
Biggest Home Defeat:	0-6 v Manchester United, 25/2/96
Biggest Away Win:	4-1 v Middlesbrough, 17/2/96
Biggest Away Defeat:	2-5 v Liverpool, 23/9/95
Biggest Home Att:	21,381 v Manchester United, 25/2/96
Smallest Home Att:	16,216 v Wimbledon, 13/1/96
Average Attendance:	18,822 (16th/20)
Leading Scorer:	6 – John McGinlay, 5 – Fabian de Freitas

Last Season: *FAPL:* 20 *FA Cup:* 4 *Coca-Cola Cup:* 4

All-Time Records

Record FAPL Win:	4-1 v Middlesbrough (away), 17/2/96
Record FAPL Defeat:	0-6 v Manchester United (home), 25/2/96
Record FL Win:	8-0 v Barnsley, Division 2, 6/10/34
Record FL Defeat:	
Record Cup Win:	13-0 v Sheffield Utd, FAC 2Rd, 1/2/1890
Record Fee Received:	£4.5m from Liverpool for Jason McAteer, 9/95
Record Fee Paid:	£1.5m to Barnsley for Gerry Taggart 8/95 and £1.5m to Partizan Belgrade for Sasa Curcic
Most FL Apps:	Eddie Hopkinson, 519, 1956-70
Most FAPL Apps:	37 – Phillips
Most FAPL Goals:	6 – McGinlay

Highest Scorer in FAPL Season: 6 – John McGinlay, 1995-96
Record Attendance (all-time): 69,912 v Man City, FAC 5Rd, 18/2/33
Record Attendance (FAPL): 21,381 v Manchester United, 25/2/96
Most FAPL Goals in Season: 29, 1995-96 – 38 games
Most FAPL Points in Season: 39, 1995-96 – 38 games

5-Year Record

	Div.	P	W	D	L	F	A	Pts	Pos	FAC	FLC
91-92	3	46	14	17	15	57	56	59	13	5	2
92-93	2	46	27	9	10	80	41	90	2	5	2
93-94	1	46	15	14	11	63	64	59	14	6	2
94-95	1	42	21	14	11	67	45	77	3	3	F
95-96	PL	38	8	5	25	39	71	29	20	4	4

Summary 1995-96

Player	Tot	St	Sb	Snu	PS	Gls	Y	R	Fa	La	Fg	Lg
BERGSSON	34	34	0	0	2	4	8	1	0	6	0	0
BLAKE	18	14	4	0	7	1	4	0	2	0	0	0
BRANAGAN	31	31	0	0	0	0	1	0	2	6	0	0
BURNETT	1	0	1	3	0	0	0	0	0	0	0	0
COLEMAN	12	12	0	0	1	1	2	0	0	0	0	0
COYLE	5	2	3	1	1	0	0	0	0	1	0	0
CURCIC	28	28	0	0	4	4	3	0	2	3	2	1
DAVISON	2	2	0	17	0	0	0	0	0	0	0	0
De FREITAS	27	17	10	3	2	5	0	0	1	3	0	0
FAIRCLOUGH	33	33	0	1	4	0	6	0	2	6	0	0
GREEN	31	26	5	6	4	3	2	0	2	5	0	0
LEE	18	9	9	2	2	1	2	0	1	4	0	0
McANESPIE	9	7	2	8	1	0	0	0	0	3	0	0
McATEER	4	4	0	0	0	0	1	0	0	0	0	0
McGINLAY	32	29	3	2	9	6	4	0	2	6	1	2
PAATELAINEN	15	12	3	6	5	1	1	0	1	1	0	0
PATTERSON	16	12	4	1	1	1	5	1	0	6	0	1
PHILLIPS	37	37	0	0	2	0	4	0	2	6	0	0
SELLARS	22	22	0	0	1	3	2	0	1	0	0	0
SMALL	1	1	0	1	0	0	0	0	0	0	0	0
SNEEKES	17	14	3	3	1	1	4	1	1	4	0	2
STRONG	1	0	1	0	0	0	0	0	0	0	0	0
STUBBS	25	24	1	1	0	4	1	0	2	3	0	0
TAGGART	11	11	0	0	1	1	6	0	2	2	0	0
TAYLOR	1	0	1	0	0	0	0	0	0	0	0	0
THOMPSON	26	23	3	2	4	1	8	0	1	5	0	1
TODD	12	9	3	1	4	2	2	0	0	4	0	0
WARD	5	5	0	0	0	0	0	0	0	0	0	0

Elite Strugglers

Bolton Wanderers' first season in the Premiership was always likely to be a tough time for the club and that task was made all the more difficult by the defection of manager Bruce Rioch to Arsenal shortly after taking the club to promotion via the play-offs and the final of the Coca Cola Cup.

Bolton turned to Roy McFarland and Colin Todd to steer the club to safety but with just two wins by the turn of the year Bolton were on course for a swift return to the Endsleigh League. The poor run of results culminated in Bolton dismissing McFarland and promoting Todd one day after a 4-2 defeat at Sheffield Wednesday. Bolton's two wins, however, were very commendable with Blackburn Rovers and Arsenal being beaten at Burnden Park. A 4-1 victory over Middlesbrough at the Riverside Stadium in mid February boosted their faint survival hopes only for a 6-0 defeat at home to Manchester United the following weekend to put the revival on hold. But come March, Bolton refused to accept what most outside Burnden Park believed to be inevitable, and with successive away wins at Leeds and Coventry closed the gap on a fast sinking QPR at the foot of the table.

A defeat at home to Spurs was followed by a win and a draw at home to Sheffield Wednesday and Manchester City respectively. The win over Wednesday lifted Bolton off the bottom but the joy was short lived as a 3-0 defeat at Everton edged Bolton closer to the drop. A home victory over Chelsea on Easter Monday still gave the club some hope of a resurrection but Bolton bowed out of the Premier with three consecutive defeats.

Any hopes supporters may have held of the club finding solace from its league form with yet another good cup campaign were quickly extinguished. In the FA Cup Bradford City were comfortably beaten 3-0 before Bolton went down at home to Leeds United in the 4th Round. A little more success was achieved in the Coca Cola Cup with Brentford and Leicester City being disposed of, the latter after an away replay, only for Wanderers to lose out at home to Norwich City in a penalty shoot out at the end of a 4th Round replay.

Although Bolton were stranded at the foot of the table for much of the campaign, they did pull off one of the bargain buys of the season with the £1.5m signing of Sasa Curcic from Partizan Belgrade in October. The club made several other forays into the transfer market during the season with Gerry Taggart, Nathan Blake, Steve McAnespie and the experienced Scott Sellars all making big money moves to Burnden Park. But it was not so much the players who came in that led to Bolton's demise, their relegation had more to do with Rioch's exit and Jason McAteer's £4.5m transfer to Liverpool. Bolton also had to contend with continual speculation surrounding the future of highly rated defender Alan Stubbs who surprised many by seeing out the whole season at Burnden Park only to make his expected big money transfer, not to reunite with his former manager at Arsenal, but to travel north to Celtic a matter of weeks after the season's end.

That Bolton were in for a long battle against relegation failed to dampen the enthusiasm of their followers as average attendances for league matches showed a massive rise over their promotion season a year earlier; 13,030 for 1994-95 against 18,822 for 1995-96. A decline in those figures below the 13,000 mark in the Endsleigh League could well force the club to part with other bright lights such as Curcic, which might rule out an equally quick return to the Premiership. ∎

Results 1995-96

Date	Opponents	Ven	Res	Pos	Atten	Scorers
19-Aug	Wimbledon	A	2-3	–	9,317	Thompson (26 pen); De Freitas (40)
22-Aug	Newcastle U.	H	1-3	–	20,243	Bergsson (51)
26-Aug	Blackburn R.	H	2-1	14	20,253	De Freitas (21); Stubbs (80)
30-Aug	Aston Villa	A	0-1	15	31,770	
09-Sep	Middlesbro'	H	1-1	16	18,376	McGinlay (24)
16-Sep	Man. United	A	0-3	18	32,812	
23-Sep	Liverpool	A	2-5	19	40,104	Todd (78); Patterson (81)
30-Sep	QPR	H	0-1	19	17,362	
14-Oct	Everton	H	1-1	19	20,427	Paatelainen (1)
21-Oct	N. Forest	A	2-3	19	25,426	Sneekes (24); De Freitas (78)
30-Oct	Arsenal	H	1-0	18	18,682	McGinlay (35)
04-Nov	Man. City	A	0-1	18	28,397	
18-Nov	West Ham	H	0-3	18	19,047	
22-Nov	Chelsea	A	2-3	19	17,495	Curcic (10); Green (67)
25-Nov	Southampton	A	0-1	20	14,404	
02-Dec	N. Forest	H	1-1	19	17,342	De Freitas (67)
09-Dec	Liverpool	H	0-1	20	21,042	
16-Dec	QPR	A	1-2	20	11,456	Sellars (43)
23-Dec	Tottenham	A	2-2	20	30,702	Green (76); Bergsson (78)
27-Dec	Leeds United	H	0-2	20	18,414	
30-Dec	Coventry C.	H	1-2	20	16,678	McGinlay (16)
01-Jan	Sheff. Wed.	A	2-4	20	24,872	Curcic (51); Taggart (77)
13-Jan	Wimbledon	H	1-0	20	16,216	McGinlay (44 pen)
20-Jan	Newcastle U.	A	1-2	20	36,534	Bergsson (19)
03-Feb	Blackburn R.	A	1-3	20	30,419	Green (29)
10-Feb	Aston Villa	H	0-2	20	18,099	
17-Feb	Middlesbro'	A	4-1	20	29,354	Blake (12); Coleman (45); De Freitas (62); Lee (73)
25-Feb	Man. United	H	0-6	20	21,381	
2-Mar	Leeds United	A	1-0	20	30,106	Bergsson (16)
16-Mar	Coventry C.	A	2-0	20	17,226	Stubbs (68, 70)
20-Mar	Tottenham	H	2-3	20	17,829	Stubbs (74); Sellars (84)
23-Mar	Sheff. Wed.	H	2-1	19	18,368	Sellars (44); Curcic (52)
30-Mar	Man. City	H	1-1	20	21,050	McGinlay (74)
6-Apr	Everton	A	0-3	20	37,974	
8-Apr	Chelsea	H	2-1	20	18,021	McGinlay (40); Curcic (44)
13-Apr	West Ham	A	0-1	20	23,086	
27-Apr	Southampton	H	0-1	20	18,795	
5-May	Arsenal	A	1-2	20	38,104	Todd (76)

FA Challenge Cup

Date	Opponents	Vn	Rnd	Res	Atten	Scorers
6-Jan	Bradford City	A	3-0	3R	10,265	McGinlay (40); Curcic (53, 66)
14-Feb	Leeds United	H	0-1	4R	16,694	

Coca-Cola League Cup

Date	Opponents	Vn	Rnd	Res	Atten	Scorers
19-Sep	Brentford	H	2R1L	1-0	5,234	Sneekes (79)
3-Oct	Brentford	A	2R2L	3-2	4,861	Patterson (58); McGinlay (66); Thompson (81)
24-Oct	Leicester City	H	3R	0-0	9,166	
8-Nov	Leicester City	A	3RR	3-2	14,884	McGinlay (39); Sneekes (61); Curcic (76)
29-Nov	Norwich City	A	4R	0-0	13,820	
20-Dec	Norwich City	H	4RR	0-0	8,736	

After extra time. Norwich won 3-2 on penalties

D1: Manchester City

Founded in 1880 as West Gorton AFC. Following ground difficulties, having lost the use of the Kirkmanshulme Cricket Ground, was relaunched as Gorton AFC in 1884. There were more ground problems before, in 1889, the club moved to Hyde Road, adopted the title of Ardwick, and employed its first professional.

Ardwick joined the Football Alliance in 1891, finishing seventh, and was founder member of Football League Division Two in 1892. Ardwick too encountered difficulties and the club was restarted as Manchester City in 1894, retaining the Football League place. In 1923 the club moved to Maine Road. Premier League founder member 1992.

Ground: Maine Road, Moss Side, Manchester, M14 7WN
Phone: 0161-226 1191/2   **Info:** 0891-12 11 91
Box Office: 0161-226 2224   **Dial-a-Seat:** 0161-227 9229
Capacity: 32,000   **Pitch:** 118 yds x 76 yds
Colours: Sky Blue, White, Sky Blue
Nickname: Blues or The Citizens

Chairman: Francis Lee   **Vice-Chairman:** Freddie Pye
Managing Director: Colin Barlow   **General Secretary:** Bernard Halford
Manager: Alan Ball   **Assistant:** Asa Hartford
First Team Coach: Tony Book   **Physio:** Eamonn Salmon

League History: 1892 Ardwick elected founder member of Division 2; 1894 Newly-formed Manchester C elected to Division 2; Division 1 1899-1902, 1903-09, 1910-26, 1928-38, 1947-50, 1951-63, 1966-83, 1985-87, 1989-92; Division 2 1902-03, 1909-10, 1926-28, 1938-47, 1950-51, 1963-66, 1983-85, 1987-89; 1992 – FA Premier League.

Honours: *Football League: Division 1 Champions:* 1936-37, 1967-68; *Runners-up:* 1903-04, 1920-21, 1976-77; *Division 2 Champions:* 1898-99, 1902-03, 1909-10, 1927-28, 1946-47, 1965-66; *Runners-up:* 1895-96, 1950-51, 1987-88. *FA Cup Winners:* 1969-70; *Runners-up:* 1973-74, 1980-81. *Cup-Winners' Cup Winners:* 1969-70.

European Competitions: CC (1): 68-69. CWC (2): 69-70 (W), 70-71. UEFA (4): 72-73, 76-77, 77-78, 78-79.

Managers: Joshua Parlby 1893-95; Sam Omerod 1895-1902; Tom Maley 1902-06; Harry Newbould 1906-12; Ernest Magnall 1912-24; David Ashworth 1924-25; Peter Hodge 1926-32; Wilf Wild 1932-46 (continued as

212

secretary to 1950); Sam Cowan 1946-47; John 'Jock' Thomson 1947-50; Leslie McDowall 1950-63; George Poyser 1963-65; Joe Mercer 1965-71 (continued as GM to 1972); Malcolm Allison 1972-73; Johnny Hart 1973; Ron Saunders 1973-74; Tony Book 1974-79; Malcolm Allison 1979-80; John Bond 1980-83; John Benson 1983; Billy McNeill 1983-86; Jimmy Frizzell 1986-87 (continued as GM); Mel Machin 1987-89; Howard Kendall 1990; *(FAPL)* Peter Reid 1990-93; Brian Horton Sept 1993-May 1995. Alan Ball July 1995-

Season 1995-96

Biggest Home Win: 2-0 v QPR, 3/2/96
Biggest Home Defeat: 2-3 v Manchester United, 6/4/96
Biggest Away Win: 1-0 v Aston Villa 25/11/95 and Leeds Utd 2/12/95
Biggest Away Defeat: 0-6 v Liverpool, 28/10/95
Biggest Home Att: 31,436 v Liverpool, 5/5/96
Smallest Home Att: 23,617 v Wimbledon, 22/11/95
Average Attendance: 27,836 (10th/20)
Leading Scorer: 9 – Uwe Rosler, 8 – Niall Quinn
Last Season: *FAPL:* 18 *FA Cup:* 5 *Coca-Cola Cup:* 3

All-Time Records

Record FAPL Win: 4-0 v Leeds United, 7/11/92 & Everton, 27/8/94
Record FAPL Defeat: 0-6 v Liverpool (away), 28/10/95
Record FL Win: 10-1 v Huddersfield Town, Division 2, 7/11/1987
Record FL Defeat: 1-9 v Everton, Division 1, 3/9/1906
Record Cup Win: 10-1 v Swindon Town, FA Cup R4, 29/1/1930
Record Fee Received: £1.7m from Tottenham H for Paul Stewart, 6/1988
Record Fee Paid: £2.5m to Wimbledon for Keith Curle, 8/1991
Most FL Appearances: Alan Oakes, 565, 1959-76
Most FAPL Apps: 131 – Keith Curle
Most FAPL Goals: 30 – Niall Quinn
Highest Scorer in FAPL season: David White, 16, 1992-93
Record Attendance (all-time): 84,569 v Stoke C, FA Cup R6, 3/3/1934
British record for any game outside London or Glasgow
Record Attendance (FAPL): 37,136 v Manchester United, 7/11/1993
Most FAPL Goals in Season: 56, 1992-93 – 42 games
Most FAPL Points in Season: 57, 1992-93 – 42 games

5-Year Record

	Div.	P	W	D	L	F	A	Pts	Pos	FAC	FLC
91-92	1	42	20	10	12	61	48	70	5	3	4
92-93	PL	42	15	12	15	56	51	57	9	6	3
93-94	PL	42	9	18	15	38	49	45	16	4	4
94-95	PL	42	12	13	17	53	64	49	17	5	5
95-96	PL	38	9	11	18	33	58	38	18	5	3

Summary 1995-96

Player	Tot	St	Sb	Snu	PS	Gls	Y	R	Fa	La	Fg	Lg
BEAGRIE	5	4	1	0	1	0	1	0	0	2	0	0
BRIGHTWELL, Ian	28	25	3	0	2	0	4	1	2	3	0	0
BROWN	21	16	5	1	3	0	5	1	5	2	0	0
CLOUGH	15	15	0	0	1	2	2	0	3	0	1	0
COTON	0	0	0	9	0	0	0	0	0	0	0	0
CREANEY	15	6	9	7	1	3	1	0	3	0	1	0
CROOKS	0	0	0	1	0	0	0	0	0	0	0	0
CURLE	32	32	0	0	0	0	7	0	5	3	0	1
EDGHILL	13	13	0	0	2	0	3	1	0	3	0	0
EKELUND	4	2	2	0	2	0	0	0	2	0	0	0
FLITCROFT	25	25	0	0	4	0	9	0	4	1	1	0
FOSTER	4	4	0	0	1	0	2	0	0	1	0	0
FRONTZECK	12	11	1	2	6	0	2	1	1	0	0	0
HILEY	5	2	3	2	1	0	0	0	0	0	0	0
IMMEL	38	38	0	0	0	0	0	0	5	3	0	0
INGRAM	5	5	0	0	1	0	0	0	1	0	0	0
KAVELASHVILI	4	3	1	2	2	1	0	0	0	0	0	0
KERNAGHAN	6	4	2	10	1	0	0	0	0	0	0	0
KERR	1	0	1	0	0	0	0	0	0	0	0	0
KINKLADZE	37	37	0	0	4	4	2	0	4	3	1	0
LOMAS	33	32	1	1	5	3	8	1	5	3	1	0
MARGETSON	0	0	0	19	0	0	1	0	0	1	0	0
MAZZARELLI	2	0	2	0	0	0	0	0	0	0	0	0
PHELAN	9	9	0	0	1	0	5	0	0	1	0	0
PHILLIPS	11	2	9	5	1	0	0	0	0	0	0	0
QUINN	31	23	8	1	5	8	4	0	4	3	2	1
ROSLER	36	34	2	0	5	9	6	0	5	3	2	2
SUMMERBEE	37	33	4	0	4	1	4	1	5	3	0	0
SYMONS	38	38	0	0	0	2	3	0	5	3	0	0
VONK	1	1	0	0	0	0	0	0	0	0	0	0
WALSH	4	4	0	0	1	0	1	0	0	0	0	0

Individual Skills Not Enough

Under their 14th manager since 1972, Manchester City were looking for a vast improvement on their form of the previous season which saw the side win just four of their final 25 Premiership matches. New manager Alan Ball splashed out over £3m on just three players, Georgi Kinkladze, Kit Symons and German goalkeeper Eike Immel who became more impressive as the season wore on. The most successful of the signings was Kinkladze who, with his exciting close control and eye for spectacular goals, gained admirers from far afield.

The season began with Uwe Rosler, top scorer the previous year, scoring an equaliser on the opening day against Tottenham but that solitary point was the sum total of City's success before taking a point off Leeds on 21 October. Eight consecutive Premiership games were lost between those two matches including a single goal defeat at Old Trafford. October ended with City being thrashed twice at Anfield, 4-0 in the Coca Cola Cup and four days later 6-0 in the Premiership. Indeed, by the end of their 11th game City had just two points in the bag and only Rosler (2), and £1.5m signing Gerry Creaney's names on the scoresheet.

Having spent ten matches at the foot of the table City's fortunes took a turn for the better when a 1-0 win over Bolton, courtesy of Nicky Summerbee's first goal since April, sparked a run of four wins in five games during which just one goal was conceded. The run looked set to continue when Kinkladze gave City the lead at Middlesbrough but eventually they went down 4-1 and began a run of just three wins in 19 Premiership matches. On New Year's Day, during a 2-1 win over West Ham, Niall Quinn became the first City player to score more than once in a league match since the previous March.

Ball sought to improve his attacking options with the £1.5m acquisition of Nigel Clough in January and two months later a similar amount took Georgian striker Mikhail Kavelashvili to Maine Road while shortly before the transfer deadline Gary Flitcroft joined Blackburn for £3.2m. The only time the goals flowed was when City led three times against the then leaders Newcastle before settling for a point on a day unfortunately best remembered for Asprilla's two clashes with Keith Curle. A win, two draws and a defeat from the next four games lifted the club to a season's high of 15th but with just one point from the next four games City were one place above the relegation positions with three games to go. More often than not, their haul of seven points from those three games would have taken them clear of the drop but, with several other lowly sides also winning, City went into the final match with Liverpool really needing victory to secure survival. At two down by half time all appeared lost. Goals from Rosler and Symons gave renewed optimism but after some bizarre time wasting tactics City trudged off the pitch to learn that it had all been in vain and for the fifth time in his managerial career Ball had suffered the pain of relegation.

During the early part of winter the Coca Cola Cup provided some relief for City as they chalked up their first win of the season with a 4-0 triumph over Wycombe but in the following round Liverpool won with ease. The FA Cup was more to City's liking with Division One promotion hopefuls Leicester being thrashed 5-0 in a replay at Maine Road. A last minute goal denied City victory at Coventry in Round Four but the job was successfully completed in the replay. City's season of struggle suffered an extra blow in the 5th Round as neighbours United closed in on the double with a 2-1 victory at Maine Road. ∎

Results 1995-96

Date	Opponents	Ven	Res	Pos	Atten	Scorers
19-Aug	Tottenham	H	1-1	–	30,827	Rosler (52)
23-Aug	Coventry C.	A	1-2	–	15,957	Rosler (82)
26-Aug	QPR	A	0-1	18	14,212	
30-Aug	Everton	H	0-2	20	28,432	
10-Sep	Arsenal	H	0-1	20	23,994	
16-Sep	Newcastle U.	A	1-3	20	36,501	Creaney (81)
23-Sep	Middlesbro'	H	0-1	20	25,865	
30-Sep	N. Forest	A	0-3	20	25,620	
14-Oct	Man. United	A	0-1	20	35,707	
21-Oct	Leeds United	H	0-0	20	26,390	
28-Oct	Liverpool	A	0-6	20	39,267	
04-Nov	Bolton Wan.	H	1-0	20	28,397	Summerbee (11)
18-Nov	Sheff. Wed.	A	1-1	20	24,422	Lomas (55)
22-Nov	Wimbledon	H	1-0	18	23,617	Quinn (90)
25-Nov	Aston Villa	H	1-0	17	28,027	Kinkladze (85)
02-Dec	Leeds United	A	1-0	15	33,249	Creaney (60)
09-Dec	Middlesbro'	A	1-4	16	29,469	Kinkladze (14)
18-Dec	N. Forest	H	1-1	16	25,660	Rosler (16)
23-Dec	Chelsea	H	0-1	17	28,668	
26-Dec	Blackburn R.	A	0-2	18	28,915	
01-Jan	West Ham	H	2-1	18	24,024	Quinn (21, 78)
13-Jan	Tottenham	A	0-1	18	31,438	
20-Jan	Coventry C.	H	1-1	18	25,710	Rosler (55)
31-Jan	Southampton	A	1-1	17	15,172	Rosler (84)
03-Feb	QPR	H	2-0	17	27,509	Clough (25); Symons (50)
10-Feb	Everton	A	0-2	18	37,354	
24-Feb	Newcastle U.	H	3-3	18	31,115	Quinn (16, 62); Rosler (77)
02-Mar	Blackburn R.	H	1-1	17	29,078	Lomas (84)
05-Mar	Arsenal	A	1-3	17	34,519	Creaney (54)
12-Mar	Chelsea	A	1-1	16	17,078	Clough (43)
16-Mar	Southampton	H	2-1	15	29,550	Kinkladze (32, 37)
23-Mar	West Ham	A	2-4	16	24,017	Quinn (76, 90)
30-Mar	Bolton Wan.	A	1-1	16	21,050	Quinn (2)
06-Apr	Man. United	H	2-3	17	29,688	Kavelashvili (39); Rosler (71)
08-Apr	Wimbledon	A	0-3	17	11,844	
13-Apr	Sheff. Wed.	H	1-0	17	30,898	Rosler (65)
27-Apr	Aston Villa	A	1-0	18	39,336	Lomas (70)
05-May	Liverpool	H	2-2	18	31,436	Rosler (71 pen); Symons (78)

FA Challenge Cup

Date	Opponents	Vn	Rnd	Res	Atten	Scorers
06-Jan	Leicester C.	A	3R	0-0	20,640	
17-Jan	Leicester C.	H	3RR	5-0	19,980	Rosler (10); Kinkladze (18); Quinn (51); Lomas (54); Creaney (80)
07-Feb	Coventry C.	A	4R	2-2	18,709	OG (Busst 33); Flitcroft (81)
14-Feb	Coventry C.	H	4RR	2-1	22,419	Clough (29); Quinn (46)
18-Feb	Man. United	A	5R	1-2	42,692	Rosler (11)

Coca-Cola League Cup

Date	Opponents	Vn	Rnd	Res	Atten	Scorers
19-Sep	Wycombe W.	A	2R1L	0-0	7,443	
04-Oct	Wycombe W.	H	2R2L	4-0	11,474	Rosler (31, 34); Quinn (60); Curle (63 pen)
	Manchester City won 4-0 on aggregate					
25-Oct	Liverpool	A	3R	0-4	29,394	

City – Premiership Fact File

- City suffered their biggest ever Premiership defeat when they lost 6-0 to Liverpool at Anfield in late October. Four days earlier they had lost 4-0 at Anfield in the Coca Cola League Cup.
- Kit Symonds and Eike Immel were the only two City players to appear in all 38 Premiership matches.
- City took a point off Spurs on the opening day of the season but failed to secure another until 21st October as they lost their next eight games. The point came in a 0-0 draw with Leeds United.
- City failed to score in eight of their opening 11 games.

D1: QPR

Founded in 1885 as St. Jude's Institute. Changed name to Queens Park Rangers in 1887; joined the London League in 1896; and turned professional in 1898. Moved to the Southern League, 1899, and were twice champions.

Led a nomadic existence in West London but in 1917 took over the home of the amateurs Shepherds Bush, Loftus Road, where, apart from a couple of seasons at White City, it has stayed. Founder members of Football League Division Three in 1920 (this becoming Division Three (South) the following season); of Division Three at the end of regionalisation in 1958; and of the Premier League, 1992.

Ground:	Loftus Road, South Africa Road, W12 7PA
Phone:	0181-743 0262 **News:** 0891 12 11 62
Box Office:	0181-749 5744 **Info:** 0181-749 7798 (24Hrs)
Capacity:	19,300 **Pitch:** 112 yds x 72 yds
Colours:	Blue/White Hoops, White, White **Nickname:** Rangers or Rs

Chairman: Clive Berlin
Secretary: Sheila Marson
Manager: Ray Wilkins MBE   **Coach:** Frank Sibley
Physio: Brian Morris

League History: 1920 Original Member of Division 3; 1921 Division 3 (S); 1948-52 Division 2; 1952-58 Division 3 (S); 1958-67 Division 3; 1967-68 Division 2; 1968-69 Division 1; 1969-73 Division 2; 1973-79 Division 1; 1979-83 Division 2; 1983-92 Division 1; 1992 – FA Premier League.

Honours: *Football League: Division 1 Runners-up:* 1975-76; *Division 2 Champions:* 1982-83; *Runners-up:* 1967-68, 1972-73; *Division 3 (S) Champions:* 1947-48; *Runners-up:* 1946-47; *Division 3 Champions:* 1966-67; *FA Cup Runners-up:* 1982; *Football League Cup Winners:* 1966-67; *Runners-up:* 1985-86. (In 1966-67 won Division 3 and Football League Cup.)

European Record: CC (0): –; CWC (0): –; UEFA (2): 76-77(QF), 84-85(2).

Managers: James Cowan 1906-13; James Howie 1913-20; Ted Liddell 1920-24; Will Wood 1924-25 (had been secretary since 1903); Bob Hewison 1925-30; John Bowman 1930-31; Archie Mitchell 1931-33; Mick O'Brien 1933-35; Billy Birrell 1935-39; Ted Vizard 1939-44; Dave Mangnall 1944-52; Jack Taylor 1952-59; Alec Stock 1959-65 (GM to 1968); Jimmy Andrews 1965; Bill Dodgin Jnr 1968; Tommy Docherty 1968; Les Allen 1969-70; Gordon Jago 1971-74; Dave Sexton 1974-77; Frank Sibley 1977-78; Steve

Burtenshaw 1978-79; Tommy Docherty 1979-80; Terry Venables 1980-84; Gordon Jago 1984; Alan Mullery 1984; Frank Sibley 1984-85; Jim Smith 1985-88; Trevor Francis 1988-90; Don Howe 1990-91; *(FAPL)* Gerry Francis June 1991-Nov 1994; Ray Wilkins Nov 1994-.

Season 1995-96

Biggest Home Win: 3-0 v Southampton 30/3/96 and West Ham 27/4/96
Biggest Home Defeat: 0-3 v Sheffield Wednesday 9/9/95
Biggest Away Win: 3-1 v Leeds Ltd 16/9/95 and Sheff. Weds 17/2/96
Biggest Away Defeat: 2-4 v Aston Villa 9/3/96
Biggest Home Att: 18,827 v West Ham United 27/4/96
Smallest Home Att: 11,189 v Coventry City 19/12/95
Average Attendance: 15,672 (18th/20)
Leading Scorer: 10 – Daniel Dichio, 8 – Kevin Gallen
Last Season: *FAPL:* 19 *FA Cup:* 4 *Coca-Cola Cup:* 4

All-Time Records

Record FAPL Win: 5-1 v Coventry City 23/10/93
Record FAPL Defeat: 0-4 v Leeds Utd 4/4/94, Blackburn Rovers 26/11/94
Record FL Win: 9-2 v Tranmere R, Division 3, 3/12/1960
Record FL Defeat: 1-8 v Mansfield Town, Division 3, 15/3/1965;
Manchester United, Division 1, 19/3/1969
Record Cup Win: 8-1 v Bristol Rvrs (away), FA Cup R1, 27/11/1937;
Crewe Alexandra, Milk Cup R1, 3/10/1983
Record Fee Received: £6m from Newcastle for Les Ferdinand, 5/94
Record Fee Paid: £1.25m to B.Dortmund for Ned Zelic, 8/95
Most FL Apps: Tony Ingham, 519, 1950-63
Most FAPL Apps: 131 – David Bardsley
Most FAPL Goals: 60 – Les Ferdinand
Highest Scorer in FAPL Season: 24, Les Ferdinand, 1994-95
Record Attendance (all-time): 35,353 v Leeds U, Division 1, 27/4/1974
Record Attendance (FAPL): 21,267 v Manchester United, 5/2/94
Most FAPL Goals in Season: 63, 1992-93 – 42 games
Most FAPL Points in Season: 63, 1992-93 – 42 games

5-Year Record

	Div.	P	W	D	L	F	A	Pts	Pos	FAC	FLC
91-92	1	42	12	18	12	48	47	54	11	3	3
92-93	PL	42	17	12	13	63	55	63	5	4	4
93-94	PL	42	16	12	14	62	61	60	9	3	4
94-95	PL	42	17	9	16	61	59	60	8	QF	3
95-96	PL	38	9	6	23	38	57	33	19	4	4

Summary 1995-96

Player	Tot	St	Sb	Snu	PS	Gls	Y	R	Fa	La	Fg	Lg
ALLEN	8	5	3	1	3	1	3	0	2	0	0	0
BARDSLEY	29	28	1	1	3	0	6	1	1	2	0	0
BARKER	33	33	0	0	4	5	10	0	0	4	0	0
BRAZIER	11	6	5	5	1	0	0	0	1	2	0	0
BREVETT	27	27	0	0	2	1	7	0	0	3	0	0
CHALLIS	11	10	1	5	2	0	1	0	2	0	0	0
CHARLES	4	0	4	0	0	0	0	0	0	0	0	0
DICHIO	29	21	8	1	2	10	7	1	1	3	0	2
DYKSTRA	0	0	0	1	0	0	0	0	0	0	0	0
GALLEN	29	26	3	5	9	8	0	0	0	2	0	1
GOODRIDGE	7	0	7	3	0	1	1	0	1	1	0	0
HATELEY	14	10	4	1	4	2	1	0	2	1	0	0
HODGE	0	0	0	1	0	0	0	0	0	0	0	0
HOLLOWAY	27	26	1	1	1	1	5	0	1	2	0	0
IMPEY	29	28	1	1	5	3	2	1	2	4	0	1
MADDIX	22	20	2	2	1	0	5	0	2	3	0	0
McDERMOTT	0	0	0	0	0	0	0	0	0	0	0	0
McDONALD	26	25	1	1	2	1	8	0	1	3	0	0
MURRAY	1	1	0	0	0	0	0	0	0	0	0	0
OSBORN	9	6	3	6	3	1	0	0	0	2	0	0
PENRICE	3	0	3	0	0	0	1	0	0	0	0	0
PLUMMER	1	0	1	3	0	0	0	0	0	0	0	0
QUASHIE	11	11	0	0	4	0	1	0	2	0	2	0
READY	21	16	5	9	3	1	7	1	1	4	0	1
ROBERTS	5	5	0	3	0	0	0	0	0	4	0	0
SINCLAIR	37	37	0	0	2	2	4	0	2	3	1	1
SOMMER	33	33	0	0	0	0	1	0	2	0	0	0
WILKINS	15	11	4	6	6	0	0	0	1	3	0	0
YATES	30	30	0	0	1	0	3	0	1	2	0	0
ZELIC	4	3	1	0	0	0	1	0	0	0	0	0
					OG	1						

Ferdinand Goals Missed

Every player has his price as Queens Park Rangers supporters discovered during the close season when Les Ferdinand was sold to Newcastle for £6m. The club made a healthy profit but the loss on the pitch was severe as manager Ray Wilkins sought to fill the void created by Ferdinand's departure. Wilkins' attempts to strengthen a side which had not finished outside the top ten during the previous three seasons included the signing of Luton goalkeeper Jurgen Sommer for £600,000, Torquay striker Greg Goodridge for an initial fee of £100,000 and midfielder Ned Zelic for £1.25m but by March Zelic was on his way to Eintracht Frankfurt.

Rangers' start to the season was less than convincing, the opening two games were lost while a win over Manchester City on 26 August was one of just three victories from their opening 17 games. To increase the attacking options Wilkins invested £1.5m on injury prone former England striker Mark Hateley, which proved to be an unpopular signing with the Loftus Road faithful but the move did fire Danny Dichio into action with the local born striker notching six goals in four games. Unfortunately for him and Rangers, though, two of those games ended in defeat. A 1-0 defeat at West Ham on 25 November edged Rangers into the relegation zone for the first time. One point from two games heightened the prospect of relegation but wins in the run up to Christmas over Bolton and Villa improved Rangers' survival chances. But just as quickly as a lifeline was grabbed it slipped from Rangers' grasp as seven defeats in succession were inflicted on Wilkins and with a run of just one win in 13 games relegation became pretty much a certainty. Even so, Rangers were not without good performances at this time, especially even during defeat at Manchester United, and to ensure that his side were in peak condition to battle against the drop Wilkins put a halt to days off between games.

The search for a three point haul ended on 17 February with a 3-1 victory at Sheffield Wednesday which included Goodridge's only goal of the season but just one point from the next three games quickly destroyed the optimism encouraged by that success. With eight games to go it was still possible for Rangers to escape with so many sides in the dogfight but when an own goal seemed to have set up a win over Manchester United at Loftus Road it was Cantona who popped up with an injury time equaliser. Simon Barker's fifth and final league goal of the season – making him the third highest scorer behind Dichio (10) and Kevin Gallen (8) – secured another point off neighbours Chelsea while resounding home wins over Southampton 3-0, Everton 3-1 and West Ham 3-0 merely showed what might have been as the win over the Hammers came on the day Rangers' demotion was confirmed by results elsewhere.

Given that Rangers struggled all season at the wrong end of the table it was hardly surprising that their cup form was also less than inspired. In the FA Cup Tranmere were defeated in Round Three but on the day Nigel Quashie came to the nation's attention with a fabulous goal against Chelsea, a missed penalty by Bradley Allen saw Rangers exit the competition. Life was hardly any easier in the Coca Cola Cup. Following a 2nd Round 1st Leg draw at Oxford United Rangers needed an extra time goal from Gallen to settle the return in London. York City, conquerors of Manchester United the previous round, fell at Loftus Road on the 3rd Round but that is where Rangers' joy ended as Aston Villa moved through to the quarter final with a single goal victory at Villa Park. ∎

Results 1995-96

Date	Opponents	Ven	Res	Pos	Atten	Scorers
19-Aug	Blackburn R.	A	0-1	–	22,860	
23-Aug	Wimbledon	H	0-3	–	11,837	
26-Aug	Man. City.	H	1-0	–	14,212	Barker (31)
30-Aug	Liverpool	A	0-1	16	37,548	
09-Sep	Sheff. Wed.	H	0-3	18	12,459	
16-Sep	Leeds United	A	3-1	15	31,504	Dichio (15, 64); Sinclair (39)
25-Sep	Tottenham	A	2-3	15	15,659	Dichio (36); Impey (46)
30-Sep	Bolton Wan.	A	1-0	12	17,362	Dichio (89)
14-Oct	Newcastle U.	H	2-3	13	18,254	Dichio (43, 68)
21-Oct	Middlesbro'	A	0-1	16	29,293	
28-Oct	N Forest	H	1-1	14	17,549	Sinclair (76)
04-Nov	Southampton	A	0-2	15	15,137	
19-Dec	Coventry C.	H	1-1	16	11,189	Barker (37)
22-Nov	Everton	A	0-2	17	30,009	
25-Nov	West Ham	A	0-1	18	21,504	
02-Dec	Middlesbro'	H	1-1	18	17,546	McDonald (15)
09-Dec	Tottenham	A	0-1	18	28,851	
16-Dec	Bolton Wan.	H	2-1	16	11,456	Osborne (40); Impey (76)
23-Dec	Aston Villa	H	1-0	16	14,778	Gallen (54)
26-Dec	Arsenal	A	0-3	17	38,259	
30-Dec	Man. United	A	1-2	18	41,890	Dichio (68)
02-Jan	Chelsea	H	1-2	19	14,904	Allen (71)
13-Jan	Blackburn R.	H	0-1	19	13,957	
20-Jan	Wimbledon	A	1-2	19	9,123	Hateley (56)
03-Feb	Man. City	A	0-2	19	27,509	
11-Feb	Liverpool	H	1-2	19	18,405	Dichio (66)
17-Feb	Sheff. Wed.	A	3-1	19	22,442	Barker (33, 67); Goodridge (87)
02-Mar	Arsenal	H	1-1	19	17,970	Gallen (20)
06-Mar	Leeds United	H	1-2	19	13,991	Gallen (30)
09-Mar	Aston Villa	A	2-4	19	28,221	Dichio (50); Gallen (59)
16-Mar	Man. United	H	1-1	19	18,817	OG (Irwin 63)
23-Mar	Chelsea	A	1-1	20	25,590	Barker (20)
30-Mar	Southampton	H	3-0	18	17,615	Brevett (25); Dichio (61); Gallen (76)
06-Apr	Newcastle U.	A	1-2	19	36,583	Holloway (53)
08-Apr	Everton	H	3-1	18	18,349	Gallen (15); Hateley (42); Impey (61)
13-Apr	Coventry C.	A	0-1	19	22,910	
27-Apr	West Ham	H	3-0	19	18,828	Ready (60); Gallen (70, 79)
05-May	N. Forest	A	0-3	19	22,910	

FA Challenge Cup

Date	Opponents	Vn	Rnd	Res	Atten	Scorers
06-Jan	Tranmere R.	A	3R	2-0	10,230	Quaishie (55); Sinclair (59)
29-Jan	Chelsea	H	4R	1-2	18,542	Quaishie (67)

Coca-Cola League Cup

Date	Opponents	Vn	Rnd	Res	Atten	Scorers
19-Sep	Oxford Utd	A	2R1L	1-1	7,477	Dichio (15)
03-Oct	Oxford Utd	H	2R2L	2-1	9,207	Ready (70); Gallen (91)
	QPR won 3-2 on aggregate					
25-Oct	York City	H	3R	3-1	12,972	Sinclair (24); Impey (55); OG (Atkin, 65)
29-Nov	Aston Villa	A	4R	0-1	24,951	

Hoops – Premiership Fact File

- Simon Barker was the only QPR player to score in their opening five matches. The goal brought a win but QPR lost the other four.
- Only three wins from the first 17 games provided Rangers with their worst ever start to a Premiership season.
- When Rangers moved back into the relegation zone on Boxing Day following a home defeat by Arsenal they never recovered from a position in the bottom three.
- Rangers relegation was confirmed on the penultimate day of the season as results went against them. Ironically the day ended with a 3-0 win for the hoops over West Ham.

CLUBS IN EUROPE 95-96

UEFA Champions' League – Blackburn Rovers

Group B Matches

Blackburn Rovers	**Spartak Moscow** Yuran (71)	**0-1**	20,290
Rosenborg Loken (29), Stensaas (86)	**Blackburn Rovers** Newell (62)	**2-1**	12,000
Legia Warsaw Podbronzy (25)	**Blackburn Rovers**	**1-0**	15,000
Blackburn Rovers	**Legia Warsaw**	**0-0**	20,897
Spartak Moscow Alenitchev (28), Nikiforiv (47), Mamedov (54)	**Blackburn Rovers**	**3-0**	25,000
Blackburn Rovers Shearer (16), Newell (31, 37, 40)	**Rosenborg**	**4-0**	20,677

Final Group Table	P	W	D	L	F	A	Pts
Spartak Moscow	6	6	0	0	15	4	18
Legia Warsaw	6	2	1	3	5	8	7
Rosenborg	6	2	0	4	11	16	6
Blackburn	6	1	1	4	5	7	4

Cup-Winners' Cup – Everton

1st Round

KR Reykjavik Bibercic (36 pen, 67 pen)	**Everton** Ebbrell (22), Unsworth (57 pen), Amokachi (88)	**2-3**	**6,000**
Everton Stuart (56), Grant (65), Rideout (87)	**KR Reykjavik** Danielsson (20)	**3-1**	**18,422**

Everton win 6-3 on aggregate

2nd Round

Everton	**Feyenoord**	**0-0**	**27,526**
Feyenoord	**Everton** Blinker (39)	**1-0**	**40,000**

Feyenoord win 1-0 on aggregate

UEFA Cup – Manchester United, Liverpool, Nottingham Forest, Leeds United

1st Round

Rotor Volgograd   **Manchester United**   0-0   39,000
Sandell (71)

Manchester United   **Rotor Volgograd**   2-2   29,724
Scholes (59), Schmeichel (89)   Nidergaus (16), Veretennikov (24)

2-2 on aggregate. Roto Volgograd win on away goals

Malmo   **Nottingham Forest**   2-1   12,486
J.Persson (59), A.Andersson (71)   Woan (36)

Nottingham Forest   **Malmo**   1-0   23,817
Roy (69)

2-2 on aggregate, Nottingham Forest win on away goals

AS Monaco   **Leeds United**   0-3   15,000
   Yeboah (2, 65, 81)

Leeds United   **AS Monaco**   0-1   24,501
   Anderson (23)

Leeds United win 3-1 on aggregate

Spartak Vladikavkaz   **Liverpool**   1-2   38,000
Kasimov (21)   McManaman (33), Redknapp (52)

Liverpool   **Spartak Vladikavkaz**   0-0   35,042

Liverpool win 2-1 on aggregate

2nd Round

Auxerre   **Nottingham Forest**   0-1   20,000
   Stone (23)

Nottingham Forest   **Auxerre**   0-0   28,063

Nottingham Forest win 1-0 on aggregate

Brondby   **Liverpool**   0-0   37,648

Liverpool   **Brondby**   0-1   35,878
   Eggen (78)

Brondby win 1-0 on aggregate

Leeds United   **PSV Eindhoven**   3-5   24,846
Speed (5), Palmer (48), McAllister (72)   Eykelkamp (11), Vink (35), Jonk (39), Nilis (83, 88)

PSV Eindhoven   **Leeds United**   3-0   28,500
Cocu (11, 74), own goal (43)

PSV Eindhoven win 8-3 on aggregate

3rd Round
Nottingham Forest McGregor (83)	Lyon	1-0	22,141
Lyon	**Nottingham Forest**	0-0	38,500

Nottingham Forest win 1-0 on aggregate

4th Round
Bayern Munich Klinsmann (16), Scholl (45)	**Nottingham Forest** Chettle (17)	2-1	38,000
Nottingham Forest Stone (84)	**Bayern Munich** Ziege (29), Strunz (43), Klinsmann (64, 79), Papin (72)	1-5	28,844

Bayern Munich win 7-2 on aggregate

UEFA CHAMPIONS' LEAGUE 1995-96

Preliminary Round

		1st	2nd	Agg	
Anderlecht* (Belgium)	Ferencvaros (Hungary)	0-1	1-1	1-2	
Dynamo Kiev (Ukraine)	Aalborg * (Denmark)	1-0	3-1	4-1	dq
Grasshopper (Switzerland) *	Maccabi Tel Aviv (Israel)	1-1	1-0	2-1	
Legia Warsaw (Poland)	IFK Gothenborg* (Sweden)	1-0	2-1	3-1	
Panathaniakos* (Greece)	Hajduk Split (Croatia)	0-0	1-1	1-1	a1
Rangers (Scotland) *	Famagusta (Cyprus)	1-0	0-0	1-0	
Rosenborg (Norway)	Besiktas* (Turkey)	3-0	1-3	4-3	
Salzburg (Austria)*	Steaua Bucharest (Romania)	0-0	0-1	0-1	

* = seeded team. a1=1st team win on away goals rule. dq = Kiev disqualified.

First Round

QUALIFIERS
Seeded Teams: Ajax (Holland), Blackburn Rovers (England), Borussia Dortmund (Germany), Juventus (Italy), Nantes (France), FC Porto (Portugal), Real Madrid (Spain) Spartak Moscow (Russia).

Prelimiary Qualifiers: Panathaniakos (Greece), Ferencvaros (Hungary), Rosenborg (Norway), Aalborg (Denmark), Steaua Bucharest (Romania), Legia Warsaw (Poland), Rangers (Scotland), Grasshopper (Switzerland).

GROUP A

Nantes	FC Porto	0-0	FC Porto	Nantes	2-2
Panathinaikos	Nantes	3-1	Aalborg	FC Porto	2-2
FC Porto	Aalborg	2-0	FC Nantes	Panathinaikos	0-0
Nantes	Aalborg	3-1			
FC Porto	Panathinaikos	0-1			
Aalborg	Panathinaikos	2-1			
Panathinaikos	FC Porto	0-0			
Aalborg	Nantes	0-2			
Panathinaikos	Aalborg	2-0			

	W	D	L	F	A	Pt
Panathinaikos	3	1	2	7	3	11
Nantes	2	1	3	8	6	9
FC Porto	1	1	4	6	5	7
Aalborg	1	4	1	5	12	4

GROUP B

Legia Warsaw	Rosenborg	3-1	Rosenborg	Legia Warsaw	4-0
Blackburn Rvrs	Spartak Moscow	0-1	Blackburn Rvrs	Rosenborg	4-1
Spartak Moscow	Legia Warsaw	2-1	Legia Warsaw	Spartak Moscow	0-1
Rosenborg	Blackburn Rvrs	2-1			
Legia Warsaw	Blackburn Rvrs	1-0			
Rosenborg	Spartak Moscow	2-4			
Spartak Moscow	Rosenborg	4-1			
Blackburn Rvrs	Legia Warsaw	0-0			
Spartak Moscow	Blackburn Rvrs	3-0			

	W	D	L	F	A	Pts
Spartak Moscow	6	0	0	15	4	18
Legia Warsaw	2	3	1	5	8	7
Rosenborg	2	4	0	11	16	6
Blackburn Rvrs	1	4	1	5	8	4

GROUP C

Bor. Dortmund	Juventus	1-3	Juventus	Bor. Dortmund	1-2
Steaua Bucharest	Rangers	1-0	Bor. Dortmund	Rangers	2-2
Rangers	Bor. Dortmund	2-2	Steaua Bucharest	Juventus	0-0
Juventus	Steaua Bucharest	3-0			
Bor. Dortmund	Steaua Bucharest	1-0			
Juventus	Rangers	4-1			
Rangers	Juventus	0-4			
Steaua Bucharest	Bor. Dortmund	0-0			
Rangers	Steaua Bucharest	1-1			

	W	D	L	F	A	Pt
Juventus	4	1	1	15	4	13
Bor. Dortmund	2	1	3	8	8	9
Steaua Bucharest	1	2	3	2	5	6
Rangers	0	3	3	6	14	3

GROUP D

Ajax	Real Madrid	1-0	Real Madrid	Ajax Amsterdam	0-2
Grasshopper	Ferencvaros	0-3	Ajax	Ferencvaros	4-0
Ferencvaros	Ajax	1-5	Grasshopper	Real Madrid	0-2
Real Madrid	Grasshopper	2-0			
Ajax	Grasshopper	3-0			
Real Madrid	Ferencvaros	6-1			
Ferencvaros	Real Madrid	1-1			
Grasshopper	Ajax	0-0			
Ferencvaros	Grasshopper	3-3			

	W	D	L	F	A	Pt
Ajax	5	0	1	15	1	16
Real Madrid	3	2	1	11	5	10
Ferencvaros	1	3	2	9	19	5
Grasshopper	0	4	2	3	13	2

Quarter Finals

		1st	2nd	Agg
Borussia Dortmund	Ajax	0-2	0-1	0-3
Legia Warsaw	Panathinaikos	0-0	0-3	0-3

		1st	2nd	Agg
Nantes	Spartak Moscow	2-0	2-2	4-2
Real Madrid	Juventus	1-0	0-2	2-1

Semi Finals

		1st	2nd	Agg
Ajax	Panathinaikos	0-1	3-0	3-1
Juventus	Nantes	2-0	2-2	4-2

Final

Wednesday, May 22 at the Olympic Stadium in Rome

Ajax	Juventus	1-1
Litmanen (41)	Ravenelli (13)	67,000

After extra time. Juventus won 4-2 on penalties.

CUP-WINNERS' CUP
1995-96

Preliminary Round

		1st	2nd	Agg	
CS Grevenmacher (Luxem.)	Reykjavik (Iceland)	3-2	0-2	3-4	
Dag-Liepaja (Latvia)	FC Lantana (Estonia)	3-0	0-0	3-0	
Dynamo Minsk (Belarus)	Molde FK (Norway)	1-1	1-2	2-3	
FC Vaduz (Liechtenstein)	Hradec Kralove (Czech)	0-5	1-9	1-14	
Hapoel Nicosia (Cyprus)	Nefski Baku (Azerbaijan)	3-0	0-0	3-0	
Katowice (Poland)	Ararat Yerevan (Armenia)	2-0	0-2	2-2	4-5
Lokomotiv Sofia (Bulgaria)	Derry City (Ireland)	0-1	2-0	2-1	
Maccabi Haifa (Israel)	Klakkxvikar (Faeroe Is.)	4-0	2-3	6-3	
Obilic (Yugoslavia)	Dynamo Batumi (Georgia)	0-1	2-2	2-3	
Shakytyor (Ukraine)	Linfield (Northern Ireland)	4-1	1-0	5-1	
Tiligul Tiraspol (Moldavia)	Sion (Switzerland)	0-0	2-3	2-3	
Turku (Finland)	FC Teuta (Albania)	1-0	0-3	1-3	
VAC Samsung (Hungary)	FC Sileks (Macedonia)	1-1	1-3	2-4	
Valetta (Malta)	Inter Bratislava (Slovakia)	0-0	2-5	2-5	
Wrexham (Wales)	Petrolul Ploiesti (Romania)	0-0	0-1	0-1	
Zalgiris Vilnius (Lithuania)	NK Mura (Slovenia)	2-0	1-2	3-2	

First Round

		1st	2nd	Agg
AEK Athens (Greece)	Sion (Switzerland)	2-0	2-2	4-2
B. Moenchengladbach (Ger.)	Sileks (Macedonia)	3-0	3-2	6-2
Deportivo de la Coruna (Spain)	Apoel Nicosia (Cyprus)	0-0	8-0	8-0
Dynamo Batumi (Georgia)	Celtic (Scotland)	2-3	0-4	2-7
Dynamo Moscow (Russia)	Ararat Yerevan (Armenia)	3-1	1-0	4-1
FC Bruges (Belgium)	Shakhtyor (Ukraine)	1-0	1-1	2-1
Hradec Kralove (Czech Rep)	Copenhagen (Denmark)	5-0	2-2	7-2
Inter Bratislava (Slovakia)	Real Zaragoza (Spain)	0-2	1-3	1-5

Liepaga (Latvia)	Feyenoord (Netherlands)	0-7	0-6	0-13	
Lokomotiv Sofia (Bulgaria)	Halmstads (Sweden)	3-1	0-2	3-3	2a
Molde (Norway)	Paris-St. Germain (France)	2-3	0-3	2-6	
Rapid Vienna (Austria)	Petrolul Ploiesti (Romania)	3-1	0-0	3-1	
Reykjavik (Iceland)	Everton (England)	3-2	1-3	3-6	
Sporting Lisbon (Portugal)	Maccabi Haifa (Israel)	4-0	0-0	4-0	
Teuta (Albania)	Parma (Italy)	0-2	0-2	0-4	
Zalgiris Vilnius (Lithuania)	Trabzonspor (Turkey)	2-2	0-1	2-3	

Second Round

		1st	2nd	Agg	
B. Moenchengladbach (Ger)	AEK Athens (Greece)	4-1	1-0	5-1	
Dynamo Moscow (Russia)	Hradec Kralove (Czech Rep)	1-0	0-1	1-1	3-1
Everton (England)	Feyenoord (Netherlands)	0-0	0-1	0-1	
Halmstads (Sweden)	Parma (Italy)	3-0	0-4	3-4	
Paris-St. Germain (France)	Celtic (Scotland)	1-0	3-0	4-0	
Real Zaragoza (Spain)	FC Bruges (Belgium)	2-1	1-0	3-1	
Sporting Lisbon (Portugal)	Rapid Vienna (Austria)	2-0	0-4	2-4	
Trabzonspor (Turkey)	Deportivo de la Coruna (Spa)	0-1	0-3	0-4	

Quarter Finals

		1st	2nd	Agg
Dynamo Moscow (Russia)	Rapid Vienna (Austria)	0-1	0-3	0-4
Parma AC (Italy)	Paris-St. Germain (France)	1-0	1-3	2-3
Deportivo de la Coruna (Spain)	Real Zaragoza (Spain)	1-0	1-1	2-1
B. Moenchengladbach (Ger)	Feyenoord (Netherlands)	2-2	0-1	2-3

Semi Finals

		1st	2nd	Agg
Feyenoord (Netherlands)	Rapid Vienna (Austria)	1-1	0-3	1-4
Deportivo de La Coruna (Spain)	Paris-St. Germain (France)	0-1	0-1	0-2

Final *Wednesday, May 8 at King Baudouin Stadium in Brussels.*

Paris St. Germain	Rapid Vienna	1-0
N'Gotty (29)		37,500

UEFA CUP 1995-96

Preliminary Round

		1st	2nd	Agg.	
Afan Lido (Wales)	RAF Riga (Latvia)	1-2	0-0	1-2	
Apollon Athens (Greece)	Olimpija Ljubljana (Slovenia)	1-0	1-3	3-2	
Bangor City (Wales)	Widzew Lodz (Poland)	0-4	0-1	0-5	
Botev Plovdiv (Bulgaria)	Dynamo Tbilisi (Georgia)	1-0	1-0	2-0	
Brondby (Denmark)	Inkaras-Grifas (Lithuania)	3-0	3-0	6-0	
Crusaders (Northern Ireland)	Silkeborg (Denmark)	1-2	1-4	2-4	
Dundalk (Ireland)	Malmo (Sweden)	0-2	0-2	0-4	
FC Kosice (Slovakia)	Ujpest Egylet (Hungary)	0-1	1-2	1-3	
FC Tirana (Albania)	Hapoel Beer Cheva (Israel)	0-1	0-2	0-3	
Fenerbahce (Turkey)	FC Partizan (Albania)	2-0	4-0	6-0	
Bordeaux (France)	Karlsruhe SC (Germany)	2-0	2-2	4-2	*
Glenavon (Northern Ireland)	FC Hafnarfjordur (Iceland)	0-0	1-0	1-0	
Hibernians FC (Malta)	Chernomorets (Ukraine)	2-5	0-2	2-7	
Jeunesse d'Esch (Luxembourg)	FC Lugano (Switzerland)	0-0	0-4	0-4	
Kapaz Ganja (Azerbaijan)	Austria Memphis (Austria)	0-4	1-5	1-9	
Levski Sofia (Bulgaria)	Dynamo Bucharest (Romania)	1-0	1-1	2-1	
Lillestroem (Nor)	Flora Tallinn (Estonia)	4-0	0-1	4-1	
Motherwell (Scotland)	MyPa-47 (Finland)	1-3	2-0	3-3	2a
Omonia Nicosia (Cyprus)	Sliema Wanderers (Malta)	3-0	2-1	5-1	
Orebro SK (Sweden)	Beggen (Luxembourg)	0-0	1-1	1-1	1a
Raith Rovers (Scotland)	Gotu Itrottarfelag (Faeroe Is)	4-0	2-2	6-2	
Red Star Belgrade (Yugoslavia)	Neuchatel Xamax (Switz.)	0-1	0-0	0-1	
Shelbourne (Ireland)	Akranes (Iceland)	0-3	0-3	0-6	
Skonto Riga (Latvia)	Branik Maribor (Slovenia)	1-0	1-2	1-2	
Slavia Sofia (Bulgaria)	Olympiakos (Greece)	0-2	0-1	0-3	
Slovan Bratislava (Slovakia)	NK Osijek (Croatia)	4-0	2-0	6-0	
Sparta Prague (Czech)	Galatasaray (Turkey)	3-1	1-1	4-1	
Sturm Graz (Austria)	Slavia Prague (Czech Rep)	0-1	1-1	1-2	
Tampere (Finland)	Viking Stavangar (Norway)	0-4	1-3	1-7	
Tirol Innsbruck (Austria)	RC Strasbourg (France)	1-1	6-1	7-2	*
Universitatea Craiova (Romania)	Dynamo Minsk (Belarus)	0-0	1-3	1-3	
Varda (Macedonia)	Samtredia (Georgia)	1-0	2-0	3-0	
Zaglebie Lubin (Poland)	Shirak Erevan (Armenia)	0-0	1-0	1-0	

*= The four clubs indicated by the two ties marked * were also playing off the InterToto Cup Semi Finals. The last four teams in the competition automatically gained entry into the Preliminary Round of the UEFA Cup.*

Scores in final column indicate penalty kick results.

1a = 1st team won on away goals rule. 2a = 2nd team won on away goals rule.

First Round

		1st	2nd	Agg	
AS Monaco	Leeds United (England)	0-3	1-0	1-3	
Avenir Beggen (Luxembourg)	Lens (France)	0-6	0-7	0-13	
Bayern Munich (Germany)	Lokomotiv Moscow (Russia)	0-1	5-0	5-1	
Brondby IF (Denmark)	Lillestroem (Norway)	3-0	0-0	3-0	
Chernomorets (Ukraine)	Widzew Lodz (Poland)	1-0	0-1	1-1	6-5
Farense (Portugal)	Olympique Lyon (France)	0-1	0-1	0-2	
FC Memphis (Austria)	Dynamo Minsk (Belarus)	1-2	0-1	1-3	
Fenerbahce (Turkey)	Real Betis (Spain)	1-2	0-2	1-4	
Freiburg (Germany)	Slavia Prague (Czech Rep)	1-2	0-0	1-2	
Glenavon (Northern Ireland)	Werder Bremen (Germany)	0-2	0-5	0-7	
Hapoel Beer Sheba (Israel)	Barcelona (Spain)	0-7	0-5	0-12	
Lazio (Italy)	Omonia Nicosia (Cyprus)	5-0	2-1	7-1	
Levski Sofia (Bulgaria)	Eendracht Aalst (Belgium)	1-2	0-1	1-3	
Lierse (Belgium)	Benfica (Portugal)	1-3	1-2	1-5	
Lugano (Switzerland)	Internazionale (Italy)	1-1	0-1	2-1	
Malmo FF (Sweden)	Nottingham Forest (England)	2-1	0-1	1-1	2a
Milan (Italy)	Zaglebie Lubin (Poland)	4-0	4-1	8-1	
MyPa-47 (Finland)	PSV Eindhoven (Netherlands)	1-1	1-7	2-8	
Neuchatel Xamax (Switzerland)	AS Roma (Italy)	1-1	0-4	1-5	
Olympiakos (Greece)	Maribor Branik (Slovenia)	2-0	3-1	5-1	
Raith Rovers (Scotland)	FC Akranes (Iceland)	3-1	0-1	3-2	
Roda JC (Netherlands)	Olimpija Ljubljana (Slovenia)	5-0	0-2	5-2	
Rotor Volgograd (Russia)	Manchester United (England)	0-0	2-2	2-2	1a
Sevilla (Spain)	Botev Plovdiv (Bulgaria)	2-0	1-1	3-1	
Slovan Bratislava (Slovakia)	Kaiserslautern (Germany)	2-1	0-3	2-4	
Sparta Prague (Czech Republic)	Silkeborg IF (Denmark)	0-1	2-1	2-2	1a
Spartak Vladikavkaz (Russia)	Liverpool (England)	1-2	0-0	1-2	
Strasbourg (France)	Ujpest Egylet (Hungary)	3-0	2-0	5-0	
Vardar (Macedonia)	Bordeaux (France)	0-2	1-1	1-3	
Viking Stavanger (Norway)	Auxerre (France)	1-1	0-1	1-2	
Vitoria Guimaraes (Portugal)	Standard Liege (Belgium)	3-1	0-0	3-1	
Zimbru Chisinau (Moldova)	Riga (Latvia)	1-0	2-1	3-1	

Second Round

		1st	2nd	Agg
AS Roma (Italy)	Eendracht Aalst (Belgium)	4-0	0-0	4-0
Auxerre (France)	Nottingham Forest (England)	0-1	0-0	0-1
Barcelona (Spain)	Vitoria Guimaraes (Portugal)	3-0	4-0	7-0
Benfica (Portugal)	Roda JC (Netherlands)	1-0	2-2	3-2
Bordeaux (France)	Rotor Volgograd (Russia)	2-1	1-0	3-1
Brondby IF (Denmark)	Liverpool (England)	0-0	1-0	1-0
Chernomorets (Ukraine)	Lens (France)	0-0	0-4	0-4
Kaiserslautern (Germany)	Real Betis (Spain)	1-3	0-1	1-4
Leeds United (England)	PSV Eindhoven (Netherlands)	3-5	0-3	3-8
Lugano (Switzerland)	Slavia Prague (Czech Rep)	1-2	0-1	1-3
Olympique Lyon (France)	Lazio (Italy)	2-1	2-0	4-1
Raith Rovers (Scotland)	Bayern Munich (Germany)	0-2	1-2	1-4

Sevilla (Spain)	Olympiakos (Greece)	1-0	1-2	2-2	1a
Sparta Prague (Czech Republic)	Zimbru Chisinau (Moldova)	4-3	2-0	6-3	
Strasbourg (France)	Milan (Italy)	0-1	1-2	1-3	
Werder Bremen (Germany)	Dynamo Minsk (Belarus)	5-0	1-2	6-2	

Third Round

		1st	*2nd*	*Agg*
Bayern Munich (Germany)	Benfica (Portugal)	4-1	3-1	7-2
Bordeaux (France)	Real Betis (Spain)	2-0	1-2	3-2
Brondby IF (Denmark)	AS Roma (Italy)	2-1	1-3	3-4
PSV Eindhoven (Netherlands)	Werder Bremen (Germany)	2-1	0-0	2-1
Sevilla (Spain)	Barcelona (Spain)	1-1	1-3	2-4
Slavia Prague (Czech Republic)	Lens (France)	0-0	1-0	1-0
Milan (Italy)	Sparta Prague (Czech Rep)	2-0	0-0	2-0
Nottingham Forest (England)	Olympique Lyon (France)	1-0	0-0	1-0

Quarter Finals

Barcelona (Spain)	PSV Eindhoven (Netherlands)	2-2	3-2	5-4	
Bayern Munich (Germany)	Nottingham Forest (England)	2-1	5-1	7-2	
Milan (Italy)	Bordeaux (France)	2-0	0-3	2-3	
Slavia Prague (Czech Rep)	AS Roma (Italy)	2-0	1-3	3-3	1a

Semi Finals

| Slavia Prague (Czech Republic) | Bordeaux (France) | 0-1 | 0-1 | 0-2 |
| Bayern Munich (Germany) | Barcelona (Spain | 2-2 | 2-1 | 4-3 |

Final

1st Leg – Wednesday, May 1 1996

Bayern Munich   Bordeaux   2-0

Helmer (35), Scholl (60)   38,323

2nd Leg – Wednesday, May 15 1996

Bordeaux   Bayern Munich   1-3

Dutuel (75)   Scholl (53), Kostadinov (66), Klinsmann (77)

Bayern Munich win 5-1 on aggregate.

Jurgen Klinsmann's goal in the 2nd leg of the final was his 15th of the season in the competition and set a new record.

FA PREMIER LEAGUE CLUB TRANSFERS 1995-96

Player	From	To	Fee
Nick Barmby	Tottenham Hotspur	Middlesbrough	£5,250,000
Andrei Kanchelskis	Manchester United	Everton	£5,000,000
Kevin Campbell	Arsenal	Nottingham Forest	£2,500,000
			(Rising to £3,000,000)
Georgi Kinkladze	Dinamo Tblisi	Manchester City	£2,000,000
Shaka Hislop	Reading	Newcastle United	£1,575,000
Gerry Taggart	Barnsley	Bolton Wanderers	£1,500,000
John Salako	Crystal Palace	Coventry City	£1,500,000
			(Rising to £3,000,000)
Ned Zelic	B Dortmund	QPR	£1,250,000
Kit Symons	Portsmouth	Manchester City	£1,200,000
			(Plus player in swap)
Igor Cvitanovic	Croatia '93	Middlesbrough	£1,000,000
Paul Williams	Derby County	Coventry City	£750,000
			(Plus player in swap)
Matt Holmes	West Ham United	Blackburn Rovers	£600,000
			(Plus player in swap)
Robbie Slater	Blackburn Rovers	West Ham United	£600,000
			(Player value in swap)
Jurgen Sommer	Luton Town	QPR	£600,000
Shaun Teale	Aston Villa	Tranmere Rovers	£500,000
Eike Immel	Stuttgart	Manchester City	£400,000
Matt Rush	West Ham United	Norwich City	£330,000
			(Rising to £500,000)
Stan Laziridis	West Adelaide	West Ham United	£300,000
Paul Beesley	Sheffield United	Leeds United	£250,000
Andy Todd	Middlesbrough	Bolton Wanderers	£250,000
Gary Walsh	Manchester United	Middlesbrough	£250,000
Sean Flynn	Coventry City	Derby County	£225,000
Adam Reed	Darlington	Blackburn Rovers	£200,000
Carl Griffiths	Manchester City	Portsmouth	£200,000
			(Player value in swap)
Fitzroy Simpson	Manchester City	Portsmouth	£200,000
			(Player value in swap)
Greg Goodridge	Torquay United	QPR	£100,000
			(Rising to £350,000)

David Eatock	Chorley	Newcastle United	£75,000
			(Rising to £300,000)
Lee Charles	Chertsey	QPR	£67,500
Ade Mike	Manchester City	Stockport County	£60,000
Paul Williams	Coventry City	Plymouth Argyle	£50,000
Steve Anthrobus	Wimbledon	Shrewsbury Town	£25,000
Dennis Bailey	QPR	Gillingham	£25,000
Andy Hill	Manchester City	Port Vale	Tribunal
Alan McCarthy	QPR	Leyton Orient	Unknown
Andy McDermot	IOW, Australia	QPR	Unknown
Greg Strong	Wigan Athletic	Bolton Wanderers	Unknown
Gary Bowyer	Nottingham Forest	Rotherham United	Free
Marvin Bryan	QPR	Blackpool	Free
John Burridge	Manchester City	Notts County	Free
Tony Carrs	Blackburn Rovers	Darlington	Free
Brian Croft	QPR	Torquay United	Free
Martin Davies	Coventry City	Cambridge United	Free
Robert Evans	Bolton Wanderers	Morecambe	Free
David Johnson	Manchester United	Bury	Free
Trevor Morley	West Ham United	Reading	Free
Nathan Murray	Newcastle United	Carlisle United	Free
Steve Pears	Middlesbrough	Liverpool	Free
Steve Reeves	Everton	Chelsea	Free

September 1995

Player	From	To	Fee
Jason McAteer	Bolton Wanderers	Liverpool	£4,500,000
Gerry Creaney	Portsmouth	Manchester City	£1,500,000
		(Including Paul Walsh valued at £500,000)	
Mark Hateley	Rangers	QPR	£1,000,000
Mark Atkins	Blackburn Rovers	Wolverhampton Wan	£1,000,000
Steve McAnespie	Raith Rovers	Bolton Wanderers	£900,000
Robert Fleck	Chelsea	Norwich City	£650,000
Paul Walsh	Manchester City	Portsmouth	£500,000
(Value in swap deal taking Gerry Creaney to Manchester City)			
Jeroen Boere	West Ham United	Crystal Palace	£375,000
		(Swap deal. Iain Dowie £125,000 plus Boere)	
Nick Culkin	York City	Manchester United	£200,000
Andy Hill	Manchester City	Port Vale	£150,000
Nil Lamptey	Anderlecht	Coventry City	£150,000
		(May rise to £450,000)	
John Williams	Coventry City	Wycombe Wanderers	£150,000
Iain Dowie	Crystal Palace	West Ham United	£125,000
(Value in swap deal that took Jeroen Boere to Crystal Palace)			

David Farrell	Aston Villa	Wycombe Wanderers	£100,000
Stuart Whitehead	Bromsgrove	Bolton Wanderers	Undisclosed
Mark Taylor	Middlesbrough	Fulham	Non-contract
Sonet Zumluta	Arsenal	Cambridge	Non-contract
Tony Brown	West Ham United	Dagenham & Redbridge	Free
Paul Davis	Arsenal	Brentford	Free
Darren Evans	Aston Villa	Hereford United	Free
Tony Gale	Blackburn Rovers	Crystal Palace	Free
Richard Flash	Manchester United	Wolverhampton Wan	Free
Paul Lyons	Manchester United	Rochdale	Free

October 1995

Player	*From*	*To*	*Fee*
Juninho	Sao Paulo (Brazil)	Middlesbrough	£4,750,000
Ruel Fox	Newcastle United	Tottenham Hotspur	£4,200,000
Darko Kovacevic	Red Star Belgrade	Sheffield Weds	£2,000,000
Dejan Stefanovic	Red Star Belgrade	Sheffield Weds	£2,000,000
Billy McKinlay	Dundee United	Blackburn Rovers	£1,750,000
Sasa Curcic	Partizan Belgrade	Bolton Wanderers	£1,500,000
Graham Fenton	Aston Villa	Blackburn Rovers	£1,500,000
Richard Jobson	Oldham Athletic	Leeds United	£1,000,000
Barry Venison	Galatasaray	Southampton	£850,000
Carl Tiler	Nottingham Forest	Aston Villa	£750,000
Lars Bohinen	Nottingham Forest	Blackburn Rovers	£700,000
Owen Coyle	Bolton Wanderers	Dundee United	£400,000
Lee Makel	Blackburn Rovers	Huddersfield Town	£300,000
Graham Coughlan	Bray Wanderers	Blackburn Rovers	£100,000
John Hills	Blackpool	Everton	£90,000
		(May rise to £500,000)	
Darren Barnard	Chelsea	Bristol City	£75,000
		(May rise to £150,000)	
Peter Whiston	Southampton	Exeter City	£50,000
Nathan Lowndes	Leeds United	Watford	£40,000
Trevor Berry	Aston Villa	Rotherham United	£20,000
Sam Shilton	Plymouth Argyle	Coventry City	£12,500
Lee Sharp	Lincoln United	QPR	Unknown
Paul Allen	Southampton	Swindon Town	Free
Cobi Jones	Coventry City	At Rentistas	Free
Craig Norman	Chelsea	Kettering Town	Free
Brian Croft	QPR	Stockport County	Non contract

November 1995

Player	From	To	Fee
Tomas Brolin	Parma	Leeds United	£4,500,000
Dan Petrescu	Sheffield Wednesday	Chelsea	£2,300,000
Klas Ingesson	Sheffield Wednesday	Bari	£900,000
Terry Phelan	Manchester City	Chelsea	£900,000
Richard Shaw	Crystal Palace	Coventry City	£650,000
		(Plus £350,000 after 40 apps)	
Andy Pearce	Sheffield Wednesday	Wimbledon	£600,000
Darren Huckerby	Lincoln City	Newcastle United	£500,000
Martin Phillips	Exeter City	Manchester City	£500,000
Stuart Barlow	Everton	Oldham Athletic	£350,000
		(May rise to £450,000)	
Gary Penrice	QPR	Watford	£300,000
Julian Darby	Coventry City	WBA	£200,000
Frank Talia	Blackburn Rovers	Swindon Town	£150,000
Kevin Sharp	Leeds United	Wigan Athletic	£100,000
Tony Grant	Leeds United	Preston North End	Free
Mark Humphries	Leeds United	Bristol City	Free
Jerome John	West Ham United	Leyton Orient	Free
Steve Nicol	Notts County	Sheffield Wednesday	Free
Micky Hazard	Tottenham Hotspur	Hitchin Town	Non contract
Chris Moors	West Ham United	Torquay United	Non contract

December 1995

Player	From	To	Fee
Chris Coleman	Crystal Palace	Blackburn Rovers	£2,800,000
Noel Whelan	Leeds United	Coventry City	£2,000,000
Slaven Bilic	Karlsruhe	West Ham United	£1,300,000
Nathan Blake	Sheffield United	Bolton Wanderers	£1,200,000
		(Including Mark Patterson in swap valued at £300,000)	
Simon Osborn	QPR	Wolverhampton Wands	£1,000,000
Scott Sellars	Newcastle United	Bolton Wanderers	£750,000
Ian Feuer	West Ham United	Luton Town	£580,000
Michael Vonk	Manchester City	Sheffield United	£350,000
Mark Patterson	Bolton Wanderers	Sheffield United	£300,000
		(Player value in swap with Blake)	
Neil Moss	Bournemouth	Southampton	£250,000
Wayne Burnett	Plymouth Argyle	Bolton Wanderers	£100,000
Paul Evans	Witts University	Leeds United	£50,000
		(May rise to £750,000)	
David Brightwell	Manchester City	Bradford City	£30,000
Leigh Jenkinson	Coventry City	St Johnstone	Unknown

Gary Bull	Nottingham Forest	Birmingham City	Free
Steve Hodge	QPR	Watford	Free
Graham Pepper	Newcastle United	Darlington	Free
Simon Webster	West Ham United	St Albans City	Free
Richard Fidler	Leeds United	Hull City	Non contract

January 1996

Player	From	To	Fee
Ilie Dumitrescu	Tottenham Hotspur	West Ham United	£1,650,000
Nigel Clough	Liverpool	Manchester City	£1,500,000
Andy Sinton	Sheffield Wednesday	Tottenham Hotspur	£1,500,000
Don Hutchison	West Ham United	Sheffield United	£1,200,000
Marc Hottiger	Newcastle United	Everton	£700,000
Tony Coton	Manchester City	Manchester United	£500,000
David White	Leeds United	Sheffield United	£500,000
Michael Frontzeck	B Moenchengladbach	Manchester City	£350,000
Gareth Hall	Chelsea	Sunderland	£300,000
Alan Fettis	Hull City	Nottingham Forest	£250,000
			(Could rise to £400,000)
Graeme Philson	Coleraine	West Ham United	£30,000
Chris Coyne	Australian IOS	West Ham United	£20,000
Nigel Spink	Aston Villa	WBA	Free
Mark Walters	Liverpool	Southampton	Free
Peter Shilton	Coventry City	West Ham United	Non-contract

February 1996

Player	From	To	Fee
Faustino Asprilla	Parma	Newcastle United	£6,700,000
David Batty	Blackburn Rovers	Newcastle United	£3,750,000
Eoin Jess	Aberdeen	Coventry City	£1,750,000
Liam Daish	Birmingham City	Coventry City	£1,500,000
Julian Joachim	Leicester City	Aston Villa	£1,500,000
Darren Caskey	Tottenham Hotspur	Reading	£700,000
Martin Allen	West Ham United	Portsmouth	£500,000
Darren Holmes	Everton	West Bromwich Albion	£80,000
Darren Currie	West Ham United	Shrewsbury Town	£70,000
Branco	Internacional	Middlesbrough	Free
Jamie Marks	Leeds United	Hull City	Free
Jan Molby	Liverpool	Swansea Town	Free
Paul Wharton	Leeds United	Hull City	Free

March 1996

Player	From	To	Fee
Garry Flitcroft	Manchester City	Blackburn Rovers	£3,200,000
Jon Newsome	Norwich City	Sheffield Wednesday	£1,600,000
Mikhail Kavelashvili	Sp Vladikavkaz	Manchester City	£1,400,000
Gary Croft	Grimsby Town	Blackburn Rovers	£1,000,000
			(Rising to £1,700,000)
Ned Zelic	QPR	Eintracht Frankfurt	£750,000
			(Rising to £1,000,000)
Niklas Gudmundsson	Halmstads	Blackburn Rovers	£750,000
Bradley Allen	QPR	Charlton Athletic	£400,000
Richard Sneekes	Bolton Wanderers	West Bromwich Albion	£400,000
Gavin Ward	Bradford City	Bolton Wanderers	£300,000
	(Plus a further £100,000 if Bolton avoided relegation)		
Regi Blinker	Feyenoord	Sheffield Wednesday	£275,000
Paul Cook	Coventry City	Tranmere Rovers	£250,000
Scott Hiley	Birmingham City	Manchester City	£250,000
Scott Taylor	Millwall	Bolton Wanderers	£150,000
Steve Cowe	Aston Villa	Swindon Town	£100,000
Steve Mautone	Canberra Cosmos	West Ham United	£30,000
Julian Watts	Sheffield Wednesday	Leicester City	Tribunal
Paul Pettinger	Leeds United	Gillingham	Free
Paul Mitchell	West Ham United	Bournemouth	Free
Terry Skiverton	Chelsea	Wycombe Wanderers	Free
Bryan Small	Aston Villa	Bolton Wanderers	Free
Paul Stewart	Liverpool	Sunderland	Free
Jonathon Sunderland	Blackpool	Scarborough	Free
Simon Wood	Coventry City	Mansfield Town	Free
Enzo Gambaro	Bolton Wanderers	Grimsby Town	Non-contract

Close Season 1996

Player	From	To	Fee
Fabrizio Ravanelli	Juventus	Middlesbrough	£7,000,000
Robert Di Matteo	Lazio	Chelsea	£4,900,000
Emerson	FC Porto	Middlesbrough	£4,000,000
Gary Speed	Leeds United	Everton	£3,500,000
Lee Bowyer	Charlton Athletic	Leeds United	£3,000,000
Andy Booth	Huddersfield Town	Sheffield Wednesday	£2,700,000
Darko Kovacevic	Sheffield Wednesday	Real Sociedad	£2,600,000
Florin Raducioiu	Espanol	West Ham United	£2,400,000
Mark Degryse	Sheffield Wednesday	PSV Eindhoven	£1,800,000
Franck Leboeuf	Strasbourg	Chelsea	£2,500,000
Ben Thatcher	Millwall	Wimbledon	£1,900,000

Dean Saunders	Galatasaray	Nottingham Forest	£1,500,000
Ole Gunnar Solskjar	Molde	Manchester United	£1,500,000
Paul Furlong	Chelsea	Birmingham City	£1,500,000
Ronny Johnsen	Besiktas	Manchester United	£1,200,000
Nikola Jerkan	Real Oviedo	Nottingham Forest	£1,000,000
Alex Rae	Millwall	Sunderland	£1,000,000
Aijosa Asanovic	Hadjuk Split	Derby County	£1,000,000
Muzzy Izzett	Chelsea	Leicester City	£800,000
Jacob Laursen	Silkeborg	Derby County	£500,000
Chris Allen	Oxford United	Nottingham Forest	£500,000
Phil Masinga	Leeds United	Zurich	£500,000
Neil Maddison	Southampton	Crystal Palace	£450,000
Gary Ablett	Everton	Birmingham City	£350,000
Steve Slade	Tottenham Hotspur	Leicester City	£350,000
Tony Coton	Manchester City	Sunderland	£350,000
Matt Clarke	Rotherham United	Sheffield Wednesday	£300,000
Barry Horne	Everton	Birmingham City	£250,000
Duncan Jupp	Fulham	Wimbledon	£200,000
Alex Chamberlain	Sunderland	Watford	£40,000
Mark Flatts	Arsenal	–	Free
Gary Monk	Torquay United	Southampton	Not disclosed
Steve Bruce	Manchester United	Birmingham City	Free
John Lukic	Leeds United	–	Free
Nigel Worthington	Leeds United	–	Free
Paul Stewart	Liverpool	Sunderland	Free
Ian Rush	Liverpool	Leeds United	Free
Gianluca Vialli	Juventus	Chelsea	Free
Nigel Spackman	Chelsea	Sheffield United	Free
Zeke Rowe	Chelsea	Brighton	Free
Espen Baardsen	Norway	Tottenham Hotspur	Not known
Erik Thorstvedt	Tottenham Hotspur	–	Free
Lee Hirst	Coventry City	–	Free
Ally Pickering	Coventry City	–	Free
Steve Morgan	Coventry City	–	Free
David Renne	Coventry City	–	Free
George Donis	Panathinaikos	Blackburn Rovers	Free
Bobby Mimms	Blackburn Rovers	–	Free
Gordon Armstrong	Sunderland	–	Free
Brian Atkinson	Sunderland	–	Free
Brett Angell	Sunderland	–	Free
John Kay	Sunderland	–	Free
Bruce Grobbelaar	Southampton	–	Free
Tommy Widdrington	Southampton	Grimsby Town	Free
Richard Hall	Southampton	West Ham United	Tribunal
Iwan Roberts	Leicester City	Wolverhampton W.	Tribunal
Mark Blake	Leicester City	–	Free
Phil Gee	Leicester City	–	Free

Paul Bedder	Leicester City	–	Free
Paul Browne	Aston Villa	Raith Rovers	Tribunal
Raimond van der Gouw			
	Vitesse Arnhem	Manchester United	Undisclosed
Steve Talboys	Wimbledon	–	Free
Roger Joseph	Wimbledon	–	Free
Gerald Dobbs	Wimbledon	–	Free
Paolo Futre	Milan	West Ham United	Free
Michael Hughes	Strasbourg	West Ham United	Tribunal
Mark Bowen	Norwich City	West Ham United	Free
Alvin Martin	West Ham United	Leyton Orient	Free
Les Sealey	West Ham United	Leyton Orient	Free
Malcolm McPherson	West Ham United	Brentford	Free
Chris Woods	Sheffield Wednesday	–	Free
Neil Webb	Nottingham Forest	–	Free
Kingsley Black	Nottingham Forest	Grimsby Town	Free
Robert Rosario	Nottingham Forest	–	Retired
Jason Kearton	Everton	–	Free
Jaime Moreno	Middlesbrough	–	Free
Paul Wilkinson	Middlesbrough	–	Free

FA PREMIER LEAGUE CLUBS
PLAYER LOANS 1995-96

August 1995

Player	*From*	*To*
David Brightwell	Manchester City	Lincoln City
Gary Bull	Nottingham Forest	Brighton & HA
Stewart Castledine	Wimbledon	Wycombe Wanderers
Robert Fleck	Chelsea	Norwich City
Shay Given	Blackburn Rovers	Swindon Town
Lance Key	Sheffield Wednesday	Lincoln City
Neil Moore	Everton	Carlisle United
Paul Pettinger	Leeds United	Rotherham United
Paul Shaw	Arsenal	Cardiff City
Paul Stewart	Liverpool	Sunderland
Simon Stewart	Sheffield Wednesday	Shrewsbury Town
Simon Tracey	Sheffield United	Nottingham Forest
Simon Webster	West Ham United	Derby County

September 1995

Player	From	To
Martin Allen	West Ham United	Portsmouth
Michael Appleton	Manchester United	Lincoln City
Richard Barker	Sheffield Wednesday	Doncaster Rovers
Trevor Berry	Aston Villa	Rotherham
Kingsley Black	Nottingham Forest	Millwall
Steve Blatherwick	Nottingham Forest	Hereford United
David Brightwell	Manchester City	Stoke City
Kenny Brown	West Ham United	Huddersfield Town
Lee Charles	QPR	Barnet
Gerald Dobbs	Wimbledon	Cardiff City
Michael Duberry	Chelsea	Bournemouth
Sieb Kykstra	QPR	Bristol City
Ian Feuer	West Ham United	Luton Town
Steve Harper	Newcastle United	Bradford City
Michael Hughes	Strasbourg	West Ham United
David Kerr	Manchester City	Mansfield
Paul McDonald	Southampton	Burnley
Jan Molby	Liverpool	Barnsley
Frank Talia	Blackburn Rovers	Swindon Town
Mark Watson	West Ham United	Leyton Orient
Peter Shilton	Southampton	Shrewsbury Town

October 1995

Player	From	To
Kenny Brown	West Ham United	Reading
Wayne Burnett	Plymouth Argyle	Bolton Wanderers
Darren Caskey	Tottenham Hotspur	Watford
Thomas Christiansen	Barcelona	Manchester City
Neil Cutler	West Bromwich Alb	Coventry City
Mark Grugel	Everton	Cliftonville
John Harkes	Derby County	West Ham United
Mike Hooper	Newcastle United	Sunderland
Phil King	Aston Villa	West Bromwich Albion
Frank Lampard	West Ham United	Swansea City
Jamie Marks	Leeds United	Linfield
Hildyard Mendes	Chelsea	Bangor
Paul Read	Arsenal	Southend United
Ben Roberts	Middlesbrough	Hartlepool United
Paul Shaw	Arsenal	Peterborough United
Mark Watson	West Ham United	Cambridge United
Paul Wilkinson	Middlesbrough	Oldham Athletic

Simon Wood	Coventry City	VS Rugby
Chris Woods	Sheffield Wednesday	Reading

November 1995

Player	From	To
Scott Canham	West Ham United	Torquay United
Darren Currie	West Ham United	Leyton Orient
Scott Fitzgerald	Wimbledon	Sheffield United
Danny Hill	Tottenham Hotspur	Birmingham City
Phil King	Aston Villa	WBA
Ben Thornley	Manchester United	Stockport County
Simon Tracey	Sheffield United	Wimbledon
Andy Turner	Tottenham Hotspur	Huddersfield Town
Michel Vonk	Manchester City	Oldham Athletic
Adrian Whitbread	West Ham United	Portsmouth
David White	Leeds United	Sheffield United

December 1995

Player	From	To
Jamie Barnwell-Edinboro	Coventry City	Swansea City
Gary Blissett	Wimbledon	Wycombe Wanderers
Jason Cundy	Tottenham Hotspur	Crystal Palace
Ronnie Ekelund	Barcelona	Manchester City
Niklas Gudmundsson	Halmstads	Blackburn Rovers *
Steve Guinan	Nottingham Forest	Darlington
Gareth Hall	Chelsea	Sunderland
Lance Key	Sheffield Wednesday	Hartlepool United
Craig Maskell	Southampton	Bristol City
Jan Molby	Liverpool	Norwich City
Aidan Newhouse	Wimbledon	Torquay United
Mark Nicolls	Chelsea	Chertsey
Ben Roberts	Middlesbrough	Wycombe Wanderers
Vinny Samways	Everton	Wolverhampton Wan
Chris Whyte	Birmingham City	Coventry City
Paul Wilkinson	Middlesbrough	Watford
Ned Zelic	QPR	Eintracht Frankfurt

Plus £50,000

January 1996

Player	From	To
Craig Armstrong	Nottingham Forest	Bristol Rovers
Richard Barker	Sheffield Wednesday	Ards
Uli Borowka	Werder Bremen	Leeds United

Scott Canham	West Ham United	Brentford
Chris Casper	Manchester United	Bournemouth
Lee Chapman	Ipswich Town	Leeds United
Terry Cooke	Manchester United	Sunderland
Dani	Sporting Lisbon	West Ham United

(Loan to end of 1995-96 season – West Ham paying £130,000 for loan)

Enzo Gambaro	AC Milan	Bolton Wanderers
Shay Given	Blackburn Rovers	Sunderland
Tony Grant	Everton	Swindon Town
Paul Holmes	Everton	WBA
Phil Jones	Liverpool	Wrexham
Ryan Jones	Sheffield Wednesday	Scunthorpe United
Jon Scargill	Sheffield Wednesday	Matlock
Matthew Smithard	Leeds United	Northampton Town
Chris Whyte	Birmingham City	West Ham United

February 1996

Player	From	To
Chris Allen	Oxford United	Nottingham Forest
Anthony Barness	Chelsea	Southend United
Jamie Barnwell-Edinboro	Coventry City	Wigan Athletic
Maro Boogers	West Ham United	Gronigen
Phil Charnock	Liverpool	Blackpool
Scott Hiley	Birmingham City	Manchester City
Danny Hill	Tottenham Hotspur	Watford
Alan Kernaghan	Middlesbrough	Bradford City
Lee Martin	Celtic	Coventry City
Kevin Pilkington	Manchester United	Rochdale
Vinny Samways	Everton	Birmingham City
John Sharpe	Manchester City	Exeter City
John Sheridan	Sheffield Wednesday	Birmingham City
Danny Shipp	West Ham United	Glenavon
Paul Tait	Birmingham City	Coventry City
Ben Thornley	Manchester United	Huddersfield Town
Vance Warner	Nottingham Forest	Grimsby Town
Mark Watson	West Ham United	Shrewsbury Town

March 1996

Player	From	To
Gary Ablett	Everton	Sheffield United
Derek Allan	Southampton	Brighton & Hove Alb.
Craig Armstrong	Nottingham Forest	Bristol Rovers
Gary Blissett	Wimbledon	Crewe Alexandra
Kenny Brown	West Ham United	Crystal Palace

Gerry Creaney	Manchester City	Oldham Athletic
Sieb Dykstra	QPR	Wycombe Wanderers
Paul Evens	Leeds United	Crystal Palace
Mark Flatts	Arsenal	Grimsby Town
Shay Given	Blackburn Rovers	Sunderland
Dale Gordon	West Ham United	Millwall
Jonathan Gould	Coventry City	Bradford City
Mustafa Izzet	Chelsea	Leicester City
Matt Jackson	Everton	Charlton Athletic
John Jensen	Arsenal	Brondby
Marc Joseph	Cambridge City	Coventry City
Jason Kearton	Everton	Preston North End
Russell Kelly	Chelsea	Leyton Orient
Lance Key	Sheffield Wednesday	Rochdale
Paul Mahorn	Tottenham Hotspur	Burnley
Brian McAllister	Wimbledon	Crewe Alexandra
Guiseppe Mazzarelli	FC Zurich	Manchester City
Scott Mean	Bournemouth	West Ham United
Neil Moore	Everton	Rotherham United
Steve Morgan	Coventry City	Bristol Rovers
Paul Murray	Carlisle	QPR
Keith O'Halloran	Middlesbrough	Scunthorpe United
Paul Pettinger	Leeds United	Gillingham
Zeke Rowe	Chelsea	Brighton & Hove Alb.
Graeme Tomlinson	Manchester United	Luton Town
Andy Turner	Tottenham Hotspur	Southend United
Paul Wilkinson	Middlesbrough	Luton Town

FA PREMIER LEAGUE CLUBS
PLAYER TRIALS 1995-96

August 1995

Player	*On Trial From*	*On Trial To*
Scott Brenchley	Liverpool	Chester City
Richard Brown	Blackburn Rovers	Blackpool
Paul Davis	Arsenal	Peterborough United
Andrew Hughes	Chelsea	Swindon Town
Matt Rawlings	Arsenal	Cardiff City

September 1995

Player	On Trial From	On Trial To
Darren Barnard	Chelsea	Birmingham City
Wayne Burnett	Plymouth Argyle	Bolton Wanderers
Nicola Carlcola	Genoa	Aston Villa
Michael Knowles	Morecambe	Blackburn Rovers
John Murphy	Aston Villa	Chester City
Antonia Pacheco	Sporting Lisbon	Aston Villa

October 1995

Player	On Trial From	On Trial To
Jon Bass	Birmingham City	Coventry City
Siobadan Dubicek	Stuttgart	Sheffield Wednesday
Mark McNally	Celtic	Manchester City
Antonio Pacheco	Sporting Lisbon	Nottingham Forest

November 1995

Player	On Trial From	On Trial To
Marcus Hahnemann	Seattle Sounders	Sheffield Wednesday
Alan Pouton	Newcastle United	Oxford United

December 1995

Player	On Trial From	On Trial To
Edmond Abazi	Benfica	Manchester City
Ralph Hanselhuttel	Casino Salzburg	Bolton Wanderers
William Prunier	Bordeaux	Manchester United
Diego Tur	Copenhagen	West Ham United

January 1996

Player	On Trial From	On Trial To
Philippe Chanlot	Toulouse	West Ham United
Igor Dobrovolski	Atletico Madrid	Everton
Ronnie Ekelund	Barcelona	Coventry City
Stefan Gislason	Fram	Arsenal
Danny Hinshelwood	Nottingham Forest	Bournemouth
Igor Korniev	Barcelona	Southampton
Tony Popovic	Sydney Croatia	Leeds United
Mark Thornton	Newcastle United	Bradford City

February 1996

Player	On Trial From	On Trial To
Carl Alford	Kettering Town	Manchester City
Emanuel Babayaro	Nigeria	West Ham United
Mark Fish	Orlando Pirates	Manchester United
Marc Joseph	Cambridge City	Coventry City
Ben Sylla	Guinea	Chelsea

March 1996

Player	On Trial From	On Trial To
Barry McConnell	Exeter City	Manchester City
Nicky Medin	Exeter City	Manchester City
Stephen Reeves	Chelsea	Oxford United
Zeke Rowe	Chelsea	Swindon Town

A-Z
FA Premier League Players
1996-97

Notes: The players are listed in alphabetical order and are those who are likely to feature in the Premiership action during the 1996-97 season. As a rule fringe players who played at least one game in 1995-96 are included. Players who did not feature in 1994-95 are included in the Ex-Players list. There are exceptions though – for instance players making a large number of appearances on the bench without actually getting on the pitch. This is true for reserve goalkeepers. *Previous Clubs Details* includes all Premiership games played to date. Specific appearance details for 1995-96 can be found in the *Club Directory* section. A club with * next to it in the *Previous Clubs Details* list indicates that the figures do not include those for the 1995-96 season. NL=Non-League. When figures are given for a non-English club they refer to the relevant country's league and cup competitions.

ADAMS Tony · Arsenal
Fullname: Anthony Alexander Adams · DOB: 10-10-66 Romford
Debut: ARSENAL v Norwich City 15/8/92
Debut Goal: ARSENAL v Newcastle Utd 18/9/94

Previous Clubs Details

Club	Signed	Fee	Tot	Start	Sub	FA	FL	Lge	FA	FL
Arsenal	Jan-84	Amateur	364	367	3	32	54	24	5	5

FAPL Summary by Club

Arsenal	1992-93 to 1995-96		118	116	2	14	20	4	4	3
Total			118	116	2	14	20	4	4	3

AGNEW Steve · Sunderland
Fullname: Stephen Mark Agnew · DOB: 09-11-65 Shipley
Debut: LEICESTER CITY v Newcastle United 21/8/94

Previous Clubs Details

Club	Signed	Fee	Tot	Start	Sub	FA	FL	Lge	FA	FL
Barnsley	Nov-83	Amateur	194	186	8	20	13	30	4	3
Blackburn Rvs	Jun-91	£700,000	2	2	0	0	2	0	0	0
Portsmouth	Nov-92	Loan	5	3	2	0	0	0	0	0
Leicester City	Feb-93	£250,000	56	52	4	2	5	4	0	0
Sunderland	Jan-95	£250,000	44	41	3	2	1	7	1	0

FAPL Summary by Club

Leicester C.	1994-95 to 1995-96		11	7	4	1	2	0	0	0
Total			11	7	4	1	2	0	0	0

ALBERT Philippe — Newcastle United

Fullname: Philippe Albert DOB: 10-08-67 Bouillon, Belgium
Debut: Leicester City v NEWCASTLE UTD 21/8/94
Debut Goal: NEWCASTLE UTD v Leicester City 10/12/94

Previous Clubs Details			*Apps*					*Goals*		
Club	Signed	Fee	Tot	Start	Sub	FA	FL	Lge	FA	FL
Anderlecht			–	–	–	–	–	–	–	–
Newcastle Utd	Aug-94	£2.65m	40	36	4	2	7	6	1	2
FAPL Summary by Club										
Newcastle Utd	1994-95 to 1995-96		40	36	4	2	7	6	1	2
Total			*40*	*36*	*4*	*2*	*7*	*6*	*1*	*2*

ALLEN Graham — Everton

Fullname: Graham Allen DOB: 08-04-77 Franworth

Previous Clubs Details			*Apps*					*Goals*		
Club	Signed	Fee	Tot	Start	Sub	FA	FL	Lge	FA	FL
Everton	Trainee		–	–	–	–	–	–	–	–

ALLEN Chris — Nottingham Forest

Fullname: Christopher Anthony Allen DOB: 18-11-72 Oxford
Debut: Sheffield W. v NOTTINGHAM FOREST 2/3/96 as sub
Debut Goal: Middlesbrough v NOTTINGHAM FOREST 16/3/96

Previous Clubs Details			*Apps*					*Goals*		
Club	Signed	Fee	Tot	Start	Sub	FA	FL	Lge	FA	FL
Oxford Utd *	May-91	Trainee	126	97	29	7	9	9	1	2
N. Forest	Feb-96	Loan	3	1	2	0	0	1	0	0
FAPL Summary by Club										
N. Forest	1995-96		3	1	2	0	0	1	0	0
Total			*3*	*1*	*2*	*0*	*0*	*1*	*0*	*0*

ALSTON Sam — Sunderland

Fullname: Sam Alston DOB:

Previous Clubs Details			*Apps*					*Goals*		
Club	Signed	Fee	Tot	Start	Sub	FA	FL	Lge	FA	FL
Newcastle Utd			0	0	0	0	0	0	0	0
Sunderland	Aug-95	Free	13	9	4	1	0	0	0	0

AMOKACHI Daniel — Everton

Fullname: Daniel Amokachi DOB: 30-12-72 Groko, Nigeria
Debut: Blackburn Rvs v EVERTON 10/9/94
Debut Goal: EVERTON v QPR 17/10/94

Previous Clubs Details			*Apps*					*Goals*		
Club	Signed	Fee	Tot	Start	Sub	FA	FL	Lge	FA	FL
FC Bruges			–	–	–	–	–	–	–	–
Everton	Aug-94	£3m	43	34	9	5	3	10	3	0

| Everton | 1994-95 to 1995-96 | 43 | 34 | 9 | 5 | 3 | 10 | 3 | 0 |
| *Total* | | *43* | *34* | *9* | *5* | *3* | *10* | *3* | *0* |

ANDERTON Darren   Tottenham Hotspur

Fullname: Darren Robert Anderton   DOB: 03-03-72 Southampton
Debut: Southampton v TOTTENHAM HOTSPUR 15/8/92
Debut Goal: TOTTENHAM HOTSPUR v Southampton 7/2/93

Previous Clubs Details

			Apps				Goals		
Club	Signed	Fee	Tot	Start	Sub	FA	FL	Lge	FA	FL
Portsmouth	Feb-90	Trainee	62	53	9	7	5	7	5	1
Tottenham H.	Jun-92	£1.75m	116	110	6	14	9	19	2	1

FAPL Summary by Club

| Tottenham H. | 1992-93 to 1995-96 | 116 | 110 | 6 | 14 | 9 | 19 | 2 | 1 |
| *Total* | | *116* | *110* | *6* | *14* | *9* | *19* | *2* | *1* |

ARDLEY Neal   Wimbledon

Fullname: Neal Christopher Ardley   DOB: 01-09-72 Epsom
Debut: WIMBLEDON v Arsenal 5/9/92 as sub
Debut Goal: WIMBLEDON v Blackburn Rvs 19/9/92

Previous Clubs Details

			Apps				Goals		
Club	Signed	Fee	Tot	Start	Sub	FA	FL	Lge	FA	FL
Wimbledon	Jul-91		71	59	12	10	11	6	0	2

FAPL Summary by Club

| Wimbledon | 1992-93 to 1995-96 | 62 | 51 | 11 | 10 | 11 | 6 | 0 | 2 |
| *Total* | | *62* | *51* | *11* | *10* | *11* | *6* | *0* | *2* |

ARMSTRONG Craig   Nottingham Forest

Fullname: Steven Craig Armstrong   DOB: 23-05-75 South Shields

Previous Clubs Details

			Apps				Goals		
Club	Signed	Fee	Tot	Start	Sub	FA	FL	Lge	FA	FL
N. Forest	Jun-92	Trainee	0	0	0	0	0	0	0	0
Burnley	Dec-94	Loan	4	4	0	0	0	0	0	0
Bristol Rvs	Jan-96	Loan	–	–	–	–	–	–	–	–

ARMSTRONG Chris   Tottenham Hotspur

Fullname: Christopher Peter Armstrong   DOB: 19-06-71 Newcastle
Debut: Manchester Utd v CRYSTAL PALACE 2/9/92
Debut Goal: CRYSTAL PALACE v Oldham Athletic 12/9/92

Previous Clubs Details

			Apps				Goals		
Club	Signed	Fee	Tot	Start	Sub	FA	FL	Lge	FA	FL
Wrexham	Mar-89		60	40	20	1	3	13	0	0
Millwall	Aug-91	£50,000	28	11	17	1	4	5	0	2
Crystal Palace	Sep-92	£1m	118	118	0	8	8	46	5	6
Tottenham H.	Jul-94	£4.5m	36	36	0	6	3	15	4	3

Club			Tot	Start	Sub	FA	FL	Lge	FA	FL
Crystal Palace		1992-93	75	75	0	6	5	23	5	5
Tottenham H.	1994-95 to 1995-96		36	36	0	6	3	15	4	3
Total			*111*	*111*	*0*	*12*	*8*	*38*	*9*	*8*

ASANOVIC Aijosa   Derby County

Fullname: Aijosa Asanovic   DOB:

Previous Clubs Details			*Apps*					*Goals*		
Club	Signed	Fee	Tot	Start	Sub	FA	FL	Lge	FA	FL
Hadjuk Split	Jul-96	£1m	–	–	–	–	–	–	–	–

ASPRILLA Tino   Newcastle United

Fullname: Faustino Asprilla   DOB: 10-11-69 Colombia
Debut: Middlesbrough v NEWCASTLE UTD 10/2/96 as sub
Debut Goal: Manchester City v NEWCASTLE UTD 24/2/96

Previous Clubs Details			*Apps*					*Goals*		
Club	Signed	Fee	Tot	Start	Sub	FA	FL	Lge	FA	FL
Parma			–	–	–	–	–	–	–	–
Newcastle Utd	Feb-96	£6.7m	14	11	3	0	0	3	0	0
FAPL Summary by Club										
Newcastle Utd		1995-96	14	11	3	0	0	3	0	0
Total			*14*	*11*	*3*	*0*	*0*	*3*	*0*	*0*

ATHERTON Peter   Sheffield Wednesday

Fullname: Peter Atherton   DOB: 06-04-70 Orrell
Debut: COVENTRY CITY v Middlesbrough 15/8/92
Debut Goal: Aston Villa v SHEFFIELD WEDNESDAY 27/11/94

Previous Clubs Details			*Apps*					*Goals*		
Club	Signed	Fee	Tot	Start	Sub	FA	FL	Lge	FA	FL
Wigan Ath	Feb-88		149	145	4	7	8	1	0	0
Coventry City	Aug-91	£300,000	114	113	1	2	4	0	0	0
Sheffield W.	Jun-94	£800,000	76	76	0	1	7	1	0	0
FAPL Summary by Club										
Coventry C.	1992-93 to 1993-94		79	78	1	2	4	0	0	0
Sheffield W.	1994-95 to 1995-96		76	76	0	4	8	1	0	0
Total			*155*	*154*	*1*	*6*	*12*	*1*	*0*	*0*

AUSTIN Dean   Tottenham Hotspur

Fullname: Dean Barry Austin   DOB: 26-04-70 Hemel Hempstead
Debut: TOTTENHAM H. v Crystal Palace 22/8/92

Previous Clubs Details			*Apps*					*Goals*		
Club	Signed	Fee	Tot	Start	Sub	FA	FL	Lge	FA	FL
Southend Utd	Mar-90	£12,000	96	96	0	2	4	2	0	0
Tottenham H.	Jun-92	£375,000	109	104	5	16	9	0	0	0

Tottenham H. 1992-93 to 1995-96	109	104	5	16	9	0	0	0
Total	*109*	*104*	*5*	*16*	*9*	*0*	*0*	*0*

BABB Phil   Liverpool

Fullname: Phillip Andrew Babb   DOB: 30-11-70 London
Debut: COVENTRY CITY v Middlesbrough 15/8/92
Debut Goal: Arsenal v COVENTRY CITY 14/8/93

Previous Clubs Details			*Apps*				*Goals*	
Club	Signed	Fee	Tot	Start	Sub	FA	FL	Lge	FA	FL
Bradford City	Aug-90		80	73	7	3	6	14	0	0
Coventry City	Jul-92	£500,000	77	70	7	2	5	3	0	1
Liverpool	Sep-94	£3.6m	62	61	1	10	11	0	0	0

FAPL Summary by Club

Coventry C. 1992-93 to 1994-95	77	70	7	2	5	3	0	1
Liverpool 1994-95 to 1995-96	62	61	1	10	11	0	0	0
Total	*139*	*131*	*8*	*12*	*16*	*3*	*0*	*1*

BALL Kevin   Sunderland

Fullname: Kevin Anthony Ball   DOB: 12-11-64 Hastings

Previous Clubs Details			*Apps*					*Goals*	
Club	Signed	Fee	Tot	Start	Sub	FA	FL	Lge	FA	FL
Coventry City		Juniors	0	0	0	0	0	0	0	0
Portsmouth	Oct-82	Free	105	96	9	8	9	4	0	0
Sunderland	Jul-90	£350,000	223	220	3	15	15	13	0	2

BARMBY Nicky   Middlesbrough

Fullname: Nicholas Jonathan Barmby   DOB: 11-02-74 Hull
Debut: Sheffield W. v TOTTENHAM HOTSPUR 7/9/92
Debut Goal: TOTTENHAM HOTSPUR v Middlesbrough 17/10/92

Previous Clubs Details			*Apps*					*Goals*	
Club	Signed	Fee	Tot	Start	Sub	FA	FL	Lge	FA	FL
Tottenham H.	Apr-91		87	81	6	13	8	20	5	1
Middlesbrough	Aug-95	£5,250,000	32	32	0	3	4	7	1	1

FAPL Summary by Club

Tottenham H. 1992-93 to 1994-95	87	81	6	13	8	20	5	1
Middlesbrough 1995-96	32	32	0	3	4	7	1	1
Total	*119*	*113*	*6*	*16*	*12*	*27*	*6*	*2*

BARNES John   Liverpool

Fullname: John Charles Bryan Barnes   DOB: 07-11-63 Jamaica
Debut: QPR v LIVERPOOL 23/11/92 as sub
Debut Goal: LIVERPOOL v Aston Villa 9/1/92

Previous Clubs Details			*Apps*					*Goals*	
Club	Signed	Fee	Tot	Start	Sub	FA	FL	Lge	FA	FL
Watford	Jul-81		233	232	1	31	21	65	11	7

251

| Liverpool | Jun-87 | £900,000 | 278 | 276 | 2 | 49 | 23 | 80 | 14 | 3 |

| Liverpool | 1992-93 to 1995-96 | 127 | 124 | 3 | 17 | 13 | 18 | 0 | 0 |
| Total | | 127 | 124 | 3 | 17 | 13 | 18 | 0 | 0 |

BARNESS Tony — Chelsea

Fullname: Anthony Barness   DOB: 25-03-73 Lewisham
Debut: CHELSEA v Norwich City 12/9/92

Previous Clubs Details			Apps					Goals		
Club	Signed	Fee	Tot	Start	Sub	FA	FL	Lge	FA	FL
Charlton Ath	Mar-91		27	21	6	3	2	1	0	0
Chelsea	Sep-92	£350,000	14	12	2	0	2	0	0	0
Middlesbrough	Aug-93	Loan	1	1	0	0	0	0	0	0
Southend Utd *	Feb-96	Loan	–	–	–	–	–	–	–	–

FAPL Summary by Club

| Chelsea | 1992-93 to 1995-96 | 14 | 12 | 2 | 0 | 2 | 0 | 0 | 0 |
| Total | | 14 | 12 | 2 | 0 | 2 | 0 | 0 | 0 |

BARNWELL Jamie — Coventry City

Fullname: James Barnwell-Edinboro   DOB: 26-12-75 Hull
Debut: Middlesbrough v COVENTRY CITY 16/9/95 as sub

Previous Clubs Details			Apps					Goals		
Club	Signed	Fee	Tot	Start	Sub	FA	FL	Lge	FA	FL
Coventry City			1	0	1	0	0	0	0	0

FAPL Summary by Club

| Coventry City | 1995-96 | 1 | 0 | 1 | 0 | 0 | 0 | 0 | 0 |
| Total | | 1 | 0 | 1 | 0 | 0 | 0 | 0 | 0 |

BARRETT Earl — Everton

Fullname: Earl Delisser Barrett   DOB: 28-04-67 Rochdale
Debut: Ipswich Town v ASTON VILLA 15/8/92
Debut Goal: ASTON VILLA v Everton 20/2/93

Previous Clubs Details			Apps					Goals		
Club	Signed	Fee	Tot	Start	Sub	FA	FL	Lge	FA	FL
Man. City	Apr-85		3	2	1	0	1	0	0	0
Chester City	Mar-86	Loan	12	12	0	0	0	0	0	0
Oldham Ath	Nov-87	£35,000	183	181	2	14	20	7	1	1
Aston Villa	Feb-92	£1.7m	119	118	1	9	15	1	0	1
Everton	Jan-95	£1.7m	25	25	0	0	2	0	0	0

FAPL Summary by Club

Aston Villa	1992-93 to 1994-95	106	105	1	9	15	1	0	0
Everton	1994-95 to 1995-96	25	25	0	0	2	0	0	0
Total		131	130	1	9	17	1	0	0

BARRON Michael   Middlesbrough

Fullname: Michael Barron   DOB: 22-12-74 Salford
Debut: MIDDLESBROUGH v Everton, 2/3/96

Previous Clubs Details			Apps					Goals		
Club	Signed	Fee	Tot	Start	Sub	FA	FL	Lge	FA	FL
Middlesbrough	Feb-93	Trainee	1	1	0	0	0	0	0	0
FAPL Summary by Club										
Middlesbrough	1995-96		1	1	0	0	0	0	0	0
Total			*1*	*1*	*0*	*0*	*0*	*0*	*0*	*0*

BART-WILLIAMS Chris   Nottingham Forest

Fullname: Christopher Gerald Bart-Williams   DOB:16-06-74 Sierra Leone
Debut: Everton v SHEFFIELD W. 15/8/92 as sub
Debut Goal: EVERTON v Coventry City 2/9/92

Previous Clubs Details			Apps					Goals		
Club	Signed	Fee	Tot	Start	Sub	FA	FL	Lge	FA	FL
Leyton Orient	Jul-91		36	34	2	0	4	2	0	0
Sheffield W.	Nov-91	£275,000	157	128	29	40	18	16	2	4
N. Forest	Jun-95	£2m	33	33	0	7	2	0	0	0
FAPL Summary by Club										
Sheffield W.	1992-93 to 1994-95		109	83	26	11	16	17	1	3
N. Forest	1995-96		33	33	0	7	2	0	0	0
Total			*142*	*116*	*26*	*18*	*18*	*17*	*1*	*3*

BARTON Warren   Newcastle United

Fullname: Warren Dean Barton   DOB: 19-03-69 Stoke Newington
Debut: Leeds Utd v WIMBLEDON 15/8/92
Debut Goal: Leeds Utd v WIMBLEDON 15/8/92

Previous Clubs Details			Apps					Goals		
Club	Signed	Fee	Tot	Start	Sub	FA	FL	Lge	FA	FL
Maidstone Utd	Jul-87	£10,000	42	41	1	3	2	0	1	0
Wimbledon	Jun-90	£300,000	180	178	2	11	16	10	0	1
Newcastle Utd	Jun-95	£4m +	31	30	1	2	5	0	0	1
FAPL Summary by Club										
Wimbledon	1992-93 to 1994-95		101	99	2	6	12	6	0	1
Newcastle Utd	1995-96		31	30	1	2	5	0	0	1
Total			*132*	*129*	*3*	*8*	*17*	*6*	*0*	*2*

BARTRAM Vince   Arsenal

Fullname: Vincent Lee Bartram   DOB: 07-08-68 Birmingham
Debut: N. Forest v ARSENAL 3/12/94   Debut Goal: (Goalkeeper)

Previous Clubs Details			Apps					Goals		
Club	Signed	Fee	Tot	Start	Sub	FA	FL	Lge	FA	FL
Wolves	Aug-85		5	5	0	3	2	0	0	0
Blackpool	Oct-89	Loan	9	9	0	0	0	0	0	0

Bournemouth	Jul-91	£65,000	132	132	0	14	10	0	0	0
Arsenal	Aug-94	£400,000	11	11	0	0	0	0	0	0
FAPL Summary by Club										
Arsenal	1994-95 to 1995-96		11	11	0	0	1	0	0	0
Total			*11*	*11*	*0*	*0*	*1*	*0*	*0*	*0*

BATTY David
Newcastle United

Fullname: David Batty DOB: 02-12-68 Leeds
Debut: LEEDS UTD v Wimbledon 15/8/92
Debut Goal: LEEDS UTD v Middlesbrough 31/1/93

| *Previous Clubs Details* | | | *Apps* | | | | | *Goals* | | |
Club	Signed	Fee	Tot	Start	Sub	FA	FL	Lge	FA	FL
Leeds Utd	Jul-87		211	201	10	12	17	4	0	0
Blackburn Rvs	Oct-93	£2.75m	54	53	1	5	6	1	0	0
Newcastle Utd	Feb-96	£3.75m	11	11	0	0	0	1	0	0
FAPL Summary by Club										
Leeds Utd	1992-93 to 1993-94		39	38	1	3	2	1	0	0
Blackburn Rvs	1993-94 to 1995-96		54	53	1	5	6	1	0	0
Newcastle Utd	1995-96		11	11	0	0	0	1	0	0
Total			*104*	*102*	*2*	*8*	*8*	*3*	*0*	*0*

BEARDSLEY Peter
Newcastle United

Fullname: Peter Andrew Beardsley DOB: 18-01-61 Newcastle
Debut: EVERTON v Sheffield W. 15/8/92
Debut Goal: Manchester Utd v EVERTON 19/8/92

| *Previous Clubs Details* | | | *Apps* | | | | | *Goals* | | |
Club	Signed	Fee	Tot	Start	Sub	FA	FL	Lge	FA	FL
Carlisle Utd	Aug-79		104	93	11	15	7	22	7	0
Vancouver	Apr-81	£275,000	–	–	–	–	–	–	–	–
Manchester Utd	Sep-82	£300,000	0	0	0	0	1	0	0	0
Vancouver	Sep-83		–	–	–	–	–	–	–	–
Newcastle Utd	Sep-83	£150,000	147	146	1	6	10	61	0	0
Liverpool	Jul-87	£1.9m	131	120	11	25	14	46	11	1
Everton	Aug-91	£1m	81	81	0	4	8	25	1	5
Newcastle Utd	Jul-93	£1.4m	104	104	0	8	10	42	3	3
FAPL Summary by Club										
Everton	1992-93		39	39	0	2	4	10	2	0
Newcastle Utd	1993-94 to 1995-96		104	104	0	8	10	42	3	3
Total			*143*	*143*	*0*	*10*	*14*	*52*	*5*	*3*

BEASANT Dave
Southampton

Fullname: David John Beasant DOB: 20-03-59 Willesden
Debut: CHELSEA v Oldham Ath 15/8/92
Debut Goal: (Goalkeeper)

Club	Signed	Fee	Apps					Goals		
			Tot	Start	Sub	FA	FL	Lge	FA	FL
Wimbledon	Aug-79	£1,000	340	340	0	27	21	0	0	0
Newcastle Utd	Jun-88	£800,000	20	20	0	2	2	0	0	0
Chelsea	Jan-89	£725,000	116	116	0	5	11	0	0	0
Grimsby Town	Oct-92	Loan	6	6	0	0	0	0	0	0
Wolves	Jan-93	Loan	4	4	0	0	1	0	0	0
Southampton	Nov-93	£300,000	74	73	1	8	4	0	0	0
FAPL Summary by Club										
Chelsea	1992-93 to 1993-94		17	17	0	0	0	0	0	0
Southampton	1993-94 to 1995-96		74	73	1	8	4	0	0	0
Total			*91*	*90*	*1*	*8*	*4*	*0*	*0*	*0*

BECKHAM David   Manchester United

Fullname: David Beckham   DOB: 02-05-75 Leytonstone
Debut: MANCHESTER UTD v Leeds Utd 2/4/95
Debut Goal:

Club	Signed	Fee	Apps					Goals		
			Tot	Start	Sub	FA	FL	Lge	FA	FL
Manchester Utd	Jan-93	Trainee	37	28	9	5	5	7	1	0
Preston NE	Feb-95	Loan	5	4	1	0	0	2	0	0
FAPL Summary by Club										
Manchester Utd	1994-95 to 1995-96		37	28	9	5	5	7	1	0
Total			*37*	*28*	*9*	*5*	*5*	*7*	*1*	*0*

BEENEY Mark   Leeds United

Fullname: Mark Beeney   DOB: 30-12-67 Tunbridge Wells
Debut: Coventry City v LEEDS UTD 8/5/93

Club	Signed	Fee	Apps					Goals		
			Tot	Start	Sub	FA	FL	Lge	FA	FL
Gillingham	Aug-86		2	2	0	0	1	0	0	0
Maidstone Utd	Feb-87		50	50	0	11	3	0	0	0
Aldershot	Mar-90	Loan	7	7	0	0	0	0	0	0
Brighton HA	Mar-91	£30,000	69	68	1	7	6	0	0	0
Leeds Utd	Apr-93	£350,000	33	33	0	4	3	0	0	0
FAPL Summary by Club										
Leeds Utd	1992-93 to 1995-96		33	33	0	4	3	0	0	0
Total			*33*	*33*	*0*	*4*	*3*	*0*	*0*	*0*

BEESLEY Paul   Leeds United

Fullname: Paul Beesley   DOB: 21-07-65 Liverpool
Debut: SHEFFIELD UTD v Manchester Utd 15/8/92
Debut Goal: SHEFFIELD UTD v Wimbledon 25/8/93

Club	Signed	Fee	Apps					Goals		
			Tot	Start	Sub	FA	FL	Lge	FA	FL
Wigan Ath	9/84	Free NL	155	153	2	6	13	3	0	0

Leyton Orient	10/89	£175,000	32	32	0	1	0	1	1	0
Sheffield Utd	10/90	£300,000	168	162	6	11	13	7	1	0
Leeds Utd	Aug-95	£250,000	10	8	2	4	5	0	0	0

FAPL Summary by Club

Sheffield Utd	1992-93 to 1994-95	64	61	3	8	5	2	1	0
Leeds Utd	1995-96	10	8	2	4	5	0	0	0
Total		*74*	*69*	*5*	*12*	*10*	*2*	*1*	*0*

BENALI Francis   Southampton

Fullname: Francis Vincent Benali   DOB: 30-12-68 Southampton
Debut: SOUTHAMPTON v Tottenham H. 15/8/92

Previous Clubs Details			*Apps*					*Goals*		
Club	Signed	Fee	Tot	Start	Sub	FA	FL	Lge	FA	FL
Southampton	Dec-86		203	180	23	18	23	0	0	0

FAPL Summary by Club

Southampton	1992-93 to 1995-96	135	126	9	7	12	0	0	0
Total		*135*	*126*	*9*	*7*	*12*	*0*	*0*	*0*

BENNETT Frank   Southampton

Fullname: Frank Bennett   DOB: 03-01-69 Birmingham
Debut: SOUTHAMPTON v Everton 14/8/93
Debut Goal: SOUTHAMPTON v Chelsea 27/12/93

Previous Clubs Details			*Apps*					*Goals*		
Club	Signed	Fee	Tot	Start	Sub	FA	FL	Lge	FA	FL
Southampton	Feb-93	£7,500	19	5	14	1	2	1	0	0

FAPL Summary by Club

Southampton	1993-94 to 1995-96	19	5	14	1	2	1	0	0
Total		*19*	*5*	*14*	*1*	*2*	*1*	*0*	*0*

BERESFORD John   Newcastle United

Fullname: John Beresford   DOB: 04-09-66 Sheffield
Debut: NEWCASTLE UTD v Tottenham H. 14/8/93

Previous Clubs Details			*Apps*					*Goals*		
Club	Signed	Fee	Tot	Start	Sub	FA	FL	Lge	FA	FL
Man. City	Sep-83		0	0	0	0	0	0	0	0
Barnsley	Aug-86	Free	88	79	9	5	7	5	1	2
Portsmouth	Mar-89	£300,000	107	102	5	11	12	8	0	2
Newcastle Utd	Jul-92	£650,000	142	141	1	12	13	1	1	0

FAPL Summary by Club

Newcastle Utd	1993-94 to 1995-96	100	99	1	8	9	0	1	0
Total		*100*	*99*	*1*	*8*	*9*	*0*	*1*	*0*

BERG Henning   Blackburn Rovers

Fullname: Henning Berg   DOB: 01-09-69 Eidsvell
Debut: BLACKBURN RVS v Crystal Palace 2/2/93
Debut Goal: BLACKBURN RVS v Chelsea 14/8/93

Previous Clubs Details			Apps					Goals		
Club	Signed	Fee	Tot	Start	Sub	FA	FL	Lge	FA	FL
KFMU Oslo			–	–	–	–	–	–	–	–
Blackburn Rvs	Dec-92	£400,000	123	118	5	8	13	2	0	0
FAPL Summary by Club										
Blackburn Rvs	1992-93 to 1995-96		123	118	5	8	13	2	0	0
Total			*123*	*118*	*5*	*8*	*13*	*2*	*0*	*0*

BERGKAMP Dennis   Arsenal

Fullname: Dennis Nicolaas Bergkamp   DOB: 18-05-69 Amsterdam
Debut: ARSENAL v Middlesbrough 20/8/95
Debut Goal: ARSENAL v Southampton 23/9/96

Previous Clubs Details			Apps					Goals		
Club	Signed	Fee	Tot	Start	Sub	FA	FL	Lge	FA	FL
Ajax	Jul-86		185	185	0	0	0	103	0	0
Internazionale	Jul-93	£12m	52	50	2	–	–	11	–	–
Arsenal	Jun-95	£7.5m	33	33	0	1	7	11	0	5
FAPL Summary by Club										
Arsenal	1995-96		33	33	0	1	7	11	0	5
Total			*33*	*33*	*0*	*1*	*7*	*11*	*0*	*5*

BILIC Slaven   West Ham United

Fullname: Slaven Bilic   DOB: 11-09-68 Croatia
Debut: Tottenham H. v WEST HAM UTD 12/2/96

Previous Clubs Details			Apps					Goals		
Club	Signed	Fee	Tot	Start	Sub	FA	FL	Lge	FA	FL
Karlsruhe			–	–	–	–	–	–	–	–
West Ham Utd	Dec-95	£1.3m	13	13	0	0	0	0	0	0
FAPL Summary by Club										
West Ham Utd	1995-96		13	13	0	0	0	0	0	0
Total			*13*	*13*	*0*	*0*	*0*	*0*	*0*	*0*

BISHOP Ian   West Ham United

Fullname: Ian William Bishop   DOB: 29-05-65 Liverpool
Debut: WEST HAM UTD v Swindon Town 11/9/93
Debut Goal: Sheffield Utd v WEST HAM UTD 28/3/94

Previous Clubs Details			Apps					Goals		
Club	Signed	Fee	Tot	Start	Sub	FA	FL	Lge	FA	FL
Everton	Jun-83		1	0	1	0	0	0	0	0
Crewe Alex	Mar-84	Loan	4	4	0	0	0	0	0	0
Carlisle Utd	Oct-84	£15,000	132	131	1	5	8	14	1	1
Bournemouth	Jul-88	£35,000	44	44	0	5	4	2	0	0
Man. City	Aug-89	£465,000	19	18	1	0	4	2	0	1
West Ham Utd	Dec-89	Exchange	222	211	11	21	16	10	3	1

West Ham Utd 1993-94 to 1995-96	102	102	0	11	9	3	1	1
Total	*102*	*102*	*0*	*11*	*9*	*3*	*1*	*1*

BJORNEBYE Stig Inge   Liverpool

Fullname: Stig Inge Bjornebye   DOB: 11-12-69 Norway
Debut: Coventry City v LIVERPOOL 19/12/92

Previous Clubs Details			*Apps*				*Goals*		
Club	Signed	Fee	Tot	Start	Sub	FA	FL	Lge	FA FL
Rosenborg (Norway)			–	–	–	–	–	–	– –
Liverpool	Dec-92	£600,000	53	50	3	9	7	0	0 0
FAPL Summary by Club									
Liverpool	1992-93 to 1995-96		53	50	3	8	8	0	0 0
Total			*53*	*50*	*3*	*8*	*8*	*0*	*0 0*

BLACKWELL Dean   Wimbledon

Fullname: Dean Robert Blackwell   DOB: 05-12-69 Camden
Debut: Leeds Utd v WIMBLEDON 15/8/92

Previous Clubs Details			*Apps*				*Goals*		
Club	Signed	Fee	Tot	Start	Sub	FA	FL	Lge	FA FL
Wimbledon	Jul-88		92	75	17	8	3	1	0 0
Plymouth A	Mar-90	Loan	15	12	2	2	0	0	0 0
FAPL Summary by Club									
Wimbledon	1992-93 to 1995-96		50	43	7	7	1	0	0 0
Total			*50*	*43*	*7*	*7*	*1*	*0*	*0 0*

BLINKER Regi   Sheffield Wednesday

Fullname: Regi Blinker   DOB: 06-04-69
Debut: Aston Villa v SHEFFIELD W. 6/3/96
Debut Goal: Aston Villa v SHEFFIELD W. 6/3/96

Previous Clubs Details			*Apps*				*Goals*		
Club	Signed	Fee	Tot	Start	Sub	FA	FL	Lge	FA FL
Feyenoord			–	–	–	–	–	–	– –
Sheffield W.	Mar-96	£275,000	9	9	0	0	0	2	0 0
FAPL Summary by Club									
Sheffield W.	1995-96		9	9	0	0	0	2	0 0
Total			*9*	*9*	*0*	*0*	*0*	*2*	*0 0*

BLISSETT Gary   Wimbledon

Fullname: Gary Paul Blissett   DOB: 29-06-64 Manchester
Debut: WIMBLEDON v QPR 27/09/93 as sub
Debut Goal: Sheffield W. v WIMBLEDON 16/10/93

Previous Clubs Details			*Apps*				*Goals*		
Club	Signed	Fee	Tot	Start	Sub	FA	FL	Lge	FA FL
Crewe Alex	Aug-83		221	112	109	4	0	39	0 3
Brentford	Mar-87	£60,000	233	220	13	14	19	79	7 9

Wimbledon	Aug-93	£350,000	31	10	21	2	2		3	0	0
Wycombe W *	Dec-95	Loan	–	–	–	–	–		–	–	–
Crewe Alex *	Mar-96	Loan	–	–	–	–	–		–	–	–

FAPL Summary by Club

| Wimbledon 1993-94 to 1995-96 | | | 31 | 10 | 21 | 2 | 2 | | 3 | 0 | 0 |
| *Total* | | | *31* | *10* | *21* | *2* | *2* | | *3* | *0* | *0* |

BLUNT Jason   Leeds United
Fullname: Jason Blunt   DOB: 16-08-77 Penzance
Debut: LEEDS UTD v Middlesbrough 30/3/96 as sub

Previous Clubs Details			*Apps*						*Goals*		
Club	Signed	Fee	Tot	Start	Sub	FA	FL		Lge	FA	FL
Leeds Utd			3	2	1	0	0		0	0	0

FAPL Summary by Club

| Leeds Utd | 1995-96 | | 3 | 2 | 1 | 0 | 0 | | 0 | 0 | 0 |
| *Total* | | | *3* | *2* | *1* | *0* | *0* | | *0* | *0* | *0* |

BODEN Chris   Derby County
Fullname: Christopher Desmond Boden   DOB: 13-10-73 Wolverhampton
Debut: Leicester City v ASTON VILLA 3/12/94 as sub

Previous Clubs Details			*Apps*						*Goals*		
Club	Signed	Fee	Tot	Start	Sub	FA	FL		Lge	FA	FL
Aston Villa	Dec-91		1	0	1	0	0		0	0	0
Barnsley	Oct-93	Loan	4	4	0	0	0		0	0	0
Derby County	Mar-95	£150,000	10	10	0	0	0		0	0	0

FAPL Summary by Club

| Aston Villa | 1994-95 to 1995-96 | | 1 | 0 | 1 | 0 | 0 | | 0 | 0 | 0 |
| *Total* | | | *1* | *0* | *1* | *0* | *0* | | *0* | *0* | *0* |

BOHINEN Lars   Blackburn Rovers
Fullname: Lars Bohinen   DOB: 08-09-69 Norway
Debut: Ipswich Town v NOTTINGHAM FOREST 20/8/94 as sub
Debut Goal: NOTTINGHAM FOREST v Sheffield W. 10/9/94

Previous Clubs Details			*Apps*						*Goals*		
Club	Signed	Fee	Tot	Start	Sub	FA	FL		Lge	FA	FL
Langes, Lillestrom			–	–	–	–	–		–	–	–
N. Forest	Oct-93	£450,000	64	59	5	1	5		6	0	2
Blackburn Rvs	Oct-95	£700,000	20	18	2	1	0		4	0	0

FAPL Summary by Club

N. Forest	1994-95 to 1995-96		41	37	4	1	5		6	0	2
Blackburn Rvs	1995-96		20	18	2	1	0		4	0	0
Total			*61*	*55*	*6*	*2*	*5*		*10*	*0*	*2*

BOLAND Willie   Coventry City
Fullname: Willie Boland   DOB: 06-08-75 Ennis, Ireland
Debut: Chelsea v COVENTRY CITY 1/5/93 as sub

Previous Clubs Details			*Apps*					*Goals*		
Club	Signed	Fee	Tot	Start	Sub	FA	FL	Lge	FA	FL
Coventry City	Nov-92		43	35	8	1	4	0	0	0
FAPL Summary by Club										
Coventry City 1992-93 to 1995-96			43	35	8	0	4	0	0	0
Total			*43*	*35*	*8*	*0*	*4*	*0*	*0*	*0*

BOOGERS Marco   West Ham United

Fullname: Marco Boogers   DOB: 12-01-67 Dordrecht
Debut: WEST HAM UTD v Leeds Utd 19/8/95 as sub

Previous Clubs Details			*Apps*					*Goals*		
Club	Signed	Fee	Tot	Start	Sub	FA	FL	Lge	FA	FL
Sparta Rotterdam										
West Ham Utd	Aug-95	£1m	4	0	4	0	0	0	0	0
FAPL Summary by Club										
West Ham Utd	1995-96		4	0	4	0	0	0	0	0
Total			*4*	*0*	*4*	*0*	*0*	*0*	*0*	*0*

BOOTH Andy   Sheffield Wednesday

Fullname: Andrew David Booth   DOB: 06-12-73 Huddersfield

Previous Clubs Details			*Apps*					*Goals*		
Club	Signed	Fee	Tot	Start	Sub	FA	FL	Lge	FA	FL
Huddersfield *	Jul-92	Trainee	80	66	14	4	7	38	1	0
Sheffield W.	Jul-96	£2.7m	0	0	0	0	0	0	0	0

BORROWS Brian   Coventry City

Fullname: Brian Borrows   DOB: 20-12-60 Liverpool
Debut: Sheffield W. v COVENTRY CITY 2/9/92
Debut Goal: COVENTRY CITY v Liverpool 19/12/92

Previous Clubs Details			*Apps*					*Goals*		
Club	Signed	Fee	Tot	Start	Sub	FA	FL	Lge	FA	FL
Everton	Apr-80		29	27	2	0	0	0	0	0
Bolton Wdrs	Mar-83	£10,000	95	95	0	4	7	0	0	0
Coventry City	Jun-85	£80,000	365	359	6	22	35	11	0	1
Bristol City	Sep-93	Loan	25	25	0	1	3	0	0	0
FAPL Summary by Club										
Coventry City 1992-93 to 1995-96			121	117	4	7	7	2	0	1
Total			*121*	*117*	*4*	*7*	*7*	*2*	*0*	*1*

BOSNICH Mark   Aston Villa

Fullname: Mark John Bosnich   DOB: 13-01-72 Sydney, Australia
Debut: Sheffield W. v ASTON VILLA 5/12/92
Debut Goal: (Goalkeeper)

Previous Clubs Details			*Apps*					*Goals*		
Club	Signed	Fee	Tot	Start	Sub	FA	FL	Lge	FA	FL
Manchester Utd	Jun-89		3	3	0	0	0	0	0	0

| Croatia Sydney | Aug-91 | | – | – | – | – | – | | – | – | – |
| Aston Villa | Feb-92 | Free | 113 | 113 | 0 | 10 | 19 | | 0 | 0 | 0 |

FAPL Summary by Club

Aston Villa	1992-93 to 1995-96		113	113	0	10	19		0	0	0
Total			*113*	*113*	*0*	*10*	*19*		*0*	*0*	*0*

BOULD Steve   Arsenal

Fullname: Stephen Andrew Bould   DOB: 16-11-62 Stoke
Debut: ARSENAL v Norwich City 15/8/92
Debut Goal: ARSENAL v Norwich City 15/8/92

Previous Clubs Details			*Apps*					*Goals*		
Club	Signed	Fee	Tot	Start	Sub	FA	FL	Lge	FA	FL
Stoke City	Nov-80		183	179	4	10	13	6	0	1
Torquay Utd	Oct-82	Loan	9	9	0	2	0	0	0	0
Arsenal	Jun-89	£390,000	211	203	8	17	28	5	0	1

FAPL Summary by Club

Arsenal	1992-93 to 1995-96		99	96	3	5	18	1	0	1
Total			*99*	*96*	*3*	*5*	*18*	*1*	*0*	*1*

BOWEN Mark   West Ham United

Fullname: Mark Rosslyn Bowen   DOB: 07-12-63 Neath
Debut: Arsenal v NORWICH CITY 15/8/92
Debut Goal: NORWICH CITY v QPR 17/10/92

Previous Clubs Details			*Apps*					*Goals*		
Club	Signed	Fee	Tot	Start	Sub	FA	FL	Lge	FA	FL
Tottenham H.	Dec-81		17	14	3	3	0	2	0	0
Norwich City*	Jul-87	£90,000	252	250	2	21	23	20	1	1
West Ham Utd	Jul-96	Free	0	0	0	0	0	0	0	0

FAPL Summary by Club

Norwich City	1992-93 to 1994-95		119	117	2	7	12	8	0	0
Total			*119*	*117*	*2*	*7*	*12*	*8*	*0*	*0*

BOWMAN Robert   Leeds United

Fullname: Robert A. Bowman   DOB: 06-08-75 Durham
Debut: Wimbledon v LEEDS UTD 6/2/93 as sub

Previous Clubs Details			*Apps*					*Goals*		
Club	Signed	Fee	Tot	Start	Sub	FA	FL	Lge	FA	FL
Leeds Utd	Nov-92		7	4	3	0	1	0	0	0

FAPL Summary by Club

Leeds Utd	1992-93 to 1995-96		7	4	3	0	1	0	0	0
Total			*7*	*4*	*3*	*0*	*1*	*0*	*0*	*0*

BOWYER Lee   Leeds United

Fullname: Lee David Bowyer   DOB: 03-01-77 London

Previous Clubs Details			Apps					Goals		
Club	Signed	Fee	Tot	Start	Sub	FA	FL	Lge	FA	FL
Charlton Ath *	Apr-94	Trainee	5	5	0	0	1	0	0	0
Leeds Utd	Jul-96	£3m	0	0	0	0	0	0	0	0

BRACEWELL Paul   Sunderland

Fullname: Paul William Bracewell   DOB: 19-07-62 Heswall
Debut: NEWCASTLE UTD v Tottenham H. 14/8/93
Debut Goal: NEWCASTLE UTD v Aston Villa 23/2/94

Previous Clubs Details			Apps					Goals		
Club	Signed	Fee	Tot	Start	Sub	FA	FL	Lge	FA	FL
Stoke City	Feb-80		129	123	6	6	6	5	0	1
Sunderland	Jul-83	£250,000	38	38	0	2	4	4	0	0
Everton	May-84	£425,000	95	95	0	21	11	7	0	2
Sunderland	Sep-89	£250,000	113	112	1	10	9	2	0	0
Newcastle Utd	Jun-92	£250,000	76	69	9	8	4	3	0	1
Sunderland	May-95	£100,000	38	38	0	4	4	0	0	0
FAPL Summary by Club										
Newcastle Utd 1993-94 to 1994-95			48	45	3	4	3	1	0	1
Total			*48*	*45*	*3*	*4*	*3*	*1*	*0*	*1*

BRANCH Michael   Everton

Fullname: Michael Branch   DOB: 18-10-72 Liverpool
Debut: Manchester Utd v EVERTON 21/2/96 as sub

Previous Clubs Details			Apps					Goals		
Club	Signed	Fee	Tot	Start	Sub	FA	FL	Lge	FA	FL
Everton			3	1	2	0	0	0	0	0
FAPL Summary by Club										
Everton	1995-96		3	1	2	0	0	0	0	0
Total			*3*	*1*	*2*	*0*	*0*	*0*	*0*	*0*

BRANCO   Middlesbrough

Fullname: Claudio Ibraim Vaz Leal   DOB: 04-04-64 Bage, Brazil
Debut: MIDDLESBROUGH v Everton 29/3/96 as sub

Previous Clubs Details			Apps					Goals		
Club	Signed	Fee	Tot	Start	Sub	FA	FL	Lge	FA	FL
Fluminense	1981									
Brescia	1986		50	–	–	–	–	4	–	–
FC Porto	1988		110	–	–	–	–	11	–	–
Genoa	1991		71	–	–	–	–	8	–	–
Fluminense	1993		–	–	–	–	–	–	–	–
Internacional	1994		–	–	–	–	–	–	–	–
Middlesbrough	Feb-96	Free	7	5	2	0	0	0	0	0
FAPL Summary by Club										
Middlesbrough		1995-96	7	5	2	0	0	0	0	0
Total			*7*	*5*	*2*	*0*	*0*	*0*	*0*	*0*

BREACKER Tim — West Ham United

Fullname: Timothy Sean Breacker DOB: 02-07-65 Bicester
Debut: WEST HAM UTD v Wimbledon 14/8/93
Debut Goal: WEST HAM UTD v Coventry City 11/12/93

Previous Clubs Details

Club	Signed	Fee	Tot	Start	Sub	FA	FL	Lge	FA	FL
Luton Town	May-83		210	204	6	21	24	3	0	0
West Ham Utd	Oct-90	£600,000	192	187	5	22	13	8	0	0

FAPL Summary by Club

West Ham Utd	1993-94 to 1995-96		95	92	3	8	7	3	0	0
Total			*95*	*92*	*3*	*8*	*7*	*3*	*0*	*0*

BRIDGES Michael — Sunderland

Fullname: Michael Bridges DOB:

Previous Clubs Details

Club	Signed	Fee	Tot	Start	Sub	FA	FL	Lge	FA	FL
Sunderland			16	2	14	0	0	4	0	0

BRIGHT Mark — Sheffield Wednesday

Fullname: Mark Abraham Bright DOB: 06-06-62 Stoke
Debut: SHEFFIELD WED v Blackburn Rvs 15/8/92
Debut Goal: SHEFFIELD WED v Blackburn Rvs 15/8/92

Previous Clubs Details

Club	Signed	Fee	Tot	Start	Sub	FA	FL	Lge	FA	FL
Port Vale	Oct-81		29	18	11	1	2	10	1	0
Leicester City	Jul-84	£33,000	42	26	16	1	4	6	0	0
Crystal Palace	Nov-86	£75,000	227	224	3	14	22	90	2	11
Sheffield W.	Sep-92	£375,000	132	112	20	13	21	50	7	11

FAPL Summary by Club

Crystal Palace	1992-93		5	5	0	0	0	0	0	0
Sheffield W.	1992-93 to 1995-96		132	112	20	13	21	50	7	11
Total			*137*	*117*	*20*	*13*	*21*	*50*	*7*	*11*

BRISCOE Lee — Sheffield Wednesday

Fullname: Lee Briscoe DOB: 30-09-75 Pontefract
Debut: Tottenham H. v SHEFFIELD WED 5/2/94 as sub

Previous Clubs Details

Club	Signed	Fee	Tot	Start	Sub	FA	FL	Lge	FA	FL
Sheffield W.	May-94		32	28	4	0	1	0	0	0

FAPL Summary by Club

Sheffield W.	1993-94 to 1995-96		32	28	4	0	1	0	0	0
Total			*32*	*28*	*4*	*0*	*1*	*0*	*0*	*0*

BROLIN Tomas — Leeds United

Fullname: Tomas Brolin DOB: 29-11-69 Hudiksvall, Sweden
Debut: Newcastle Utd v LEEDS UTD 25/11/95 as sub

Debut Goal: Sheffield Wed. v LEEDS UTD, 16/12/95

Previous Clubs Details			*Apps*					*Goals*		
Club	Signed	Fee	Tot	Start	Sub	FA	FL	Lge	FA	FL
GIF Sundsvall	1987		51	–	–	–	–	13	–	–
Norrkoping	1990		11	–	–	–	–	7	–	–
Parma	1990									
Leeds Utd	Nov-95	£4.5m	19	17	2	2	4	4	0	0
FAPL Summary by Club										
Leeds Utd	1995-96		19	17	2	2	4	4	0	0
Total			*19*	*17*	*2*	*2*	*4*	*4*	*0*	*0*

BROWN Kenny   West Ham United

Fullname: Kenneth James Brown   DOB: 11-07-67 Barking
Debut: Newcastle Utd v WEST HAM UTD 25/9/93

Previous Clubs Details			*Apps*					*Goals*		
Club	Signed	Fee	Tot	Start	Sub	FA	FL	Lge	FA	FL
Norwich City	Jul-85	Juniors	25	24	1	0	0	0	0	0
Plymouth A	Aug-88	Free	126	126	0	6	9	4	0	0
West Ham Utd	Aug-91	£175,000	63	55	8	9	2	5	1	0
Huddersfield *	Sep-95	Loan	–	–	–	–	–	–	–	–
Reading *	Oct-95	Loan	–	–	–	–	–	–	–	–
C. Palace *	Mar-96	Loan	–	–	–	–	–	–	–	–
FAPL Summary by Club										
West Ham Utd	1993-94 to 1995-96		21	17	4	4	1	0	1	0
Total			*21*	*17*	*4*	*4*	*1*	*0*	*1*	*0*

BURLEY Craig   Chelsea

Fullname: Craig William Burley   DOB: 24-09-71 Irvine
Debut: Tottenham H. v CHELSEA 5/12/92
Debut Goal: CHELSEA v Everton 3/1/94

Previous Clubs Details			*Apps*					*Goals*		
Club	Signed	Fee	Tot	Start	Sub	FA	FL	Lge	FA	FL
Chelsea	Sep-89		82	59	23	13	5	5	3	0
FAPL Summary by Club										
Chelsea	1992-93 to 1995-96		73	53	20	13	2	5	3	0
Total			*73*	*53*	*20*	*13*	*2*	*5*	*3*	*0*

BURROWS David   Coventry City

Fullname: David Burrows   DOB: 25-10-68 Dudley
Debut: N. Forest v WEST HAM UTD 16/8/92
Debut Goal: WEST HAM UTD v Coventry City 11/12/93

Previous Clubs Details			*Apps*					*Goals*		
Club	Signed	Fee	Tot	Start	Sub	FA	FL	Lge	FA	FL
WBA	Oct-86		46	37	9	2	4	1	0	0
Liverpool	Oct-88	£550,000	146	135	11	17	16	3	0	0
West Ham Utd	Sep-93	Swap	29	29	0	3	3	1	0	1

Everton	Sep-94	Swap +	19	19	0	2	2	0	0	0
Coventry City	Mar-95	£1.1m	24	24	0	1	0	0	0	0

FAPL Summary by Club

Club			Tot	Start	Sub	FA	FL	Lge	FA	FL
Liverpool	1992-93 to 1993-94		30	29	1	0	5	2	0	0
West Ham Utd	1993-94 to 1994-95		29	29	0	3	3	1	0	1
Everton	1994-95		19	19	0	2	2	0	0	0
Coventry City	1994-95 to 1995-96		24	24	0	1	0	0	0	0
Total			*102*	*101*	*1*	*6*	*10*	*3*	*0*	*1*

BUSST David   Coventry City

Fullname: David John Busst   DOB: 30-06-67 Birmingham
Debut: Norwich City v COVENTRY CITY 16/1/93
Debut Goal: COVENTRY CITY v Everton 20/8/94

Previous Clubs Details			*Apps*					*Goals*		
Club	Signed	Fee	Tot	Start	Sub	FA	FL	Lge	FA	FL
Coventry City	Jan-92	Free	50	48	2	4	3	2	0	1

FAPL Summary by Club

Coventry City	1992-93 to 1995-96		50	48	2	4	6	4	0	1
Total			*50*	*48*	*2*	*4*	*6*	*4*	*0*	*1*

BUTT Nicky   Manchester United

Fullname: Nicholas Butt   DOB: 21-01-75 Manchester
Debut: MANCHESTER UTD v Oldham Ath 21/11/92
Debut Goal: Southampton v MANCHESTER UTD 31/12/94

Previous Clubs Details			*Apps*					*Goals*		
Club	Signed	Fee	Tot	Start	Sub	FA	FL	Lge	FA	FL
Manchester Utd	Jan-93		56	42	14	11	3	3	1	0

FAPL Summary by Club

Manchester Utd	1992-93 to 1995-96		56	42	14	12	3	3	1	0
Total			*56*	*42*	*14*	*12*	*3*	*3*	*1*	*0*

CALDERWOOD Colin   Tottenham Hotspur

Fullname: Colin Calderwood   DOB: 20-01-65 Stranraer
Debut: Newcastle Utd v TOTTENHAM H. 14/8/93
Debut Goal: TOTTENHAM H. v Sheffield Wed 10/12/94

Previous Clubs Details			*Apps*					*Goals*		
Club	Signed	Fee	Tot	Start	Sub	FA	FL	Lge	FA	FL
Mansfield T	Mar-82		100	97	3	6	4	1	1	0
Swindon Town	Jul-85	£30,000	330	328	2	17	35	20	1	0
Tottenham H.	Jul-93	£1.25m	91	87	4	13	9	2	0	0

FAPL Summary by Club

Tottenham H.	1993-94 to 1995-96		91	87	4	13	9	2	0	0
Total			*91*	*87*	*4*	*13*	*9*	*2*	*0*	*0*

CAMPBELL Andy — Middlesbrough

Fullname: Andrew Campbell DOB:
Debut: MIDDLESBROUGH v Sheffield W. 5/4/96 as sub

Previous Clubs Details			*Apps*					*Goals*		
Club	Signed	Fee	Tot	Start	Sub	FA	FL	Lge	FA	FL
Middlesbrough			2	1	1	0	0	0	0	0
FAPL Summary by Club										
Middlesbrough	1995-96		2	1	1	0	0	0	0	0
Total			*2*	*1*	*1*	*0*	*0*	*0*	*0*	*0*

CAMPBELL Sol — Tottenham Hotspur

Fullname: Sulzeer Campbell DOB: 18-09-74 Newham
Debut: TOTTENHAM H. v Chelsea 5/12/92 as sub
Debut Goal: TOTTENHAM H. v Chelsea 5/12/92

Previous Clubs Details			*Apps*					*Goals*		
Club	Signed	Fee	Tot	Start	Sub	FA	FL	Lge	FA	FL
Tottenham H.	Sep-92		96	87	9	12	9	1	0	1
FAPL Summary by Club										
Tottenham H.	1992-93 to 1995-96		96	87	9	12	9	2	0	1
Total			*96*	*87*	*9*	*12*	*9*	*2*	*0*	*1*

CAMPBELL Kevin — Nottingham Forest

Fullname: Kevin Joseph Campbell DOB: 04-02-70 Lambeth
Debut: ARSENAL v Norwich City 15/8/92
Debut Goal: ARSENAL v Norwich City 15/8/92

Previous Clubs Details			*Apps*					*Goals*		
Club	Signed	Fee	Tot	Start	Sub	FA	FL	Lge	FA	FL
Arsenal	Feb-88		166	124	42	19	14	46	2	6
Leyton Orient	Jan-89	Loan	16	16	0	0	0	9	0	0
Leicester City	Nov-89	Loan	11	11	0	0	0	5	0	0
N. Forest	Jun-95	£2.5m	21	21	0	7	0	3	3	0
FAPL Summary by Club										
Arsenal	1992-93 to 1994-95		97	79	18	12	18	22	1	6
N. Forest	1995-96		21	21	0	7	0	3	3	0
Total			*118*	*100*	*18*	*19*	*18*	*25*	*4*	*6*

CANTONA Eric — Manchester United

Fullname: Eric Cantona DOB: 24-05-66 Paris, France
Debut: MANCHESTER UTD v Wimbledon 15/8/92
Debut Goal: Middlesbrough v MANCHESTER UTD 22/8/92

Previous Clubs Details			*Apps*					*Goals*		
Club	Signed	Fee	Tot	Start	Sub	FA	FL	Lge	FA	FL
Auxerre			81	–	–	–	–	23	–	–
Martiques	Loan		–	–	–	–	–	–	–	–
Marseille	1988	£2.2m	55	–	–	–	–	13	–	–

266

			Apps					Goals		
Bordeaux	Loan		11	–	–	–	–	6	–	–
Montpellier	Loan		33	–	–	–	–	10	–	–
Nimes	1991	£1m	–	–	–	–	–	–	–	–
Leeds Utd	Feb-92	£900,000	28	18	10	0	1	9	0	0
Manchester Utd	Nov-92	£1.2m	107	106	1	14	6	53	10	1

FAPL Summary by Club

		Apps					Goals		
Leeds Utd	1992-93	13	12	1	0	1	6	0	0
Manchester Utd	1992-93 to 1995-96	107	106	1	14	6	53	10	1
Total		*120*	*118*	*2*	*14*	*7*	*59*	*10*	*1*

CARBON Matt   Derby County

Fullname: Matthew Carbon   DOB: 08-06-75 Nottingham

Previous Clubs Details			Apps					Goals		
Club	Signed	Fee	Tot	Start	Sub	FA	FL	Lge	FA	FL
Lincoln City *	Apr-93		43	40	3	3	3	7	0	1
Derby County	Mar-96	£400,000	5	2	3	0	0	0	0	0

CAREY Brian   Leicester City

Fullname: Brian Patrick Carey   DOB: 31-05-68 Cork
Debut: Wimbledon v LEICESTER CITY 10/9/94

Previous Clubs Details			Apps					Goals		
Club	Signed	Fee	Tot	Start	Sub	FA	FL	Lge	FA	FL
Manchester Utd	Sep-89	£100,000	0	0	0	0	0	0	0	0
Wrexham	Jan-91	Loan	3	3	0	0	0	0	0	0
Wrexham	Dec-91	Loan	13	13	0	3	0	1	0	0
Leicester City	Jul-93	£250,000	58	51	7	1	3	1	0	0

FAPL Summary by Club

		Apps					Goals		
Leicester City	1994-95	12	11	1	0	0	0	0	0
Total		*12*	*11*	*1*	*0*	*0*	*0*	*0*	*0*

CARR Franz   Aston Villa

Fullname: Franz Alexander Carr   DOB: 24-09-66 Preston
Debut: Coventry City v SHEFFIELD UTD 24/3/93
Debut Goal: Manchester Utd v SHEFFIELD UTD 6/2/93

Previous Clubs Details			Apps					Goals		
Club	Signed	Fee	Tot	Start	Sub	FA	FL	Lge	FA	FL
Blackburn Rvs	Jul-84		0	0	0	0	0	0	0	0
N. Forest	Aug-84	£100,000	131	122	9	4	18	17	0	5
Sheffield W.	Dec-89	Loan	12	9	3	2	0	0	0	0
West Ham Utd	Mar-91	Loan	3	1	2	0	0	0	0	0
Newcastle Utd	May-91	£250,000	24	20	4	0	4	3	0	0
Sheffield Utd	Jan-93	£120,000	18	18	0	4	0	4	0	0
Leicester City	Sep-94	£100,000	13	12	1	0	0	1	0	0
Aston Villa	Dec-95	£250,000 +	4	3	1	1	0	0	1	0

CARSLEY Lee Derby County

Fullname: Lee Carsley   DOB: 28-04-74 Birmingham

Previous Clubs Details			*Apps*				*Goals*		
Club	Signed	Fee	Tot	Start	Sub	FA	FL	Lge	FA	FL
Derby County	May-95		58	53	5	1	6	3	0	0

CASTLEDINE Stewart Wimbledon

Fullname: Stewart Mark Castledine   DOB: 22-01-73 Wandsworth
Debut: Coventry City v WIMBLEDON 2/4/94
Debut Goal: Coventry City v WIMBLEDON 2/4/94

Previous Clubs Details			*Apps*				*Goals*		
Club	Signed	Fee	Tot	Start	Sub	FA	FL	Lge	FA	FL
Wimbledon	Jul-91		15	10	5	2	0	3	0	0
Wycombe W	Aug-95	Loan								

FAPL Summary by Club

		Tot	Start	Sub	FA	FL	Lge	FA	FL
Wimbledon	1993-94 to 1995-96	13	10	3	2	0	3	0	0
Total		*13*	*10*	*3*	*2*	*0*	*3*	*0*	*0*

CHARLES Gary Aston Villa

Fullname: Gary Andrew Charles   DOB: 13-04-70 Newham
Debut: Manchester Utd v ASTON VILLA 4/2/95
Debut Goal: –

Previous Clubs Details			*Apps*				*Goals*		
Club	Signed	Fee	Tot	Start	Sub	FA	FL	Lge	FA	FL
N. Forest	Nov-87	Trainee	56	54	2	10	9	1	0	1
Leicester City	Mar-89	Loan	8	5	3	0	0	0	0	0
Derby County	Jul-93	£750,000	43	43	0	1	3	1	0	0
Aston Villa	Jan-95	£2.9m +	50	48	2	5	8	1	0	0

FAPL Summary by Club

		Tot	Start	Sub	FA	FL	Lge	FA	FL
N. Forest	1992-93	14	14	0	0	0	0	0	0
Aston Villa	1994-95 to 1995-96	50	48	2	5	8	1	0	0
Total		*64*	*62*	*2*	*5*	*8*	*1*	*0*	*0*

CHARLTON Simon Southampton

Fullname: Simon Thomas Charlton   DOB: 25-10-71 Huddersfield
Debut: SOUTHAMPTON v Everton 14/8/93
Debut Goal: SOUTHAMPTON v Chelsea 27/12/93

Previous Clubs Details			*Apps*				*Goals*		
Club	Signed	Fee	Tot	Start	Sub	FA	FL	Lge	FA	FL
Huddersfield	Jul-89	Trainee	124	121	3	10	9	1	0	1

Southampton	Aug-93	£250,000	84	78	6	8	5	2	0	0
FAPL Summary by Club										
Southampton	1993-94 to 1995-96		84	78	6	8	5	2	0	0
Total			*84*	*78*	*6*	*8*	*5*	*2*	*0*	*0*

CHARNOCK Phil — Liverpool

Fullname: Philip Charnock   DOB: 14-02-75 Southport

Previous Clubs Details			*Apps*					*Goals*		
Club	Signed	Fee	Tot	Start	Sub	FA	FL	Lge	FA	FL
Liverpool	May-92		0	0	0	0	1	0	0	0
Blackpool *	Feb-96	Loan								

CHETTLE Steve — Nottingham Forest

Fullname: Stephen Chettle   DOB: 27-09-68 Nottingham

Debut: N. Forest v Liverpool 16/8/92

Previous Clubs Details			*Apps*					*Goals*		
Club	Signed	Fee	Tot	Start	Sub	FA	FL	Lge	FA	FL
N. Forest	Aug-86	Trainee	293	280	13	32	41	7	0	1
FAPL Summary by Club										
N. Forest	1992-93 to 1995-96		108	108	0	13	10	0	0	0
Total			*108*	*108*	*0*	*13*	*10*	*0*	*0*	*0*

CHRISTIE Isyeden — Coventry City

Fullname: Isyeden Christie   DOB: 14-11-76

Debut: Blackburn Rvrs v COVENTRY CITY 23/9/95 as sub

Previous Clubs Details			*Apps*					*Goals*		
Club	Signed	Fee	Tot	Start	Sub	FA	FL	Lge	FA	FL
Coventry City			1	0	1	0	0	0	0	0
FAPL Summary by Club										
Coventry City	1995-96		1	0	1	0	1	0	0	0
Total			*1*	*0*	*1*	*0*	*1*	*0*	*0*	*0*

CLARK Lee — Newcastle United

Fullname: Lee Robert Clark   DOB: 27-10-72 Wallsend

Debut: NEWCASTLE UTD v Tottenham H. 14/8/93

Debut Goal: Swindon Town v NEWCASTLE UTD 18/9/93

Previous Clubs Details			*Apps*					*Goals*		
Club	Signed	Fee	Tot	Start	Sub	FA	FL	Lge	FA	FL
Newcastle Utd	Nov-89	Trainee	160	134	26	13	16	22	2	0
FAPL Summary by Club										
Newcastle Utd	1993-94 to 1995-96		76	60	16	7	8	5	1	0
Total			*76*	*60*	*16*	*7*	*8*	*5*	*1*	*0*

CLARKE Adrian — Arsenal

Fullname: Adrian Clarke   DOB: 28-09-74

Debut: ARSENAL v QPR 31/12/94 as sub

Previous Clubs Details			Apps					Goals		
Club	Signed	Fee	Tot	Start	Sub	FA	FL	Lge	FA	FL
Arsenal	Trainee		7	4	3	2	0	0	0	0
FAPL Summary by Club										
Arsenal	1994-95 to 1995-96		7	4	3	2	0	0	0	0
Total			*7*	*4*	*3*	*2*	*0*	*0*	*0*	*0*

CLARKE Steve   Chelsea
Fullname: Stephen Clarke   DOB: 29-08-63 Saltcoats
Debut: CHELSEA v Oldham Ath 15/8/92

Previous Clubs Details			Apps					Goals		
Club	Signed	Fee	Tot	Start	Sub	FA	FL	Lge	FA	FL
St Mirren	1981	Free	151	151	0	20	21	6	0	0
Chelsea	Jan-87	£422,000	251	247	4	20	16	6	1	1
FAPL Summary by Club										
Chelsea	1992-93 to 1995-96		110	107	3	20	7	0	0	0
Total			*110*	*107*	*3*	*20*	*7*	*0*	*0*	*0*

CLARKE Andy   Wimbledon
Fullname: Andrew Weston Clarke   DOB: 22-07-67 Islington
Debut: Leeds Utd v WIMBLEDON 15/8/92
Debut Goal: WIMBLEDON v Aston Villa 3/10/92

Previous Clubs Details			Apps					Goals		
Club	Signed	Fee	Tot	Start	Sub	FA	FL	Lge	FA	FL
From NL Barnet										
Wimbledon	Feb-91	£250,000	145	69	76	12	16	16	2	3
FAPL Summary by Club										
Wimbledon	1992-93 to 1995-96		99	49	50	7	5	10	2	1
Total			*99*	*49*	*50*	*7*	*5*	*10*	*2*	*1*

COLE Andy   Manchester United
Fullname: Andrew Alexander Cole   DOB: 15-10-71 Nottingham
Debut: NEWCASTLE UTD v Tottenham H. 14/8/93
Debut Goal: Manchester Utd v NEWCASTLE UTD 21/8/93

Previous Clubs Details			Apps					Goals		
Club	Signed	Fee	Tot	Start	Sub	FA	FL	Lge	FA	FL
Arsenal	Oct-89	Trainee	1	0	1	0	0	0	0	0
Fulham	May-91	Loan	13	13	0	0	0	3	0	0
Bristol City	Mar-92	£500,000	41	41	0	0	0	20	0	0
Newcastle Utd	Mar-93	£1.75m	70	69	1	4	7	54	1	8
Manchester Utd	Jan-95	£7m +	52	49	3	7	1	23	2	0
FAPL Summary by Club										
Newcastle Utd	1993-94 to 1994-95		58	58	0	4	7	43	1	8
Manchester Utd	1994-95 to 1995-96		52	49	3	7	1	23	2	0
Total			*110*	*107*	*3*	*11*	*8*	*66*	*3*	*8*

COLEMAN Chris — Blackburn Rovers

Fullname: Christopher Coleman DOB: 10-06-70 Swansea
Debut: CRYSTAL PALACE v Blackburn Rvs 15/8/92
Debut Goal: Coventry City v CRYSTAL PALACE 3/12/92

Previous Clubs Details

Club	Signed	Fee	Tot	Start	Sub	FA	FL	Lge	FA	FL
			Apps					*Goals*		
Swansea City	Sep-87	Man.C.Jnrs	160	159	1	13	8	2	1	0
Crystal Palace	Jul-91	£275,000	154	143	11	8	26	13	1	2
Blackburn Rvs	Dec-95	£2.8m	20	19	1	2	0	0	0	0

FAPL Summary by Club

Crystal Palace	1992-93 to 1994-95		73	66	7	7	14	6	1	2
Blackburn Rvs	1995-96		20	19	1	2	0	0	0	0
Total			*93*	*85*	*8*	*9*	*14*	*6*	*1*	*2*

COLLYMORE Stan — Liverpool

Fullname: Stanley Victor Collymore DOB: 22-01-71 Stone
Debut: CRYSTAL PALACE v Southampton 26/9/92 as sub
Debut Goal: N. Forest v Manchester Utd 22/8/94

Previous Clubs Details

Club	Signed	Fee	Tot	Start	Sub	FA	FL	Lge	FA	FL
			Apps					*Goals*		
Crystal Palace	Jan-91	£100,000	20	4	16	0	5	1	0	0
Southend Utd	Nov-92	£100,000	30	30	0	3	0	15	3	0
N. Forest	Jul-93	£2.1m	65	64	1	2	9	41	1	7
Liverpool	Jul-95	£8.5m	30	29	1	7	4	14	5	0

FAPL Summary by Club

Crystal Palace	1992-93		2	0	2	0	2	0	0	0
N. Forest	1993-94 to 1994-95		37	37	0	2	4	23	1	2
Liverpool	1995-96		30	29	1	7	4	14	5	0
Total			*69*	*66*	*3*	*9*	*10*	*37*	*6*	*2*

COOKE Terry — Manchester United

Fullname: Terry Cooke DOB: 05-08-76 Marston Green
Debut: MANCHESTER UTD v Bolton Wdrs 16/9/95

Previous Clubs Details

Club	Signed	Fee	Tot	Start	Sub	FA	FL	Lge	FA	FL
			Apps					*Goals*		
Manchester Utd			4	1	3	0	2	0	0	0
Sunderland	Jan-96	Loan	6	6	0	0	0	0	0	0

FAPL Summary by Club

Manchester Utd	1994-95		4	1	3	0	2	0	0	0
Total			*4*	*1*	*3*	*0*	*2*	*0*	*0*	*0*

COOPER Colin — Nottingham Forest

Fullname: Colin Terence Cooper DOB: 28-02-67 Durham
Debut: Ipswich Town v N. Forest 20/8/94
Debut Goal: Everton v N. Forest 30/8/94

Previous Clubs Details			Apps					Goals		
Club	Signed	Fee	Tot	Start	Sub	FA	FL	Lge	FA	FL
Middlesbrough	Jul-84		189	183	6	13	18	6	0	0
Millwall	Jul-91	£300,000	77	77	0	2	6	6	0	0
N. Forest	Jun-93	£1.5m	109	108	1	8	10	13	1	1
FAPL Summary by Club										
N. Forest	1994-95 to 1995-96		72	72	0	6	6	6	0	0
Total			*72*	*72*	*0*	*6*	*6*	*6*	*0*	*0*

COOPER Kevin Derby County

Fullname: Kevin Lee Cooper   DOB: 08-02-75 Derby

Previous Clubs Details			Apps					Goals		
Club	Signed	Fee	Tot	Start	Sub	FA	FL	Lge	FA	FL
Derby County	02-93	Trainee	2	0	2	0	0	0	0	0

COTON Tony Sunderland

Fullname: Anthony Philip Coton   DOB: 19-05-61 Tamworth
Debut: Man. City v QPR 17/8/92   Debut Goal: (Goalkeeper)

Previous Clubs Details			Apps					Goals		
Club	Signed	Fee	Tot	Start	Sub	FA	FL	Lge	FA	FL
Birmingham C	Oct-78		94	94	0	10	10	0	0	0
Watford	Sep-84	£300,000	233	233	0	32	18	0	0	0
Man. City	Jul-90	£1m	163	162	1	11	16	0	0	0
Manchester Utd	Jan-96	£500,000	0	0	0	0	0	0	0	0
Sunderland	Jul-96	£350,000								
FAPL Summary by Club										
Man. City	1992-93 to 1995-96		93	92	1	4	9	0	0	0
Total			*93*	*92*	*1*	*4*	*9*	*0*	*0*	*0*

COTTEE Tony West Ham United

Fullname: Anthony Richard Cottee   DOB: 11-07-65 West Ham
Debut: Blackburn Rvs v EVERTON 15/9/92
Debut Goal: Blackburn Rvs v EVERTON 15/9/92

Previous Clubs Details			Apps					Goals		
Club	Signed	Fee	Tot	Start	Sub	FA	FL	Lge	FA	FL
West Ham Utd	Sep-82	Trainee	212	203	9	24	19	92	11	14
Everton	Aug-88	£2.3m	184	161	23	21	23	72	11	4
West Ham Utd	Sep-94	£300,000+	64	61	3	5	6	23	1	3
FAPL Summary by Club										
Everton	1992-93 to 1994-95		68	64	4	2	8	28	3	0
West Ham Utd	1994-95 to 1995-96		64	61	3	5	6	23	1	3
Total			*132*	*125*	*7*	*7*	*14*	*51*	*4*	*3*

COUZENS Andy Leeds United

Fullname: Andrew Couzens   DOB: 04-06-75 Shipley
Debut: LEEDS UTD v Coventry City 18/3/95 as sub

Previous Clubs Details   Apps   Goals

Club	Signed	Fee	Tot	Start	Sub	FA	FL	Lge	FA	FL
Leeds Utd			18	10	8	0	2	0	0	0
FAPL Summary by Club										
Leeds Utd	1994-95 to 1995-96		18	10	8	0	2	0	0	1
Total			*18*	*10*	*8*	*0*	*2*	*0*	*0*	*1*

COX Neil   Middlesbrough

Fullname: Neil James Cox   DOB: 08-10-71 Scunthorpe
Debut: Sheffield W. v ASTON VILLA 5/12/92
Debut Goal: ASTON VILLA v Everton 20/2/93

Previous Clubs Details   Apps   Goals

Club	Signed	Fee	Tot	Start	Sub	FA	FL	Lge	FA	FL
Scunthorpe Utd	Mar-90	Trainee	17	17	0	4	0	1	0	0
Aston Villa	Feb-91	£400,000	7	4	3	0	0	0	0	0
Middlesbrough	Jul-94	£850,000	75	74	1	2	8	3	0	0
FAPL Summary by Club										
Aston Villa	1992-93 to 1993-94		35	22	13	6	7	3	0	0
Middlesbrough	1995-96		35	35	0	2	5	2	0	0
Total			*70*	*57*	*13*	*8*	*12*	*5*	*0*	*0*

CRAWFORD Jimmy   Newcastle United

Fullname: James Crawford   DOB: Chicago, USA

Previous Clubs Details   Apps   Goals

Club	Signed	Fee	Tot	Start	Sub	FA	FL	Lge	FA	FL
Bohemians (Ire)			–	–	–	–	–	–	–	–
Newcastle Utd	Mar-95	£75,000	0	0	0	0	1	0	0	0

CROFT Gary   Blackburn Rovers

Fullname: Gary Croft   DOB: 17-02-74 Burton on Trent

Previous Clubs Details   Apps   Goals

Club	Signed	Fee	Tot	Start	Sub	FA	FL	Lge	FA	FL
Grimsby Town	Jul-92	Trainee	113	103	10	5	5	2	1	0
Blackburn Rvs	Mar-96	£1m	0	0	0	0	0	0	0	0

CROSSLEY Mark   Nottingham Forest

Fullname: Mark Geoffrey Crossley   DOB: 16-06-69 Barnsley
Debut: N. Forest v Liverpool 16/8/92   Debut Goal: (Goalkeeper)

Previous Clubs Details   Apps   Goals

Club	Signed	Fee	Tot	Start	Sub	FA	FL	Lge	FA	FL
N. Forest	Jul-87	Trainee	238	237	1	29	31	0	0	0
FAPL Summary by Club										
N. Forest	1992-93 to 1995-96		117	117	0	9	6	0	0	0
Total			*117*	*117*	*0*	*9*	*6*	*0*	*0*	*0*

CUNDY Jason — Tottenham Hotspur

Fullname: Jason Victor Cundy DOB: 12-11-69 Wandsworth
Debut: Southampton v TOTTENHAM H. 15/8/92
Debut Goal: Ipswich Town v TOTTENHAM H. 30/8/92

Previous Clubs Details			*Apps*					*Goals*		
Club	Signed	Fee	Tot	Start	Sub	FA	FL	Lge	FA	FL
Chelsea	Aug-88		41	40	1	6	6	2	0	0
Tottenham H.	Mar-92	£750,000	26	23	3	0	2	1	0	0
Crystal Palace	*Dec-95	Loan	–	–	–	–	–	–	–	–
FAPL Summary by Club										
Tottenham H. 1992-93 to 1995-96			16	13	3	0	2	1	0	0
Total			*16*	*13*	*3*	*0*	*2*	*1*	*0*	*0*

CUNNINGHAM Kenny — Wimbledon

Fullname: Kenneth Edward Cunningham DOB: 28-06-71 Dublin
Debut: WIMBLEDON v Newcastle Utd 19/11/94

Previous Clubs Details			*Apps*					*Goals*		
Club	Signed	Fee	Tot	Start	Sub	FA	FL	Lge	FA	FL
Millwall	Sep-89		121	117	4	1	8	1	0	0
Wimbledon	Nov-94	£1.3m +	61	60	1	11	2	0	0	0
FAPL Summary by Club										
Wimbledon 1994-95 to 1995-96			61	60	1	11	2	0	0	0
Total			*61*	*60*	*1*	*11*	*2*	*0*	*0*	*0*

DAISH Liam — Coventry City

Fullname: Liam Sean Daish DOB: 23-09-68 Portsmouth
Debut: COVENTRY CITY v Middlesbrough 24/2/96
Debut Goal: Everton v COVENTRY CITY 9/3/96

Previous Clubs Details			*Apps*					*Goals*		
Club	Signed	Fee	Tot	Start	Sub	FA	FL	Lge	FA	FL
Portsmouth	Aug-86	Apprentice	1	1	0	0	0	0	0	0
Cambridge Utd	Jul-88	Free	139	138	1	17	11	5	0	0
Birmingham C.	Jan-94	£50,000	56	56	0	5	3	3	0	1
Coventry City	Feb-95	£1.5m	11	11	0	0	0	1	0	0
FAPL Summary by Club										
Coventry City	1995-96		11	11	0	0	0	1	0	0
Total			*11*	*11*	*0*	*0*	*0*	*1*	*0*	*0*

DAVIES Simon — Manchester United

Fullname: Simon Davies DOB: 23-04-74 Winsford
Debut: MANCHESTER UTD v Crystal Palace 19/11/94

Previous Clubs Details			*Apps*					*Goals*		
Club	Signed	Fee	Tot	Start	Sub	FA	FL	Lge	FA	FL
Manchester Utd	Jul-92	Trainee	11	4	7	0	1	0	0	0
Exeter City	Dec-93	Loan	6	5	1	1	0	1	0	0

FAPL Summary by Club

		Tot	Start	Sub	FA	FL	Lge	FA	FL
Manchester Utd	1994-95 to 1995-96	11	4	7	0	4	0	0	0
Total		*11*	*4*	*7*	*0*	*4*	*0*	*0*	*0*

DAVIS Neil   Aston Villa

Fullname: Neil Davis   DOB: 15-08-73 Bloxwich
Debut: ASTON VILLA v Middlesbrough 19/3/96 as sub

Previous Clubs Details			*Apps*				*Goals*		
Club	Signed	Fee	Tot	Start	Sub	FA	FL	Lge	FA	FL
Aston Villa	1991	From NL	2	0	2	1	0	0	0	0

FAPL Summary by Club

		Tot	Start	Sub	FA	FL	Lge	FA	FL
Aston Villa	1995-96	2	0	2	1	0	0	0	0
Total		*2*	*0*	*2*	*1*	*0*	*0*	*0*	*0*

DAY Chris   Tottenham Hotspur

Fullname: Christopher Day   DOB: 28-07-75 Whipps Cross
Debut Goal: (Goalkeeper)

Previous Clubs Details			*Apps*				*Goals*		
Club	Signed	Fee	Tot	Start	Sub	FA	FL	Lge	FA	FL
Tottenham	1992	Trainee	0	0	0	0	0	0	0	0

DEANE Brian   Leeds United

Fullname: Brian Christopher Deane   DOB: 07-02-68 Leeds
Debut: LEEDS UTD v Manchester Utd 15/8/93
Debut Goal: LEEDS UTD v Manchester Utd 15/8/93

Previous Clubs Details			*Apps*				*Goals*		
Club	Signed	Fee	Tot	Start	Sub	FA	FL	Lge	FA	FL
Doncaster Rvs	Dec-85	Junior	66	59	7	3	3	12	1	0
Sheffield Utd	Jul-88	£30,000	197	197	0	24	16	93	11	11
Leeds Utd	Jul-93	£2.7m	110	104	6	11	12	27	3	2

FAPL Summary by Club

		Tot	Start	Sub	FA	FL	Lge	FA	FL
Sheffield Utd	1992-93	41	41	0	6	4	15	3	2
Leeds Utd	1993-94 to 1995-96	110	104	6	12	10	27	3	2
Total		*151*	*145*	*6*	*18*	*14*	*42*	*6*	*4*

DI MATTEO Roberto   Chelsea

Fullname: Roberto Di Matteo   DOB: 29-05-70 Sciaffusa (Swit)

Previous Clubs Details			*Apps*				*Goals*		
Club	Signed	Fee	Tot	Start	Sub	FA	FL	Lge	FA	FL
Schaffhausen	1988		50	–	–	–	–	2	–	–
Zurich (Swi)	1991		34	–	–	–	–	6	–	–
Aarau (Swi)	1992		31	–	–	–	–	1	–	–
Lazio (Ita)	1993		–	–	–	–	–	–	–	–
Chelsea	Jul-96	£4.9m								

DICKOV Paul — Arsenal

Fullname: Paul Dickov
DOB: 01-11-72 Livingstone
Debut: ARSENAL v Southampton 20/3/93
Debut Goal: ARSENAL v Crystal Palace 8/5/93

Previous Clubs Details			Apps					Goals		
Club	Signed	Fee	Tot	Start	Sub	FA	FL	Lge	FA	FL
Arsenal	Dec-90		22	6	14	0	4	3	0	0
Luton Town	Oct-93	Loan	15	8	7	0	0	1	0	0
Brighton HA	10-Mar	Loan	8	8	0	0	0	5	0	0
FAPL Summary by Club										
Arsenal	1992-93 to 1995-96		20	6	14	0	4	3	0	3
Total			*20*	*6*	*14*	*0*	*4*	*3*	*0*	*3*

DICKS Julian — West Ham United

Fullname: Julian Andrew Dicks
DOB: 08-08-68 Bristol
Debut: WEST HAM UTD v Wimbledon 14/8/93
Debut Goal: Everton v LIVERPOOL 14/8/93

Previous Clubs Details			Apps					Goals		
Club	Signed	Fee	Tot	Start	Sub	FA	FL	Lge	FA	FL
Birmingham C.	Apr-86		89	83	6	5	6	1	0	0
West Ham Utd	Mar-88	£300,000	159	159	0	14	19	29	2	5
Liverpool	Sep-93	£1.6m	24	24	0	1	3	3	0	0
West Ham Utd	Oct-94	£500,000+	63	63	0	5	5	15	0	1
FAPL Summary by Club										
West Ham Utd	1993-94		7	7	0	0	0	1	0	0
Liverpool	1993-94 to 1994-95		24	24	0	1	3	3	0	0
West Ham Utd	1994-95 to 1995-96		63	63	0	5	5	15	0	1
Total			*94*	*94*	*0*	*6*	*8*	*19*	*0*	*1*

DIXON Lee — Arsenal

Fullname: Lee Michael Dixon
DOB: 17-03-64 Manchester
Debut: ARSENAL v Norwich City 15/8/92
Debut Goal: ARSENAL v Norwich City 1/4/95

Previous Clubs Details			Apps					Goals		
Club	Signed	Fee	Tot	Start	Sub	FA	FL	Lge	FA	FL
Burnley	Jul-82		4	4	0	0	1	0	0	0
Chester City	Feb-84	Free	57	56	1	1	2	1	0	0
Bury	Jul-85	Free	45	45	0	8	4	6	1	0
Stoke City	Jul-86	£40,000	71	71	0	7	6	5	0	0
Arsenal	Jan-88	£400,000	254	251	3	26	32	16	1	0
FAPL Summary by Club										
Arsenal	1992-93 to 1995-96		139	138	1	15	23	3	0	0
Total			*139*	*138*	*1*	*15*	*23*	*3*	*0*	*0*

DONALDSON O'Neill — Sheffield Wednesday

Fullname: O'Neill Donaldson   DOB: 24-11-69
Debut: Man. City v SHEFFIELD WED 18/3/95 as sub
Debut Goal: QPR v SHEFFIELD W. 9/9/95

Previous Clubs Details			*Apps*				*Goals*		
Club	Signed	Fee	Tot	Start	Sub	FA	FL	Lge	FA	FL
Sheffield W.			4	2	2	0	0	1	0	0
FAPL Summary by Club										
Sheffield W.	1994-95 to 1995-96		4	1	3	0	0	1	0	0
Total			*4*	*1*	*3*	*0*	*0*	*1*	*0*	*0*

DONIS George — Blackburn Rovers

Fullname: Georgio Donis   DOB:

Previous Clubs Details			*Apps*				*Goals*		
Club	Signed	Fee	Tot	Start	Sub	FA	FL	Lge	FA	FL
Panathinaikos (Greece)			–	–	–	–	–	–	–	–
Blackburn Rvs	Jul-96	Free								

DORIGO Tony — Leeds United

Fullname: Anthony Robert Dorigo   DOB: 31-12-65 Melbourne
Debut: LEEDS UTD v Wimbledon 15/8/92
Debut Goal: LEEDS UTD v Ipswich Town 27/2/93

Previous Clubs Details			*Apps*				*Goals*		
Club	Signed	Fee	Tot	Start	Sub	FA	FL	Lge	FA	FL
Aston Villa	Jul-83		111	106	5	7	15	1	0	0
Chelsea	May-87	£475,000	146	146	0	4	14	11	0	0
Leeds Utd	May-91	£1.3m	153	153	0	12	13	5	0	0
FAPL Summary by Club										
Leeds Utd	1992-93 to 1995-96		115	115	0	11	8	2	0	0
Total			*115*	*115*	*0*	*11*	*8*	*2*	*0*	*0*

DOW Andy — Chelsea

Fullname: Andrew Dow   DOB: 07-02-73 Dundee
Debut: CHELSEA v Blackburn Rvs 14/8/93 as sub

Previous Clubs Details			*Apps*				*Goals*		
Club	Signed	Fee	Tot	Start	Sub	FA	FL	Lge	FA	FL
Dundee	Nov-90		–	–	–	–	–	–	–	–
Chelsea	Aug-93		15	14	1	1	2	0	0	0
Bradford City	Sep-94	Loan	5	0	0	0	0	0	0	0
FAPL Summary by Club										
Chelsea	1993-94 to 1995-96		15	14	1	1	2	0	0	0
Total			*15*	*14*	*1*	*1*	*2*	*0*	*0*	*0*

DOWIE Iain — West Ham United

Fullname: Iain Dowie   DOB: 09-01-65 Hatfield
Debut: QPR v SOUTHAMPTON 19/8/92

Debut Goal: Crystal Palace v SOUTHAMPTON 26/9/92

Previous Clubs Details

Club	Signed	Fee	Apps					Goals		
			Tot	Start	Sub	FA	FL	Lge	FA	FL
Luton Town	Dec-88	£30k NL	66	53	13	3	4	15	0	0
Fulham	Sep-89	Loan	5	5	0	0	0	1	0	0
West Ham Utd	Mar-91	£480,000	12	12	0	0	0	4	0	0
Southampton	Sep-91	£500,000	122	115	7	6	11	30	1	1
Crystal Palace	Jan-95	£400,000	15	15	0	6	0	4	4	0
West Ham Utd	Sep-95	£125,000 + 33	33	33	0	3	3	8	1	0

FAPL Summary by Club

		Apps					Goals		
Southampton	1992-93 to 1994-95	92	90	2	2	7	21	1	1
Crystal Palace	1994-95 to 1995-96	15	15	0	6	0	4	4	0
West Ham Utd	1995-96	33	33	0	3	3	8	1	0
Total		*140*	*138*	*2*	*11*	*10*	*33*	*6*	*1*

DOZZELL Jason   Tottenham Hotspur

Fullname: Jason Alvin Winans Dozzell   DOB: 09-12-67 Ipswich
Debut: IPSWICH TOWN v Aston Villa 15/8/92
Debut Goal: IPSWICH TOWN v Liverpool 25/8/92

Previous Clubs Details

Club	Signed	Fee	Apps					Goals		
			Tot	Start	Sub	FA	FL	Lge	FA	FL
Ipswich Town	Dec-84		291	271	20	18	23	45	10	3
Tottenham H.	Aug-93	£1.9m	67	58	9	5	8	11	1	0

FAPL Summary by Club

		Apps					Goals		
Ipswich Town	1992-93	41	41	0	4	7	7	2	0
Tottenham H.	1993-94 to 1995-96	67	58	9	5	8	11	1	0
Total		*108*	*99*	*9*	*9*	*15*	*18*	*3*	*0*

DRAPER Mark   Aston Villa

Fullname: Mark Draper   DOB: 11-11-70 Long Eaton
Debut: LEICESTER CITY v Newcastle Utd 21/8/94
Debut Goal: Everton v LEICESTER CITY 24/9/94

Previous Clubs Details

Club	Signed	Fee	Apps					Goals		
			Tot	Start	Sub	FA	FL	Lge	FA	FL
Notts County	Dec-88		222	206	16	10	15	40	1	1
Leicester City	Jul-94	£1.25m	39	39	0	2	2	5	0	0
Aston Villa	Jul-95	£3.25m	36	36	0	5	8	2	2	1

FAPL Summary by Club

		Apps					Goals		
Leicester City	1994-95	39	39	0	2	2	5	0	0
Aston Villa	1995-96	36	36	0	5	8	2	2	1
Total		*75*	*75*	*0*	*7*	*10*	*7*	*2*	*1*

DUBERRY Michael   Chelsea

Fullname: Michael Wayne Duberry   DOB: 14-10-75 London
Debut: CHELSEA v Coventry City 4/5/94

Previous Clubs Details			Apps					Goals		
Club	Signed	Fee	Tot	Start	Sub	FA	FL	Lge	FA	FL
Chelsea	Jun-93		23	23	0	8	0	0	2	0
FAPL Summary by Club										
Chelsea	1993-94 to 1995-96		23	23	0	8	0	0	2	0
Total			*23*	*23*	*0*	*8*	*0*	*0*	*2*	*0*

DUBLIN Dion — Coventry City

Fullname: Dion Dublin DOB: 22-04-69 Leicester
Debut: Sheffield Utd v MANCHESTER UTD 15/8/92 as sub
Debut Goal: Southampton v MANCHESTER UTD 24/8/92

Previous Clubs Details			Apps					Goals		
Club	Signed	Fee	Tot	Start	Sub	FA	FL	Lge	FA	FL
Norwich City	Mar-88		0	0	0	0	0	0	0	0
Cambridge Utd	Aug-88		156	133	23	21	10	53	11	5
Manchester Utd	Jul-92	£1m	12	4	8	2	2	2	0	1
Coventry City	Sep-94	£2m	0	65	65	7	5	27	3	2
FAPL Summary by Club										
Manchester Utd	1992-93 to 1994-95		12	4	8	2	2	2	0	1
Coventry City	1994-95 to 1995-96		65	65	0	7	5	27	3	2
Total			*77*	*69*	*8*	*9*	*7*	*29*	*3*	*3*

DUMITRESCU Ilie — West Ham United

Fullname: Ilie Dumitrescu DOB: 06-01-69 Romania
Debut: Sheffield Wed v TOTTENHAM H. 20/8/94
Debut Goal: TOTTENHAM H. v Ipswich Town 30/8/94

Previous Clubs Details			Apps					Goals		
Club	Signed	Fee	Tot	Start	Sub	FA	FL	Lge	FA	FL
Steaua Buc.	Jun-87		2	2	0	0	0	0	0	0
Olt Scornicesti	Jul-87		32	32	0	1	0	1	0	0
Steaua Buc.	Jul-88		164	164	0	16	0	71	4	0
Tottenham H.	Aug-94	£2.6m	31	29	2	0	2	9	0	0
FC Seville	Dec-94	Loan	–	–	–	–	–	–		
West Ham Utd	Jan-95	£1.65m	3	2	1	0	0	0	0	0
FAPL Summary by Club										
Tottenham H.	1994-95 to 1995-96		18	16	2	0	2	5	0	0
West Ham Utd	1995-96		3	2	1	0	0	0	0	0
Total			*21*	*18*	*3*	*0*	*2*	*5*	*0*	*0*

EARLE Robbie — Wimbledon

Fullname: Robert Gerald Earle DOB: 27-01-65 Newcastle-u-Lyme
Debut: Leeds Utd v WIMBLEDON 15/8/92
Debut Goal: WIMBLEDON v Arsenal 5/9/92

Previous Clubs Details			Apps					Goals		
Club	Signed	Fee	Tot	Start	Sub	FA	FL	Lge	FA	FL
Port Vale	Jul-82		294	284	10	21	23	77	4	4

Wimbledon	Jul-91	£775,000	160	160	0	21	14	41	3	5
FAPL Summary by Club										
Wimbledon	1992-93 to 1995-96		130	130	0	19	12	27	3	5
Total			*130*	*130*	*0*	*19*	*12*	*27*	*3*	*5*

EBBRELL John   Everton

Fullname:	John Keith Ebbrell	DOB: 01-10-69 Bromborough

Debut: EVERTON v Sheffield W. 15/8/92
Debut Goal: Blackburn Rvs v EVERTON 15/9/92

Previous Clubs Details			*Apps*					*Goals*		
Club	Signed	Fee	Tot	Start	Sub	FA	FL	Lge	FA	FL
Everton	Nov-86		210	200	10	20	16	13	3	1
FAPL Summary by Club										
Everton	1992-93 to 1995-96		114	113	1	10	7	9	1	0
Total			*114*	*113*	*1*	*10*	*7*	*9*	*1*	*0*

EDINBURGH Justin   Tottenham Hotspur

Fullname:	Justin Charles Edinburgh	DOB: 18-12-69 Brentwood

Debut: Southampton v TOTTENHAM H. 15/8/92
Debut Goal:

Previous Clubs Details			*Apps*					*Goals*		
Club	Signed	Fee	Tot	Start	Sub	FA	FL	Lge	FA	FL
Southend Utd	Jul-88		62	60	2	5	6	0	0	0
Tottenham H.	Jul-90	£150,000	149	135	14	21	19	1	0	0
FAPL Summary by Club										
Tottenham H.	1992-93 to 1995-96		110	99	11	16	11	0	0	0
Total			*110*	*99*	*11*	*16*	*11*	*0*	*0*	*0*

EHIOGU Ugo   Aston Villa

Fullname:	Ugochuku Ehiogu	DOB: 03-11-72 Hackney

Debut: ASTON VILLA v Southampton 22/8/92
Debut Goal: Tottenham H. v ASTON VILLA 23/8/95

Previous Clubs Details			*Apps*					*Goals*		
Club	Signed	Fee	Tot	Start	Sub	FA	FL	Lge	FA	FL
WBA	Jul-89		2	0	2	0	0	0	0	0
Aston Villa	Jul-91	£40,000	103	92	11	9	13	1	0	1
FAPL Summary by Club										
Aston Villa	1992-93 to 1995-96		96	89	7	8	13	1	0	1
Total			*96*	*89*	*7*	*8*	*13*	*1*	*0*	*1*

EKOKU Efan   Wimbledon

Fullname:	Efangwu Goziem Ekoku	DOB: 08-06-67 Manchester

Debut: NORWICH CITY v Manchester Utd 5/4/93 as sub
Debut Goal: Tottenham H. v NORWICH CITY 9/4/93

Previous Clubs Details			Apps					Goals		
Club	Signed	Fee	Tot	Start	Sub	FA	FL	Lge	FA	FL
Bournemouth	May-90		62	43	19	7	7	21	2	0
Norwich City	Mar-93	£500,000	37	26	11	2	3	15	0	1
Wimbledon	Oct-94	£800,000	55	52	3	10	1	16	3	0
FAPL Summary by Club										
Norwich City	1992-93 to 1994-95		37	26	11	1	3	15	0	2
Wimbledon	1994-95 to 1995-96		55	52	3	10	1	16	3	0
Total			*92*	*78*	*14*	*11*	*4*	*31*	*3*	*2*

ELKINS Gary — Wimbledon

Fullname: Gary Elkins DOB: 04-05-66 Wallingford
Debut: Leeds Utd v WIMBLEDON 15/8/92
Debut Goal: WIMBLEDON v Liverpool 4/4/94

Previous Clubs Details			Apps					Goals		
Club	Signed	Fee	Tot	Start	Sub	FA	FL	Lge	FA	FL
Fulham	Dec-83		104	100	4	4	6	2	0	0
Exeter City	Dec-89	Loan	5	5	0	0	0	0	0	0
Wimbledon	Aug-90	£20,000	110	100	10	7	8	3	1	0
FAPL Summary by Club										
Wimbledon	1992-93 to 1995-96		82	75	7	7	7	2	0	0
Total			*82*	*75*	*7*	*7*	*7*	*2*	*0*	*0*

ELLIOTT Robert — Newcastle United

Fullname: Robert James Elliott DOB: 25-12-73 Newcastle
Debut: Oldham Ath v NEWCASTLE UTD 23/2/94
Debut Goal: Leicester City v NEWCASTLE UTD 21/8/94 as sub

Previous Clubs Details			Apps					Goals		
Club	Signed	Fee	Tot	Start	Sub	FA	FL	Lge	FA	FL
Newcastle Utd	Apr-91		50	42	8	7	3	2	0	0
FAPL Summary by Club										
Newcastle Utd	1993-94 to 1995-96		35	28	7	7	2	2	0	0
Total			*35*	*28*	*7*	*7*	*2*	*2*	*0*	*0*

EMERSON — Middlesbrough

Fullname: Emerson Moises Costa DOB: 12-04-72 Rio de Janeiro

Previous Clubs Details			Apps					Goals		
Club	Signed	Fee	Tot	Start	Sub	FA	FL	Lge	FA	FL
Flamengo (Brazil)	1989									
Curtiba (Brazil)	1991									
Beleneses (Portugal)	1992									
FC Porto (Portugal)	1994									
Middlesbrough	Jul-96	£4m								

EUELL Jason   Wimbledon

Fullname: Jason Euell   DOB: 06-02-77 South London
Debut: WIMBLEDON v Southampton, 28/10/95
Debut Goal: WIMBLEDON v Southampton, 28/10/95

Previous Clubs Details   *Apps*   *Goals*

Club	Signed	Fee	Tot	Start	Sub	FA	FL	Lge	FA	FL
Wimbledon			9	4	5	6	0	2	0	0
FAPL Summary by Club										
Wimbledon	1995-96		9	4	5	6	0	2	0	0
Total			*9*	*4*	*5*	*6*	*0*	*2*	*0*	*0*

FARRELLY Gareth   Aston Villa

Fullname: Gareth Farrelly   DOB: 28-08-75 Dublin
Debut: ASTON VILLA v Leeds Utd 3/2/96 as sub

Previous Clubs Details   *Apps*   *Goals*

Club	Signed	Fee	Tot	Start	Sub	FA	FL	Lge	FA	FL
Aston Villa	Jan-92	Trainee	4	1	3	0	1	0	0	0
Rotherham Utd	Mar-95	Loan	10	9	1	0	0	2	0	0
FAPL Summary by Club										
Aston Villa	1995-96		4	1	3	0	1	0	0	0
Total			*4*	*1*	*3*	*0*	*1*	*0*	*0*	*0*

FEAR Peter   Wimbledon

Fullname: Peter Stanley Fear   DOB: 10-09-73 Sutton
Debut: Arsenal v WIMBLEDON 10/2/93
Debut Goal: WIMBLEDON v Leeds Utd 26/3/94

Previous Clubs Details   *Apps*   *Goals*

Club	Signed	Fee	Tot	Start	Sub	FA	FL	Lge	FA	FL
Wimbledon	Jul-92		45	37	8	3	5	2	0	0
FAPL Summary by Club										
Wimbledon	1992-93 to 1995-96		45	37	8	3	5	2	0	0
Total			*45*	*37*	*8*	*3*	*5*	*2*	*0*	*0*

FENTON Graham   Blackburn Rovers

Fullname: Graham Anthony Fenton   DOB: 22-05-74 Wallsend
Debut: ASTON VILLA v Man. City 22/2/94
Debut Goal: Sheffield Utd v ASTON VILLA 16/4/94

Previous Clubs Details   *Apps*   *Goals*

Club	Signed	Fee	Tot	Start	Sub	FA	FL	Lge	FA	FL
Aston Villa	Feb-92		32	16	16	0	7	3	0	0
WBA	Jan-94	Loan	7	7	0	0	0	3	0	0
Blackburn Rvs	Dec-95	£1.5m	14	4	10	0	0	6	0	0

		Tot	Start	Sub	FA	FL	Lge	FA	FL
Aston Villa	1993-94 to 1995-96	32	16	16	0	7	3	0	0
Blackburn Rvs	1995-96 to 1995-96	14	4	10	0	0	6	0	0
Total		*46*	*20*	*26*	*0*	*7*	*9*	*0*	*0*

FERDINAND Les — Newcastle United

Fullname: Leslie Ferdinand
Debut: Man. City v QPR 17/8/92   DOB: 18-12-66 Acton
Debut Goal: QPR v Southampton 19/8/92

Previous Clubs Details			*Apps*				*Goals*		
Club	Signed	Fee	Tot	Start	Sub	FA	FL	Lge	FA	FL
QPR	Apr-87	£15,000	163	152	11	8	13	80	3	7
Brentford	Mar-88	Loan	3	3	0	0	0	0	0	0
Besiktas	Jun-88	Loan	–	–	–	–	–	–	–	-
Newcastle Utd	Jun-95	£6m	37	37	0	2	5	25	1	3

FAPL Summary by Club									
QPR	1992-93 to 1994-95	110	109	1	7	8	60	3	5
Newcastle Utd	1995-96	37	37	0	2	5	25	1	3
Total		*147*	*146*	*1*	*9*	*13*	*85*	*4*	*8*

FERDINAND Rio — West Ham United

Fullname: Rio Ferdinand
Debut: WEST HAM UTD v Sheffield W. 5/5/96 as sub   DOB:

Previous Clubs Details			*Apps*				*Goals*		
Club	Signed	Fee	Tot	Start	Sub	FA	FL	Lge	FA	FL
West Ham Utd			1	0	1	0	0	0	0	0

FAPL Summary by Club									
West Ham Utd	1995-96	1	0	1	0	0	0	0	0
Total		*1*	*0*	*1*	*0*	*0*	*0*	*0*	*0*

FERGUSON Duncan — Everton

Fullname: Duncan Ferguson
Debut: EVERTON v Coventry City 15/10/94   DOB: 27-12-71 Stirling
Debut Goal: EVERTON v Liverpool 21/11/94

Previous Clubs Details			*Apps*				*Goals*		
Club	Signed	Fee	Tot	Start	Sub	FA	FL	Lge	FA	FL
Dundee Utd	Feb-90	From NL	77	75	2	8	3	28	6	2
Rangers	Jul-93	£4m	35	35	0	3	2	5	0	0
Everton	Dec-94	£4m +	41	38	3	6	1	12	3	0

FAPL Summary by Club									
Everton	1994-95 to 1995-96	41	38	3	6	1	12	3	0
Total		*41*	*38*	*3*	*6*	*1*	*12*	*3*	*0*

FILAN John   Coventry City

Fullname: John Filan   DOB: 08-02-70 Sydney
Debut: Tottenham H. v COVENTRY CITY 9/5/95
Debut Goal: (Goalkeeper)

Previous Clubs Details			*Apps*					*Goals*		
Club	Signed	Fee	Tot	Start	Sub	FA	FL	Lge	FA	FL
Sydney, Budapest			–	–	–	–	–	–	–	–
Cambridge Utd	Mar-93	£40,000	52	52	0	3	4	0	0	0
N. Forest	Dec-94	Loan	0	0	0	0	0	0	0	0
Coventry City	Mar-95	£300,000	15	15	0	0	2	0	0	0
FAPL Summary by Club										
Coventry City	1994-95 to 1995-96		15	15	0	0	2	0	0	0
Total			*15*	*15*	*0*	*0*	*2*	*0*	*0*	*0*

FINN Neil   West Ham United

Fullname: Neil Finn   DOB:
Debut: Man. City v WEST HAM UTD 1/1/96
Debut Goal: (Goalkeeper)

Previous Clubs Details			*Apps*					*Goals*		
Club	Signed	Fee	Tot	Start	Sub	FA	FL	Lge	FA	FL
West Ham Utd			1	1	0	0	0	0	0	0
FAPL Summary by Club										
West Ham Utd	1995-96		1	1	0	0	0	0	0	0
Total			*1*	*1*	*0*	*0*	*0*	*0*	*0*	*0*

FITZGERALD Scott   Wimbledon

Fullname: Scott Brian Fitzgerald   DOB: 13-08-69 Westminster
Debut: Leeds Utd v WIMBLEDON 15/8/92

Previous Clubs Details			*Apps*					*Goals*		
Club	Signed	Fee	Tot	Start	Sub	FA	FL	Lge	FA	FL
Wimbledon	Jul-87		106	95	11	9	8	13	0	0
Sheffield Utd *	Mar-96	Loan								
FAPL Summary by Club										
Wimbledon	1992-93 to 1995-96		69	61	8	6	11	0	0	0
Total			*69*	*61*	*8*	*6*	*11*	*0*	*0*	*0*

FJORTOFT Jan-Aage   Middlesbrough

Fullname: Jan-Aage Fjortoft   DOB: 10-01-67 Aalesund, Norway
Debut: Sheffield Utd v SWINDON TOWN 14/8/93
Debut Goal: SWINDON TOWN v Tottenham H. 22/1/94

Previous Clubs Details			*Apps*					*Goals*		
Club	Signed	Fee	Tot	Start	Sub	FA	FL	Lge	FA	FL
Rapid Vienna			–	–	–	–	–	–	–	–
Swindon Town	Aug-93	£500,000	36	26	10	2	1	12	1	0
Middlesbrough	Mar-95	£1.3m	36	35	1	0	6	9	0	2

		Tot	Start	Sub	FA	FL	Lge	FA	FL
Swindon Town	1993-94	36	26	10	2	1	12	1	0
Middlesbrough	1995-96	28	27	1	0	6	6	0	2
Total		*64*	*53*	*11*	*2*	*7*	*18*	*1*	*2*

FLEMING Curtis   **Middlesbrough**

Fullname: Curtis Fleming   DOB: 08-10-68 Manchester
Debut: Tottenham Hot v MIDDLESBROUGH 17/10/92 as sub
Debut Goal: MIDDLESBROUGH v Wimbledon 13/4/96

Previous Clubs Details			*Apps*				*Goals*		
Club	Signed	Fee	Tot	Start	Sub	FA	FL	Lge	FA	FL
Middlesbrough	Aug-91	£50,000	127	115	12	9	10	1	0	0

FAPL Summary by Club

		Tot	Start	Sub	FA	FL	Lge	FA	FL
Middlesbrough	1992-93 to 1995-96	38	36	2	2	1	1	0	0
Total		*38*	*36*	*2*	*2*	*1*	*1*	*0*	*0*

FLITCROFT Garry   **Blackburn Rovers**

Fullname: Gary William Flitcroft   DOB: 06-11-72 Bolton
Debut: Man. City v Oldham Ath 29/8/92
Debut Goal: Ipswich Town v Man. City 12/12/92

Previous Clubs Details			*Apps*				*Goals*		
Club	Signed	Fee	Tot	Start	Sub	FA	FL	Lge	FA	FL
Man. City	Jul-91		115	109	6	10	11	13	2	0
Bury	Mar-92	Loan	12	12	0	0	0	0	0	0
Blackburn Rvs	Mar-96	£3.2m	3	3	0	0	0	0	0	0

FAPL Summary by Club

		Tot	Start	Sub	FA	FL	Lge	FA	FL
Man. City	1992-93 to 1995-96	115	109	6	14	12	13	2	0
Blackburn Rvs	1995-96	3	3	0	0	0	0	0	0
Total		*118*	*112*	*6*	*14*	*12*	*13*	*2*	*0*

FLOWERS Tim   **Blackburn Rovers**

Fullname: Timothy David Flowers   DOB: 03-02-67 Kenilworth
Debut: SOUTHAMPTON v Tottenham H. 15/8/92
Debut Goal: (Goalkeeper)

Previous Clubs Details			*Apps*				*Goals*		
Club	Signed	Fee	Tot	Start	Sub	FA	FL	Lge	FA	FL
Wolves	Aug-84		63	63	0	2	5	0	0	0
Southampton	Jun-86	£70,000	192	192	0	16	26	0	0	0
Swindon Town	Mar-87	Loan	2	2	0	0	0	0	0	0
Swindon Town	Nov-87	Loan	5	5	0	0	0	0	0	0
Blackburn Rvs	Nov-93	£2.4m	105	105	0	8	7	0	0	0

FAPL Summary by Club

		Tot	Start	Sub	FA	FL	Lge	FA	FL
Southampton	1992-93 to 1993-94	54	54	0	1	5	0	0	0
Blackburn Rvs	1993-94 to 1995-96	105	105	0	4	11	0	0	0
Total		*159*	*159*	*0*	*5*	*16*	*0*	*0*	*0*

FLYNN Sean   Derby County

Fullname: Sean Michael Flynn   DOB: 13-03-68 Birmingham
Debut: COVENTRY CITY v Middlesbrough 15/8/92
Debut Goal: Arsenal v COVENTRY CITY 14/8/93

Previous Clubs Details   *Apps*   *Goals*

Club	Signed	Fee	Tot	Start	Sub	FA	FL	Lge	FA	FL
Coventry City	Mar-91	£20,000NL	97	90	7	3	5	9	0	1
Derby County	Aug-95	£225,000	42	29	13	1	3	2	0	0

FAPL Summary by Club

Coventry City 1992-93 to 1994-95			75	69	6	3	5	7	0	1
Total			*75*	*69*	*6*	*3*	*5*	*7*	*0*	*1*

FORD Mark   Leeds United

Fullname: Mark Ford   DOB: 10-10-75 Pontefract
Debut: Swindon Town v LEEDS UTD 7/5/94 as sub

Previous Clubs Details   *Apps*   *Goals*

Club	Signed	Fee	Tot	Start	Sub	FA	FL	Lge	FA	FL
Leeds Utd			12	11	1	5	4	0	0	0

FAPL Summary by Club

Leeds Utd 1993-94 to 1995-96			12	11	1	5	4	0	0	0
Total			*12*	*11*	*1*	*5*	*4*	*0*	*0*	*0*

FORRESTER Jamie   Leeds United

Fullname: Jamie Forrester   DOB: 01-11-74 Bradford
Debut: N. Forest v LEEDS UTD 21/3/93

Previous Clubs Details   *Apps*   *Goals*

Club	Signed	Fee	Tot	Start	Sub	FA	FL	Lge	FA	FL
Auxerre (France)			–	–	–	–	–	–	–	–
Leeds Utd	Oct-92	£120,000	9	7	2	2	0	0	0	0
Southend Utd	Sep-94	Loan	5	3	2	0	0	0	0	0

FAPL Summary by Club

Leeds Utd 1992-93 to 1995-96			9	7	2	2	0	0	0	0
Total			*9*	*7*	*2*	*2*	*0*	*0*	*0*	*0*

FOWLER Robbie   Liverpool

Fullname: Robert Bernard Fowler   DOB: 09-04-75 Liverpool
Debut: Chelsea v LIVERPOOL 25/9/93
Debut Goal: LIVERPOOL v Oldham Ath 16/10/93

Previous Clubs Details   *Apps*   *Goals*

Club	Signed	Fee	Tot	Start	Sub	FA	FL	Lge	FA	FL
Liverpool	Apr-92		108	105	3	15	17	65	6	11

FAPL Summary by Club

Liverpool 1993-94 to 1995-96			108	105	3	15	17	65	6	11
Total			*108*	*105*	*3*	*15*	*17*	*65*	*6*	*11*

FOX Ruel   Tottenham Hotspur
Fullname: Ruel Adrian Fox   DOB: 14-01-68 Ipswich
Debut: Arsenal v NORWICH CITY 15/8/92
Debut Goal: Arsenal v NORWICH CITY 15/8/92

Previous Clubs Details			*Apps*					*Goals*		
Club	Signed	Fee	Tot	Start	Sub	FA	FL	Lge	FA	FL
Norwich City	Jan-86		172	148	24	13	16	22	0	3
Newcastle Utd	Feb-94	£2.25m	58	56	2	5	3	12	0	1
Tottenham H.	Dec-95	£4.2m	26	26	0	6	0	6	0	0
FAPL Summary by Club										
Norwich City	1992-93 to 1993-94		59	57	2	4	5	11	0	2
Newcastle Utd	1993-94 to 1995-96		58	56	2	5	3	12	0	1
Tottenham H.	1995-96		26	26	0	6	0	6	0	0
Total			*143*	*139*	*4*	*15*	*8*	*29*	*0*	*3*

FREESTONE Chris   Middlesbrough
Fullname: Christopher Freestone   DOB: 09-04-71
Debut: MIDDLESBROUGH v Sheffield W. 5/4/96
Debut Goal: MIDDLESBROUGH v Sheffield W. 5/4/96

Previous Clubs Details			*Apps*					*Goals*		
Club	Signed	Fee	Tot	Start	Sub	FA	FL	Lge	FA	FL
Middlesbrough	Nov-94	£10,000NL	4	2	2	1	0	1	0	0
FAPL Summary by Club										
Middlesbrough	1995-96		3	2	1	1	0	1	0	0
Total			*3*	*2*	*1*	*1*	*0*	*1*	*0*	*0*

FUTRE Paulo   West Ham United
Fullname: Dos Santos Futre Jorge Paulo   DOB: 28-02-66 Montijo (Por)

Previous Clubs Details			*Apps*					*Goals*		
Club	Signed	Fee	Tot	Start	Sub	FA	FL	Lge	FA	FL
Sporting Lisbon	1983		21	–	–	–	–	3	–	–
FC Porto	1984		81	–	–	–	–	25	–	–
Atletico Madrid	1987		162	–	–	–	–	38	–	–
Benfica	Feb-93		11	–	–	–	–	3	–	–
Marseille	1993		8	–	–	–	–	2	–	–
Reggiana	Nov-93		–	–	–	–	–	–	–	–
Milan			–	–	–	–	–	–	–	–
West Ham Utd	Jul-96	Free								

GABBIADINI Marco   Derby County
Fullname: Marco Gabbiadini   DOB: 20-01-68 Nottingham

Previous Clubs Details			*Apps*					*Goals*		
Club	Signed	Fee	Tot	Start	Sub	FA	FL	Lge	FA	FL
York City	May-85		60	42	18	0	7	14	0	1
Sunderland	Sep-87	£80,000	157	155	2	5	14	75	0	9

Crystal Palace	Oct-91	£1.8m	15	15	0	1	6	5	0	1
Derby County	Jan-92	£1m	174	158	16	9	12	50	3	7

GALLACHER Kevin   Blackburn Rovers
Fullname: Kevin William Gallacher   DOB: 23-11-66 Clydebank
Debut: COVENTRY CITY v Blackburn Rvs 29/8/92
Debut Goal: Oldham Ath v COVENTRY CITY 5/9/92

Previous Clubs Details			*Apps*					*Goals*		
Club	Signed	Fee	Tot	Start	Sub	FA	FL	Lge	FA	FL
Coventry City	Jan-90		100	99	1	4	11	28	0	7
Blackburn Rvs	Mar-93	£1.6m	56	51	5	6	4	15	1	0
FAPL Summary by Club										
Coventry City	1992-93 to 1993-94		20	19	1	1	2	6	0	0
Blackburn Rvs	1992-93 to 1994-95		56	51	5	6	4	15	1	0
Total			*76*	*70*	*6*	*7*	*6*	*21*	*1*	*0*

GAYLE Marcus   Wimbledon
Fullname: Marcus Anthony Gayle   DOB: 27-09-70 Hammersmith
Debut: WIMBLEDON v Leeds Utd 26/3/94
Debut Goal: N. Forest v WIMBLEDON 17/10/94

Previous Clubs Details			*Apps*					*Goals*		
Club	Signed	Fee	Tot	Start	Sub	FA	FL	Lge	FA	FL
Brentford	Jul-89		156	118	38	8	9	22	2	0
Wimbledon	Mar-94	£250,000	67	53	14	8	4	7	0	1
FAPL Summary by Club										
Wimbledon	1993-94 to 1995-96		67	53	14	8	4	7	0	1
Total			*67*	*53*	*14*	*8*	*4*	*7*	*0*	*1*

GEMMILL Scot   Nottingham Forest
Fullname: Scot Gemmill   DOB: 02-01-71 Paisley
Debut: N. Forest v Liverpool 16/8/92
Debut Goal: Tottenham H. v NOTTM FOREST 28/10/92

Previous Clubs Details			*Apps*					*Goals*		
Club	Signed	Fee	Tot	Start	Sub	FA	FL	Lge	FA	FL
N. Forest	Jan-90		157	149	8	17	23	23	1	3
FAPL Summary by Club										
N. Forest	1992-93 to 1995-96		83	78	5	13	7	3	1	0
Total			*83*	*78*	*5*	*13*	*7*	*3*	*1*	*0*

GIGGS Ryan   Manchester United
Fullname: Ryan Joseph Giggs   DOB: 29-11-73 Cardiff
Debut: Sheffield Utd v MANCHESTER UTD 18/8/92
Debut Goal: N. Forest v MANCHESTER UTD 29/8/92

Previous Clubs Details			*Apps*					*Goals*		
Club	Signed	Fee	Tot	Start	Sub	FA	FL	Lge	FA	FL
Manchester Utd	Dec-90		177	164	13	26	27	37	5	7

		Tot	Start	Sub	FA	FL	Lge	FA	FL
Manchester Utd 1992-93 to 1995-96	141	131	10	23	12	34	5	3
Total		*141*	*131*	*10*	*23*	*12*	*34*	*5*	*3*

GILLESPIE Keith   Newcastle United

Fullname: Keith Gillespie   DOB: 18-02-75 Bangor
Debut: Sheffield W. v MANCHESTER UTD 8/10/94
Debut Goal: MANCHESTER UTD v Newcastle Utd 29/10/94 as sub

Previous Clubs Details			*Apps*					*Goals*		
Club	Signed	Fee	Tot	Start	Sub	FA	FL	Lge	FA	FL
Manchester Utd	Feb-93	Trainee	0	0	0	2	3	0	1	0
Wigan Ath	Sep-93	Loan	8	8	0	0	0	4	0	0
Newcastle Utd	Jan-95	£1m +	45	41	4	3	4	4	2	1

FAPL Summary by Club

		Tot	Start	Sub	FA	FL	Lge	FA	FL
Manchester Utd 1994-95 to 1994-95	9	3	6	0	3	1	0	0
Newcastle Utd 1994-95 to 1995-96	45	41	4	3	4	6	2	1
Total		*54*	*44*	*10*	*3*	*7*	*7*	*2*	*1*

GINOLA David   Newcastle United

Fullname: David Ginola   DOB: 25-01-67 Gassin, nr St. Tropez
Debut: NEWCASTLE UTD v Coventry City 19/8/95
Debut Goal: Sheffield Weds v NEWCASTLE UTD 27/8/95

Previous Clubs Details			*Apps*					*Goals*		
Club	Signed	Fee	Tot	Start	Sub	FA	FL	Lge	FA	FL
PSG (France)			–	–	–	–	–	–	–	–
Newcastle Utd	Jul-95	£2.5m	34	34	0	2	4	5	0	0

FAPL Summary by Club

		Tot	Start	Sub	FA	FL	Lge	FA	FL
Newcastle Utd	1995-96	34	34	0	2	4	5	0	0
Total		*34*	*34*	*0*	*2*	*4*	*5*	*0*	*0*

GIVEN Shay   Blackburn Rovers

Fullname: Shay Given   DOB: 20-04-76 Lifford
Debut Goal: (Goalkeeper)

Previous Clubs Details			*Apps*					*Goals*		
Club	Signed	Fee	Tot	Start	Sub	FA	FL	Lge	FA	FL
Blackburn Rvs		From Celtic	0	0	0	0	0	0	0	0
Swindon		Loan	–	–	–	–	–	–	–	–
Sunderland	Jan-96	Loan	17	17	0	0	0	0	0	0

GOODMAN Jon   Wimbledon

Fullname: Jonathan Goodman   DOB: 02-06-71 Walthamstow
Debut: WIMBLEDON v Newcastle Utd 19/11/94
Debut Goal: Ipswich Town v WIMBLEDON 16/12/94

Previous Clubs Details			*Apps*					*Goals*		
Club	Signed	Fee	Tot	Start	Sub	FA	FL	Lge	FA	FL
Millwall	Aug-90	£50,000NL	94	82	12	6	6	27	0	0

Wimbledon Nov-94 £1.3m + 46 22 24 4 1 10 3 0
FAPL Summary by Club
Wimbledon 1994-95 to 1995-96 46 22 24 4 1 10 3 0
Total 46 22 24 4 1 10 3 0

GRANT Tony — Everton

Fullname: Anthony Grant   DOB: 14-11-74 Liverpool
Debut: Newcastle Utd v EVERTON 1/2/95 as sub
Debut Goal: Middlesbrough v EVERTON 2/3/96

Previous Clubs Details			Apps					Goals		
Club	Signed	Fee	Tot	Start	Sub	FA	FL	Lge	FA	FL
Everton			18	12	6	1	2	1	0	0
Swindon *	Jan-96	Loan								
FAPL Summary by Club										
Everton	1994-95 to 1995-96		18	12	6	1	2	1	0	0
Total			18	12	6	1	2	1	0	0

GRAY Andy — Leeds United

Fullname: Andrew Gray   DOB: 15-11-77 Harrogate
Debut: LEEDS UTD v West Ham Utd 13/1/96 as sub

Previous Clubs Details			Apps					Goals		
Club	Signed	Fee	Tot	Start	Sub	FA	FL	Lge	FA	FL
Leeds Utd			15	12	3	2	2	0	0	0
FAPL Summary by Club										
Leeds Utd	1995-96		15	12	3	2	2	0	0	0
Total			15	12	3	2	2	0	0	0

GRAY Michael — Sunderland

Fullname: Michael Gray   DOB: 03-08-74 Sunderland

Previous Clubs Details			Apps					Goals		
Club	Signed	Fee	Tot	Start	Sub	FA	FL	Lge	FA	FL
Sunderland	Jul-92	Trainee	111	95	16	4	9	7	0	0

GRAY Martin — Sunderland

Fullname: Martin David Gray   DOB: 17-08-71 Stockton

Previous Clubs Details			Apps					Goals		
Club	Signed	Fee	Tot	Start	Sub	FA	FL	Lge	FA	FL
Sunderland	Feb-90	Trainee	64	46	18	3	8	1	0	0
Aldershot	Jan-91	Loan	5	3	2	0	0	0	0	0
Fulham	Oct-95	Loan								

GRAY Phil — Sunderland

Fullname: Philip Gray   DOB: 14-01-93 Belfast

Previous Clubs Details			Apps					Goals		
Club	Signed	Fee	Tot	Start	Sub	FA	FL	Lge	FA	FL
Tottenham H.	Aug-86	Apprentice	9	4	5	1	0	0	0	0

Barnsley	Jan-90	Loan	3	3	0	1	0	0	0	0
Fulham	Nov-90	Loan	3	3	0	0	0	0	0	0
Luton Town	Aug-91	£275,000	59	54	5	2	4	22	1	3
Sunderland	Jul-93	£800,000	115	108	7	8	9	34	3	4

GRAYSON Simon   Leicester City

Fullname: Simon Nicholas Grayson   DOB: 16-12-69 Ripon
Debut: LEICESTER CITY v Newcastle Utd 21/8/94

Previous Clubs Details			*Apps*					*Goals*		
Club	Signed	Fee	Tot	Start	Sub	FA	FL	Lge	FA	FL
Leeds Utd	Jun-88	Trainee	2	2	0	0	0	0	0	0
Leicester City	Mar-92	£50,000	152	139	13	16	11	2	0	0
FAPL Summary by Club										
Leicester City	1994-95		34	34	0	3	2	0	0	0
Total			*34*	*34*	*0*	*3*	*2*	*0*	*0*	*0*

GUDMUNDSSON Niklas   Blackburn Rovers

Fullname: Niklas Gudmundsson   DOB: 29-02-72 Halmstad
Debut: BLACKBURN RVRS v Sheffield W. 20/1/96 as sub

Previous Clubs Details			*Apps*					*Goals*		
Club	Signed	Fee	Tot	Start	Sub	FA	FL	Lge	FA	FL
Halstads			–	–	–	–	–	–	–	–
Blackburn Rvs	Mar-96	£750,000	4	1	3	0	0	0	0	0
FAPL Summary by Club										
Blackburn Rvs	1995-96		4	1	3	0	0	0	0	0
Total			*4*	*1*	*3*	*0*	*0*	*0*	*0*	*0*

GUINAN Steve   Nottingham Forest

Fullname: Stephen Guinan   DOB: 24-12-75 Birmingham
Debut: Wimbledon v N. Forest 30/3/96

Previous Clubs Details			*Apps*					*Goals*		
Club	Signed	Fee	Tot	Start	Sub	FA	FL	Lge	FA	FL
N. Forest			2	1	1	0	0	0	0	0
Darlington *	Dec-95	Loan								
FAPL Summary by Club										
N. Forest	1995-96		2	1	1	0	0	0	0	0
Total			*2*	*1*	*1*	*0*	*0*	*0*	*0*	*0*

GULLIT Ruud   Chelsea

Fullname: Dil Ruud Gullit   DOB: 01-09-62 Amsterdam
Debut: CHELSEA v Everton 19/8/95
Debut Goal: CHELSEA v Southampton 16/9/95

Previous Clubs Details			*Apps*					*Goals*		
Club	Signed	Fee	Tot	Start	Sub	FA	FL	Lge	FA	FL
Haarlem	Jul-79		91	–	–	–	–	32	–	–

Feyenoord	Jul-82		85	–	–	–	–	30	–	–
PSV	Jul-85		68	–	–	–	–	46	–	–
Milan	Jul-87		117	–	–	–	–	35	–	–
Sampdoria	Jul-93		–	–	–	–	–	–	–	–
Chelsea	May-95	Free	21	21	0	7	2	3	3	0

FAPL Summary by Club

Chelsea	1995-96	31	31	0	7	2	3	3	0
Total		*31*	*31*	*0*	*7*	*2*	*3*	*3*	*0*

HAALAND Alf-Inge   Nottingham Forest

Fullname: Alf-Inge Haaland   DOB: 23-11-72 Stavanger, Norway
Debut: Southampton v N. Forest 17/9/94
Debut Goal: N. Forest v Ipswich Town 10/12/94

Previous Clubs Details			*Apps*					*Goals*		
Club	Signed	Fee	Tot	Start	Sub	FA	FL	Lge	FA	FL
N. Forest			40	33	7	3	1	1	0	0

FAPL Summary by Club

N. Forest	1994-95 to 1995-96	37	30	7	3	1	1	0	0
Total		*37*	*30*	*7*	*3*	*1*	*1*	*0*	*0*

HALL Gareth   Sunderland

Fullname: Gareth David Hall   DOB: 20-03-69 Croydon
Debut: CHELSEA v Oldham Ath 15/8/92
Debut Goal: CHELSEA v Ipswich Town 17/10/92

Previous Clubs Details			*Apps*					*Goals*		
Club	Signed	Fee	Tot	Start	Sub	FA	FL	Lge	FA	FL
Chelsea	May-86		138	120	18	6	13	4	0	0
Sunderland	Jan-96	£300,000	14	8	6	0	0	0	0	0

FAPL Summary by Club

Chelsea	1992-93 to 1995-96	55	49	6	0	6	3	0	0
Total		*55*	*49*	*6*	*0*	*6*	*3*	*0*	*0*

HALL Marcus   Coventry City

Fullname: Marcus Hall   DOB: 24-03-76
Debut: COVENTRY CITY v Tottenham H. 31/12/94 as sub

Previous Clubs Details			*Apps*					*Goals*		
Club	Signed	Fee	Tot	Start	Sub	FA	FL	Lge	FA	FL
Coventry City			30	26	4	2	4	0	0	0

FAPL Summary by Club

Coventry City	1994-95 to 1995-96	30	26	4	2	4	0	0	0
Total		*30*	*26*	*4*	*2*	*4*	*0*	*0*	*0*

HALL Richard   West Ham United

Fullname: Richard Anthony Hall   DOB: 14-03-72 Ipswich
Debut: SOUTHAMPTON v Tottenham H. 15/8/92
Debut Goal: Oldham Ath v SOUTHAMPTON 31/10/92

Previous Clubs Details			*Apps*					*Goals*		
Club	Signed	Fee	Tot	Start	Sub	FA	FL	Lge	FA	FL
Scunthorpe Utd	Mar-90		22	22	0	3	2	3	0	0
Southampton	Feb-91	£200,000	126	119	7	12	14	11	3	1
West Ham Utd	Jul-96	£1.9m								
FAPL Summary by Club										
Southampton	1992-93 to 1995-96		99	98	1	10	7	9	1	1
Total			*99*	*98*	*1*	*10*	*7*	*9*	*1*	*1*

HARFORD Mick   Wimbledon

Fullname: Michael Gordon Harford   DOB: 12-02-59 Sunderland
Debut: CHELSEA v Oldham Ath 15/8/92
Debut Goal: CHELSEA v Oldham Ath 15/8/92

Previous Clubs Details			*Apps*					*Goals*		
Club	Signed	Fee	Tot	Start	Sub	FA	FL	Lge	FA	FL
Lincoln City	Jul-77		115	109	6	3	8	41	0	5
Newcastle Utd	Dec-80	£180,000	19	18	1	0	0	4	0	0
Bristol City	Aug-81	£160,000	30	30	0	5	5	11	2	1
Birmingham C.	Mar-82	£100,000	92	92	0	7	10	25	2	6
Luton Town	Dec-84	£250,000	139	135	4	27	16	57	11	10
Derby County	Jan-90	£450,000	58	58	0	1	7	15	0	3
Luton Town	Sep-91	£325,000	29	29	0	0	1	12	0	0
Chelsea	Aug-92	£300,000	28	27	1	5	1	9	2	0
Sunderland	Mar-93	£250,000	11	10	1	0	0	2	0	0
Coventry City	Jul-93	£200,000	1	0	1	0	0	1	0	0
Wimbledon	Aug-94	£70,000	48	34	14	11	4	8	1	1
FAPL Summary by Club										
Chelsea	1992-93 to 1995-96		28	27	1	1	5	9	0	2
Coventry City	1993-94		1	0	1	0	0	1	0	0
Wimbledon	1994-95 to 1995-96		48	34	14	11	4	8	1	1
Total			*77*	*61*	*16*	*12*	*9*	*18*	*1*	*3*

HARKES John   Derby County

Fullname: John Andrew Harkes   DOB: 08-03-67 New Jersey, USA
Debut: SHEFFIELD WED v N. Forest 19/8/92 as sub
Debut Goal: Chelsea v SHEFFIELD W. 30/1/93

Previous Clubs Details			*Apps*					*Goals*		
Club	Signed	Fee	Tot	Start	Sub	FA	FL	Lge	FA	FL
Sheffield W.	Oct-90	£70,000	81	59	22	13	17	7	1	3
Derby County	Aug-93		74	67	7	0	5	2	0	0
West Ham Utd	Oct-95	Loan	10	6	4	2	0	0	0	0
FAPL Summary by Club										
Sheffield W.	1992-93		29	23	6	7	7	2	1	2
West Ham Utd	1995-96		10	6	4	2	0	0	0	0
Total			*39*	*29*	*10*	*9*	*7*	*2*	*1*	*2*

HARKNESS Steve — Liverpool

Fullname: Steven Harkness   DOB: 27-08-71 Carlisle
Debut: Ipswich Town v LIVERPOOL 25/8/92
Debut Goal: LIVERPOOL v Tottenham H. 8/5/93

Previous Clubs Details			Apps					Goals		
Club	Signed	Fee	Tot	Start	Sub	FA	FL	Lge	FA	FL
Carlisle Utd	Mar-89		13	12	1	0	0	0	0	0
Liverpool	Jul-89	£75,000	64	57	7	4	9	2	0	1
Huddersfield	Sep-93	Loan	5	5	0	0	0	0	0	0
Southend Utd	Feb-95	Loan	6	6	0	0	0	0	0	0
FAPL Summary by Club										
Liverpool	1992-93 to 1995-96		53	50	3	2	7	3	0	1
Total			*53*	*50*	*3*	*2*	*7*	*3*	*0*	*1*

HARTE Ian — Leeds United

Fullname: Ian Harte   DOB: 31-08-77 Drogheda
Debut: LEEDS UTD v West Ham Utd 13/1/96

Previous Clubs Details			Apps					Goals		
Club	Signed	Fee	Tot	Start	Sub	FA	FL	Lge	FA	FL
Leeds Utd			4	2	2	0	1	0	0	0
FAPL Summary by Club										
Leeds Utd	1995-96		4	2	2	0	1	0	0	0
Total			*4*	*2*	*2*	*0*	*1*	*0*	*0*	*0*

HARTSON John — Arsenal

Fullname: John Hartson   DOB: 05-04-75 Swansea
Debut: ARSENAL v Everton 14/1/95
Debut Goal: Coventry City v ARSENAL 21/1/95

Previous Clubs Details			Apps					Goals		
Club	Signed	Fee	Tot	Start	Sub	FA	FL	Lge	FA	FL
Luton Town	Dec-92		34	21	13	5	1	6	0	1
Arsenal	Jan-95	£2.5m	34	29	5	1	3	11	0	1
FAPL Summary by Club										
Arsenal	1994-95 to 1995-96		34	29	5	1	3	11	0	1
Total			*34*	*29*	*5*	*1*	*3*	*11*	*0*	*1*

HEALD Paul — Wimbledon

Fullname: Paul Andrew Heald   DOB: 20-09-68 Wath-on-Dearne
Debut: SWINDON TOWN v Sheffield W. 4/2/94 as sub
Debut Goal: (Goalkeeper)

Previous Clubs Details			Apps					Goals		
Club	Signed	Fee	Tot	Start	Sub	FA	FL	Lge	FA	FL
Sheffield Utd	Jun-87	Trainee	0	0	0	0	0	0	0	0
Leyton Orient	Dec-88	Unkown	176	176	0	9	13	0	0	0
Coventry City	Mar-92	Loan	2	2	0	0	0	0	0	0

Swindon Town	Mar-94	Loan	2	1	1	0	0		0	0	0
Wimbledon	Aug-95	£125,000	18	18	0	0	2		0	0	0
FAPL Summary by Club											
Swindon T	1993-94		3	2	1	0	0		1	0	0
Wimbeldon	1995-96		18	18	0	0	2		0	0	0
Total			*21*	*20*	*1*	*0*	*2*		*1*	*0*	*0*

HEANEY Neil   Southampton

Fullname: Neil Andrew Heaney   DOB: 03-11-71 Middlesbrough
Debut: ARSENAL v Liverpool 31/1/93
Debut Goal: Newcastle Utd v SOUTHAMPTON 22/3/95 as sub

Previous Clubs Details			Apps						Goals		
Club	Signed	Fee	Tot	Start	Sub	FA	FL		Lge	FA	FL
Arsenal	Nov-89		7	4	3	0	1		0	0	0
Hartlepool Utd	Jan-91	Loan	3	2	1	0	0		0	0	0
Cambridge Utd	Jan-92	Loan	13	9	4	1	0		2	0	0
Southampton	Mar-94	£300,000	53	38	15	6	5		4	2	1
FAPL Summary by Club											
Arsenal	1992-93 to 1993-94		6	4	2	0	1		0	0	0
Southampton	1993-94 to 1995-96		59	40	19	6	5		4	2	1
Total			*65*	*44*	*21*	*6*	*6*		*4*	*2*	*1*

HELDER Glenn   Arsenal

Fullname: Glenn Helder   DOB: 28-10-68 Leiden, Holland
Debut: ARSENAL v N. Forest 21/2/95
Debut Goal: Middlesbrough v ARSENAL 13/1/96

Previous Clubs Details			Apps						Goals		
Club	Signed	Fee	Tot	Start	Sub	FA	FL		Lge	FA	FL
Sparta Rotterdam	1989		93	–	–	–	–		9	–	–
Vitesse Arnhem	1993		52	–	–	–	–		12	–	–
Arsenal	Feb-95	£2.3m	37	27	10	2	6		1	0	0
FAPL Summary by Club											
Arsenal	1994-95 to 1995-96		37	27	10	2	6		1	0	0
Total			*37*	*27*	*10*	*2*	*6*		*1*	*0*	*0*

HENDRIE John   Middlesbrough

Fullname: John Hendrie   DOB: 24-10-63 Lennoxtown
Debut: Coventry City v MIDDLESBROUGH 15/8/92
Debut Goal: MIDDLESBROUGH v Leeds Utd 22/8/92

Previous Clubs Details			Apps						Goals		
Club	Signed	Fee	Tot	Start	Sub	FA	FL		Lge	FA	FL
Coventry City	May-81	Apprentice	21	15	6	0	2		2	0	0
Hereford Utd	Jan-84	Loan	6	6	0	0	0		0	0	0
Bradford City	Jul-84	Free	173	173	0	11	17		46	6	4
Newcastle Utd	Jun-88	£500,000	34	34	0	4	2		4	0	1

Club	Signed	Fee	Tot	Start	Sub	FA	FL	Lge	FA	FL
Leeds Utd	Jun-89	£600,000	27	22	5	1	1	5	0	0
Middlesbrough	Jul-90	£550,000	192	181	11	10	23	45	2	6
FAPL Summary by Club										
Middlesbrough 1992-93 to 1995-96			45	38	7	0	3	10	0	0
Total			*45*	*38*	*7*	*0*	*3*	*10*	*0*	*0*

HENDRY Colin   Blackburn Rovers

Fullname: Edward Colin James Hendry   DOB: 07-12-65 Keith
Debut: Crystal Palace v BLACKBURN RVS 15/8/92
Debut Goal: BLACKBURN RVS v Coventry City 26/1/93

Previous Clubs Details			*Apps*					*Goals*		
Club	Signed	Fee	Tot	Start	Sub	FA	FL	Lge	FA	FL
Dundee	1983	From NL	51	17	24	5	0	2	1	0
Blackburn Rvs	Mar-87	£30,000	102	99	3	3	4	22	0	0
Man. City	Nov-89	£700,000	63	57	6	5	5	5	2	1
Blackburn Rvs	Nov-91	£700,000	162	157	5	12	20	10	0	0
FAPL Summary by Club										
Blackburn Rvs 1992-93 to 1995-96			135	134	1	11	20	6	0	0
Total			*135*	*134*	*1*	*11*	*20*	*6*	*0*	*0*

HESKEY Emile   Leicester City

Fullname: Emile Heskey   DOB: 11-01-78 Leicester
Debut: QPR v LEICESTER CITY 8/3/95

Previous Clubs Details			*Apps*					*Goals*		
Club	Signed	Fee	Tot	Start	Sub	FA	FL	Lge	FA	FL
Leicester City			31	21	10	0	2	7	0	0
FAPL Summary by Club										
Leicester City	1994-95		1	1	0	0	0	0	0	0
Total			*1*	*1*	*0*	*0*	*0*	*0*	*0*	*0*

HIGNETT Craig   Middlesbrough

Fullname: Craig Hignett   DOB: 12-01-70 Prescot
Debut: Oldham Ath v MIDDLESBROUGH 28/11/92
Debut Goal: Aston Villa v MIDDLESBROUGH 17/1/93

Previous Clubs Details			*Apps*					*Goals*		
Club	Signed	Fee	Tot	Start	Sub	FA	FL	Lge	FA	FL
Liverpool	Trainee		0	0	0	0	0	0	0	0
Crewe Alex	May-88	Free	121	108	13	12	10	42	8	4
Middlesbrough	Nov-92	£500,000	98	79	19	4	11	22	0	8
FAPL Summary by Club										
Middlesbrough 1992-93 to 1995-96			43	35	8	1	4	9	0	2
Total			*43*	*35*	*8*	*1*	*4*	*9*	*0*	*2*

HILL Colin   Leicester City

Fullname: Colin Frederick Hill   DOB: 12-11-63 Uxbridge
Debut: LEICESTER CITY v Newcastle Utd 21/8/94

Previous Clubs Details			Apps					Goals		
Club	Signed	Fee	Tot	Start	Sub	FA	FL	Lge	FA	FL
Arsenal	Aug-81	Apprentice	46	46	0	1	4	1	0	0
Maritime (Por)		Free	–	–	–	–	–	–	–	–
Colchester Utd	Oct-87	Free	69	64	5	7	2	0	2	0
Sheffield Utd	Aug-89	£85,000	82	77	5	12	5	1	0	0
Leicester City	Mar-92	Loan	10	10	0	0	0	0	0	0
Leicester City	Jul-92	£200,000	128	124	4	8	10	0	1	0
FAPL Summary by Club										
Leicester City	1994-95		24	24	0	3	0	0	0	0
Total			*24*	*24*	*0*	*3*	*0*	*0*	*0*	*0*

HILLIER David
Arsenal

Fullname: David Hillier DOB: 19-12-69 Blackheath
Debut: ARSENAL v Norwich City 15/8/92
Debut Goal: ARSENAL v Sheffield Utd 9/1/93

Previous Clubs Details			Apps					Goals		
Club	Signed	Fee	Tot	Start	Sub	FA	FL	Lge	FA	FL
Arsenal	Feb-88		102	82	20	15	15	2	0	0
FAPL Summary by Club										
Arsenal	1992-93 to 1995-96		59	46	13	10	13	1	0	0
Total			*59*	*46*	*13*	*10*	*13*	*1*	*0*	*0*

HINCHCLIFFE Andy
Everton

Fullname: Andrew George Hinchcliffe DOB: 05-02-69 Manchester
Debut: EVERTON v Sheffield W. 15/8/92
Debut Goal: EVERTON v N. Forest 13/3/93

Previous Clubs Details			Apps					Goals		
Club	Signed	Fee	Tot	Start	Sub	FA	FL	Lge	FA	FL
Man. City	Jun-86		112	107	5	12	11	8	1	1
Everton	Jul-90	£800,000	275	247	28	20	23	88	7	11
FAPL Summary by Club										
Everton	1992-93 to 1995-96		108	101	7	9	13	5	1	1
Total			*108*	*101*	*7*	*9*	*13*	*5*	*1*	*1*

HIRST David
Sheffield Wednesday

Fullname: David Eric Hirst DOB: 07-12-67 Cudworth
Debut: Everton v SHEFFIELD W. 15/8/92
Debut Goal: SHEFFIELD WED v N. Forest 19/8/92

Previous Clubs Details			Apps					Goals		
Club	Signed	Fee	Tot	Start	Sub	FA	FL	Lge	FA	FL
Barnsley	Nov-85		28	26	2	0	1	9	0	0
Sheffield W.	Aug-86	£200,000	263	238	25	17	34	100	6	11
FAPL Summary by Club										
Sheffield W.	1992-93 to 1995-96		74	70	4	7	12	28	1	4
Total			*74*	*70*	*4*	*7*	*12*	*28*	*1*	*4*

HISLOP Shaka   **Newcastle United**

Fullname: Neil Hislop   DOB: 22-02-69 London
Debut: NEWCASTLE UTD v Coventry City, 19 Aug 95
Debut Goal: (Goalkeeper)

Previous Clubs Details			*Apps*					*Goals*		
Club	Signed	Fee	Tot	Start	Sub	FA	FL	Lge	FA	FL
Reading	Sep-92		104	104	0	3	10	0	0	0
Newcastle Utd	Aug-95	£1.575m	24	24	0	0	4	0	0	0
FAPL Summary by Club										
Newcastle Utd		1995-96	24	24	0	0	4	0	0	0
Total			*24*	*24*	*0*	*0*	*4*	*0*	*0*	*0*

HITCHCOCK Kevin   **Chelsea**

Fullname: Kevin Joseph Hitchcock   DOB: 05-10-62 Canning Town
Debut: Man. City v CHELSEA 20/9/92
Debut Goal: (Goalkeeper)

Previous Clubs Details			*Apps*					*Goals*		
Club	Signed	Fee	Tot	Start	Sub	FA	FL	Lge	FA	FL
N. Forest	Aug-83	£15,000	0	0	0	0	0	0	0	0
Mansfield T	Feb-84	Loan	14	14	0	0	0	0	0	0
Mansfield T	Jun-84	£140,000	168	168	0	10	12	0	0	0
Chelsea	Mar-88	£250,000	69	68	1	5	8	0	0	0
Northampton T	Dec-90	Loan	17	17	0	0	0	0	0	0
FAPL Summary by Club										
Chelsea	1992-93 to 1995-96		46	45	1	8	6	0	0	0
Total			*46*	*45*	*1*	*8*	*6*	*0*	*0*	*0*

HODGES Glyn   **Derby County**

Fullname: Glyn Peter Hodges   DOB: 30-04-63 Streatham
Debut: SHEFFIELD UTD v Manchester Utd 15/8/92
Debut Goal: SHEFFIELD UTD v Wimbledon 25/8/92

Previous Clubs Details			*Apps*					*Goals*		
Club	Signed	Fee	Tot	Start	Sub	FA	FL	Lge	FA	FL
Wimbledon	Feb-81		232	200	32	15	16	49	2	3
Newcastle Utd	Jul-87	£200,000	7	7	0	0	0	0	0	0
Watford	Oct-87	£300,000	86	82	4	8	5	15	1	2
Crystal Palace	Jul-90	£410,000	7	5	2	0	4	0	0	1
Sheffield Utd	Jan-91	£450,000	125	101	24	13	5	16	3	0
Derby County	Feb-96	Free	8	7	1	0	0	0	0	0
FAPL Summary by Club										
Sheffield Utd	1992-93 to 1993-94		62	47	15	15	9	6	4	2
Total			*62*	*47*	*15*	*15*	*9*	*6*	*4*	*2*

HOLDSWORTH Dean   **Wimbledon**

Fullname: Dean Christopher Holdsworth   DOB: 08-11-68 London
Debut: Leeds Utd v WIMBLEDON 15/8/92

Debut Goal: WIMBLEDON v Coventry City 22/8/92

Previous Clubs Details

Club	Signed	Fee	Tot	Start	Sub	FA	FL	Lge	FA	FL
Watford	Nov-86	Apprentice	16	2	14	0	0	3	0	0
Carlisle Utd	Feb-88	Loan	4	4	0	0	0	1	0	0
Port Vale	Mar-88	Loan	6	6	0	0	0	2	0	0
Swansea City	Aug-88	Loan	5	4	1	0	0	1	0	0
Brentford	Oct-88	Loan	7	2	5	0	0	1	0	0
Brentford	Sep-89	£125,000	110	106	4	6	8	53	7	6
Wimbledon	Jul-92	£720,000	139	134	5	14	13	53	5	9

FAPL Summary by Club

Wimbledon	1992-93 to 1995-96		139	134	5	14	13	53	5	9
Total			*139*	*134*	*5*	*14*	*13*	*53*	*5*	*9*

HOLMES Matty — Blackburn Rovers
Fullname: Matthew Jason Holmes   DOB: 01-08-69 Luton
Debut: WEST HAM UTD v Wimbledon 14/8/93
Debut Goal: WEST HAM UTD v Man. City 1/11/93

Previous Clubs Details

Club	Signed	Fee	Tot	Start	Sub	FA	FL	Lge	FA	FL
Bournemouth	22/9/88	Trainee	114	105	9	10	7	8	0	0
Cardiff City	23/3/89	Loan	1	0	1	0	0	0	0	0
West Ham Utd	19/8/92	£40,000	76	63	13	6	4	5	0	0
Blackburn Rvs	Aug-95	£1.2m +	8	7	1	0	0	1	0	0

FAPL Summary by Club

West Ham Utd	1993-94 to 1994-95		58	57	1	5	4	4	0	0
Blackburn Rvs	1995-96		8	7	1	0	0	1	0	0
Total			*66*	*64*	*2*	*5*	*4*	*5*	*0*	*0*

HOPKIN David — Chelsea
Fullname: David Hopkin   DOB: 21-08-70 Greenock
Debut: Liverpool v CHELSEA 10/2/92
Debut Goal: Everton v CHELSEA 3/5/95

Previous Clubs Details

Club	Signed	Fee	Tot	Start	Sub	FA	FL	Lge	FA	FL
Morton	1989	From NL	48	33	15	2	2	4	2	1
Chelsea	Sep-92	£300,000	40	21	19	5	1	2	0	0

FAPL Summary by Club

Chelsea	1992-93 to 1994-95		40	21	19	5	1	2	0	0
Total			*40*	*21*	*19*	*5*	*1*	*2*	*0*	*0*

HOTTIGER Marc — Everton
Fullname: Marc Hottiger   DOB: 07-11-67 Lausanne
Debut: Leicester City v NEWCASTLE UTD 21/8/94
Debut Goal: Chelsea v NEWCASTLE UTD 1/4/95

Previous Clubs Details			*Apps*					*Goals*		
Club	Signed	Fee	Tot	Start	Sub	FA	FL	Lge	FA	FL
Sion	–	–	–	–	–	–	–	–	–	–
Newcastle Utd	Aug-94	£600,000	39	38	1	4	7	1	1	0
Everton	Jan-96	£700,000	9	9	0	0	0	1	0	0
FAPL Summary by Club										
Newcastle Utd 1994-95 to 1995-96			39	38	1	4	7	1	1	0
Everton		1995-96	9	9	0	0	0	1	0	0
Total			*48*	*47*	*1*	*4*	*7*	*2*	*1*	*0*

HOULT Russell — Derby County

Fullname: Russell Hoult DOB: 28-03-91 Leicester
Debut Goal: (Goalkeeper)

Previous Clubs Details			*Apps*					*Goals*		
Club	Signed	Fee	Tot	Start	Sub	FA	FL	Lge	FA	FL
Leicester City	Mar-91		10	10	0	0	3	0	0	0
Lincoln City	Aug-91	Loan	2	2	0	0	1	0	0	0
Bolton W.	Nov-93	Loan	4	3	1	0	0	0	0	0
Derby County	Mar-95	£200,000	56	55	1	1	2	0	0	0

HOWE Stephen — Nottingham Forest

Fullname: Stephen Robert Howe DOB: 06-11-73 Annitsford
Debut: NOTTINGHAM F. v Manchester Utd 27/11/95
Debut Goal: Sheffield W. v NOTTINGHAM F. 2/3/96

Previous Clubs Details			*Apps*					*Goals*		
Club	Signed	Fee	Tot	Start	Sub	FA	FL	Lge	FA	FL
N. Forest			13	6	7	0	1	2	0	0
FAPL Summary by Club										
N. Forest		1995-96	9	4	5	0	0	2	0	0
Total			*9*	*4*	*5*	*0*	*0*	*2*	*0*	*0*

HOWELLS David — Tottenham Hotspur

Fullname: David Howells DOB: 15-12-67 Guildford
Debut: Southampton v TOTTENHAM H. 15/8/92
Debut Goal: Blackburn Rvs v TOTTENHAM H. 7/11/92

Previous Clubs Details			*Apps*					*Goals*		
Club	Signed	Fee	Tot	Start	Sub	FA	FL	Lge	FA	FL
Tottenham H.	Jan-85		225	192	33	20	26	20	1	4
FAPL Summary by Club										
Tottenham H. 1992-93 to 1995-96			91	86	5	11	7	6	0	2
Total			*91*	*86*	*5*	*11*	*7*	*6*	*0*	*2*

HOWEY Steve — Newcastle United

Fullname: Stephen Norman Howey DOB: 26-10-71 Sunderland
Debut: NEWCASTLE UTD v Tottenham H. 14/8/93
Debut Goal: NEWCASTLE UTD v Leicester City 10/12/94

300

Previous Clubs Details			Apps					Goals		
Club	Signed	Fee	Tot	Start	Sub	FA	FL	Lge	FA	FL
Newcastle Utd	Dec-89		146	127	19	13	14	5	0	1
FAPL Summary by Club										
Newcastle Utd	1993-94 to 1995-96		72	70	2	5	9	2	0	0
Total			*72*	*70*	*2*	*5*	*9*	*2*	*0*	*0*

HOWEY Lee   Sunderland
Fullname: Lee Matthew Howey   DOB: 01-04-69 Sunderland

Previous Clubs Details			Apps					Goals		
Club	Signed	Fee	Tot	Start	Sub	FA	FL	Lge	FA	FL
Sunderland	Mar-93	Free NL	57	30	27	6	5	8	1	2

HUCKERBY Darren   Newcastle United
Fullname: Darren Carl Huckerby   DOB: 27-04-76 Nottingham
Debut: NEWCASTLE UTD v Bolton Wdrs 20/1/96 as sub

Previous Clubs Details			Apps					Goals		
Club	Signed	Fee	Tot	Start	Sub	FA	FL	Lge	FA	FL
Lincoln City *	Jul-93	Trainee	13	4	8	0	0	3	0	0
Newcastle Utd	Nov-95	£500,000	1	0	1	1	0	0	0	0
FAPL Summary by Club										
Newcastle Utd	1995-96		1	0	1	1	0	0	0	0
Total			*1*	*0*	*1*	*1*	*0*	*0*	*0*	*0*

HUGHES Mark   Chelsea
Fullname: Leslie Mark Hughes   DOB: 01-11-63 Wrexham
Debut: Sheffield Utd v MANCHESTER UTD 15/8/92
Debut Goal: Sheffield Utd v MANCHESTER UTD 15/8/92

Previous Clubs Details			Apps					Goals		
Club	Signed	Fee	Tot	Start	Sub	FA	FL	Lge	FA	FL
Manchester Utd	Nov-80		89	85	4	10	6	37	4	4
Barcelona	Jul-86	£2.5m	–	–	–	–	–	–	–	–
Bayern Munich	Oct-87	Loan	–	–	–	–	–	–	–	–
Manchester Utd	Jul-88	£1.5m	256	251	5	36	32	83	9	7
Chelsea	Jun-95	£1.5m	31	31	0	6	2	8	4	0
FAPL Summary by Club										
Manchester Utd	1992-93 to 1994-95		111	110	1	15	11	35	6	6
Chelsea	1995-96		31	31	0	6	2	8	4	0
Total			*142*	*141*	*1*	*21*	*13*	*43*	*10*	*6*

HUGHES Stephen   Arsenal
Fullname: Stephen John Hughes   DOB: 18-09-76
Debut: ARSENAL v Aston Villa 26/12/94

Previous Clubs Details			Apps					Goals		
Club	Signed	Fee	Tot	Start	Sub	FA	FL	Lge	FA	FL
Arsenal		Trainee	2	1	1	0	1	0	0	0

FAPL Summary by Club
Arsenal   1994-95 to 1995-96   2   1   1   0   1   0   0   0
Total   *2*   *1*   *1*   *0*   *1*   *0*   *0*   *0*

HUGHES David   Southampton

Fullname: David Robert Hughes   DOB: 30-12-72 St Albans
Debut: Oldham Ath v SOUTHAMPTON 5/12/94 as sub
Debut Goal: QPR v SOUTHAMPTON 28/12/94 as sub

Previous Clubs Details			*Apps*				*Goals*		
Club	Signed	Fee	Tot	Start	Sub	FA	FL	Lge	FA	FL
Southampton	Jul-91	Juniors	25	8	17	5	2	3	1	0

FAPL Summary by Club

| Southampton | 1993-94 to 1995-96 | 25 | 8 | 17 | 5 | 2 | 3 | 1 | 0 |
| *Total* | | *25* | *8* | *17* | *5* | *2* | *3* | *1* | *0* |

HUGHES Michael   West Ham United

Fullname: Michael Eamon Hughes   DOB: 02-08-71 Larne
Debut: QPR v WEST HAM UTD 4/12/94
Debut Goal: WEST HAM UTD v N. Forest 31/12/94

Previous Clubs Details			*Apps*				*Goals*		
Club	Signed	Fee	Tot	Start	Sub	FA	FL	Lge	FA	FL
Strasbourg			–	–	–	–	–	–	–	–
West Ham Utd	Nov-94	Loan	45	43	2	5	2	2	1	0

FAPL Summary by Club

| West Ham Utd | 1994-95 to 1995-96 | 45 | 43 | 2 | 5 | 2 | 2 | 1 | 0 |
| *Total* | | *45* | *43* | *2* | *5* | *2* | *2* | *1* | *0* |

HUMPHRIES Ritchie   Sheffield Wednesday

Fullname: Ritchie Humphries   DOB:
Debut: QPR v SHEFFIELD W. 9/9/95

Previous Clubs Details		*Apps*				*Goals*		
Club	Signed	Fee	Tot	Start	Sub	FA	FL	Lge	FA	FL
Sheffield W.			5	1	4	0	0	0	0	0

FAPL Summary by Club

| Sheffield W. | 1995-96 | 5 | 1 | 4 | 0 | 0 | 0 | 0 | 0 |
| *Total* | | *5* | *1* | *4* | *0* | *0* | *0* | *0* | *0* |

HYDE Graham   Sheffield Wednesday

Fullname: Graham Hyde   DOB: 10-11-70 Doncaster
Debut: Everton v SHEFFIELD W. 15/8/92
Debut Goal: N. Forest v SHEFFIELD WED 3/10/92

Previous Clubs Details			*Apps*				*Goals*		
Club	Signed	Fee	Tot	Start	Sub	FA	FL	Lge	FA	FL
Sheffield W.	May-88		130	97	33	13	19	8	1	2

		Tot	Start	Sub	FA	FL	Lge	FA	FL
Sheffield W.	1992-93 to 1995-96	117	88	29	11	18	8	1	2
Total		*117*	*88*	*29*	*11*	*18*	*8*	*1*	*2*

IRVING Richard   Nottingham Forest

Fullname: Richard Irving   DOB: 10-09-75 Halifax
Debut: N. Forest v Manchester Utd 27/11/95

Previous Clubs Details			*Apps*				*Goals*		
Club	Signed	Fee	Tot	Start	Sub	FA	FL	Lge	FA	FL
Manchester Utd			0	0	0	0	0	0	0	0
N. Forest	Jul-95	£75,000	0	0	1	0	0	0	0	0

FAPL Summary by Club

		Tot	Start	Sub	FA	FL	Lge	FA	FL
N. Forest	1995-96	1	0	1	0	0	0	0	0
Total		*1*	*0*	*1*	*0*	*0*	*0*	*0*	*0*

IRWIN Dennis   Manchester United

Fullname: Dennis Joseph Irwin   DOB: 31-10-65 Cork
Debut: Sheffield Utd v MANCHESTER UTD 15/8/92
Debut Goal: MANCHESTER UTD v Ipswich Town 22/8/92

Previous Clubs Details			*Apps*				*Goals*		
Club	Signed	Fee	Tot	Start	Sub	FA	FL	Lge	FA	FL
Leeds Utd	Oct-83		72	72	0	3	5	1	0	0
Oldham Ath	May-86		167	166	1	13	19	4	0	3
Manchester Utd	Jun-90	£625,000	225	223	2	29	30	14	4	0

FAPL Summary by Club

		Tot	Start	Sub	FA	FL	Lge	FA	FL
Manchester Utd	1992-93 to 1995-96	153	153	0	23	15	10	6	0
Total		*153*	*153*	*0*	*23*	*15*	*10*	*6*	*0*

IZZET Muzzy   Leicester City

Fullname: Mustafa Izzet   DOB: 31-10-74 Mile End, London

Previous Clubs Details			*Apps*				*Goals*		
Club	Signed	Fee	Tot	Start	Sub	FA	FL	Lge	FA	FL
Chelsea			0	0	0	0	0	0	0	0
Leicester City	Feb-96	Loan	9	8	1	0	0	1	0	0
Leicester City	Jul-96	£800,000								

JACKSON Mark   Leeds United

Fullname: Mark Jackson   DOB: 30-09-77 Leeds
Debut: LEEDS UTD v Middlesbrough 30/3/96

Previous Clubs Details			*Apps*				*Goals*		
Club	Signed	Fee	Tot	Start	Sub	FA	FL	Lge	FA	FL
Leeds Utd			1	0	1	0	0	0	0	0

FAPL Summary by Club

		Tot	Start	Sub	FA	FL	Lge	FA	FL
Leeds Utd	1995-96	1	0	1	0	0	0	0	0
Total		*1*	*0*	*1*	*0*	*0*	*0*	*0*	*0*

JACKSON Matthew   Everton

Fullname: Matthew Alan Jackson   DOB: 19-10-71 Leeds
Debut: Sheffield W. v EVERTON 15/8/92
Debut Goal: Crystal Palace v EVERTON 9/1/93

Previous Clubs Details

Club	Signed	Fee	Tot	Start	Sub	FA	FL	Lge	FA	FL
Luton Town	Jul-90		9	7	2	0	2	0	0	0
Preston NE	Mar-91	Loan	4	3	1	0	0	0	0	0
Everton	Oct-91	£600,000	138	132	6	14	9	4	2	0
Charlton Ath*	Mar-96	Loan								

FAPL Summary by Club

Everton	1992-93 to 1995-96		108	102	6	12	9	3	2	0
Total			*108*	*102*	*6*	*12*	*9*	*3*	*2*	*0*

JAMES David   Liverpool

Fullname: David Benjamin James   DOB: 01-08-70 Welwyn Garden C.
Debut: N. Forest v LIVERPOOL 16/892
Debut Goal: (Goalkeeper)

Previous Clubs Details

Club	Signed	Fee	Tot	Start	Sub	FA	FL	Lge	FA	FL
Watford	Jul-88		89	89	0	2	6	0	0	0
Liverpool	Jun-92	£1m	123	122	1	14	13	0	0	0

FAPL Summary by Club

Liverpool	1992-93 to 1995-96		123	122	1	15	12	0	0	0
Total			*123*	*122*	*1*	*15*	*12*	*0*	*0*	*0*

JERKAN Nikola   Nottingham Forest

Fullname: Nikola Jerkan   DOB:

Previous Clubs Details

Club	Signed	Fee	Tot	Start	Sub	FA	FL	Lge	FA	FL
Real Oviedo			–	–	–	–	–	–	–	–
N. Forest	Jul-96	£1m								

JESS Eoin   Coventry City

Fullname: Eoin Jess   DOB: 13-12-70
Debut: COVENTRY CITY v Middlesbrough 24/2/96
Debut Goal: COVENTRY CITY v QPR 13/4/96

Previous Clubs Details

Club	Signed	Fee	Tot	Start	Sub	FA	FL	Lge	FA	FL
Aberdeen			–	–	–	–	–	–	–	–
Coventry City	Feb-96	£1.75m	12	9	3	0	0	1	0	0

FAPL Summary by Club

Coventry City	1995-96		12	9	3	0	0	1	0	0
Total			*12*	*9*	*3*	*0*	*0*	*1*	*0*	*0*

JOACHIM Julian   Aston Villa

Fullname: Julian Kevin Joachim   DOB: 12-09-74 Peterborough
Debut: LEICESTER CITY v Newcastle Utd 21/8/94
Debut Goal: LEICESTER CITY v Newcastle Utd 21/8/94

Previous Clubs Details			*Apps*					*Goals*		
Club	Signed	Fee	Tot	Start	Sub	FA	FL	Lge	FA	FL
Leicester City	Sep-92	Trainee	99	77	22	5	9	25	1	3
Aston Villa	Feb-96	£1.5m	11	4	7	0	0	1	0	0
FAPL Summary by Club										
Leicester City	1994-95		15	11	4	0	2	3	0	0
Aston Villa	1995-96		11	4	7	0	0	1	0	0
Total			*26*	*15*	*11*	*0*	*2*	*4*	*0*	*0*

JOBSON Richard   Leeds United

Fullname: Richard Ian Jobson   DOB: 09-05-63 Holderness
Debut: Chelsea v OLDHAM ATH 15/8/92
Debut Goal: Man. City v OLDHAM ATH 29/8/92

Previous Clubs Details			*Apps*					*Goals*		
Club	Signed	Fee	Tot	Start	Sub	FA	FL	Lge	FA	FL
Watford	Nov-82	£22,000	28	26	2	1	2	4	0	0
Hull City	Feb-85	£40,000	221	219	2	13	12	17	1	0
Oldham Ath *	Sep-90	£460,000	177	176	1	13	13	10	0	1
Leeds Utd	Oct-95	£1m	12	12	0	1	0	1	0	0
FAPL Summary by Club										
Oldham Ath	1992-93 to 1993-94		77	77	0	9	7	7	0	0
Leeds Utd	1995-96		12	12	0	1	0	1	0	0
Total			*89*	*89*	*0*	*10*	*7*	*8*	*0*	*0*

JOHNSEN Erland   Chelsea

Fullname: Erland Johnsen   DOB: 05-04-67 Fredrikstad, Norway
Debut: N. Forest v CHELSEA 16/1/93
Debut Goal: CHELSEA v Blackburn Rvs 14/8/93

Previous Clubs Details			*Apps*					*Goals*		
Club	Signed	Fee	Tot	Start	Sub	FA	FL	Lge	FA	FL
Chelsea	Nov-89	£306,000	127	121	6	16	6	1	0	0
FAPL Summary by Club										
Chelsea	1992-93 to 1995-96		96	91	5	12	6	1	0	0
Total			*96*	*91*	*5*	*12*	*6*	*1*	*0*	*0*

JOHNSEN Ronnie   Manchester United

Fullname: Ronald Johnsen   DOB:

Previous Clubs Details			*Apps*					*Goals*		
Club	Signed	Fee	Tot	Start	Sub	FA	FL	Lge	FA	FL
Besiktas			–	–	–	–	–	–	–	–
Manchester Utd	Jul-96	£1.2m								

JOHNSON Tommy   Aston Villa

Fullname: Thomas Johnson   DOB: 15-01-71 Newcastle
Debut: ASTON VILLA v QPR 14/1/95
Debut Goal: ASTON VILLA v Wimbledon 11/2/95

Previous Clubs Details			*Apps*				*Goals*		
Club	Signed	Fee	Tot	Start	Sub	FA	FL	Lge	FA	FL
Notts County	Jan-89		118	100	18	5	9	47	5	1
Derby County	Mar-92	£1.3m	84	77	7	5	6	23	2	1
Aston Villa	Jan-95	£2.9m +	39	30	9	5	4	9	1	2
FAPL Summary by Club										
Aston Villa	1994-95 to 1995-96		39	30	9	5	4	9	1	2
Total			*39*	*30*	*9*	*5*	*4*	*9*	*1*	*2*

JONES Rob   Liverpool

Fullname: Robert Marc Jones   DOB: 05-11-71 Wrexham
Debut: LIVERPOOL v Sheffield Utd 19/8/92

Previous Clubs Details			*Apps*				*Goals*		
Club	Signed	Fee	Tot	Start	Sub	FA	FL	Lge	FA	FL
Crewe Alex	Dec-88		75	59	16	3	9	2	0	0
Liverpool	Oct-91	£300,000	160	160	0	27	19	0	0	0
FAPL Summary by Club										
Liverpool	1992-93 to 1995-96		132	132	0	18	19	0	0	0
Total			*132*	*132*	*0*	*18*	*19*	*0*	*0*	*0*

JONES Vinny   Wimbledon

Fullname: Vincent Peter Jones   DOB: 05-01-65 Watford
Debut: CHELSEA v Oldham Ath 15/8/92
Debut Goal: Sheffield W. v CHELSEA 22/8/92

Previous Clubs Details			*Apps*				*Goals*		
Club	Signed	Fee	Tot	Start	Sub	FA	FL	Lge	FA	FL
Wimbledon	Nov-86	£10,000NL	77	77	0	13	8	9	1	0
Leeds Utd	Jun-89	£650,000	46	44	2	1	2	5	0	0
Sheffield Utd	Sep-90	£700,000	35	35	0	1	4	2	0	0
Chelsea	Aug-91	£575,000	42	42	0	4	1	4	1	0
Wimbledon	Sep-92	£700,000	124	120	4	11	13	9	0	2
FAPL Summary by Club										
Chelsea	1992-93		7	7	0	0	0	1	0	0
Wimbledon	1992-93 to 1995-96		124	120	4	11	13	9	0	2
Total			*131*	*127*	*4*	*11*	*13*	*10*	*0*	*2*

JUNINHO   Middlesbrough

Fullname: Juninho   DOB: 22-02-73 Sao Paulo, Brazil
Debut: MIDDLESBROUGH v Leeds Utd 4/11/95
Debut Goal: MIDDLESBROUGH v Man. City 9/12/95

<table>
<thead>
<tr><th rowspan="2">Previous Clubs Details
Club</th><th rowspan="2">Signed Fee</th><th colspan="5">Apps</th><th colspan="3">Goals</th></tr>
<tr><th>Tot</th><th>Start</th><th>Sub</th><th>FA</th><th>FL</th><th>Lge</th><th>FA</th><th>FL</th></tr>
</thead>
<tbody>
<tr><td>Sao Paulo</td><td>From Ituano</td><td>–</td><td>–</td><td>–</td><td>–</td><td>–</td><td>–</td><td>–</td><td>–</td></tr>
<tr><td>Middlesbrough Oct-95</td><td>£4.75m</td><td>21</td><td>20</td><td>1</td><td>3</td><td>2</td><td>2</td><td>0</td><td>0</td></tr>
<tr><td colspan="11">FAPL Summary by Club</td></tr>
<tr><td>Middlesbrough</td><td>1995-96</td><td>21</td><td>20</td><td>1</td><td>3</td><td>2</td><td>2</td><td>0</td><td>0</td></tr>
<tr><td>Total</td><td></td><td>21</td><td>20</td><td>1</td><td>3</td><td>2</td><td>2</td><td>0</td><td>0</td></tr>
</tbody>
</table>

KANCHELSKIS Andrei — Everton

Fullname: Andrei Kanchelskis   DOB: 23-01-69 Kirovograd, USSR
Debut: Sheffield Utd v MANCHESTER UTD 15/8/93
Debut Goal: MANCHESTER UTD v Leeds Utd 6/9/93

<table>
<thead>
<tr><th rowspan="2">Previous Clubs Details
Club</th><th rowspan="2">Signed Fee</th><th colspan="5">Apps</th><th colspan="3">Goals</th></tr>
<tr><th>Tot</th><th>Start</th><th>Sub</th><th>FA</th><th>FL</th><th>Lge</th><th>FA</th><th>FL</th></tr>
</thead>
<tbody>
<tr><td>Shakhtyor Donezts</td><td></td><td>–</td><td>–</td><td>–</td><td>–</td><td>–</td><td>–</td><td>–</td><td>–</td></tr>
<tr><td>Manchester Utd Mar-91</td><td>£1.1m</td><td>123</td><td>96</td><td>27</td><td>12</td><td>16</td><td>27</td><td>4</td><td>3</td></tr>
<tr><td>Everton Jul-95</td><td>£5m</td><td>32</td><td>32</td><td>0</td><td>4</td><td>0</td><td>16</td><td>0</td><td>0</td></tr>
<tr><td colspan="11">FAPL Summary by Club</td></tr>
<tr><td>Manchester Utd 1992-93 to 1994-95</td><td></td><td>88</td><td>67</td><td>21</td><td>11</td><td>15</td><td>23</td><td>3</td><td>1</td></tr>
<tr><td>Everton 1995-96 to 1995-96</td><td></td><td>32</td><td>32</td><td>0</td><td>4</td><td>0</td><td>16</td><td>0</td><td>0</td></tr>
<tr><td>Total</td><td></td><td>120</td><td>99</td><td>21</td><td>15</td><td>15</td><td>39</td><td>3</td><td>1</td></tr>
</tbody>
</table>

KAVANAGH Graham — Middlesbrough

Fullname: Graham Anthony Kavanagh   DOB: 03-12-73 Dublin
Debut: MIDDLESBROUGH v N. Forest 21/10/92
Debut Goal: Leeds Utd v MIDDLESBROUGH 30/3/96

<table>
<thead>
<tr><th rowspan="2">Previous Clubs Details
Club</th><th rowspan="2">Signed Fee</th><th colspan="5">Apps</th><th colspan="3">Goals</th></tr>
<tr><th>Tot</th><th>Start</th><th>Sub</th><th>FA</th><th>FL</th><th>Lge</th><th>FA</th><th>FL</th></tr>
</thead>
<tbody>
<tr><td>Home Farm (Ire)</td><td></td><td>–</td><td>–</td><td>–</td><td>–</td><td>–</td><td>–</td><td>–</td><td>–</td></tr>
<tr><td>Middlesbrough Aug-91</td><td></td><td>35</td><td>22</td><td>13</td><td>4</td><td>1</td><td>3</td><td>0</td><td>0</td></tr>
<tr><td>Darlington</td><td>Loan</td><td>5</td><td>5</td><td>0</td><td>0</td><td>0</td><td>0</td><td>0</td><td>0</td></tr>
<tr><td colspan="11">FAPL Summary by Club</td></tr>
<tr><td>Middlesbrough 1992-93 to 1995-96</td><td></td><td>17</td><td>12</td><td>5</td><td>0</td><td>0</td><td>1</td><td>0</td><td>0</td></tr>
<tr><td>Total</td><td></td><td>17</td><td>12</td><td>5</td><td>0</td><td>0</td><td>1</td><td>0</td><td>0</td></tr>
</tbody>
</table>

KAVANAGH Jason — Derby County

Fullname: Jason Colin Kavanagh   DOB: 23-11-71 Birmingham

<table>
<thead>
<tr><th rowspan="2">Previous Clubs Details
Club</th><th rowspan="2">Signed Fee</th><th colspan="5">Apps</th><th colspan="3">Goals</th></tr>
<tr><th>Tot</th><th>Start</th><th>Sub</th><th>FA</th><th>FL</th><th>Lge</th><th>FA</th><th>FL</th></tr>
</thead>
<tbody>
<tr><td>Derby County Dec-88</td><td></td><td>99</td><td>74</td><td>25</td><td>7</td><td>5</td><td>1</td><td>0</td><td>0</td></tr>
</tbody>
</table>

KEANE Roy — Manchester United

Fullname: Roy Maurice Keane   DOB: 10-08-71 Cork
Debut: NOTTINGHAM FOREST v Liverpool 16/8/92
Debut Goal: Leeds Utd v NOTTINGHAM FOREST 5/12/92

Previous Clubs Details			Apps					Goals		
Club	Signed	Fee	Tot	Start	Sub	FA	FL	Lge	FA	FL
Cobh Ramblers			–	–	–	–	–	–	–	–
N. Forest	May-90	£10,000	114	114	0	18	17	22	3	6
Manchester Utd	Jul-93	£3.75m	90	86	4	20	9	13	1	0
FAPL Summary by Club										
N. Forest	1992-93		40	40	0	4	5	6	1	1
Manchester Utd	1993-94 to 1995-96		91	86	5	20	9	13	1	0
Total			*131*	*126*	*5*	*24*	*14*	*19*	*2*	*1*

KELLY Gary — Leeds United

Fullname: Gary Kelly
DOB: 09-07-74 Drogheda
Debut: Man. City v LEEDS UTD 14/8/93

Previous Clubs Details			Apps					Goals		
Club	Signed	Fee	Tot	Start	Sub	FA	FL	Lge	FA	FL
Leeds Utd	Sep-91		118	118	0	12	12	0	0	0
FAPL Summary by Club										
Leeds Utd	1993-94 to 1995-96		118	118	0	12	12	0	0	0
Total			*118*	*118*	*0*	*12*	*12*	*0*	*0*	*0*

KELLY David — Sunderland

Fullname: David Thomas Kelly
DOB: 25-11-65 Birmingham

Previous Clubs Details			Apps					Goals		
Club	Signed	Fee	Tot	Start	Sub	FA	FL	Lge	FA	FL
Walsall	Dec-83	Free NL	147	115	32	14	12	63	3	4
West Ham Utd	Aug-88	£600,000	41	29	12	6	14	7	0	5
Leicester City	Mar-90	£300,000	66	63	3	1	6	22	0	1
Newcastle Utd	Dec-91	£250,000	70	70	0	5	4	35	1	2
Wolves *	Jun-93	£750,000	78	73	5	11	5	26	6	2
Sunderland			10	9	1	1	1	2	0	0

KENNA Jeff — Blackburn Rovers

Fullname: Jeffrey Jude Kenna
DOB: 27-08-70 Dublin
Debut: QPR v SOUTHAMPTON 19/8/92
Debut Goal: SOUTHAMPTON v Sheffield Utd 27/2/92

Previous Clubs Details			Apps					Goals		
Club	Signed	Fee	Tot	Start	Sub	FA	FL	Lge	FA	FL
Southampton	Apr-89		114	110	4	11	4	4	0	0
Blackburn Rvs	Mar-95	£1.5m	41	41	0	2	4	1	0	0
FAPL Summary by Club										
Southampton	1992-93 to 1994-95		98	95	3	7	4	4	0	0
Blackburn Rvs	1994-95 to 1995-96		41	41	0	2	4	1	0	0
Total			*139*	*136*	*3*	*9*	*8*	*5*	*0*	*0*

KENNEDY Mark   Liverpool

Fullname: Mark Kennedy   DOB: 15-05-76 Dublin
Debut: LIVERPOOL v Leeds Utd 9/4/95 as sub

Previous Clubs Details

Club	Signed	Fee	Tot	Start	Sub	FA	FL	Lge	FA	FL
				Apps					Goals	
Millwall	May-92	Trainee								
Liverpool	Mar-95	£1.5m +	10	5	5	0	1	0	0	0

FAPL Summary by Club

Liverpool	1994-95 to 1995-96	10	5	5	0	1	0	0	0
Total		*10*	*5*	*5*	*0*	*1*	*0*	*0*	*0*

KEOWN Martin   Arsenal

Fullname: Martin Raymond Keown   DOB: 24-07-66 Oxford
Debut: EVERTON v Coventry City 17/10/92
Debut Goal: N. Forest v ARSENAL 3/12/94

Previous Clubs Details

Club	Signed	Fee	Tot	Start	Sub	FA	FL	Lge	FA	FL
				Apps					Goals	
Arsenal	Jan-84		22	22	0	5	0	0	0	0
Brighton HA	Feb-85	Loan	23	21	2	0	2	1	0	1
Aston Villa	Jun-86	£200,000	112	109	3	6	13	3	0	0
Everton	Jun-89	£750,000	96	92	4	12	11	0	0	0
Arsenal	Feb-93	£2m	114	96	18	7	13	1	0	1

FAPL Summary by Club

Everton	1992-93	13	13	0	2	4	0	0	0
Arsenal	1992-93 to 1995-96	114	96	18	7	13	1	0	1
Total		*127*	*109*	*18*	*9*	*17*	*1*	*0*	*1*

KERSLAKE David   Tottenham Hotspur

Fullname: David Kerslake   DOB: 19-06-66 Stepney
Debut: LEEDS UTD v Man. City 13/3/93

Previous Clubs Details

Club	Signed	Fee	Tot	Start	Sub	FA	FL	Lge	FA	FL
				Apps					Goals	
QPR	Jun-83		58	38	20	4	8	6	0	4
Swindon Town	Nov-89	£110,000	135	133	2	8	12	1	0	0
Leeds Utd	Mar-93	£500,000	8	8	0	0	0	0	0	0
Tottenham H.	Sep-93	£450,000	37	34	3	2	5	0	0	0

FAPL Summary by Club

Leeds Utd	1992-93 to 1993-94	8	8	0	0	0	0	0	0
Tottenham H.	1993-94 to 1995-96	37	34	3	2	5	0	0	0
Total		*45*	*42*	*3*	*2*	*5*	*0*	*0*	*0*

KERWELL Harry   Leeds United

Fullname: Harold Kerwell   DOB: 22-09-78 Australia
Debut: LEEDS UTD v Middlesbrough 30/3/96

Previous Clubs Details			Apps					Goals		
Club	Signed	Fee	Tot	Start	Sub	FA	FL	Lge	FA	FL
Leeds Utd			2	2	0	0	0	0	0	0
FAPL Summary by Club										
Leeds Utd	1995-96		2	2	0	0	0	0	0	0
Total			*2*	*2*	*0*	*0*	*0*	*0*	*0*	*0*

KEY Lance · Sheffield Wednesday

Fullname: Lance Key · DOB: 13-05-68 Kettering

Previous Clubs Details			Apps					Goals		
Club	Signed	Fee	Tot	Start	Sub	FA	FL	Lge	FA	FL
Sheffield W.	Apr-90	£10,000NL	0	0	0	1	0	0	0	0
Oldham Ath	Oct-93	Loan	2	2	0	0	0	0	0	0
Lincoln City *	Aug-95	Loan							
Hartlepool *	Dec-95	Loan							

KHARINE Dimitri · Chelsea

Fullname: Dimitri Kharine · DOB: 16-08-68 Moscow
Debut: QPR v CHELSEA 27/1/93
Debut Goal: (Goalkeeper)

Previous Clubs Details			Apps					Goals		
Club	Signed	Fee	Tot	Start	Sub	FA	FL	Lge	FA	FL
CSKA Moscow	–	–	–	–	–	–	–	–	–	–
Chelsea	Dec-92	£200,000	102	102	0	12	8	0	0	0
FAPL Summary by Club										
Chelsea	1992-93 to 1995-96		102	102	0	12	8	0	0	0
Total			*102*	*102*	*0*	*12*	*8*	*0*	*0*	*0*

KIMBLE Alan · Wimbledon

Fullname: Alan Frank Kimble · DOB: 06-08-66 Dagenham
Debut: West Ham Utd v WIMBLEDON 14/8/93

Previous Clubs Details			Apps					Goals		
Club	Signed	Fee	Tot	Start	Sub	FA	FL	Lge	FA	FL
Charlton Ath	Aug-84		6	6	0	0	0	0	0	0
Exeter City	Aug-85	Loan	1	1	0	0	1	0	0	0
Cambridge Utd	Aug-86	Free	299	295	4	29	24	24	1	0
Wimbledon	Jul-93	£175,000	71	71	0	11	6	0	0	0
FAPL Summary by Club										
Wimbledon	1993-94 to 1995-96		71	71	0	11	6	0	0	0
Total			*71*	*71*	*0*	*11*	*6*	*0*	*0*	*0*

KING Phil · Aston Villa

Fullname: Philip Geoffrey King · DOB: 28-01-67 Bristol
Debut: Everton v SHEFFIELD W. 15/8/92
Debut Goal: SHEFFIELD W. v Southampton 12/4/93

Previous Clubs Details | | | *Apps* | | | | | *Goals* | | |
Club	Signed	Fee	Tot	Start	Sub	FA	FL	Lge	FA	FL
Exeter City	Jan-85		27	24	3	0	1	0	0	0
Torquay Utd	Jul-86	£3,000	24	24	0	1	2	3	0	0
Swindon Town	Feb-87	£15,000	116	112	4	5	11	4	0	0
Sheffield Wed	Nov-89	£400,000	139	124	15	9	17	2	0	0
Notts County	Oct-93	Loan	6	6	0	0	0	0	0	0
Aston Villa	Aug-94	£250,000	16	13	3	0	3	0	0	0
WBA *	Oct-95	Loan								

FAPL Summary by Club

Sheffield W.	1992-93 to 1993-94		22	18	4	1	4	1	0	0
Aston Villa	1994-95		16	13	3	0	3	0	0	0
Total			*38*	*31*	*7*	*1*	*7*	*1*	*0*	*0*

KITSON Paul   Newcastle United

Fullname: Paul Kitson   DOB: 09-01-71 Peterlee
Debut: Aston Villa v NEWCASTLE UTD 1/10/94
Debut Goal: NEWCASTLE UTD v QPR 5/11/94

Previous Clubs Details | | | *Apps* | | | | | *Goals* | | |
Club	Signed	Fee	Tot	Start	Sub	FA	FL	Lge	FA	FL
Leicester City	Dec-88		50	39	11	2	5	6	3	1
Derby County	Mar-92	£1.3m	97	97	0	5	7	34	3	1
Newcastle Utd	Sep-94	£2.25m	33	26	7	7	3	10	3	1

FAPL Summary by Club

Newcastle Utd	1994-95 to 1995-96		33	26	7	7	3	10	3	1
Total			*33*	*26*	*7*	*7*	*3*	*10*	*3*	*1*

KIWOMYA Chris   Arsenal

Fullname: Christopher Mark Kiwomya   DOB: 02-12-69 Huddersfield
Debut: IPSWICH TOWN v Aston Villa 15/8/92
Debut Goal: Manchester Utd v IPSWICH TOWN 23/8/92

Previous Clubs Details | | | *Apps* | | | | | *Goals* | | |
Club	Signed	Fee	Tot	Start	Sub	FA	FL	Lge	FA	FL
Ipswich Town	Mar-87		226	197	29	14	14	50	2	8
Arsenal	Jan-95	£1.55m +	14	5	9	0	0	3	0	0

FAPL Summary by Club

Ipswich Town	1992-93		90	85	5	6	8	18	1	7
Arsenal	1994-95		14	5	9	0	0	3	0	0
Total			*104*	*90*	*14*	*6*	*8*	*21*	*1*	*7*

KJELDBERG Jakob   Chelsea

Fullname: Jakob Kjeldberg   DOB: 21-10-69 Denmark
Debut: Wimbledon v CHELSEA 17/8/93
Debut Goal: CHELSEA v Sheffield Utd 7/5/94

| *Previous Clubs Details* | | | *Apps* | | | | | *Goals* | | |
Club	Signed	Fee	Tot	Start	Sub	FA	FL	Lge	FA	FL
Silkeborg (Denmark)			–	–	–	–	–	–	–	–
Chelsea	Aug-93	£400,000	52	52	0	8	5	2	0	0
FAPL Summary by Club										
Chelsea	1993-94 to 1994-95		52	52	0	8	5	24	0	0
Total			*52*	*52*	*0*	*8*	*5*	*24*	*0*	*0*

KUBICKI Dariusz   Sunderland

Fullname: Dariusz Kubicki   DOB: 06-06-63 Warsaw, Poland
Debut: Swindon Town v ASTON VILLA 30/10/93

| *Previous Clubs Details* | | | *Apps* | | | | | *Goals* | | |
Club	Signed	Fee	Tot	Start	Sub	FA	FL	Lge	FA	FL
Legia Warsaw			0	0	0	0	0	0	0	0
Aston Villa	Aug-91	£200,000	25	24	1	5	3	0	0	0
Sunderland	Mar-94	£100,000	107	107	0	5	6	0	0	0
FAPL Summary by Club										
Aston Villa	1993-94		2	1	1	0	0	0	0	0
Total			*2*	*1*	*1*	*0*	*0*	*0*	*0*	*0*

LAMPARD Jnr Frank   West Ham United

Fullname: Frank Lampard   DOB: 21-06-78 Romford
Debut: WEST HAM UTD v Coventry City 31/1/96 as sub

| *Previous Clubs Details* | | | *Apps* | | | | | *Goals* | | |
Club	Signed	Fee	Tot	Start	Sub	FA	FL	Lge	FA	FL
West Ham Utd		Trainee	0	0	2	0	0	0	0	0
Swansea City*	Oct-95	Loan								
FAPL Summary by Club										
West Ham Utd	1995-96		2	0	2	0	0	0	0	0
Total			*2*	*0*	*2*	*0*	*0*	*0*	*0*	*0*

LAMPTEY Nil   Coventry City

Fullname: Nil Odartey Lamptey   DOB: 10-12-74 Accra, Ghana
Debut: Blackburn Rvs v ASTON VILLA 24/9/94 as sub

| *Previous Clubs Details* | | | *Apps* | | | | | *Goals* | | |
Club	Signed	Fee	Tot	Start	Sub	FA	FL	Lge	FA	FL
Anderlecht			–	–	–	–	–	–	–	–
Aston Villa	Aug-94	£1m	6	1	5	0	3	0	0	3
Udinese										
Coventry City	Sep-95	£150,000+	6	3	3	1	4	0	0	2
FAPL Summary by Club										
Aston Villa	1994-95 to 1995-96		6	1	5	0	3	0	0	3
Coventry City	1995-96		6	3	3	1	4	0	0	2
Total			*12*	*4*	*8*	*1*	*7*	*0*	*0*	*5*

LAURSEN Jacob   Derby County

Fullname: Jacob Laursen   DOB:

Previous Clubs Details			Apps					Goals		
Club	Signed	Fee	Tot	Start	Sub	FA	FL	Lge	FA	FL
Silkeborg			–	–	–	–	–	–	–	–
Derby County		£500,000								

LAWRENCE Jamie   Leicester City

Fullname: James Hubert Lawrence   DOB: 08-03-70 Balham
Debut: Crystal Palace v LEICESTER CITY 14/1/95
Debut Goal: LEICESTER CITY v Wimbledon 1/4/95 as sub

Previous Clubs Details			Apps					Goals		
Club	Signed	Fee	Tot	Start	Sub	FA	FL	Lge	FA	FL
Sunderland	Oct-93	From NL	4	2	2	0	1	0	0	0
Doncaster Rvs	Mar-94	£20,000	25	16	9	1	2	3	0	0
Leicester City	Jan-95	£125,000	32	19	13	0	0	1	0	0
FAPL Summary by Club										
Leicester City	1994-95		17	9	8	0	0	1	0	0
Total			*17*	*9*	*8*	*0*	*0*	*1*	*0*	*0*

LAZIRIDIS Stan   West Ham United

Fullname: Stanley Laziridis   DOB:
Debut: Arsenal v WEST HAM UTD 16/9/95 as sub

Previous Clubs Details			Apps					Goals		
Club	Signed	Fee	Tot	Start	Sub	FA	FL	Lge	FA	FL
West Adelaide (Aus)			–	–	–	–	–	–	–	–
West Ham Utd	Aug-95	£300,000	4	2	2	1	1	0	0	0
FAPL Summary by Club										
West Ham Utd	1995-96		4	2	2	1	1	0	0	0
Total			*4*	*2*	*2*	*1*	*1*	*0*	*0*	*0*

LE SAUX Graeme   Blackburn Rovers

Fullname: Graeme Pierre Le Saux   DOB: 17-10-68 Jersey
Debut: CHELSEA v Ipswich Town 17/10/92
Debut Goal: Chelsea v BLACKBURN RVS 14/8/93

Previous Clubs Details			Apps					Goals		
Club	Signed	Fee	Tot	Start	Sub	FA	FL	Lge	FA	FL
Chelsea	Dec-87		90	77	13	8	13	8	0	1
Blackburn Rvs	Mar-93	Swap	104	102	2	6	10	6	0	0
FAPL Summary by Club										
Chelsea	1992-93		14	10	4	1	4	0	0	0
Blackburn Rvs	1992-93 to 1995-96		104	102	5	6	10	6	0	0
Total			*118*	*112*	*6*	*7*	*14*	*6*	*0*	*0*

LE TISSIER Matthew   Southampton

Fullname: Matthew Paul Le Tissier   DOB: 14-10-68 Guernsey
Debut: SOUTHAMPTON v Tottenham H. 15/8/92
Debut Goal: QPR v SOUTHAMPTON 19/8/92

Previous Clubs Details

Club	Signed	Fee	Tot	Start	Sub	FA	FL	Lge	FA	FL
Southampton	Oct-86		326	296	30	29	36	127	12	20
FAPL Summary by Club										
Southampton	1992-93 to 1995-96		153	153	0	13	10	67	7	9
Total			*153*	*153*	*0*	*13*	*10*	*67*	*7*	*9*

LEBOEUF Franck   Chelsea

Fullname: Franck Leboeuf   DOB:

Previous Clubs Details

Club	Signed	Fee	Tot	Start	Sub	FA	FL	Lge	FA	FL
Strasbourg			–	–	–	–	–	–	–	–
Chelsea	Jul-96	£2.5m								

LEE David   Chelsea

Fullname: David John Lee   DOB: 26-11-69 Kingswood
Debut: Aston Villa v CHELSEA 2/9/92
Debut Goal: CHELSEA v Manchester Utd 19/12/92

Previous Clubs Details

Club	Signed	Fee	Tot	Start	Sub	FA	FL	Lge	FA	FL
Chelsea	Jun-88		149	117	32	14	17	10	0	1
Reading	Jan-92	Loan	5	5	0	0	0	5	0	0
Plymouth A	Mar-92	Loan	9	9	0	0	0	1	0	0
Portsmouth	Aug-94	Loan	5	4	1	0	0	0	0	0
FAPL Summary by Club										
Chelsea	1992-93 to 1995-96		77	64	13	9	10	4	0	0
Total			*77*	*64*	*13*	*9*	*10*	*4*	*0*	*0*

LEE Robert   Newcastle United

Fullname: Robert Martin Lee   DOB: 01-02-66 West Ham
Debut: NEWCASTLE UTD v Tottenham H. 14/8/93
Debut Goal: NEWCASTLE UTD v Swindon Town 12/3/94

Previous Clubs Details

Club	Signed	Fee	Tot	Start	Sub	FA	FL	Lge	FA	FL
Charlton Ath	Jul-83		298	274	24	14	19	58	2	1
Newcastle Utd	Sep-92	£700,000	184	184	0	12	12	34	3	3
FAPL Summary by Club										
Newcastle Utd	1993-94 to 1995-96		112	112	0	8	9	24	1	2
Total			*112*	*112*	*0*	*8*	*9*	*24*	*1*	*2*

LEE Jason   Nottingham Forest
Fullname: Jason Benedict Lee   DOB: 09-05-71 Newham
Debut: Ipswich Town v N. Forest 20/8/94
Debut Goal: Newcastle Utd v NOTTIM FOREST 11/2/95 as sub

Previous Clubs Details			Apps				Goals		
Club	Signed	Fee	Tot	Start	Sub	FA	FL	Lge	FA	FL
Charlton Ath	Jun-89	Trainee	1	0	1	0	0	0	0	0
Stockport Co	Feb-91	Loan	2	2	0	0	0	0	0	0
Lincoln City	Mar-91	£35,000	93	86	7	3	6	21	1	0
Southend Utd	Jul-93	undisclosed	24	18	6	1	1	3	0	0
N. Forest	Mar-94	£200,000	63	36	27	4	3	11	0	0
FAPL Summary by Club										
N. Forest	1994-95 to 1995-96		50	26	24	4	3	11	0	0
Total			*50*	*26*	*24*	*4*	*3*	*11*	*0*	*0*

LENNON Neil   Leicester City
Fullname: Neil Francis Lennon   DOB: 25-06-71 Lurgan

Previous Clubs Details			Apps				Goals		
Club	Signed	Fee	Tot	Start	Sub	FA	FL	Lge	FA	FL
Man. City	Aug-89	Trainee	1	1	0	0	0	0	0	0
Crewe Alex	Sep-90	Free	122	117	5	7	4	13	1	1
Leicester City			15	14	1	0	0	1	0	0

LEONHARDSEN Oyvind   Wimbledon
Fullname: Oyvind Leonhardsen   DOB: 17-08-70
Debut: WIMBLEDON v Aston Villa 9/11/94
Debut Goal: WIMBLEDON v Aston Villa 9/11/94

Previous Clubs Details			Apps				Goals		
Club	Signed	Fee	Tot	Start	Sub	FA	FL	Lge	FA	FL
Rosenborg			–	–	–	–	–	–	–	–
Wimbledon	Jan-95	£650,000	49	46	3	10	2	8	2	0
FAPL Summary by Club										
Wimbledon	1994-95 to 1995-96		49	46	3	10	2	8	2	0
Total			*49*	*46*	*3*	*10*	*2*	*8*	*2*	*0*

LEWIS Neil   Leicester City
Fullname: Neil Anthony Lewis   DOB: 28-06-74 Wolverhampton
Debut: Wimbledon v LEICESTER CITY 10/9/94

Previous Clubs Details			Apps				Goals		
Club	Signed	Fee	Tot	Start	Sub	FA	FL	Lge	FA	FL
Leicester City	Jul-92	Trainee	45	36	9	1	3	1	0	0
FAPL Summary by Club										
Leicester City	1994-95		16	13	3	1	2	0	0	0
Total			*16*	*13*	*3*	*1*	*2*	*0*	*0*	*0*

LIDDLE Craig — Middlesbrough

Fullname: Craig George Liddle DOB: 21-10-71 Chester le Street
Debut: MIDDLESBROUGH v Leeds Utd 4/11/95

Previous Clubs Details

Club	Signed	Fee	Tot	Start	Sub	FA	FL	Lge	FA	FL
				Apps					*Goals*	
Middlesbrough	Jul-94	Free NL	14	14	0	1	3	0	0	0

FAPL Summary by Club

| Middlesbrough | 1995-96 | | 13 | 13 | 0 | 1 | 3 | 0 | 0 | 0 |
| *Total* | | | *13* | *13* | *0* | *1* | *3* | *0* | *0* | *0* |

LIMPAR Anders — Everton

Fullname: Anders Limpar DOB: 24-09-65 Sweden
Debut: ARSENAL v Norwich City 15/8/92
Debut Goal: Liverpool v ARSENAL 23/8/92

Previous Clubs Details

Club	Signed	Fee	Tot	Start	Sub	FA	FL	Lge	FA	FL
				Apps					*Goals*	
Arsenal	Jul-90	£1m	96	76	20	7	9	18	2	0
Everton	Mar-94	£1.6m	63	49	14	10	1	5	1	0

FAPL Summary by Club

Arsenal	1992-93 to 1993-94		33	21	12	2	6	2	0	0
Everton	1993-94 to 1995-96		64	50	14	10	1	14	1	0
Total			*97*	*71*	*26*	*12*	*7*	*16*	*1*	*0*

LINIGHAN Andy — Arsenal

Fullname: Andrew Linighan DOB: 18-06-62 Hartlepool
Debut: Sheffield Utd v ARSENAL 19/9/92
Debut Goal: Oldham Ath v ARSENAL 20/2/93

Previous Clubs Details

Club	Signed	Fee	Tot	Start	Sub	FA	FL	Lge	FA	FL
				Apps					*Goals*	
Hartlepool Utd	Sep-80		110	110	0	8	8	4	0	1
Leeds Utd	May-84	£200,000	66	66	0	2	6	3	0	1
Oldham Ath	Jan-86	£65,000	87	87	0	3	8	6	0	2
Norwich City	Mar-88	£350,000	86	86	0	10	6	8	0	0
Arsenal	Jun-90	£1.25m	107	91	16	14	14	4	1	1

FAPL Summary by Club

| Arsenal | 1992-93 to 1995-96 | | 80 | 69 | 11 | 10 | 12 | 4 | 1 | 1 |
| *Total* | | | *80* | *69* | *11* | *10* | *12* | *4* | *1* | *1* |

LYTTLE Des — Nottingham Forest

Fullname: Desmond Lyttle DOB: 24-09-71 Wolverhampton
Debut: Ipswich Town v N. Forest 20/8/94
Debut Goal: Aston Villa v N. Forest 23/9/95

Previous Clubs Details

Club	Signed	Fee	Tot	Start	Sub	FA	FL	Lge	FA	FL
				Apps					*Goals*	
Swansea City	Jul-92	£12,500	46	46	0	5	2	1	0	0

N. Forest	Jul-93	£375,000	108	107	1	11	12		2	0	0

FAPL Summary by Club

N. Forest	1994-95 to 1995-96	71	70	1	9	6		1	0	0
Total		*71*	*70*	*1*	*9*	*6*		*1*	*0*	*0*

MABBUTT Gary   Tottenham Hotspur

Fullname: Gary Vincent Mabbutt   DOB: 23-08-61 Bristol
Debut: Wimbledon v TOTTENHAM HOTSPUR 25/10/92
Debut Goal: TOTTENHAM HOTSPUR v Nottm Forest 18/12/92

Previous Clubs Details			*Apps*					*Goals*		
Club	Signed	Fee	Tot	Start	Sub	FA	FL	Lge	FA	FL
Bristol Rvs	Jan-79		131	122	9	6	10	10	1	1
Tottenham H.	Aug-82	£105,000	462	449	13	46	61	27	4	2

FAPL Summary by Club

Tottenham H.	1992-93 to 1995-96	123	123	0	16	10	2	1	0
Total		*123*	*123*	*0*	*16*	*10*	*2*	*1*	*0*

MAGILTON Jim   Southampton

Fullname: James Magilton   DOB: 06-05-69 Belfast
Debut: SOUTHAMPTON v Liverpool 14/2/94
Debut Goal: Arsenal v SOUTHAMPTON 19/11/94

Previous Clubs Details			*Apps*					*Goals*		
Club	Signed	Fee	Tot	Start	Sub	FA	FL	Lge	FA	FL
Liverpool	May-86		0	0	0	0	0	0	0	0
Oxford Utd	Oct-90	£100,000	150	150	0	8	9	34	4	1
Southampton	Feb-94	£600,000	88	88	0	11	6	9	3	0

FAPL Summary by Club

Southampton	1993-94 to 1995-96	88	88	0	11	6	9	3	0
Total		*88*	*88*	*0*	*11*	*6*	*9*	*3*	*0*

MARSH Mike   Coventry City

Fullname: Michael Andrew Marsh   DOB: 21-07-69 Liverpool
Debut: LIVERPOOL v Arsenal 23/8/92
Debut Goal: LIVERPOOL v Crystal Palace 28/11/92

Previous Clubs Details			*Apps*					*Goals*		
Club	Signed	Fee	Tot	Start	Sub	FA	FL	Lge	FA	FL
Liverpool	Aug-87		69	42	27	8	11	2	0	3
West Ham	Sep-93	Swap	49	46	3	6	6	1	1	0
Coventry City	Dec-94	£500,000	15	15	0	4	0	2	0	0

FAPL Summary by Club

Liverpool	1992-93 to 1993-94	30	22	8	2	6	2	0	3
West Ham U.	1993-94 to 1994-95	49	46	3	6	6	1	1	0
Coventry City	1994-95	15	15	0	4	0	2	0	0
Total		*94*	*83*	*11*	*12*	*12*	*5*	*1*	*3*

MARSHALL Scott   Arsenal

Fullname: Scott Roderick Marshall   DOB: 01-05-73 Edinburgh
Debut: Sheffield Wednesday v ARSENAL 6/5/93
Debut Goal: ARSENAL v Newcastle Utd 23/3/96

Previous Clubs Details

Club	Signed	Fee	Tot	Start	Sub	FA	FL	Lge	FA	FL
Arsenal	Mar-91		13	12	1	0	0	0	0	0
Rotherham Utd	Dec-93	Loan	10	10	0	0	0	0	0	0
Sheffield Utd	Aug-94	Loan	17	17	0	0	0	0	0	0

FAPL Summary by Club

Arsenal	1992-93 to 1995-96		13	12	1	0	0	1	0	0
Total			*13*	*12*	*1*	*0*	*0*	*1*	*0*	*0*

MASKELL Craig   Southampton

Fullname: Craig Dell Maskell   DOB: 10-04-68 Aldershot
Debut: Sheffield Utd v SWINDON TOWN 14/8/93
Debut Goal: Southampton v SWINDON TOWN 25/8/93

Previous Clubs Details

Club	Signed	Fee	Tot	Start	Sub	FA	FL	Lge	FA	FL
Southampton	Apr-86	Apprentice	6	2	4	0	0	1	0	0
Huddersfield	May-88	£20,000	87	86	1	8	6	43	3	4
Reading	Aug-90	£250,000	72	60	12	6	2	27	0	0
Swindon Town	Jul-92	£225,000	47	40	7	3	4	21	0	1
Southampton	Feb-94	£250,000	17	8	9	2	0	1	0	0
Bristol City *	Dec-95	Loan								

FAPL Summary by Club

Swindon Tn	1993-94		14	8	6	2	2	3	0	0
Southampton	1993-94 to 1995-96		17	8	9	2	0	1	0	0
Total			*31*	*16*	*15*	*4*	*2*	*4*	*0*	*0*

MATTEO Dominic   Liverpool

Fullname: Dominic Matteo   DOB: 28-04-74 Dumfries
Debut: Manchester City v LIVERPOOL 23/10/93

Previous Clubs Details

Club	Signed	Fee	Tot	Start	Sub	FA	FL	Lge	FA	FL
Liverpool	May-92		23	18	5	1	2	0	0	0

FAPL Summary by Club

Liverpool	1993-94 to 1995-96		23	7	16	1	2	0	0	0
Total			*23*	*7*	*16*	*1*	*2*	*0*	*0*	*0*

MAY David   Manchester United

Fullname: David May   DOB: 24-06-70 Oldham
Debut: Crystal Palace v BLACKBURN ROVERS 15/8/92
Debut Goal: Everton v BLACKBURN ROVERS 3/3/93

Club	Signed	Fee	Apps					Goals		
			Tot	Start	Sub	FA	FL	Lge	FA	FL
Blackburn Rvs	Jun-88		122	122	0	10	13	3	1	2
Manchester U.	Jul-94	£1.4m	35	26	9	3	2	3	0	1
FAPL Summary by Club										
Blackburn Rvs1992-93 to 1993-94			74	74	0	7	10	2	1	2
Manchester U. 1994-95 to 1995-96			35	26	9	3	2	3	0	1
Total			*109*	*100*	*9*	*10*	*12*	*5*	*1*	*3*

MAYBURY Alan   Leeds United

Fullname: Alan Maybury   DOB: 08-08-78 Dublin
Debut: Aston Villa v LEEDS UNITED 3/2/96

Previous Clubs Details			Apps					Goals		
Club	Signed	Fee	Tot	Start	Sub	FA	FL	Lge	FA	FL
Leeds Utd			1	1	0	0	0	0	0	0
FAPL Summary by Club										
Leeds Utd		1995-96	1	1	0	0	0	0	0	0
Total			*1*	*1*	*0*	*0*	*0*	*0*	*0*	*0*

McALLISTER Brian   Wimbledon

Fullname: Brian McAllister   DOB: 30-11-70 Glasgow
Debut: Sheffield Utd v WIMBLEDON 25/8/92

Previous Clubs Details			Apps					Goals		
Club	Signed	Fee	Tot	Start	Sub	FA	FL	Lge	FA	FL
Wimbledon	Feb-89		55	51	4	3	5	0	0	0
Plymouth A.	Dec-90	Loan	8	7	1	0	0	0	0	0
Crewe Alex *	Mar-96	Loan								
FAPL Summary by Club										
Wimbledon	1992-93 to 1995-96		42	41	1	3	5	0	0	0
Total			*42*	*41*	*1*	*3*	*5*	*0*	*0*	*0*

McALLISTER Gary   Coventry City

Fullname: Gary McAllister   DOB: 25-12-64 Motherwell
Debut: LEEDS UNITED v Wimbledon 15/8/92
Debut Goal: LEEDS UNITED v Liverpool 29/8/92

Previous Clubs Details			Apps					Goals		
Club	Signed	Fee	Tot	Start	Sub	FA	FL	Lge	FA	FL
Leicester City	Aug-85	£125,000	201	199	2	5	15	46	2	3
Leeds Utd	Jun-90	£1m	231	230	1	24	26	32	6	4
Coventry City	Jul-96	£3m	0	0	0	0	0	0	0	0
FAPL Summary by Club										
Leeds Utd 1992-93 to 1995-96			151	151	0	17	15	25	5	2
Total			*151*	*151*	*0*	*17*	*15*	*25*	*5*	*2*

McATEER Jason   Liverpool

Fullname: Jason McAteer   DOB: 18-06-71 Birkenhead
Debut: Wimbledon v BOLTON WANDERERS 19/8/95

Previous Clubs Details   *Apps*   *Goals*

Club	Signed	Fee	Tot	Start	Sub	FA	FL	Lge	FA	FL
Bolton W.	Jan-92		113	108	5	11	11	9	3	2
Liverpool	Sep-95	£4m	29	27	2	7	4	0	3	0

FAPL Summary by Club

Bolton Wanderers		1995-96	4	4	0	0	0	0	0	0
Liverpool		1995-96	29	27	2	7	4	0	3	0
Total			*33*	*31*	*2*	*7*	*4*	*0*	*3*	*0*

McCLAIR Brian   Manchester United

Fullname: Brian John McClair   DOB: 08-12-63 Bellshill
Debut: Sheffield Utd v MANCHESTER UNITED 15/8/92
Debut Goal: Everton v MANCHESTER UNITED 12/9/92

Previous Clubs Details   *Apps*   *Goals*

Club	Signed	Fee	Tot	Start	Sub	FA	FL	Lge	FA	FL
Celtic	Jul-83		0	0	0	0	0	0	0	0
Manchester U.	Jul-87	£850,000	320	290	30	39	42	89	14	18

FAPL Summary by Club

Manchester U.	1992-93 to 1995-96		130	100	30	15	14	18	3	5
Total			*130*	*100*	*30*	*15*	*14*	*18*	*3*	*5*

McGOLDRICK Eddie   Arsenal

Fullname: Edward John Paul McGoldrick   DOB: 30-04-65 Islington
Debut: CRYSTAL PALACE v Blackburn Rvs 15/8/92
Debut Goal: Oldham Athletic v CRYSTAL PALACE 19/8/92

Previous Clubs Details   *Apps*   *Goals*

Club	Signed	Fee	Tot	Start	Sub	FA	FL	Lge	FA	FL
Northampton	Aug-86	£10,000	107	97	10	7	9	9	1	0
Crystal Palace	Jan-89	£200,000	147	139	8	5	22	11	0	2
Arsenal	Jul-93	£1m	38	32	6	2	9	0	0	0

FAPL Summary by Club

Crystal Palace		1992-93	42	42	0	1	8	8	0	2
Arsenal	1993-94 to 1995-96		38	32	6	2	9	0	0	0
Total			*80*	*74*	*6*	*3*	*17*	*8*	*0*	*2*

McGOWAN Gavin   Arsenal

Fullname: Gavin McGowan   DOB: 16-01-76 Blackheath
Debut: Sheffield Wednesday v ARSENAL 6/5/93 as sub

Previous Clubs Details   *Apps*   *Goals*

Club	Signed	Fee	Tot	Start	Sub	FA	FL	Lge	FA	FL
Arsenal			4	2	2	1	0	0	0	0

Arsenal	1992-93 to 1995-96	4	2	2	1	0		0	0	0
Total		*4*	*2*	*2*	*1*	*0*		*0*	*0*	*0*

McGRATH Paul   Aston Villa

Fullname: Paul McGrath   DOB: 04-12-59 Ealing
Debut: ASTON VILLA v Ipswich Town 15/8/92
Debut Goal: ASTON VILLA v Nottingham Forest 12/12/92

Previous Clubs Details			*Apps*					*Goals*		
Club	Signed	Fee	Tot	Start	Sub	FA	FL	Lge	FA	FL
Manchester U.	Apr-82	£30,000	163	159	4	17	13	12	2	2
Aston Villa	Jul-89	£400,000	262	247	15	24	30	8	1	0

FAPL Summary by Club

Aston Villa	1992-93 to 1995-96	142	137	5	12	21		6	0	1
Total		*142*	*137*	*5*	*12*	*21*		*6*	*0*	*1*

McGREGOR Paul   Nottingham Forest

Fullname: Paul Anthony McGregor   DOB: 17-12-74 Liverpool
Debut: NOTTM FOREST v Ipswich Town 10/12/94 as sub
Debut Goal: West Ham Utd v NOTTM FOREST 31/12/94 as sub

Previous Clubs Details			*Apps*					*Goals*		
Club	Signed	Fee	Tot	Start	Sub	FA	FL	Lge	FA	FL
Nottingham Forest			24	7	17	2	0	3	0	0

FAPL Summary by Club

N. Forest	1994-95 to 1995-96	24	7	17	2	0		3	0	0
Total		*24*	*7*	*17*	*2*	*0*		*3*	*0*	*0*

McKINLAY Billy   Blackburn Rovers

Fullname: William McKinlay   DOB: 22-04-69 Glasgow
Debut: West Ham Utd v BLACKBURN ROVERS 21/10/95 as sub
Debut Goal: Nottingham Forest v BLACKBURN ROVERS 13/4/96

Previous Clubs Details			*Apps*					*Goals*		
Club	Signed	Fee	Tot	Start	Sub	FA	FL	Lge	FA	FL
Dundee Utd			–	–	–	–	–	–	–	–
Blackburn Rvs	Oct-95	£1.75m	19	13	6	2	1	2	0	0

FAPL Summary by Club

Blackburn Rvs	1995-96	19	13	6	2	1		2	0	0
Total		*19*	*13*	*6*	*2*	*1*		*2*	*0*	*0*

McMAHON Gerry   Tottenham Hotspur

Fullname: Gerard McMahon   DOB: 29-12-73 Belfast
Debut: TOTTENHAM HOTSPUR v Coventry City 9/5/95

Previous Clubs Details			*Apps*					*Goals*		
Club	Signed	Fee	Tot	Start	Sub	FA	FL	Lge	FA	FL
Glenavon			–	–	–	–	–	–	–	–
Tottenham H.	Jul-92	£100,000	16	9	7	1	3	0	0	0

Barnet	Oct-94	Loan	10	10	0	2	0	2	1	0

FAPL Summary by Club

Tottenham H.	1994-95 to 1995-96		16	9	7	1	3	0	0	0
Total			*16*	*9*	*7*	*1*	*3*	*0*	*0*	*0*

McMAHON Sam   Leicester City

Fullname: Samuel Keiron McMahon   DOB: 09-02-76 Newark
Debut: LEICESTER CITY v Wimbledon 1/4/95 as sub
Debut Goal:

Previous Clubs Details			Apps					Goals		
Club	Signed	Fee	Tot	Start	Sub	FA	FL	Lge	FA	FL
Leicester City	Jul-94	Trainee	4	1	3	0	1	1	0	0

FAPL Summary by Club

Leicester City	1994-95		1	0	1	0	0	0	0	0
Total			*1*	*0*	*1*	*0*	*0*	*0*	*0*	*0*

McMANAMAN Steve   Liverpool

Fullname: Steven McManaman   DOB: 11-02-72 Bootle
Debut: Nottingham Forest v LIVERPOOL 16/8/92
Debut Goal: LIVERPOOL v Wimbledon 26/9/92

Previous Clubs Details			Apps					Goals		
Club	Signed	Fee	Tot	Start	Sub	FA	FL	Lge	FA	FL
Liverpool	Feb-90		171	160	11	26	24	24	5	8

FAPL Summary by Club

Liverpool	1992-93 to 1995-96		139	134	5	17	19	19	2	5
Total			*139*	*134*	*5*	*17*	*19*	*19*	*2*	*5*

MELVILLE Andy   Sunderland

Fullname: Andrew Roger Melville   DOB: 29-11-68 Swansea

Previous Clubs Details			Apps					Goals		
Club	Signed	Fee	Tot	Start	Sub	FA	FL	Lge	FA	FL
Swansea City	Jul-86	Trainee	175	165	10	15	10	22	5	0
Oxford Utd	Jul-90	£275,000	135	135	0	6	12	13	0	1
Sunderland	Aug-93		120	120	0	7	11	9	0	0

MERSON Paul   Arsenal

Fullname: Paul Charles Merson   DOB: 20-03-68 Harlesden
Debut: ARSENAL v Norwich City 15/8/92
Debut Goal: ARSENAL v Sheffield Wednesday 29/8/92

Previous Clubs Details			Apps					Goals		
Club	Signed	Fee	Tot	Start	Sub	FA	FL	Lge	FA	FL
Arsenal	Nov-85		295	257	38	28	37	71	4	9
Brentford	Jan-87	Loan	7	6	1	0	0	0	0	0

FAPL Summary by Club

Arsenal	1992-93 to 1995-96		128	118	10	13	22	22	1	3
Total			*128*	*118*	*10*	*13*	*22*	*22*	*1*	*3*

MIKLOSKO Ludek   West Ham United

Fullname: Ludek Miklosko   DOB: 09-12-61 Protesov, Czechoslovakia
Debut: WEST HAM UNITED v Wimbledon 14/8/93
Debut Goal: (Goalkeeper)

Previous Clubs Details			Apps				Goals		
Club	Signed	Fee	Tot	Start	Sub	FA	FL	Lge	FA	FL
Banik Ostrava			–	–	–	–	–	–	–	–
West Ham U.	Feb-90	£300,000	266	266	0	23	20	0	0	0

FAPL Summary by Club

		Apps				Goals		
West Ham U. 1993-94 to 1995-96	120	120	0	11	10	0	0	0
Total	*120*	*120*	*0*	*11*	*10*	*0*	*0*	*0*

MILLER Alan   Middlesbrough

Fullname: Alan John Miller   DOB: 29-03-70 Epping
Debut: Leeds Utd v ARSENAL 21/11/92
Debut Goal: (Goalkeeper)

Previous Clubs Details			Apps				Goals		
Club	Signed	Fee	Tot	Start	Sub	FA	FL	Lge	FA	FL
Arsenal	May-88		8	6	2	0	0	0	0	0
Plymouth A.	Nov-88	Loan	13	13	0	2	0	0	0	0
WBA	Aug-91	Loan	3	3	0	0	0	0	0	0
Birmingham C.	Dec-91	Loan	15	15	0	0	0	0	0	0
Middlesbrough	Aug-94	£500,000	47	47	0	2	1	0	0	0

FAPL Summary by Club

		Apps				Goals		
Arsenal	1992-93 to 1993-94	8	6	2	0	0	0	0	0
Middlesbrough	1995-96	6	6	0	0	0	0	0	0
Total		*14*	*12*	*2*	*0*	*0*	*0*	*0*	*0*

MILOSEVIC Savo   Aston Villa

Fullname: Savo Milosevic   DOB:
Debut: ASTON VILLA v Manchester Utd, 19/8/95
Debut Goal: Blackburn Rvs v ASTON VILLA 9/9/95

Previous Clubs Details			Apps				Goals		
Club	Signed	Fee	Tot	Start	Sub	FA	FL	Lge	FA	FL
Partizan Belgrade			–	–	–	–	–	–	–	–
Aston Villa	Jun-95	£3.5m	37	36	1	5	7	12	1	1

FAPL Summary by Club

		Apps				Goals		
Aston Villa	1995-96	37	36	1	5	7	12	1	1
Total		*37*	*36*	*1*	*5*	*7*	*12*	*1*	*1*

MINTO Scott   Chelsea

Fullname: Scott Christopher Minto   DOB: 06-08-71 Heswall
Debut: Nottingham Forest v CHELSEA 19/11/94

Previous Clubs Details			Apps					Goals		
Club	Signed	Fee	Tot	Start	Sub	FA	FL	Lge	FA	FL
Charlton Ath	Feb-89		180	171	9	10	8	6	0	2
Chelsea	Jun-94	£775,000	29	29	0	2	1	0	0	0
FAPL Summary by Club										
Chelsea	1994-95 to 1995-96		29	29	0	2	1	0	0	0
Total			*29*	*29*	*0*	*2*	*1*	*0*	*0*	*0*

MONCUR John   West Ham United

Fullname: John F Moncur   DOB: 22-09-66 Stepney
Debut: Sheffield Utd v SWINDON TOWN 14/8/93
Debut Goal: Sheffield Utd v SWINDON TOWN 14/8/93

Previous Clubs Details			Apps					Goals		
Club	Signed	Fee	Tot	Start	Sub	FA	FL	Lge	FA	FL
Tottenham H.	Aug-84		21	10	11	0	3	1	0	0
Doncaster Rvs	Sep-86	Loan	4	4	0	0	0	0	0	0
Cambridge Utd	Mar-87	Loan	4	3	1	0	0	0	0	0
Portsmouth	Mar-89	Loan	7	7	0	0	0	0	0	0
Brentford	Oct-89	Loan	5	5	0	0	0	0	0	0
Ipswich Town	Oct-91	Loan	6	5	1	0	0	0	0	0
N. Forest	Feb-92	Loan	0	0	0	0	0	0	0	0
Swindon Town	Mar-92	£80,000	58	53	5	1	4	5	0	0
West Ham U.	Aug-94	£1m	50	49	1	3	6	2	1	2
FAPL Summary by Club										
Swindon Tn		1993-94	41	41	0	1	3	4	0	0
West Ham U.	1994-95 to 1995-96		50	49	1	3	6	2	1	2
Total			*91*	*90*	*1*	*4*	*9*	*6*	*1*	*2*

MONKOU Ken   Southampton

Fullname: Kenneth John Monkou   DOB: 29-11-64 Necare, Surinam
Debut: SOUTHAMPTON v Manchester Utd 24/8/92
Debut Goal: SOUTHAMPTON v Sheffield Wednesday 28/12/92

Previous Clubs Details			Apps					Goals		
Club	Signed	Fee	Tot	Start	Sub	FA	FL	Lge	FA	FL
Chelsea	Mar-89	£100,000	94	92	2	3	12	2	0	0
Southampton	Aug-92	£750,000	131	130	1	13	10	8	0	1
FAPL Summary by Club										
Southampton	1992-93 to 1995-96		131	130	1	13	10	8	0	1
Total			*131*	*130*	*1*	*13*	*10*	*8*	*0*	*1*

MOORE Alan   Middlesbrough

Fullname: Alan Moore   DOB: 25-11-74 Dublin
Debut: MIDDLESBROUGH v Everton 10/4/92

Previous Clubs Details			Apps					Goals		
Club	Signed	Fee	Tot	Start	Sub	FA	FL	Lge	FA	FL
Middlesbrough	Dec-91	Trainee	93	82	11	3	9	15	2	0

Middlesbrough 1992-93 to 1995-96	14	5	9	0	3	0	0	0
Total	*14*	*5*	*9*	*0*	*3*	*0*	*0*	*0*

MORRIS Chris   Middlesbrough

Fullname: Christopher Barry Morris   DOB: 24-12-63 Newquay
Debut: Coventry City v MIDDLESBROUGH 15/8/92
Debut Goal: MIDDLESBROUGH v Wimbledon 21/11/92

Previous Clubs Details			*Apps*					*Goals*		
Club	Signed	Fee	Tot	Start	Sub	FA	FL	Lge	FA	FL
Sheffield W.	Oct-92		74	61	13	12	10	1	0	1
Celtic	Aug-87	£125,000	170	154	16	22	17	8	1	0
Middlesbrough	Aug-92	£450,000 +	78	72	6	6	10	3	0	0

FAPL Summary by Club

Middlesbrough 1992-93 to 1995-96	48	44	4	2	4	27	0	0
Total	*48*	*44*	*4*	*2*	*4*	*27*	*0*	*0*

MORRIS Jody   Chelsea

Fullname: Jody Morris   DOB:
Debut: CHELSEA v Middlesbrough, 4/2/96 as sub

Previous Clubs Details			*Apps*					*Goals*		
Club	Signed	Fee	Tot	Start	Sub	FA	FL	Lge	FA	FL
Chelsea			1	0	1	0	0	0	0	0

FAPL Summary by Club

Chelsea	1995-96	1	0	1	0	0	0	0	0
Total	*1*	*0*	*1*	*0*	*0*	*0*	*0*	*0*

MORROW Steve   Arsenal

Fullname: Stephen Joseph Morrow   DOB: 02-07-70 Bangor
Debut: ARSENAL v Oldham Athletic 26/8/92
Debut Goal: Blackburn Rvs v ARSENAL 8/3/95

Previous Clubs Details			*Apps*					*Goals*		
Club	Signed	Fee	Tot	Start	Sub	FA	FL	Lge	FA	FL
Arsenal	May-88		48	34	14	5	8	1	0	2
Reading	Jan-91	Loan	10	10	0	0	0	0	0	0
Watford	Aug-91	Loan	8	7	1	0	0	0	0	0
Reading	Oct-91	Loan	3	3	0	0	0	0	0	0
Barnet	Mar-92	Loan	1	1	0	0	0	0	0	0

FAPL Summary by Club

Arsenal	1992-93 to 1995-96	46	34	12	5	9	1	0	2
Total	*46*	*34*	*12*	*5*	*9*	*1*	*0*	*2*

MULLIN John   Sunderland

Fullname: John Mullin   DOB: 11-08-75 Bury

Previous Clubs Details

Club	Signed	Fee	Tot	Start	Sub	FA	FL	Lge	FA	FL
					Apps				Goals	
Burnley	Aug-92	Trainee	18	11	7	2	0	2	0	0
Sunderland	Aug-95	£40,000	10	5	5	1	1	1	0	0

MURRAY Scott   Aston Villa

Fullname: Scott Murray   DOB: 26-05-74 Aberdeen

Debut: ASTON VILLA v Middlesbrough, 19/3/96

Previous Clubs Details

Club	Signed	Fee	Tot	Start	Sub	FA	FL	Lge	FA	FL
					Apps				Goals	
Aston Villa			3	3	0	0	0	0	0	0
FAPL Summary by Club										
Aston Villa	1995-96		3	3	0	0	0	0	0	0
Total			*3*	*3*	*0*	*0*	*0*	*0*	*0*	*0*

MUSTOE Robbie   Middlesbrough

Fullname: Robin Mustoe   DOB: 28-08-68 Witney

Debut: Coventry City v MIDDLESBROUGH 15/8/92

Debut Goal: Tottenham H. v MIDDLESBROUGH 17/10/92

Previous Clubs Details

Club	Signed	Fee	Tot	Start	Sub	FA	FL	Lge	FA	FL
					Apps				Goals	
Oxford Utd	Jul-86	Junior	91	78	13	2	2	10	0	0
Middlesbrough	Jul-90	£375,000	177	171	6	1	3	13	0	2
FAPL Summary by Club										
Middlesbrough 1992-93 to 1995-96			44	42	2	0	3	2	0	1
Total			*44*	*42*	*2*	*0*	*3*	*2*	*0*	*1*

MYERS Andy   Chelsea

Fullname: Andrew John Myers   DOB: 03-11-73 Hounslow

Debut: Wimbledon v CHELSEA 28/12/92

Previous Clubs Details

Club	Signed	Fee	Tot	Start	Sub	FA	FL	Lge	FA	FL
					Apps				Goals	
Chelsea	Jun-91		53	47	6	9	2	1	0	0
FAPL Summary by Club										
Chelsea	1992-93 to 1995-96		39	38	1	7	1	0	0	0
Total			*39*	*38*	*1*	*7*	*1*	*0*	*0*	*0*

NDLOVU Peter   Coventry City

Fullname: Peter Ndlovu   DOB: 25-02-73 Bulawayo, Zimbabwe

Debut: Tottenham H. v COVENTRY CITY 19/8/92 as sub

Debut Goal: Sheffield Wednesday v COVENTRY CITY 2/9/92

Previous Clubs Details

Club	Signed	Fee	Tot	Start	Sub	FA	FL	Lge	FA	FL
					Apps				Goals	
Coventry City	Jul-91	£10,000	125	104	21	5	7	31	1	1

Coventry City 1992-93 to 1995-96	134	122	12	6	8	34	1	2
Total	*134*	*122*	*12*	*6*	*8*	*34*	*1*	*2*

NEILSON Alan   Southampton

Fullname: Alan Bruce Neilson   DOB: 26-09-72 Wegburg, Germany
Debut: Ipswich Town v NEWCASTLE UNITED 31/8/93 as sub

Previous Clubs Details			*Apps*			*Goals*		
Club	Signed	Fee	Tot	Start	Sub	FA	FL	Lge FA FL
Newcastle Utd	Feb-91	Trainee	74	62	12	1	8	6	0	1
Southampton	18	15	3	2	0	0	0	0

FAPL Summary by Club

Newcastle Utd 1993-94 to 1994-95	20	15	5	0	1	0	0	0
Southampton	1995-96	18	15	3	2	0	0	0	0
Total		*38*	*30*	*8*	*2*	*1*	*0*	*0*	*0*

NETHERCOTT Stuart   Tottenham Hotspur

Fullname: Stuart David Nethercott   DOB: 21-03-73 Ilford
Debut: TOTTENHAM HOTSPUR v Norwich City 9/4/93 as sub

Previous Clubs Details			*Apps*			*Goals*		
Club	Signed	Fee	Tot	Start	Sub	FA	FL	Lge FA FL
Tottenham H.	Jul-91		45	29	16	8	0	0	1	0
Maidstone Utd	Sep-91	Loan	13	13	0	0	0	1	0	0
Barnet	Feb-92	Loan	3	3	0	0	0	0	0	0

FAPL Summary by Club

Tottenham H. 1992-93 to 1995-96	45	29	16	8	0	0	1	0
Total	*45*	*29*	*16*	*8*	*0*	*0*	*1*	*0*

NEVILLE Gary   Manchester United

Fullname: Gary Alexander Neville   DOB: 18-02-75 Bury
Debut: MANCHESTER UNITED v Crystal Palace 19/11/94

Previous Clubs Details			*Apps*			*Goals*		
Club	Signed	Fee	Tot	Start	Sub	FA	FL	Lge FA FL
Manchester U.	Jan-93	Trainee	49	46	3	10	4	0	0	0

FAPL Summary by Club

Manchester U.1994-95 to 1995-96	49	46	3	10	4	0	0	0
Total	*49*	*46*	*3*	*10*	*4*	*0*	*0*	*0*

NEVILLE Phil   Manchester United

Fullname: Philip John Neville   DOB: 21-01-77 Bury
Debut: Manchester City v MANCHESTER UNITED 11/2/95

Previous Clubs Details			*Apps*			*Goals*		
Club	Signed	Fee	Tot	Start	Sub	FA	FL	Lge FA FL
Manchester U.	26	22	4	8	2	0	0	0

Manchester U.1994-95 to 1995-96	26	22	4	8	2	0	0	0
Total	*26*	*22*	*4*	*8*	*2*	*0*	*0*	*0*

NEWSOME Jon   Sheffield Wednesday

Fullname: Jonathan Newsome   DOB: 06-09-70 Sheffield
Debut: LEEDS UNITED v Wimbledon 15/8/92
Debut Goal: LEEDS UNITED v Blackburn Rvs 23/10/93

Previous Clubs Details			*Apps*				*Goals*		
Club	Signed	Fee	Tot	Start	Sub	FA	FL	Lge	FA	FL
Sheffield Wed	Jul-81		7	6	1	0	3	0	0	0
Leeds Utd	Jun-91	£150,000	76	62	14	4	3	3	0	0
Norwich City *	Jun-94	£1m	35	35	0	4	4	3	0	0
Sheffield W.	Mar-96	£1.6m	8	8	0	0	0	1	0	0

FAPL Summary by Club

Leeds Utd	1992-93 to 1993-94	66	55	11	4	3	1	0	0
Norwich City	1994-95	35	35	0	4	4	3	0	0
Sheffield W.	1995-96	8	8	0	0	0	1	0	0
Total		*109*	*98*	*11*	*8*	*7*	*5*	*0*	*0*

NEWTON Eddie   Chelsea

Fullname: Edward John Ikem Newton   DOB: 13-12-71 Hammersmith
Debut: Norwich City v CHELSEA 19/8/92
Debut Goal: CHELSEA v Sheffield Wednesday 22/8/92

Previous Clubs Details			*Apps*				*Goals*		
Club	Signed	Fee	Tot	Start	Sub	FA	FL	Lge	FA	FL
Chelsea	May-90		125	108	17	12	13	8	0	1
Cardiff City	Jan-92	Loan	18	18	0	0	0	4	0	0

FAPL Summary by Club

Chelsea	1992-93 to 1995-96	124	108	16	12	13	7	0	0
Total		*124*	*108*	*16*	*12*	*13*	*7*	*0*	*0*

NICOL Steve   Sheffield Wednesday

Fullname: Stephen Nicol   DOB: 01-12-61 Irvine
Debut: Nottingham Forest v LIVERPOOL 16/8/92
Debut Goal: QPR v LIVERPOOL 18/8/93

Previous Clubs Details			*Apps*				*Goals*		
Club	Signed	Fee	Tot	Start	Sub	FA	FL	Lge	FA	FL
Liverpool	Oct-81	£300,000	342	328	15	50	42	36	3	4
Notts County *	Jan-95	Free	19	19	0	0	0	0	0	0
Sheffield W.	Nov-95	Free	19	18	1	0	0	0	0	0

FAPL Summary by Club

Liverpool	1992-93 to 1994-95	67	63	4	3	7	1	0	0
Sheffield W.	1995-96	19	18	1	0	0	0	0	0
Total		*86*	*81*	*5*	*3*	*7*	*1*	*0*	*0*

NOLAN Ian
Sheffield Wednesday

Fullname: Ian Robert Nolan
DOB: 09-07-70 Liverpool
Debut: SHEFFIELD WED v Tottenham H. 20/8/94
Debut Goal: Liverpool v SHEFFIELD WEDNESDAY 1/10/94

Previous Clubs Details			Apps				Goals		
Club	Signed	Fee	Tot	Start	Sub	FA	FL	Lge	FA	FL
Preston	From NL		0	0	0	0	0	0	0	0
Tranmere Rvs	Aug-91	£10,000	88	87	1	7	10	1	1	0
Sheffield W.	Aug-94	£1.5m	71	71	0	4	8	3	0	0
FAPL Summary by Club										
Sheffield W.	1994-95 to 1995-96		71	71	0	4	8	3	0	0
Total			*71*	*71*	*0*	*4*	*8*	*3*	*0*	*0*

O'CONNOR Jon
Everton

Fullname: Jonathon O'Connor
DOB: 29-10-76 Darlington
Debut: Manchester Utd v EVERTON 21/2/96

Previous Clubs Details			Apps				Goals		
Club	Signed	Fee	Tot	Start	Sub	FA	FL	Lge	FA	FL
Everton	Oct-93		4	3	1	0	0	0	0	0
FAPL Summary by Club										
Everton	1995-96		4	3	1	0	0	0	0	0
Total			*4*	*3*	*1*	*0*	*0*	*0*	*0*	*0*

O'HALLORAN Keith
Middlesbrough

Fullname: Keith James O'Halloran
DOB: 11-10-75
Debut: Southampton v MIDDLESBROUGH 20/1/96 as sub

Previous Clubs Details			Apps				Goals		
Club	Signed	Fee	Tot	Start	Sub	FA	FL	Lge	FA	FL
Cherry Orchard			–	–	–	–	–	–	–	–
Middlesbrough	Sep-94		4	2	2	2	0	0	0	0
Scunthorpe *	Mar-96	Loan	–	–	–	–	–	–	–	–
FAPL Summary by Club										
Middlesbrough	1995-96		3	2	1	2	0	0	0	0
Total			*3*	*2*	*1*	*2*	*0*	*0*	*0*	*0*

O'KANE John
Manchester United

Fullname: John Andrew O'Kane
DOB: 15-11-74 Nottingham
Debut: Aston Villa v MANCHESTER UTD 19/8/95 as sub

Previous Clubs Details			Apps				Goals		
Club	Signed	Fee	Tot	Start	Sub	FA	FL	Lge	FA	FL
Manchester U.	Jan-93	Trainee	1	1	0	0	0	0	0	0
FAPL Summary by Club										
Manchester U.	1995-96		1	0	1	0	0	0	0	0
Total			*1*	*0*	*1*	*0*	*0*	*0*	*0*	*0*

OAKLEY Matthew   **Southampton**

Fullname: Matthew Oakley   DOB: 17-08-77
Debut: Everton v TOTTENHAM HOTSPUR 6/5/95 as sub

Previous Clubs Details			Apps					Goals		
Club	Signed	Fee	Tot	Start	Sub	FA	FL	Lge	FA	FL
Southampton			11	5	6	3	0	0	1	0
FAPL Summary by Club										
Southampton 1994-95 to 1995-96			11	5	6	3	0	0	1	0
Total			*11*	*5*	*6*	*3*	*0*	*0*	*1*	*0*

OGRIZOVIC Steve   **Coventry City**

Fullname: Steven Ogrizovic   DOB: 12-09-57 Mansfield
Debut: COVENTRY CITY v Middlesbrough 15/8/92
Debut Goal: (Goalkeeper)

Previous Clubs Details			Apps					Goals		
Club	Signed	Fee	Tot	Start	Sub	FA	FL	Lge	FA	FL
Chesterfield	Jul-77		16	16	0	0	2	0	0	0
Liverpool	Nov-77	£70,000	4	4	0	0	0	0	0	0
Shrewsbury T.	Aug-82	£70,000	84	84	0	5	7	0	0	0
Coventry City	Jun-84	£72,000	440	440	0	28	41	1	0	0
FAPL Summary by Club										
Coventry City 1992-93 to 1995-96			124	124	0	9	9	0	0	0
Total			*124*	*124*	*0*	*9*	*9*	*0*	*0*	*0*

ORD Richard   **Sunderland**

Fullname: Richard John Ord   DOB: 03-03-70 Murton

Previous Clubs Details			Apps					Goals		
Club	Signed	Fee	Tot	Start	Sub	FA	FL	Lge	FA	FL
Sunderland	Jul-87	Trainee	196	177	19	10	19	5	1	0
York City	Feb-90	Loan	3	3	0	0	0	0	0	0

PALLISTER Gary   **Manchester United**

Fullname: Gary Andrew Pallister   DOB: 30-06-65 Ramsgate
Debut: Sheffield Utd v MANCHESTER UNITED 15/8/92
Debut Goal: MANCHESTER UNITED v Blackburn Rvs 3/5/93

Previous Clubs Details			Apps					Goals		
Club	Signed	Fee	Tot	Start	Sub	FA	FL	Lge	FA	FL
Middlesbrough	Nov-84		156	156	0	10	10	5	1	0
Darlington	Oct-85	Loan	7	7	0	0	0	0	0	0
Manchester U.	Aug-89	£2.3m	257	254	3	34	36	9	2	0
FAPL Summary by Club										
Manchester U.1992-93 to 1995-96			146	146	0	20	16	5	2	0
Total			*146*	*146*	*0*	*20*	*16*	*5*	*2*	*0*

PALMER Carlton   **Leeds United**

Fullname: Carlton Lloyd Palmer   DOB: 05-12-65 Rowley Regis
Debut: Everton v SHEFFIELD WEDNESDAY 15/8/92
Debut Goal: SHEFFIELD WEDNESDAY v Oldham Athlteic 17/10/92

Previous Clubs Details			*Apps*					*Goals*		
Club	Signed	Fee	Tot	Start	Sub	FA	FL	Lge	FA	FL
WBA	Dec-84		121	114	7	4	8	4	0	1
Sheffield W.	Feb-89	£750,000	205	204	1	18	31	14	2	1
Leeds Utd	Aug-94	£2.8m	74	74	0	9	10	5	1	0
FAPL Summary by Club										
Sheffield W.	1992-93 to 1993-94		71	70	1	11	16	6	2	1
Leeds Utd	1994-95 to 1995-96		74	74	0	9	10	5	1	0
Total			*145*	*144*	*1*	*20*	*26*	*11*	*3*	*1*

PARKER Garry   **Leicester City**

Fullname: Garry Stuart Parker   DOB: 07-09-65 Oxford
Debut: Ipswich Town v ASTON VILLA 15/8/92
Debut Goal: Sheffield Utd v ASTON VILLA 29/8/92

Previous Clubs Details			*Apps*					*Goals*		
Club	Signed	Fee	Tot	Start	Sub	FA	FL	Lge	FA	FL
Luton Town	May-83		42	31	11	8	4	3	0	1
Hull City	Feb-86	£72,000	84	82	2	4	5	8	0	0
N. Forest	Mar-88	£260,000	97	93	4	16	23	17	5	4
Aston Villa	Nov-91	£650,000	81	79	2	10	8	11	1	0
Leicester City	Feb-95	£550,000 +	54	50	4	3	4	5	0	0
FAPL Summary by Club										
Aston Villa	1992-93 to 1994-95		70	66	4	5	12	11	0	0
Leicester City	1994-95		14	14	0	1	0	2	0	0
Total			*84*	*80*	*4*	*6*	*12*	*13*	*0*	*0*

PARKINSON Joe   **Everton**

Fullname: Joseph S Parkinson   DOB: 11-06-71 Eccles
Debut: EVERTON v Aston Villa 20/8/94 as sub
Debut Goal: Manchester City v EVERTON 30/8/95

Previous Clubs Details			*Apps*					*Goals*		
Club	Signed	Fee	Tot	Start	Sub	FA	FL	Lge	FA	FL
Wigan Athletic	Apr-89		119	115	4	9	11	6	0	1
Bournemouth	Jul-93	£35,000	30	30	0	4	4	1	0	1
Everton	Mar-94	£25,000	62	60	2	8	3	3	1	0
FAPL Summary by Club										
Everton	1994-95 to 1995-96		62	60	2	8	3	3	1	0
Total			*62*	*60*	*2*	*8*	*3*	*3*	*1*	*0*

PARLOUR Ray   **Arsenal**

Fullname: Raymond Parlour   DOB: 07-03-73 Romford
Debut: ARSENAL v Sheffield Wednesday 29/8/92

Debut Goal: ARSENAL v Sheffield Wednesday 29/8/92

Previous Clubs Details			Apps					Goals		
Club	Signed	Fee	Tot	Start	Sub	FA	FL	Lge	FA	FL
Arsenal	Mar-91		106	84	22	9	15	4	1	0
FAPL Summary by Club										
Arsenal	1992-93 to 1995-96		100	82	18	9	15	3	1	0
Total			*100*	*82*	*18*	*9*	*15*	*3*	*1*	*0*

PEACOCK Darren   Newcastle United

Fullname: Darren Peacock   DOB: 03-02-68 Bristol
Debut: Manchester City v QPR 17/8/92
Debut Goal: QPR v Coventry City 20/2/93

Previous Clubs Details			Apps					Goals		
Club	Signed	Fee	Tot	Start	Sub	FA	FL	Lge	FA	FL
Newport Co.	Feb-86		28	24	4	1	2	0	0	0
Hereford Utd	Mar-89		59	56	3	6	6	5	0	1
QPR	Dec-90	£200,000	126	123	3	3	12	6	0	1
Newcastle Utd	Mar-94	£2.7m	78	77	1	6	9	1	0	2
FAPL Summary by Club										
QPR	1992-93 to 1993-94		68	65	3	2	8	5	0	1
Newcastle Utd	1993-94 to 1995-96		78	77	1	6	9	1	0	2
Total			*146*	*142*	*4*	*8*	*17*	*6*	*0*	*3*

PEACOCK Gavin   Chelsea

Fullname: Gavin Keith Peacock   DOB: 18-11-67 Welling, Kent
Debut: CHELSEA v Blackburn Rvs 14/8/92
Debut Goal: CHELSEA v Blackburn Rvs 14/8/92

Previous Clubs Details			Apps					Goals		
Club	Signed	Fee	Tot	Start	Sub	FA	FL	Lge	FA	FL
QPR	Nov-84		17	7	10	1	0	1	0	0
Gillingham	Oct-87	£40,000	70	69	1	2	4	11	0	0
Bournemouth	Aug-89	£250,000	56	56	0	2	6	8	0	0
Newcastle Utd	Nov-90	£150,000	106	102	4	6	6	35	2	5
Chelsea	Aug-93	£1.25m	103	92	11	18	6	17	9	1
FAPL Summary by Club										
Newcastle Utd	1992-93		32	29	3	4	4	12	2	2
Chelsea	1993-94 to 1995-96		103	92	11	18	6	17	9	1
Total			*135*	*121*	*14*	*22*	*10*	*29*	*11*	*3*

PEARCE Ian   Blackburn Rovers

Fullname: Ian Anthony Pearce   DOB: 07-05-74 Bury St Edmunds
Debut: CHELSEA v Liverpool 5/9/92 as sub
Debut Goal: West Ham Utd v BLACKBURN ROVERS 27/4/94

Previous Clubs Details			Apps					Goals		
Club	Signed	Fee	Tot	Start	Sub	FA	FL	Lge	FA	FL
Chelsea	Aug-91		4	0	4	0	0	0	0	0

| Blackburn Rvs | Oct-93 | £300,000 | 45 | 35 | 10 | 3 | 6 | 2 | 0 | 1 |

Chelsea	1992-93 to 1993-94	1	0	1	0	0	0	0	0
Blackburn Rvs	1993-94 to 1995-96	45	35	10	3	6	2	0	1
Total		*46*	*35*	*11*	*3*	*6*	*2*	*0*	*1*

PEARCE Stuart   Nottingham Forest

Fullname: Stuart Pearce   DOB: 24-04-62 Shepherds Bush
Debut: NOTTINGHAM FOREST v Liverpool 16/8/92
Debut Goal: Oldham Athletic v NOTTINGHAM FOREST 22/8/92

Previous Clubs Details

Club	Signed	Fee	Tot	Start	Sub	FA	FL	Lge	FA	FL
Coventry City	Oct-83	£25,000	52	52	0	2	0	4	0	0
N. Forest	Jun-85	£200,000	368	368	0	35	58	58	9	10

FAPL Summary by Club

| N. Forest | 1992-93 to 1995-96 | 90 | 90 | 0 | 8 | 9 | 13 | 2 | 3 |
| *Total* | | *90* | *90* | *0* | *8* | *9* | *13* | *2* | *3* |

PEARCE Andy   Wimbledon

Fullname: Andrew John Pearce   DOB: 20-04-66 Bradford on Avon
Debut: COVENTRY CITY v Middlesbrough 15/8/92
Debut Goal: COVENTRY CITY v Crystal Palace 3/10/92

Previous Clubs Details

Club	Signed	Fee	Tot	Start	Sub	FA	FL	Lge	FA	FL
Coventry City	May-90	£15,000	71	68	3	3	6	4	0	0
Sheffield W.	Aug-93	£500,000	69	66	3	7	12	3	1	0
Wimbledon	Nov-96	£600,000	7	6	1	2	0	0	0	0

FAPL Summary by Club

Coventry City	1992-93	24	21	3	1	2	1	0	0
Sheffield W.	1993-94 to 1995-96	69	66	3	7	12	3	0	1
Wimbledon	1995-96	7	6	1	2	0	0	0	0
Total		*100*	*93*	*7*	*10*	*14*	*4*	*0*	*1*

PEARS Stephen   Liverpool

Fullname: Stephen Pears   DOB: 22-01-62 Brandon
Debut: Coventry City v MIDDLESBROUGH 15/8/92
Debut Goal: (Goalkeeper)

Previous Clubs Details

Club	Signed	Fee	Tot	Start	Sub	FA	FL	Lge	FA	FL
Manchester U.	Jan-79	Apprentice	4	4	0	0	1	0	0	0
Middlesbrough	Nov-83	Loan	12	12	0	2	0	0	0	0
Middlesbrough	Jul-85	£80,000	327	327	0	23	32	0	0	0
Liverpool	Aug-95	Free								

			Tot	Start	Sub	FA	FL		Lge	FA	FL
Middlesbrough	1992-93		26	26	0	0	0		0	0	0
Total			*26*	*26*	*0*	*0*	*0*		*0*	*0*	*0*

PEARSON Nigel   Middlesbrough

Fullname: Nigel Graham Pearson   DOB: 21-08-63 Nottingham
Debut: Everton v SHEFFIELD WEDNESDAY 15/8/92
Debut Goal: Everton v SHEFFIELD WEDNESDAY 15/8/92

Previous Clubs Details			*Apps*						*Goals*		
Club	Signed	Fee	Tot	Start	Sub	FA	FL		Lge	FA	FL
Shrewsbury T.	Nov-81	£5,000	153	153	0	6	19		5	0	0
Sheffield W.	Oct-87	£250,000	180	176	4	15	19		14	1	5
Middlesbrough	Jul-94	£750,000	45	42	3	3	5		0	0	0

FAPL Summary by Club

			Tot	Start	Sub	FA	FL		Lge	FA	FL
Sheffield W.	1992-93 to 1993-94		21	17	4	2	5		1	0	0
Middlesbrough	1995-96		36	36	0	3	5		0	0	0
Total			*57*	*53*	*4*	*5*	*10*		*1*	*0*	*0*

PEMBERTON John   Leeds United

Fullname: John Matthew Pemberton   DOB: 18-11-64 Oldham
Debut: Norwich City v SHEFFIELD UNITED 21/11/92

Previous Clubs Details			*Apps*						*Goals*		
Club	Signed	Fee	Tot	Start	Sub	FA	FL		Lge	FA	FL
Rochdale	Sep-84		1	1	0	0	0		0	0	0
Crewe Alex	Mar-85		121	116	5	3	7		1	0	1
Crystal Palace	Mar-88	£80,000	78	76	2	8	7		2	0	0
Sheffield Utd	Jul-90	£300,000	68	67	1	4	4		0	0	0
Leeds Utd	Nov-93	£250,000	53	44	9	6	4		0	0	0

FAPL Summary by Club

			Tot	Start	Sub	FA	FL		Lge	FA	FL
Sheffield Utd	1992-93 to 1993-94		19	19	0	4	0		0	0	0
Leeds Utd	1993-94 to 1995-96		53	44	9	6	4		0	0	1
Total			*72*	*63*	*9*	*10*	*4*		*0*	*0*	*1*

PEMBRIDGE Mark   Sheffield Wednesday

Fullname: Mark Anthony Pembridge DOB: 29-11-70 Merthyr Tydfil
Debut: Liverpool v SHEFFIELD UNITED 19/8/95
Debut Goal: SHEFFIELD W. v Blackburn Rvrs 23/8/95

Previous Clubs Details			*Apps*						*Goals*		
Club	Signed	Fee	Tot	Start	Sub	FA	FL		Lge	FA	FL
Luton Town	Jul-89	Trainee	60	60	0	4	2		6	0	0
Derby County	Jun-92	£1.25m	110	108	2	6	9		28	3	1
Sheffield W.	Jul-95	£900,000	25	24	1	0	3		2	0	0

FAPL Summary by Club

			Tot	Start	Sub	FA	FL		Lge	FA	FL
Sheffield W.	1995-96		25	24	1	0	3		2	0	1
Total			*25*	*24*	*1*	*0*	*3*		*2*	*0*	*1*

PERRY Chris   Wimbledon

Fullname: Christopher John Perry   DOB: 26-04-73 Surrey
Debut: WIMBLEDON v Liverpool 4/4/94 as sub

Previous Clubs Details			Apps					Goals		
Club	Signed	Fee	Tot	Start	Sub	FA	FL	Lge	FA	FL
Wimbledon	Jul-91		59	51	8	10	3	0	0	0
FAPL Summary by Club										
Wimbledon	1993-94 to 1995-96		59	51	8	10	3	0	0	0
Total			59	51	8	10	3	0	0	0

PETRESCU Dan   Chelsea

Fullname: Dan Vasile Petrescu   DOB: 22-12-67 Bucharest
Debut: SHEFFIELD WED v Tottenham H. 20/8/94
Debut Goal: SHEFFIELD WED v Tottenham H. 20/8/94

Previous Clubs Details			Apps					Goals		
Club	Signed	Fee	Tot	Start	Sub	FA	FL	Lge	FA	FL
Steaua Buch.	Jun-86		2	2	0	0	0	0	0	0
Olt Scornicesti	Jul-86		24	24	0	1	0	0	0	0
Steaua Buch.	Jul-87		93	93	0	14	0	27	3	0
Foggia (Italy)	Jul-91		55	55	0	6	0	7	0	0
Genoa (Italy)	Jul-93		24	24	0	1	0	1	0	0
Sheffield W.	Aug-94	£1.3m	37	28	9	2	2	3	0	0
Chelsea	Nov-95	£2.3m	24	22	2	7	0	2	1	0
FAPL Summary by Club										
Sheffield W.	1994-95 to 1995-96		37	28	9	2	2	3	0	0
Chelsea	1995-96		24	22	2	7	0	2	1	0
Total			61	50	11	9	2	5	1	0

PHELAN Terry   Chelsea

Fullname: Terence M Phelan   DOB: 16-03-67 Manchester
Debut: MANCHESTER CITY v Norwich City 26/8/92
Debut Goal: MANCHESTER CITY v Southampton 28/12/93

Previous Clubs Details			Apps					Goals		
Club	Signed	Fee	Tot	Start	Sub	FA	FL	Lge	FA	FL
Leeds Utd	Aug-84		14	12	2	0	3	0	0	0
Swansea City	Jul-86	Free	45	45	0	5	4	0	0	0
Wimbledon	Jul-87	£100,000	159	155	4	16	15	1	2	0
Man. City	Aug-92	£2.5m	102	101	1	8	11	1	1	0
Chelsea	Nov-95	£900,000	12	12	0	8	0	0	0	0
FAPL Summary by Club										
Man. City	1992-93 to 1995-96		103	102	1	8	11	1	1	0
Chelsea	1995-96		12	12	0	8	0	0	0	0
Total			115	114	1	16	11	1	1	0

PHILLIPS David — Nottingham Forest

Fullname: David Owen Phillips   DOB: 29-07-63 Wegberg, Germany
Debut: Arsenal v NORWICH CITY 15/8/92
Debut Goal: Arsenal v NORWICH CITY 15/8/92

Previous Clubs Details			Apps					Goals		
Club	Signed	Fee	Tot	Start	Sub	FA	FL	Lge	FA	FL
Plymouth A.	Aug-81		73	65	8	13	3	15	0	0
Man. City	Aug-84	£65,000	81	81	0	5	8	13	0	0
Coventry City	Jun-86	£150,000	100	93	7	9	8	8	1	0
Norwich City	Jun-89	£525,000	152	152	0	14	12	17	1	0
N. Forest	Aug-93	£600,000	99	92	7	10	12	5	0	0
FAPL Summary by Club										
Norwich City 1992-93 to 1995-96			42	42	0	2	2	8	0	0
N. Forest 1994-95 to 1995-96			56	52	4	8	5	1	0	0
Total			*98*	*94*	*4*	*10*	*7*	*9*	*0*	*0*

PILKINGTON Kevin — Manchester United

Fullname: Kevin Pilkington   DOB: 08-03-74 Hitchin
Debut: MANCHESTER UTD v Crystal Palace 19/11/94 as sub
Debut Goal: (Goalkeeper)

Previous Clubs Details			Apps					Goals		
Club	Signed	Fee	Tot	Start	Sub	FA	FL	Lge	FA	FL
Manchester U.	Jul-92	Trainee	4	3	1	1	1	0	0	0
Rochdale *	Feb-96	Loan	–	–	–	–	–	–	–	–
FAPL Summary by Club										
Manchester U.1994-95 to 1995-96			4	2	2	1	1	0	0	0
Total			*4*	*2*	*2*	*1*	*1*	*0*	*0*	*0*

PLATT David — Arsenal

Fullname: David Andrew Platt   DOB: 10-06-66 Oldham
Debut: ARSENAL v Middlesbrough, 20/8/95
Debut Goal: Everton v ARSENAL, 23/8/95

Previous Clubs Details			Apps					Goals		
Club	Signed	Fee	Tot	Start	Sub	FA	FL	Lge	FA	FL
Crewe Alex	Jan-85		134	134	0	0	0	55	0	0
Aston Villa	Feb-88		121	121	0	0	0	50	0	0
Bari			29	–	–	–	–	11	–	–
Juventus			16	–	–	–	–	3	–	–
Sampdoria			29	–	–	–	–	9	–	–
Arsenal	Jul-95	£4.75m	29	27	2	1	3	6	0	0
FAPL Summary by Club										
Arsenal	1995-96		29	27	2	1	3	6	0	0
Total			*29*	*27*	*2*	*1*	*3*	*6*	*0*	*0*

PLATTS Mark   Sheffield Wednesday

Fullname: Mark Platts   DOB:
Debut: SHEFFIELD W. v Wimbledon 10/2/96 as sub

Previous Clubs Details			Apps					Goals		
Club	Signed	Fee	Tot	Start	Sub	FA	FL	Lge	FA	FL
Sheffield W.			2	0	2	0	0	0	0	0
FAPL Summary by Club										
Sheffield W.		1995-96	2	0	2	0	0	0	0	0
Total			*2*	*0*	*2*	*0*	*0*	*0*	*0*	*0*

POLLOCK Jamie   Middlesbrough

Fullname: Jamie Pollock   DOB: 16-02-74 Stockton
Debut: MIDDLESBROUGH v Leeds Utd 22/8/92 as sub
Debut Goal: Sheffield Wednesday v MIDDLESBROUGH 1/5/93

Previous Clubs Details			Apps					Goals		
Club	Signed	Fee	Tot	Start	Sub	FA	FL	Lge	FA	FL
Middlesbrough	Dec-91	Trainee	155	144	11	14	19	18	1	1
FAPL Summary by Club										
Middlesbrough	1992-93 to 1995-96		51	46	5	3	6	2	1	0
Total			*51*	*46*	*5*	*3*	*6*	*2*	*1*	*0*

POOLE Kevin   Leicester City

Fullname: Kevin Poole   DOB: 21-07-63 Bromsgrove
Debut: Nottingham Forest v LEICESTER CITY 27/8/94
Debut Goal: (Goalkeeper)

Previous Clubs Details			Apps					Goals		
Club	Signed	Fee	Tot	Start	Sub	FA	FL	Lge	FA	FL
Aston Villa	Jun-81	Apprentice	28	28	0	1	2	0	0	0
Northampton	Nov-84	Loan	3	3	0	0	0	0	0	0
Middlesbrough	Aug-87		34	34	0	2	4	0	0	0
Hartlepool Utd	Mar-91	Loan	12	12	0	0	0	0	0	0
Leicester City	Jul-91	£40,000	156	156	0	8	9	0	0	0
FAPL Summary by Club										
Leicester City		1994-95	36	36	0	3	2	0	0	0
Total			*36*	*36*	*0*	*3*	*2*	*0*	*0*	*0*

PORIC Adem   Sheffield Wednesday

Fullname: Adem Poric   DOB: 22-04-73 Australia
Debut: Everton v SHEFFIELD WEDNESDAY 26/12/94 as sub

Previous Clubs Details			Apps					Goals		
Club	Signed	Fee	Tot	Start	Sub	FA	FL	Lge	FA	FL
St George (Australia)			–	–	–	–	–	–	–	–
Sheffield W.	Oct-93	£60,000	5	4	1	0	0	0	0	0
FAPL Summary by Club										
Sheffield W.	1994-95 to 1995-96		5	2	3	0	0	0	0	0
Total			*5*	*2*	*3*	*0*	*0*	*0*	*0*	*0*

POTTS Steve   West Ham United

Fullname: Steven John Potts   DOB: 07-05-67 Hartford, USA
Debut: WEST HAM UNITED v Wimbledon 14/8/93

Previous Clubs Details   *Apps*   *Goals*

Club	Signed	Fee	Tot	Start	Sub	FA	FL	Lge	FA	FL
West Ham U.	Jul-83		312	302	10	34	37	1	0	0

FAPL Summary by Club

West Ham U. 1993-94 to 1995-96			117	117	0	11	10	0	0	0
Total			*117*	*117*	*0*	*11*	*10*	*0*	*0*	*0*

POWELL Darryl   Derby County

Fullname: Darryl Anthony Powell   DOB: 15-11-71 Lambeth

Previous Clubs Details   *Apps*   *Goals*

Club	Signed	Fee	Tot	Start	Sub	FA	FL	Lge	FA	FL
Portsmouth	Dec-88	Trainee	132	83	49	10	14	16	0	3
Derby County	Aug-95	(not known)	37	37	0	0	2	5	0	0

POWELL Chris   Derby County

Fullname: Christopher George Robin Powell   DOB: 08-09-69 Lambeth

Previous Clubs Details   *Apps*   *Goals*

Club	Signed	Fee	Tot	Start	Sub	FA	FL	Lge	FA	FL
Crystal Palace	Dec-87	Trainee	3	2	1	0	1	0	0	0
Aldershot	Jan-90	Loan	11	11	0	0	0	0	0	0
Southend Utd *	Aug-90	Free	221	219	2	7	11	3	0	0
Derby County	Jan-96	£800,000	19	19	0	0	0	0	0	0

PREECE David   Derby County

Fullname: David William Preece   DOB: 28-05-63 Bridgnorth

Previous Clubs Details   *Apps*   *Goals*

Club	Signed	Fee	Tot	Start	Sub	FA	FL	Lge	FA	FL
Walsall	Jul-80	Apprentice	110	107	4	6	18	5	1	5
Luton Town	Dec-84	£150,000	336	328	8	27	23	21	2	3
Derby County	Aug-95	Free	13	10	3	0	2	1	0	0
Birmingham C.	Nov-95	Loan	–	–	–	–	–	–	–	–
Swindon Town	Mar-96	Loan	–	–	–	–	–	–	–	–

PRESSLEY Steve   Coventry City

Fullname: Steven Pressley   DOB: 11-10-73 Elgin
Debut: Arsenal v COVENTRY CITY 23/10/94
Debut Goal: COVENTRY CITY v Manchester Utd 1/5/95

Previous Clubs Details   *Apps*   *Goals*

Club	Signed	Fee	Tot	Start	Sub	FA	FL	Lge	FA	FL
Rangers	Aug-90	From NL	32	25	7	2	3	1	0	0
Coventry City	Oct-94	£600,000	19	18	1	3	0	1	0	0

Coventry City 1994-95 to 1995-96	19	18	1	3	0		1	0	0
Total	*19*	*18*	*1*	*3*	*0*		*1*	*0*	*0*

PRESSMAN Kevin   Sheffield Wednesday
Fullname: Kevin Paul Pressman   DOB: 06-11-67 Fareham
Debut: SHEFFIELD WEDNESDAY v Southampton 12/4/92
Debut Goal: (Goalkeeper)

Previous Clubs Details			*Apps*					*Goals*		
Club	Signed	Fee	Tot	Start	Sub	FA	FL	Lge	FA	FL
Sheffield W.	Nov-85		158	158	0	8	25	0	0	0
Stoke City	Mar-92	Loan	4	4	0	0	0	0	0	0

FAPL Summary by Club

Sheffield W. 1992-93 to 1995-96	99	99	0	8	16		0	0	0
Total	*99*	*99*	*0*	*8*	*16*		*0*	*0*	*0*

RADEBE Lucas   Leeds United
Fullname: Lucas Radebe   DOB: 12-04-69 Johannesburg
Debut: Sheffield Wednesday v LEEDS UNITED 26/9/94 as sub

Previous Clubs Details			*Apps*					*Goals*		
Club	Signed	Fee	Tot	Start	Sub	FA	FL	Lge	FA	FL
Kaiser Chiefs			–	–	–	–	–	–	–	–
Leeds Utd	Aug-94	£250,000	25	19	6	6	4	0	0	0

FAPL Summary by Club

Leeds Utd 1994-95 to 1995-96	25	19	6	6	4		0	0	0
Total	*25*	*19*	*6*	*6*	*4*		*0*	*0*	*0*

RADUCIOIU Florin   West Ham United
Fullname: Florin Raducioiu   DOB:

Previous Clubs Details			*Apps*					*Goals*		
Club	Signed	Fee	Tot	Start	Sub	FA	FL	Lge	FA	FL
Espanyol			–	–	–	–	–	–	–	–
West Ham U.	Jul-96	£2.4m	0	0	0	0	0	0	0	0

RAE Alex   Sunderland
Fullname: Alexander Scott Rae   DOB: 30-09-69 Glasgow

Previous Clubs Details			*Apps*					*Goals*		
Club	Signed	Fee	Tot	Start	Sub	FA	FL	Lge	FA	FL
Falkirk	1987	From NL	83	71	12	3	5	20	0	1
Millwall *	Aug-90	£100,000	181	168	13	11	13	50	4	0
Sunderland	Jul-96	£1m	0	0	0	0	0	0	0	0

RAVANELLI Fabio   Middlesbrough
Fullname: Fabrizio Ravanelli   DOB: 11-12-68 Perugia, Italy
Previous Clubs Details

Club	Signed	Fee	Tot	Start	Sub	FA	FL	Lge	FA	FL
					Apps				*Goals*	
Perugia (Ita)	1986		90	–	–	–	–	41	–	–
Avellino (Ita)	1989		7	–	–	–	–	0	–	–
Castertana (Ita)	Oct-89	Loan	27	–	–	–	–	12	–	–
Reggiana (Ita)	1990		66	–	–	–	–	24	–	–
Juventus	1992		–	–	–	–	–	–	–	–
Middlesbrough	Jul-96	£7m	0	0	0	0	0	0	0	0

REDKNAPP Jamie   Liverpool
Fullname: Jamie Frank Redknapp   DOB: 25-06-73 Barton on Sea
Debut: Leeds Utd v LIVERPOOL 29/8/92
Debut Goal: LIVERPOOL v Chelsea 5/9/92
Previous Clubs Details

Club	Signed	Fee	Tot	Start	Sub	FA	FL	Lge	FA	FL
					Apps				*Goals*	
Bournemouth	Jun-90		13	6	7	3	3	0	0	0
Liverpool	Jan-91	£350,000	233	116	17	13	21	13	0	4
FAPL Summary by Club										
Liverpool	1992-93 to 1995-96		127	111	16	11	21	12	0	4
Total			*127*	*111*	*16*	*11*	*21*	*12*	*0*	*4*

REEVES Alan   Wimbledon
Fullname: Alan Reeves   DOB: 19-11-67 Birkenhead
Debut: WIMBLEDON v Leicester City 10/9/94
Debut Goal: QPR v WIMBLEDON 24/9/94
Previous Clubs Details

Club	Signed	Fee	Tot	Start	Sub	FA	FL	Lge	FA	FL
					Apps				*Goals*	
Norwich City	Sep-88	From NL	0	0	0	0	0	0	0	0
Chester City	Aug-89	£10,000	40	31	9	3	2	2	0	0
Rochdale	Jul-91	Free	116	114	2	6	10	9	1	0
Wimbledon	Sep-94	£300,000	57	53	4	8	0	4	0	0
FAPL Summary by Club										
Wimbledon	1994-95 to 1995-96		57	53	4	8	0	4	0	0
Total			*57*	*53*	*4*	*8*	*0*	*4*	*0*	*0*

RICHARDSON Kevin   Coventry City
Fullname: Kevin Richardson   DOB: 04-12-62 Newcastle
Debut: Ipswich Town v ASTON VILLA 15/8/92
Debut Goal: ASTON VILLA v Chelsea 2/9/92
Previous Clubs Details

Club	Signed	Fee	Tot	Start	Sub	FA	FL	Lge	FA	FL
					Apps				*Goals*	
Everton	Dec-80		109	95	14	13	13	16	1	3
Watford	Sep-86	£225,000	39	39	0	7	3	2	0	0

Club	Signed	Fee	Tot	Start	Sub	FA	FL	Lge	FA	FL
Arsenal	Aug-87	£200,000	96	88	8	9	16	5	1	2
Real Sociedad	Jun-90	£750,000	–	–	–	–	–	–	–	–
Aston Villa	Aug-91	£450,000	143	142	1	12	15	14	0	3
Coventry City	Feb-95	£300,000	47	47	0	3	4	0	0	1
FAPL Summary by Club										
Aston Villa	1992-93 to 1994-95		101	100	1	7	13	8	0	3
Coventry City	1994-95 to 1995-96		47	47	0	3	4	0	0	1
Total			*148*	*147*	*1*	*10*	*17*	*8*	*0*	*4*

RIDEOUT Paul   Everton

Fullname: Paul David Rideout   DOB: 14-08-64 Bournemouth
Debut: EVERTON v Sheffield Wednesday 15/8/92
Debut Goal: Nottingham Forest v EVERTON 7/11/92

Previous Clubs Details			Apps					Goals		
Club	Signed	Fee	Tot	Start	Sub	FA	FL	Lge	FA	FL
Swindon Town	Aug-81		95	90	5	7	3	38	1	2
Aston Villa	Jun-83	£200,000	54	50	4	2	6	19	0	3
Bari (Italy)	Jul-85	£400,000	0	0	0	0	0	0	0	0
Southampton	Jul-88	£430,000	75	68	7	7	13	19	0	2
Swindon Town	Mar-91	Loan	9	9	0	0	0	1	0	0
Notts County	Sep-91	£250,000	11	9	2	1	2	3	0	0
Rangers	Jan-92	£500,000								
Everton	Aug-92	£500,000	102	82	20	9	11	29	3	6
FAPL Summary by Club										
Everton	1992-93 to 1995-96		102	82	20	9	11	29	3	6
Total			*102*	*82*	*20*	*9*	*11*	*29*	*3*	*6*

RIEPER Marc   West Ham United

Fullname: Marc Rieper   DOB: 05-06-63 Rodoure, Denmark
Debut: Leeds Utd v WEST HAM UNITED 10/12/94
Debut Goal: WEST HAM UNITED v Blackburn Rvs 30/4/95

Previous Clubs Details			Apps					Goals		
Club	Signed	Fee	Tot	Start	Sub	FA	FL	Lge	FA	FL
Brondby			–	–	–	–	–	–	–	–
West Ham U.	Dec-94	£500,000	57	52	5	3	3	3	0	0
FAPL Summary by Club										
West Ham U.	1994-95 to 1995-96		57	52	5	3	3	3	0	0
Total			*57*	*52*	*5*	*3*	*3*	*3*	*0*	*0*

RIPLEY Stuart   Blackburn Rovers

Fullname: Stuart Edward Ripley   DOB: 20-11-67 Middlesbrough
Debut: Crystal Palace v BLACKBURN ROVERS 15/8/92
Debut Goal: Crystal Palace v BLACKBURN ROVERS 15/8/92

Previous Clubs Details			Apps					Goals		
Club	Signed	Fee	Tot	Start	Sub	FA	FL	Lge	FA	FL
Middlesbrough	Nov-85		249	210	39	18	23	26	1	3

Bolton W.	Feb-86	Loan	5	5	0	0	0		0	0	0
Blackburn Rvs	Jul-92	£1.3m	144	141	3	11	18		11	2	0
FAPL Summary by Club											
Blackburn Rvs	1992-93 to 1995-96		144	141	3	11	18		11	2	0
Total			*144*	*141*	*3*	*11*	*18*		*11*	*2*	*0*

ROBERTS Iwan   Leicester City

Fullname: Iwan Wyn Roberts   DOB: 26-08-68 Bangor, Wales
Debut: LEICESTER CITY v Newcastle Utd 21/8/94 as sub
Debut Goal: LEICESTER CITY v Coventry City 3/10/94

Previous Clubs Details			*Apps*						*Goals*		
Club	Signed	Fee	Tot	Start	Sub	FA	FL		Lge	FA	FL
Watford	Jul-86	Trainee	63	40	23	7	8		9	0	3
Huddersfield	Aug-90	£275,000	142	141	1	12	14		51	4	6
Leicester City	Nov-93	£100,000	100	92	8	5	5		41	2	1
FAPL Summary by Club											
Leicester City	1994-95		37	32	5	3	2		9	2	0
Total			*37*	*32*	*5*	*3*	*2*		*9*	*2*	*0*

ROBERTSON Sandy   Coventry City

Fullname: Alexander Robertson   DOB: 26-04-71 Edinburgh
Debut: COVENTRY CITY v QPR 22/1/94 as sub

Previous Clubs Details			*Apps*						*Goals*		
Club	Signed	Fee	Tot	Start	Sub	FA	FL		Lge	FA	FL
Rangers			–	–	–	–	–		–	–	–
Coventry City	Jan-94	£250,000	4	0	4	0	0		0	0	0
FAPL Summary by Club											
Coventry City	1993-94 to 1994-95		4	0	4	0	0		0	0	0
Total			*4*	*0*	*4*	*0*	*0*		*0*	*0*	*0*

ROBINS Mark   Leicester City

Fullname: Mark Gordon Robins   DOB: 22-12-69 Ashton-under-Lyne
Debut: Arsenal v NORWICH CITY 15/8/92
Debut Goal: Arsenal v NORWICH CITY 15/8/92

Previous Clubs Details			*Apps*						*Goals*		
Club	Signed	Fee	Tot	Start	Sub	FA	FL		Lge	FA	FL
Manchester U.	Dec-86	Apprentice	48	19	29	8	7		11	3	2
Norwich City	Aug-92	£800,000	50	43	7	0	5		16	0	1
Leicester City	Jan-95	£1m	48	35	13	2	5		11	0	4
FAPL Summary by Club											
Norwich City	1992-93 to 1994-95		67	57	10	2	7		20	0	1
Leicester City	1994-95		17	16	1	2	0		5	0	0
Total			*84*	*73*	*11*	*4*	*7*		*25*	*0*	*1*

ROBINSON Matt — Southampton

Fullname: Matthew Robinson DOB: 23-12-74 Exeter
Debut: TOTTENHAM HOTSPUR v Sheff Wed 29/4/95 as sub

Previous Clubs Details			Apps					Goals		
Club	Signed	Fee	Tot	Start	Sub	FA	FL	Lge	FA	FL
Southampton	Jul-93	Trainee	7	0	7	2	0	0	0	0
FAPL Summary by Club										
Southampton	1994-95 to 1995-96		7	0	7	2	0	0	0	0
Total			*7*	*0*	*7*	*2*	*0*	*0*	*0*	*0*

ROCASTLE David — Chelsea

Fullname: David Carlyle Rocastle DOB: 02-05-67 Lewisham
Debut: Ipswich Town v LEEDS UNITED 3/10/93 as sub
Debut Goal: LEEDS UNITED v Manchester City 13/3/93

Previous Clubs Details			Apps					Goals		
Club	Signed	Fee	Tot	Start	Sub	FA	FL	Lge	FA	FL
Arsenal	Dec-84		218	204	14	20	33	24	4	6
Leeds Utd	Jul-92	£2m	25	17	8	3	3	2	0	0
Man. City	Dec-93	Swap	21	21	0	2	0	2	0	0
Chelsea	Aug-94	£1.25m	29	27	2	1	3	1	0	1
FAPL Summary by Club										
Leeds Utd	1992-93 to 1993-94		25	17	8	3	3	2	0	0
Man. City	1993-94		21	21	0	2	0	2	0	0
Chelsea	1994-95 to 1995-96		29	27	2	1	3	1	0	1
Total			*75*	*65*	*10*	*6*	*6*	*5*	*0*	*1*

ROLLING Franck — Leicester City

Fullname: Franck Rolling DOB:

Previous Clubs Details			Apps					Goals		
Club	Signed	Fee	Tot	Start	Sub	FA	FL	Lge	FA	FL
Ayr Utd			–	–	–	–	–	–	–	–
Leicester City	Oct-95	£100,000	17	17	0	1	3	0	0	0

ROSE Matthew — Arsenal

Fullname: Matthew Rose DOB: 24-09-75 Dartford
Debut: QPR v ARSENAL, 2/3/96 as sub

Previous Clubs Details			Apps					Goals		
Club	Signed	Fee	Tot	Start	Sub	FA	FL	Lge	FA	FL
Arsenal		Trainee	4	1	3	0	0	0	0	0
FAPL Summary by Club										
Arsenal	1995-96		4	1	3	0	0	0	0	0
Total			*4*	*1*	*3*	*0*	*0*	*0*	*0*	*0*

ROSENTHAL Ronny — Tottenham Hotspur

Fullname: Ronny Rosenthal DOB: 11-10-63 Haifa, Israel
Debut: Nottingham Forest v LIVERPOOL 16/8/92 as sub

Debut Goal: LIVERPOOL v Aston Villa 19/9/92

Previous Clubs Details

Club	Signed	Fee	Apps					Goals		
			Tot	Start	Sub	FA	FL	Lge	FA	FL
Liverpool	Mar-90	£1m	74	32	42	8	9	21	1	1
Tottenham H.	Jan-94	£250,000	68	51	17	9	3	3	6	1

FAPL Summary by Club

Liverpool	1992-93 to 1993-94		30	16	14	1	3	6	0	1
Tottenham H.	1993-94 to 1995-96		68	51	17	9	3	3	6	1
Total			*98*	*67*	*31*	*10*	*6*	*9*	*6*	*2*

ROWETT Gary   Derby County

Fullname: Gary Rowett   DOB: 06-03-74 Bromsgrove
Debut: Sheffield Wednesday v EVERTON 2/4/94 as sub

Previous Clubs Details

Club	Signed	Fee	Apps					Goals		
			Tot	Start	Sub	FA	FL	Lge	FA	FL
Cambridge Utd	Sep-91		63	51	12	7	7	9	0	1
Everton	Feb-94	£200,000	4	2	2	0	0	0	0	0
Blackpool	Jan-95	Loan	18	18	0	0	0	0	0	0
Derby County			35	34	1	1	2	0	0	0

FAPL Summary by Club

Everton	1993-94 to 1994-95		4	2	2	0	0	0	0	0
Total			*4*	*2*	*2*	*0*	*0*	*0*	*0*	*0*

ROWLAND Keith   West Ham United

Fullname: Keith Rowland   DOB: 01-09-71 Portadown
Debut: Norwich City v COVENTRY CITY 16/1/93 as sub

Previous Clubs Details

Club	Signed	Fee	Apps					Goals		
			Tot	Start	Sub	FA	FL	Lge	FA	FL
Bournemouth	Oct-89		72	65	7	8	5	2	0	0
Coventry City	Jan-93	Loan	2	0	2	0	0	0	0	0
West Ham U.	Aug-93	£110,000	58	46	12	6	3	0	0	0

FAPL Summary by Club

Coventry City	1992-93		2	0	2	0	0	0	0	0
West Ham U.	1993-94 to 1995-96		58	46	12	6	3	0	0	0
Total			*60*	*46*	*14*	*6*	*3*	*0*	*0*	*0*

ROY Bryan   Nottingham Forest

Fullname: Bryan Roy   DOB: 12-02-70 Amsterdam
Debut: Ipswich Town v NOTTINGHAM FOREST 20/8/94
Debut Goal: Ipswich Town v NOTTINGHAM FOREST 20/8/94

Previous Clubs Details

Club	Signed	Fee	Apps					Goals		
			Tot	Start	Sub	FA	FL	Lge	FA	FL
Ajax	Jul-87		126	–	–	–	–	17	–	–
Foggia	Nov-92		20	–	–	–	–	3	–	–
N. Forest	Aug-94	£2.5m	65	62	3	8	5	21	1	1

RUDDOCK Neil   Liverpool

Fullname:	Neil Ruddock	DOB: 09-05-68 Wandsworth
Debut:	Southampton v TOTTENHAM HOTSPUR 15/8/92	
Debut Goal:	TOTTENHAM HOTSPUR v Liverpool 31/10/92	

Previous Clubs Details			*Apps*				*Goals*		
Club	Signed	Fee	Tot	Start	Sub	FA	FL	Lge	FA	FL
Millwall	Mar-86		0	0	0	0	0	0	0	0
Tottenham H.	Apr-86	£50,000	9	7	2	2	0	0	1	0
Millwall	Jun-88	£300,000	2	0	2	0	2	1	0	3
Southampton	Feb-89	£250,000	107	100	7	10	15	9	3	1
Tottenham H.	May-92	£750,000	38	38	0	5	4	3	0	0
Liverpool	Jul-93	£2.5m	96	94	2	2	17	10	0	1

FAPL Summary by Club									
Tottenham H.	1992-93	38	38	0	5	4	3	0	0
Liverpool	1993-94 to 1995-96	96	94	2	2	17	10	0	1
Total		*134*	*132*	*2*	*7*	*21*	*13*	*0*	*1*

RUSH Ian   Leeds United

Fullname:	Ian James Rush	DOB: 20-10-61 St Asaph
Debut:	Nottingham Forest v LIVERPOOL 16/8/92	
Debut Goal:	Manchester Utd v LIVERPOOL 18/10/92	

Previous Clubs Details			*Apps*				*Goals*		
Club	Signed	Fee	Tot	Start	Sub	FA	FL	Lge	FA	FL
Chester City	Jul-79		34	33	1	5	0	14	3	0
Liverpool	Apr-80	£300,000	224	224	0	24	47	139	19	25
Juventus (Italy)	Jun-87	£3.8m	–	–	–	–	–	–	–	–
Liverpool	Aug-88	£2.2m	245	223	22	36	31	90	18	21
Leeds Utd	Jun-96	Free	0	0	0	0	0	0	0	0

FAPL Summary by Club									
Liverpool	1992-93 to 1995-96	130	118	12	14	18	45	3	12
Total		*130*	*118*	*12*	*14*	*18*	*45*	*3*	*12*

RUSSELL Craig   Sunderland

Fullname:	Craig Stewart Russell	DOB: 04-02-74 South Shields

Previous Clubs Details			*Apps*				*Goals*		
Club	Signed	Fee	Tot	Start	Sub	FA	FL	Lge	FA	FL
Sunderland	Jul-92	Trainee	118	93	25	7	7	27	2	1

SALAKO John   Coventry City

Fullname:	John Akin Salako	DOB: 11-02-69 Nigeria
Debut:	CRYSTAL PALACE v Blackburn Rvs 15/8/92	
Debut Goal:	Arsenal v CRYSTAL PALACE 1/10/94	

Club	Signed	Fee	Apps Tot	Start	Sub	FA	FL	Goals Lge	FA	FL
Previous Clubs Details			*Apps*					*Goals*		
Crystal Palace	Mar-86	Apprentice	176	133	43	12	17	19	2	4
Swansea City	14/8/89	Loan	13	13	0	0	0	3	0	0
Coventry City	Aug-95	£1.5m +	37	34	3	3	3	3	1	1
FAPL Summary by Club										
Crystal Palace	1992-93 to 1994-95		52	51	1	8	10	4	2	3
Coventry City	1995-96		37	34	3	3	3	3	1	1
Total			89	85	4	11	13	7	3	4

SAMWAYS Vinny　　　　　　　　　　　　　　　　　Everton

Fullname: Vincent Samways　　　　　　　DOB: 27-10-68 Bethnal Green
Debut: Southampton v TOTTENHAM HOTSPUR 15/8/92
Debut Goal: TOTTENHAM HOTSPUR v Liverpool 18/12/93

Club	Signed	Fee	Apps Tot	Start	Sub	FA	FL	Goals Lge	FA	FL
Previous Clubs Details			*Apps*					*Goals*		
Tottenham H.	Oct-85		193	165	28	16	30	11	2	4
Everton	Jul-94	£2m	23	17	6	0	3	2	0	1
Wolves.	Dec-95	Loan	–	–	–	–	–	–	–	–
Birmingham C	Feb-96	Loan	–	–	–	–	–	–	–	–
FAPL Summary by Club										
Tottenham H.	1992-93 to 1993-94		73	73	0	8	8	3	2	1
Everton	1994-95 to 1995-96		23	17	6	0	3	2	0	1
Total			96	90	6	8	11	5	2	2

SAUNDERS Dean　　　　　　　　　　　　　　　Coventry City

Fullname: Dean Nicholas Saunders　　　　　DOB: 21-06-64 Swansea
Debut: LIVERPOOL v Nottingham Forest 16/8/92
Debut Goal: LIVERPOOL v Chelsea 5/9/92

Club	Signed	Fee	Apps Tot	Start	Sub	FA	FL	Goals Lge	FA	FL
Previous Clubs Details			*Apps*					*Goals*		
Swansea City	Jun-82		49	42	7	1	3	12	0	0
Cardiff City	Mar-85	Loan	4	3	1	0	0	0	0	0
Brighton HA	Aug-85		72	66	6	7	4	20	5	0
Oxford Utd	Mar-87	£60,000	59	57	2	2	10	22	2	8
Derby County	Oct-88	£1m	106	106	0	4	12	42	0	1
Liverpool	Jul-91	£2.9m	42	42	0	8	5	11	2	2
Aston Villa	Sep-92	£2.3m	72	71	1	7	12	23	3	6
Galatasaray	Jul-95	£1.5m	–	–	–	–	–	–	–	–
Coventry City	Jul-96		0	0	0	0	0	0	0	0
FAPL Summary by Club										
Liverpool	1992-93		6	6	0	0	0	1	0	0
Aston Villa	1992-93 to 1994-95		112	111	1	9	15	38	4	7
Total			118	117	1	9	15	39	4	7

SCALES John   Liverpool

Fullname: John Robert Scales   DOB: 04-07-66 Harrogate
Debut: Leeds Utd v WIMBLEDON 15/8/92
Debut Goal: WIMBLEDON v Middlesbrough 9/3/93

Previous Clubs Details			*Apps*				*Goals*		
Club	Signed	Fee	Tot	Start	Sub	FA	FL	Lge	FA	FL
Bristol Rvs	Jul-85		72	68	4	6	3	2	0	0
Wimbledon	Jul-87	£70,000	240	235	5	21	19	11	1	0
Liverpool	Sep-94	£3m +	62	62	0	14	9	2	0	2
FAPL Summary by Club										
Wimbledon	1992-93 to 1994-95		72	72	0	8	7	1	1	0
Liverpool	1994-95 to 1995-96		62	62	0	14	9	2	0	2
Total			*134*	*134*	*0*	*22*	*16*	*3*	*1*	*2*

SCHMEICHEL Peter   Manchester United

Fullname: Peter Boleslaw Schmeichel DOB: 18-11-68 Glodsone, Den.
Debut: Sheffield Utd v MANCHESTER UNITED 15/8/92
Debut Goal: (Goalkeeper)

Previous Clubs Details			*Apps*				*Goals*		
Club	Signed	Fee	Tot	Start	Sub	FA	FL	Lge	FA	FL
Manchester U.	Aug-91	£550,000	190	190	0	26	17	0	0	0
FAPL Summary by Club										
Manchester U.	1992-93 to 1995-96		150	150	0	23	11	0	0	0
Total			*150*	*150*	*0*	*23*	*11*	*0*	*0*	*0*

SCHOLES Paul   Manchester United

Fullname: Paul Scholes   DOB: 16-11-74 Salford
Debut: Ipswich Town v MANCHESTER UTD 24/9/94 as sub
Debut Goal: Ipswich Town v MANCHESTER UTD 24/9/94 as sub

Previous Clubs Details			*Apps*				*Goals*		
Club	Signed	Fee	Tot	Start	Sub	FA	FL	Lge	FA	FL
Manchester U.	Jan-93	Trainee	43	22	21	5	4	15	1	4
FAPL Summary by Club										
Manchester U.	1994-95 to 1995-96		43	22	21	5	4	15	1	4
Total			*43*	*22*	*21*	*5*	*4*	*15*	*1*	*4*

SCIMECA Ricky   Aston Villa

Fullname: Riccardo Scimeca   DOB: 13-08-75 Leamington
Debut: ASTON VILLA v Manchester Utd 19/8/95 as sub

Previous Clubs Details			*Apps*				*Goals*		
Club	Signed	Fee	Tot	Start	Sub	FA	FL	Lge	FA	FL
Aston Villa	Jul-93		17	7	10	2	3	0	0	0
FAPL Summary by Club										
Aston Villa	1995-96		17	7	10	2	3	0	0	0
Total			*17*	*7*	*10*	*2*	*3*	*0*	*0*	*0*

SCOTT Martin   Sunderland

Fullname: Martin Scott   DOB: 07-01-68 Sheffield

Previous Clubs Details

Club	Signed	Fee	Apps					Goals		
			Tot	Start	Sub	FA	FL	Lge	FA	FL
Rotherham Utd	Jan-86	Apprentice	94	93	1	9	11	3	0	2
Bristol City	Dec-90	£200,000	171	171	0	10	10	14	0	1
Sunderland	Dec-94	£750,000	67	67	0	5	3	6	0	0

SCOTT Kevin   Tottenham Hotspur

Fullname: Kevin Watson Scott   DOB: 17-12-66 Easington
Debut: NEWCASTLE UNITED v Tottenham H. 14/8/93
Debut Goal: NEWCASTLE UNITED v Sheffield Wednesday 5/3/94

Previous Clubs Details

Club	Signed	Fee	Apps					Goals		
			Tot	Start	Sub	FA	FL	Lge	FA	FL
Newcastle Utd	Dec-84		227	227	0	16	18	8	1	0
Tottenham H.	Feb-94	£850,000	18	16	2	0	1	1	0	0
Port Vale	Jan-95	Loan	17	17	0	0	0	1	0	0
FAPL Summary by Club										
Newcastle Utd		1993-94	18	18	0	1	2	0	0	0
Tottenham H.	1993-94 to 1995-96		18	16	2	0	1	1	0	0
Total			*36*	*34*	*2*	*1*	*3*	*1*	*0*	*0*

SEAMAN David   Arsenal

Fullname: David Andrew Seaman   DOB: 19-09-63 Rotherham
Debut: ARSENAL v Norwich City 15/8/92
Debut Goal: (Goalkeeper)

Previous Clubs Details

Club	Signed	Fee	Apps					Goals		
			Tot	Start	Sub	FA	FL	Lge	FA	FL
Leeds Utd	Sep-81		0	0	0	0	0	0	0	0
Peterborough	Aug-82	£4,000	91	91	0	5	10	0	0	0
Birmingham C.	Oct-84	£100,000	75	75	0	5	4	0	0	0
QPR	Aug-86	£225,000	141	141	0	17	13	0	0	0
Arsenal	May-90	£1.3m	227	227	0	30	28	0	0	0
FAPL Summary by Club										
Arsenal	1992-93 to 1995-96		147	147	0	15	27	0	0	0
Total			*147*	*147*	*0*	*15*	*27*	*0*	*0*	*0*

SEGERS Hans   Wimbledon

Fullname: Johannes Segers   DOB: 30-10-71 Eindhoven
Debut: Leeds Utd v WIMBLEDON 15/8/92
Debut Goal: (Goalkeeper)

Previous Clubs Details

Club	Signed	Fee	Apps					Goals		
			Tot	Start	Sub	FA	FL	Lge	FA	FL
N. Forest	Aug-84	£50,000	58	58	0	5	4	0	0	0
Stoke City	Feb-87	Loan	1	1	0	0	0	0	0	0

				Apps					Goals		
Sheffield Utd	Nov-87	Loan	10	10	0	0	0		0	0	0
Dunfermline A.	Mar-88	Loan	0	0	0	0	0		0	0	0
Wimbledon	Sep-88	£180,000	267	265	2	22	26		0	0	0
FAPL Summary by Club											
Wimbledon	1992-93 to 1995-96	118	116	2	12	13		0	0	0
Total			*118*	*116*	*2*	*12*	*13*		*0*	*0*	*0*

SELLEY Ian   Arsenal

Fullname: Ian Selley   DOB: 14-06-74 Chertsey
Debut: ARSENAL v Blackburn Rvs 12/9/92

Previous Clubs Details			*Apps*					*Goals*		
Club	Signed	Fee	Tot	Start	Sub	FA	FL	Lge	FA	FL
Arsenal	May-92		40	35	5	3	6	0	0	0
FAPL Summary by Club										
Arsenal	1992-93 to 1994-95	40	35	5	3	6	0	0	0
Total			*40*	*35*	*5*	*3*	*6*	*0*	*0*	*0*

SHARPE Lee   Manchester United

Fullname: Lee Stuart Sharpe   DOB: 27-05-71 Halesowen
Debut: Aston Villa v MANCHESTER UNITED 7/11/92
Debut Goal: MANCHESTER UNITED v Coventry City 28/12/92

Previous Clubs Details			*Apps*					*Goals*		
Club	Signed	Fee	Tot	Start	Sub	FA	FL	Lge	FA	FL
Torquay Utd		Trainee	14	9	5	0	0	3	0	0
Manchester U.	Jun-88	£185,000	193	160	33	29	23	21	3	9
FAPL Summary by Club										
Manchester U.	1992-93 to 1995-96	116	100	16	19	8	17	3	2
Total			*116*	*100*	*16*	*19*	*8*	*17*	*3*	*2*

SHAW Richard   Coventry City

Fullname: Richard Edward Shaw   DOB: 11-09-68 Brentford
Debut: CRYSTAL PALACE v Blackburn Rvs 15/8/92
Debut Goal:

Previous Clubs Details			*Apps*					*Goals*		
Club	Signed	Fee	Tot	Start	Sub	FA	FL	Lge	FA	FL
Crystal Palace	Sep-86	Apprentice	207	193	14	18	30	3	0	0
Hull City	Dec-89	Loan	4	4	0	0	0	0	0	0
Coventry City	Nov-95	£650,000	21	21	0	3	0	0	0	0
FAPL Summary by Club										
Crystal Palace	1992-93 to 1994-95	74	73	1	9	11	0	0	0
Coventry City	1995-96	21	21	0	3	0	0	0	0
Total			*95*	*94*	*1*	*12*	*11*	*0*	*0*	*0*

SHAW Paul   Arsenal

Fullname: Paul Shaw   DOB: 04-09-73 Burnham
Debut: Nottingham Forest v ARSENAL 3/12/94 as sub

Previous Clubs Details			*Apps*					*Goals*		
Club	Signed	Fee	Tot	Start	Sub	FA	FL	Lge	FA	FL
Arsenal			4	0	4	0	0	0	0	0
Burnley	Mar-95	Loan	9	8	1	0	0	1	0	0
FAPL Summary by Club										
Arsenal	1994-95 to 1995-96		4	0	4	0	0	0	0	0
Total			*4*	*0*	*4*	*0*	*0*	*0*	*0*	*0*

SHEARER Alan   Blackburn Rovers
Fullname: Alan Shearer   DOB: 13-08-70 Newcastle
Debut: Crystal Palace v BLACKBURN ROVERS 15/8/92
Debut Goal: Crystal Palace v BLACKBURN ROVERS 15/8/92

Previous Clubs Details			*Apps*					*Goals*		
Club	Signed	Fee	Tot	Start	Sub	FA	FL	Lge	FA	FL
Southampton	Apr-88		118	105	13	14	18	23	4	11
Blackburn Rvs	Jul-92	£3.3m	138	132	6	8	16	112	2	12
FAPL Summary by Club										
Blackburn Rvs	1992-93 to 1995-96		138	132	6	8	16	112	2	12
Total			*138*	*132*	*6*	*8*	*16*	*112*	*2*	*12*

SHERIDAN John   Sheffield Wednesday
Fullname: John Joseph Sheridan   DOB: 01-10-64 Manchester
Debut: SHEFFIELD WED v Blackburn Rvs 31/10/92
Debut Goal: SHEFFIELD WED v Manchester Utd 26/12/92

Previous Clubs Details			*Apps*					*Goals*		
Club	Signed	Fee	Tot	Start	Sub	FA	FL	Lge	FA	FL
Leeds Utd	Mar-82		230	225	5	12	14	47	1	3
N. Forest	Jul-89	£650,000	0	0	0	0	1	0	0	0
Sheffield W.	Nov-89	£500,000	195	187	8	18	24	25	3	3
Birmingham C.	Feb-96	Loan								
FAPL Summary by Club										
Sheffield W.	1992-93 to 1995-96		98	91	7	11	13	7	1	2
Total			*98*	*91*	*7*	*11*	*13*	*7*	*1*	*2*

SHERINGHAM Teddy   Tottenham Hotspur
Fullname: Edward Paul Sheringham   DOB: 02-04-66 Walthamstow
Debut: NOTTINGHAM FOREST v Liverpool 16/8/92
Debut Goal: NOTTINGHAM FOREST v Liverpool 16/8/92

Previous Clubs Details			*Apps*					*Goals*		
Club	Signed	Fee	Tot	Start	Sub	FA	FL	Lge	FA	FL
Millwall	Jan-84		220	205	15	12	17	93	5	8
Aldershot	Feb-85	Loan	5	4	1	0	0	0	0	0
N. Forest	Jul-91	£2m	42	42	0	4	10	14	2	5
Tottenham H.	Aug-92	£2.1m	137	134	3	17	11	68	13	8

N. Forest	1992-93	3	3	0	0	0	1	0	0
Tottenham H. 1992-93 to 1995-96		137	134	3	22	15	68	17	11
Total		*140*	*137*	*3*	*22*	*15*	*69*	*17*	*11*

SHERWOOD Tim   Blackburn Rovers

Fullname: Timothy Alan Sherwood   DOB: 06-02-69 St Albans
Debut: Crystal Palace v BLACKBURN ROVERS 15/8/92
Debut Goal: BLACKBURN ROVERS v Norwich City 3/10/92

Previous Clubs Details			*Apps*				*Goals*		
Club	Signed	Fee	Tot	Start	Sub	FA	FL	Lge	FA	FL
Watford	Feb-87		30	23	7	9	5	2	0	0
Norwich City	Jul-87	£175,000	71	66	5	4	7	10	0	1
Blackburn Rvs	Feb-92	£500,000	159	154	5	11	19	15	1	0

FAPL Summary by Club

Blackburn Rvs 1992-93 to 1995-96		149	148	1	11	18	15	1	0
Total		*149*	*148*	*1*	*11*	*18*	*15*	*1*	*0*

SHIPPERLEY Neil   Southampton

Fullname: Neil Shipperley   DOB: 30-10-74 Chatham
Debut: Southampton v CHELSEA 10/4/93 as sub
Debut Goal: CHELSEA v Wimbledon 12/4/93

Previous Clubs Details			*Apps*				*Goals*		
Club	Signed	Fee	Tot	Start	Sub	FA	FL	Lge	FA	FL
Chelsea	Sep-92		37	26	11	3	6	7	1	1
Watford	Dec-94	Loan	–	–	–	–	–	–	–	–
Southampton	Jan-95	£1.25m	56	56	0	10	4	12	5	2

FAPL Summary by Club

Chelsea	1992-93 to 1994-95	37	26	11	3	6	7	1	1
Southampton	1994-95 to 1995-96	56	56	0	10	4	12	5	2
Total		*93*	*82*	*11*	*13*	*10*	*19*	*6*	*3*

SHORT Craig   Everton

Fullname: Craig Jonathan Short   DOB: 25-06-68 Bridlington
Debut: Nottingham Forest v EVERTON 17/9/95
Debut Goal: EVERTON v Middlesbrough 26/12/95

Previous Clubs Details			*Apps*				*Goals*		
Club	Signed	Fee	Tot	Start	Sub	FA	FL	Lge	FA	FL
Scarborough	Oct-87	From NL	63	61	2	2	6	7	0	0
Notts County	Jul-89	£100,000	128	128	0	8	6	6	1	1
Derby County	Sep-92	£2.5m	118	118	0	7	11	9	4	0
Everton	Jul-95	£2.5m	23	22	1	3	2	2	0	0

FAPL Summary by Club

Everton	1995-96	23	22	1	3	2	2	0	0
Total		*23*	*22*	*1*	*3*	*2*	*2*	*0*	*0*

SILENZI Andrea   Nottingham Forest

Fullname: Andrea Silenzi   DOB: Sierra Leone
Debut: Coventry City v NOTTINGHAM F. 9/9/95 as sub

Previous Clubs Details			Apps					Goals		
Club	Signed	Fee	Tot	Start	Sub	FA	FL	Lge	FA	FL
Lodigiani	1984		49	–	–	–	–	15	–	–
Arezzo	1987		19	–	–	–	–	0	–	–
Reggiana	1988		67	–	–	–	–	32	–	–
Napoli	1990		39	–	–	–	–	6	–	–
Torino	1992		–	–	–	–	–	–	–	–
N. Forest	Jul-95	£2.5m	10	3	7	3	1	0	1	1
FAPL Summary by Club										
N. Forest	1995-96		10	3	7	3	1	0	1	1
Total			10	3	7	3	1	0	1	1

SIMPSON Paul   Derby County

Fullname: Paul David Simpson   DOB: 26-07-66 Carlisle

Previous Clubs Details			Apps					Goals		
Club	Signed	Fee	Tot	Start	Sub	FA	FL	Lge	FA	FL
Man. City	Aug-83	Apprentice	121	99	22	12	11	18	2	4
Oxford Utd	Oct-88	£200,000	142	138	6	9	10	43	2	3
Derby County	Feb-92	£500,000	166	133	33	5	11	46	1	5

SINCLAIR Frank   Chelsea

Fullname: Frank Mohammed Sinclair   DOB: 03-12-71 Lambeth
Debut: Manchester City v CHELSEA 20/9/92
Debut Goal: Wimbledon v CHELSEA 10/4/95

Previous Clubs Details			Apps					Goals		
Club	Signed	Fee	Tot	Start	Sub	FA	FL	Lge	FA	FL
Chelsea	May-90		131	126	5	12	13	1	1	1
WBA	Dec-91	Loan	6	6	0	0	0	1	0	0
FAPL Summary by Club										
Chelsea	1992-93 to 1995-96		115	114	1	11	13	4	1	1
Total			115	114	1	11	13	4	1	1

SINTON Andy   Tottenham Hotspur

Fullname: Andrew Sinton   DOB: 19-03-66 Newcastle
Debut: Manchester City v QPR 17/8/92
Debut Goal: Manchester City v QPR 17/8/92

Previous Clubs Details			Apps					Goals		
Club	Signed	Fee	Tot	Start	Sub	FA	FL	Lge	FA	FL
Cambridge Utd	Apr-83		93	90	3	3	6	13	0	1
Brentford	Dec-85	£25,000	149	149	0	11	8	28	1	3
QPR	Mar-89	£350,000	160	160	0	13	14	22	2	0
Sheffield W.	Aug-93	£2.75m	60	54	6	9	9	3	0	0

Tottenham H.	Jan-96	£1.5m	9	8	1	0	0	0	0	0

QPR	1992-93	36	36	0	2	4	7	0	0
Sheffield W.	1993-94 to 1995-96	60	54	6	4	10	3	0	0
Tottenham H.	1995-96	9	8	1	0	0	0	0	0
Total		*105*	*98*	*7*	*6*	*14*	*10*	*0*	*0*

SKINNER Justin   Wimbledon

Fullname: Justin James Skinner   DOB: 17-09-72 Dorking
Debut: Liverpool v WIMBLEDON 26/9/92

Previous Clubs Details			*Apps*					*Goals*		
Club	Signed	Fee	Tot	Start	Sub	FA	FL	Lge	FA	FL
Wimbledon	Jul-91	Trainee	2	1	1	0	0	0	0	0
Bournemouth	Mar-94	Loan	16	16	0	0	0	0	0	0
Wycombe W.	Feb-95	Loan	10	8	2	0	0	0	0	0
FAPL Summary by Club										
Wimbledon	1992-93 to 1995-96		2	1	1	0	0	0	0	0
Total			*2*	*1*	*1*	*0*	*0*	*0*	*0*	*0*

SLADE Steve   Leicester City

Fullname: Steve Slade   DOB: 06-10-75 Romford
Debut: Wimbledon v TOTTENHAM H. 16/12/95 as sub
Debut Goal:

Previous Clubs Details			*Apps*					*Goals*		
Club	Signed	Fee	Tot	Start	Sub	FA	FL	Lge	FA	FL
Tottenham H.			5	1	4	2	1	0	0	0
Leicester City	Jul-96	£350,000	0	0	0	0	0	0	0	0
FAPL Summary by Club										
Tottenham H.	1995-96		5	1	4	2	1	0	0	0
Total			*5*	*1*	*4*	*2*	*1*	*0*	*0*	*0*

SLATER Robbie   West Ham United

Fullname: Robert David Slater   DOB: 22-11-64 Skelmersdale
Debut: Southampton v BLACKBURN ROVERS 20/8/94
Debut Goal: Blackburn Rvs v WEST HAM UTD 2/12/95

Previous Clubs Details			*Apps*					*Goals*		
Club	Signed	Fee	Tot	Start	Sub	FA	FL	Lge	FA	FL
Lens			–	–	–	–	–	–	–	–
Blackburn Rvs	Apr-94	£300,000	18	12	6	1	1	0	0	0
West Ham U.	Aug-95	£600,000	22	16	6	1	2	2	0	0
FAPL Summary by Club										
Blackburn Rvs	1994-95		18	12	6	1	1	0	0	0
West Ham U.	1995-96		22	16	6	1	2	2	0	0
Total			*40*	*28*	*12*	*2*	*3*	*2*	*0*	*0*

SMITH Paul — Nottingham Forest

Fullname: Paul Smith DOB: 25-01-76

Previous Clubs Details

Club	Signed	Fee	Tot	Start	Sub	FA	FL	Lge	FA	FL
			|← Apps →|					|← Goals →|		
N. Forest	Jan-95	£50,000NL	0	0	0	0	0	0	0	0

SMITH Martin — Sunderland

Fullname: Martin Geoffrey Smith DOB: 13-11-74 Sunderland

Previous Clubs Details

Club	Signed	Fee	Tot	Start	Sub	FA	FL	Lge	FA	FL
Sunderland	Sep-92	Trainee	85	70	15	8	6	20	1	0

SOLSKAR Ole Gunnar — Manchester United

Fullname: Ole Gunnar Solskar DOB:

Previous Clubs Details

Club	Signed	Fee	Tot	Start	Sub	FA	FL	Lge	FA	FL
Molde			–	–	–	–	–	–	–	–
Manchester U.	Jul-96	£1.5m	0	0	0	0	0	0	0	0

SOUTHALL Neville — Everton

Fullname: Neville Southall DOB: 16-09-58 Llandudno
Debut: EVERTON v Sheffield Wednesday 15/8/92
Debut Goal: (Goalkeeper)

Club	Signed	Fee	Tot	Start	Sub	FA	FL	Lge	FA	FL
Bury	Jun-80	£6,000	39	39	0	5	0	0	0	0
Everton	Jul-81	£150,000	491	491	0	62	61	0	0	0
Port Vale	Jan-83	Loan	9	9	0	0	0	0	0	0
FAPL Summary by Club										
Everton	1992-93 to 1995-96	161	161	0	13	15	0	0	0	
Total			*161*	*161*	*0*	*13*	*15*	*0*	*0*	*0*

SOUTHGATE Gareth — Aston Villa

Fullname: Gareth Southgate DOB: 03-09-70 Watford
Debut: CRYSTAL PALACE v Blackburn ROVERS 15/8/92
Debut Goal: CRYSTAL PALACE v Blackburn ROVERS 15/8/92

Club	Signed	Fee	Tot	Start	Sub	FA	FL	Lge	FA	FL
Crystal Palace	Jan-89		110	106	4	1	17	12	0	5
Aston Villa	Jun-95	£2.5m	141	137	4	5	25	13	0	6
FAPL Summary by Club										
Crystal Palace	1992-93 to 1994-95	75	75	0	8	13	4	0	4	
Aston Villa	1995-96	31	31	0	4	8	1	0	1	
Total			*106*	*106*	*0*	*12*	*21*	*5*	*0*	*5*

SPEED Gary   Everton
Fullname: Gary Andrew Speed   DOB: 08-09-69 Hawarden
Debut: LEEDS UNITED v Wimbledon 15/8/92
Debut Goal: Aston Villa v LEEDS UNITED 19/8/92

Previous Clubs Details			Apps					Goals		
Club	Signed	Fee	Tot	Start	Sub	FA	FL	Lge	FA	FL
Leeds Utd	Jun-88		248	231	17	15	26	39	5	11
Everton	Jul-96	£3.5m	0	0	0	0	0	0	0	0
FAPL Summary by Club										
Leeds Utd	1992-93 to 1995-96		143	142	1	11	14	22	5	5
Total			*143*	*142*	*1*	*11*	*14*	*22*	*5*	*5*

SPENCER John   Chelsea
Fullname: John Spencer   DOB: 11-09-70 Glasgow
Debut: Norwich City v CHELSEA 19/8/92 as sub
Debut Goal: CHELSEA v Manchester City 9/1/93

Previous Clubs Details			Apps					Goals		
Club	Signed	Fee	Tot	Start	Sub	FA	FL	Lge	FA	FL
Rangers	1986	Juniors	13	7	6	0	2	2	0	0
Morton	Mar-89	Loan	4	4	0	0	0	1	0	0
Chelsea	Aug-92	£450,000	99	75	24	20	6	36	4	0
FAPL Summary by Club										
Chelsea	1992-93 to 1995-96		99	75	24	20	6	36	4	0
Total			*99*	*75*	*24*	*20*	*6*	*36*	*4*	*0*

SRNICEK Pavel   Newcastle United
Fullname: Pavel Srnicek   DOB: 10-03-68 Ostrava, Czechoslovakia
Debut: NEWCASTLE UNITED v Tottenham H. 14/8/93
Debut Goal: (Goalkeeper)

Previous Clubs Details			Apps					Goals		
Club	Signed	Fee	Tot	Start	Sub	FA	FL	Lge	FA	FL
Banik Ostrava			–	–	–	–	–	–	–	–
Newcastle Utd	Feb-91	£350,000	126	125	1	12	10	0	0	0
FAPL Summary by Club										
Newcastle Utd	1993-94 to 1995-96		74	73	1	7	8	0	0	0
Total			*74*	*73*	*1*	*7*	*8*	*0*	*0*	*0*

STAMP Phillip   Middlesbrough
Fullname: Phillip Lawrence Stamp   DOB: 12-12-75 Middlesbrough
Debut: Wimbledon v MIDDLESBROUGH 18/11/95
Debut Goal: MIDDLESBROUGH v Manchester City 9/12/95

Previous Clubs Details			Apps					Goals		
Club	Signed	Fee	Tot	Start	Sub	FA	FL	Lge	FA	FL
Middlesbrough	Feb-93	Trainee	22	19	3	2	4	2	0	0

Middlesbrough	1995-96	12	11	1	1	2	2	0	0
Total		*12*	*11*	*1*	*1*	*2*	*2*	*0*	*0*

STAUNTON Steve Aston Villa

Fullname: Stephen Staunton   DOB: 19-01-69 Drogheda
Debut: Ipswich Town v ASTON VILLA 15/8/92
Debut Goal: ASTON VILLA v Crystal Palace 5/9/92

Previous Clubs Details			*Apps*				*Goals*		
Club	Signed	Fee	Tot	Start	Sub	FA	FL	Lge	FA	FL
Liverpool	Sep-86	£20,000	65	55	10	16	8	0	1	4
Bradford City	Nov-87	Loan	8	7	1	0	2	0	0	0
Aston Villa	Aug-91	£1.1m	151	148	3	14	18	14	0	1

FAPL Summary by Club

Aston Villa	1992-93 to 1995-96	114	111	3	10	16	10	0	1
Total		*114*	*111*	*3*	*10*	*16*	*10*	*0*	*1*

STEFANOVIC Dejan Sheffield Wednesday

Fullname: Dejan Stefanovic   DOB:
Debut: Nottingham Forest v SHEFFIELD W. 26/12/95

Previous Clubs Details			*Apps*				*Goals*		
Club	Signed	Fee	Tot	Start	Sub	FA	FL	Lge	FA	FL
Red Star Belgrade			–	–	–	–	–	–	–	–
Sheffield W.	Oct-95	£2m	6	5	1	1	0	0	0	0

FAPL Summary by Club

Sheffield W.	1995-96	6	5	1	1	0	0	0	0
Total		*6*	*5*	*1*	*1*	*0*	*0*	*0*	*0*

STEIN Mark Chelsea

Fullname: Mark Eral Sean Stein   DOB: 28-01-66 South Africa
Debut: CHELSEA v Oldham Athletic 30/10/93
Debut Goal: Southampton v CHELSEA 27/12/93

Previous Clubs Details			*Apps*				*Goals*		
Club	Signed	Fee	Tot	Start	Sub	FA	FL	Lge	FA	FL
Luton Town	Jan-84		54	41	13	9	5	19	3	0
Aldershot	Jan-86	Loan	2	2	0	0	0	1	0	0
QPR	Aug-88	£300,000	33	20	13	3	4	4	1	2
Oxford Utd	Sep-89	Swap	82	72	10	3	4	18	0	0
Stoke City	Sep-91	£100,000	94	94	0	4	8	50	0	8
Chelsea	Oct-93	£1.5m	50	46	4	9	1	21	2	0

FAPL Summary by Club

Chelsea	1993-94 to 1995-96	50	46	4	9	1	21	2	0
Total		*50*	*46*	*4*	*9*	*1*	*21*	*2*	*0*

STEWART Paul　　　　　　　　　　　　　　　Sunderland

Fullname:　Paul Andrew Stewart　　　　　DOB: 07-10-64 Manchester
Debut:　　Nottingham Forest v LIVERPOOL 16/8/92
Debut Goal: LIVERPOOL v Sheffield Utd 19/8/92

Previous Clubs Details			Apps					Goals		
Club	Signed	Fee	Tot	Start	Sub	FA	FL	Lge	FA	FL
Blackpool	Oct-81		191	188	3	7	11	56	2	3
Man. City	Mar-87	£200,000	51	51	0	4	6	27	1	2
Tottenham H.	Jun-88	£1.7m	131	126	5	9	23	28	2	7
Liverpool	Jul-92	£2.3m	32	28	4	1	6	1	0	0
Crystal Palace	Jan-94	Loan	18	18	0	0	0	3	0	0
Wolves	Sep-94	Loan	8	5	3	0	0	2	0	0
Burnley	Feb-95	Loan	6	6	0	0	0	0	0	0
Sunderland	Aug-95	Free	12	11	1	0	0	1	0	0
FAPL Summary by Club										
Liverpool	1992-93 to 1993-94		32	28	4	1	6	1	0	0
Total			*32*	*28*	*4*	*1*	*6*	*1*	*0*	*0*

STIMAC Igor　　　　　　　　　　　　　　Derby County

Fullname:　Igor Stimac　　　　　　　　　　DOB: 09-06-67

Previous Clubs Details			Apps					Goals		
Club	Signed	Fee	Tot	Start	Sub	FA	FL	Lge	FA	FL
Hadjuk Split			–	–	–	–	–	–	–	–
Cadiz			–	–	–	–	–	–	–	–
Hadjuk Split			–	–	–	–	–	–	–	–
Derby County	Oct-95	£1.5m	27	27	0	1	0	1	0	0

STONE Steve　　　　　　　　　　　　Nottingham Forest

Fullname:　Steven Brian Stone　　　　　DOB: 20-08-71 Gateshead
Debut:　　Middlesbrough v NOTTINGHAM FOREST 20/2/92
Debut Goal: Middlesbrough v NOTTINGHAM FOREST 20/2/92

Previous Clubs Details			Apps					Goals		
Club	Signed	Fee	Tot	Start	Sub	FA	FL	Lge	FA	FL
N. Forest	May-89		133	131	2	10	12	18	0	0
FAPL Summary by Club										
N. Forest	1992-93 to 1995-96		87	86	1	8	7	13	0	0
Total			*87*	*86*	*1*	*8*	*7*	*13*	*0*	*0*

STRACHAN Gordon　　　　　　　　　　　Coventry City

Fullname:　Gordon David Strachan　　　　DOB: 09-02-57 Edinburgh
Debut:　　LEEDS UNITED v Wimbledon 15/8/92
Debut Goal: QPR v LEEDS UNITED 24/10/92

Previous Clubs Details			Apps					Goals		
Club	Signed	Fee	Tot	Start	Sub	FA	FL	Lge	FA	FL
Manchester U.	Aug-84	£500,000	160	155	5	22	13	33	2	1
Leeds Utd	Mar-89	£300,000	197	188	9	14	19	37	2	3

Coventry City	Mar-95	Free	17	10	7	2	3		0	0	0

FAPL Summary by Club

Leeds Utd	1992-93 to 1994-95		70	62	8	7	6		7	1	1
Coventry City	1994-95 to 1995-96		17	10	7	2	3		0	0	0
Total			*87*	*72*	*15*	*9*	*9*		*7*	*1*	*1*

STUART Graham   Everton

Fullname: Graham Charles Stuart   DOB: 24-10-70 Tooting
Debut: CHELSEA v Oldham Athletic 15/8/92
Debut Goal: Norwich City v CHELSEA 19/8/92

			Apps					Goals			
Previous Clubs Details											
Club	Signed	Fee	Tot	Start	Sub	FA	FL		Lge	FA	FL
Chelsea	Jun-89		87	70	17	7	11		14	1	2
Everton	Aug-93	£850,000	87	73	14	11	5		15	5	2

FAPL Summary by Club

Chelsea	1992-93		39	31	8	1	6		9	0	1
Everton	1993-94 to 1995-96		87	73	14	11	5		15	5	2
Total			*126*	*104*	*22*	*12*	*11*		*24*	*5*	*3*

STURRIDGE Dean   Derby County

Fullname: Dean Constantine Sturridge   DOB: 27-07-73 Birmingham

			Apps					Goals			
Previous Clubs Details											
Club	Signed	Fee	Tot	Start	Sub	FA	FL		Lge	FA	FL
Derby County	Jul-91	Trainee	62	49	13	0	1		21	0	0
Torquay Utd	Dec-94	Loan	10	10	0	0	0		5	0	0

SULLIVAN Neil   Wimbledon

Fullname: Neil Sullivan   DOB: 24-02-70 Sutton
Debut: Southampton v WIMBLEDON 17/10/92

			Apps					Goals			
Previous Clubs Details											
Club	Signed	Fee	Tot	Start	Sub	FA	FL		Lge	FA	FL
Wimbledon	Jul-88		32	31	1	8	0		0	0	0
Crystal Palace	May-92	Loan	1	1	0	0	0		0	0	0

FAPL Summary by Club

Wimbledon	1992-93 to 1995-96		30	29	1	8	0		0	0	0
Total			*30*	*29*	*1*	*8*	*0*		*0*	*0*	*0*

SUMMERBELL Mark   Middlesbrough

Fullname: Mark Sumerbell   DOB:
Debut: Tottenham H. v MIDDLESBROUGH 8/4/96 as sub

			Apps					Goals			
Previous Clubs Details											
Club	Signed	Fee	Tot	Start	Sub	FA	FL		Lge	FA	FL
Middlesbrough			1	0	1	0	0		0	0	0

FAPL Summary by Club

Middlesbrough	1995-96		1	0	1	0	0		0	0	0
Total			*1*	*0*	*1*	*0*	*0*		*0*	*0*	*0*

SUTTON Wayne   Derby County
Fullname: Wayne Frank Sutton   DOB: 01-10-75 Derby

Previous Clubs Details			*Apps*					*Goals*		
Club	Signed	Fee	Tot	Start	Sub	FA	FL	Lge	FA	FL
Derby County	May-94	Trainee	1	1	0	0	0	0	0	0

SUTTON Steve   Derby County
Fullname: Stephen John Sutton   DOB: 16-04-61 Hartington
Debut Goal: (Goalkeeper)

Previous Clubs Details			*Apps*					*Goals*		
Club	Signed	Fee	Tot	Start	Sub	FA	FL	Lge	FA	FL
N. Forest	Apr-79	Apprentice	199	199	0	14	33	0	0	0
Mansfield T.	Mar-81	Loan	0	8	8	0	0	0	0	0
Derby County	Jan-85	Loan	14	14	0	0	0	0	0	0
Coventry City	Feb-91	Loan	1	1	0	0	0	0	0	0
Luton Town	Nov-91	Loan	0	14	14	0	0	0	0	0
Derby County	Mar-92	£300,000	61	60	1	0	0	0	0	0
Reading *	Jan-96	Loan	–	–	–	–	–	–	–	–

SUTTON Chris   Blackburn Rovers
Fullname: Christopher Roy Sutton   DOB: 10-03-73 Nottingham
Debut: Arsenal v NORWICH CITY 15/8/92
Debut Goal: NORWICH CITY v QPR 17/10/92

Previous Clubs Details			*Apps*					*Goals*		
Club	Signed	Fee	Tot	Start	Sub	FA	FL	Lge	FA	FL
Norwich City	Jul-91		102	89	13	10	9	35	5	3
Blackburn Rvs	Jul-94	£5m	53	49	4	2	7	15	2	1
FAPL Summary by Club										
Norwich City 1992-93 to 1993-94			79	73	6	4	7	33	2	3
Blackburn Rvs1994-95 to 1995-96			53	49	4	2	7	15	2	1
Total			*132*	*122*	*10*	*6*	*14*	*48*	*4*	*4*

TAYLOR Ian   Aston Villa
Fullname: Ian Kenneth Taylor   DOB: 04-06-68 Birmingham
Debut: SHEFFIELD WED v Tottenham H. 20/8/94
Debut Goal: SHEFFIELD WEDNESDAY v Newcastle Utd 22/10/94

Previous Clubs Details			*Apps*					*Goals*		
Club	Signed	Fee	Tot	Start	Sub	FA	FL	Lge	FA	FL
Port Vale	Jul-92		83	83	0	6	4	28	1	2
Sheffield W.	Jun-94	£1m	14	9	5	0	4	1	0	1
Aston Villa	Dec-94	£1m	47	46	1	5	6	4	1	1
FAPL Summary by Club										
Sheffield W.	1994-95		14	9	5	0	4	1	0	1
Aston Villa	1994-95 to 1995-96		47	46	1	5	6	4	1	1
Total			*61*	*55*	*6*	*5*	*10*	*5*	*1*	*2*

TAYLOR Scott   Leicester City
Fullname: Scott Dean Taylor   DOB: 28-11-70 Portsmouth

Previous Clubs Details   *Apps*   *Goals*

Club	Signed	Fee	Tot	Start	Sub	FA	FL	Lge	FA	FL
Reading	Jun-89	Trainee	207	164	43	13	12	24	3	1
Leicester City	Aug-95	£500,000	39	39	0	1	3	6	0	0

TELFER Paul   Coventry City
Fullname: Paul Norman Telfer   DOB: 12-10-91 Edinburgh
Debut: Newcastle Utd v COVENTRY CITY 19/8/95
Debut Goal: COVENTRY CITY v Manchester City 23/8/95

Previous Clubs Details   *Apps*   *Goals*

Club	Signed	Fee	Tot	Start	Sub	FA	FL	Lge	FA	FL
Luton Town	Nov-88	Trainee	98	81	7	10	3	10	2	0
Coventry City	Jun-95	£1.15m	31	31	0	3	4	1	1	0

FAPL Summary by Club

Coventry City		1995-96	31	31	0	3	4	1	1	0
Total			*31*	*31*	*0*	*3*	*4*	*1*	*1*	*0*

THATCHER Ben   Wimbldeon
Fullname: Benjamin David Thatcher   DOB: 30-11-75 Swindon

Previous Clubs Details   *Apps*   *Goals*

Club	Signed	Fee	Tot	Start	Sub	FA	FL	Lge	FA	FL
Millwall *	Jun-96	Trainee	48	46	2	5	4	1	0	0
Wimbledon	Jul-96	£1.9m	0	0	0	0	0	0	0	0

THOMAS Michael   Liverpool
Fullname: Michael Lauriston Thomas   DOB: 24-08-67 Lambeth
Debut: LIVERPOOL v Southampton 1/9/92
Debut Goal: LIVERPOOL v Norwich City 25/10/92

Previous Clubs Details   *Apps*   *Goals*

Club	Signed	Fee	Tot	Start	Sub	FA	FL	Lge	FA	FL
Arsenal	Dec-84		163	149	14	17	23	24	1	5
Portsmouth	Dec-86	Loan	3	3	0	0	0	0	0	0
Liverpool	Dec-91	£1.5m	82	57	25	17	5	5	2	1

FAPL Summary by Club

Liverpool		1992-93 to 1995-96	65	41	24	12	5	2	0	1
Total			*65*	*41*	*24*	*12*	*5*	*2*	*0*	*1*

THORN Andy   Wimbledon
Fullname: Andrew Charles Thorn   DOB: 12-11-66 Carshalton
Debut: CRYSTAL PALACE v Blackburn Rvs 15/8/92
Debut Goal: CRYSTAL PALACE v Leeds Utd 20/12/92

Previous Clubs Details   *Apps*   *Goals*

Club	Signed	Fee	Tot	Start	Sub	FA	FL	Lge	FA	FL
Wimbledon	Nov-84		107	106	1	9	7	2	0	0

Club	Signed	Fee	Tot	Start	Sub	FA	FL	Lge	FA	FL
Newcastle Utd	Aug-88	£850,000	36	36	0	0	4	2	0	1
Crystal Palace	Dec-89	£650,000	128	128	0	10	19	3	0	4
Wimbledon	Oct-94	Free	37	33	4	3	3	1	0	0

FAPL Summary by Club

Club			Tot	Start	Sub	FA	FL	Lge	FA	FL
Crystal Palace	1992-93		34	34	0	0	5	1	0	1
Wimbledon	1994-95 to 1995-96		37	33	4	3	3	1	0	0
Total			71	67	4	3	8	2	0	1

THORNLEY Ben   Manchester United

Fullname: Benjamin Thornley   DOB: 21-04-75 Bury
Debut: West Ham Utd v MAN UNITED 26/2/94 as sub

Previous Clubs Details			Apps					Goals		
Club	Signed	Fee	Tot	Start	Sub	FA	FL	Lge	FA	FL
Manchester U.	Jan-93	Trainee	2	0	2	0	0	0	0	0
Stockport Co. *	Nov-95	Loan	–	–	–	–	–	–	–	–
Huddersfield *	Feb-96	Loan	–	–	–	–	–	–	–	–

FAPL Summary by Club

Manchester U.	1993-94 to 1995-96		2	0	2	0	0	0	0	0
Total			2	0	2	0	0	0	0	0

THORSTVEDT Erik   Tottenham Hotspur

Fullname: Erik Thorstvedt   DOB: 28-10-62 Stavanger, Norway
Debut: TOTTENHAM HOTSPUR v Coventry City 19/8/92
Debut Goal: (Goalkeeper)

Previous Clubs Details			Apps					Goals		
Club	Signed	Fee	Tot	Start	Sub	FA	FL	Lge	FA	FL
Eik, Viking (Nor)			–	–	–	–	–	–	–	–
Borussia Monchengladbach			–	–	–	–	–	–	–	–
IFK (Swe)			–	–	–	–	–	–	–	–
Tottenham H.	Dec-88	£400,000	173	171	2	14	25	0	0	0

FAPL Summary by Club

Tottenham H.	1992-93 to 1995-96		60	58	2	6	7	0	0	0
Total			60	58	2	6	7	0	0	0

TILER Carl   Aston Villa

Fullname: Carl Tiler   DOB: 11-01-70 Sheffield
Debut: Blackburn Rvs v NOTTINGHAM FOREST 5/9/93

Previous Clubs Details			Apps					Goals		
Club	Signed	Fee	Tot	Start	Sub	FA	FL	Lge	FA	FL
Barnsley	Aug-88	Trainee	71	67	4	5	4	3	0	0
N. Forest	May-91	£1.4m	69	67	2	6	11	1	0	0
Swindon Town	Nov-94	Loan	2	2	0	0	0	0	0	0
Aston Villa	Oct-95	£750,000	1	1	0	0	0	0	0	0

TINKLER Mark   Leeds United

Fullname: Mark Roland Tinkler   DOB: 24-10-74 Bishop Auckland
Debut: Sheffield Utd v LEEDS UNITED 6/4/93

Previous Clubs Details			*Apps*				*Goals*		
Club	Signed	Fee	Tot	Start	Sub	FA	FL	Lge	FA	FL
Leeds Utd	Nov-91		22	13	9	0	1	0	0	0

FAPL Summary by Club

Leeds Utd	1992-93 to 1995-96	22	13	9	0	1	0	0	0
Total		*22*	*13*	*9*	*0*	*1*	*0*	*0*	*0*

TISDALE Paul   Southampton

Fullname: Paul Tisdale   DOB: 14-01-73 Malta
Debut: Sheff Wed v TOTTENHAM HOTSPUR 2/1/95 as sub
Debut Goal: Manchester City v SOUTHAMPTON 16/3/96

Previous Clubs Details			*Apps*				*Goals*		
Club	Signed	Fee	Tot	Start	Sub	FA	FL	Lge	FA	FL
Southampton	Jun-91	Junior	15	5	10	1	1	1	0	0
Northampton	Mar-92	Loan	5	5	0	0	0	0	0	0

FAPL Summary by Club

Southampton	1994-95 to 1995-96	15	5	10	1	1	1	0	0
Total		*15*	*5*	*10*	*1*	*1*	*1*	*0*	*0*

TOWNSEND Andy   Aston Villa

Fullname: Andrew David Townsend   DOB: 23-07-63 Maidstone
Debut: CHELSEA v Oldham Athletic 15/8/92
Debut Goal: CHELSEA v Norwich City 12/9/92

Previous Clubs Details			*Apps*				*Goals*		
Club	Signed	Fee	Tot	Start	Sub	FA	FL	Lge	FA	FL
Southampton	Jan-85	£35,000	83	77	6	5	8	5	0	0
Norwich City	Aug-88	£300,000	71	66	5	10	4	8	2	0
Chelsea	Jul-90	£1.2m	110	110	0	7	17	12	0	7
Aston Villa	Jul-93	£2.1m	95	94	1	9	18	6	0	2

FAPL Summary by Club

Chelsea	1992-93	41	41	0	1	6	4	0	3
Aston Villa	1993-94 to 1995-96	95	94	1	9	18	6	0	2
Total		*136*	*135*	*1*	*10*	*24*	*10*	*0*	*5*

TROLLOPE Paul   Derby County

Fullname: Paul Jonathan Trollope   DOB: 03-06-72 Swindon

Previous Clubs Details			Apps					Goals		
Club	Signed	Fee	Tot	Start	Sub	FA	FL	Lge	FA	FL
Swindon Town	Dec-89	Trainee	0	0	0	0	0	0	0	0
Torquay Utd	Mar-92	Free	88	85	3	7	3	12	0	1
Derby County	Dec-94	Loan	5	4	1	0	0	1	0	0
Derby County	Jan-95	£100,000	36	26	10	1	2	3	0	0

UNSWORTH David   Everton

Fullname: David G Unsworth   DOB: 16-10-73 Chorley
Debut: EVERTON v Liverpool 7/12/92
Debut Goal: EVERTON v Arsenal 29/10/94

Previous Clubs Details			Apps					Goals		
Club	Signed	Fee	Tot	Start	Sub	FA	FL	Lge	FA	FL
Everton	May-92		82	76	6	7	5	6	0	0
FAPL Summary by Club										
Everton	1992-93 to 1995-96		80	75	5	7	5	5	0	0
Total			*80*	*75*	*5*	*7*	*5*	*5*	*0*	*0*

VAN DER GOUW Raimond   Manchester United

Fullname: Raimond Van der Gouw   DOB:

Previous Clubs Details			Apps					Goals		
Club	Signed	Fee	Tot	Start	Sub	FA	FL	Lge	FA	FL
Vitesse Arnhem			–	–	–	–	–	–	–	–
Manchester U.	Jul-96	undisclosed	0	0	0	0	0	0	0	0

Van Der LAAN Robin   Derby County

Fullname: Robertus Van Der Laan   DOB: 05-09-68 Schiedam, Holland

Previous Clubs Details			Apps					Goals		
Club	Signed	Fee	Tot	Start	Sub	FA	FL	Lge	FA	FL
Wageningen			–	–	–	–	–	–	–	–
Port Vale	Feb-91	£80,000	132	111	21	8	8	19	1	1
Derby County	Aug-95	£475,000	39	39	0	1	3	6	0	0

VENISON Barry   Southampton

Fullname: Barry Venison   DOB: 16-08-64 Consett
Debut: NEWCASTLE UNITED v Tottenham H. 14/8/93
Debut Goal: NEWCASTLE UNITED v Aston Villa 25/2/95

Previous Clubs Details			Apps					Goals		
Club	Signed	Fee	Tot	Start	Sub	FA	FL	Lge	FA	FL
Sunderland	Jan-82	Apprentice	173	169	4	8	21	2	0	0
Liverpool	Jul-86	£200,000	110	103	7	21	17	1	0	0
Newcastle Utd	Jul-92	£250,000	109	108	1	11	9	1	0	0
Galatasaray	Jun-95	£750,000	–	–	–	–	–	–	–	–
Southampton	Oct-95	£850,000	22	21	1	3	2	0	0	0

VIALLI Gianluca   Chelsea

Fullname: Gianluca Vialli   DOB: 09-07-64 Cremona

Previous Clubs Details			*Apps*					*Goals*		
Club	Signed	Fee	Tot	Start	Sub	FA	FL	Lge	FA	FL
Cremonese	1980		105	–	–	–	–	23	–	–
Sampdoria	1984		223	–	–	–	–	82	–	–
Juventus	1992		–	–	–	–	–	–	–	–
Chelsea	Jun-96	Free	0	0	0	0	0	0	0	0

VICKERS Steve   Middlesbrough

Fullname: Stephen Vickers   DOB: 13-10-67 Bishop Auckland

Debut: Arsenal v MIDDLESBROUGH 20/8/95

Debut Goal: MIDDLESBROUGH v Coventry City 16/9/95

Previous Clubs Details			*Apps*					*Goals*		
Club	Signed	Fee	Tot	Start	Sub	FA	FL	Lge	FA	FL
Tranmere Rvs	Sep-85		311	310	1	19	21	11	3	5
Middlesbrough	Dec-93	£700,000	58	57	1	5	6	4	0	1

FAPL Summary by Club

		Tot	Start	Sub	FA	FL	Lge	FA	FL
Middlesbrough	1995-96	32	32	0	3	6	1	0	1
Total		*32*	*32*	*0*	*3*	*6*	*1*	*0*	*1*

WADDLE Chris   Sheffield Wednesday

Fullname: Christopher Roland Waddle   DOB: 14-12-60 Felling

Debut: Everton v SHEFFIELD WEDNESDAY 15/8/92

Debut Goal: SHEFFIELD WEDNESDAY v Everton 6/2/93

Previous Clubs Details			*Apps*					*Goals*		
Club	Signed	Fee	Tot	Start	Sub	FA	FL	Lge	FA	FL
Newcastle Utd	Jul-80	£1,000	170	169	1	12	8	46	4	2
Tottenham H.	Jun-85	£590,000	138	137	1	14	21	33	5	4
Marseille	Jul-89	£4.25m	0	0	0	0	0	0	0	0
Sheffield W.	Jun-92	£1m	109	94	15	13	20	10	3	0

FAPL Summary by Club

		Tot	Start	Sub	FA	FL	Lge	FA	FL
Sheffield W.	1992-93 to 1995-96	109	94	15	13	19	10	3	0
Total		*109*	*94*	*15*	*13*	*19*	*10*	*3*	*0*

WALKER Ian   Tottenham Hotspur

Fullname: Ian Michael Walker   DOB: 31-10-71 Watford

Debut: Southampton v TOTTENHAM HOTSPUR 15/8/92

Debut Goal: (Goalkeeper)

Previous Clubs Details

Club	Signed	Fee	Tot	Start	Sub	FA	FL	Lge	FA	FL
				Apps					*Goals*	
Tottenham H.	Dec-89		126	125	1	14	5	0	0	0
Oxford Utd	Sep-90	Loan	2	2	0	0	1	0	0	0

FAPL Summary by Club

| Tottenham H. | 1992-93 to 1995-96 | | 107 | 106 | 1 | 14 | 8 | 0 | 0 | 0 |
| *Total* | | | *107* | *106* | *1* | *14* | *8* | *0* | *0* | *0* |

WALKER Des   Sheffield Wednesday

Fullname: Desmond Sinclair Walker   DOB: 26-11-65 Hackney
Debut: SHEFFIELD WEDNESDAY v Aston Villa 18/8/93

Previous Clubs Details

Club	Signed	Fee	Tot	Start	Sub	FA	FL	Lge	FA	FL
				Apps					*Goals*	
N. Forest	Nov-83		264	259	5	27	40	1	0	0
Sampdoria	May-92	£1.5m	–	–	–	–	–	–	–	–
Sheffield W.	Aug-93	£2.75m	116	116	0	8	14	0	0	0

FAPL Summary by Club

| Sheffield W. | 1993-94 to 1995-96 | | 116 | 116 | 0 | 8 | 14 | 0 | 0 | 0 |
| *Total* | | | *116* | *116* | *0* | *8* | *14* | *0* | *0* | *0* |

WALLACE Rod   Leeds United

Fullname: Rodney Seymour Wallace   DOB: 02-10-69 Greenwich
Debut: LEEDS UNITED v Wimbledon 15/8/92
Debut Goal: LEEDS UNITED v Tottenham H. 25/8/92

Previous Clubs Details

Club	Signed	Fee	Tot	Start	Sub	FA	FL	Lge	FA	FL
				Apps					*Goals*	
Southampton	Apr-88		128	111	17	10	19	44	3	6
Leeds Utd	Jun-91	£1.6m	158	141	17	13	12	40	1	3

FAPL Summary by Club

| Leeds Utd | 1992-93 to 1995-96 | | 125 | 107 | 18 | 12 | 9 | 29 | 1 | 1 |
| *Total* | | | *125* | *107* | *18* | *12* | *9* | *29* | *1* | *1* |

WALSH Gary   Middlesbrough

Fullname: Gary Walsh   DOB: 21-03-68 Wigan
Debut: Ipswich Town v MANCHESTER UNITED 24/9/94
Debut Goal: (Goalkeeper)

Previous Clubs Details

Club	Signed	Fee	Tot	Start	Sub	FA	FL	Lge	FA	FL
				Apps					*Goals*	
Manchester U.	Apr-85	Juniors	50	49	1	0	7	0	0	0
Airdrieonians	Jan-88	Loan	3	3	0	0	3	0	0	0
Oldham A.	Nov-93	Loan	6	6	0	0	0	0	0	0
Middlesbrough	Aug-95	£250,000	31	31	0	3	6	0	0	0

		Tot	Start	Sub	FA	FL	Lge	FA	FL
Manchester U.	1994-95	10	10	0	0	3	0	0	0
Middlesbrough	1995-96	31	31	0	3	6	0	0	0
Total		*41*	*41*	*0*	*3*	*9*	*0*	*0*	*0*

WALSH Steve   Leicester City

Fullname: Steven Walsh   DOB: 03-11-64 Preston
Debut: LEICESTER CITY v Newcastle Utd 21/8/94

Previous Clubs Details			*Apps*					*Goals*		
Club	Signed	Fee	Tot	Start	Sub	FA	FL	Lge	FA	FL
Wigan Athletic	Sep-82	Juniors	125	123	2	6	7	4	0	0
Leicester City	Jun-86	£100,000	287	285	2	9	23	44	0	3

FAPL Summary by Club

		Tot	Start	Sub	FA	FL	Lge	FA	FL
Leicester City	1994-95	5	5	0	0	0	0	0	0
Total		*5*	*5*	*0*	*0*	*0*	*0*	*0*	*0*

WALTERS Mark   Southampton

Fullname: Mark Everton Walters   DOB: 02-06-64 Birmingham
Debut: Nottingham Forest v LIVERPOOL 16/8/92
Debut Goal: LIVERPOOL v Sheffield Utd 19/8/92

Previous Clubs Details			*Apps*					*Goals*		
Club	Signed	Fee	Tot	Start	Sub	FA	FL	Lge	FA	FL
Aston Villa	May-82		181	168	13	12	21	39	1	6
Rangers	Dec-87	£500,000	–	–	–	–	–	–	–	–
Liverpool	Aug-91	£1.25m	93	58	53	8	12	14	0	4
Stoke City	Mar-94	Loan	9	9	0	0	0	2	0	0
Wolves	Sep-94	Loan	11	11	0	0	0	3	0	0
Southampton	Jan-96	Free	4	4	0	4	0	0	0	0

FAPL Summary by Club

		Tot	Start	Sub	FA	FL	Lge	FA	FL
Liverpool	1992-93 to 1994-95	68	40	28	5	8	11	0	2
Southampton	1995-96	4	4	0	4	0	0	0	0
Total		*72*	*44*	*28*	*9*	*8*	*11*	*0*	*2*

WARD Ashley   Derby County

Fullname: Ashley Stuart Ward   DOB: 24-11-70 Manchester
Debut: NORWICH CITY v Chelsea 10/12/94
Debut Goal: NORWICH CITY v Chelsea 10/12/94

Previous Clubs Details			*Apps*					*Goals*		
Club	Signed	Fee	Tot	Start	Sub	FA	FL	Lge	FA	FL
Man. City	Aug-89	Trainee	0	0	1	2	0	0	0	0
Wrexham	Jan-91	Loan	4	4	0	0	0	2	0	0
Leicester City	Jul-91	£80,000	10	2	8	1	3	0	0	0
Blackpool	Nov-92	Loan	2	2	0	0	0	1	0	0
Crewe Alex	Dec-92	£80,000	61	58	3	2	4	25	4	2
Norwich City *	Dec-94	£500,000	25	25	0	0	0	8	0	0
Derby County	Mar-96	£1m	7	5	2	0	0	1	0	0

Norwich City	1994-95	25	25	0	0	0	8	0	0
Total		*25*	*25*	*0*	*0*	*0*	*8*	*0*	*0*

WARHURST Paul   Blackburn Rovers

Fullname: Paul Warhurst   DOB: 26-09-69 Stockport
Debut: Everton v SHEFFIELD WEDNESDAY 15/8/92
Debut Goal: Nottingham Forest v SHEFFIELD WED 12/9/92

Previous Clubs Details

			Apps					Goals		
Club	Signed	Fee	Tot	Start	Sub	FA	FL	Lge	FA	FL
Man. City	Jun-88		0	0	0	0	0	0	0	0
Oldham Ath	Oct-88	£10,000	67	60	7	9	8	2	0	0
Sheffield W.	Jul-91	£750,000	66	60	6	8	9	6	4	5
Blackburn Rvs	Sep-93	£2.7m	46	25	21	2	8	2	0	0

FAPL Summary by Club

Sheffield W.	1992-93 to 1993-94	33	29	4	7	7	6	5	3
Blackburn Rvs	1993-94 to 1995-96	46	25	21	9	15	2	5	3
Total		*79*	*54*	*25*	*16*	*22*	*8*	*10*	*6*

WARREN Christer   Southampton

Fullname: Christer Warren   DOB: 10-10-74 Bournemouth
Debut: Arsenal v SOUTHAMPTON 23/9/95 as sub

Previous Clubs Details

			Apps					Goals		
Club	Signed	Fee	Tot	Start	Sub	FA	FL	Lge	FA	FL
Southampton	Aug-95	£40,000NL	7	1	6	0	1	0	0	0

FAPL Summary by Club

Southampton	1995-96	7	1	6	0	1	0	0	0
Total		*7*	*1*	*6*	*0*	*1*	*0*	*0*	*0*

WASSALL Darren   Derby County

Fullname: Darren Paul Wassall   DOB: 27-06-68 Birmingham

Previous Clubs Details

			Apps					Goals		
Club	Signed	Fee	Tot	Start	Sub	FA	FL	Lge	FA	FL
N. Forest	Jun-86	Apprentice	27	17	10	4	8	0	0	0
Hereford Utd	Oct-87	Loan	5	5	0	1	0	0	0	0
Bury	Mar-89	Loan	7	7	0	0	0	1	0	0
Derby County	Jun-92	£600,000	98	90	8	4	9	0	0	0

WATSON Dave   Everton

Fullname: David Watson   DOB: 20-11-61 Liverpool
Debut: EVERTON v Sheffield Wednesday 15/8/92
Debut Goal: Middlesbrough v EVERTON 10/4/93

Previous Clubs Details

			Apps					Goals		
Club	Signed	Fee	Tot	Start	Sub	FA	FL	Lge	FA	FL
Liverpool	May-79		0	0	0	0	0	0	0	0
Norwich City	Nov-80	£100,000	212	212	0	18	21	11	1	3

Club	Signed	Fee	Tot	Start	Sub	FA	FL	Lge	FA	FL
Everton	Aug-86	£900,000	340	338	2	42	35	23	5	6

FAPL Summary by Club

Everton	1992-93 to 1995-96		140	139	1	12	12	5	2	1
Total			*140*	*139*	*1*	*12*	*12*	*5*	*2*	*1*

WATSON Mark   West Ham United

Fullname: Mark Watson   DOB: 28-12-73 Birmingham
Debut: QPR v WEST HAM UTD 27/4/96 as sub

Previous Clubs Details			*Apps*					*Goals*		
Club	Signed	Fee	Tot	Start	Sub	FA	FL	Lge	FA	FL
West Ham U.		from NL	0	0	1	0	0	0	0	0

FAPL Summary by Club

West Ham U.	1995-96		1	0	1	0	0	0	0	0
Total			*1*	*0*	*1*	*0*	*0*	*0*	*0*	*0*

WATSON Steve   Newcastle United

Fullname: Stephen Craig Watson   DOB: 01-04-74 North Shields
Debut: NEWCASTLE UNITED v Tottenham H. 14/8/93
Debut Goal: NEWCASTLE UNITED v Swindon Town 12/3/94

Previous Clubs Details			*Apps*					*Goals*		
Club	Signed	Fee	Tot	Start	Sub	FA	FL	Lge	FA	FL
Newcastle Utd	Jul-90		136	112	24	8	12	10	0	1

FAPL Summary by Club

Newcastle Utd	1993-94 to 1995-96		82	66	16	3	12	9	0	1
Total			*82*	*66*	*16*	*3*	*12*	*9*	*0*	*1*

WATSON Gordon   Southampton

Fullname: Gordon William George Watson   DOB: 20-03-71 Sidcup
Debut: Everton v SHEFFIELD WEDNESDAY 15/8/92 as sub
Debut Goal: Oldham Athletic v SHEFFIELD WEDNESDAY 7/4/93

Previous Clubs Details			*Apps*					*Goals*		
Club	Signed	Fee	Tot	Start	Sub	FA	FL	Lge	FA	FL
Charlton Ath.	Apr-89		31	20	11	1	2	7	0	7
Sheffield W.	Feb-91	£250,000	43	24	19	6	8	13	2	3
Southampton	Mar-95	£1.2m	37	30	7	5	3	6	1	2

FAPL Summary by Club

Sheffield W.	1992-93 to 1993-94		57	24	33	6	10	15	2	3
Southampton	1994-95 to 1995-96		37	30	7	5	3	6	1	2
Total			*94*	*54*	*40*	*11*	*13*	*21*	*3*	*5*

WATTS Julian   Leicester City

Fullname: Julian D Watts   DOB: 17-03-71 Sheffield
Debut: Liverpool v SHEFFIELD WEDNESDAY 3/3/93
Debut Goal: SHEFFIELD W. v Wimbledon, 10/2/96 as sub

Club	Signed	Fee	Apps					Goals		
			Tot	Start	Sub	FA	FL	Lge	FA	FL
Rotherham Utd	Jul-90		20	17	3	4	1	1	0	0
Sheffield W.	Mar-92	£80,000	16	12	4	0	1	1	0	0
Shrewsbury	Dec-92	Loan	9	9	0	0	0	0	0	0
Leicester City	Mar-96		9	9	0	0	0	0	0	0
FAPL Summary by Club										
Sheffield W.	1992-93		15	12	3	0	1	1	0	0
Total			*15*	*12*	*3*	*0*	*1*	*1*	*0*	*0*

WEGERLE Roy   Coventry City

Fullname: Roy Connon Wegerle   DOB: 19-03-64 Johannesburg
Debut: Coventry City v BLACKBURN ROVERS 29/8/92
Debut Goal: BLACKBURN ROVERS v Norwich City 3/10/92

Previous Clubs Details

Club	Signed	Fee	Apps					Goals		
			Tot	Start	Sub	FA	FL	Lge	FA	FL
Tampa Bay (USA)			–	–	–	–	–	–	–	–
Chelsea	Jun-86	£100,000	23	15	8	2	0	3	1	0
Swindon Town	Mar-88	Loan	7	7	0	0	0	1	0	0
Luton Town	Jul-88	£75,000	45	39	6	1	10	10	0	8
QPR	Dec-89	£1m	75	71	4	11	5	29	1	1
Blackburn Rvs	Mar-92	£1.2m	34	20	14	5	6	6	2	4
Coventry City	Mar-93	£1m	54	47	7	5	5	9	1	1
FAPL Summary by Club										
Blackburn Rvs	1992-93		22	11	11	5	6	4	2	4
Coventry City	1992-93 to 1994-95		54	47	7	10	11	15	3	5
Total			*76*	*58*	*18*	*15*	*17*	*19*	*5*	*9*

WETHERALL David   Leeds United

Fullname: David Wetherall   DOB: 14-03-71 Sheffield
Debut: Southampton v LEEDS UNITED 19/9/92
Debut Goal: LEEDS UNITED v Chelsea 24/3/93

Previous Clubs Details

Club	Signed	Fee	Apps					Goals		
			Tot	Start	Sub	FA	FL	Lge	FA	FL
Sheffield W.	Jul-89	Trainee	0	0	0	0	0	0	0	0
Leeds Utd	Jul-91	£125,000	118	116	2	15	13	9	3	0
FAPL Summary by Club										
Leeds Utd	1992-93 to 1995-96		117	116	1	15	13	9	3	0
Total			*117*	*116*	*1*	*15*	*13*	*9*	*3*	*0*

WHELAN Noel   Coventry City

Fullname: Noel Whelan   DOB: 30-12-74 Leeds
Debut: Sheffield Wednesday v LEEDS UNITED 4/5/93
Debut Goal: LEEDS UNITED v Arsenal 23/8/94 as sub

Previous Clubs Details			Apps					Goals		
Club	Signed	Fee	Tot	Start	Sub	FA	FL	Lge	FA	FL
Leeds Utd	Mar-93		48	28	20	2	5	7	0	1
Coventry City	Dec-95	£2m	21	21	0	3	0	8	1	0
FAPL Summary by Club										
Leeds Utd	1992-93 to 1995-96		48	28	20	2	5	7	0	1
Coventry City	1995-96		21	21	0	3	0	8	1	0
Total			69	49	20	5	5	15	1	1

WHELAN Phil
Middlesbrough

Fullname: Philip James Whelan DOB: 07-03-72 Stockport
Debut: IPSWICH TOWN v Aston Villa 15/8/92
Debut Goal: Tottenham H. v MIDDLESBROUGH 8/4/96

Previous Clubs Details			Apps					Goals		
Club	Signed	Fee	Tot	Start	Sub	FA	FL	Lge	FA	FL
Ipswich Town	Jul-90		69	64	5	3	7	2	0	0
Middlesbrough	Mar-95	£300,000	13	9	4	3	3	1	0	0
FAPL Summary by Club										
Ipswich Town	1992-93 to 1993-94		61	56	5	3	7	0	0	0
Middlesbrough	1995-96		13	9	4	3	3	1	0	0
Total			74	65	9	6	10	1	0	0

WHITBREAD Adrian
West Ham United

Fullname: Adrian Richard Whitbread DOB: 22-10-71 Epping
Debut: Sheffield Utd v SWINDON TOWN 14/8/93
Debut Goal: SWINDON TOWN v Tottenham H. 22/1/94

Previous Clubs Details			Apps					Goals		
Club	Signed	Fee	Tot	Start	Sub	FA	FL	Lge	FA	FL
Leyton Orient	Nov-89		125	125	0	11	11	2	1	0
Swindon Town	Aug-93	£500,000	35	34	1	2	0	1	0	0
West Ham U.	Aug-94	Swap +	10	3	7	1	3	0	0	0
Portsmouth	Nov-95	Loan								
FAPL Summary by Club										
Swindon Town	1993-94		35	34	1	2	0	1	0	0
West Ham U.	1994-95 to 1995-96		10	3	7	1	3	0	0	0
Total			45	37	8	3	3	1	0	0

WHITLOW Mike
Leicester City

Fullname: Michael William Whitlow DOB: 13-01-68 Liverpool
Debut: LEICESTER CITY v Newcastle Utd 21/8/94
Debut Goal: Manchester Utd v LEICESTER CITY 28/12/94

Previous Clubs Details			Apps					Goals		
Club	Signed	Fee	Tot	Start	Sub	FA	FL	Lge	FA	FL
Leeds Utd	Nov-88	£10,000NL	77	62	15	5	5	4	0	0
Leicester City	Mar-92	£250,000	130	127	3	6	8	6	0	1

WHITTINGHAM Guy · Sheffield Wednesday

Fullname: Guy Whittingham · DOB: 10-11-64 Evesham
Debut: ASTON VILLA v Manchester Utd 23/8/93 as sub
Debut Goal: Everton v ASTON VILLA 31/8/93

Previous Clubs Details			*Apps*					*Goals*		
Club	Signed	Fee	Tot	Start	Sub	FA	FL	Lge	FA	FL
Portsmouth	Jun-89		160	149	11	10	9	88	10	3
Aston Villa	Jul-93	£1.2m	18	13	5	0	2	3	0	0
Wolves	Feb-94	Loan	13	13	0	1	0	8	0	0
Sheffield W.	Dec-94	£700,000	50	43	7	4	4	15	0	1
FAPL Summary by Club										
Aston Villa	1993-94 to 1994-95		25	17	8	0	5	5	0	1
Sheffield W.	1994-95 to 1995-96		50	43	7	4	4	15	0	1
Total			*75*	*60*	*15*	*4*	*9*	*20*	*0*	*2*

WHYTE Derek · Middlesbrough

Fullname: Derek Whyte · DOB: 31-08-68 Glasgow
Debut: Coventry City v MIDDLESBROUGH 15/8/92

Previous Clubs Details			*Apps*					*Goals*		
Club	Signed	Fee	Tot	Start	Sub	FA	FL	Lge	FA	FL
Celtic			216	211	5	26	19	7	0	0
Middlesbrough	Aug-92		138	136	2	2	11	2	0	0
FAPL Summary by Club										
Middlesbrough	1992-93 to 1995-96		60	58	2	0	3	0	0	0
Total			*60*	*58*	*2*	*0*	*3*	*0*	*0*	*0*

WILCOX Jason · Blackburn Rovers

Fullname: Jason Malcolm Wilcox · DOB: 15-03-71 Farnworth
Debut: BLACKBURN ROVERS v Arsenal 18/8/92
Debut Goal: Middlesbrough v BLACKBURN ROVERS 5/12/92

Previous Clubs Details			*Apps*					*Goals*		
Club	Signed	Fee	Tot	Start	Sub	FA	FL	Lge	FA	FL
Blackburn Rvs	Jun-89		170	158	12	11	14	22	1	0
FAPL Summary by Club										
Blackburn Rvs	1992-93 to 1995-96		103	99	4	11	12	18	1	0
Total			*103*	*99*	*4*	*11*	*12*	*18*	*1*	*0*

WILLEMS Ron · Derby County

Fullname: Ron Willems · DOB:

Previous Clubs Details			*Apps*					*Goals*		
Club	Signed	Fee	Tot	Start	Sub	FA	FL	Lge	FA	FL
Grasshopper Club			–	–	–	–	–	–	–	–

| Derby County | | | 33 | 31 | 2 | 1 | 2 | 11 | 0 | 1 |

WILLIAMS Paul   Coventry City

Fullname: Paul Darren Williams   DOB: 26-03-71 Burton
Debut: Newcastle Utd v COVENTRY CITY, 19/8/95
Debut Goal: COVENTRY CITY v Tottenham H., 4/11/95

Previous Clubs Details			Apps					Goals		
Club	Signed	Fee	Tot	Start	Sub	FA	FL	Lge	FA	FL
Derby County	Jul-89	Trainee	160	153	7	8	12	25	3	2
Lincoln City	Nov-89	Loan	3	3	0	2	0	0	0	0
Coventry City	Aug-95	£750,000+plr	32	30	2	1	4	1	0	1
FAPL Summary by Club										
Coventry City		1995-96	32	30	2	1	4	2	0	1
Total			*32*	*30*	*2*	*1*	*4*	*2*	*0*	*1*

WILLIAMS Mike   Sheffield Wednesday

Fullname: Michael Anthony Williams   DOB: 21-11-69 Bradford
Debut: SHEFFIELD WEDNESDAY v Southampton 12/4/93
Debut Goal: SHEFFIELD WEDNESDAY v Ipswich Town 14/5/95

Previous Clubs Details			Apps					Goals		
Club	Signed	Fee	Tot	Start	Sub	FA	FL	Lge	FA	FL
Sheffield W.	Feb-91		17	14	3	0	2	1	0	0
Halifax Town	Dec-92	Loan	9	9	0	0	0	1	0	0
FAPL Summary by Club										
Sheffield W.	1992-93 to 1995-96		22	16	6	0	4	1	0	0
Total			*22*	*16*	*6*	*0*	*4*	*1*	*0*	*0*

WILLIAMSON Danny   West Ham United

Fullname: Daniel Williamson   DOB: 05-12-73 Newham
Debut: Arsenal v WEST HAM UNITED 30/4/94 as sub
Debut Goal: WEST HAM UNITED v Southampton 7/5/94

Previous Clubs Details			Apps					Goals		
Club	Signed	Fee	Tot	Start	Sub	FA	FL	Lge	FA	FL
West Ham U.			36	34	2	3	1	5	0	0
FAPL Summary by Club										
West Ham U.	1993-94 to 1995-96		36	34	2	3	1	5	0	0
Total			*36*	*34*	*2*	*3*	*1*	*5*	*0*	*0*

WILLIS Jimmy   Leicester City

Fullname: James Anthony Willis   DOB: 12-07-68 Liverpool
Debut: Blackburn Rvs v LEICESTER CITY 23/8/94
Debut Goal: LEICESTER CITY v Wimbledon 1/4/95

Previous Clubs Details			Apps					Goals		
Club	Signed	Fee	Tot	Start	Sub	FA	FL	Lge	FA	FL
Halifax Tn			0	0	0	0	0	0	0	0
Stockport Co.	Dec-87	Free	10	10	0	0	0	0	0	0

Club	Signed	Fee	Tot	Start	Sub	FA	FL	Lge	FA	FL
Darlington	Mar-88	£12,000	90	90	0	5	5	6	0	0
Leicester City	Dec-91	£100,000	61	59	2	6	3	3	0	0
Bradford City	Mar-92	Loan	9	9	0	0	0	1	0	0
FAPL Summary by Club										
Leicester City	1994-95		29	29	0	2	2	2	0	0
Total			*29*	*29*	*0*	*2*	*2*	*2*	*0*	*0*

WILSON Clive — Tottenham Hotspur

Fullname: Clive Euclid Aklana Wilson
DOB: 13-11-61 Manchester
Debut: Manchester City v QPR 17/8/92
Debut Goal: QPR v Manchester City 6/8/92

Previous Clubs Details			Apps					Goals		
Club	Signed	Fee	Tot	Start	Sub	FA	FL	Lge	FA	FL
Man. City	Dec-79		109	107	2	2	10	9	0	2
Chester City	Sep-82	Loan	21	21	0	0	0	2	0	0
Chelsea	Mar-87	£250,000	81	68	13	4	6	5	0	0
QPR	Jul-90	£450,000	172	170	2	8	16	10	1	1
Tottenham H.	Jun-95	Free	28	28	0	5	2	0	1	0
FAPL Summary by Club										
QPR	1992-93 to 1994-95		119	119	0	6	10	6	1	1
Tottenham H.	1995-96		28	28	0	5	2	0	1	0
Total			*147*	*147*	*0*	*11*	*12*	*6*	*2*	*1*

WINTERBURN Nigel — Arsenal

Fullname: Nigel Winterburn
DOB: 11-12-63 Nuneaton
Debut: ARSENAL v Norwich City 15/8/92
Debut Goal: ARSENAL v Oldham Athletic 26/8/92

Previous Clubs Details			Apps					Goals		
Club	Signed	Fee	Tot	Start	Sub	FA	FL	Lge	FA	FL
Wimbledon	Aug-83		165	164	1	12	13	8	0	0
Arsenal	May-87	£407,000	308	307	1	31	42	7	0	3
FAPL Summary by Club										
Arsenal	1992-93 to 1995-96		138	138	0	14	23	3	0	1
Total			*138*	*138*	*0*	*14*	*23*	*3*	*0*	*1*

WISE Dennis — Chelsea

Fullname: Dennis Frank Wise
DOB: 15-12-66 Kensington
Debut: CHELSEA v Blackburn Rvs 26/8/92
Debut Goal: Aston Villa v CHELSEA 2/9/92

Previous Clubs Details			Apps					Goals		
Club	Signed	Fee	Tot	Start	Sub	FA	FL	Lge	FA	FL
Wimbledon	Mar-85		135	127	8	11	14	26	3	0
Chelsea	Jul-90	£1.6m	187	184	3	18	21	40	3	6
FAPL Summary by Club										
Chelsea	1992-93 to 1995-96		116	114	2	13	12	20	1	3
Total			*116*	*114*	*2*	*13*	*12*	*20*	*1*	*3*

WOAN Ian   Nottingham Forest
Fullname: Ian Simon Woan   DOB: 14-12-67 Heswall
Debut: NOTTINGHAM FOREST v Liverpool 16/8/92
Debut Goal: Coventry City v NOTTINGHAM FOREST 9/1/93
Previous Clubs Details   *Apps*   *Goals*
Club	Signed	Fee	Tot	Start	Sub	FA	FL	Lge	FA	FL
N. Forest	Mar-90	£80,000NL	155	147	8	18	13	29	4	1
FAPL Summary by Club
| N. Forest | 1992-93 to 1995-96 | | 98 | 95 | 3 | 12 | 6 | 16 | 3 | 0 |
| *Total* | | | *98* | *95* | *3* | *12* | *6* | *16* | *3* | *0* |

WRACK Darren   Derby County
Fullname: Darren Wrack   DOB: 05-05-76 Cleethorpes
Previous Clubs Details   *Apps*   *Goals*
Club	Signed	Fee	Tot	Start	Sub	FA	FL	Lge	FA	FL
Derby County	Jul-94	Trainee	10	2	8	1	3	0	0	0

WRIGHT Mark   Liverpool
Fullname: Mark Wright   DOB: 01-08-63 Dorchester on Thames
Debut: Nottingham Forest v LIVERPOOL 16/8/92
Debut Goal: LIVERPOOL v Southampton 1/9/92
Previous Clubs Details   *Apps*   *Goals*
Club	Signed	Fee	Tot	Start	Sub	FA	FL	Lge	FA	FL
Oxford Utd	Aug-80		10	8	2	1	0	0	0	0
Southampton	Mar-82	£80,000	170	170	0	17	25	7	1	2
Derby County	Aug-87	£760,000	144	144	0	5	15	10	0	0
Liverpool	Jul-91	£2.2m	119	117	2	16	13	5	0	0
FAPL Summary by Club
| Liverpool | 1992-93 to 1995-96 | | 98 | 96 | 2 | 7 | 12 | 5 | 0 | 1 |
| *Total* | | | *98* | *96* | *2* | *7* | *12* | *5* | *0* | *1* |

WRIGHT Ian   Arsenal
Fullname: Ian Edward Wright   DOB: 03-11-63 Woolwich
Debut: ARSENAL v Norwich City 15/8/92
Debut Goal: Liverpool v ARSENAL 23/8/92
Previous Clubs Details   *Apps*   *Goals*
Club	Signed	Fee	Tot	Start	Sub	FA	FL	Lge	FA	FL
Crystal Palace	Aug-85		225	206	19	11	19	90	3	9
Arsenal	Sep-91	£2.5m	162	160	2	14	25	95	12	23
FAPL Summary by Club
| Arsenal | 1992-93 to 1995-96 | 132 | 130 | 2 | 14 | 22 | 71 | 12 | 21 |
| *Total* | | *132* | *130* | *2* | *14* | *22* | *71* | *12* | *21* |

WRIGHT Alan   Aston Villa
Fullname: Alan Geoffrey Wright   DOB: 28-09-71 Ashton-under-Lyme

Debut: Crystal Palace v BLACKBURN ROVERS 15/8/92
Debut Goal: Middlesbrough v ASTON VILLA 1/1/96

Previous Clubs Details

Club	Signed	Fee	Tot	Start	Sub	FA	FL	Lge	FA	FL
				Apps					*Goals*	
Blackpool	Apr-89		98	91	7	8	12	0	0	0
Blackburn Rvs	Oct-91	£400,000	69	63	6	5	8	1	0	0
Aston Villa	Mar-95	£1m	46	46	0	5	8	2	0	0
FAPL Summary by Club										
Blackburn Rvs	1992-93 to 1994-95		41	35	6	4	8	0	0	0
Aston Villa	1994-95 to 1995-96		46	46	0	5	8	2	0	0
Total			*87*	*81*	*6*	*9*	*16*	*2*	*0*	*0*

YATES Dean   Derby County
Fullname: Dean Richard Yates   DOB: 26-10-67 Leicester

Previous Clubs Details

Club	Signed	Fee	Tot	Start	Sub	FA	FL	Lge	FA	FL
				Apps					*Goals*	
Notts County	Jun-85	Apprentice	293	291	2	20	20	33	0	0
Derby County	Jan-95	£350,000	49	49	0	1	3	3	0	0

YEBOAH Anthony   Leeds United
Fullname: Anthony Yeboah   DOB: 06-06-66 Kumasi, Ghana
Debut: LEEDS UNITED v QPR 24/1/95 as sub
Debut Goal: LEEDS UNITED v Everton 22/2/95

Previous Clubs Details

Club	Signed	Fee	Tot	Start	Sub	FA	FL	Lge	FA	FL
				Apps					*Goals*	
Eintracht Frankfurt			–	–	–	–	–	–	–	–
Leeds Utd	Jan-95	£3.4m	41	39	2	8	7	24	2	3
FAPL Summary by Club										
Leeds Utd	1994-95 to 1995-96		41	39	2	8	7	24	2	3
Total			*41*	*39*	*2*	*8*	*7*	*24*	*2*	*3*

YORKE Dwight   Aston Villa
Fullname: Dwight Yorke   DOB: 03-11-71 Tobago, WI
Debut: ASTON VILLA v Leeds Utd 19/8/92
Debut Goal: ASTON VILLA v Crystal Palace 5/9/92

Previous Clubs Details

Club	Signed	Fee	Tot	Start	Sub	FA	FL	Lge	FA	FL
				Apps					*Goals*	
Aston Villa	Nov-89	£120,000	163	127	36	20	19	41	9	7
FAPL Summary by Club										
Aston Villa	1992-93 to 1995-96		111	92	19	13	16	28	5	7
Total			*111*	*92*	*19*	*13*	*16*	*28*	*5*	*7*

A-Z PREMIER LEAGUE MANAGERS

	Start	Finish	P	W	D	L	F	A	Pts	PG
ARDILES, Ossie										
Tottenham Hot.	19-Jun-93	30-Oct-94	54	16	14	24	75	83	62	1.15
ATKINSON, Ron										
Aston Villa	Jun-91	10-Nov-94	98	38	27	33	118	114	141	1.44
Coventry City	15-Feb-95	current	52	16	14	22	52	67	62	1.19
BALL, Alan										
Southampton	20-Jan-94	Jul-95	60	19	22	19	87	93	79	1.32
Manchester City	Jul-95	current	38	9	11	18	33	58	38	1.00
BASSETT, Dave										
Sheffield United	21-Jan-88	12-Dec-95	84	22	28	34	96	113	94	1.12
BONDS, Billy										
West Ham United	23-Apr-90	10-Aug-94	42	13	13	16	47	58	52	1.24
BRANFOOT, Ian										
Southampton	Jun-91	11-Jan-94	66	18	14	34	77	97	68	1.03
BURLEY, George										
Ipswich Town	28-Dec-94	–	22	4	2	16	16	53	14	0.64
CLARK, Frank										
Nottingham F.	12-May-93	current	80	37	24	19	122	97	135	1.69
CLOUGH, Brian										
Nottingham F.	6-Jan-75	1-May-93	42	10	10	22	41	62	40	0.95
COPPELL, Steve										
Crystal Palace	1984	20-May-93	42	11	16	15	48	61	49	1.17
DALGLISH, Kenny										
Blackburn Rovers	Oct-91	May-95	126	72	28	26	211	121	244	1.94
DEEHAN, John										
Norwich City	7-Jan-94	1995	61	12	23	26	66	89	59	0.97
EVANS, Roy										
Liverpool	28-Jan-94	current	96	46	24	26	150	94	162	1.69

	Start	Finish	P	W	D	L	F	A	Pts	PG

FERGUSON, Alex
Manchester Utd 6-Nov-86 current 164 102 34 186 297 132 346 2.11

FRANCIS, Gerry
QPR Jun-91 11-Nov-94 56 24 14 18 88 76 86 1.54
Tottenham Hot. 15-Nov-94 current 67 27 25 15 95 70 106 1.58

FRANCIS, Trevor
Sheffield Wed. 17-Jun-91 20-May-95 126 44 42 40 180 162 174 1.38

GORMAN, John
Swindon Town 4-Jun-93 21-Nov-94 42 5 15 22 47 100 30 0.71

GOULD, Bobby
Coventry City 24-Jun-92 23-Oct-93 54 16 19 19 66 73 67 1.24

GRAHAM, George
Arsenal 14-May-86 21-Feb-95 112 41 38 33 132 98 161 1.44

GULLITT, Ruud
Chelsea 1-Jun-96 current – – – – – – – –

HARFORD, Ray
Blackburn Rovers May-95 current 38 18 7 13 61 47 61 1.61

HODDLE, Glenn
Chelsea 4-Jun-93 31-May-96 122 38 41 43 145 152 155 1.27

HORTON, Brian
Manchester City 27-Aug-93 16-May-95 80 21 30 29 90 108 93 1.16

KEEGAN, Kevin
Newcastle United 5-Feb-92 current 122 67 26 29 215 125 227 1.86

KENDALL, Howard
Everton Nov-90 4-Dec-93 60 22 11 27 73 78 77 1.28

KINNEAR, Joe
Wimbledon 19-Jan-92 current 164 57 45 62 215 243 216 1.32

LAWRENCE, Lennie
Middlesbrough 10-Jul-91 2-May-94 42 11 11 20 54 75 44 1.05

LITTLE, Brian
Leicester City May-91 22-Nov-94 14 2 3 9 14 26 9 0.64
Aston Villa 25-Nov-94 current 65 26 20 19 84 64 98 1.51

LIVERMORE/CLEMENCE, Doug/Ray
Tottenham H. 27-May-92 Jun-93 42 16 11 15 60 66 59 1.40

	Start	Finish	P	W	D	L	F	A	Pts	PG
LYALL, John										
Ipswich Town	11-May-90	5-Dec-94	101	24	34	43	101	146	106	1.05
McFARLAND, Roy										
Bolton Wanderers	Jun-95	Jan-96	22	2	4	16	21	44	10	0.45
McGHEE, Mark										
Leicester City	14-Dec-94	Dec-95	24	3	7	14	26	47	16	0.67
MERRINGTON, Dave										
Southampton	Jul-95	Jun-96	38	9	11	18	34	52	38	1.00
NEAL, Phil										
Coventry City	23-Oct-93	14-Feb-95	58	18	18	22	54	69	72	1.24
O'NEILL, Martin										
Leicester City	Dec-93	current	–	–	–	–	–	–	–	–
PLEAT, David										
Sheffield Wed.	Jun-95	current	38	10	10	18	48	61	40	1.05
PORTERFIELD, Ian										
Chelsea	1991	15-Feb-93	29	9	10	10	32	36	37	1.28
REDKNAPP, Harry										
West Ham United	10-Aug-94	current	80	27	20	33	87	100	101	1.26
REID, Peter										
Manchester City	1990	26-Aug-93	46	15	13	18	57	56	58	1.26
RIOCH, Bruce										
Arsenal	8-Jun-95	current	38	17	12	9	49	32	63	1.66
ROBSON, Bryan										
Middlesbrough	May-94	current	38	11	10	17	35	50	43	1.13
ROYLE, Joe										
Oldham Athletic	14-Jul-82	10-Nov-94	84	22	23	39	105	142	89	1.06
Everton	10-Nov-94	current	66	27	22	17	99	71	103	1.56
SMITH, Alan										
Crystal Palace	3-Jun-93	15-May-95	42	11	12	19	34	49	45	1.07
SMITH, Jim										
Derby County	Aug-95	current	–	–	–	–	–	–	–	–

	Start	Finish	P	W	D	L	F	A	Pts	PG
SOUNESS, Graeme										
Liverpool	1991	28-Jan-94	68	28	18	22	106	87	102	1.50
Southampton	Jul-95	current								
TODD, Colin										
Bolton Wanderers	2-Jan-96	current	16	6	1	9	18	27	19	1.19
WALKER, Mike										
Norwich City	1-Jun-92	7-Jan-94	65	25	16	18	97	91	109	1.68
Everton	7-Jan-94	8-Nov-94	31	6	9	16	29	52	27	0.87
WEBB, David										
Chelsea	15-Feb-93	11-May-93	13	5	4	4	19	18	19	1.46
WILKINS, Ray										
QPR	15-Nov-94	current	108	35	25	48	136	156	130	1.20
WILKINSON, Howard										
Leeds United	10-Oct-88	current	164	62	51	51	221	196	237	1.45

CARETAKER MANAGERS

	Start	Finish	P	W	D	L	F	A	Pts	PG
BARRON, Jim										
Aston Villa	10-Nov-94	25-Nov-94	1	1	0	0	4	3	3	3.00
EVANS, Allan										
Leicester City	22-Nov-94	13-Dec-94	4	1	1	2	5	7	4	1.00
GODDARD, Paul										
Ipswich Town	5-Dec-94	28-Dec-94	3	0	2	1	4	7	2	0.67
HARVEY, Colin										
Everton	4-Dec-93	6-Jan-94	7	0	1	6	2	12	1	0.14
HOUSTON, Stuart										
Arsenal	21-Feb-95	8-Jun-95	14	5	2	7	13	17	17	1.21
MORTIMORE, John										
Southampton	11-Jan-94	20-Jan-94	1	1	0	0	1	0	3	3.00
PERRYMAN, Steve										
Tottenham H.	1-Nov-94	14-Nov-94	1	0	0	1	0	2	0	0.00

PG=Points per Game average

FA Carling Premiership
Stadium Guide

Arsenal

Arsenal Stadium, Highbury, London N5

Nickname: Gunners

All-seater Capacity: 39,497

Colours: Red/White sleeves, White, Red

Pitch: 110 yds x 71 yds

Directions:

From North: M1, J2 follow sign for the City. After Holloway Road station (c 6 miles) take third left into Drayton Park. Then right into Aubert Park after ¾ mile and 2nd left into Avenell Road.

From South: Signs for Bank of England then Angel from London Bridge. Right at traffic lights towards Highbury roundabout. Follow Holloway Road then third right into Drayton Park, thereafter as above. *From West:* A40(M) to A501 ring road. Left at Angel to Highbury roundabout, then as above.

Rail: Drayton Park/Finsbury Park.   Tube (Piccadilly line): Arsenal.

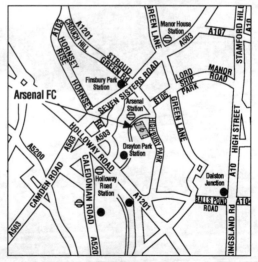

Club: 0171 704 4000 Recorded: 0171 704 4242

Aston Villa

Villa Park, Trinity Rd, Birmingham, B6 6HE

Nickname: The Villains
All-seater Capacity: 40,530

Colours: Claret/Blue, White, Blue/Claret
Pitch: 115 yds x 75 yds

Directions:

M6 J6, follow signs for Birmingham NE. third exit at roundabout then right into Ashton Hall Rd after ¹/₂ mile.
Rail: Witton.

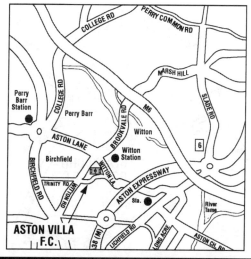

Club: 0121 327 2299 Ticket Info: 0891 121848

Blackburn Rovers

Ewood Park, Blackburn, BB2 4JF

Nickname: Blue and Whites
All-seater Capacity: 30,591

Colours: Blue/White, White, Blue
Pitch: 115yds x 76yds

Directions:

From North, South & West: M6 J31 follow signs for Blackburn then Bolton Road.
Turn left after 1½ miles into Kidder Street.
From East: A677 or A679 following signs for Bolton Road, then as above.
Rail: Blackburn Central.

Club: 01254 698888 Ticket Info: 0891 121179

Chelsea

Stamford Bridge, London SW6

Nickname: The Blues   **Colours:** Royal Blue, Royal Blue, White
All-seater Capacity: 31,791 (Rising to 41,000)   **Pitch:** 110 yds x 72 yds

Directions:

From North & East: A1 or M1 to central London and Hyde Park corner. Follow signs for Guildford (A3) and then Knightsbridge (A4). After a mile turn left into Fulham Road. *From South:* A219 Putney Bridge then follow signs for West End joining A308 and then into Fulham Road. *From West:* M4 then A4 to central London. Follow A3220 to Westminster, after ¾ mile right at crossroads into Fulham Road.

Rail/Tube: Fulham Broadway (District line).

Club: 0171 385 5545 Ticket Info: 0891 121011

Coventry City

Highfield Road Stadium, King Richard Street, Coventry, CV2 4FW

Nickname: Sky Blues
All-seater Capacity: 24,021

Colours: All Sky Blue
Pitch: 110 yds x 75 yds

Directions:

From North & West: M6 J3, after 3½ miles turn left into Eagle Street and straight on to Swan Lane. *From South & East:* M1 to M45 then A45 to Ryton-on-Dunsmore where third exit at roundabout is A423. After one mile turn right into B4110. Left at T-junction then right into Swan Lane.

Rail: Coventry.

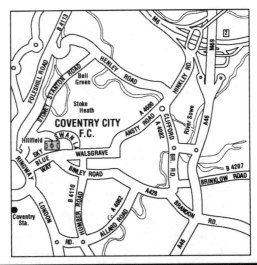

Club: 01203 234000 Box Office 01203 23020

Derby County

The Baseball Ground, Shaftesbury Crescent, Derby, DE23 8NB

Nickname: The Rams
Capacity: 19,500 (15,000 seated)

Colours: White and Black
Pitch: 110yds x 71 yds

Directions:

From South & North – M1 Motorway: M1 J24. At roundabout take 2nd exit towards Derby – A6. Follow A6 for about 7 miles passing through Shadlow and Alvaston. Turn onto Ring Road following 'Football Traffic' signs. At next roundabout – the Spider Bridge roundabout – take 3rd exit (s/p City Centre) into Osmaston Road (A514). Shaftesbury Crescent about one mile on left.
From North: A38 and continue towards Buxton. A38 becomes Derby Ring Road. Cross over River Derwent and at next roundabout turn left (s/p Ring Road/M1 South). Continue for about 4 miles to Spider Bridge roundabout. Take 3rd exit (s/p City Centre) into Osmaston Road (A514). Shaftesbury Crescent one mile on left.

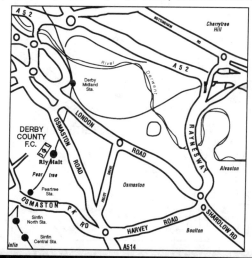

Club: 01332 340105

Everton

Goodison Park, Liverpool, L4 4EL

Nickname: The Toffees
All-seater Capacity: 40,160

Colours: Royal Blue, White, Blue
Pitch: 112 yds x 78 yds

Directions:

From North: M6 J8 take A58 to A580 and follow into Walton Hall Avenue.
From South & East: M6 J21A to M62, turn right into Queen's Drive then, after 4 miles, left into Walton Hall Avenue.
From West: M53 through Wallasey Tunnel, follow signs for Preston on A580. Walton Hall Avenue is signposted.
Rail: Liverpool Lime Street

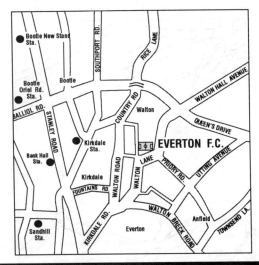

Club: 0151 521 2020 Ticket Info: 0891 121599

Leeds United

Elland Road, Leeds, LS11 0ES

Nickname: United
All-seater Capacity: 39,704

Colours: All White
Pitch: 117 yds x 76 yds

Directions:

From North & East: A58, A61, A63 or A64 into city centre and then onto M621.
Leave motorway after 1½ miles onto A643 and Elland Road.
From West: take M62 to M621 then as above.
From South: M1 then M621 then as above.
Rail: Leeds City.

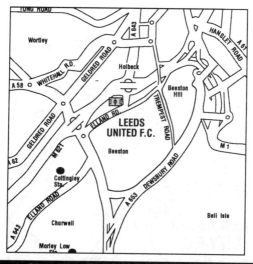

Club: 0113 271 6037 Info: 0891 121180

Leicester City

City Stadium. Filbert Street, Leicester, LE2 7FL

Nickname: Foxes or Fiberts
Capacity: 22,517

Colours: All Blue
Pitch: 112 yds x 75 yds

Directions:
From North: Leave M1 J22, or take A46, A607 to town centre. Towards Rugby via Almond Road, Aylestone Road, and then left into Walnut Street and Filbert Street for the ground. *From South:* M1 or M69 and then A46 to Upperton Road and Filbert Street. *From East:* A47 into town centre, then right along Oxford Street to Aylestone Road and as North. *From West:* M69 and A50 to Aylestone Road, and then as North.
Rail: Leicester

Club: 0115 255 5000 Tickets: 0116 291 5232

Liverpool

Anfield Road, Liverpool 4 0TH

Nickname: Reds or Pool
All-seater Capacity: 41,000

Colours: All Red/White Trim
Pitch: 110 yds x 75 yds

Directions:

From North: M6 J8, follow A58 to Walton Hall Avenue and pass Stanley Park turning left into Anfield Road. *From South/East:* To end of M62 and right into Queens Drive (A5058). After three miles turn left into Utting Avenue and right after one mile into Anfield Road. *From West:* M53 through Wallasey Tunnel, follow signs for Preston then turn into Walton Hall Avenue and right into Anfield Road before Stanley Park. *Rail:* Liverpool Lime Street.

Club: 0151 263 2361 Match: 0151 260 9999

Manchester United

Old Trafford, Manchester, M16 0RA

Nickname: Red Devils
All-seater Capacity: 53,050

Colours: Red Shirts, White Shorts
Pitch: 116 yds x 76 yds

Directions:

From North: From the M63 Junction 4 follow the signs for Manchester (A5081).
Turn right after 2½ miles into Warwick Road.
From South: From the M6 Junction 19 follow the A556 then the A56 (Altrincham).
From Altrincham follow the signs for Manchester turning left into Warwick Road
after six miles.
From East: From the M62 Junction 17 take the A56 to Manchester. Follow the
signs South and then to Chester. Turn right into Warwick Road after two miles.

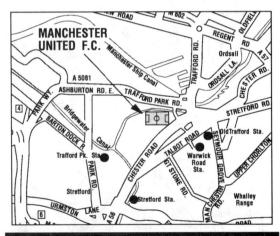

Club: 0161 872 1661 Tickets: 0161 872 0199

Middlesbrough

Cellnet Riverside Stadium, Middlesbrough, TS3 6RS

Nickname: The Boro

All-seater Capacity: 31,000
(expanding to 34,000 during 1996-97)

Colours: Red with White/Black,
White, Red/Black

Pitch: 115 yds x 75 yds

Directions:

From South: A1 (M) onto A19. Follow signs to Teesside/Middlesbrough. After approx 31 miles exit onto A66. Keep following signs to Middlesbrough (A66 Middlesbrough By-Pass). At first roundabout (2.5 miles) turn left. New stadium link road off of second roundabout (due for completion by start 1996-97 season).
From North: Take A19 towards Teesside/Middlesbrough. Cross Tees Bridge and join A66 eastbound. Turn left at first roundabout (approx 3 miles). New stadium link road of second roundabout (due for completion by start 1996-97 season).
Rail: Middlesbrough (600 yards).

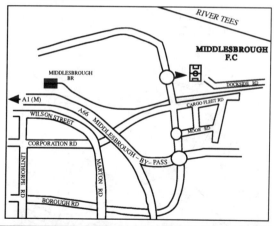

Club: 01642 819659 Tickets: 01642 815996

Newcastle United

St James' Park, Newcastle-upon-Tyne, NE1 4ST

Nickname: Magpies
All-seater Capacity: 36,401

Colours: Black/White, Black, Black
Pitch: 115 yds x 75 yds.

Directions:

From South: Follow A1, A68 then A6127 to cross the Tyne. At roundabout, first exit into Moseley Street. Left into Neville Street, right at end for Clayton Street and then Newgate Street. Left for Leaze Park Road. *From West:* A69 towards city centre. Left into Clayton Street for Newgate Street, left again for Leaze Park Road. *From North:* A1 then follow signs for Hexham until Percy Street. Right into Leaze Park Road.

Rail: Newcastle Central (1/2 mile).

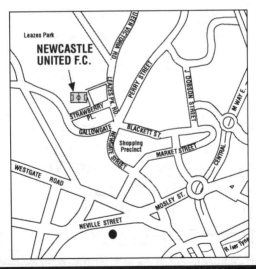

Club: 0191 232 8361 Info: 0891 121190

Nottingham Forest

City Ground, Nottingham, NG2 5FJ

Nickname: The Reds or Forest
All-seater Capacity: 30,539

Colours: Red, White, Red
Pitch: 115 yds x 78 yds

Directions:

From North: Leave the M1 J26 for the A610 and the A606. Left into Radcliffe Road for the ground. *From South:* Leave the M1 J24 to Trent Bridge, turning right into Radcliffe Road. *From East:* A52 to West Bridgeford and right for the ground. *From West:* A52 to A606 and then as for the North.
Rail: Nottingham.

Sheffield Wednesday

Hillsborough, Sheffield, S6 1SW

Nickname: The Owls
All-seater Capacity: 36,020

Colours: Blue/White, Blue, Blue
Pitch: 115 yds x 75 yds

Directions:

From North: M1 J34 then A6109 to Sheffield. At roundabout after 1½ miles take third exit then turn left after three miles into Harries Road.

From South & East: M1 J31 or 33 to A57. At roundabout take Prince of Wales Road exit. A further six miles then turn left into Herries Road South.

From West: A57 to A6101 then turn left after four miles at T junction into Penistone Road.

Rail: Sheffield Midland.

Club: 0114 243 3122 Tickets: 0114 233 7233

Southampton

The Dell, Milton Road, Southampton, SO9 4XX

Nickname: The Saints
All-seater Capacity: 15,288

Colours: Red/White, Black, Black
Pitch: 110 yds x 72 yds

Directions:

From North: A33 into The Avenue then right into Northlands Road. Right at the end into Archer's Road. *From East:* M27 then A334 and signs for Southampton along A3024. Follow signs for the West into Commercial Road, right into Hill Lane then first right into Milton Road.

From West: Take A35 then A3024 towards city centre. Left into Hill Lane and first right into Milton Road.

Rail: Southampton Central.

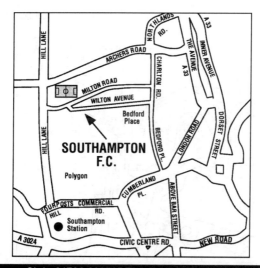

Club: 01703 220505 Tickets: 01703 228575

Sunderland

Roker Park, Sunderland, SR6 9SW

Nickname: Rokermen
Capacity: 22,657

Colours: Red & White stripes. Black, Red
Pitch: 113 yds x 74 yds

Directions:

From South: A1 J64 towards Washington A195. Follow signs to Tyne Tunnel A182 and Sunderland A1231 onto the Washington Highway. Continue following signs for Sunderland A1231. Once on A1231 follow signs for City Centre. At major junction keep to left and follow signs towards Roker B1289. Enter one-way system following signs to Roker. At Wheatsheaf pub turn left and ground is on left hand side.

From North: From junction of A194M (formerly A19) and A184 follow signs towards Tyne Tunnel A184 and then towards Sunderland A184. Continue through Bolden towards City Centre (A1018). Continue into Newcastle Road. Turn left at traffic lights into Charlton Road towards Roker Park. At next lights turn tight into Fulwell Road. Ground on left-hand side.

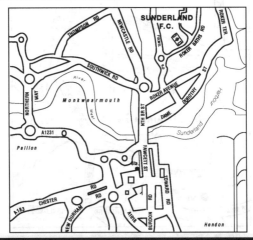

Club: 0191 514 0332

Tottenham Hotspur

748 High Road, Tottenham, London, N17 0AP

Nickname: Spurs
All-seater Capacity: 30,246

Colours: White, Navy Blue, White
Pitch: 110 yds x 73 yds

Directions:

A406 North Circular to Edmonton. At traffic lights follow signs for Tottenham along A1010 then Fore Street for ground.
Rail: White Hart Lane (adjacent).
Tube: Seven Sisters (Victoria Line) or Manor House (Piccadilly Line).

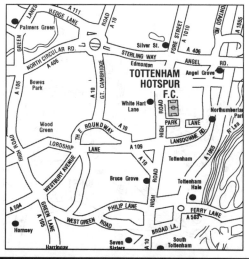

Club: 0181 365 5000 Tickets: 0181 365 5050

West Ham United

Boleyn Ground, Green Street, Upton Park, London E13

Nickname: The Hammers
All-seater Capacity: 24,500

Colours: Claret, White, White
Pitch: 112 yds x 72 yds

Directions:

From North & West: North Circular to East Ham then Barking Rd for 1½ miles until traffic lights. Turn right into Green Street.
From South: Blackwall Tunnel then A13 to Canning Town. Then A124 to East Ham, Green Street on left after two miles.
From East: A13 then A117 and A124. Green Street on right after ¾ miles.
Rail/Tube: Upton Park (¼ mile).

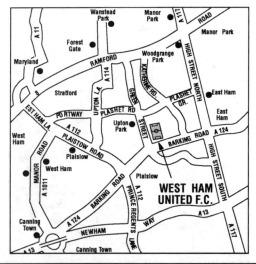

Club: 0181 548 2748 Tickets: 0181 548 2700

Wimbledon

Selhurst Park, South Norwood, London E5

Nickname: The Dons
All-seater Capacity: 26,995

Colours: All Blue with Yellow trim
Pitch: 110 yds x 74 yds

Directions:

From North: M1/A1 to North Circular A406 and Chiswick. Follow South Circular A205 to Wandsworth then A3 and A214 towards Streatham and A23. Then left onto B273 for one mile and turn left at end into High Street and Whitehorse Lane.
From South: On A23 follow signs for Crystal Palace along B266 going through Thornton Heath into Whitehorse Lane. *From East:* A232 Croydon Road to Shirley joining A215, Norwood Road. Turn left after 2½ miles into Whitehorse Lane.
From West: M4 to Chiswick then as above.
Rail: Selhurst, Norwood Junction or Thornton Heath.

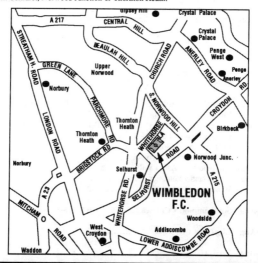

Club: 0181 771 2233 Tickets: 0181 771 8841

Form 'n Encounter Guide

Our unique *Form 'n Encounter Guide* will allow you to plan your season's FA Carling Premiership schedule by providing you with a form guide which helps you to predict what are likely to be the most exciting games to attend on a day-by-day basis. Listed are the results from the previous Premiership encounters for the matches. Please do check that the game you are looking to attend is on before you set out. Match dates and ko times are all subject to change to cope with TV schedules and the like.

Cup matches and World Cup qualifiers for the home countries are shown in italic type.

Dates given for the European club competitions are based on the Wednesday of the week – however, this date is normally reserved exclusively for UEFA Champions' League fixtures, UEFA Cup matches are generally played on the Tuesday and Cup-Winners' Cup ties on the Thursdays. Clubs involved in the latter may move subsequent league matches to the Sunday.

Matches to be shown live on Sky Sports are shown in **bold** type.

Date	Match /Event 92-93	93-94	94-95	95-96
07-Aug	*European Preliminary Round 1st Legs*			
11-Aug	*Littlewoods Pools FA Charity Shield*			
	Manchester United v Newcastle			
17-Aug	Arsenal v West Ham ....–	0-2	0-1	1-0
17-Aug	Blackburn R. v Tottenham H. 0-2	1-0	2-0	2-1
17-Aug	Coventry C. v N. Forest 0-1	–	0-0	1-1
17-Aug	Derby County v Leeds U. ....–	–	–	–
17-Aug	Everton v Newcastle U. ....–	0-2	2-0	1-3
17-Aug	Middlesbrough v Liverpool 1-2	–	–	2-1
17-Aug	Sheffield W. v Aston Villa............1-2	0-0	1-2	2-0
17-Aug	Sunderland v Leicester ....-	–	–	–
17-Aug	Wimbledon v Man. Utd 1-2	1-0	0-1	2-4
18-Aug	**Southampton v Chelsea 1-0**	**3-1**	**0-1**	**2-3**
19-Aug	**Liverpool v Arsenal 0-2**	**0-0**	**3-0**	**3-1**
20-Aug	Leeds U. v Sheffield W.................3-1	2-1	0-1	2-0

Date	Match	92-93	93-94	94-95	95-96
21-Aug	*European Preliminary Round 2nd Legs*				
	Coca Cola-Cup 1st Round 1st Leg				
21-Aug	Aston Villa v Blackburn R. 0-0	0-1	0-1	2-0	
21-Aug	Chelsea v Middlesbrough ....–	–	–	5-0	
21-Aug	Leicester C. v Southampton ....–	4-0	–	–	
21-Aug	Man. Utd v Everton 0-3	1-0	2-0	2-0	
21-Aug	Newcastle U. v Wimbledon ....–	4-0	2-1	6-1	
21-Aug	N. Forest v Sunderland ....–	–	–	–	
21-Aug	Tottenham H. v Derby ....–	–	–	–	
21-Aug	West Ham v Coventry C. ....–	3-2	0-1	3-2	
24-Aug	Aston Villa v Derby ....–	–	–	–	
24-Aug	Chelsea v Coventry C. 2-1	1-2	2-2	2-2	
24-Aug	Leicester C. v Arsenal ....–	–	2-1	–	
24-Aug	Liverpool v Sunderland ....–	–	–	–	
24-Aug	Newcastle U. v Sheffield W. ....–	4-2	2-1	2-0	
24-Aug	N. Forest v Middlesbrough ....–	–	–	1-0	
24-Aug	Tottenham H. v Everton 2-1	3-2	2-1	0-0	
24-Aug	West Ham v Southampton ....–	3-3	2-0	2-1	
25-Aug	**Man. Utd v Blackburn R. 3-1**	**1-1**	**1-0**	**1-0**	
26-Aug	**Leeds U. v Wimbledon 2-1**	**4-0**	**3-1**	**1-1**	
28-Aug	*Coca Cola-Cup 1st Round 2nd Leg*				
31-Aug	*World Cup Qualifier: Austria v Scotland, Wales v San Marino,*				
	Liechtenstein v Rep of Ireland, N.Ireland v Ukraine				
1-Sep	*World Cup Qualifier: Moldova v England*				
2-Sep	**Sheffield W. v Leicester ....–**	**–**	**1-0**	**–**	
3-Sep	Arsenal v Chelsea 2-1	1-0	3-1	1-1	
3-Sep	Blackburn R. v Leeds U. 3-1	2-1	1-1	1-0	
3-Sep	Sunderland v Newcastle U. ....–	–	–	–	
3-Sep	Wimbledon v Tottenham H. 1-1	2-1	1-2	0-1	
4-Sep	Coventry C. v Liverpool..............5-1	1-0	1-1	1-0	
4-Sep	Derby County v Man. Utd ....–	–	–	–	
4-Sep	Everton v Aston Villa..................1-0	0-1	2-2	1-0	

Date	Match	92-93	93-94	94-95	95-96
4-Sep	Middlesbrough v West Ham ....–		–	–	4-2
4-Sep	Southampton v N. Forest 1-2			1-1	3-4
7-Sep	Aston Villa v Arsenal 1-0		0-4	1-1	
7-Sep	Leeds U. v Man. Utd 0-0		0-2	2-1	3-1
7-Sep	Liverpool v Southampton 1-1		4-2	3-1	1-1
7-Sep	Middlesbrough v Coventry C. 0-2		–		2-1
7-Sep	N. Forest v Leicester ....–			2-4	–
7-Sep	Sheffield W. v Chelsea 3-3		3-1	1-1	0-0
7-Sep	Tottenham H. v Newcastle U. ....–		1-2	4-2	1-1
7-Sep	Wimbledon v Everton 1-3		1-1	2-1	2-3
8-Sep	**Sunderland v West Ham ....–**		**–**	**–**	**–**
9-Sep	**Blackburn R. v Derby County ......–**		**–**	**–**	**–**
11-Sep	*European Competitions First Round 1st Legs*				
14-Sep	Coventry C. v Leeds U. 3-3		0-2	2-1	0-0
14-Sep	Derby County v Sunderland ....–		–	–	–
14-Sep	Everton v Middlesbrough ....–		–	–	4-0
14-Sep	Leicester C. v Liverpool ....–		–	1-2	–
14-Sep	Man. Utd v N. Forest 2-0		–	1-2	5-0
14-Sep	Newcastle U. v Blackburn R. ....–		1-1	1-1	1-0
14-Sep	Southampton v Tottenham H. 0-0		1-0	4-3	0-0
14-Sep	West Ham v Wimbledon ....–		0-2	3-0	1-1
15-Sep	**Chelsea v Aston Villa 0-1**		**1-1**	**1-0**	**1-2**
16-Sep	**Arsenal v Sheffield W. 2-1**		**1-0**	**0-0**	**4-2**
28-Sep	*Coca Cola-Cup 2nd Round 1st Leg*				
21-Sep	Aston Villa v Man. Utd 1-0		1-2	1-2	3-1
21-Sep	Blackburn R. v Everton 2-3		2-0	3-0	0-3
21-Sep	Leeds U. v Newcastle U. ....–		1-1	0-0	0-1
21-Sep	Liverpool v Chelsea 2-1		2-1	–	2-0
21-Sep	Middlesbrough v Arsenal 1-0		–	–	2-3
21-Sep	N. Forest v West Ham ....–		–	1-1	1-1
21-Sep	Sheffield W. v Derby..................–		–	–	–
21-Sep	Sunderland v Coventry C. ....–		–	–	–

Date	Match	92-93	93-94	94-95	95-96
22-Sep	**Tottenham H. v Leicester** ....–	–	**0-0**	–
23-Sep	**Wimbledon v Southampton** 1-2	**1-0**	**0-2**	**1-2**
25-Sep	*European Competitions First Round 2nd Legs*				
28-Sep	Arsenal v Sunderland.....................–	–	–	–
28-Sep	Chelsea v N. Forest 0-0	–	0-2	1-0
28-Sep	Coventry C. v Blackburn R. 0-2	2-1	1-1	5-0
28-Sep	Derby County v Wimbledon ....–	–	–	–
28-Sep	Everton v Sheffield W. 1-1	0-2	1-4	2-2
28-Sep	Leicester C. v Leeds ....–	–	1-3	–
28-Sep	Southampton v Middlesbrough ....–	–	–	2-1
28-Sep	West Ham v Liverpool ....–	1-2	0-0	0-0
29-Sep	**Man. Utd v Tottenham H.** 4-1	**2-1**	**0-0**	**1-0**
30-Sep	**Newcastle U. v Aston Villa** ....–	**5-1**	**3-1**	**1-0**
2-Oct	*Coca Cola-Cup 2nd Round 2nd Leg*				
2-Oct	*World Cup Qualifiers: Latvia v Scotland, Wales v Holland, N.Ireland v Armenia*				
12-Oct	Blackburn R. v Arsenal 1-0	1-1	3-1	1-1
12-Oct	Derby County v Newcastle U. ....–	–	–	–
12-Oct	Everton v West Ham ....–	0-1	1-0	3-0
12-Oct	Leeds U. v N. Forest 1-4	–	1-0	1-3
12-Oct	Leicester C. v Chelsea ....–	–	1-1	–
12-Oct	Man. Utd v Liverpool..................2-2	1-0	2-0	2-2
12-Oct	Tottenham H. v Aston Villa 0-0	1-1	3-4	0-1
12-Oct	Wimbledon v Sheffield W.............1-1	2-1	0-1	2-2
13-Oct	**Coventry C. v Southampton** 2-0	**1-1**	**1-3**	**1-1**
14-Oct	**Sunderland v Middlesbrough** ....–	–	–	–
16-Oct	*European Competitions Second Round 1st Legs*				

Date	Match	92-93	93-94	94-95	95-96
19-Oct	Arsenal v Coventry C. 3-0		0-3	2-1	1-1
19-Oct	Aston Villa v Leeds U. 1-1		1-0	0-0	3-0
19-Oct	Chelsea v Wimbledon 4-2		2-0	1-1	1-2
19-Oct	Liverpool v Everton 1-0		2-1	0-0	1-2
19-Oct	Middlesbrough v Tottenham H. 3-0		–	–	0-1
19-Oct	N. Forest v Derby County ....–		–	–	–
19-Oct	Sheffield W. v Blackburn R. 0-0		1-2	0-1	2-1
19-Oct	Southampton v Sunderland ....–		–	–	–
19-Oct	West Ham v Leicester ....–		–	0-1	–
20-Oct	**Newcastle U. v Man. Utd..............–**		**1-1**	**1-1**	**0-1**
23-Oct	*Coca Cola-Cup 3rd Round*				
26-Oct	Arsenal v Leeds U. 0-0		2-1	1-3	2-1
26-Oct	Chelsea v Tottenham H. 1-1		4-3	1-1	0-0
26-Oct	Coventry C. v Sheffield W. 1-0		1-1	2-0	0-1
26-Oct	Leicester C. v Newcastle U. ....–		–	1-3	–
26-Oct	Middlesbrough v Wimbledon.........2-0		–	–	1-2
26-Oct	Southampton v Man. Utd 0-1		1-3	2-2	3-1
26-Oct	Sunderland v Aston Villa ....–		–	–	–
26-Oct	West Ham v Blackburn R................–		1-2	2-0	1-1
27-Oct	**Liverpool v Derby County ....–**		**–**	**–**	**–**
28-Oct	**N. Forest v Everton 0-1**		**–**	**2-1**	**3-2**
30-Oct	*European Competitions Second Round 2nd Legs*				
2-Nov	Aston Villa v N. Forest 2-1		–	0-2	1-1
2-Nov	Blackburn R. v Liverpool 4-1		2-0	3-2	2-3
2-Nov	Derby County v Leicester ....–		–	–	–
2-Nov	Leeds U. v Sunderland ....–		–	–	–
2-Nov	Man. Utd v Chelsea 3-0		0-1	0-0	1-1
2-Nov	Sheffield W. v Southampton 5-2		2-0	1-1	2-2
2-Nov	Tottenham H. v West Ham ....–		1-4	3-1	0-1
2-Nov	Wimbledon v Arsenal..................3-2		0-3	1-3	0-3
3-Nov	**Newcastle U. v Middlesbrough ......–**		**–**	**–**	**1-0**

Date	Match	92-93	93-94	94-95
4-Nov	**Everton v Coventry C. 1-1**	**0-0**	**0-2**	**2-2**

9-Nov *World Cup Qualifiers: Georgia v England, Holland v Wales, Germany v N.Ireland*

10-Nov *World Cup Qualifiers: Scotland v Sweden, Rep of Ireland v Iceland*

Date	Match	92-93	93-94	94-95
16-Nov	Aston Villa v Leicester ....–	–	4-4	–
16-Nov	Blackburn R. v Chelsea 2-0	2-0	2-1	3-0
16-Nov	Everton v Southampton 2-1	1-0	0-0	2-0
16-Nov	Leeds U. v Liverpool 2-2	2-0	0-2	1-0
16-Nov	Man. Utd v Arsenal 0-0	1-0	3-0	1-0
16-Nov	Newcastle U. v West Ham...............–	2-0	2-0	3-0
16-Nov	Tottenham H. v Sunderland ....–	–	–	–
16-Nov	Wimbledon v Coventry C. 1-2	1-2	2-0	0-2

Date	Match	92-93	93-94	94-95
17-Nov	**Derby County v Middlesbrough......–**	**–**	**–**	**–**

Date	Match	92-93	93-94	94-95
18-Nov	**Sheffield W. v N. Forest 2-0**	**–**	**1-7**	**1-3**

20-Nov *European Competitions Third Round 1st Legs*

Date	Match	92-93	93-94	94-95
23-Nov	Chelsea v Newcastle U. ....–	1-0	1-1	1-0
23-Nov	Coventry C. v Aston Villa 3-0	0-1	0-1	0-3
23-Nov	Leicester C. v Everton ....–	–	2-2	–
23-Nov	Liverpool v Wimbledon 2-3	1-1	3-0	2-2
23-Nov	Middlesbrough v Man. Utd 1-1	–	–	0-3
23-Nov	N. Forest v Blackburn R. 1-3	–	0-2	1-5
23-Nov	Southampton v Leeds U. 1-1	0-2	1-3	1-1
23-Nov	Sunderland v Sheffield W...............–	–	–	–
23-Nov	West Ham v Derby County ....–	–	–	–

Date	Match	92-93	93-94	94-95
24-Nov	**Arsenal v Tottenham H. 1-3**	**1-1**	**1-1**	**0-0**

27-Nov *Coca Cola-Cup 4th Round*

Date	Match	92-93	93-94	94-95
30-Nov	Aston Villa v Middlesbrough ....–	–	–	0-0
30-Nov	Blackburn R. v Southampton 0-0	2-0	3-2	2-1
30-Nov	Derby County v Coventry ....–	–	–	–
30-Nov	Everton v Sunderland ....–	–	–	–

Date	Match	92-93	93-94	94-95	95-96
30-Nov	Man. Utd v Leicester	–	–	1-1	–
30-Nov	Newcastle U. v Arsenal	–	2-0	1-0	2-0
30-Nov	Sheffield W. v West Ham	–	5-0	1-0	0-1
30-Nov	Wimbledon v N. Forest	1-0	–	2-2	1-0
1-Dec	**Leeds U. v Chelsea**	**1-1**	**4-1**	**2-3**	**1-0**
2-Dec	**Tottenham H. v Liverpool**	**2-0**	**3-3**	**0-0**	**1-3**
4-Dec	*European Competitions Third Round 2nd Legs*				
7-Dec	Arsenal v Derby County	–	–	–	–
7-Dec	Chelsea v Everton	2-1	4-2	0-1	0-0
7-Dec	Coventry C. v Tottenham H.	1-0	1-0	0-4	2-3
7-Dec	Leicester C. v Blackburn R.	–	–	1-1	–
7-Dec	Liverpool v Sheffield W.	1-0	2-0	4-1	1-0
7-Dec	Middlesbrough v Leeds U.	–	–	–	1-1
7-Dec	Southampton v Aston Villa	2-0	4-1	2-1	0-1
7-Dec	Sunderland v Wimbledon	–	–	–	–
8-Dec	**West Ham v Man. Utd**	**–**	**2-2**	**1-1**	**0-1**
9-Dec	**N. Forest v Newcastle U.**	**–**	**–**	**0-0**	**1-1**
14-Dec	*World Cup Qualifiers: Wales v Turkey (or Sun 15), N.Ireland v Albania*				
14-Dec	Arsenal v Southampton	4-3	1-0	1-1	4-2
14-Dec	Coventry C. v Newcastle U.	–	2-1	0-0	0-1
14-Dec	Derby County v Everton	–	–	–	–
14-Dec	Leeds U. v Tottenham H.	5-0	2-0	1-1	1-3
14-Dec	Liverpool v N. Forest	0-0	–	1-0	4-2
14-Dec	Middlesbrough v Leicester	4-1	–	–	–
14-Dec	Sheffield W. v Man. Utd	3-3	2-3	1-0	0-0
14-Dec	West Ham v Aston Villa	–	0-0	1-0	1-4
14-Dec	Wimbledon v Blackburn R.	1-1	4-1	0-3	1-1
15-Dec	**Sunderland v Chelsea**	**–**	**–**	**–**	**–**

Date	Match	92-93	93-94	94-95	95-96
21-Dec	Blackburn R. v Middlesbrough ....–	–	–	–	1-0
21-Dec	Chelsea v West Ham ....–		2-0	1-2	1-2
21-Dec	Everton v Leeds U......................2-0		1-1	3-0	2-0
21-Dec	Leicester C. v Coventry C. ....–		–	2-2	–
21-Dec	Man. Utd v Sunderland ....–		–	–	–
21-Dec	N. Forest v Arsenal...................0-1		–	2-2	0-1
21-Dec	Southampton v Derby County ....–		–	–	–
21-Dec	Tottenham H. v Sheffield W. 0-2		1-3	3-1	1-0
22-Dec	**Aston Villa v Wimbledon............1-0**	**0-1**	**7-1**	**2-0**
23-Dec	**Newcastle U. v Liverpool...............–**	**3-0**	**1-1**	**2-1**
26-Dec	Aston Villa v Chelsea..................1-3		1-0	3-0	0-1
26-Dec	Blackburn R. v Newcastle U. ....–		1-0	0-0	2-1
26-Dec	Leeds U. v Coventry C. 2-2		1-0	3-0	3-1
26-Dec	Liverpool v Leicester				
26-Dec	Middlesbrough v Everton 1-2		–	–	0-2
26-Dec	N. Forest v Man. Utd 0-2		–	1-1	1-1
26-Dec	**Sheffield W. v Arsenal 1-0**	**0-1**	**3-1**	**1-0**
26-Dec	Sunderland v Derby County				
26-Dec	Tottenham H. v Southampton 4-2		3-0	1-2	1-0
26-Dec	Wimbledon v West Ham ....–		1-2	1-0	0-1
28-Dec	Arsenal v Aston Villa..................0-1		1-2	0-0	2-0
28-Dec	Chelsea v Sheffield W. 0-2		1-1	1-1	0-0
28-Dec	Coventry C. v Middlesbrough				0-0
28-Dec	Derby County v Blackburn R.				
28-Dec	Everton v Wimbledon 0-0		3-2	0-0	2-4
28-Dec	Leicester C. v N. Forest				
28-Dec	Man. Utd v Leeds U. 2-0		0-0	0-0	1-0
28-Dec	Newcastle U. v Tottenham H. ....–		0-1	3-3	1-1
28-Dec	Southampton v Liverpool 2-1		4-2	0-2	1-3
28-Dec	West Ham v Sunderland				
1-Jan	Arsenal v Middlesbrough 1-1		–	–	1-1
1-Jan	Chelsea v Liverpool 0-0		1-0	0-0	2-2
1-Jan	Coventry C. v Sunderland				
1-Jan	Derby County v Sheffield W.				

Date	Match	92-93	93-94	94-95	95-96
1-Jan	**Everton v Blackburn R. 2-1**	**0-3**	**1-2**	**1-0**	
1-Jan	Leicester C. v Tottenham H. ....–		–	3-1	–
1-Jan	Man. Utd v Aston Villa 1-1	3-1	1-0	0-0	
1-Jan	Newcastle U. v Leeds U. ....–	1-1	1-2	2-1	
1-Jan	Southampton v Wimbledon 2-2	1-0	2-3	0-0	
1-Jan	West Ham v N. Forest ....–	–	3-1	1-0	
4-Jan	*FA Cup Third Round*				
8-Jan	*Coca Cola-Cup 5th Round*				
11-Jan	Aston Villa v Newcastle U. ....–	0-2	0-2	1-1	
11-Jan	Blackburn R. v Coventry C. 2-5	2-1	4-0	5-1	
11-Jan	Leeds U. v Leicester ....–	–	3-1	–	
11-Jan	Liverpool v West Ham ....–	2-0	0-0	2-0	
11-Jan	Middlesbrough v Southampton 2-1	–	–	0-0	
11-Jan	N. Forest v Chelsea 3-0	–	0-1	0-0	
11-Jan	Sheffield W. v Everton 3-1	5-1	0-0	2-5	
11-Jan	Sunderland v Arsenal ....–	–	–	–	
11-Jan	Tottenham H. v Man. Utd 1-1	0-1	0-1	4-1	
11-Jan	Wimbledon v Derby County ....–	–	–	–	
18-Jan	Arsenal v Everton 2-0	2-0	1-1	1-2	
18-Jan	Chelsea v Derby County ....–	–	–	–	
18-Jan	Coventry C. v Man. Utd................0-1	0-1	2-3	0-4	
18-Jan	Leicester C. v Wimbledon...............–	–	3-4	–	
18-Jan	Liverpool v Aston Villa 1-2	2-1	3-2	3-0	
18-Jan	Middlesbrough v Sheffield W. 1-1	–	–	3-1	
18-Jan	N. Forest v Tottenham H. 2-1	–	2-2	2-1	
18-Jan	Southampton v Newcastle U. ....–	2-1	3-1	1-0	
18-Jan	Sunderland v Blackburn R. ....–	–	–	–	
18-Jan	West Ham v Leeds U. ....–	0-1	0-0	1-2	
4-Jan	*FA Cup Fourth Round*				
1-Feb	Aston Villa v Sunderland............–	–	–	–	
1-Feb	Blackburn R. v West Ham...............–	0-2	4-2	4-2	
1-Feb	Derby County v Liverpool...............–	–	–	–	
1-Feb	Everton v N. Forest 3-0	–	1-2	3-0	
1-Feb	Leeds U. v Arsenal 3-0	2-1	1-0	0-3	
1-Feb	Man. Utd v Southampton 2-1	2-0	2-1	4-1	

Date	Match	92-93	93-94	94-95	95-96
1-Feb	Newcastle U. v Leicester ....–	–	3-1	–
1-Feb	Sheffield W. v Coventry C. 1-2	0-0	5-1	4-3
1-Feb	Tottenham H. v Chelsea...............1-2	1-1	0-0	1-1
1-Feb	Wimbledon v Middlesbrough ....–	–	–	0-0
12-Feb	*World Cup Qualifiers: England v Italy*				
15-Feb	*FA Cup Fifth Round*				
15-Feb	Aston Villa v Coventry C. 0-0	–	0-0	4-1
15-Feb	Blackburn R. v N. Forest 4-1	–	3-0	7-0
15-Feb	Derby County v West Ham ....–	–	–	–
15-Feb	Everton v Leicester ....–	–	1-1	–
15-Feb	Leeds U. v Southampton 2-1	0-0	0-0	1-0
15-Feb	Man. Utd v Middlesbrough ....–	–	–	2-0
15-Feb	Newcastle U. v Chelsea...............–	0-0	4-2	2-0
15-Feb	Sheffield W. v Sunderland..............–	–	–	–
15-Feb	Tottenham H. v Arsenal 1-0	0-1	1-0	2-1
15-Feb	Wimbledon v Liverpool 2-0	1-1	0-0	1-0
19-Feb	*Coca Cola-Cup Semi Final 1st Leg*				
23-Feb	*Coca Cola-Cup Semi Final 1st Leg*				
22-Feb	Arsenal v Wimbledon..................0-1	1-1	0-0	1-3
22-Feb	Chelsea v Man. Utd 1-1	1-0	2-3	1-4
22-Feb	Coventry C. v Everton 0-1	2-1	0-0	2-1
22-Feb	Leicester C. v Derby County ....–	–	–	–
22-Feb	Liverpool v Blackburn R. 2-1	0-1	–	3-0
22-Feb	Middlesbrough v Newcastle U. ....–	–	–	1-2
22-Feb	N. Forest v Aston Villa 0-1	–	1-2	1-1
22-Feb	Southampton v Sheffield W. 1-2	1-1	0-0	0-1
22-Feb	Sunderland v Leeds U. ....–	–	–	–
22-Feb	West Ham v Tottenham H. ....–	1-3	1-2	1-1
1-Mar	Aston Villa v Liverpool 4-2	2-1	2-0	0-2
1-Mar	Blackburn R. v Sunderland ....–	–	–	–
1-Mar	Derby County v Chelsea ....–	–	–	–
1-Mar	Everton v Arsenal 0-0	1-1	1-1	0-2
1-Mar	Leeds U. v West Ham ....–	1-0	2-2	2-0

Date	Match	92-93	93-94	94-95	95-96
1-Mar	Man. Utd v Coventry C. 5-0		0-0	2-0	1-0
1-Mar	Newcastle U. v Southampton	–	1-2	5-1	1-0
1-Mar	Sheffield W. v Middlesbrough	–		–	0-1
1-Mar	Tottenham H. v N. Forest 2-1		–	1-4	0-1
1-Mar	Wimbledon v Leicester	–		2-1	–
4-Mar	Arsenal v Man. Utd 0-1		0-0	0-0	1-0
4-Mar	Sunderland v Tottenham	–	–	–	–
5-Mar	*European Competitions Quarter Finals 1st Legs*				
5-Mar	Chelsea v Blackburn R. 0-0		1-2	1-2	2-3
5-Mar	Coventry C. v Wimbledon 0-2		1-2	1-1	3-3
5-Mar	Leicester C. v Aston Villa	–	–	1-1	–
5-Mar	Liverpool v Leeds U. 2-0		2-0	0-1	5-0
5-Mar	Middlesbrough v Derby County ......-	–	–	–	–
5-Mar	N. Forest v Sheffield W. 1-2		–	4-1	1-0
5-Mar	Southampton v Everton 0-0		0-2	2-0	2-2
5-Mar	West Ham v Newcastle U................	–	2-4	1-3	2-0
8-Mar	*FA Cup Sixth Round*				
8-Mar	Arsenal v N. Forest.....................1-1		–	1-0	1-1
8-Mar	Coventry C. v Leicester.................	–	–	4-2	–
8-Mar	Derby County v Southampton	–			
8-Mar	Leeds U. v Everton....................2-0		3-0	1-0	2-2
8-Mar	Liverpool v Newcastle U.	–	0-2	2-0	4-3
8-Mar	Middlesbrough v Blackburn R. 3-2		–	–	2-0
8-Mar	Sheffield W. v Tottenham H. 2-0		1-0	3-4	1-3
8-Mar	Sunderland v Man. Utd	–	–	–	–
8-Mar	West Ham v Chelsea	–	1-0	1-2	1-3
8-Mar	Wimbledon v Aston Villa 2-3		2-2	4-3	3-3
12-Mar	*Coca Cola-Cup Semi Final 2nd Leg*				
15-Mar	Aston Villa v West Ham	–	3-1	0-2	1-1
15-Mar	Blackburn R. v Wimbledon 0-0		3-0	2-1	3-2
15-Mar	Chelsea v Sunderland	–	–	–	–
15-Mar	Everton v Derby County	–	–	–	–
15-Mar	Leicester C. v Middlesbrough ....-	–	–	–	–
15-Mar	Man. Utd v Sheffield W. 2-1		5-0	1-0	2-2

Date	Match	92-93	93-94	94-95	95-96
15-Mar	Newcastle U. v Coventry C. ....–		4-0	4-0	3-0
15-Mar	N. Forest v Liverpool 1-0		–	1-1	1-0
15-Mar	Southampton v Arsenal 2-0		0-4	1-0	0-0
15-Mar	Tottenham H. v Leeds U. 4-0		1-1	1-1	2-1

16-Mar *Coca Cola-Cup Semi Final 2nd Leg*

19-Mar *European Competitions Quarter Finals 2nd Legs*

Date	Match	92-93	93-94	94-95	95-96
22-Mar	Arsenal v Liverpool 0-1		1-0	0-1	0-0
22-Mar	Blackburn R. v Aston Villa 3-0		1-0	3-1	1-1
22-Mar	Coventry C. v West Ham ....–		1-1	2-0	2-2
22-Mar	Derby County v Tottenham H. ....–		–	–	–
22-Mar	Everton v Man. Utd 0-2		0-1	1-0	2-3
22-Mar	Middlesbrough v Chelsea 0-0		–	–	2-0
22-Mar	Sheffield W. v Leeds U. 1-1		3-3	1-1	6-2
22-Mar	Southampton v Leicester ....–		–	4-3	–
22-Mar	Sunderland v N. Forest ....–		–	–	–
22-Mar	Wimbledon v Newcastle U. ....–		4-2	3-2	3-3

29-Mar *World Cup Qualifiers: Scotland v Estonia, Wales v Belgium,*
        N.Ireland v Portugal

Date	Match	92-93	93-94	94-95	95-96
29-Mar	Aston Villa v Sheffield W. 2-0		2-2	1-1	3-2
29-Mar	Chelsea v Southampton 1-1		2-0	0-2	3-0
29-Mar	Leeds U. v Derby County ....–		–	–	–
29-Mar	Leicester C. v Sunderland ....–		–	–	–
29-Mar	Liverpool v Middlesbrough ....–		–	–	1-0
29-Mar	Man. Utd v Wimbledon 0-1		3-1	3-0	3-1
29-Mar	Newcastle U. v Everton ....–		1-0	2-0	1-0
29-Mar	N. Forest v Coventry C. 1-1		–	2-0	0-0
29-Mar	Tottenham H. v Blackburn R. 1-2		0-2	3-1	2-3
29-Mar	West Ham v Arsenal ....–		0-0	0-2	0-1

2-Apr *World Cup Qualifiers: Scotland v Austria, Macedonia v Rep of*
       Ireland, Ukraine v N.Ireland

Date	Match	92-93	93-94	94-95	95-96
5-Apr	Aston Villa v Everton 2-1		0-0	0-0	1-0
5-Apr	Chelsea v Arsenal 1-0		0-2	2-1	1-0
5-Apr	Leeds U. v Blackburn R. 5-2		3-3	1-1	0-0

5-Apr	Leicester C. v Sheffield W. ....–	–	0-1	–
5-Apr	Liverpool v Coventry C.............4-0	1-0	2-3	0-0
5-Apr	Man. Utd v Derby County ....–	–	–	–
5-Apr	Newcastle U. v Sunderland ....–	–	–	–
5-Apr	N. Forest v Southampton 1-2	–	3-0	1-0
5-Apr	Tottenham H. v Wimbledon 1-1	1-1	1-2	3-1
5-Apr	West Ham v Middlesbrough ....–	–	–	2-0

6-Apr   *Coca Cola-Cup Final*

9-Apr   *European Competitions Semi Finals 1st Legs*

12-Apr	Arsenal v Leicester ....–	–	1-1	–
12-Apr	Blackburn R. v Man. Utd 0-0	2-0	2-4	1-2
12-Apr	Coventry C. v Chelsea 1-2	1-1	2-2	1-0
12-Apr	Derby County v Aston Villa ....–	–	–	–
12-Apr	Everton v Tottenham H. 1-2	0-1	0-0	1-1
12-Apr	Middlesbrough v N. Forest...........1-2	–	–	1-1
12-Apr	Sheffield W. v Newcastle U. ....–	0-1	0-0	0-2
12-Apr	Southampton v West Ham..............–	0-2	1-1	0-0
12-Apr	Sunderland v Liverpool ....–	–	–	–
12-Apr	Wimbledon v Leeds U. 1-0	1-0	0-0	2-4

13-Apr   *FA Cup Semi Finals*

19-Apr	Arsenal v Blackburn R. 0-1	1-0	0-0	0-0
19-Apr	Aston Villa v Tottenham H. 0-0	1-0	1-0	2-1
19-Apr	Chelsea v Leicester ....–	–	4-0	–
19-Apr	Liverpool v Man. Utd.................1-2	3-3	2-0	2-0
19-Apr	Middlesbrough v Sunderland...........–	–	–	–
19-Apr	Newcastle U. v Derby County ....–	–	–	–
19-Apr	N. Forest v Leeds U. 1-1	–	3-0	2-1
19-Apr	Sheffield W. v Wimbledon...........1-1	2-2	0-1	2-1
19-Apr	Southampton v Coventry C. 2-2	1-0	0-0	1-0
19-Apr	West Ham v Everton ....–	0-1	2-2	2-1
22-Apr	Blackburn R. v Sheffield W. 1-0	1-1	3-1	3-0
22-Apr	Leeds U. v Aston Villa 1-1	2-0	1-0	2-0
22-Apr	Sunderland v Southampton ....–	–	–	–
22-Apr	Wimbledon v Chelsea 0-0	1-1	1-1	1-1

23-Apr   *European Competitions Semi Finals 2nd Legs*

23-Apr	Coventry C. v Arsenal 0-2	1-0	0-1	0-0
23-Apr	Derby County v N. Forest ....–	–	–	–
23-Apr	Everton v Liverpool 2-1	2-0	2-0	1-1
23-Apr	Leicester C. v West Ham ....–		1-2	–
23-Apr	Man. Utd v Newcastle U. ....–	1-1	2-0	2-0
23-Apr	Tottenham H. v Middlesbrough.........–	–	–	1-1

30-Apr *World Cup Qualifiers: England v Georgia, Sweden v Scotland, Romania v Rep of Ireland, Armenia v N.Ireland*

3-May	Arsenal v Newcastle U. ....–	2-1	2-3	2-0
3-May	Chelsea v Leeds U...................1-0	1-1	0-3	4-1
3-May	Coventry C. v Derby County ....–	–	–	–
3-May	Leicester C. v Man. Utd.................–	–	0-4	–
3-May	Liverpool v Tottenham H. 6-2	1-2	1-1	0-0
3-May	Middlesbrough v Aston Villa.........2-3	–	–	0-2
3-May	N. Forest v Wimbledon 1-1	–	3-1	4-1
3-May	Southampton v Blackburn R. 1-1	3-1	1-1	1-0
3-May	Sunderland v Everton ....–	–	–	–
3-May	West Ham v Sheffield W. ....–	2-0	0-2	1-1

7-May *UEFA Cup Final First Leg*

11-May	Aston Villa v Southampton 1-1	0-2	1-1	3-0
11-May	Blackburn R. v Leicester ....–	–	3-0	–
11-May	Derby County v Arsenal ....–	–	–	–
11-May	Everton v Chelsea 0-1	4-2	3-3	1-1
11-May	Leeds U. v Middlesbrough ....–	–	–	0-1
11-May	Man. Utd v West Ham ....–	3-0	1-0	2-1
11-May	Newcastle U. v N. Forest ....–	–	2-1	3-1
11-May	Sheffield W. v Liverpool 1-1	3-1	1-2	1-1
11-May	Tottenham H. v Coventry C. 0-2	1-2	1-3	3-1
11-May	Wimbledon v Sunderland ....–	–	–	–

14-May *European Cup-Winners Cup Final*

14-May *Play-off Semi Finals*

17-May *FA Cup Final*

21-May *UEFA Cup Final 2nd Leg*

24-May	*Div 3 Play-off Final*
25-May	*Div 2 Play-off Final*
26-May	*Div 1 Play-off Final*
28-May	*European Cup Final*
31-May	*World Cup Qualifier: Poland v England*
7-Jun	*World Cup Qualifier: Rep of Ireland v Liechtenstein*
8-Jun	*World Cup Qualifier: Belarus v Scotland*

FA Carling
PREMIERSHIP
97-98
Pocket Annual

The 5th edition of the
Premiership *bible* will be
available in August 1997.
Reserve your copy now.